SCOTLAND

BED & BREAKFAST

Friendly, economical bed-and-breakfasting is one of the best ways you can choose to get to know Scotland – and the Scots. It's a great combination – good food, comfortable bedrooms, a holiday atmosphere – and all in the setting of a family home, where the owner's touch makes all the difference. Much more personal than a hotel, a bed and breakfast adds up to superb value.

There's a wide and varied range of bed and breakfasts to choose from, around the country. Welcoming doors are opened in country cottages, superior suites, city drawing rooms, farmhouse kitchens, warm with baking, even in mansions with trout streams in the grounds.

A bed and breakfast is perfect for a short break – a weekend in the country, or a theatre stop in Edinburgh or Glasgow. It's the perfect place to stop on a touring holiday to take in the history and scenery that make Scotland famous. It's the ideal place to unwind after a day's business or travel – always relaxing, never too grand for comfort.

Start making your choices now. Just reading this book will put you in the holiday mood – and once you get here, we don't think you'll be disappointed !

Where to Stay...?

Over 1500 answers to the age-old question!

Revised annually, this is the most comprehensive guide to bed and breakfast establishments in Scotland.

Every property in the guide has been graded and classified by Scottish Tourist Board inspectors. See page vi for details of this reliable quality assessment scheme.

Accommodation is listed

- by location (in the case of isolated country properties, this is the nearest town or village)

- in alphabetical order

The maps on pages xxxv to xl show all the locations around Scotland which have entries in the guide.

Learn to use the symbols in each entry - they contain a mine of information! There is a key on the back flap. You can use them to check on facilities from four-poster beds to swimming pools, from babysitting services to access for disabled visitors. Naturally, it is always advisable to confirm with the establishment that a particular facility is still available.

Prices in the guide are quoted per person and represent the minimum and maximum charges expected to apply to most rooms in the establishment. They include VAT at the appropriate rate and service charges where applicable.

The prices of accommodation, services and facilities are supplied to us by the operators and were, to the best of

binding contract which must be fulfilled on both sides. Should you fail to take up accommodation, you may not only forfeit any deposit already paid, but may also have to compensate the establishment if the accommodation cannot be re-let.

our knowledge, correct at the time of going to press. However, prices can change at any time during the lifetime of the publication, and you should check again when you book.

Bookings can be made direct to the establishment, through a travel agent, or through a local Tourist Information Centre (more details on page xix).

Remember, when you accept accommodation by telephone or in writing, you are entering a legally

QUALITY HOLIDAY ACCOMMODATION

To ensure you find the right place to stay, we have visited nearly 10,000 individual establishments.

Every year, Scottish Tourist Board inspectors travel the country, staying in hotels, guest houses and bed and breakfasts and visiting self catering holiday homes, to assess them for the standards expected by visitors to our country and ensure your needs are met.

Using our Grading and Classification Scheme they assess all the important factors that contribute to the comforts of your accommodation and highlight the range of facilities and services offered.

GRADING for QUALITY of facilties and services

DELUXE	An overall EXCELLENT quality standard
HIGHLY COMMENDED	An overall VERY GOOD quality standard
COMMENDED	An overall GOOD quality standard
APPROVED	An overall ACCEPTABLE quality standard

Quality grades are awarded by the Scottish Tourist Board inspectors only after they have slept in the beds, sampled meals and talked to staff. They are based on a wide ranging assessment of quality and service aspects, including the warmth of welcome, atmosphere and efficiency of service, as well as the quality of furnishings, fittings and decor. Each establishment is assessed on its own merits, irrespective of the range of facilities on offer.

CROWN CLASSIFICATION for RANGE of facilities and services

When you book a hotel, guest house or bed and breakfast with the following crown classification you will receive at least the facilities and services indicated.

NOTE: Each level includes all the facilities and equipment listed underneath.

👑 👑 👑 👑 👑	All bedrooms with full ensuite facilities. Restaurant serving breakfast, lunch and dinner. Night porter and room service. 24 hour lounge service.
👑 👑 👑 👑	Evening meal, choice of dishes and selection of wine. Colour TV, radio and telephone in bedrooms. Laundry services, toiletries. Quiet seating area.
👑 👑 👑	Evening meal. Hairdryer. Shoe cleaning equipment. Ironing facilities and tea and coffee making facilities.
👑 👑	Colour TV. Early morning tea. Minimum of 20% bedrooms with ensuite/private facilities.
👑	Your own bedroom key. Shared lounge area. Washbasins in bedrooms or in private bathrooms.
Listed	Clean and comfortable accommodation. Cooked or continental breakfast. Adequate heating at no extra charge. Clean towels and fresh soap. Bedding clean and in sound condition. Hot water with no extra charge for baths or showers.

Classification covers the range of facilities and services offered, from LISTED to 5 CROWNS. More crowns mean more facilities.

Look out for this distinctive sign of
Quality Assured Accommodation

For full details of the scheme contact The Quality Assurance Department, Visitor Services Division, Scottish Tourist Board, Thistle House, Beechwood Park North, Inverness IV2 3ED. Telephone: (01463) 716996.

Over 4,000 serviced establishments are members of the Grading and Classification Scheme and they are to be found in all parts of Scotland.

Où loger?

Plus de 1500 réponses à l'éternelle question!

Ce livre révisé chaque année est le guide le plus complet des Bed & Breakfasts en Ecosse.

Chaque établissement dans ce guide a été noté et classé par les inspecteurs du Scottish Tourist Board. Reportez-vous à la page x pour plus de détails sur ce système fiable d'évaluation de la qualité.

Les modes d'hébergement sont répertoriés

• par emplacement (dans le cas des établissements ruraux isolés, c'est la ville ou le village le plus proche)

• par ordre alphabétique

Les cartes des pages xxxv à xl montrent les endroits en Ecosse qui figure dans ce guide.

Familiarisez-vous avec les symboles dans chaque annonce. Ce sont des mines d'informations! Vous pouvez les utiliser pour vérifier quels sont les aménagements proposés, des lits à baldaquin aux piscines, et des services de garde d'enfants à l'accès pour les visiteurs handicapés. Evidemment, il est toujours conseillé de vérifier auprès de l'établissement qu'un aménagement particulier est toujours disponible.

Les prix dans ce guide s'entendent par personne et représentent le prix minimum et le prix maximum auxquels s'attendre dans la plupart des chambres de l'établissement. La TVA au taux approprié et le service (le cas échéant) sont compris.

par l'intermédiaire d'une agence de voyages ou d'un Tourist Information Centre local (pour plus de détails, reportez-vous à la page xix).

Souvenez-vous qu'accepter une chambre par téléphone ou par écrit revient à passer un contrat légal qui lie les deux parties et doit être exécuté par celles-ci. Si vous ne prenez pas la chambre, vous risquez non seulement de perdre les arrhes éventuellement versées, mais aussi de devoir indemniser l'établissement s'il ne peut relouer la chambre.

Les prix de l'hébergement, du service et des aménagements nous ont été fournis par les organisateurs et étaient, à notre connaissance, corrects au moment d'imprimer. Cependant, les prix sont susceptibles de changer à tout moment pendant la durée de vie de la publication et il est donc bon de les revérifier au moment de réserver.

Les réservations peuvent être effectuées directement auprès de l'établissement,

UN HÉBERGEMENT DE QUALITÉ

Pour que vous soyez sûr de trouver l'hébergement qui vous convient, nous avons inspecté près de 10000 établissements différents.

Chaque année les inspecteurs de l'Office de Tourisme écossais sillonnent le pays, séjournent dans les hôtels, les pensions et les B&B et inspectent les locations meublées pour les évaluer en fonction des niveaux de qualité auxquels peuvent s'attendre les touristes en vacances en Ecosse, et pour s'assurer qu'ils répondent à vos besoins.

En appliquant le Système de Classement et de Classification de l'Office de Tourisme écossais, ils évaluent tous les facteurs importants qui contribuent au confort de l'hébergement et mettent en relief la gamme d'aménagements et de prestations de service offerte.

CLASSEMENT en fonction de la **QUALITÉ** des aménagements et prestations de service

DELUXE	EXCELLENT niveau global de qualité.
HIGHLY COMMENDED	TRÈS BON niveau global de qualité.
COMMENDED	BON niveau global de qualité.
APPROVED	Niveau global de qualité ACCEPTABLE.

Les inspecteurs de l'Office de Tourisme écossais n'attribuent ces mentions qu'après avoir dormi dans les lits, goûté aux repas et bavardé avec le personnel. Ces mentions reposent sur une évaluation générale de la qualité et des prestations de service offertes par chaque établissement - dont la chaleur de l'accueil, l'ambiance et la compétence du service, ainsi que la qualité de l'ameublement, des installations et du décor. Chaque établissement est évalué selon ses propres mérites, quelle que soit la gamme d'équipements offerte.

x

CLASSIFICATION PAR COURONNES en fonction de la **GAMME** d'aménagements
et de prestations de service

Si vous réservez une chambre dans un hôtel, une pension ou un B&B ayant reçu une des classifications suivantes, vous serez sûr de bénéficier au moins des aménagements et des prestations de service indiqués.

NB: Chaque niveau comprend tous les aménagements et installations des niveaux précédents.

👑👑👑👑👑	Salle de bains dans toutes les chambres. Restaurant servant petit déjeuner, déjeuner et dîner. Portier de nuit et service à l'étage. Service au salon 24h sur 24.
👑👑👑👑	Dîner, choix de plats et carte des vins. TV couleurs, radio et téléphone dans les chambres. Service de blanchisserie, produits de toilette. Coin salon tranquille.
👑👑👑	Dîner. Sèche-cheveux. Nécessaire de cirage de chaussurs. Possibilité de repassage et nécessaire pour préparer des boissons chaudes.
👑👑	TV couleurs. Thé servé au réveil. 20% des chambres, au moins, ont les WC ou une baignoire ou douche.
👑	Chambres fermant à clef. Salon réservé aux clients. Lavabos dans chambres ou dans salles de bains privées.
LISTED	Hébergement propre et confortable. Petit déjeuner à l'anglaise ou continental. Chauffage suffisant sans supplément. Serviettes propres et savon neuf. Literie propre et en bon état. Eau chaude sans supplément pour bains et douches.

Chaque niveau de classification, de LISTED (Répertorié) à 5 COURONNES, est attribué en fonction de la gamme d'aménagements et de prestations de service offerte. Plus il y a de couronnes plus la gamme d'aménagements et de prestations de service est importante.

Pour recevoir des informations complètes sur ce système contactez The Quality Assurance Department, Visitor Services Division, Scottish Tourist Board, Thistle House, Beechwood Park North, Inverness IV2 3ED. Téléphone: (01463) 716996.

Plus de 4000 établissements hôteliers partout en Ecosse sont membres du système de classement et de classification.

Recherchez ce signe caractéristique
d'un hébergement de qualité garantie

ÜBER DIESES BUCH

Unterkunftsmöglichkeiten...

Über 1500 Angebote, aus denen Sie auswählen können!

Hierbei handelt es sich um den umfassendsten Führer zu "Bed & Breakfast"-Unterkünften in Schottland; dieser wird jedes Jahr überarbeitet.

Jede Unterkunft in diesem Führer wurde von Inspektoren des Scottish Tourist Board gradiert und klassifiziert. Einzelheiten zu diesem zuverlässigen Qualitätssicherungsschema auf Seite xiv.

Die Aufführung von Unterkünften erfolgt

- nach jeweiligem Ort (bei abgelegenen Unterkünften auf dem Land ist das die nächste Stadt oder das nächste Dorf)

- in alphabetischer Reihenfolge

Die Karten auf den Seiten xxxv bis xl zeigen alle in diesem Führer enthaltenen Orte in ganz Schottland.

Machen Sie sich mit den Symbolen in jedem Eintrag vertraut, denn sie enthalten eine Vielzahl von Informationen! Sie können damit die jeweiligen Einrichtungen überprüfen, angefangen von Himmelbetten zu Swimmingpools, von Babysitterdiensten bis Zugangsmöglichkeiten für Behinderte. Es ist natürlich immer ratsam, sich von einer Unterkunft die Verfügbarkeit einer bestimmten Einrichtung bestätigen zu lassen.

Die Preise in diesem Führer gelten pro Person und stellen die Mindest- bzw. Höchstbeträge dar, mit denen man für die meisten Zimmer in dieser Unterkunft rechnen muß. Die Preise enthalten ggf. Bedienung und Mehrwertsteuer zum jeweils geltenden Tarif.

Ort vorgenommen werden (nähere Einzelheiten auf Seite xix).

Bitte beachten Sie, daß Sie bei telefonischer oder schriftlicher Unterkunftsannahme einen rechtsgültigen Vertrag eingehen, der von beiden Parteien zu erfüllen ist. Bei Nichtanspruchnahme der Unterkunft verfällt unter Umständen nicht nur eine bereits getätigte Anzahlung, sondern ist auch Schadenersatz zu leisten, falls eine anderweitige Vermietung der Unterkunft nicht möglich ist.

Die Preise für Unterbringung, Leistungen und Einrichtungen werden uns von den Veranstaltern mitgeteilt und waren nach unserer Kenntnis korrekt zum Zeitpunkt der Drucklegung. Die Preise können sich jedoch jederzeit nach Veröffentlichung ändern, und Sie sollten sich daher bei der Buchung nochmals erkundigen.

Buchungen können direkt bei der Unterkunft, über ein Reisebüro oder über ein Tourist Information Centre vor

QUALITÄTSURLAUBSUNTERKÜNFTE

Um zu gewährleisten, daß Sie die richtige Unterbringungsmöglichkeit finden, haben wir nahezu 10.000 individuelle Unterkünfte besucht.

Jedes Jahr reisen Prüfer des Scottish Tourist Board durch Schottland und wohnen in Hotels, Pensionen sowie "Bed & Breakfast"-Unterkünften und besuchen Ferienwohnungen für Selbstversorger, um diese auf deren Standards, die von Besuchern unseres Landes erwartet werden, hin zu beurteilen und um zu gewährleisten, daß Ihre Anforderungen erfüllt werden. Anhand unseres Gradierungs- und Klassifikationsschemas bewerten unsere Prüfer alle wichtige Faktoren, die zum Komfort Ihrer Unterkunft beitragen, und heben die Auswahl an Einrichtungen und den angebotenen Service hervor.

QUALITÄTSGRADIERUNG von Einrichtungen und Leistungen

DELUXE	Ein insgesamt AUSGEZEICHNETER Qualitätsstandard.
HIGHLY COMMENDED	Ein insgesamt SEHR GUTER Qualitätsstandard.
COMMENDED	Ein insgesamt GUTER Qualitätsstandard.
APPROVED	Ein insgesamt ANGEMESSENER Qualitätsstandard.

Qualitätsgradierungen werden von den Prüfern des Scottish Tourist Board erst verliehen, nachdem sie in den Unterkünften übernachtet, gegessen und sich mit dem Personal unterhalten haben. Diese Gradierungen basieren auf eine umfassende Bewertung von Qualität und Leistungen, wie z.B. ein herzliches Willkommen, Atmosphäre und effizienter Service sowie die Qualität von Möbeln, Einrichtung und Ausstattung. Jede Unterkunft wird nach ihren eigenen Leistungen beurteilt, unabhängig von der angebotenen Auswahl an Einrichtungen.

KRONENKLASSIFIKATION für ANGEBOTENE Einrichrtungen und Service

Wenn Sie ein Hotel, eine Pension oder eine "Bed & Breakfast"- Unterkunft mit folgender Klassifikation buchen, werden Sie mindestens die angegebenen Einrichtungen und Leistungen vorfinden.

HINWEIS: Jede Stufe enthält alle Einrichtungen und Ausstattung der vorherigen Stufen.

👑 👑 👑 👑 👑	Alle Zimmer mit eigenem Bad. Restaurant, in dem Frühstück, Mittag– und Abendessen serviert werden. Nachtportier und Zimmerservice. 24-stündiger Service in der Lounge.
👑 👑 👑 👑	Abendessen, Menüwahl und Auswahl an Weinen. Farbfernsehen, Radio und Telefon in Zimmern. Wäschedienst, Toilettenartikel. Ruhiger Sitzbereich.
👑 👑 👑	Abendessen. Fon. Schuhputzzeug. Bügelmöglichkeiten und Vorrichtungen zur Tee-/Kaffeebereitung.
👑 👑	Farbfernsehen. Tee vor dem Frühstück. Mindestens 20% der Zimmer mit eigenem Bad.
👑	Eigener Zimmerschlüssel. Gemeinschaftlicher Lounge-Bereich. Zimmer mit Waschbecken oder eigenem Bad.
Listed	Saubere und bequeme Unterkunft. Warmes oder kontinentales Frühstück. Angemessene Heizung ohne Aufpreis. Saubere Handtücher und frische Seife. Bettwäsche sauber und in gutem Zustand. Heißes Wasser ohne Aufpreis für Bäder oder Duschbäder.

Die Klassifikation gibt den Umfang der angebotenen Einrichtungen und Leistungen an. Die Klassifikationen reichen von LISTED bis zu 5 KRONEN. Mehr Kronen bedeuten mehr Einrichtungen.

Achten Sie auf dieses
unverwechselbare Zeichen
für Qualitätsunterkünfte

Für ausführliche Einzelheiten zu diesem Schema wenden Sie sich bitte an: The Quality Assurance Department, Visitor Services Division, Scottish Tourist Board, Thistle House, Beechwood Park North, Inverness IV2 3ED. Tel.: (01463) 716996.

Über 4000 von Bedienungspersonal versorgte Unterkünften in allen Landesteilen Schottlands sind Mitglieder des Gradierungs- und Klassifikationsschemas.

SCOTLAND WELCOMES VISITORS WITH DISABILITIES

We want visitors with a disability to get around Scotland and enjoy its attractions, secure in the knowledge that comfortable, suitable accommodation is waiting at the end of the day. Obviously, you need to know in advance just what kind of access and facilities will be available in the accommodation you choose.

Along with the quality grading and classification schemes that apply to all establishments in Scottish Tourist Board guides, we operate a national accessibility scheme. Through it, we can identify and promote places that meet the needs of visitors with a disability.

The three categories of accessibility – drawn up in close consultation with specialist organisations – are:

 Unassisted wheelchair access for residents

 Assisted wheelchair access for residents

 Access for residents with mobility difficulties

Look out for these symbols in establishments, in advertising and brochures. They assure you that entrances, ramps, passageways, doors, restaurant facilities, bathrooms and toilets, as well as kitchens in self-catering properties, have been inspected. Write or telephone for details of the standards in each category – address on page vii.

For more information about travel, accommodation and organisations to help you, write (or ask at a Tourist Information Centre) for the Scottish Tourist Board booklet "Practical Information for Visitors with Disabilities."

Useful advice and information can also be obtained from:

Disability Scotland
Information Department
Princes House
5 Shandwick Place
EDINBURGH EH2 4RG
Tel: (0131) 229 8632

Holiday Care Service
2nd Floor
Imperial Buildings
Victoria Road
Horley, Surrey RH6 7PZ
Tel: (01293) 774535

You can be sure of a warm welcome where you see the Welcome Host sign displayed.

Welcome Host is one of the most exciting and far reaching customer programmes ever developed for the tourism industry. The aim of Welcome Host is to raise the standards of hospitality offered to you during your stay. You will see the Welcome Host badge being worn by a wide variety of people in Scotland (people who have taken part in STB's Welcome Host training programme and have given a personal commitment to providing quality service during your stay). In many organisations you will also see the Welcome Host certificate, displaying an organisation's commitment to the provision of this quality service.

Welcome Hosts are everywhere, from Shetland to Coldstream and from Peterhead to Stornoway and all places in between.

Scotland is famous for its warm welcome and Welcome Hosts will ensure you receive first class service throughout your stay. Look out for the Welcome sign.

From Scotland's natural larder comes a wealth of fine flavours.

The sea yields crab and lobster, mussels and oysters, haddock and herring to be eaten fresh or smoked. From the lochs and rivers come salmon and trout.

Scotch beef and lamb, venison and game are of prime quality, often adventurously combined with local vegetables or with wild fruits such as redcurrants and brambles. Raspberries and strawberries are cultivated to add their sweetness to trifles and shortcakes, and to the home-made jams that are an essential part of Scottish afternoon tea.

The Scots have a sweet tooth, and love all kinds of baking – rich, crisp shortbread, scones, fruit cakes and gingerbreads. Crumbly oatcakes make the ideal partner for Scottish cheeses, which continue to develop from their ancient farming origins into new – and very successful – styles.

And in over a hundred distilleries, barley, yeast and pure spring water come together miraculously to create malt whisky – the water of life.

Many Scottish hotels and restaurants pride themselves on the use they make of these superb natural ingredients – over 300 are members of the Taste of Scotland Scheme which encourages the highest culinary standards, use of Scottish produce, and a warm welcome to visitors. Look for the Stockpot symbol at establishments, or write to Taste of Scotland for a copy of their guide (£5.50 by post or £4.95 in shops).

Taste of Scotland Scheme
33 Melville Street
EDINBURGH
EH3 7JF
Tel: (0131) 220 1900

SCOTLAND'S TOURIST AREAS

1. **South of Scotland**

2. **Edinburgh and Lothians**

3. **Glasgow and The Clyde**

4. **Perthshire, Dundee, Angus
   and the Kingdom of Fife**

5. **West Highlands and Islands,
   Loch Lomond, Stirling and Trossachs**

6. **Grampian Highlands, Aberdeen
   and the North East Coast**

7. **The Highlands and Skye**

8. **Outer Islands**

Area Tourist Boards
Important note: While the information on
pages xix – xxix is correct at the time of
going to press, there will be changes made
to Scotland's Area Tourist Board Network
in 1996. If you have difficulty with any of the
information here, please contact The Scottish
Tourist Board's Central Information
Department: telephone 0131 332 2433

SOUTH OF SCOTLAND
AYRSHIRE AND ARRAN TOURIST BOARD

AYR ✉
Burns' House
16 Burns Statue
Square
Ayr
KA7 1UP
Tel: (01292) 288688
Jan-Dec

BRODICK ✉
The Pier
Brodick
Isle of Arran
Tel: (01770)
302140/302401
Jan-Dec

GIRVAN
Bridge Street
Girvan
Ayrshire
Tel: (01465) 714950
Apr-Oct

IRVINE
New Street
Irvine
KA12 8DG
Tel: (01294) 313886
Jan-Dec

KILMARNOCK ✉
62 Bank Street
Kilmarnock
Ayrshire
Tel: (01563) 539090
Jan-Dec

LARGS ✉
Promenade
Largs
Ayrshire
KA30 8BG
Tel: (01475) 673765
Jan-Dec

LOCHRANZA
The Pier
Lochranza
Isle of Arran
Tel: (01770) 830320
May-Oct

MAUCHLINE
National Burns
Memorial Tower
Kilmarnock Road
Mauchline
Ayrshire
Tel: (01290) 551916
Jan-Dec

MILLPORT ♿
28 Stuart Street
Millport
Isle of Cumbrae
Tel: (01475) 530753
Easter-Sept

TROON
Municipal Buildings
South Beach
Troon
Ayrshire
Tel: (01292) 317696
Easter-Sept

SCOTTISH BORDERS TOURIST BOARD

COLDSTREAM ♿
Town Hall
High Street
Coldstream
Tel: (01890) 882607
Apr-Oct

EYEMOUTH ♿
Auld Kirk
Market Square
Eyemouth
Tel: (018907) 50678
Apr-Oct

GALASHIELS ♿
3 St Johns Street
Galashiels
Tel: (01896) 755551
Apr-Oct

HAWICK
Drumlanrig's Tower
High Street
Hawick
TD9 9EN
Tel: (01450) 372547
Jan-Dec

JEDBURGH ⊠ &
Murray's Green
Jedburgh
TD8 6BE
Tel: (01835) 863435
Jan-Dec

KELSO &
Town House
The Square
Kelso
Tel:(01573) 223464
Apr-Oct

MELROSE
Abbey House
Abbey Street
Melrose
Kelso
Tel: (01896) 822555
Apr-Oct

PEEBLES &
High Street
Peebles
Kelso
Tel: (01721) 720138
Apr-Nov

SELKIRK &
Halliwells House
Selkirk
Tel: (01750) 20054
Apr-Oct

DUMFRIES AND GALLOWAY TOURIST BOARD

CASTLE DOUGLAS
Markethill
Castle Douglas
Tel: (01556) 502611
Easter-Oct

DALBEATTIE
Town Hall
Dalbeattie
Tel: (01556) 610117
Easter-early Oct

DUMFRIES ⊠
Whitesands
Dumfries
Tel: (01387) 253862
Jan-Dec

GATEHOUSE OF
FLEET
Car Park
Gatehouse of Fleet
Tel: (01557) 814212
Easter-Oct

GRETNA
Gateway to Scotland
M74 Service Area
DG16 5HQ
Tel: (01461) 338500
Jan-Dec

GRETNA GREEN &
Old Headless Cross
Gretna Green
Tel: (01461) 337834
Easter-Oct

KIRKCUDBRIGHT &
Harbour Square
Kirkcudbright
Tel: (01557) 330494
Easter-Oct

LANGHOLM
Kilngreen
Langholm
Tel: (01387) 380976
Easter-early Oct

MOFFAT &
Church Gate
Moffat
Tel: (01683) 20620
Easter-Oct

NEWTON STEWART
Dashwood Square
Newton Stewart
Tel. (01671) 402431

SANQUHAR &
Tolbooth
High Street
Sanquhar
Tel: (01659) 50185
Easter-early Oct

STRANRAER &
1 Bridge Street
Stanraer
Tel: (01776) 702595
Easter-Oct

EDINBURGH AND LOTHIANS

DUNBAR ✉ ♿
143 High Street
Dunbar
TEL: (01368) 863353
Jan-Dec

DALKEITH
The Library
White Hart Street
Dalkeith
Midlothian
Tel: (0131) 663 2083
Jan-Dec

**EDINBURGH AND
SCOTLAND
INFORMATION
CENTRE** ✉ ♿
3 Princes Street
Edinburgh
EH2 2QP
Tel: (0131) 557 1700
Jan-Dec

**EDINBURGH
AIRPORT** ♿
Tourist Information
Desk
Main Concourse
next to Bureau de
Change
Edinburgh Airport
Edinburgh
EH12 9DN
Tel: (0131) 333 2167
Jan-Dec

LINLITHGOW ✉
Burgh Halls
The Cross
Linlithgow
Tel: (01506) 844600
Jan-Dec

MUSSELBURGH ♿
Brunton Hall
Musselburgh
East Lothian
Tel: (0131) 665 6597
June-end Sept

NEWTONGRANGE
Scottish Mining
Museum
Lady Victoria Colliery
Newtongrange
Tel: (0131) 663 4262
April-Oct

NORTH BERWICK
✉ ♿
Quality Street
North Berwick
Dunbar
Tel: (01620) 892197
Jan-Dec

OLDCRAIGHALL
✉ ♿
Granada Service Area
A1
Oldcraighall
Musselburgh
Tel: (0131) 653 6172
Jan-Dec

PENCRAIG
A1
By East Linton
East Lothian
Tel: (01620) 860063
Apr-end Sept

PENICUIK
Edinburgh Crystal
Visitor Centre
Penicuik
Midlothian
Tel: (01968) 673846
May-Oct

GLASGOW AND THE CLYDE

ABINGTON
Welcome Break
Service Area
Junction 13, M74
Abington
Tel: (01864) 502436
Jan-Dec

BIGGAR ♿
155 High Street
Biggar
Lanarkshire
Tel: (01899) 21066
Easter-Oct

COATBRIDGE
The Time Capsule
Buchanan Street
Coatbridge
Tel: (01236) 431133
Apr-Oct

GLASGOW ✉
35 St Vincent Place
Glasgow
G1 2ER
Tel: (0141) 204 4400
Jan-Dec

HAMILTON ♿
Road Chef Services
M74 Northbound
Hamilton
Tel: (01698) 285590
Jan-Dec

PAISLEY
Town Hall
Abbey Close
Paisley
Tel: (0141) 889 0711
Apr-Nov

GLASGOW AIRPORT
Tourist Information
Desk
Glasgow Airport
Paisley
Tel: (0141) 848 4440
Jan-Dec

LANARK ✉ ♿
Horsemarket
Ladyacre Road
Lanark
ML11 7LQ
Tel: (01555) 661661
Jan-Dec

GOUROCK
Pierhead
Gourock
Tel: (01475) 639467
Apr-Sept

MOTHERWELL ✉
Motherwell Library
Hamilton Road
Motherwell
Tel: (01698) 267676
Jan-Dec

PERTHSHIRE, DUNDEE, ANGUS AND THE KINGDOM OF FIFE
ANGUS AND CITY OF DUNDEE TOURIST BOARD

ARBROATH ✉
Market Place
Arbroath
Angus DD11 1HR
Tel: (01241) 872609
Jan-Dec

DUNDEE ✉ ♿
4 City Square
Dundee
DD1 3BA
Tel: (01382) 434664
Jan-Dec

MONTROSE
Bridge Street
Montrose
Tel: (01674) 672000
Apr-early Oct

BRECHIN
St Ninians Place
Brechin
Angus
Tel: (01356) 623050

FORFAR
40 East High Street
Forfar
Tel: (01307) 467876
Apr-early Oct

CARNOUSTIE
High Street
Carnoustie
Tel: (01241) 852258
Apr-early Oct

KIRRIEMUIR
1 Cumberland Close
Kirriemuir
Tel: (01575) 574097
Apr-early Oct

KINGDOM OF FIFE TOURIST BOARD

ANSTRUTHER
Scottish Fisheries
Museum
Anstruther
Tel: (01333) 311073
Easter, May-Sept

BURNTISLAND ⊠
4 Kirkgate
Burntisland
Tel: (01592) 872667
Jan-Dec

CRAIL
Museum & Heritage
Centre
Marketgate
Crail
Tel: (01333) 450869
June-Sept

CUPAR ♿
Coal Road
Cupar
Fife
Tel: (01334) 652874
Jun-Sept

DUNFERMLINE
13/15 Maygate
Dunfermline
KY12 7NE
Tel: (01383) 720999
Jan-Dec

FORTH ROAD
BRIDGE
Queensferry Lodge
Hotel
St Margarets Head
North Queensferry
Tel: (01383) 417759
Jan-Dec (unstaffed
Nov-Mar)

GLENROTHES
Rothes Halls
Rothes Square
Glenrothes
Fife
KY7 5NX
Tel: (01592) 754954
Jan-Dec

KIRKCALDY ⊠
19 Whytescauseway
Kirkcaldy
Tel: (01592) 267775
Jan-Dec

LEVEN ⊠
The Beehive
Durie Street
Leven
Tel: (01333) 429464
Jan-Dec

ST ANDREWS ⊠
70 Market Street
St Andrews
KY16 9NU
Tel: (01334) 472021
Jan-Dec

PERTHSHIRE TOURIST BOARD

ABERFELDY ♿
The Square
Aberfeldy
Tel: (01887) 820276
Jan-Dec

AUCHTERARDER
90 High Street
Auchterarder
Tel: (01764) 664235
Jan-Dec

BLAIRGOWRIE ♿
26 Wellmeadow
Blairgowrie
Perthshire
Tel: (01250)
872960/873701
Jan-Dec

CRIEFF ♿
Town Hall
High Street
Crieff
Tel: (01764) 652578
Jan-Dec

DUNKELD ♿
The Cross
Dunkeld
Perthshire
Tel: (01350) 727688
March-Oct

KINROSS ♿
Service Area Junction
6 M90
Kinross
Tel: (01577) 863680
Jan-Dec

PERTH ✉ ♿
45 High Street
Perth
PH1 5TJ
Tel: (01738) 638353
Jan-Dec

PERTH -
Inveralmond ♿
Inveralmond
A9 Western City By-pass
Perth
Tel: (01738) 638481
Easter-Oct

PITLOCHRY ✉ ♿
22 Atholl Road
Pitlochry
Perthshire
PH16 5BX
Tel: (01796)
472215/472751
Jan-Dec

WEST HIGHLANDS AND ISLANDS, LOCH LOMOND, STIRLING & TROSSACHS

ABERFOYLE ♿
Main Street
Aberfoyle
Perthshire
FK8 3TH
Tel: (01877) 382352
Apr-Oct

ALVA
Scotland's Mill Trail
Visitor Centre
Glentana Mills
West Stirling Street
Alva
Tel: (01259) 769696
Jan-Dec

BALLOCH ♿
Balloch Road
Balloch
Dunbartonshire
Tel: (01389) 753533
March-Nov

BO'NESS
62 Union Street
Bo'ness
Tel: (01506) 826626
Easter-Sept

BOWMORE
The Square
Bowmore
Isle of Islay
Tel: (01496) 810254
Jan-Dec

CALLANDER ♿
Rob Roy & Trossachs
Visitor Centre
Ancaster Square
Callander
Perthshire
Tel: (01877) 330784
March-Dec

CAMPBELTOWN ✉
Mackinnon House
The Pier
Campbeltown
Tel: (01586) 552056
Jan-Dec

CRAIGNURE
The Pierhead
Craignure
Isle of Mull
Tel: (01680) 812377
Jan-Dec

DRYMEN
The Square
Drymen
Tel: (01360) 660068
Jan-Oct

DUMBARTON
A82 Northbound
Milton
Dumbarton
Tel: (01389) 742306
Apr-Oct

DUNBLANE ♿
Stirling Road
Dunblane
Stirlingshire
Tel: (01786) 824428
May-Sept

DUNOON ✉
7 Alexandra Parade
Dunoon
PA23 9AB
Tel: (01369) 703785
Jan-Dec

FALKIRK ✉
2-4 Glebe Street
Falkirk
Tel: (01324) 620244
Jan-Dec

HELENSBURGH &
The Clock Tower
Helensburgh
Dunbartonshire
Tel: (01436) 672642
Apr-Oct

INVERARAY
Front Street
Inveraray
Argyll
Tel: (01499) 302063
Jan-Dec

KILLIN &
Main Street
Killin
Perthshire
Tel: (01567) 820254
Apr-Oct

KINCARDINE
BRIDGE
Pine 'N' Oak Lay-by
Airth
by Falkirk
Tel: (01324) 831422
Easter-Sept

LOCHGILPHEAD
Lochnell Street
Lochgilphead
Argyll
Tel: (01564) 602344
April-Oct

OBAN ✉ &
Boswell House
Argyll Square
Oban
Tel: (01631) 63122
Jan-Dec

ROTHESAY ✉
15 Victoria Street
Rothesay
Isle of Bute
PA20 0AJ
Tel: (01700) 502151
Jan-Dec

STIRLING ✉ &
Dumbarton Road
Stirling
FK8 2QQ
Tel: (01786) 475019
Jan-Dec

STIRLING ✉ &
Royal Burgh of Stirling
Visitor Centre
Stirling
Tel: (01786) 479901
Jan-Dec

STIRLING &
Pirnhall Motorway
Service Area, Jct 9
(M9)
Pirnhall
By Stirling
Tel: (01786) 814111
March-Nov

TARBERT - LOCH
LOMOND
Main Street
Tarbert
Dunbartonshire
Tel: (01301) 70260
April-Oct

TARBERT
Harbour Street
Tarbert
Argyll
Tel: (01880) 820429
April-Oct

TOBERMORY
Main Street
Tobermory
Isle of Mull
Tel: (01688) 302182
Jan-Dec

TYNDRUM
Main Street
Tyndrum
Perthshire
Tel: (01838) 400246
Apr-Oct

GRAMPIAN HIGHLANDS, ABERDEEN & THE NORTH EAST COAST

ABERDEEN ✉ &
St Nicholas House
Broad Street
Aberdeen
AB9 1DE
Tel: (01224) 632727
Jan-Dec

ABOYNE
Ballater Road Car Park
Aboyne
Tel: (013398) 86060
Apr-Oct

ADEN
Aden Country Park
Mintlaw
Tel: (01771) 623037
Apr-Oct

ALFORD ♿
Railway Museum
Station Yard
Alford AB3 8AD
Tel: (019755) 62052
Mid Apr-Oct

BALLATER
Station Square
Ballater
Tel: (013397) 55306
Apr-End Oct

BANCHORY ✉
Bridge Street
Banchory
AB31 3SX
Tel: (01330) 822000
Jan-Dec

BANFF ✉
Collie Lodge
Banff AB45 1AU
Tel: (01261) 812419
Apr-Oct

BRAEMAR ✉
The Mews
Mar Road
Braemar
Tel: (013397) 41600
Jan-Dec

BUCKIE
Cluny Square
Buckie
Tel: (01542) 834853
Mid May-Sept

CRATHIE
Car Park
Balmoral Castle
Crathie
Tel: (013397) 42414
Apr-Sept

CULLEN
20 Seafield Street
Cullen
Tel: (01542) 840757
Mid May-Sept

DUFFTOWN
Clock Tower
The Square
Dufftown
Tel: (01340) 820501
Easter-Nov

ELGIN ✉
17 High Street
Elgin
IV30 1EG
Tel: (01343) 542666
Jan-Dec

ELLON
Market Street Car Park
Ellon AB4 8JD
Tel: (01358) 720730
Late March-Oct

FORRES
116 High Street
Forres
Tel: (01309) 672938
Easter-Oct

FRASERBURGH
Saltoun Square
Fraserburgh
Tel: (01346) 518315
Apr-Oct

HUNTLY ♿
7a The Square
Huntly
AB5 5AE
Tel: (01466) 792255

INVERURIE
Town Hall
Market Place
Inverurie
AB5 9SN
Tel: (01467) 620600
Mid Apr-Oct

KEITH
Church Road
Keith
Tel: (01542) 882634
Mid May-Sept

PETERHEAD
54 Broad Street
Peterhead
Tel: (01779) 471904
Apr-Oct

STONEHAVEN
66 Allardice Street
Stonehaven
Tel: (01569) 762806
Mid Apr-Oct

TOMINTOUL
The Square
Tomintoul
Tel: (01807) 580285
Easter-Oct

TURRIFF
High Street
Turriff
Tel: (01888) 563001
Apr-Oct

AVIEMORE ✉ ♿
Grampian Road
Aviemore
Inverness-shire
Tel: (01479) 810363
Jan-Dec

BALLACHULISH
Ballachulish
Argyll
Tel: (01855)811296
Apr-Oct

BETTYHILL ♿
Clachan
Bettyhill
Sutherland
Tel: (01641) 521342
Apr-Sept

BROADFORD
Car Park
Broadford
Isle of Skye
Tel: (01471) 822361
Apr-Oct

CARRBRIDGE
Main Street
Carrbridge
Inverness-shire
Tel: (01479) 841630
May-Sept

DAVIOT WOOD
A9
By Inverness
Tel: (01463) 772203
Apr-Oct

DORNOCH ✉
The Square
Dornoch
Sutherland
IV25 3SD
Tel: (01862) 810400
Jan-Dec

DURNESS ♿
Sango
Durness
Sutherland
Tel: (01971) 511259
Apr-Oct

FORT AUGUSTUS
The Car Park
Fort Augustus
Tel: (01320) 366367
Apr-Oct

FORT WILLIAM ✉ ♿
Cameron Square
Fort William
Tel: (01397) 703781
Jan-Dec

GAIRLOCH ✉ ♿
Auchtercairn
Gairloch
Ross-shire
Tel: (01445) 712130
Jan-Dec

GRANTOWN-ON-
SPEY ♿
High Street
Grantown-on-Spey
Morayshire
Tel: (01479) 872773
Apr-Oct

HELMSDALE ♿
Coupar Park
Helmsdale
Sutherland
Tel: (01431) 820640
Apr-Sept

INVERNESS ✉
Castle Wynd
Inverness
IV2 3BJ
Tel: (01463) 234353
Jan-Dec

JOHN O'GROATS
Country Road
John O'Groats
Tel: (01955) 611373
Apr-Sept

KILCHOAN
Argyll
Tel: (01972) 510222
Apr-Sept

KINGUSSIE
King Street
Kingussie
Tel: (01540) 661297
May-Sept

KYLE OF LOCHALSH
Car Park
Kyle of Lochalsh
Ross-shire
Tel: (01599) 534276
Apr-Oct

LAIRG
Ferrycroft
Lairg
Sutherland
Tel: (01549) 402160
Easter-Oct

LOCHCARRON ♿
Main Street
Lochcarron
Ross-shire
Tel:(01520) 722357
April-Oct

LOCHINVER ♿
Main Street
Lochinver
Sutherland
Tel: (01571) 844330
Apr-Oct

MALLAIG ✉ ♿
Mallaig
Inverness-shire
Tel: (01687) 462170
Apr-Sept

NAIRN
62 King Street
Nairn
Tel: (01667) 452753
Apr-Oct

NORTH KESSOCK
✉ ♿
North Kessock
Ross-shire
Tel: (01463) 731505
Jan-Dec

PORTREE ✉
Meall House
Portree
Isle of Skye
IV51 9BZ
Tel: (01478) 612137
Jan-Dec

RALIA ♿
A9, Nr Newtonmore
Inverness-shire
Tel: (01540) 673253
Apr-Oct

SHIEL BRIDGE
Glenshiel
Kyle of Lochalsh
Ross-shire
Tel: (01599) 511264
Apr-Sept

SPEAN BRIDGE
Spean Bridge
Inverness-shire
Tel: (01397) 712576
Apr-Sept

STRONTIAN
Strontian
Argyll
Tel: (01967) 402131
April-Oct

THURSO
Riverside
Thurso
Tel: (01847) 892371
Apr-Oct

UIG
Ferry Terminal
The Pier
Uig
Tel: (01470) 542404
Easter-Oct

ULLAPOOL
Argyle Street
Ullapool
Tel: (01854) 612135
Easter-Nov

WICK ✉
Whitechapel Road
Wick
KW1 4EA
Tel: (01955) 602596
Jan-Dec

OUTER ISLANDS
ORKNEY TOURIST BOARD

KIRKWALL ✉
6 Broad Street
Kirkwall
Orkney
Tel: (01856) 872856
Jan-Dec

STROMNESS
Ferry Terminal
Building
Stromness
Orkney
Tel: (01856) 850716
Jan-Dec

SHETLAND ISLANDS TOURISM

LERWICK ⊠
Market Cross
Lerwick
Shetland ZE1 0LU
Tel: (01595) 693434
Jan-Dec

WESTERN ISLES TOURIST BOARD

CASTLEBAY
Main Street
Castlebay
Isle of Barra
Tel: (01871) 810336
Easter-Oct

LOCHMADDY
Pier Road
Lochmaddy
Isle of North Uist
Tel: (01876) 500231
Easter-Oct

LOCHBOISDALE
Pier Road
Lochboisdale
Isle of South Uist
Tel: (01878) 700286
Easter-Oct

STORNOWAY ⊠
4 South Beach Street
Stornoway
Isle of Lewis
PA87 2DD
Tel: (01851) 703088
Jan-Dec

Getting around

Scotland is a small country and travel is easy. There are direct air links with UK cities, with Europe and North America. There is also an internal air network bringing the islands of the North and West within easy reach.

Scotland's rail network not only includes excellent cross-border InterCity services but also a good internal network. All major towns are linked by rail and there are also links to the western seaboard at Mallaig and Kyle of Lochalsh (for ferry connections to Skye and the Western Isles) and to Inverness, Thurso and Wick for ferries to Orkney and Shetland.

All the usual discount cards are valid but there are also ScotRail Rovers (multi journey tickets allowing you to save on rail fares) and the Freedom of Scotland Travelpass, a combined rail and ferry pass allowing unlimited travel on ferry services to the islands and all of the rail network. In addition Travelpass also offers discounts on bus services and some air services.

InterCity services are available from all major centres, for example: Birmingham, Carlisle, Crewe, Manchester, Newcastle, Penzance, Peterborough, Preston, Plymouth, York and many others.

There are frequent InterCity departures from Kings Cross and Euston stations to Edinburgh and Glasgow. The journey time from Kings Cross to Edinburgh is around 4 hours and from Euston to Glasgow around 5 hours.

Coach connections include express services to Scotland from all over the UK; local bus companies in Scotland offer explorer tickets and discount cards. Postbuses (normally minibuses) take passengers on over 130 rural routes throughout Scotland.

Ferries to and around the islands are regular and reliable, most ferries carry vehicles, although some travelling to smaller islands convey only passengers.

Contact the Information Department, Scottish Tourist Board, PO Box 705, Edinburgh EH4 3EU, or any Tourist Information Centre, for details of travel and transport.

Many visitors choose to see Scotland by road – distances are short and driving on the quiet roads of the Highlands is a new and different experience. In remoter areas, some roads are still single track, and passing places must be used. When vehicles approach from different directions, the car nearest to a passing place must stop in or opposite it. Please do not use passing places to park in!

Speed limits on Scottish roads: Dual carriageways 70mph/112kph; single carriageways 60mph/96kph; built-up areas 30mph/48kph.

The driver and front-seat passenger in a car must wear seatbelts; rear seatbelts, if fitted, must be used. Small children and babies must at all times be restrained in a child seat or carrier.

Opening times

Public holidays: Christmas and New Year's Day are holidays in Scotland, taken by almost everyone. Scottish banks, and many offices, will close in 1996 on 1 and 2 January, 5 and 8 April, 6 and 27 May, 26 August, 25 and 26 December. Scottish towns also take Spring and Autumn holidays which may vary from place to place, but are usually on a Monday.

Banking hours: In general, banks open Monday to Friday, 0930 to 1600, with some closing later on a Thursday. Banks in cities, particularly in or near the main shopping centres, may be open at weekends. Cash machines in hundreds of branches allow you to withdraw cash outside banking hours, using the appropriate cards.

Pubs and restaurants: Licensing laws in Scotland generally allow bars to service alcoholic drinks between 1100 and 1430, and from 1700 to 2300, Monday to Saturday. Most are also licensed to open on Sundays; some open in the afternoon, or later at night. Hotel bars have the same hours as pubs except for Sunday, when they open 1230 to 1430, and 1830 to 2300. Residents in hotels may have drinks served at any time.

Telephone codes

If you are calling from abroad, first dial your own country's international access code (usually 00, but do please check). Next, dial the UK code, 44, then the area code except for the first 0, then the remainder of the number as normal.

Quarantine regulations

If you are coming to Scotland from overseas, please do not attempt to bring your pet on holiday with you. British quarantine regulations are stringently enforced, and anyone attempting to contravene them will incur severe penalties as well as the loss of the animal.

In the same way that you want to be sure of the standard of accommodation you choose to stay in while on holiday in Scotland, you also want to be sure you make the most of your time.

The Scottish Tourist Board has introduced a quality assurance scheme for Visitor Attractions which provides valuable information on the quality of such attractions as castles, museums, gardens, nature reserves, leisure centres and much more.

The Scottish Tourist Board awards provide you with an assurance that an attraction has been independently verified by one of our inspectors, who have assessed the condition and standard of facilities and services provided.

The three Quality grades are;

 acceptable quality standard

 good quality standard

 very good quality standard

The Scottish Tourist Board Quality Assurance Scheme for Visitor Attractions is integrated with our Accommodation Scheme so you can follow the STB quality trail night and day.

PASSPORT TO THE ISLANDS

Staying on an island is a very special experience – the ferry crossing, even if it's only a few minutes long, adds a special magic to any trip.

To find accommodation in island locations in this guide, you need to look under the name of the island itself (if it is one of the smaller ones), or under the name of the appropriate town on the island (if it is larger). On Arran, for example, locations to check include Brodick, Lamlash, Whiting Bay and so on. This index tells you the names to look up for the island that interests you, together with references for the maps on pages xxxv to xl.
Happy hunting!

MAPS

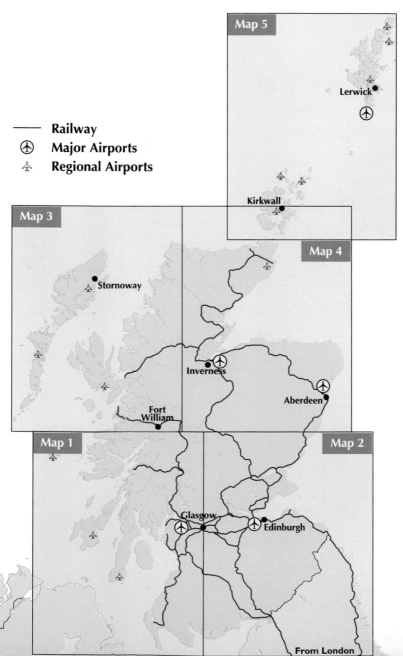

Map 5

Map 3

Map 4

Map 1

Map 2

—— Railway
⊕ Major Airports
⊁ Regional Airports

Lerwick

Kirkwall

Stornoway

Inverness

Aberdeen

Fort
William

Glasgow

Edinburgh

From London

MAP 1

These maps are for "Bed & Breakfast" location only. Holiday attractions and touring routes can be found on the Scotland Touring Map published by the Scottish Tourist Board.

Car ferries and terminals:

Brodick - - - - Rothesay

Scale 1:1 300 000

0   10   20 miles

© Bartholomew, 1995

MAP 2

1 2 3 4 5 6 7 8 9 10 11 12

A B C D E F G H

Pitlochry · Ballintuim · Kirriemuir · Lunan
gall · Aberfeldy · Alyth · Forfar
Kenmore · Blairgowrie · Glamis
an · Dunkeld · Meigle · Arbroath
· Coupar Angus

Amulree · Cargill · Burrelton · Carnoustie
Bankfoot · Stanley
Luncarty · Scone · Dundee · Newport-on-Tay
· Perth

ie · Crieff · Newburgh · St Andrews
Abernethy

Auchterarder · Cupar · Kingsbarns
Blackford · Auchtermuchty · Freuchie · Peat Inn · Crail
· Milnathort · Falkland · Anstruther
e · Dunblane · Kinross · Glenrothes · Markinch
ir Drummond · Scotlandwell · St Monans
· Ballingry · Elie

Tillicoultry · Lassodie · Kirkcaldy
Saline · Burntisland
Dunfermline · North Berwick
Newmills · Aberdour · Whitekirk
Falkirk · Dalgety Bay · Gullane · Dunbar
Grangemouth · Inverkeithing · East
Bonnybridge · Bo'ness · South Queensferry · Longniddry · Linton
Cumbernauld · Linlithgow · Cockburnspath
bridge · Uphall · Ratho · Tranent · St Abbs
Livingston · EDINBURGH · Musselburgh · Haddington · Coldingham · Eyemouth
Airdrie · East · Lasswade · Dalkeith · Gifford · Reston · Burnmouth
Calder · Loanhead · Pathhead · Ayton
Penicuik · Gorebridge · Duns · Berwick-upon-Tweed

Kirkmuirhill · West · Lauder · Leitholm
aven · Linton · Peebles · Eccles · Coldstream
Lanark · Walkerburn · Earlston · Birgham
Biggar · Innerleithen · Galashiels · Melrose · Kelso
uglas · Ettrickbridge · Newtown · Yetholm
· Selkirk · St Boswells · Morebattle
Abington · Jedburgh
Crawford · Hawick · Denholm

nquhar · Moffat
Thornhill · Beattock

Newcastleton
Lockerbie · Canonbie
Dumfries · Eaglesfield · Newcastle upon Tyne · Sunderland
Ecclefechan · Kirkpatrick Fleming
Dalbeattie · Gretna Green · Gretna
Kippford · Kirkbean · Carlisle · Middlesbrough
holm · Rockcliffe
udbright · Auchencairn

NORTH SEA

Solway Firth

Firth of Forth
Firth of Tay

MAP 3

These maps are for "Bed & Breakfast" location only. Holiday attractions and touring routes can be found on the Scotland Touring Map published by the Scottish Tourist Board.

MAP 3   MAP 4

OUTER HEBRIDES

LEWIS

Port of Ness

South Shawbost

Back

Callanish   Stornoway   Aignish

Achmore

Scourie

Drumbeg   Kyles

Lochinver

Ullapool

HARRIS

Tarbert

Scadabay

Leverburgh

The Minch

Berneray

Otternish

Sollas

Lochmaddy

NORTH UIST

Grimsay

Glendale

Liniclate   BENBECULA

SOUTH UIST

Lochboisdale

Ludag
Eriskay

BARRA

Castlebay

Kilmuir

Uig

Glenhinnisdale

Treaslane   Kensaleyre

Bernisdale

Dunvegan

Portree

Struan   RAASAY

Raasay

Sconser

SKYE

Aultbea   Laide

Dundonnell

Poolewe

Gairloch   Badachro

Loch Maree

Diabaig

Shieldaig   Torridon

Kishorn

Lochcarron

Plockton   Stromeferry

Duirinish   Ardelve

Balmacara

Kyle of Lochalsh   Dornie

Broadford   Glenelg

Breakish

Kylerhea

Ord   Isleornsay

Elgol   Teangue

Armadale   Kilmore

CANNA

RUM

EIGG   Loch Morar

MUCK

Mallaig

Morar

Arisaig

Ardnamurchan   Acharacle

Kilchoan

Kinlochewe

Strathcarron

Glenshiel

Invergarry

Invergloy

Corpach
Fort William

Onich   Kinlochleven

MAP 4

MAP 5

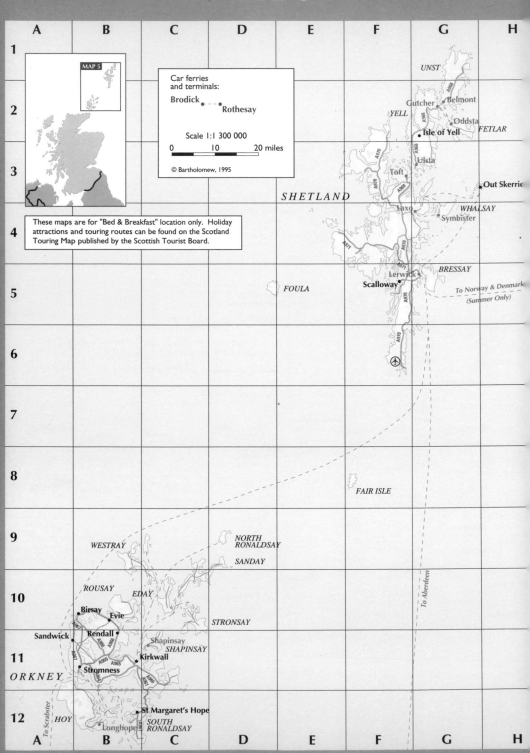

MAP 5

Car ferries
and terminals:

Brodick •- - -• Rothesay

Scale 1:1 300 000

0   10   20 miles

© Bartholomew, 1995

These maps are for "Bed & Breakfast" location only. Holiday
attractions and touring routes can be found on the Scotland
Touring Map published by the Scottish Tourist Board.

UNST

YELL Gutcher • Belmont

• Oddsta

• Isle of Yell *FETLAR*

Ulsta

Toft

SHETLAND • Out Skerrie

Laxo *WHALSAY*

• Symbister

BRESSAY

Lerwick •

Scalloway • To Norway & Denmark
(Summer Only)

FOULA

FAIR ISLE

WESTRAY *NORTH
RONALDSAY*

SANDAY

ROUSAY *EDAY*

Birsay • Evie *STRONSAY*

Sandwick Rendall •

Shapinsay *SHAPINSAY*

Kirkwall •

Stromness •

ORKNEY

To Scrabster *HOY* St Margaret's Hope

Longhope *SOUTH
RONALDSAY*

To Aberdeen

SCOTLAND

BED & BREAKFAST
1996

ABERCHIRDER, by Huntly **Banffshire** Mrs E Gregor Skeibhill Farm Aberchirder Banffshire AB54 5TT Tel: (Aberchirder) 01466 780301	Map 4 F8	COMMENDED Listed	2 Family	1 Pub Bath/Show	B&B per person from £12.50 Single from £11.50 Double	Open Jan-Dec Dinner 1800-2000 B&B + Eve. Meal £18.50

Home cooking and baking on friendly working family farm.
Close to Castle and Whisky Trails. 8 miles (13kms) from Banff; 11 miles (17kms) from Huntly.

ABERDEEN Abbotswell Guest House 28 Abbotswell Crescent Aberdeen AB1 5AR Tel: (Aberdeen) 01224 871788 Fax: 01224 891257	Map 4 G10	COMMENDED Listed	4 Single 2 Twin 5 Double 1 Family	7 En Suite fac 3 Pub Bath/Show	B&B per person £20.00-£25.00 Single £16.00-£20.00 Double	Open Jan-Dec Dinner at 1800 B&B + Eve. Meal £26.00-£35.00

Recently modernised bungalow with garden.
Close to industrial estate and only 1.5 miles (2.5kms) from city centre.

Aberdeen Nicoll's Guest House 63 Springbank Terrace Aberdeen AB1 2JZ Tel: (Aberdeen) 01224 572867	COMMENDED Listed	3 Twin 1 Double 2 Family	2 En Suite fac 2 Pub Bath/Show	B&B per person £18.00-£20.00 Single £14.00-£16.00 Double	Open Jan-Dec

Family run, granite terraced guest house. Centrally located within
0.25 miles (0.5km) of city centre shops; 1 mile (2kms) from Duthie Park.

The Angel Islington Guest House 191 Bon Accord Street Aberdeen AB1 2UA Tel: (Aberdeen) 01224 587043	COMMENDED Listed	2 Single 1 Twin 2 Double 1 Family	1 En Suite fac 3 Pub Bath/Show	B&B per person £18.00-£25.00 Single £15.00-£20.00 Double	Open Jan-Dec

Semi-detached granite built Victorian house in residential area on south side of city.
Shops, railway station and Duthie Park within 1 mile (2kms).

Antrim Guest House 157 Crown Street Aberdeen AB1 2HT Tel: (Aberdeen) 01224 590987 Fax: 01224 575826	APPROVED Listed	3 Single 3 Twin 1 Family	3 Pub Bath/Show	B&B per person £20.00-£22.00 Single £14.00-£15.00 Double	Open Jan-Dec

Situated close to city centre, railway and bus stations. Private parking.

Arkaig Guest House 43 Powis Terrace Aberdeen AB2 3PP Tel: (Aberdeen) 01224 638872 Fax: 01224 622189	COMMENDED	4 Single 2 Twin 2 Double 1 Family	7 En Suite fac 1 Pub Bath/Show	B&B per person £17.00-£26.00 Single £19.00-£20.00 Double	Open Jan-Dec Dinner 1700-1830 B&B + Eve. Meal £25.50-£34.50

Traditional granite house; city centre 0.5 mile (1km).
Convenient to places of interest, station, harbour, airport, both universities and hospital.

Bimini 69 Constitution Street Aberdeen AB2 1ET Tel: (Aberdeen) 01224 646912 Fax: 01224 646912	COMMENDED	1 Single 4 Twin 1 Double 1 Family	2 Pub Bath/Show	B&B per person £18.00-£20.00 Single £17.00-£19.00 Double	Open Jan-Dec

Personally run guest house. In residential area close to centre and all local amenities.
Car park to rear.

Bracadale Guest House 391 Holburn Street Aberdeen AB1 6DR Tel: (Aberdeen) 01224 573036	COMMENDED Listed	1 Single 3 Twin 2 Double	2 En Suite fac 2 Pub Bath/Show	B&B per person £20.00-£25.00 Single £18.00-£20.00 Double	Open Jan-Dec

Warm and friendly welcome to this family run guest house in centre of city.
Close to shops, museums, and theatre also main tourist routes

Campbell's Guest House 444 King Street Aberdeen AB2 3BS Tel: (Aberdeen) 01224 625444/ 0831 162201 (mobile) Fax: 01224 624556	COMMENDED	1 Single 2 Twin 1 Double 2 Family	4 En Suite fac 1 Pub Bath/Show	B&B per person £22.00-£30.00 Single £17.00-£20.00 Double	Open Jan-Dec

Semi-detached house, own car park and on main bus route. City centre 1 mile (2kms).
Close to golf links, sandy beach, leisure centre and University.

John Crawford Hayfield Equestrian Centre Hazlehead Park Aberdeen AB1 8BB Tel: (Aberdeen) 01224 313834 Fax: 01224 313834	APPROVED Listed	4 Single 2 Twin 2 Double 2 Family	8 Priv.NOT ensuite 2 Pub Bath/Show	B&B per person £15.00-£25.00 Single £15.00-£20.00 Double Room only per person £15.00-£20.00	Open Jan-Dec Dinner 1730-1830 B&B + Eve. Meal £20.00-£25.00	

Accommodation at one of Scotland's premier riding centres offering pleasure riding or holiday courses for all ages.

The Four Bees Guest House 356 Holburn Street Aberdeen AB1 6DX Tel: (Aberdeen) 01224 585110	COMMENDED Listed	1 Single 2 Twin 2 Double 2 Family	1 En Suite fac 2 Pub Bath/Show	B&B per person £14.00-£18.00 Single £14.00-£18.00 Double Room only per person £14.00-£18.00	Open Jan-Dec	

Traditional granite house with long garden, set back from the road. Convenient for city centre and all amenities. On main bus routes.

FURAIN GUEST HOUSE

North Deeside Road, Peterculter, Aberdeen AB1 0QN
Telephone: 01224 732189

FURAIN GUEST HOUSE, on the A93, 8 miles west of Aberdeen centre, close to several historic castles and convenient for touring some of the most beautiful countryside in the UK. We give a full Scottish breakfast with choice, special diets catered for.

Furain Guest House 92 North Deeside Road Peterculter Aberdeen AB1 0QN Tel: (Aberdeen) 01224 732189	COMMENDED	1 Single 3 Twin 2 Double 2 Family	8 En Suite fac 1 Pub Bath/Show	B&B per person £27.00-£30.00 Single £18.50-£21.00 Double	Open Jan-Dec Dinner 1900-2100 B&B + Eve. Meal £29.00-£40.00	

Late Victorian house built of red granite. Family run, convenient for town, Royal Deeside and the Castle Trail. Private car parking.

Kingswood House 422 Great Western Road Aberdeen AB1 6NQ Tel: (Aberdeen) 01224 323368	COMMENDED Listed	2 Single 1 Double 2 Family	1 Limited ensuite 1 Pub Bath/Show	B&B per person £20.00-£24.00 Single £15.00-£18.00 Double	Open Jan-Dec	

Granite-built Victorian town house, personally run and situated a short distance from town centre; on main bus route.

Klibreck Guest House 410 Great Western Road Aberdeen AB1 6NR Tel: (Aberdeen) 01224 316115	COMMENDED	1 Single 3 Twin 1 Double 1 Family	2 Pub Bath/Show	B&B per person from £20.00 Single from £15.00 Double	Open Jan-Dec	

Granite building, corner site in residential area in city's West End. On main bus route to city centre and Royal Deeside. Off-road parking.

Mrs Margaret Laing 20 Louisville Avenue Aberdeen AB1 6TX Tel: (Aberdeen) 01224 319812	COMMENDED	1 Single 1 Twin 1 Family	1 Pub Bath/Show	B&B per person £16.00-£18.00 Single £15.00-£17.00 Double	Open Jan-Dec	

Terraced granite house in quiet residential area 2 miles (3 kms) from city centre. Close to main Inverness, Braemar and Perth roads.

Mrs Macklin Regency Rooms 89 Crown Street Aberdeen AB1 2HH Tel: (Aberdeen) 01224 211600 Fax: 01224 211884	COMMENDED Listed	4 Single 4 Twin 1 Double	9 En Suite fac 1 Pub Bath/Show	B&B per person to £34.90 Single to £17.45 Double	Open Jan-Dec	

Beautifully appointed rooms with first class facilities. City centre location.

ABERDEEN, continued	Map 4 G10					
Norman & Mary Marshall Manorville 252 Great Western Road Aberdeen AB1 6PJ Tel: (Aberdeen) 01224 594190 Fax: 01224 594190	COMMENDED 👑👑	1 Twin 1 Double 1 Family	3 En Suite fac	B&B per person £25.00-£28.00 Single £18.00-£22.00 Double	Open Jan-Dec	

Granite dwelling house in close proximity to town centre on main bus route to Deeside.
All rooms ensuite.

| Mrs Vera Naughton Miller 5 Cairnvale Crescent Aberdeen AB1 5JB Tel: (Aberdeen) 01224 874163 | COMMENDED Listed | 1 Single 1 Double | 1 Pub Bath/Show | B&B per person £16.00-£17.00 Single £13.50-£14.00 Double | Open Jan-Dec | |

Semi-detached non-smoking family house in quiet residential street.
2 miles (3 kms) from city centre. On main bus route. Convenient for Deeside.

| Royal Crown Guest House 111 Crown Street Aberdeen AB1 2HH Tel: (Aberdeen) 01224 586461 | COMMENDED Listed | 2 Single 2 Twin 2 Double 2 Family | 2 En Suite fac 3 Limited ensuite 2 Pub Bath/Show | B&B per person £18.00-£32.00 Single £16.00-£22.00 Double | Open Jan-Dec | |

Traditional granite townhouse, centrally situated within walking distance
of all amenities. Car parking.

Salisbury Guest House

12 SALISBURY TERRACE, ABERDEEN AB1 6QH
Telephone: 01224 590447

Detached, granite, family-run guest house, B&B, evening meal, central
heating, electric blankets, cot, tea/coffee facilities, colour TV in bedrooms.
TV lounge, personal attention.

Single BB £16   Double/Twin £30   Dinner £6.

COMMENDED 👑👑

| Salisbury Guest House 12 Salisbury Terrace Aberdeen AB1 6QH Tel: (Aberdeen) 01224 590447 | COMMENDED 👑👑 | 1 Single 1 Twin 1 Double 1 Family | 3 Pub Bath/Show | B&B per person from £17.00 Single from £16.00 Double | Open Jan-Dec Dinner 1700-1800 B&B + Eve. Meal from £23.00 | |

Family run guest house in quiet street near to city centre and to main bus routes.
Home cooking.

Scottish Agricultural College

CRAIBSTONE ESTATE, BUCKSBURN, ABERDEEN AB2 9TR
Telephone: 01224 715018   Fax: 01224 712758

Craibstone Estate is an 800 acre working farm offering
woodland and hill walks. Accommodation is in **Mackie**, **Hunter**
or **Sutton Halls** providing a relaxed peaceful atmosphere at
affordable prices. Golfing holidays can be arranged.
Only five miles from City Centre.

| Scottish Agricultural College Crabstone Estate, Bucksburn Aberdeen AB2 9TR Tel: (Aberdeen) 01224 712532 Fax: 01224 712758 | APPROVED Listed | 103 Single 18 Twin | 60 En Suite fac 5 Pub Bath/Show | B&B per person £18.00-£25.00 Single from £16.00 Double | Open mid March-mid April July-Sept Dinner 1730-1900 B&B + Eve. Meal £23.50-£35.00 | |

Halls of Residence, set in extensive country park on outskirts of Aberdeen,
with easy access to all amenities.

Skala Guest House 2 Springbank Place Aberdeen AB1 2LW Tel: (Aberdeen) 01224 572260	COMMENDED Listed	4 Single 3 Twin 2 Family	2 Pub Bath/Show	B&B per person £18.50-£21.00 Single £15.00-£18.00 Double	Open Jan-Dec

Personally run, offering comfortable accommodation. Centrally situated to all amenities. Pets welcome.

St ELMO
64 HILTON DRIVE, ABERDEEN AB2 2NP
Telephone: 01224 483065   Mobile: 0585 849776
e.mail k.watt@aberdeen.ac.uk.
This clean, comfortable, smoke-free family accommodation is ideal for guests looking for a small, quiet place to stay, but yet on a city centre bus route, close to airport, university and hospital. Each room has self-catering facilities (microwave, fridge, etc). CTV. *Special weekly rates.* On/off-street car parking available.

Mrs A Watt St Elmo, 64 Hilton Drive Aberdeen AB2 2NP Tel: (Aberdeen) 01224 483065/ 0585 849776 (mobile)	APPROVED Listed	2 Twin 1 Double	1 Pub Bath/Show	B&B per person £17.00-£21.00 Single £14.00-£15.00 Double	Open Jan-Dec

Detached bungalow in residential area with frequent bus service. City centre 2 miles (3kms). No smoking.

BY ABERDEEN Mrs Goudriaan Blackdog Heights Bridge of Don, Aberdeen Aberdeenshire AB23 8BT Tel: (Aberdeen) 01224 704287	Map 4 G10 COMMENDED Listed	2 Single 1 Twin 1 Double	1 Pub Bath/Show	B&B per person £16.00-£18.00 Single £15.00-£17.00 Double	Open Jan-Dec

Large modern bungalow in own grounds 5 miles (8kms) from Aberdeen, 2 miles (3kms) from Exhibition Centre. Handy for main A92 and near the beach.

ABERDOUR Fife	Map 2 C4				

HAWKCRAIG HOUSE
Hawkcraig Point, Aberdour, Fife KY3 0TZ
Telephone: 01383 860335
Old ferryman's house at water's edge overlooking Aberdour Harbour and Inchcolm. Only 30 minutes from Edinburgh by road or rail. Accommodation on ground floor comprises one twin (shower ensuite), one double (bath ensuite), sitting room and conservatory. Taste of Scotland dinners (pre-booked), residents and non-residents.

Mrs E Barrie Hawkcraig House Hawkcraig Point Aberdour Fife KY3 0TZ Tel: (Aberdour) 01383 860335	DELUXE	1 Twin 1 Double	2 En Suite fac	B&B per person £25.00-£27.00 Single £20.00-£22.00 Double	Open mid Mar-Oct Dinner 1900-2030 B&B + Eve. Meal £39.50-£46.50

Old ferryman's house situated at water's edge overlooking Aberdour Harbour and Inchcolm Island. Steep access. Taste of Scotland member.

Forth View Hawkcraig Point Aberdour Fife KY3 0TZ Tel: (Aberdour) 01383 860402	APPROVED	1 Single 2 Twin 1 Double 1 Family	3 En Suite fac 1 Pub Bath/Show	B&B per person £20.00-£30.00 Single £19.00-£25.00 Double	Open Apr-Oct Dinner at 1900

Secluded hotel at Hawkcraig Point, on seashore with impressive views. Near Silversands Beach. Local golf course. Home cooking a speciality.

Mrs S Knott Dunraggie, Murrell Road Aberdour Fife KY3 0XN Tel: (Aberdour) 01383 860136	COMMENDED	1 Single 2 Double	1 En Suite fac 1 Priv.NOT ensuite 2 Pub Bath/Show	B&B per person £18.00-£20.00 Single £17.00-£19.00 Double	Open Apr-Sep

Comfortable, warm and quiet; ideal for all ages. Lovely views over River Forth.

ABERDOUR continued

Mrs Janet Lonie
Flock House, Seaside Place
Aberdour
Fife
KY3 0TX
Tel: (Aberdour) 01383 860777

Map 2 C4

COMMENDED
Listed

1 Twin   1 Pub Bath/Show
1 Family

B&B per person
£17.00-£18.00 Single
£16.00-£17.00 Double

Open Jan-Dec

Traditional, listed cottage in quiet private road, close to attractive beach
and golf course. Good base for sporting activities and touring.

ABERFELDY
Perthshire

Map 2 A1

Balnearn House
Crieff Road
Aberfeldy
Perthshire
PH15 2BJ
Tel: (Aberfeldy) 01887 820431

COMMENDED

4 Twin   8 En Suite fac
4 Double   2 Priv. NOT ensuite
2 Family
Suite avail

B&B per person
from £25.00 Single
£18.50-£27.50 Double

Open Apr-Dec

Substantial stone-built house surrounded by attractive garden. Mountain view.
Large car park, close to the renowned "Birks Walk".

Mrs Bassett-Smith
Handa, Taybridge Road
Aberfeldy
Perthshire
PH15 2BH
Tel: (Aberfeldy) 01887 820334

COMMENDED

1 Twin   2 En Suite fac
1 Double

B&B per person
£16.00-£17.00 Single

Open Jan-Dec
Dinner 1800-1930
B&B + Eve. Meal
£22.50-£23.50

Semi-detached house with fine views over Wade's Bridge to Weem Rock.
Putting green next door, golf course and tennis court 100 yards.

Dunolly House
Taybridge Drive
Aberfeldy
Perthshire
PH15 2BP
Tel: (Aberfeldy) 01887 820298

APPROVED
Listed

1 Single   6 En Suite fac
2 Twin   1 Limited ensuite
5 Double   6 Pub Bath/Show
8 Family

B&B per person
£16.00-£20.00 Single
£11.00-£17.50 Double

Open Jan-Dec
Dinner 1800-2030

Large house on the outskirts of town beside the Tay.
Ideal for groups and families. All year activity holidays.

Fernbank House
Kenmore Street
Aberfeldy
Perthshire
PH15 2BL
Tel: (Aberfeldy) 01887 820345

HIGHLY
COMMENDED

1 Single   7 En Suite fac
2 Twin
3 Double
1 Family

B&B per person
£23.50-£33.50 Single
£21.50-£24.50 Double

Open Jan-Dec

Quiet, comfortable, non-smoking Victorian country house set in own grounds with private parking.
All rooms en-suite. Quality guest house.

Mrs Malcolm
Novar, 2 Home Street
Aberfeldy
Perthshire
PH15 2AJ
Tel: (Aberfeldy) 01887 820779

COMMENDED
Listed

1 Twin   1 En Suite fac
1 Family   1 Priv. NOT ensuite

B&B per person
£16.00-£18.00 Single

Open Apr-Oct

Stone-built villa with attractive, well-maintained garden in residential area.
Private parking. Convenient for town centre.

Mr & Mrs P Nunn
Mavisbank, Taybridge Drive
Aberfeldy
Perthshire
PH15 2BP
Tel: (Aberfeldy) 01887 820223

COMMENDED

1 Twin   1 Pub Bath/Show
1 Double

B&B per person
£15.00-£16.00 Double

Open Mar-Oct

Friendly welcome in peaceful setting on outskirts of small country town.
Beautiful views. Convenient for golfing, fishing, walking and birdwatching.

Tigh'n Eilean Guest House
Taybridge Drive
Aberfeldy
Perthshire
PH15 2BP
Tel: (Aberfeldy) 01887 820109

HIGHLY
COMMENDED

1 Twin   2 En Suite fac
2 Double   1 Priv. NOT ensuite

B&B per person
£17.00-£20.00 Single
£17.00-£20.00 Double

Open Jan-Dec
Dinner 1800-1900
B&B + Eve. Meal
£27.00-£30.00

Elegant Victorian house overlooking the river.
Warm and comfortable; homecooking. One room with jacuzzi.

BY ABERFELDY **Perthshire** Mrs C Campbell Weem Farm, Weem Aberfeldy Perthshire PH15 2LD Tel: (Aberfeldy) 01887 820228	**Map 2** A1	**APPROVED** ♕	1 Double 1 Family	1 En Suite fac 1 Pub Bath/Show	B&B per person £14.00-£16.00 Single £13.00-£15.00 Double	Open Apr-Sep	

Traditional stone-built farm house situated on roadside.
Ideal location for golfing, touring and all outdoor activities.

BY ABERFOYLE **Perthshire**	**Map 1** H3

Creag-Ard House B&B
MILTON, NEAR ABERFOYLE, STIRLING FK8 3TQ
Telephone: 01877 382297
Nestling in three acres of beautiful gardens, this lovely
Victorian house enjoys some of the most magnificent scenery
in Scotland. Overlooking *Loch Ard*, with long distance views
to *Ben Lomond* and surrounded by tree-clad mountains.
Own trout fishing and boat hire available. Secure car parking.
Centrally situated for touring Scotland.

Andrew and Pauline Carter Creag-Ard House B&B Milton, near Aberfoyle Perthshire FK8 3TQ Tel: (Aberfoylc) 01877 382297	**COMMENDED** ♕ ♕	1 Single 3 Twin 2 Double 1 Family	4 En Suite fac 1 Pub Bath/Show	B&B per person £20.00-£60.00 Single £17.50-£30.00 Double	Open Jan-Dec

Detached Victorian house with superb views over Loch Ard and
Ben Lomond beyond. Private fishing and boating. Most bedrooms ensuite.

Mrs A Wilson Dalchon Kinlochard, by Aberfoyle Perthshire FK8 3TL Tel: (Kinlochard) 01877 387305	**COMMENDED** Listed	2 Double	1 Pub Bath/Show	B&B per person £16.00-£18.00 Single £13.00-£14.00 Double	Open Jan-Dec

Modern, detached bungalow in peaceful setting overlooking Loch Ard
with views of Ben Lomond. Easy access to Queen Elizabeth Forest walks.

ABERLOUR **Banffshire** Mrs E J Mitchell Roys Croft Aberlour Banffshire AB38 9NR Tel: (Aberlour) 01340 871408	**Map 4** D8 **COMMENDED** Listed	1 Single 1 Twin 1 Double	1 Pub Bath/Show	B&B per person £12.50-£14.00 Single £12.50-£14.00 Double Room only per person £9.50-£11.00	Open Jan-Dec

Small working croft in the heart of the Whisky Trail near the
delightful village of Charlestown of Aberlour in Speyside.

ABERNETHY **Perthshire** Mrs MacKenzie Gattaway Farm Abernethy Perthshire PH2 9LQ Tel: (Abernethy) 01738 850746	**Map 2** C3 **COMMENDED** ♕ ♕ ♕	2 Twin 1 Double	2 En Suite fac 1 Pub Bath/Show	B&B per person to £15.15 Single to £15.50 Double	Open Jan-Dec Dinner 1800-2100

Georgian/Victorian farmhouse in a quiet rural location.
Spectacular views. Ideal for touring and all outdoor activities.

BY ABERNETHY Perthshire	Map 2 C3

EASTER CLUNIE FARMHOUSE

Newburgh, Fife KY14 6EJ
Telephone: 01337 840218

19th-century comfortable centrally heated farmhouse
with panoramic views over the River Tay.
Tea and coffee-making facilities. Walled garden.
Enjoy a relaxing holiday. Close to Perth and St Andrews.

| Mrs K Baird
Easter Clunie Farmhouse
Newburgh
Fife
KY14 6EJ
Tel: (Newburgh) 01337 840218 | COMMENDED
👑👑 | 2 Twin
1 Family | 1 En Suite fac
2 Priv. NOT ensuite | B&B per person
£14.00-£16.00 Single
£14.00-£16.00 Double | Open Apr-Oct | |

19th-century farmhouse on working farm. Quiet setting.
Splendid Victorian walled garden. Convenient for main routes to Edinburgh and the Highlands.

| **ABINGTON**
Lanarkshire
Mrs C Craig
Townfoot
Roberton, by Abington
Lanarkshire
ML12 6RS
Tel: (Lamington) 018995 655 | Map 2
B7
COMMENDED
Listed | 2 Twin | 1 Pub Bath/Show | B&B per person
£14.00 Single
£14.00 Double | Open Jan-Dec
Dinner 1800-2000
B&B + Eve. Meal
£20.00-£22.00 | |

In a delightfully quiet position, set back from the main road, small and friendly
with comfortable rooms. Some annexe accommodation for self-catering.

| Mrs Mary Hodge
Craighead Farm
Abington, by Biggar
Lanarkshire
ML12 6SQ
Tel: (Crawford) 01864 502356
Fax: 01864 502356 | COMMENDED
👑👑 | 1 Twin
1 Double | 2 Priv. NOT ensuite
2 Pub Bath/Show | B&B per person
£15.50-£16.50 Single
£15.50-£16.50 Double | Open May-Oct
Dinner 1800-1900
B&B + Eve. Meal
£21.00-£23.00 | |

Stone-built 18th-century farmhouse, on working farm in peaceful rural location.
Friendly, relaxed atmosphere. Evening meals.

| Mrs J Hyslop
Glentewing Farm
Crawfordjohn, by Abington
Lanarkshire
ML12 6ST
Tel: (Crawfordjohn)
01864 504221 | HIGHLY
COMMENDED
👑👑👑 | 1 Twin
1 Double | 2 En Suite fac | B&B per person
£15.00-£19.00 Single
£15.00-£19.00 Double | Open Jan-Dec
Dinner 1830-1930 | |

Early 20th-century farmhouse set in a glen with view towards Tinto Hill. Far from
the madding crowd yet only 5 miles (8kms) from M74. Home-cooking a speciality.

| Mrs Lillias Hyslop
Netherton Farmhouse
Abington, by Biggar
Lanarkshire
ML12 6RU
Tel: (Crawford) 01864 502321 | COMMENDED
👑👑 | 1 Twin
1 Double
1 Family | 1 En Suite fac
2 Pub Bath/Show | B&B per person
£13.00-£16.00 Single
£13.00-£16.00 Double
Room only per person
£10.00-£15.00 | Open Jan-Dec
Dinner 1800-2000
B&B + Eve. Meal
£20.00-£22.00 | |

Formerly a shooting lodge for Edward VII, this large mixed stock farm
is set amidst rolling hill country. Conveniently located for all major roads.

| ABOYNE | Map 4 |
| Aberdeenshire | F11 |

ARBOR LODGE
Ballater Road, Aboyne AB34 5HY
Telephone: 013398 86951

ARBOR LODGE is a large luxury home set in a woodland garden in the picturesque village of Aboyne. All bedrooms have en-suite bathrooms, tea-making facilities and television. Ideally located for touring Royal Deeside. Activities include golf, fishing, bowling, tennis, gliding, water skiing, swimming, squash and hill-walking.

Arbor Lodge	DELUXE	3 Twin	3 En Suite fac	B&B per person	Open Mar-Oct
Ballater Road				£22.00 Single	
Aboyne				£22.00 Double	
Aberdeenshire					
AB34 5HY					
Tel: (Aboyne) 013398 86951					
Fax: 013398 86951					

A newly built spacious house of character with large landscaped garden, front and rear. Near centre of village. All bedrooms en-suite.

ALLTDINNIE
Birse, Aboyne, Aberdeenshire AB34 5ES
Telephone: 013398 86323

Delightful country house set in secluded grounds close to Aboyne. Whether you want to explore the castle trail, whisky trail, hillwalk or play our golf courses assistance is on hand with routes planned and tee times arranged. Alternatively relax and enjoy warm Scottish hospitality.

Mrs Eileen Barton	HIGHLY COMMENDED	1 Single	2 Priv. NOT ensuite	B&B per person	Open Apr-Oct
Alltdinnie, Birse		1 Twin	1 Pub Bath/Show	to £22.00 Single	Dinner 1900-2000
Aboyne		1 Double		to £22.00 Double	B&B + Eve. Meal
Aberdeenshire					£36.00-£40.00
AB34 5ES					
Tel: (Aboyne) 013398 86323					

Historic, Victorian country house, peacefully located with large attractive garden. Owners can advise on golf, fishing, walking, gliding etc.

Hazelhurst Lodge, Restaurant &	DELUXE	1 Twin	3 En Suite fac	B&B per person	Open Jan-Dec
Hazelhurst Art Gallery		2 Double		£27.00-£45.00 Single	Dinner 1930-2130
Ballater Road				£27.00-£35.00 Double	
Aboyne					
Aberdeenshire					
AB34 5HY					
Tel: (Aboyne) 013398 86921					
Fax: 013398 86660					

Former Coachman's Lodge to Aboyne Castle with small restaurant and large garden. Ideal for touring Royal Deeside.

WELCOME

Whenever you are in Scotland, you can be sure of a warm welcome at your nearest Tourist Information Centre.

For guide books, maps, souvenirs, our Centres provide a service second to none – many now offer bureau-de-change facilities. And, of course, Tourist Information Centres offer free, expert advice on what to see and do, route-planning and accommodation for everyone – visitors and residents alike!

ABOYNE continued	Map 4 F11

STRUAN HALL

Ballater Road, Aboyne AB34 5HY
Telephone/Fax: 013398 87241

We provide quality accommodation in a lovely village in the heart of Royal Deeside. Struan Hall is ideally situated for touring the area bounded by Perth, Inverness and Aberdeen. Quiet roads provide access to wonderful scenery, distilleries, castles, gardens and a full range of sporting and outdoor activities.

Phyllis & Michael Ingham Struan Hall, Ballater Road Aboyne Aberdeenshire AB34 5HY Tel: (Aboyne) 013398 87241 Fax: 013398 87241	**DELUXE** 👑👑	2 Twin 1 Double	3 En Suite fac	B&B per person £22.00-£27.00 Single £20.00-£22.00 Double	Open Feb-Nov	
		Stone-built house c.1870, situated near centre of village, recently refurbished to a high standard, with a warm and friendly welcome.				
Mrs E L Thorburn Birkwood Lodge, Gordon Crescent Aboyne Aberdeenshire AB34 5HJ Tel: (Aboyne) 013398 86347	**HIGHLY COMMENDED** 👑👑👑	2 Twin 1 Double	2 En Suite fac 1 Priv. NOT ensuite	B&B per person £25.00 Single £20.00 Double	Open Jan-Dec Dinner 1900-2030 B&B + Eve. Meal £35.00-£40.00	
		Personal attention, fresh country produce and a high standard of comfort combine to provide a memorable experience of Royal Deeside.				

ACHARACLE, Ardnamurchan Argyll	Map 3 F12

BELMONT

Acharacle, Ardnamurchan, Argyll PH36 4JT
Telephone: 01967 431266

Good food and a warm welcome await you at Belmont, a converted manse overlooking Loch Shiel and the Moidart Hills. This family run establishment is the ideal centre for exploring the unspoilt Ardnamurchan Peninsula, with its abundant wildlife, excellent beaches and numerous walks. En-suite facilities. Children welcome.

Mrs C L Learmouth Belmont Acharacle, Ardnamurchan Argyll PH36 4JT Tel: (Salen) 01967 431266	**COMMENDED** 👑👑	1 Single 1 Twin 1 Double	2 En Suite fac 1 Priv. NOT ensuite	B&B per person £16.00-£19.00 Single £16.00-£19.00 Double	Open Jan-Dec Dinner 1800-2100 B&B + Eve. Meal £27.00-£30.00	
		Former Manse, overlooking Loch Shiel towards hills of Moidart. Good home cooking.				

ACHMORE Lewis, Western Isles Mrs W Golder Lochview, 35b Achmore Achmore Lewis, Western Isles PA86 9DU Tel: (Crossbost) 01851 860205	Map 3 D5 **COMMENDED** 👑	1 Twin 2 Double	2 Pub Bath/Show	B&B per person from £15.00 Single from £15.00 Double	Open Jan-Dec Dinner 1800-1900 B&B + Eve. Meal £23.00	
		Detached bungalow in a rural location overlooking Loch Achmore. Callanish Standing Stones about 5 miles (8kms). Good touring centre for west coast.				

AIGNISH, Point **Lewis, Western Isles** Mrs L G MacDonald Ceol-Na-Mara, 1A Aignish Point Lewis, Western Isles HS2 0PB Tel: (Garrabost) 01851 870339	Map 3 E4	COMMENDED ♕	1 Twin 1 Double 1 Family	2 Pub Bath/Show	B&B per person £16.00 Single £15.00 Double	Open Jan-Dec Dinner 1830-2000 B&B + Eve. Meal £23.00-£24.00	

Comfortable modern home in pleasant rural Stornoway across
the causeway on the Eye Peninsula. Home cooking and baking.

AIRDRIE **Lanarkshire** Mrs E Hunter Easter Glentore Farm Greengairs, by Airdrie Lanarkshire ML6 7TJ Tel: (Greengairs) 01236 830243	Map 2 A5	HIGHLY COMMENDED ♕♕	3 Double	1 En Suite fac 1 Pub Bath/Show	B&B per person £22.00-£27.00 Single £18.00-£22.00 Double	Open Jan-Dec Dinner 1700-2000	

Working stock-rearing farm only 15 miles (24kms) from the centre of Glasgow.
Warm welcome, home cooking and homely atmosphere.

Rosslee Guest House 107 Forrest Street Airdrie Lanarkshire ML6 7AR Tel: (Airdrie) 01236 765865		COMMENDED ♕♕♕	2 Single 3 Twin 1 Family	3 En Suite fac 2 Pub Bath/Show	B&B per person £20.00-£25.00 Single £20.00-£25.00 Double	Open Jan-Dec Dinner 1730-1830 B&B + Eve. Meal £27.00-£35.00	

Former church manse, now family run guest house with comfortable rooms.
Central situation for Edinburgh or Glasgow.

ALFORD **Aberdeenshire** Mrs Iris Henderson 13 Montgarrie Road Alford Aberdeenshire AB33 8AE Tel: (Alford) 019755 62159	Map 4 F10	COMMENDED Listed	1 Twin 1 Double	1 Pub Bath/Show	B&B per person from £15.00 Single from £14.00 Double	Open Mar-Oct	

Friendly welcome in comfortable accommodation.
Within walking distance to local park, museums and village amenities.

BY ALFORD **Aberdeenshire** Mrs C E Braiden Macbrae Lodge Montgarrie, Alford Aberdeenshire AB33 8AX Tel: (Alford) 019755 63421	Map 4 F10	COMMENDED Listed	1 Twin 1 Double 1 Family	2 Pub Bath/Show	B&B per person £15.00 Single £15.00 Double Room only per person £15.00	Open Jan-Dec	

In quiet position, with lovely views of open countryside.
Comfortable accommodation and home-baking. Ideal for Castle and Whisky Trails.

ALNESS **Ross-shire** Mrs Dorothy MacDougall Averon Bank Cottage, Ardross Road Alness Ross-shire IV17 0QA Tel: (Alness) 01349 882392	Map 4 B7	COMMENDED ♕	3 Twin	3 En Suite fac	B&B per person from £18.00 Single £16.00-£18.00 Double	Open Jan-Dec	

Detached cottage in small cul-de-sac on the outskirts of the village
with private garden area.

ALYTH
Perthshire — Map 2 C1

Airlie Mount Holiday Services
2 Albert Street
Alyth, Blairgowrie
Perthshire
PH11 8AX
Tel: (Alyth) 01828 632986
Fax: 01828 632563

COMMENDED Listed

1 Single	3 En Suite fac	B&B per person	Open Jan-Dec
2 Twin	1 Limited ensuite	from £20.00 Single	Dinner 1900-2200
2 Double	1 Priv. NOT ensuite	from £20.00 Double	B&B + Eve. Meal
2 Family	3 Pub Bath/Show	Room only per person	£32.00-£35.00
		from £15.00	

A warm welcome at this Victorian mansion, quietly located in peaceful Alyth.

Mrs Ann Ferguson
Bruceton Farm
Alyth, Blairgowrie
Perthshire
PH11 8JT
Tel: (Craigton) 01575 530201

COMMENDED

1 Single	1 En Suite fac	B&B per person	Open Mar-Nov
1 Twin	2 Priv. NOT ensuite	to £17.50 Single	
1 Double		to £17.50 Double	
		Room only per person	
		to £12.00	

Secluded farmhouse, large rooms with panoramic views,
within easy reach of the picturesque glens of Perthshire and Angus.

Mrs McBain
Old Stables, 2 Losset Road
Alyth
Perthshire
PH11 8BT
Tel: (Alyth) 01828 632547

HIGHLY COMMENDED

2 Twin	3 En Suite fac	B&B per person	Open Jan-Dec
1 Family		£16.00-£21.00 Single	
		£16.00-£21.00 Double	

Warm and friendly welcome assured in this striking conversion of 19C stable.
Log fireplace and sauna. Private car park close to town centre.

Mrs Jean Rimmer
Lintrathen, St Ninians Road
Alyth
Perthshire
PH11 8AR
Tel: (Alyth) 01828 632785

COMMENDED Listed

1 Single	1 Pub Bath/Show	B&B per person	Open Mar-Nov
1 Double		£12.00-£14.00 Single	
		£12.00-£14.00 Double	

Modern bungalow at the edge of the town. Good touring area. Ample car parking.

AMULREE
Perthshire — Map 2 A2

Mrs M P Lush
Scotston
Trochry, by Dunkeld
Perthshire
PH8 0ED
Tel: (Amulree) 01350 725225

APPROVED

1 Double	1 En Suite fac	B&B per person	Open Jan-Dec
1 Family	1 Priv. NOT ensuite	£14.00-£15.50 Single	Dinner 1800-2100
		£13.50-£15.00 Double	B&B + Eve. Meal
		Room only per person	£20.50-£22.00
		£12.00-£13.50	

Traditional stone-built working farmhouse. Convenient for touring
local places of interest. Evening meal available.

ANSTRUTHER
Fife — Map 2 D3

The Hermitage
Ladywalk
Anstruther
Fife
KY10 3EX
Tel: (Anstruther) 01333 310909

HIGHLY COMMENDED

1 Twin	2 Pub Bath/Show	B&B per person	Open Jan-Dec
3 Double		£25.00-£35.00 Single	Dinner from 1900
		£20.00-£25.00 Double	B&B + Eve. Meal
			£30.00-£45.00

19th-century Listed East Neuk town house with secluded south-facing garden.
Comfortable accommodation furnished to a high standard. Private parking.

Mrs E MacGeachy
The Dykes
69 Pittenweem Road
Anstruther
Fife
KY10 3DT
Tel: (Anstruther) 01333 310537

COMMENDED

1 Double	1 Pub Bath/Show	B&B per person	Open Mar-Sep
1 Family		from £20.00 Single	
		from £15.00 Double	

Detached bungalow on edge of village. Views over golf course to the sea.
Attractive well maintained garden. Non-smoking house.

| Mrs B Ritchie
The Sheiling,
32 Glenogil Gardens
Anstruther, Fife
KY10 3ET
Tel: (Anstruther) 01333 310697 | | COMMENDED
♔ | 2 Double | 1 Pub Bath/Show | B&B per person
£20.00-£22.00 Single
£13.50-£15.50 Double | Open Apr-Sep | |

Pretty, white semi-detached bungalow in quiet area near harbour.
Attractive gardens. Homemade shortbread, jams and marmalade.

The Spindrift
Pittenweem Road, Anstruther, Fife KY10 3DT
Telephone and Fax: 01333 310573

Set on the western edge of Anstruther, The Spindrift has established a growing reputation for its unique brand of comfort, hospitality, freshly prepared food and service. Convenient for golf, walking, bird watching or exploring the picturesque and historic East Neuk. Please contact Eric and Moyra McFarlane for reservations.

| The Spindrift
Pittenweem Road
Anstruther
Fife
KY10 3DT
Tel: (Anstruther) 01333 310573
Fax: 01333 310573 | | HIGHLY
COMMENDED
♔♔♔ | 2 Twin
3 Double
3 Family | 8 En Suite fac | B&B per person
£30.00-£40.00 Single
£25.00-£28.00 Double
Room only per person
£25.00-£35.00 | Open Jan-Dec
Dinner 1800-1930
B&B + Eve. Meal
£36.00-£40.00 | |

Stone-built Victorian house with wealth of original features, set in fishing village.
Short walk from town centre. Ideal touring base. Non-smoking.

| APPIN
Argyll
Mrs B MacLeod
Lurignish
Appin
Argyll
PA38 4BN
Tel: (Appin) 01631 730365 | Map 1
E1 | COMMENDED
Listed | 1 Double
1 Family | 1 Pub Bath/Show | B&B per person
£16.00-£18.00 Double | Open mid May-Sep
Dinner 1800-1900
B&B + Eve. Meal
£26.00-£28.00 | |

Modern bungalow on 1000 acre hill farm. Traditional Highland hospitality,
home cooking, baking. Half-way between Fort William and Oban.

| BY APPIN
Argyll | Map 1
E1 | | | | | | |

LOCHSIDE COTTAGE
Fasnacloich, Appin, Argyll PA38 4BJ   **Tel: 01631 730216**

Enjoy the West Highlands and Islands. The tranquil setting of Lochside Cottage (wonderful walks from cottage garden), combined with the friendly atmosphere of the Broadbents' home, ensures a pleasant relaxing holiday away from the hurly burly of modern life. Comfortable, attractive bedrooms, sittingroom and delicious home cooking. Local information readily available.

| Mrs Stella M Broadbent
Lochside Cottage
Fasnacloich, Appin
Argyll
PA38 4BJ
Tel: (Oban) 01631 730216
Fax: 01631 730216 | | HIGHLY
COMMENDED
♔♔♔ | 2 Twin
1 Double | 2 En Suite fac
1 Priv. NOT ensuite | B&B per person
£18.00-£20.00 Single
£18.00-£20.00 Double | Open Jan-Dec
Dinner from 1930
B&B + Eve. Meal
£33.00-£35.00 | |

Set in the beauty and the grandeur of the Highland Glen where the historic
Campbell/Stewart rivalry inspired R.L. Stevenson's "Kidnapped".

ARBROATH **Angus** Mrs S M Fergusson 6 Monkbarns Drive Arbroath Angus DD11 2DS Tel: (Arbroath) 01241 873991	Map 2 D1	COMMENDED ♔	3 Twin 1 Family	2 Pub Bath/Show	B&B per person from £15.00 Single £14.00-£15.00 Double	Open Apr-Sep

Spacious family house in quiet cul-de-sac with sea views, off-road parking.
Gaelic spoken. Non-smoking.

Sandhutton Guest House 16 Addison Place Arbroath Angus DD11 2AX Tel: (Arbroath) 01241 872007		HIGHLY COMMENDED ♔ ♔	2 Twin 1 Double	1 Priv. NOT ensuite 2 Pub Bath/Show	B&B per person £19.00 Single £16.00-£18.00 Double	Open Apr-Oct

Victorian villa offering a warm welcome and comfortable non-smoking accommodation
with modern facilities. Centrally located for amenities

ARDELVE, by Dornie
Ross-shire — Map 3 F9

'AR DACHAIDH'
Ardelve, Kyle of Lochalsh, Ross-shire IV40 8DY
Telephone: 01599 555363
A pleasant family run home on Inverness to Kyle of
Lochalsh road A87 past Eileen Donan Castle at Sallachy
junction. Nearby Kyle is where the ferries leave for Outer
Isles. Also car ferry from Glenelg to Skye. Handy for hill
walking, pleasant forest walk and gardens at Claick.

Mrs E Inglis Ar Dachaidh Ardelve, by Dornie Ross-shire Tel: (Dornie) 01599 555363	COMMENDED Listed	1 Twin 1 Family	1 Pub Bath/Show	B&B per person to £14.00 Double	Open Easter-Sep

18th-century house, formerly a manse, in own grounds.
Near to Eilean Donan Castle; good base for climbing, walking and touring.

ARDEN, by Luss **Dunbartonshire** Mrs P McNair North Polnaberoch Arden, by Luss Dunbartonshire G83 8RQ Tel: (Arden) 01389 850615	Map 1 G4	HIGHLY COMMENDED ♔ ♔	1 Double 1 Family	2 En Suite fac .	B&B per person £19.00-£21.00 Double	Open May-Oct Dinner from 2000

In tranquil rural setting with large garden. Short distance from Loch Lomond,
Golf courses and country walks.

ARDFERN
Argyll — Map 1 E3

Lunga Estate
Ardfern, Argyll PA31 8QR
Telephone: 01852 500237 Fax 01852 500639
Lunga, a 17th Century mansion overlooking Firth of Lorne and
Sound of Jura, home to the MacDougalls for over 300 years, who
offer comfortable rooms for B & B and self-catering flats or
cottages. Join us for our famous candle-lit dinners and share the
facilities of this beautiful 3000-acre coastal estate.

C Lindsay-MacDougall of Lunga Lunga Ardfern, by Lochgilphead Argyll PA31 8QR Tel: (Barbreck) 01852 500237 Fax: 01852 500639	APPROVED ♔ ♔ ♔	1 Single 1 Twin 2 Double	4 En Suite fac 1 Pub Bath/Show	B&B per person £15.00-£18.00 Single £15.00-£18.00 Double	Open Jan-Dec Dinner from 2000

18th-century mansion house on 3000 acre estate. Riding, fishing, sailing and
hill-walking available. Annexe accommodation.

ARDGAY **Sutherland** Mrs W J Munro Corvost Ardgay Sutherland IV24 3BP Tel: (The Craigs) 01863 755317	Map 4 A6	COMMENDED ♛	1 Single 1 Twin 1 Double	2 Pub Bath/Show	B&B per person £12.00-£14.00 Single £12.00-£14.00 Double Room only per person from £8.00	Open Jan-Dec Dinner from 1900 B&B + Eve. Meal £20.00-£22.00

Set in a beautiful and historical Highland Strath, this modern bungalow
on working croft has many interesting farm animals, including deer. Golfing area.

ARDNAMURCHAN **Argyll**	Map 3 E12

Feorag House

GLENBORRODALE, ACHARACLE, ARGYLL PH36 4JP
Telephone: 01972 500248

Set within 13 acres and having the benefit of a private shoreline,
Feorag House is the perfect setting to relax
and enjoy excellent cuisine, warm friendly hospitality and
comfortable surroundings. All bedrooms have superb seaviews
and bathrooms ensuite. Abundant wildlife including otters,
wildcat, buzzards and eagles. Fishing, walking and sailing.

Feorag House Glenborrodale Acharacle Argyll PH36 4JP Tel: (Glenborrodale) 01972 500248		DELUXE ♛♛♛	1 Twin 2 Double	3 En Suite fac	B&B per person £25.00-£35.00 Single £25.00-£35.00 Double	Open Jan-Dec Dinner 1930-2100 B&B + Eve. Meal £43.00-£53.00

Delightful country house on shores of Loch Sunart.
Peace and tranquillity, warm and friendly atmosphere with imaginative cuisine.
Ideal central location for exploring Ardnamurchan.

ARDRISHAIG, by Lochgilphead **Argyll** Allt-Na-Craig Tarbert Road Ardrishaig Argyll PA30 8EP Tel: (Lochgilphead) 01546 603245	Map 1 E4	HIGHLY COMMENDED ♛♛♛	1 Single 2 Twin 2 Double 1 Family	6 En Suite fac	B&B per person £25.00-£30.00 Single £25.00-£30.00 Double Room only per person £20.00-£25.00	Open Jan-Dec, ex Xmas/New Year Dinner 1930-2030 B&B + Eve. Mea £40.00-£45.00

Large, Victorian house in spacious grounds with panoramic views over Loch Fyne.
Home cooking using fresh ingredients.

ARISAIG **Inverness-shire** Kinloid Farm Guest House Kinloid, Kilmartin Arisaig Inverness-shire PH39 4NS Tel: (Arisaig) 01687 450366 Fax: 01687 450366	Map 3 F11	COMMENDED ♛♛♛	1 Twin 2 Double	3 En Suite fac 1 Pub Bath/Show	B&B per person from £20.00 Double	Open Apr-Oct Dinner at 1830

Bungalow style farmhouse on working farm about 0.5 miles (1km) from the village.
Magnificent sea and mountain views.

Scotland for Golf . . .

Find out more about golf in Scotland. There's more to it than
just the championship courses so get in touch with us now for
information on the hidden gems of Scotland.
Write to: **Information Unit, Scottish Tourist Board,
23 Ravelston Terrace, Edinburgh EH4 3EU
or call: 0131-332 2433**

| ARROCHAR | Map 1 |
| Dunbartonshire | G3 |

FERRY COTTAGE
ARROCHAR, DUNBARTONSHIRE G83 7AH
Tel: 01301 702428   Fax: 01301 702699

This 200-year-old house, fully refurbished by a local craftsman, is central for touring and all outdoor activities. Our scenic views across Loch Long and the Arrochar Alps are second to none. Bedroom facilities include tea/coffee, hairdryers, en-suites and firm beds to ensure a restful night. One features a "FOUR POSTER WATER BED". Central heating throughout. Cosy lounge and PAY PHONE. For your peace of mind there is private parking and a Fire Certificate.

★ OPEN MOST OF THE YEAR.
★ Colour TV in all bedrooms.
5 minutes drive from Loch Lomond.
NON-SMOKING ESTABLISHMENT!
Situated 1 mile south of Arrochar on the A814.

| Mrs C Bennetton
Ferry Cottage
Ardmay, Arrochar
Dunbartonshire
G83 7AH
Tel: (Arrochar) 01301 702428
Fax: 01301 702699 | COMMENDED 👑👑👑 | 1 Twin
1 Double
1 Family | 3 En Suite fac | B&B per person
£18.50-£22.50 Double | Open Jan-Dec
Dinner at 1930
B&B + Eve. Meal
£28.50-£32.50 | |
| Refurbished 200-year-old house with attractive bedrooms and en-suite shower-rooms. Scenic views across Loch Long. | | | | | | |

| Mrs J R Hetherington
5 Admiralty Cottage
Arrochar
Dunbartonshire
G83 7AQ
Tel: (Arrochar) 01301 702427 | APPROVED Listed | 2 Twin
1 Double | 1 Pub Bath/Show | B&B per person
£14.00-£16.00 Single
£12.00-£14.00 Double | Open Jan-Dec | |
| Small, family house, situated by roadside, overlooking Loch Long. Ideal location for all outdoor activities. | | | | | | |

| Lochside Guest House
Arrochar
Dunbartonshire
G83 7AA
Tel: (Arrochar) 01301 702467
Fax: 01301 702467 | APPROVED 👑👑 | 1 Single
1 Twin
3 Double
2 Family | 3 En Suite fac
1 Priv. NOT ensuite
3 Pub Bath/Show | B&B per person
£16.00-£20.00 Single
£16.00-£20.00 Double
Room only per person
£16.00-£20.00 | Open Jan-Dec
Dinner from 1830
B&B + Eve. Meal
£25.00-£29.00 | |
| Friendly atmosphere in this guest house on the shore of Loch Long with view across the Loch to the Cobbler. Evening meals by arrangement. | | | | | | |

| AUCHENCAIRN,
by Castle Douglas
Kirkcudbrightshire | Map 2
A10 |

THE ROSSAN
Auchencairn, Castle Douglas, Kirkcudbrightshire DG7 1QR
Telephone: 01556 640269

Former Victorian Manse. Large and beautiful garden. Ample parking. Dogs welcome, evening meal available. Wholefood, mostly organic. Meat/Vegetarian. Gluten-free meals always available. Other medical diets by arrangement. Ideal centre for birdwatching, hillwalking. Two sandy beaches. Golf 7 miles, riding locally. No smoking.
Contact Mrs Bardsley for brochure. Listed and Approved.

| Mrs Bardsley
The Rossan
Auchencairn
by Castle Douglas
Kirkcudbrightshire
DG7 1QR
Tel: (Auchencairn)
01556 640269 | APPROVED Listed | 3 Family | 2 Pub Bath/Show | B&B per person
£12.00-£17.00 Single
from £12.00 Double | Open Jan-Dec
Dinner from 1900
B&B + Eve. Meal
£20.00-£25.00 | |
| Former Victorian manse, with large gardens, on outskirts of the village. Convenient for touring. Vegetarian, gluten-free and special diets available. Budget accommodation. | | | | | | |

Mrs E Hendry Rascarrel Cottage Auchencairn by Castle Douglas Kirkcudbrightshire DG7 1RJ Tel: (Auchencairn) 01556 640214		**HIGHLY COMMENDED** 👑👑	2 Twin 1 Double	2 En Suite fac 1 Pub Bath/Show	B&B per person £16.00-£18.00 Double Room only per person £15.00-£17.00	Open Mar-Oct	

Attractive cottage with open rural and sea views. Coastal and forest walks nearby.
Only 2 miles (3 kms) from village where good meals are available.

AUCHTERARDER **Perthshire** Mrs S Robertson Nether Coul Auchterarder Perthshire PH3 1ET Tel: (Auchterarder) 01764 663119	Map 2 B3	**COMMENDED** 👑👑	1 Single 1 Twin 1 Family	2 Priv. NOT ensuite 1 Pub Bath/Show	B&B per person £14.00-£16.00 Single £14.00-£16.00 Double	Open Jan-Dec Dinner 1800-1900 B&B + Eve. Meal £22.50-£24.00	

Renovated stone cottage with large garden and stream.
Both rooms with private facilities. Friendly atmosphere,
home cooking, fresh produce.

Mrs Margaret West The Parsonage 111 High Street Auchterarder Perthshire PH3 1AA Tel: (Auchterarder) 01764 662392		**COMMENDED** 👑👑	2 Twin 2 Family	1 En Suite fac 2 Pub Bath/Show	B&B per person £18.00-£22.00 Single £17.00-£20.00 Double	Open Jan-Dec	

Personally run guest house in the centre of Auchterarder.
Convenient for golf courses, restaurants and all amenities.
Lovely views from all bedrooms.

BY AUCHTERARDER **Perthshire** Mrs Janice Scougall Raith Farm Madderty, by Crieff Perthshire PH7 3RJ Tel: (Madderty) 01764 683262	Map 2 B3	**COMMENDED** 👑👑	2 Family	2 En Suite fac	B&B per person £18.00-£20.00 Single	Open Apr-Oct	

Traditional farmhouse situated in beautiful countryside. Convenient for touring,
walking, golfing, fishing and parachuting. Children welcome.

AUCHTERMUCHTY **Fife** Donald & Isobel Steven Ardchoille Farmhouse Dunshalt Auchtermuchty Fife KY14 7EY Tel: (Auchtermuchty) 01337 828414/ 0589 988174 (mobile) Fax: 01337 828414	Map 2 C3	**HIGHLY COMMENDED** 👑👑👑	3 Twin	3 En Suite fac	B&B per person £25.00-£35.00 Double	Open Jan-Dec Dinner 1830-1930	

A warm welcome at a well-appointed farmhouse with superb views to the
Lomond Hills. Taste of Scotland award with home cooking and
baking a speciality. All rooms have private facilities. Non-smoking.

AULTBEA **Ross-shire** Cartmel Guest House Birchburn Road Aultbea Ross-shire IV22 2HZ Tel: (Aultbea) 01445 731375	Map 3 F6	**COMMENDED** 👑👑	2 Twin 2 Double	2 En Suite fac 1 Pub Bath/Show	B&B per person £16.00-£19.00 Double	Open Jan-Dec Dinner from 1830 B&B + Eve. Meal £26.00-£29.00	

Comfortable bungalow guest house set in 1.5 acres of mature garden.
Personally run. Vegetarians very welcome. Regret no smoking.

AULTBEA continued	Map 3 F6

SANDALE

Commended ♕♕♕

5 PIER ROAD, IV22 2JQ   Telephone: 01445 731336

Comfortable non-smoking accommodation set in a colourful garden with residents' lounge overlooking Loch Ewe. All rooms ensuite. Ideal centre for hillwalkers or just relaxing. Inverewe Gardens nearby. Home baking, evening meals, ample parking. *True Highland Hospitality.*

Mrs A MacLennan Sandale, 5 Pier Road Aultbea Ross-shire IV22 2JQ Tel: (Aultbea) 01445 731336	COMMENDED ♕♕♕	1 Double 2 Family	3 En Suite fac	B&B per person from £14.00 Single from £14.00 Double	Open Mar-Nov Dinner 1800-2000 B&B + Eve. Meal from £24.00
		House with sun lounge and views over Loch Ewe, set in a colourful garden. Traditional Scottish hospitality. Good home cooking.			
Mrs H McLeod The Croft Aultbea Ross-shire IV22 2JA Tel: (Aultbea) 01445 731352	COMMENDED Listed	1 Twin 2 Double	1 Pub Bath/Show	B&B per person from £16.00 Single from £14.50 Double	Open Jan-Dec Dinner 1800-2000 B&B + Eve. Meal from £24.50
		Detached house situated in elevated position overlooking Aultbea and Loch Ewe with views of Torridon Hills. Scottish cooking & hospitality.			
Mellondale Guest House 47 Mellon Charles Aultbea Ross-shire IV22 2JL Tel: (Aultbea) 01445 731326	HIGHLY COMMENDED ♕♕♕	2 Twin 3 Double	5 En Suite fac 2 Pub Bath/Show	B&B per person £17.00-£21.00 Single £17.00-£21.00 Double	Open Feb-Nov Dinner from 1830 B&B + Eve. Meal £25.00-£30.00
		Modern family guest house set in 4 acres with views of Loch Ewe. 9 miles (14.4 kms) from Inverewe Gardens. Ideal walking centre.			
AVIEMORE **Inverness-shire** A'Anside Guest House off Grampian Road Aviemore Inverness-shire PH22 1QD Tel: (Aviemore) 01479 810871	Map 4 C10 COMMENDED ♕♕	1 Twin 3 Double 1 Family	5 En Suite fac	B&B per person £16.00-£25.00 Single £16.00-£20.00 Double	Open Jan-Dec
		Modern bungalow sitting above the town. Stunning views over the town to the Cairngorm Mountains. Most rooms ensuite facilities.			
Ardlogie Guest House Dalfaber Road Aviemore Inverness-shire PH22 1PU Tel: (Aviemore) 01479 810747	COMMENDED Listed	1 Twin 4 Double	4 En Suite fac 1 Priv. NOT ensuite	B&B per person £16.00-£18.00 Double	Open Jan-Dec
		Semi-detached house in quiet road, 5 minutes walk from centre with its many facilities. Ideal for skiing, walking and touring.			
Mr R Bruce Hame, Dalfaber Road Aviemore Inverness-shire PH22 1PY Tel: (Aviemore) 01479 810822/ 0836 560174 (mobile)	APPROVED Listed	1 Twin 2 Double	1 Pub Bath/Show	B&B per person £15.00-£18.00 Single £13.00-£15.00 Double	Open Jan-Dec
		Traditional Scottish hospitality in friendly home, situated in quiet location but only 5 minutes walk from all amenities.			
Mrs Burgon Ardenlea, 13 Craig-na-Gower Aviemore Inverness-shire PH22 1RN Tel: (Aviemore) 01479 811738	COMMENDED Listed	1 Twin 1 Double	2 En Suite fac	B&B per person £18.00-£20.00 Single £13.50-£15.50 Double	Open Jan-Dec
		Traditional Scottish hospitality in friendly family home. Ideal base for touring beautiful Strathspey.			

Cairngorm Guest House Grampian Road Aviemore Inverness-shire PH22 1RP Tel: (Aviemore) 01479 810630 Fax: 01479 810630	COMMENDED 👑👑	3 Twin 5 Double 1 Family	9 En Suite fac	B&B per person £18.00-£20.00 Single £16.00-£20.00 Double	Open Jan-Dec	

Detached stone villa within 5 minutes walk of the centre and 10 minutes from bus and rail stations.

Mr and Mrs S Carruthers Iona, 18 Morlich Place Aviemore Inverness-shire PH22 1TH Tel: (Aviemore) 01479 810941	COMMENDED 👑👑	2 Twin 1 Double	1 En Suite fac 1 Pub Bath/Show	B&B per person £16.50-£20.50 Single £14.50-£18.50 Double	Open Jan-Dec, exc Xmas	

Friendly bed and breakfast in new house situated towards the north end of the village at the end of a quiet cul-de-sac. Facilities for outdoor activities.

Mrs E Clark Sonas, 19 Muirton Aviemore Inverness-shire PH22 1SF Tel: (Aviemore) 01479 810409	HIGHLY COMMENDED Listed	1 Twin 2 Double	2 Pub Bath/Show	B&B per person from £17.50 Single from £15.00 Double	Open Jan-Dec	

Modern detached bungalow in quiet residential area of village. All bedrooms have washbasins, colour TVs and tea/coffee making facilities.

Mrs A M Ferguson Cairn Eilrig, Glenmore Aviemore Inverness-shire PH22 1QU Tel: (Cairngorm) 01479 861223	COMMENDED Listed	1 Twin 1 Family	1 Pub Bath/Show	B&B per person from £12.50 Double	Open Jan-Dec	

Bungalow situated in Glenmore Forest Park with superb open views of the Cairngorms. Warm Highland hospitality guaranteed. Ski lifts 2 miles (3 kms).

Ms D J Harris Junipers, 5 Dell Mhor Aviemore Inverness-shire PH22 1QW Tel: (Aviemore) 01479 810405/ 0850 183397	COMMENDED Listed	1 Single 1 Double 1 Family	1 En Suite fac 1 Pub Bath/Show	B&B per person £14.00-£15.00 Single Room only per person £16.00	Open Jan-Dec	

Comfortable home with large sun room and Alpine garden, midway between Aviemore and Coylumbridge.

KINAPOL GUEST HOUSE
Dalfaber Road, Aviemore, Inverness-shire PH22 1PY
Tel: 01479 810513 Commended 👑
Small modern guest house in quiet situation, only 5 minutes' walk to station, buses and Aviemore Centre. All bedrooms have H&C, electric blankets, tea/coffee trays etc., and most have views of Cairngorm Mountains. Large bright guests' lounge with TV and hot drinks trolley. Large garden with access to river. Drying cupboard and ski store. Mountain bikes for hire. Reduced rates for week bookings and continental breakfasts. *Major credit cards accepted*

Kinapol Guest House Dalfaber Road Aviemore Inverness-shire PH22 1PY Tel: (Aviemore) 01479 810513	COMMENDED 👑	1 Twin 3 Double 1 Family	2 Pub Bath/Show	B&B per person £14.00-£20.00 Single £13.50-£14.00 Double Room only per person £11.00-£18.00	Open Jan-Dec	

Friendly welcome at modern house in large garden with views of Cairngorms. Quiet location but only 5 minutes walk to the town centre.

Lynwilg House Aviemore Inverness-shire PH22 1PZ Tel: (Aviemore) 01479 811685	HIGHLY COMMENDED 👑👑👑	1 Single 1 Twin 2 Double	3 En Suite fac 1 Priv. NOT ensuite	B&B per person £22.00-£30.00 Single £22.00-£30.00 Double	Open Jan-Nov Dinner 1900-2000 B&B + Eve. Meal £37.00-£47.00	

1930s country house set in 4 acres of landscaped gardens overlooking the Cairngorms, approximately 1 mile (2kms) south of Aviemore.

AVIEMORE continued	Map 4 C10					

Ravenscraig Guest House

Grampian Road, Aviemore, Inverness-shire PH22 1RP
Telephone: 01479 810278

This family run guest house is ideally situated for touring the Highlands and provides accommodation and full Scottish breakfast. The aim at Ravenscraig is to make you feel at home in informal and comfortable surroundings. Robert and Christine look forward to extending a warm Highland welcome to you.

| Ravenscraig Guest House Grampian Road Aviemore Inverness-shire PH22 1RP Tel: (Aviemore) 01479 810278 | COMMENDED 👑👑 | 1 Single 4 Twin 5 Double 2 Family | 12 En Suite fac | B&B per person £18.00-£36.00 Single £18.00-£20.00 Double | Open Jan-Dec | |

Situated on edge of village, within a few minutes walk of Aviemore centre. All rooms en suite. Some ground-floor annexe accommodation.

AYR	Map 1 G7					
Mr & Mrs H W Anton Clyde Cottage, 1 Arran Terrace Ayr KA7 1JF Tel: (Ayr) 01292 267368	COMMENDED 👑👑	1 Twin 1 Double 1 Family	1 En Suite fac 1 Pub Bath/Show	B&B per person £16.00 Single £14.00-£15.00 Double	Open Jan-Dec Dinner from 1800 B&B + Eve. Meal £19.00-£21.00	

Homely welcome at Listed stone-built house with large garden in Conservation Area. 200 yards from seafront, easy walk to town. Private parking.

| Armadale Guest House 33 Bellevue Crescent Ayr KA7 2DP Tel: (Ayr) 01292 264320 | COMMENDED Listed | 1 Twin 1 Double 1 Family | 2 En Suite fac 1 Pub Bath/Show | B&B per person from £16.00 Single from £16.00 Double | Open Jan-Dec | |

Personally run Edwardian terraced house; some ensuite rooms; convenient for beach, town centre and railway station.

| Mrs W Campbell Ferguslea, 98 New Road Ayr Ayrshire KA8 8JG Tel: (Ayr) 01292 268551 | COMMENDED 👑👑 | 1 Single 2 Twin | 1 Priv. NOT ensuite 1 Pub Bath/Show | B&B per person £14.00-£16.00 Single £14.00-£16.00 Double Room only per person £11.00-£13.00 | Open Jan-Dec | |

Traditional Scottish hospitality in comfortable family home, within 10 minutes walk of town centre and all amenities.

| Crescent Guest House 26 Bellevue Crescent Ayr KA7 2DR Tel: (Ayr) 01292 287329/ 0585 585223 (mobile) Fax: 01292 286779 | DELUXE 👑👑 | 2 Twin 2 Double | 4 En Suite fac | B&B per person £28.00-£35.00 Single £20.00-£25.00 Double | Open Jan-Nov | |

Refurbished Victorian terrace house in quiet location with easy access for town centre and beach.

Scotland for Golf . . .

Find out more about golf in Scotland. There's more to it than just the championship courses so get in touch with us now for information on the hidden gems of Scotland.

Write to: **Information Unit, Scottish Tourist Board, 23 Ravelston Terrace, Edinburgh EH4 3EU or call: 0131-332 2433**

VAT is shown at 17.5%: changes in this rate may affect prices. Prices shown are for guidance only. Please send SAE with each enquiry.

| Dargil Guest House
7 Queen's Terrace
Ayr
KA7 1DU
Tel: (Ayr) 01292 261955 | COMMENDED
👑👑 | 1 Twin
2 Double
1 Family | 1 En Suite fac
2 Pub Bath/Show | B&B per person
£15.00-£17.00 Double
Room only per person
£18.00-£20.00 | Open Jan-Dec
Dinner 1700-1730
B&B + Eve. Meal
from £23.00 |

Small, friendly guest house with sea front location.
Only a few minutes walk from the town centre. Private parking.

| Daviot Guest House
12 Queen's Terrace
Ayr
KA7 1DU
Tel: (Ayr) 01292 269678 | COMMENDED
👑👑 | 1 Single
1 Twin
1 Double
1 Family | 1 En Suite fac
2 Pub Bath/Show | B&B per person
from £17.00 Single
from £17.00 Double | Open Jan-Dec
Dinner from 1700 |

Friendly welcome at this quietly situated terraced house only a few minutes walk
from the seafront and town centre.

| Mrs M Ferguson
Kilkerran, 15 Prestwick Road
Ayr
KA8 8LD
Tel: (Ayr) 01292 266477 | COMMENDED
👑👑 | 1 Single
2 Twin
1 Double
1 Family | 2 En Suite fac
1 Pub Bath/Show | B&B per person
£14.00-£15.00 Single
£14.00-£17.00 Double | Open Jan-Dec |

Family run guest house on main road from Ayr to Prestwick airport.
Two minutes drive from town centre and convenient for Burns Country.

| Mrs T Filippi
Coilbank Villa
32 Castlehill Road
Ayr
KA7 2HZ
Tel: (Ayr) 01292 262936 | COMMENDED
Listed | 1 Single
2 Twin | 2 Pub Bath/Show | B&B per person
£16.00 Single
£15.00 Double | Open Apr-Sep |

Stone built Victorian town house with large garden, convenient for
town centre and beach. Near railway station.

| Mrs Agnes Gemmell
Dunduff Farm, Dunure
Ayr
Ayrshire
KA7 4LH
Tel: (Dunure) 01292 500225
Fax: 01292 500222 | HIGHLY
COMMENDED
👑👑👑 | 1 Twin
2 Double | 2 En Suite fac
1 Priv. NOT ensuite
1 Pub Bath/Show | B&B per person
£25.00-£30.00 Single
£18.00-£22.50 Double | Open Apr-Oct |

17C farmhouse on working farm in elevated position 5 miles (8kms) south of Ayr,
with fine views over Firth of Clyde to Arran. Private trout loch.

| The Grasmere
2 Eglinton Terrace
Ayr
KA7 1JJ
Tel: (Ayr) 01292 611033 | COMMENDED
👑👑 | 1 Single
2 Double | 1 En Suite fac
1 Limited ensuite
1 Pub Bath/Show | B&B per person
£15.00-£25.00 Single
£15.00-£25.00 Double
Room only per person
£15.00-£25.00 | Open Mar-Oct |

Victorian terraced house conveniently situated in quiet location
between town centre and seafront. Television in bedrooms.

| Iona Guest House
27 St Leonards Road
Ayr
KA7 2PS
Tel: (Ayr) 01292 269541 | COMMENDED
👑👑 | 2 Single
1 Twin
1 Double | 2 En Suite fac
1 Pub Bath/Show | B&B per person
£15.00-£17.00 Single
£15.00-£18.00 Double | Open Feb-Nov
Dinner 1830-1930
B&B + Eve. Meal
£22.00-£26.00 |

Traditional family home in residential area, ideally situated for
both the business and holiday traveller.

| Langley Bank Guest House
39 Carrick Road
Ayr
KA7 2RD
Tel: (Ayr) 01292 264246
Fax: 01292 282628 | HIGHLY
COMMENDED
Listed | 1 Single
2 Twin
2 Double
1 Family | 4 En Suite fac
2 Pub Bath/Show | B&B per person
£15.00-£40.00 Single
£15.00-£25.00 Double | Open Jan-Dec |

Elegantly refurbished Victorian house close to all amenities. Most rooms
have private facilities and telephones. Good base for touring Ayrshire.

	Map 1 G7						
AYR continued Mrs J B Mair Laggan, 42 Craigie Road Ayr KA8 0EZ Tel: (Ayr) 01292 264947		COMMENDED	1 Double 1 Family	1 Pub Bath/Show	B&B per person £15.00-£16.00 Single £15.00-£16.00 Double	Open Apr-Sep	

Semi-detached villa in residential area, close to racecourse, woodland and riverside walks, and public parks. 15 minutes walk from town centre and its amenities.

Mrs Wilson Deanbank, 44 Ashgrove Street Ayr KA7 3BG Tel: (Ayr) 01292 263745		HIGHLY COMMENDED	1 Double 1 Family	1 Pub Bath/Show	B&B per person from £17.00 Single from £16.00 Double	Open Jan-Dec	

Friendly, semi-detached home with many additional comforts. In a quiet residential situation, yet convenient for town centre. Close to numerous golf courses.

	Map 2 F5						
AYTON, by Eyemouth **Berwickshire** Mrs N Ferguson Towerwoods, The Crofts Ayton Berwickshire TD14 5QT Tel: (Coldingham) 018907 81529		COMMENDED Listed	1 Single 2 Twin	1 En Suite fac 2 Pub Bath/Show	B&B per person from £15.00 Double	Open Jan-Dec	

Modern family home quietly set in small friendly village. Convenient for A1. 2.5 miles (4kms) from the beach.

Mrs Riach Ayton Mains Farm House Ayton Berwickshire TD14 5RE Tel: (Ayton) 018907 81336		COMMENDED Listed	2 Single 1 Twin 1 Double	2 Pub Bath/Show	B&B per person £15.00-£16.00 Single £14.00-£15.00 Double	Open Apr-Oct	

On the main Eyemouth to Ayton road, this traditional farmhouse built in 1840 has delightful gardens. A non-smoking house.

Mrs Stevens Springbank Cottage, Beanburn Ayton Berwickshire TD14 5QZ Tel: (Ayton) 018907 81263		COMMENDED Listed	1 Twin 1 Family	1 Pub Bath/Show	B&B per person £15.00-£20.00 Double	Open Jan-Dec	

Victorian cottage set in attractive gardens in peaceful village convenient for A1. Ideal centre for touring Borders. Close to coastal Nature Reserve.

	Map 3 E4						
BACK **Lewis, Western Isles** Mrs M Fraser Seaside Villa Back Lewis, Western Isles PA86 Tel: (Back) 01851 820208		COMMENDED	1 Twin 1 Double 1 Family	1 En Suite fac 1 Limited ensuite 1 Pub Bath/Show	B&B per person from £16.00 Single from £15.00 Double	Open Jan-Dec Dinner from 1800	

Modern house on working croft, friendly atmosphere with home baking and cooking, 7 miles (11kms) from Stornoway. Lovely sea views.

	Map 3 F7						
BADACHRO **Ross-shire** Mrs D Moore Hazel Cottage, Leacnasaide Badachro, Gairloch Ross-shire Tel: (Badachro) 01445 741300		COMMENDED	1 Twin 2 Double	2 En Suite fac 1 Priv. NOT ensuite	B&B per person to £16.00 Double	Open May-Sep	

Modern detached house with garden. On quiet wooded road. 1 mile (2kms) Badachro. 4 miles (6kms) Gairloch.

Mr & Mrs G Willey Harbour View Badachro Ross-shire IV21 2AA Tel: (Badachro) 01445 741316		COMMENDED	2 Double 1 Family	3 En Suite fac 1 Pub Bath/Show	B&B per person £17.00-£19.00 Single £17.00-£19.00 Double	Open Mar-Oct Dinner at 1900 B&B + Eve. Meal £26.00-£28.00	

With superb views over Badachro Bay, this extended fisherman's cottage, having small rooms and coombed ceilings, retains its original period charm.

BALLACHULISH Argyll	Map 1 F1

Craiglinnhe Guest House

BALLACHULISH, ARGYLL PA39 4JX   Tel: 01855 811270

Craiglinnhe, situated close to the water's edge amidst magnificent scenery, provides an excellent touring base for the Western Highlands. Set in beautiful gardens, this small, personally managed guest house offers traditional Scottish hospitality in extremely well-appointed accommodation. An ideal setting in which to relax and unwind.

Brochure on request.   Commended 👑👑👑

Craiglinnhe Guest House Ballachulish Argyll PA39 4JX Tel: (Ballachulish) 01855 811270	COMMENDED 👑👑👑	4 Twin 2 Double	6 En Suite fac	B&B per person £19.00-£20.00 Double	Open Dec-Oct Dinner from 1900 B&B + Eve. Meal £28.00-£30.00
	Family run guest house overlooking Loch Linnhe and the mountains beyond. Hill walking and mountaineering in the area. Good centre for touring.				
Mrs Dow Tigh-ard, Brecklet Ballachulish Argyll PA39 4JG Tel: (Ballachulish) 01855 811328	COMMENDED Listed	1 Twin 1 Double	2 Pub Bath/Show	B&B per person £14.00-£15.00 Double	Open Apr-Oct
	Family home on edge of village, with magnificent views across Loch Leven to hills beyond. 12 miles (19 kms) from Fort William.				
Fern Villa Guest House Ballachulish Argyll PA39 4JE Tel: (Ballachulish) 01855 811393	COMMENDED 👑👑👑	2 Twin 3 Double	5 En Suite fac	B&B per person £17.00-£20.00 Single £17.00-£20.00 Double	Open Jan-Dec Dinner from 1900 B&B + Eve. Meal £26.00-£29.00
	Granite-built house in lochside village amidst spectacular scenery, convenient for Fort William. Excellent touring base. Table licence.				
Lyn-Leven Guest House Ballachulish Argyll PA39 4JP Tel: (Ballachulish) 01855 811392 Fax: 01855 811600	COMMENDED 👑👑👑	4 Twin 3 Double 1 Family	8 En Suite fac 1 Pub Bath/Show	B&B per person £18.00-£25.00 Single £16.00-£18.50 Double Room only per person £18.00-£25.00	Open Jan-Dec Dinner from 1830 B&B + Eve. Meal £25.00-£34.00
	Family run modern guest house in Ballachulish village and overlooking Loch Leven. All home cooking.				
Mr & Mrs M MacAskill Park View, 18 Park Road Ballachulish Argyll, PA39 4JS Tel: (Ballachulish) 01855 811560	COMMENDED 👑	1 Twin 2 Double	2 Pub Bath/Show	B&B per person £11.00-£15.00 Double	Open Jan-Dec
	Family house in quiet residential situation overlooking a small park. Convenient for Glencoe and Fort William.				

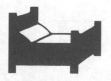

Book your accommodation anywhere in Scotland the easy way – through your nearest Tourist Information Centre.

A booking fee of £2.75 is charged, and you will be asked for a small deposit.

Local bookings are usually free, or a small fee will be charged.

BALLACHULISH continued	Map 1 F1

Ballachulish Home Farm

Highly Commended 👑👑👑

BALLACHULISH, ARGYLL PA39 4JX

This is a brand new, traditional style farmhouse, situated on an elevated site amid naturally wooded parkland, giving a sense of peace and quietness. Accommodation includes three double rooms, all en-suite, bright spacious lounge, separate dining room and drying facilities. Very central for touring West Highlands.

For details contact Mrs J McLauchlan. Tel: 01855 811792.

Joan McLauchlan Ballachulish Home Farm Ballachulish Argyll PA39 4JX Tel: (Ballachulish) 01855 811792	**HIGHLY COMMENDED** 👑👑👑	1 Twin 2 Double	3 En Suite fac	B&B per person £22.00-£25.00 Double	Open Jan-Oct
		New, traditional style farmhouse, situated on an elevated site amid naturally wooded parkland, giving a sense of peace and quietness. Open view across Loch Leven.			
Mrs J Watt Riverside House Ballachulish Argyll, PA39 4JE Tel: (Ballachulish) 01855 811473	**COMMENDED** 👑👑	1 Twin 2 Double	1 En Suite fac 2 Pub Bath/Show	B&B per person from £16.00 Single from £14.00 Double	Open Mar-Oct
		Modern family house in quiet location in centre of village. 1 mile from Glencoe, 15 miles (24 kms) from Fort William.			
BALLANTRAE **Ayrshire** Mrs J Campbell Craigalbert Farm Ballantrae Ayrshire KA26 0PD Tel: (Ballantrae) 01465 831289	Map 1 F9 **COMMENDED Listed**	1 Twin 2 Double	1 En Suite fac 2 Pub Bath/Show	B&B per person from £15.00 Single from £15.00 Double Room only per person from £15.00	Open May-Oct
		Bungalow style farmhouse on 180-acre beef and sheep farm 2 miles (3kms) from village. Rural and sea views. Good base for touring and walking.			

ARDSTINCHAR COTTAGE

Main Street, Ballantrae, Ayrshire KA26 0NA
Telephone: 01465 831343

This tastefully furnished family home is situated adjacent to the ruined Ardstinchar Castle and enjoys panoramic views over the Stinchar estuary. Accommodation offers good value, home from home comforts. Perfectly situated for touring beautiful Galloway and exploring "Burns" country and offers an ideal stop-off for Irish ferry traffic.

Mrs Drummond Ardstinchar Cottage Main Street, Ballantrae Ayrshire KA26 0NA Tel: (Ballantrae) 01465 831343	**COMMENDED** 👑	1 Twin 2 Double	1 Pub Bath/Show	B&B per person £15.00-£20.00 Single £13.00-£16.00 Double	Open Jan-Dec
		Comfortable accommodation in family home, within 20 minutes drive from Irish ferries.			
Mrs E McIntyre Downan Farm Ballantrae Ayrshire KA26 0PB Tel: (Ballantrae) 01465 831226	**COMMENDED Listed**	1 Double 1 Family	1 Pub Bath/Show	B&B per person £14.00-£16.00 Single £14.00-£16.00 Double Room only per person £10.00-£12.00	Open May-Oct
		100-acre stock farm situated on coast just south of Ballantrae with fine views over Firth of Clyde towards Kintyre and Arran.			

VAT is shown at 17.5%: changes in this rate may affect prices. Prices shown are for guidance only. Please send SAE with each enquiry.

Mrs Georgina McKinley Laggan Farm Ballantrae, Girvan Ayrshire KA26 0JZ Tel: (Ballantrae) 01465 831402	COMMENDED	1 Double 1 Family	1 En Suite fac 1 Pub Bath/Show	B&B per person £14.00-£17.00 Single £14.00-£17.00 Double	Open May-Oct Dinner 1700-1900 B&B + Eve. Meal £22.00-£25.00	

Family run dairy farm 0.5 miles (1km) south of Ballantrae on the Ayrshire coast. Woodland walks, fishing by arrangement.

Mrs J Sloan The Haven 75 Main Street Ballantrae Ayrshire KA26 0NA Tel: (Girvan) 01465 831306	COMMENDED	1 Twin 1 Family	2 Priv. NOT ensuite	B&B per person from £16.00 Double	Open Jan-Dec	

Characteristic bungalow in elevated private position overlooking River Stincher, Ballantrae Bay, Irish Sea and hills of Glenapp.

BALLATER
Aberdeenshire   Map 4 / E11

Averill Chalmers Bank House, Station Square Ballater Tel: (Ballater) 013397 55996 Fax: 013397 55996	HIGHLY COMMENDED	1 Twin 1 Double 2 Family	4 En Suite fac	B&B per person £22.00 Single £19.50 Double	Open Jan-Dec	

Central, convenient to all amenities. Recently refurbished, family run, offering excellent views over village, and Royal Deeside beyond.

Evelyn M Gray "Dee Valley" 26 Viewfield Road Ballater Aberdeenshire AB35 5RD Tel: (Ballater) 013397 55408	COMMENDED	1 Twin 2 Double 1 Family	1 En Suite fac 2 Pub Bath/Show	B&B per person £20.00-£23.00 Single £15.00-£18.00 Double	Open Apr-Nov	

Detached house in quiet residential area, close to village centre, bus station and golf course. Excellent base for touring.

Mrs A P Henchie Morven Lodge 29 Braemar Road Ballater Aberdeenshire AB35 5RQ Tel: (Ballater) 013397 55373	COMMENDED	1 Twin 1 Double 1 Family	1 Priv. NOT ensuite 2 Pub Bath/Show	B&B per person £15.00-£17.00 Double	Open May-Oct	

Former rectory situated close to the town centre. Convenient base for touring Deeside.

Moorside Guest House Braemar Road Ballater Aberdeenshire AB35 5RL Tel: (Ballater) 013397 55492 Fax: 013397 55492	COMMENDED	3 Twin 3 Double 3 Family	9 En Suite fac	B&B per person £20.00-£25.00 Single £17.00-£19.00 Double	Open Mar-Nov	

Friendly personally run guest house. All rooms ensuite, TV and courtesy tray. Large garden and car park. Excellent restaurants nearby.

Netherley Guest House 2 Netherley Place Ballater Aberdeenshire AB35 5QE Tel: (Ballater) 013397 55792	COMMENDED	2 Single 2 Twin 2 Double 3 Family	4 En Suite fac 2 Pub Bath/Show	B&B per person £17.50-£18.50 Single £15.50-£20.00 Double	Open Feb-Oct	

Family run guest house in a quiet location in the centre of a renowned village. Close to shops and amenities.

Mrs C J Strachan Osborne House 4 Dundarroch Road Ballater Aberdeenshire AB35 5RP Tel: (Ballater) 013397 56031	HIGHLY COMMENDED	2 Twin 1 Double	3 En Suite fac	B&B per person £29.00-£34.00 Single £20.00-£25.00 Double	Open May-Oct	

Late Victorian granite house with feature portico; private grounds and parking. Quiet residential area close to centre and golf course. No smoking.

BY BALLINGRY, nr Loch Leven Fife	Map 2 C3

NAVITIE HOUSE

Commended

Ballingry, Nr Loch Leven, Fife, KY5 8LR
Telephone: 01592 860295 Fax: 01592 869769

This period mansion, set in 4 acres of ground, offers large rooms with en-suite facilities, home cooking, sauna and excellent views over the Forth Valley. Situated 4 miles off the M90 and only 25 minutes drive from Edinburgh. Many golf courses within a short drive.
B&B from £20 per night. Discounts for children.

Navitie House by Ballingry, nr Loch Leven Fife KY5 8LR Tel: (Ballingry) 01592 860295 Fax: 01592 869769	COMMENDED	1 Single 2 Twin 3 Double 3 Family	7 En Suite fac 2 Priv. NOT ensuite 1 Pub Bath/Show	B&B per person from £22.00 Single £20.00-£37.00 Double	Open Jan-Dec Dinner 1900-2100 B&B + Eve. Meal £29.00-£31.00

Detached house in its own grounds overlooking Ballingry village.
Only 4 miles (6kms) from the Edinburgh to Perth motorway.

BALLINTUIM, by Blairgowrie Perthshire Mrs Alison J Constable Tomlea Farm Ballintuim, by Blairgowrie Perthshire PH10 7NL Tel: (Strathardle) 01250 881383	Map 2 B1 COMMENDED Listed	2 Twin	1 Priv. NOT ensuite 2 Pub Bath/Show	B&B per person £15.00-£16.00 Single £13.00-£15.00 Double	Open Jan-Dec Dinner 1830-2000

Working farm set in heart of Scottish Glen with superb views.
Private fishing and hill walking.

BALLOCH Dunbartonshire Mrs M Brown 6 McLean Crescent Lomond Road Estate Balloch Dunbartonshire G83 8HW Tel: (Alexandria) 01389 752855	Map 1 G4 COMMENDED Listed	1 Twin 1 Double	1 Pub Bath/Show	B&B per person £16.50-£17.50 Single £14.50-£15.50 Double	Open Jan-Dec Dinner from 1800 B&B + Eve. Meal £21.00-£22.50

Modern family villa in quiet residential area, offering a warm and friendly welcome.
30 minute drive from Glasgow Airport.

Mrs Margaret Campbell Gowanlea Guest House Drymen Road Balloch Dunbartonshire G83 8HS Tel: (Alexandria) 01389 752456	HIGHLY COMMENDED	1 Twin 2 Double	3 En Suite fac	B&B per person £16.00-£25.00 Single £16.00-£20.00 Double	Open Jan-Dec

Situated in residential area of Balloch, close to world-famous Loch Lomond.
Friendly welcome, all rooms ensuite.

Mrs Janice Elder Kinnoul, Drymen Road Balloch Dunbartonshire G83 8HS Tel: (Alexandria) 01389 721116	COMMENDED	2 Double 2 Family	2 En Suite fac 2 Priv. NOT ensuite	B&B per person £23.00-£25.00 Single £16.00-£18.00 Double	Open Jan-Dec Dinner 1900-2000 B&B + Eve. Meal £27.50-£29.50

Spacious detached stone-built Victorian villa in quiet residential area only
minutes from Loch Lomond and Balloch Country Park.

Mrs Margot Foulger Beulah, Fisherwood Road Balloch Dunbartonshire G83 8SW Tel: (Alexandria) 01389 753022	COMMENDED	1 Twin 1 Double	2 En Suite fac	B&B per person £16.00-£19.00 Single £16.00-£19.00 Double	Open Jan-Dec

Family home set in secluded mature garden. Private parking
and convenient for shops and railway station to Glasgow.

Mrs E Oultram Westville, Riverside Lane Balloch G83 8LF Tel: (Alexandria) 01389 752307	COMMENDED	1 Double 1 Family	1 Pub Bath/Show	B&B per person £17.00-£19.00 Single £17.00-£19.00 Double Room only per person £15.00-£17.00	Open Jan-Dec

Mature bungalow, situated in quiet area of Balloch. Private parking.
Overlooking the marina at River Leven. Ideal location for touring.

Mr Thomas Patrick Woodvale, Drymen Road Balloch Dunbartonshire G83 Tel: (Alexandria) 01389 755771	APPROVED Listed	2 Double 1 Family	3 En Suite fac	B&B per person £12.00-£17.00 Double Room only per person £13.00-£18.00	Open Jan-Dec Dinner 1730-1900

Family home in centre of Balloch. Short walk to all amenities.
Ideal base for touring.

Mrs Margo J Ross Glyndale, 6 McKenzie Drive Lomond Rd Est. Balloch Dunbartonshire G83 8HL Tel: (Alexandria) 01389 758238	COMMENDED Listed	1 Twin 1 Double	1 Pub Bath/Show	B&B per person £14.50-£15.50 Double	Open Jan-Dec

Modern family home in residential area, two minutes walk from Loch Lomond
and 30 minutes drive from Glasgow Airport.

Mr C Tait 240 Main Street Jamestown Balloch Dunbartonshire Tel: (Balloch) 01389 752473	COMMENDED	1 Family	1 En Suite fac	B&B per person from £22.50 Single from £14.50 Double	Open Mar-Oct Dinner 1730-1930 B&B + Eve. Meal from £20.50

Self-contained, serviced flat in family home. Personal attention from your hosts.
Ideal for touring Loch Lomond and the Trossachs.

Jeanette Wilson Shieldaig Farm, Upper Stoneymollen Road Balloch Dunbartonshire G83 8QY Tel: (Alexandria) 01389 752459	HIGHLY COMMENDED	1 Twin 1 Double	1 En Suite fac 1 Priv. NOT ensuite	B&B per person £25.00-£30.00 Single £17.50-£20.00 Double	Open Jan-Dec Dinner 1930-2030 B&B + Eve. Meal £30.00-£42.50

Totally refurbished farm buildings in secluded setting. Conveniently situated for
touring Loch Lomond & Trossachs. Easy access to A82.

BALLYGRANT Isle of Islay, Argyll	Map 1 C5	

Kilmeny Farmhouse

Ballygrant, Isle of Islay, Argyll PA45 7QW
Telephone: 01496 840668

In the heart of a 300 acre beef farm, Kilmeny Farmhouse commands
magnificent views of surrounding hills and glen. This family business
places its emphasis on quality and personal service. En-suite bedrooms
with bath shower etc are elegantly furnished. Public rooms are
charming with a country house influence. Four-course dinner menu.

Mrs Margaret Rozga Kilmeny Farmhouse Ballygrant Isle of Islay, Argyll PA45 7QW Tel: (Port Askaig) 01496 840668	DELUXE	1 Twin 2 Double	3 En Suite fac	B&B per person from £28.00 Single from £28.00 Double	Open Jan-Dec Dinner 1830-2000 B&B + Eve. Meal from £45.00

On working farm, with excellent views over surrounding farmland. Friendly
atmosphere and home cooking with a choice of menus. Two ground floor bedrooms.

BALMACARA Ross-shire Mrs A Gordon Ashgrove, Balmacara Square Balmacara, by Kyle of Lochalsh Ross-shire IV40 8DJ Tel: (Balmacara) 01599 566259	Map 3 F9 COMMENDED	1 Twin 1 Double 1 Family	1 En Suite fac 1 Pub Bath/Show	B&B per person £15.00-£17.00 Double	Open Jan-Dec

Traditional village cottage, off main road to Skye.
3 miles (5kms) from Kyle of Lochalsh and the new Skye Bridge.

| BALMACARA continued | Map 3 F9 |

Old Post Office House

Balmacara, by Kyle of Lochalsh IV40 8DH
Telephone: 01599 566200 Fax: 01599 555322

Our comfortable family home has successfully operated as a guesthouse for ten years. We are open all year, offering the good and simple comforts to travellers. Situated on the village street beside shops, pub, restaurant, petrol station and opposite the jetty into Lochalsh!

Miss Anne F McGlennon Old Post Office House Balmacara by Kyle of Lochalsh Tel: (Balmacara) 01599 566200 Fax: 01599 555322	COMMENDED Listed	2 Twin 1 Double	2 Pub Bath/Show	B&B per person £15.00-£20.00 Single £15.00-£20.00 Double	Open Jan-Dec

Modernised and renovated former post office situated on shores of Loch Alsh. With fine views southwards to Kylerhea and Isle of Skye.

BALMAHA, by Drymen Stirlingshire Mrs E Craik Lomond Bank Balmaha Stirlingshire G63 0JQ Tel: (Balmaha) 01360 870213	Map 1 G4 HIGHLY COMMENDED	2 Double	1 En Suite fac 1 Priv. NOT ensuite	B&B per person £25.00 Single £20.00-£25.00 Double	Open Apr-Oct

Comfortable, Victorian country house, on the shores of Loch Lomond. Magnificent views and extensive grounds. One bedroom ensuite.

Mrs K MacFadyen Dunleen Milton of Buchanan Balmaha Stirlingshire G63 0JE Tel: (Balmaha) 01360 870274	HIGHLY COMMENDED	1 Twin 1 Double	1 Pub Bath/Show	B&B per person £17.00-£18.00 Double	Open May-Oct

Comfortable modern bungalow situated in a quiet spot within easy reach of Loch Lomond. Friendly atmosphere.

Mrs F MacLuskie Critreoch Rowardennan Road Balmaha Stirlingshire G63 0AW Tel: (Balmaha) 01360 870309	COMMENDED	1 Single 1 Twin 1 Double	1 Pub Bath/Show	B&B per person £16.00-£16.50 Single £16.00-£16.50 Double	Open Apr-Oct

Friendly, family home in beautiful location, close to shore of Loch Lomond, with magnificent views. Warm welcome assured.

Mrs Margaret Maxwell Cashel Farm Balmaha Drymen Glasgow G63 0AW Tel: (Balmaha) 01360 870229	COMMENDED	2 Family	1 En Suite fac 1 Pub Bath/Show	B&B per person £17.00-£20.00 Single	Open Mar-Sep

Working farm with Galloway cows and black face sheep. Quiet location overlooking Loch Lomond. On West Highland Way.

BALQUHIDDER Perthshire Mrs Lesley Blain Calea Sona Balquhidder Perthshire FK19 8NY Tel: (Strathyre) 01877 384260	Map 1 H2 COMMENDED	1 Twin 1 Double	1 En Suite fac 1 Priv. NOT ensuite	B&B per person £20.00 Double	Open Jan-Dec

Cottage, an interesting blend of old and new, peacefully situated with superb views. Good walking area.

Craigruie Farmhouse

Craigruie Farm, Balquhidder, By Lochearnhead, Perthshire FK19 8PQ
Telephone: 01877 384262

Craigruie Farmhouse is set in the beautiful braes of Balquhidder overlooking Loch Voil. Enjoy personally organised sporting activities including fishing, stalking and shooting on this family run hill farm. Excellent traditional fayre in very comfortable surroundings. Warm welcome to all.

Mrs Marshall Craigruie Farmhouse Balquhidder, by Lochearnhead Perthshire FK19 8PQ Tel: (Balquhidder) 01877 384262	**COMMENDED** Listed	1 Twin 2 Family	1 En Suite fac 1 Pub Bath/Show	B&B per person from £21.00 Single £18.00-£20.00 Double	Open Jan-Dec Dinner 1800-2130 B&B + Eve. Meal £28.00-£34.00

Tastefully renovated farmhouse, overlooking Loch Voil, peacefully situated 2 miles (3kms) from Balquhidder. Personally organised sporting and fishing.

BANCHORY **Kincardineshire** Kathleen Balsamo Towerbank, 93 High Street Banchory Kincardineshire Tel: (Banchory) 01330 824798/822657	Map 4 F11 **HIGHLY COMMENDED**	2 Twin	2 En Suite fac	B&B per person from £20.00 Single from £17.00 Double	Open Jan-Dec

Centrally situated Victorian house, south facing with splendid views towards the Deeside hills.

Mrs Hampson The Old Police House 3 Bridge Street Banchory Kincardineshire AB31 3SX Tel: (Banchory) 01330 824000	**HIGHLY COMMENDED**	1 Twin 1 Double	2 En Suite fac	B&B per person from £20.00 Single from £17.00 Double	Open Jan-Dec

Banchory's original Police Station and Prison. House of great character and warmth. Centrally located and close to all amenities.

The Old West Manse

71 Station Road, Banchory, Kincardineshire AB31 3UD
Telephone: 01330 822202

Luxuriously refurbished Victorian manse set in the heart of Royal Deeside amidst the famous *Castle* and *Whisky* trails. Deluxe accommodation, tastefully designed by Laura Ashley and furnished to the very highest standard. Expansive gardens and ample private parking. Golf and fishing by prior arrangement. A real *Home from Home* experience.

Mr & Mrs Taylor The Old West Manse B&B 71 Station Road Banchory Kincardineshire AB31 3UD Tel: (Banchory) 01330 822202	**DELUXE**	2 Twin 2 Double	2 En Suite fac 2 Priv. NOT ensuite	B&B per person £20.00-£28.00 Single £20.00-£24.00 Double	Open Jan-Dec

A former manse. A real home-from-home experience in a relaxed and informal atmosphere. Fine views over River Dee and hills beyond.

Village Guest House 83 High Street Banchory Kincardineshire AB31 3TJ Tel: (Banchory) 01330 823307	**HIGHLY COMMENDED** Listed	2 Twin 2 Double Suites avail	1 Priv. NOT ensuite 3 Pub Bath/Show	B&B per person £18.00-£25.00 Single £19.00-£20.00 Double Room only per person to £18.00	Open Jan-Dec Dinner 1900-2000 B&B + Eve. Meal £30.00-£32.00

Charming Victorian house in centre of Royal Deeside village. Fountain patio. Warm Scottish welcome.

BY BANCHORY **Kincardineshire** Caroline Collen Knappach Toll Steading Knappach, by Banchory Kincardineshire AB31 3JA Tel: (Crathes) 01330 844425	Map 4 F11	HIGHLY COMMENDED Listed	1 Twin 1 Double	1 Pub Bath/Show	B&B per person from £20.00 Single from £17.00 Double	Open Jan-Dec Dinner 1930-2030 B&B + Eve. Meal from £35.00	

Renovated steading in beautiful countryside, all home cooking and non-smoking.

Mrs Jean Flavell The Mill of Eslie by Banchory Kincardineshire AB31 3LD Tel: (Banchory) 01330 823875		HIGHLY COMMENDED	1 Twin 1 Double	2 En Suite fac	B&B per person £20.00 Single £17.00 Double	Open Jan-Dec	

Granite-built converted mill in peaceful location with fine views of spectacular scenery of Royal Deeside, 4 miles (6kms) south of Banchory. Non-smoking.

Mrs P Law Monthammock Farm Durris, by Banchory Kincardineshire AB31 3DX Tel: (Drumoak) 01330 811421		COMMENDED	1 Twin 1 Double	1 En Suite fac 1 Pub Bath/Show	B&B per person to £20.00 Single to £17.00 Double	Open Jan-Dec Dinner 1800-1930	

Tranquillity and a warm welcome at this sympathetically converted steading with spectacular views over Deeside.

Mrs Irene Taylor Wester Knockhill, Strachan Banchory Kincardineshire AB31 3LL Tel: (Banchory) 01330 824328		HIGHLY COMMENDED Listed	1 Twin 2 Double	1 En Suite fac 1 Pub Bath/Show	B&B per person £22.00-£25.00 Single £18.00-£20.00 Double Room only per person £15.00-£20.00	Open Jan-Dec	

Spacious modernised house on small farm. Large garden bounded by a stream. Peaceful setting in beautiful Royal Deeside.

BANFF Dorothy & Alec Clark Montcoffer House, Montcoffer Banff AB45 3LJ Tel: (Banff) 01261 812979	Map 4 F7	APPROVED	1 Single 1 Double 1 Family	2 En Suite fac 1 Priv. NOT ensuite	B&B per person from £16.00 Single from £16.00 Double	Open Jan-Dec Dinner 1800-2000 B&B + Eve. Meal from £23.50	

Listed 17th-century mansion, overlooking Deveron Valley. Ideal centre for walking, golf, fishing, Castle and Whisky trails.

LOOK FOR THE SIGNS OF THE WELCOME HOSTS

Welcome Host

MORAYHILL
Bellevue Road, Banff AB45 1BJ
Telephone: 01261 815956

This comfortable family home is situated in Banff, an historic coastal town with many fine buildings including Duff House, a Country House Gallery. There are many good golf courses including Duff House Royal close by. The castle and coastal trails are also within easy reach.

Mrs Wilkie Morayhill, Bellevue Road Banff AB45 1BJ Tel: (Banff) 01261 815956		COMMENDED 👑👑👑	2 Twin 1 Double	2 En Suite fac 1 Pub Bath/Show	B&B per person from £15.00 Single from £15.00 Double	Open Jan-Dec	

Large Victorian house, centrally situated for town, golf, and fishing. Warm and friendly welcome assured.

BY BANFF Mrs Arjes North Sandlaw Farmhouse Alvah, by Banff Banffshire AB45 3UD Tel: (Eden) 01261 821252	Map 4 F7	COMMENDED Listed	1 Single 1 Twin 1 Double	1 Priv. NOT ensuite 2 Pub Bath/Show	B&B per person £15.00-£17.50 Single £15.00-£17.50 Double	Open Apr-Oct Dinner to 1900 B&B + Eve. Meal £22.00-£24.50	

Substantial farmhouse, differently furnished in beautiful peaceful surroundings near River Deveron. Languages spoken.

BANKFOOT **Perthshire** Mrs C McKay Blair House, Main Street Bankfoot Perthshire PH1 4AB Tel: (Bankfoot) 01738 787338	Map 2 B2	COMMENDED 👑👑	1 Twin 1 Double	2 En Suite fac 2 Pub Bath/Show	B&B per person from £16.00 Double	Open Jan-Dec	

A friendly welcome at this personally run B & B. Private parking; ideal location for touring the Perthshire area. Fishing, golfing within easy reach.

BARRHILL **Ayrshire** Mrs Hughes Blair Farm Barrhill, Girvan Ayrshire KA26 0RD Tel: (Barrhill) 01465 821247	Map 1 G9	COMMENDED 👑👑	1 Twin 2 Double	1 En Suite fac 1 Pub Bath/Show	B&B per person £14.50-£18.00 Single £14.50-£18.00 Double	Open Easter-Oct Dinner from 1800 B&B + Eve. Meal from £22.50	

Traditional farmhouse, convenient for Glen Trool Country Park and Ayrshire coast. Fishing available.

BEATTOCK **Dumfriesshire** Mrs F Bell Cogries Farm Beattock Dumfriesshire DG10 9PP Tel: (Johnstone Bridge) 01576 470320	Map 2 B8	COMMENDED 👑	1 Double 3 Family	1 Pub Bath/Show	B&B per person from £14.50 Double	Open Feb-Nov	

Dairy and mixed farm (275 acres) quietly situated yet convenient for the A74 and Moffat. Good centre for touring.

BEAULY **Inverness-shire** George & Pat Borland Knoydart, Windhill Beauly Inverness-shire IV4 7AS Tel: (Inverness) 01463 782353	Map 4 A8	HIGHLY COMMENDED 👑👑👑	1 Twin 2 Double	3 En Suite fac 1 Pub Bath/Show	B&B per person from £20.00 Single Room only per person from £17.00	Open Easter-Sep	

Luxurious modern home set in beautiful rural area. Ideally situated for touring. Warm welcome assured.

BEAULY continued	Map 4 A8					
Heathmount Guest House Station Road Beauly Inverness-shire IV4 7EQ Tel: (Beauly) 01463 782411		COMMENDED	2 Single 1 Double 2 Family	1 Pub Bath/Show	B&B per person £15.00-£18.00 Single £15.00-£18.00 Double	Open Jan-Dec
			Formerly a merchant's house, c1892, now a family run guest house situated near the centre of Beauly, with off-road parking.			
Mrs MacKay Ellangowan, Croyard Road Beauly Inverness-shire IV4 7DJ Tel: (Beauly) 01463 782273		COMMENDED	1 Twin 1 Double 1 Family	3 Limited ensuite 1 Pub Bath/Show	B&B per person £13.00-£15.00 Double	Open Apr-Oct
			Comfortable, centrally heated home near Priory. Ideal base for touring.			
Mrs C Munro Wester Moniack Farm Kirkhill, by Inverness Inverness-shire IV5 7PQ Tel: (Drumchardine) 01463 831237		COMMENDED Listed	1 Double 1 Family	1 Pub Bath/Show	B&B per person £14.00-£16.00 Single £14.00-£15.00 Double B&B + Eve. Meal £21.00-£22.00	Open Jan-Dec Dinner 1830-2000
			Farmhouse with family atmosphere in a peaceful setting, next to Castle and Winery. Conveniently situated for Inverness and touring the Highlands.			
Mrs M Ritchie Rheindown Farm Beauly Inverness-shire IV4 7AB Tel: (Beauly) 01463 782461		COMMENDED	1 Double 1 Family	1 Pub Bath/Show	B&B per person £13.50-£14.50 Double	Open Apr-Oct Dinner from 1815 B&B + Eve. Meal £20.50-£22.50
			Farmhouse on working farm in elevated position overlooking Beauly and the Firth beyond. Home cooking.			
BEITH Ayrshire	Map 1 G6					

SHOTTS FARM

BEITH, AYRSHIRE KA15 1LB
TELEPHONE: 01505 502273

Comfortable friendly accommodation is offered on this 160-acre dairy farm, one mile from the A736, well situated to visit golf courses, country parks and leisure centre. Also ideal for the ferry to Arran or Millport and for many good shopping centres all around.

Mrs Gillan Shotts Farm Barrmill, Beith Ayrshire KA15 1LB Tel: (Beith) 01505 502273	COMMENDED Listed	1 Double 1 Family	2 Pub Bath/Show	B&B per person from £12.00 Single from £11.00 Double	Open Jan-Dec Dinner 1830-2230 B&B + Eve. Meal from £18.00
		Family run farmhouse accommodation on a 160-acre dairy farm. Ideal base for Burns Country, Arran and cultural Glasgow.			
Mrs E Workman Meikle Auchengree Glengarnock Beith Ayrshire KA14 3BU Tel: (Dalry) 01294 832205	COMMENDED	1 Twin 2 Double	1 En Suite fac 2 Pub Bath/Show	B&B per person from £16.50 Single from £15.50 Double	Open Jan-Dec
		Modern comfortable farmhouse, with friendly atmosphere, on dairy farm. Central for Largs, Ayr and Glasgow. Large games room with indoor bowls.			

BENDERLOCH, by Connel **Argyll** Mrs June Currie Hawthorn Benderloch, by Connel Argyll PA37 1QS Tel: (Ledaig) 01631 720452	Map 1 E2	COMMENDED ♛	1 Twin 1 Double	1 Pub Bath/Show	B&B per person from £13.00 Double	Open Mar-Oct Dinner 1830-2000	
Bungalow in peaceful rural setting 9 miles (14kms) from Oban, and 5 minutes walk from Tralee beach. Own restaurant adjacent.							

BERNERAY **North Uist, Western Isles** D A McKillop Burnside Croft Berneray North Uist, Western Isles Tel: (Berneray) 01876 540235 Fax: 01876 540230	Map 3 B7	COMMENDED ♛♛♛	1 Twin 2 Double	2 En Suite fac 1 Priv. NOT ensuite	B&B per person £19.00-£23.00 Single £19.00-£23.00 Double Room only per person £19.00-£23.00	Open Jan-Dec Dinner 1800-2030 B&B + Eve. Meal £25.00-£30.00	
A fine example of traditional Highland hospitality. You quickly become one of the family enjoying Gloria's good food and Don Alick's wide ranging conversation.							

BERNISDALE, by Portree **Isle of Skye, Inverness-shire** Mrs Sharon Brotherhood Donmar, Post Office House, 43 Bernisdale Bernisdale, by Portree Isle of Skye, Inverness-shire IV51 9NS Tel: (Skeabost Bridge) 01470 532204	Map 3 D8	COMMENDED Listed	1 Single 2 Family	2 Pub Bath/Show	B&B per person £13.00-£15.00 Single £13.00-£15.00 Double	Open Jan-Dec Dinner 1830-2000 B&B + Eve. Meal £21.00-£23.00	
Detached house in quiet area of Bernisdale township between Portree and Dunvegan overlooking Loch Snizort. Central location for touring in Skye.							

BY BETTYHILL **Sutherland** Mrs H I McPherson 7 Borgie Skerray Sutherland KW14 7TH Tel: (Bettyhill) 01641 521428	Map 4 B3	COMMENDED ♛	2 Family	2 En Suite fac	B&B per person £21.00-£23.00 Single £16.00-£18.00 Double	Open Jan-Dec Dinner 1830-1930 B&B + Eve. Meal £27.00-£34.00	
A warm Highland welcome assured at this stone-built croft house. Home cooking, salmon a speciality. On main A836. Parking available.							

BIGGAR **Lanarkshire** Mrs Margaret E Kirby Walston Mansion Farmhouse Walston, Carnwath Lanarkshire ML11 8NF Tel: (Dunsyre) 01899 81338	Map 2 B6	COMMENDED ♛♛♛	1 Twin 1 Double 1 Family	2 En Suite fac 2 Pub Bath/Show	B&B per person £13.00-£15.00 Single £13.00-£15.00 Double Room only per person £13.00-£15.00	Open Jan-Dec Dinner 1800-2000 B&B + Eve. Meal £20.00-£22.00	
19th-century stone-built farmhouse situated in small village at south west end of Pentland Hills. 5 miles (8kms) from Biggar.							

BIGGAR continued	Map 2 B6		

LINDSAYLANDS HOUSE
BIGGAR, LANARKSHIRE ML12 6NR
TELEPHONE: 01899 220033/221221   FAX: 01899 221009
THIS LOVELY LISTED COUNTRY HOUSE IS SET IN ITS OWN GROUNDS SURROUNDED BY 94 ACRES OF ITS OWN FARMLAND. SITUATED OFF MAIN ROAD 1 MILE WEST OF BIGGAR. 3 LARGE BEDROOMS WITH PRIVATE FACILITIES, GUEST LOUNGE AND DINING ROOM. IDEAL BASE FOR TOURING GLASGOW, EDINBURGH, BORDERS OR JUST RELAXING.

Mrs M E Stott Lindsaylands House Biggar Lanarkshire Tel: (Biggar) 01899 220033/221221 Fax: 01899 221009	**HIGHLY COMMENDED**	1 Twin 2 Double	2 En Suite fac 1 Priv. NOT ensuite	B&B per person £26.00-£29.00 Single £22.00-£25.00 Double	Open Mar-Nov Dinner 1930-2030 B&B + Eve. Meal £34.50-£39.00

Attractive country house, set in 6 acres of garden, amidst lovely countryside, with views to Border Hills. Hard tennis court.

BY BIGGAR Lanarkshire Skirling House Skirling by Biggar Lanarkshire ML12 6HD Tel: (Skirling) 01899 860274 Fax: 01899 860255	Map 2 B6 **HIGHLY COMMENDED**	2 Twin 1 Double	3 En Suite fac	B&B per person £35.00 Single £25.00-£30.00 Double	Open March-Dec Dinner 1930-2000

Open fires, peaceful gardens, rolling hills, fine cuisine.
Unique Arts & Crafts house by village green.
All rooms overlooking secluded gardens and woods.

BIRGHAM, by Coldstream Berwickshire Mrs K Boyle Appleacre Birgham, by Coldstream Berwickshire TD12 4NF Tel: (Birgham) 01890 830306	Map 2 E6 **COMMENDED**	1 Twin 1 Double	1 Pub Bath/Show	B&B per person to £15.00 Double	Open May-Sep

Comfortable bungalow, with attractive garden, within easy walking distance of old village pub.

BIRSAY Orkney Mrs Balderstone Heatherlea Birsay Orkney KW17 2LR Tel: (Birsay) 01856 721382	Map 5 B10 **APPROVED**	1 Twin 1 Double	1 Pub Bath/Show	B&B per person £14.50-£15.00 Single £14.50-£15.00 Double	Open Apr-Oct

Beautiful situation overlooking the Loch of Boardhouse. Free trout angling.
Boat for hire. Close to RSPB reserves and archaeological areas.

Mrs Clouston Primrose Cottage Birsay Orkney KW17 2NB Tel: (Birsay) 01856 721384	**COMMENDED**	1 Single 2 Double	1 Pub Bath/Show	B&B per person £13.00-£14.00 Single £13.00-£14.00 Double	Open Jan-Dec Dinner 1800-2000 B&B + Eve. Meal £19.00-£21.00

In quiet location overlooking Marwick Bay, close to RSPB reserves.
Local produce used whenever possible, fresh fish and shellfish.

BLACKFORD Perthshire Mrs R Robertson Yarrow House, Moray Street Blackford Perthshire PH4 1PY Tel: (Blackford) 01764 682358	Map 2 A3 **COMMENDED**	1 Single 1 Twin 1 Family	1 En Suite fac 1 Pub Bath/Show	B&B per person £15.00-£16.00 Single £15.00-£16.00 Double Room only per person £10.00-£12.00	Open Jan-Dec Dinner from 1800

Comfortable home in the centre of village with good walks in the surrounding countryside. Convenient for the A9.

BLACKWATERFOOT Isle of Arran Mrs G Arthur Broombrae Kilpatrick Isle of Arran Tel: (Shiskine) 01770 860435	Map 1 E7	HIGHLY COMMENDED	2 Twin	1 Pub Bath/Show	B&B per person £16.00 Single £16.00 Double	Open Mar-Nov Dinner 1930-2130 B&B + Eve. Meal £27.00

About 1 mile (2kms) from Blackwaterfoot on the Lagg Rd.
Quietly situated, with magnificent views to Kintyre from the sun-lounge.

Mrs Sherwood Morvern Blackwaterfoot Isle of Arran KA27 8EU Tel: (Shiskine) 01770 860254	APPROVED	1 Twin 2 Double	1 En Suite fac 1 Pub Bath/Show	B&B per person £16.00-£18.00 Single £16.00-£18.00 Double	Open Jan-Dec Dinner from 1830 B&B + Eve. Meal £27.00-£28.00

Former bank house now a family home in the heart of the village.

BLAIR ATHOLL Perthshire Dalgreine off St Andrew's Crescent Blair Atholl Perthshire PH18 5SX Tel: (Blair Atholl) 01796 481276	Map 4 C12	COMMENDED	1 Single 2 Twin 2 Double 1 Family	2 En Suite fac 1 Priv.NOT ensuite 1 Pub Bath/Show	B&B per person £14.00-£17.50 Single £14.00-£17.50 Double	Open Jan-Dec Dinner 1830-1930 B&B + Eve. Meal £23.00-£26.50

Well-appointed guest house, convenient for Blair Castle, Pitlochry Festival Theatre
and the many local activities and attractions. Good home cooking.

THE FIRS
St Andrews Crescent, Blair Atholl
Perthshire PH18 5TA
Telephone: 01796 481256

A warm, friendly family run guest house in this peaceful village close to Pitlochry.

Blair Atholl is a quiet holiday centre in the heart of Highland Perthshire. With famous Blair Castle, shops, folk museum, water mill, bowling and fishing etc., the village caters for all. Extensive woodland, riverside and hill walks around the village.

All rooms en-suite, with colour TV and tea/coffee-making facilities. Excellent weekly terms.

Kirstie and Geoff Crerar look forward to welcoming you.

The Firs St Andrews Crescent Blair Atholl Perthshire PH18 5TA Tel: (Blair Atholl) 01796 481256	COMMENDED	1 Twin 1 Double 2 Family	4 En Suite fac	B&B per person £21.50-£23.50 Single £16.50-£18.50 Double	Open Mar-Nov Dinner from 1930 B&B + Eve. Meal £25.50-£34.00

Friendly family home with half an acre of garden, in a tranquil setting.
Fine touring centre, close to Blair Castle.

E MacKenzie Moraybank St Andrews Crescent Blair Atholl Perthshire PH18 5TA Tel: (Blair Atholl) 01796 481612	COMMENDED	1 Twin 1 Double	1 Pub Bath/Show	B&B per person £12.50-£14.00 Single	Open Jan-Dec Dinner 1800-2000 B&B + Eve. Meal from £18.00

80-year-old house, situated in Blair Atholl. Ideal location for touring, golfing,
hill-walking, fishing and all outdoor pursuits.

BY BLAIR ATHOLL
Perthshire — Map 4 C12

APPROVED Listed

Mrs Thomson
Bailenabruaich
Glen Fender, Blair Atholl
Perthshire
PH18 5TU
Tel: (Blair Atholl) 01796 481329

1 Single	1 Pub Bath/Show	B&B per person	Open Mar-Oct
1 Twin		from £15.00 Single	
1 Double		from £15.00 Double	

Warm and comfortable converted croft deep in Strathblair country amidst breathtaking scenery. Ideal for walking and birdwatching.

BLAIR DRUMMOND
Perthshire — Map 2 A3

COMMENDED 👑👑

Mrs P Darby
The Linns, Kirk Lane
Blair Drummond, by Stirling
Perthshire
FK9 4AN
Tel: (Doune) 01786 841679

1 Twin	1 En Suite fac	B&B per person	Open Apr-Oct
2 Double	1 Priv. NOT ensuite	£16.50-£17.50 Single	
	2 Pub Bath/Show	£15.50-£17.50 Double	

19th-century cottage with modern extension in rural setting. 4 miles from Stirling. Next to Safari Park.

BLAIRGOWRIE
Perthshire — Map 2 B1

DRYFESANDS

Burnhead Road, Blairgowrie Perthshire PH10 6SY   Tel: 01250 873417
Haven for Non-smokers.   Open all year.
Ideally placed for golf, hill-walking, skiing and touring or just relax and be spoilt by our superb Cordon Bleu cuisine, personal service and spacious, luxurious accommodation.
All bedrooms are en-suite at £30 pp half board or £20 pp B&B.
Our STB **Deluxe** 👑👑👑 rating is your guarantee of satisfaction.

Dryfesands Guest House
Burnhead Road
Blairgowrie
Perthshire
PH10 6SY
Tel: (Blairgowrie)
01250 873417
Fax: 01250 873417

DELUXE 👑👑👑

1 Twin	3 En Suite fac	B&B per person	Open Jan-Dec
2 Double		to £25.00 Single	Dinner from 1900
		to £20.00 Double	B&B + Eve. Meal to £34.00

Modern bungalow, ensuite facilities, in quiet residential area. Non-smokers' haven; mainly fresh produce; regret no children/pets. Ideal for touring and golf.

DUAN VILLA
Perth Road, Blairgowrie, Perthshire PH10 6EQ
Telephone: 01250 873053

Detached attractive Victorian villa – many of original features intact – providing relaxing atmosphere to enjoy your stay in Blairgowrie. An ideal base for sight-seeing, touring, walking, golfing, ski-ing or fishing. There is ample parking and garden for guests' enjoyment. Situated 10 minutes' walk from centre of town.

Duan Villa
Perth Road
Blairgowrie
Perthshire
PH10 6EQ
Tel: (Blairgowrie)
01250 873053

COMMENDED 👑👑

1 Twin	1 En Suite fac	B&B per person	Open Jan-Dec
1 Double	1 Pub Bath/Show	£15.50-£20.00 Single	Dinner 1830-1930
1 Family		£15.50-£18.50 Double	B&B + Eve. Meal £24.00-£27.00

Traditional, sandstone, detached house retaining original cornices and wood panelling. On access route to Glenshee.

Glenshieling House

HATTON ROAD, BLAIRGOWRIE, PERTHSHIRE PH10 7HZ
Telephone: 01250 874605

Located away from main Balmoral Road in two acres of tranquillity.
Central heating, ensuite facilities, colour TVs. Outstanding food –
chef/owner – trained Gleneagles and France, mouth-watering choices
for breakfast and dinner, plus good wine list. Ideal touring centre,
approximately one hour – Edinburgh, Aberdeen, Glasgow.
Great golfing centre. *Access and Visa welcome.*

Glenshieling House Hatton Road, Rattray Blairgowrie Perthshire PH10 7HZ Tel: (Blairgowrie) 01250 874605	HIGHLY COMMENDED 	1 Single 2 Twin 2 Double 2 Family	4 En Suite fac 2 Pub Bath/Show	B&B per person £21.00-£26.50 Single £21.00-£26.50 Double	Open Jan-Dec Dinner 1800-2100 B&B + Eve. Meal £37.95-£43.45	
		Lovely Victorian house tranquilly set in 2 acres of garden and woodland near Blairgowrie. Chef/Proprietor trained in Gleneagles and France.				
Mr & Mrs Grant Norwood House, Park Drive Blairgowrie Perthshire PH10 6PA Tel: (Blairgowrie) 01250 874146	COMMENDED 	1 Twin 1 Double 1 Family	1 Pub Bath/Show	B&B per person £15.00-£17.00 Single £15.00 Double	Open Jan-Dec Dinner 1800-2000 B&B + Eve. Meal £21.00-£23.00	
		Comfortable Victorian family house in residential area. Good home cooking; golfers, walkers and skiers welcome. Private parking. Ideal for touring Perthshire.				
The Laurels Guest House Golf Course Road, Rosemount Blairgowrie Perthshire PH10 6LH Tel: (Blairgowrie) 01250 874920	HIGHLY COMMENDED 	1 Single 3 Twin 2 Double	4 En Suite fac 1 Pub Bath/Show	B&B per person £17.50-£18.50 Single £17.50-£18.50 Double	Open Jan-Nov Dinner 1830-1900	
		Originally a farmhouse dating from 1873, set back from main road, on outskirts of Blairgowrie with own large garden and ample parking.				

Your key to quality accommodation in Scotland:

The Scottish Tourist Board's
Grading and Classification Scheme

BLAIRGOWRIE continued

Map 2
B1

Duncraggan

Perth Road, Blairgowrie PH10 6EJ
Telephone: 01250 872082

Duncraggan House of character offers peace and relaxation in comfortable and beautiful surroundings with meals of high standard and off-road parking. Ideally situated for tourists, hillwalkers, golfers and skiers alike or just relax in our acre of garden with 9-hole putting green. Four poster bed in double room with private facilities (not en-suite).

Commended 👑👑👑   AA QQQ

Mrs C McClement Duncraggan, Perth Road Blairgowrie Perthshire PH10 6EJ Tel: (Blairgowrie) 01250 872082	COMMENDED 👑👑👑	1 Single 1 Twin 1 Double	2 En Suite fac 1 Priv. NOT ensuite 2 Pub Bath/Show	B&B per person from £18.00 Single from £18.00 Double	Open Jan-mid Dec Dinner from 1900
		Stone-built house of interesting design with large garden, conveniently situated on the main Perth to Blairgowrie road. Town centre 0.5 miles (1km).			
Mrs Murray Eildon Bank, Perth Road Blairgowrie Perthshire PH10 6ED Tel: (Blairgowrie) 01250 873648	COMMENDED 👑👑	1 Twin 2 Double	1 En Suite fac 1 Pub Bath/Show	B&B per person £14.00-£15.00 Single £14.00-£15.00 Double	Open Jan-Dec
		Comfortable family home, near to town centre, with ample private parking. Television in bedrooms. Good base for touring.			
BY BLAIRGOWRIE **Perthshire** Mrs M B Crichton Lunanbrae Essendy, by Blairgowrie Perthshire PH10 6RA Tel: (Essendy) 01250 884224	Map 2 B1 HIGHLY COMMENDED Listed	1 Twin 1 Double	2 Priv. NOT ensuite 1 Pub Bath/Show	B&B per person from £20.00 Single from £17.50 Double	Open May-Sep Dinner 1900-2100
		Spacious and peacefully located bungalow with spectacular views, and large beautifully maintained garden. Ideal location for golfing, fishing, touring and walking.			
Mrs H Wightman Bankhead, Clunie Blairgowrie Perthshire PH10 6SG Tel: (Essendy) 01250 884281	COMMENDED 👑	1 Twin 1 Family	1 Pub Bath/Show	B&B per person to £16.00 Single to £14.00 Double	Open Jan-Dec Dinner 1830-1900
		Farmhouse on working family farm between Loch Marlee and Clunie. Ideal for touring, local fishing, golfing and skiing. All home cooking.			
BOAT OF GARTEN **Inverness-shire** Avingormack Guest House Boat of Garten Inverness-shire PH24 3BT Tel: (Boat of Garten) 01479 831614	Map 4 C10 HIGHLY COMMENDED 👑👑👑	1 Twin 2 Double 1 Family	2 En Suite fac 2 Pub Bath/Show	B&B per person from £17.00 Single	Open Jan-Dec Dinner 1900-2000 B&B + Eve. Meal from £30.00
		Former croft recently redecorated and refurbished, enjoying panoramic views of Cairngorms. Mountain bike hire. No smoking. Vegetarian menu available.			

STEORNABHAGH

Deshar Road, Boat of Garten, Inverness-shire PH24 3BN
Telephone: 01479 831371

A Highland welcome awaits you at the home of Bryan and Mattie Cunningham. From its peaceful setting a wide range of activities are available. Ideal for golfing at the 18-hole golf club, bird life at Abernethy reserve, walking on the many forest trails and water sports nearby.

Mrs M Cunningham Steornabhagh, Deshar Road Boat of Garten Inverness-shire PH24 3BN Tel: (Boat of Garten) 01479 831371	HIGHLY COMMENDED 😾😾😾	1 Twin 1 Double 1 Family	3 En Suite fac	B&B per person from £18.00 Single from £17.00 Double	Open Jan-Dec Dinner 1830-1900 B&B + Eve. Meal from £29.00

Attractive comfortable bungalow just off main street, in peaceful garden setting.
Ideal touring base. Bedrooms en-suite or with private facilities.

"LOCHEIL"

BOAT OF GARTEN, INVERNESS-SHIRE PH24 3BX
Telephone: 01479 831603

John and Barbara Davison offer all-year Bed and Breakfast accommodation in their comfortable home 1 mile from the "Osprey Village" on the A95 road midway between Aviemore and Grantown-on-Spey. Dinners and packed lunches on prior notice. Residents' CTV lounge. 1-acre garden, ample parking. *Brochure on request.*

Mrs B A Davison Locheil Boat of Garten Inverness-shire PH24 3BX Tel: (Boat of Garten) 01479 831603	COMMENDED 😾	2 Single 1 Twin 1 Double	1 Pub Bath/Show	B&B per person £14.00-£15.50 Single £14.00-£15.50 Double	Open Jan-Dec Dinner from 1900 B&B + Eve. Meal £23.00-£24.50

Stone-built house with new guest sitting room.
Comfortable bed and breakfast accommodation. Evening meals by arrangement.

Granlea Guest House Boat of Garten Inverness-shire PH24 3BN Tel: (Boat of Garten) 01479 831601	COMMENDED 😾😾😾	1 Twin 2 Double 1 Family	2 En Suite fac 1 Pub Bath/Show	B&B per person £16.00-£18.00 Single £16.00-£18.00 Double	Open Jan-Dec Dinner 1830-2000

Stone-built Edwardian house, in village centre,
close to Osprey reserve and golf course. Ideal touring base.

MOORFIELD HOUSE

Deshar Road, Boat-of-Garten, Inverness-shire PH24 3BN
Telephone: 01479 831646

Quietly situated in the village. Moorfield is a Victorian House, AA/RAC acclaimed. Warm comfortable rooms all with private facilities, TV, tea/coffee makers. Licensed hospitality bar in cosy residents' lounge. Private parking. Traditional home-cooked dinners. Within easy reach of most Highland attractions, suited to those seeking peace and tranquillity.

Moorfield House Deshar Road Boat of Garten Inverness-shire PH24 3BN Tel: (Boat of Garten) 01479 831646	COMMENDED 😾😾😾	1 Single 1 Twin 1 Double 1 Family	3 En Suite fac 1 Priv. NOT ensuite	B&B per person £22.00 Single £19.00 Double	Open Jan-Dec Dinner 1830-1900 B&B + Eve. Meal £29.00-£32.00

Personally run hotel in centre of peaceful Highland village.
Ideally situated for walking, golfing, fishing, etc. Home cooking.

BOAT OF GARTEN continued

Map 4 C10

Ryvoan Guest House
Kinchurdy Road
Boat of Garten
Inverness-shire
PH24 3BP
Tel: (Boat of Garten)
01479 831654

HIGHLY COMMENDED

1 Twin   2 En Suite fac
1 Double   2 Pub Bath/Show
1 Family

B&B per person
from £17.00 Single

Open Jan-Dec
Dinner at 1900
B&B + Eve. Meal
from £29.00

Victorian house set in mature woodland with period accommodation and modern facilities. Near RSPB reserve, golf club and Cairngorms.

CROFTSIDE
STREET OF KINCARDINE, BOAT OF GARTEN PH24 3BY
Telephone: 01479 831431

Letti and Mel invite you to enjoy the numerous attractions of Speyside, whilst experiencing real Highland hospitality, in the comfort of their modern home. Croftside is on the B970 road, 1 mile from the village and golf course, adjacent to the River Spey, and close to the Abernethy Bird Reserve.

Mrs L Sim
Croftside, Street of Kincardine
Boat of Garten
Inverness-shire
PH24 3BY
Tel: (Boat of Garten)
01479 831431

HIGHLY COMMENDED

2 Twin   3 En Suite fac
1 Double

B&B per person
from £17.00 Single

Open Jan-Oct

Warm welcome at modern house overlooking River Spey with views of Cairngorms and close to site of Osprey nest.

BO'NESS
West Lothian
Mrs Nancy Findlay
Gamrie, 63 Dean Road
Bo'ness
West Lothian
EH51 9BA
Tel: (Bo'ness) 01506 824563

Map 2 B4

COMMENDED Listed

1 Single   1 Pub Bath/Show
1 Twin
1 Double

B&B per person
from £14.00 Single

Open Jan-Dec,
exc Xmas/New Year

Centrally situated comfortable accommodation on major express bus route to Edinburgh. Private parking.

Mrs J A Harwood
The Knowe, Erngath Road
Bo'ness
West Lothian
EH51 9EN
Tel: (Bo'ness) 01506
825254/828226
Fax: 01506 828226

COMMENDED Listed

1 Single   2 Pub Bath/Show
1 Twin
1 Family

B&B per person
£17.00-£22.00 Single
£16.00-£20.00 Double

Open Jan-Dec
Dinner 1800-2000
B&B + Eve. Meal
£23.00-£30.00

Detached Victorian house retaining many original features, standing in own grounds in elevated position with fine views over River Forth.

BONNYBRIDGE
Stirlingshire
Mrs Jean Forrester
Bandominie Farm, Walton Road
Bonnybridge
Stirlingshire
FK4 2HP
Tel: (Banknock) 01324 840284

Map 2 A4

COMMENDED Listed

1 Single   1 Pub Bath/Show
1 Twin
1 Double

B&B per person
£15.00-£16.00 Single
£15.00-£16.00 Double

Open Jan-Dec

Working farm 2 miles (3kms) from A80 at Castle Cary (B816). Easy travel to Glasgow, Edinburgh and the North. Lovely views.

BRAEMAR
Aberdeenshire
Clunie Lodge
Clunie Bank Road
Braemar
Aberdeenshire
AB35 5YP
Tel: (Braemar) 013397 41330

Map 4 D11

COMMENDED

1 Twin   3 En Suite fac
2 Double   1 Priv. NOT ensuite
2 Family   1 Pub Bath/Show

B&B per person
£15.00-£17.50 Single
£15.00-£17.50 Double

Open Dec-Oct
Dinner 1800-2000
B&B + Eve. Meal
£25.00-£27.00

Family run, Victorian, former manse in the centre of Braemar. Home cooking. 5 day midweek break; ideal for skiing and hill walking.

Cranford Guest House & Wishing Well Restaurant 15 Glenshee Road Braemar Aberdeenshire AB35 5YQ Tel: (Braemar) 013397 41675		COMMENDED ♛♛♛	2 Twin 1 Double	3 En Suite fac	B&B per person £16.00-£17.50 Double	Open Jan-Oct Dinner 1800-2030

Traditional B & B with the best of local Scottish produce and homebaking tastefully served in our licensed restaurant from 6.00pm.

BREAKISH **Isle of Skye, Inverness-shire** Mrs M A B Macgregor Langdale House Waterloo, Breakish Isle of Skye, Inverness-shire IV42 8QE Tel: (Broadford) 01471 822376	Map 3 F10	COMMENDED ♛♛♛	1 Twin 2 Double	3 En Suite fac	B&B per person £20.00 Double	Open Mar-Nov Dinner 1900-2000 B&B & Eve. Meal £35.00

Superb views of sea and mountains from most rooms. Nature watch. Vegetarian and Coeliac food by arrangement.

BRECHIN Angus	Map 4 F12

Wood of Auldbar Farmhouse
WOOD OF AULDBAR, ABERLEMNO, BRECHIN DD9 6SZ
Telephone: 01307 830218
Award-winning farmhouse. A warm welcome awaits you at our family farm. Excellent food and accommodation. Tea facilities in all bedrooms. Smoke alarms throughout. Food Hygiene Certificate held. Ideal for touring Glens of Angus, Royal Deeside, Balmoral. Glamis within easy reach. Nature walks, bird-watching, fishing, golf; leisure centres nearby. Aberlemno Standing Stones can be viewed. Aberdeen, Dundee, St Andrews and Edinburgh all within easy reach.
B&B from £14.50. EM from £9. Reduced terms for children.

Mrs J Stewart Wood of Auldbar Brechin Angus DD9 6SZ Tel: (Aberlemno) 01307 830218	COMMENDED Listed	1 Single 1 Twin 1 Family	2 Pub Bath/Show	B&B per person from £15.50 Single from £14.50 Double	Open Jan-Dec Dinner 1800-2000 B&B + Eve. Meal from £23.00

Farmhouse with large south-facing garden on working mixed arable and stock farm in pleasant countryside. All home cooking, baking and preserves.

FARMHOUSE BED & BREAKFAST
TILLYGLOOM FARM, BRECHIN, ANGUS DD9 7PE
Telephone: 01356 622953
Enjoy the atmosphere of our working farm. Golf courses, country walks, nearby Angus glens and castles. TV lounge, home cooking. Prices from £12.50 per night B&B per person; DB&B from £18.50.
Contact Mrs Lorna Watson

Mrs L Watson Tillygloom Farm Brechin Angus DD9 7PE Tel: (Brechin) 01356 622953	COMMENDED Listed	1 Twin 1 Family	1 Pub Bath/Show	B&B per person £13.00-£15.00 Single £12.50-£13.00 Double	Open Apr-Oct Dinner 1800-2000 B&B + Eve. Meal £19.00-£22.00

Friendly farmhouse welcome awaits guests at our home near Brechin. In quiet, pleasant surroundings. Easy access to a host of local activities.

BY BRECHIN Angus Mrs R Beatty Brathinch Farm by Brechin Angus DD9 7QX Tel: (Edzell) 01356 648292 Fax: 01356 648003	Map 4 F12	COMMENDED Listed	1 Twin 2 Double	1 En Suite fac 1 Priv. NOT ensuite 2 Pub Bath/Show	B&B per person £15.00-£20.00 Single £13.50-£16.00 Double Room only per person £12.00-£14.00	Open Jan-Dec

18th-century farmhouse on a family run working arable farm, with large garden. Easy access to Angus Glens.

BRIDGEND, by Brechin Angus Mrs L Gibb The Post House Glen Lethnot, by Brechin Angus DD9 7UQ Tel: (Menmuir) 01356 660277	Map 4 F12	COMMENDED Listed	1 Twin	1 Pub Bath/Show	B&B per person from £12.00 Double	Open Nov-Jul Dinner 1900-2100 B&B + Eve. Meal from £17.00	
			Within easy distance of all Angus glens and Royal Deeside. Good food and a warm welcome awaits.				

BRIG O' TURK Perthshire	Map 1 H3						

Dundarroch
Country House

Brig O' Turk, Trossachs, Perthshire FK17 8HT
Tel: 01877 376200 Fax: 01877 376202

This luxuriously appointed Victorian Country House peacefully nestling in quiet river meadows amidst the Trossachs Mountains enjoys a long-established reputation for excellence. We offer a delightful combination of warm hospitality in a relaxed informal atmosphere. The elegant Lounge and Breakfast Room are furnished with tapestries, paintings and fine antiques. Beautiful en-suite bedrooms, each with stunning view, have every facility thoughtfully provided. Add a quaint bar restaurant in the grounds of *Dundarroch* and you have a splendid base from which to explore this area of outstanding scenic beauty.

STB 👑👑👑👑 Highly Commended
AA QQQQQ "Premier Selected"
Internationally Acclaimed.

Dundarroch Country House Brig O' Turk Perthshire FK17 8HT Tel: (Trossachs) 01877 376200/ 0585 584806 (mobile) Fax: 01877 376202		HIGHLY COMMENDED 👑👑👑	1 Twin 2 Double	3 En Suite fac	B&B per person £39.75-£46.75 Single £29.75-£37.75 Double	Open Apr-Oct Dinner 1800-2100	
			Extensive breakfast menu, served in this beautifully appointed Victorian country house set in 14 acres of tranquil countryside, spectacular mountain views.				

BROADFORD Isle of Skye, Inverness-shire Mrs J Donaldson Fairwinds, Elgol Road Broadford Isle of Skye, Inverness-shire IV49 9AB Tel: (Broadford) 01471 822270	Map 3 E10	COMMENDED 👑👑	1 Twin 2 Double	3 En Suite fac	B&B per person £17.00-£20.00 Single £17.00-£20.00 Double	Open Mar-Oct	
			Peacefully situated bungalow in extensive garden overlooking Broadford River and the mountains. Bicycles for hire.				

ASHGROVE

Black Park, Broadford, Isle of Skye IV49 9AE
Telephone: 01471 822327

Comfortable accommodation in three-bedroomed bungalow. Two bedrooms with WHB, one bedroom with WHB, shower and toilet en-suite. Colour TV lounge, tea-making facilities. Cot available. Eight miles from Kyle ferry. Turn off main road at Lime Park/Black Park junction.
From £13 to £18 per person.   👑 Commended

Mrs M Fletcher Ashgrove, 11 Black Park Broadford Isle of Skye, Inverness-shire IV49 9AE Tel: (Broadford) 01471 822327		COMMENDED 👑	1 Twin 1 Double 1 Family	1 En Suite fac 1 Pub Bath/Show	B&B per person £13.00-£18.00 Double	Open Jan-Dec	
			Modern bungalow with fine views of sea and mountains.				

Ptarmigan

Broadford, Isle of Skye IV49 9AQ
Telephone: 01471 822744 Fax: 01471 822745

A warm welcome awaits you at Ptarmigan. En-suite bedrooms on ground floor with panoramic views across Broadford Bay. 15 metres from seashore. Ideal bird/otter watching – binoculars supplied. Excellent base for touring Skye and S.W. Ross-shire. Minutes walk from pubs/restaurants. Ample parking.

Mrs D MacPhie Ptarmigan Broadford Isle of Skye, Inverness-shire IV49 9AQ Tel: (Broadford) 01471 822744 Fax: 01471 822745	HIGHLY COMMENDED	1 Twin 2 Double	3 En Suite fac 1 Pub Bath/Show	B&B per person £20.00-£25.00 Double	Open Jan-Dec
Modern family home on seashore of Broadford Bay. **Panoramic views across islands to mainland.**					
Mrs D Robertson Westside, Elgol Road Broadford Isle of Skye, Inverness-shire IV49 9AB Tel: (Broadford) 01471 822320	HIGHLY COMMENDED	1 Single 1 Twin 1 Double	3 En Suite fac 1 Pub Bath/Show	B&B per person £16.00-£18.00 Single £16.00-£18.00 Double	Open Jan-Dec
A warm welcome and good food at this modern bungalow in a quiet lane, **with views across to Beinn Na Cailleach.**					
Mrs M Robertson Earsary, 7-8 Harrapool Broadford Isle of Skye, Inverness-shire IV49 9AQ Tel: (Broadford) 01471 822697	HIGHLY COMMENDED	1 Twin 1 Double 1 Family	3 En Suite fac	B&B per person £16.00-£22.00 Double	Open Jan-Dec Dinner 1730-1900 B&B + Eve. Meal £26.00-£30.00
Modern house with high standard of accommodation on working croft. **Panoramic views over Broadford Bay.**					
Mrs Robertson Tigh a Croisean, 4 Black Park Broadford Isle of Skye, Inverness-shire IV49 9AE Tel: (Broadford) 01471 822338	HIGHLY COMMENDED	1 Twin 2 Double	2 En Suite fac 1 Pub Bath/Show	B&B per person £14.00-£18.00 Double	Open Apr-Sep
Comfortable family home in quiet location in Broadford village. **All rooms with private facilities.**					
Mrs Scott Tigh-na-Mara Lower Harrapool, Broadford Isle of Skye, Inverness-shire IV49 9AB Tel: (Broadford) 01471 822475	COMMENDED	1 Family	1 Priv. NOT ensuite 1 Pub Bath/Show	B&B per person £15.00-£17.00 Double	Open Apr-Oct
Family room in 150-year-old cottage on the sea shore. **8 miles from Skye Bridge. Own sitting room.**					

Highly Commended

CORRY LODGE

LIVERAS, BROADFORD, ISLE OF SKYE IV49 9AA
Telephone: 01471 822235   Fax: 01471 822318

This is a comfortable 18th-century family house situated on the outskirts of Broadford. Ideal centre for touring the Isle of Skye. Ample parking, large garden. *Brochure available.*

Home of the Liveras Fold of Highland Cattle.

Talisker Award for Highest Quality Accommodation (1994).

Jane Wilcken Corry Lodge, Liveras Broadford Isle of Skye, Inverness-shire IV49 9AA Tel: (Broadford) 01471 822235 Fax: 01471 822318	HIGHLY COMMENDED	2 Twin 2 Double	4 En Suite fac	B&B per person £17.50-£25.00 Double	Open Jan-Dec Dinner at 2000 B&B + Eve. Meal £32.50-£40.00
Late 18th-century shooting lodge, totally restored to its former splendour **on 80-acre estate stretching to the shoreline.**					

BY BROADFORD **Isle of Skye, Inverness-shire** Mrs Flora A MacLeod Hazelwood Cottage, Heaste by Broadford Isle of Skye, Inverness-shire IV42 8QF Tel: (Broadford) 01471 822294	Map 3 E10	COMMENDED Listed	1 Twin 2 Double	1 Pub Bath/Show	B&B per person from £14.00 Double		Open May-Oct

Modern bungalow on working croft, with panoramic views over
Loch Eishort towards the hills of Knoydart.

BRODICK **Isle of Arran** Carrick Lodge Brodick Isle of Arran KA27 8BH Tel: (Brodick) 01770 302550	Map 1 F6	COMMENDED	1 Single 2 Twin 2 Double 1 Family	5 En Suite fac 1 Priv. NOT ensuite	B&B per person £17.00-£21.00 Single £17.00-£21.00 Double Room only per person £15.00-£19.00	Open Feb-Oct Dinner from 1900 B&B + Eve. Meal £27.00-£31.00	

Sandstone built, former manse in its own gardens. Panoramic views over
Brodick Bay from sitting room. Convenient for ferry terminal.

Glen Cloy Farmhouse

Glen Cloy, Brodick, Isle of Arran KA27 8DA
Telephone: 01770 302351

Glen Cloy Farmhouse is a beautiful sandstone house set in its own grounds
in a quiet glen close to Brodick. Golf, Castle and mountains nearby. All the
rooms are tastefully furnished and a log fire burns warmly. We grow most
of our own vegetables and use quality local produce.

Glencloy Farm House Brodick Isle of Arran KA27 8DA Tel: (Brodick) 01770 302351	COMMENDED	1 Single 2 Twin 2 Double	2 En Suite fac 1 Pub Bath/Show	B&B per person £20.00-£26.00 Single £20.00-£26.00 Double	Open Mar-Nov Dinner 1900-1930 B&B + Eve. Meal £33.00-£38.00

Farmhouse, set in peaceful glen with views of hills and sea.
Within easy reach of Brodick ferry. Chef/proprietor; fresh, homegrown produce.

Ms Smith Tigh-na-mara Guest House The Sea Front Brodick Isle of Arran KA27 8AJ Tel: (Brodick) 01770 302538	COMMENDED	2 Twin 3 Double 2 Family	2 En Suite fac 3 Pub Bath/Show	B&B per person £15.00-£17.00 Double	Open Apr-Oct

Villa in a central position on the beachfront with views over
Brodick Bay to Goat Fell.

BRORA **Sutherland** Mrs J Ballantyne Clynelish Farm Brora Sutherland KW9 6LR Tel: (Brora) 01408 621265 Fax: 01408 621265	Map 4 C6	COMMENDED	1 Twin 1 Double 1 Family	2 En Suite fac 1 Priv. NOT ensuite	B&B per person £15.00-£18.00 Single £15.00-£18.00 Double	Open Jan-Dec

Family home, on working farm, in rural setting about a mile (2 kms) from
Brora and beaches.

John & Ishbel Clarkson Tigh Fada, Golf Road Brora Sutherland KW9 6QS Tel: (Brora) 01408 621332 Fax: 01408 621332	COMMENDED	2 Twin 1 Double	1 En Suite fac 2 Priv. NOT ensuite	B&B per person £15.50-£20.00 Double	Open Jan-Dec

Fine sea views and peat fires, home baking and a real Highland welcome.
Ideal halfway house between Inverness and John O'Groats.

LYNWOOD

Golf Road, Brora, Sutherland KW9 6QS
Telephone: 01408 621226   Fax: 01408 621226

*Take advantage of the area's excellent facilities with Brora golf
course only yards away. Enjoy our 4 or 7 days golfing holidays,
B&B and evening meals, choice of menu, combined with traditional
home cooking to suit everyone's tastes. Other local activities include
fishing, bowls, walking and birdwatching.*

Mrs M Cooper Lynwood, Golf Road Brora Sutherland KW9 6QS Tel: (Brora) 01408 621226 Fax: 01408 621226		HIGHLY COMMENDED	2 Twin 1 Double 1 Family	3 En Suite fac 1 Pub Bath/Show	B&B per person £18.00-£23.00 Single £16.00-£20.00 Double	Open Mar-Dec Dinner 1900-2000 B&B + Eve. Meal £26.00-£30.00
			Family home in substantial Edwardian house in its own grounds overlooking Brora harbour. Home cooking. Annexe garden room available on ground floor.			
Mrs Fraser Craiglyn, Victoria Road Brora Sutherland KW9 6QN Tel: (Brora) 01408 621124 Fax: 01408 621124		COMMENDED	1 Twin 1 Family	2 Pub Bath/Show	B&B per person £13.00-£14.00 Single £13.00-£14.00 Double	Open Mar-Dec
			Comfortable accommodation in friendly bed and breakfast. Ideal touring base. Ample private parking.			
BUCKIE **Banffshire** Mrs Norma Pirie Rosemount 62 East Church Street Buckie Banffshire AB56 1ER Tel: (Buckie) 01542 833434	Map 4 E7	HIGHLY COMMENDED	2 Twin 1 Double	2 En Suite fac 1 Priv. NOT ensuite	B&B per person £20.00-£22.50 Single £15.00-£20.00 Double	Open Jan-Dec
			Modernised Victorian detached house, centrally situated overlooking harbour. Ideal for fishing and golf.			
BY BUCKIE **Banffshire** Mrs Catherine Crawford Glenelg, 26 Richmond Terrace Portgordon, Buckie Banffshire AB56 2RA Tel: (Buckie) 01542 833221	Map 4 E7	COMMENDED Listed	1 Single 1 Double 1 Family	2 Pub Bath/Show	B&B per person £12.00-£12.50 Single £12.00-£12.50 Double Room only per person from £9.00	Open Jan-Dec Dinner 1730-1900 B&B + Eve. Meal from £17.00
			Detached Victorian house in quiet residential area, with fine views overlooking the Moray Firth.			
BUNESSAN **Isle of Mull, Argyll** Mrs S Campbell Uisken Croft Bunessan Isle of Mull, Argyll PA67 6DS Tel: (Fionnphort) 01681 700307	Map 1 C3	COMMENDED	1 Double 1 Family	1 Pub Bath/Show	B&B per person from £14.00 Single from £14.00 Double Room only per person to £14.00	Open Apr-Oct Dinner 1830-1930 B&B + Eve. Meal from £21.00
			Working croft in sandy bay with island views. 5 miles (8kms) from Iona Ferry. Abundant wildlife. Evening meals, with local salmon a speciality.			

BURGHEAD **Moray** Mrs Anne Smith Norland, 26 Granary Street Burghead, Elgin Moray IV30 2UJ Tel: (Burghead) 01343 835212	Map 4 D7	COMMENDED Listed	1 Twin 2 Double	1 Pub Bath/Show	B&B per person from £13.00 Single from £12.50 Double	Open Jan-Dec

Traditional Scottish hospitality in friendly bed and breakfast situated in quiet fishing village.

BURNMOUTH, Eyemouth **Berwickshire** Mr & Mrs R Goff Greystonelees Farm House Burnmouth Berwickshire TD14 5SZ Tel: (Ayton) 018907 81709	Map 2 F5	COMMENDED ♕♕	1 Single 1 Twin 1 Double	2 En Suite fac 1 Pub Bath/Show	B&B per person £15.00-£25.00 Single £15.00-£18.00 Double	Open Jan-Dec Dinner 1800-2000 B&B + Eve. Meal £23.00-£33.00

Georgian farmhouse in quiet countryside 200 yards from A1. Good walking country.
St Abbs Head 5 miles (8kms); Eyemouth 2 miles (3kms); Home baking.

BURNTISLAND **Fife** Jean & Angus Bowman Gruinard, 148 Kinghorn Road Burntisland Fife KY3 9JU Tel: (Burntisland) 01592 873877	Map 2 C4	COMMENDED ♕♕	1 Double 1 Family	1 En Suite fac 1 Priv. NOT ensuite	B&B per person £16.00-£25.00 Single £16.00-£18.50 Double	Open Jan-Dec Dinner 1830-2000 B&B + Eve. Meal £22.00-£24.00

Very well appointed traditional stone house, close to town centre.
Garden with views across the Firth of Forth.

BURRELTON, Blairgowrie **Perthshire**	Map 2 C2	

"SHOCARJEN"
BED & BREAKFAST

THE GREEN, BURRELTON
BLAIRGOWRIE PH13 9NU
Telephone: 01828 670223

Shocarjen is situated in the centre of the village of Burrelton. Ideal for your enjoyment of Perthshire. There are castles and stately homes to be visited in the surrounding district. Good theatres locally. Sporting persons can enjoy golfing, fishing, ski-ing all within easy distance.
Locally: Perth – 12 miles; Dundee – 17 miles; Pitlochry – 25 miles.

Mrs Shonaidh Beattie Shocarjen, The Green Burrelton, Blairgowrie Perthshire PH13 9NU Tel: (Burrelton) 01828 670223		COMMENDED ♕♕	2 Double 1 Family	3 En Suite fac	B&B per person from £19.00 Single from £16.50 Double	Open Jan-Dec

Renovated traditional house in centre of friendly village.
Good touring base for the Perthshire Highlands.

CAIRNRYAN **Wigtownshire** Mrs A Gray Albannach, Loch Ryan Cairnryan Wigtownshire DG9 8QX Tel: (Cairnryan) 01581 200624	Map 1 F10	APPROVED ♕♕♕	1 Single 2 Twin 1 Family	3 En Suite fac 1 Priv. NOT ensuite	B&B per person to £17.50 Single to £17.50 Double Room only per person to £14.00	Open Jan-Dec Dinner from 1800 B&B + Eve. Meal £22.00-£25.00

Former manse, on the shores of Loch Ryan.
Ideal location for Cairnryan and Stranraer ferries to Ireland.

	Map 1 H3						
CALLANDER **Perthshire** Abbotsford Lodge Stirling Road Callander Perthshire FK17 8DA Tel: (Callander) 01877 330066	COMMENDED 👑👑👑	1 Single 4 Twin 5 Double 8 Family	10 En Suite fac 4 Pub Bath/Show	B&B per person £23.50-£28.00 Single £17.50-£22.00 Double	Open Jan-Dec Dinner from 1900 B&B + Eve. Meal £29.50-£34.00	
		Family run Victorian house in its own grounds with private parking, some ground-floor rooms. Close to town centre. Home cooking and baking.				
Mrs O Aitken Achray House 4 Achray Avenue Callander Perthshire FK17 8JZ Tel: (Callander) 01877 330104	COMMENDED 👑	1 Single 1 Twin 1 Double	2 Pub Bath/Show	B&B per person £14.00-£16.00 Single £14.00-£16.00 Double	Open Apr-Oct Dinner at 1830 B&B + Eve. Meal £22.00-£24.00	
		Modern family villa in quiet residential area near the edge of town. Private parking. Non-smoking establishment.				
Annfield Guest House North Church Street Callander Perthshire FK17 8EG Tel: (Callander) 01877 330204	COMMENDED 👑👑👑	1 Single 2 Twin 4 Double 1 Family	4 En Suite fac 2 Pub Bath/Show	B&B per person £16.00-£18.00 Single £16.00-£18.00 Double	Open Jan-Dec	
		Centrally situated in a quiet area of the town in close proximity to shops and restaurants. Stepping stone to the Highlands.				
Arden House Guest House Bracklinn Road Callander Perthshire FK17 8EQ Tel: (Callander) 01877 330235	HIGHLY COMMENDED 👑👑👑	1 Single 2 Twin 2 Double 1 Family	6 En Suite fac	B&B per person £18.00-£25.00 Single £18.00-£21.00 Double	Open Mar-Nov Dinner from 1900 B&B + Eve. Meal £28.00-£30.00	
		Family run, peacefully situated in its own grounds. Superb panoramic views to Ben Ledi and the Trossachs. A non-smoking house.				

ARRAN LODGE DELUXE 👑👑👑

Leny Road, Callander FK17 8AJ　　Telephone: 01877 330976

An enchanting period bungalow, luxuriously appointed on the banks of the River Leny by Callander's western outskirts. Relax in tranquil riverside gardens. Delight in luxurious 4-poster bedrooms and enjoy mouth-watering cuisine in our elegant Victorian dining room. A warm welcome and private parking. A non-smoking home.

RAC "Highly Acclaimed".　　AA "Premier Selected". QQQQQ.

Arran Lodge Leny Road Callander Perthshire FK17 8AJ Tel: (Callander) 01877 330976	DELUXE 👑👑👑	4 Double	3 En Suite fac 1 Priv. NOT ensuite	B&B per person £24.00-£34.00 Double	Open Marb-Oct Dinner at 1930 B&B + Eve. Meal £39.00-£52.50	
		Delightful, period bungalow on A84 with tranquil riverside garden. Friendly welcome, quality cuisine and private parking. A non-smoking home.				
Craig Villa Guest House Craig Villa, Leny Road Callander Perthshire FK17 8AW Tel: (Callander) 01877 330871	COMMENDED 👑👑	4 Double	4 En Suite fac	B&B per person £30.00 Single Room only per person £25.00	Open Apr-Nov	
		Stone-built villa in main street, 5 minutes walk from shops and Rob Roy Centre. Own car park with easy access to ground floor bedroom.				

CALLANDER continued	Map 1 H3

East Mains Guest House
East Mains House, Bridgend
Callander FK17 8AG   Tel: 01877 330535

East Mains is a family run 18th-century guest house set in its own grounds, ideally situated to tour central Scotland. Offering a high standard of accommodation with impressive Georgian lounge (log fire). All rooms have private facilities, colour TV and tea/coffee-making. Private parking available.

East Mains House Bridgend Callander FK17 8AG Tel: (Callander) 01877 330535	COMMENDED ✿✿✿	1 Single 3 Double 1 Family	4 En Suite fac 1 Pub Bath/Show	B&B per person £16.00-£25.00 Single £17.00-£19.00 Double	Open Apr-Oct

Fine, 18th-century mansion house, with impressive lounge, situated in its own grounds. Close to town centre and River Teith.

INVERTROSSACHS COUNTRY HOUSE
Invertrossachs, by Callander, Perthshire FK17 8HG
Telephone: 01877 331126 Fax: 01877 331229

At this splendid lochside Edwardian Mansion we are pleased to offer a superior accommodation and breakfast service complemented with a discreet level of personal attention.

Our Loch Room with private bath, shower and wc is a large double or twin with commanding views over Loch Venachar. Our Victoria Suite in its own private wing sleeps up to 4 in a choice of bedrooms (double, small double and single) with private bath, shower and wc. Both Loch and Victoria have colour TV, d/dial phone, trouser press, hairdryers, video, CD and tea-making facilities. Prices include 5-course Scottish breakfast served in our conservatory. Optional dinner service available.

Leisurely walking, cycling, fishing on site. Golf/Water sports close by. Ideal touring base for freedom, flexibility and a complete escape. – *Advance booking recommended.* **As featured in BBC's "Summer Holiday" 1995. Please quote EBB**

Invertrossachs Country House Invertrossachs, by Callander Perthshire FK17 8HG Tel: (Callander) 01877 331126 Fax: 01877 331229	HIGHLY COMMENDED ✿✿✿	1 Twin 2 Double Suite avail	3 En Suite fac 1 Pub Bath/Show	B&B per person £35.00-£75.00 Single £35.00-£55.00 Double	Open Jan-Dec

Edwardian mansion in its own 28 acres of mature woodlands overlooking Loch Venachar. Quiet rural setting 4 miles (6kms) up a private drive.

The Knowe Ancaster Road Callander Perthshire FK17 8EL Tel: (Callander) 01877 330076 Fax: 01877 331776	COMMENDED ✿✿✿	2 Twin 3 Double	5 En Suite fac	– B&B per person £18.00-£20.00 Double	Open Jan-Dec Dinner from 1830 B&B + Eve. Meal £29.00-£31.00

Family run with a friendly welcome and good cooking. Quietly situated off the main road with magnificent views. Ideal for a peaceful holiday.

Mrs A Lochans The Lochans, 5 Lubnaig Drive Callander Perthshire FK17 8JT Tel: (Callander) 01877 330627	COMMENDED ✿	1 Twin 1 Family	2 En Suite fac	B&B per person £20.00-£21.50 Single £17.00-£18.50 Double	Open Apr-Oct Dinner 1830-1930 B&B + Eve. Meal £26.00-£29.00

Detached chalet bungalow in quiet residential area on south side of town, 1/2 mile (1km) from town centre. Both bedrooms with en suite facilities.

Mrs E MacKenzie Lamorna, Ancaster Road Callander Perthshire FK17 8EL Tel: (Callander) 01877 330868	COMMENDED	1 Twin 1 Double	1 Pub Bath/Show	B&B per person £15.00-£16.00 Double	Open Apr-Oct

Family run, detached bungalow in a quiet area.
Comfortable rooms, warm, friendly atmosphere. Private parking.

CRAIGROYSTON

4 Bridge Street, Callander FK17 8AA
Telephone: 01877 331395

Family run bed and breakfast near shops and meadows. Ideal touring base. Good home cooking, dinner on request. Television, tea/coffee facilities. All rooms en-suite.
Children and dogs welcome.

Ken and Betty Macleod Craigroyston, 4 Bridge Street Callander Perthshire FK17 8AA Tel: (Callander) 01877 331395	APPROVED	1 Single 1 Double 1 Family	3 En Suite fac	B&B per person £18.50-£20.00 Single £16.50-£17.50 Double	Open Jan-Dec exc Nov

Terraced house conveniently situated in town centre. All rooms ensuite.
Dinner by arrangement.

Riverview House

LENY ROAD, CALLANDER FK17 8AL
Telephone: 01877 330635

Detached Victorian house set in its own grounds near parklands, yet close to shops and other venues. Private facilities in all rooms including colour TV and tea-making. Good home cooking with choice on menu. Ample parking in own grounds.

Riverview House Leny Road Callander Perthshire FK17 8AL Tel: (Callander) 01877 330635	COMMENDED	1 Single 1 Twin 3 Double	4 En Suite fac 1 Limited ensuite 1 Pub Bath/Show	B&B per person £19.00 Single £19.00 Double	Open Apr-Nov Dinner 1900-1915 B&B + Eve. Meal £31.00-£31.50

19th-century house situated back from the main route north out of Callander.
All meals with choice of menu, using fresh produce in season.

Tulipan Lodge Guest House Tulipan Crescent Callander Perthshire FK17 8AR Tel: (Callander) 01877 330572	COMMENDED	2 Twin 3 Double	5 En Suite fac	B&B per person £25.00-£27.00 Single £18.00-£20.00 Double	Open Apr-Oct Dinner 1830-1900 B&B + Eve. Meal £28.50-£37.50

Substantial stone villa on edge of village with level walking to shops
and all amenities. Evening meals available.

CALLANISH **Lewis, Western Isles** Eshcol Guest House 21 Breascleit Callanish Lewis, Western Isles PA86 9ED Tel: (Callanish) 01851 621357	Map 3 D4	HIGHLY COMMENDED	2 Twin 1 Double	2 En Suite fac 1 Priv. NOT ensuite	B&B per person £20.00-£22.00 Single £20.00-£22.00 Double	Open Mar-Oct Dinner 1700-1900 B&B + Eve. Meal from £36.00

Modern detached house with superb views. Near to Callanish Standing Stones
and Carloway Broch. Ensuite facilites. Brochure available.

Catherine Morrison 27 Callanish Callanish Lewis, Western Isles PA86 9DY Tel: (Callanish) 01851 621392	COMMENDED	1 Twin 1 Double	1 Priv. NOT ensuite 1 Pub Bath/Show	B&B per person to £17.00 Single	Open Mar-Sep

Comfortable accommodation on working croft close to the standing stones
and overlooking the sea loch.

| CAMPBELTOWN | Map 1 |
| Argyll | E7 |

WESTBANK GUEST HOUSE
DELL ROAD, CAMPBELTOWN PA28 6JG
Telephone: 01586 553660
A Victorian villa in a quiet residential area near all town amenities. Ideal base for Machrihanish Golf Club and surrounding countryside for birdwatching etc.
A warm welcome awaits you from proprietors:
Hilary and Ralph Shepherd.
AA and RAC Listed

Westbank Guest House Dell Road Campbeltown Argyll PA28 6JG Tel: (Campbeltown) 01586 553660	COMMENDED 👑👑	3 Twin 5 Double	2 En Suite fac 2 Pub Bath/Show	B&B per person from £22.00 Single from £17.00 Double	Open Jan-Dec Dinner 1730-1800

A well-maintained Victorian villa in quiet residential area,
near to Machrihanish Golf Course, and an ideal base for touring.

| CANNICH | Map 3 |
| Inverness-shire | H9 |

Kerrow House
Cannich, Strathglass, Inverness-shire IV4 7NA
Telephone: 01456 415243 Fax: 01456 415425
Magnificent country house offering warm hospitality. Comfortable stylish rooms with private facilities. Wine and dine in licensed restaurant enjoying superb cuisine. Relax in peaceful family atmosphere of beautiful house and grounds. Also self-catering. Open all year and close to Glens of Affric and Cannich. Prices from £15 to £20.

Mr & Mrs Doyle Kerrow House Cannich, Strathglass Inverness-shire IV4 7NA Tel: (Cannich) 01456 415243 Fax: 01456 415425	COMMENDED 👑👑	1 Twin 1 Double 1 Family	3 Priv. NOT ensuite	B&B per person £15.00-£20.00 Single £15.00-£20.00 Double	Open Jan-Dec Dinner 1900-2130 B&B + Eve. Meal £28.00-£35.00

Large country house 200 years old with many period features.
Set in wooded grounds on banks of River Glass.
Bedrooms with own bathrooms.

CANONBIE, by Langholm **Dumfriesshire** Mr & Mrs Carruthers Watchknowe, Watchhill Road Canonbie Dumfriesshire DG14 0TA Tel: (Canonbie) 013873 71805	Map 2 D9	COMMENDED 👑👑	1 Double 1 Family	2 Priv. NOT ensuite	B&B per person £15.00-£16.00 Single £15.00-£16.00 Double	Open Apr-Sep

Renovated 1930's bungalow set in 1 acre of secluded gardens.
Open views of rolling countryside.

Scotland for Golf . . .
Find out more about golf in Scotland. There's more to it than just the championship courses so get in touch with us now for information on the hidden gems of Scotland.
Write to: Information Unit, Scottish Tourist Board,
23 Ravelston Terrace, Edinburgh EH4 3EU
or call: 0131-332 2433

CARDROSS
Dunbartonshire

Map 1
G4

KIRKTON HOUSE

Tel: 01389 841951
Fax: 01389 841868

Darleith Road, Cardross G82 5EZ
COUNTRY HOUSE GUEST ACCOMMODATION
Glasgow Airport 14 miles, Dumbarton & Helensburgh each 4 miles.

OLD WORLD CHARMS WITH MODERN AMENITIES

18/19th-century converted farmstead with superb Clyde views. Tranquil rural setting. Informal guest lounge and dining rooms with original stone walls and fireplaces. Drinks licence. Convivial, home cooked dinners by oil lamplight. Real open fire in the guest lounge.

Kirkton House Darleith Road Cardross Dunbartonshire G82 5EZ Tel: (Cardross) 01389 841951 Fax: 01389 841868	HIGHLY COMMENDED	2 Twin 4 Family	6 En Suite fac	B&B per person £32.50-£37.50 Single £27.00-£29.50 Double	Open Jan-Dec Dinner 1930-2030 B&B + Eve. Meal £44.50-£55.00	

Built around central courtyard in a quiet, elevated rural position commanding magnificent views of the River Clyde.

Mrs A C G Russell Lea Farm Cardross Dunbartonshire G82 5EW Tel: (Cardross) 01389 763035	COMMENDED Listed	1 Twin 1 Family	1 Pub Bath/Show	B&B per person £16.00-£18.00 Single £14.00-£16.00 Double	Open Jan-Dec	

Farmhouse on working farm with panoramic views over the Clyde.
Ideal centre for touring. Friendly family atmosphere.

CARGILL, by Perth
Perthshire

Map 2
B2

Cargil House

Cargill, by Perth PH2 6DT
Telephone: 01250 883334

Far from the madding crowd . . . Cargil House is an elegant period mansion, set in mature grounds on the banks of the River Tay – the ideal spot for a peaceful holiday, with good company and personal service. The rooms are beautifully appointed, very comfortably furnished, with twin/double beds. All have wash-hand basin and tea/coffee-making equipment. En-suite bath and shower facilities are available. Breakfast and optional Evening Meal are taken in a quiet dining room overlooking the river.

Cargil is perfectly situated for a golfing, fishing, hillwalking, sightseeing or ski-ing holiday – or if you simply want to relax.

Miss C Dorrell Cargil House Cargill, by Perth Perthshire PH2 6DT Tel: (Meikleour) 01250 883334	COMMENDED	1 Single 1 Twin 1 Family	1 En Suite fac 1 Pub Bath/Show	B&B per person £18.00-£19.50 Single £18.00-£19.50 Double Room only per person from £18.00	Open Jan-Nov Dinner 1930-2100 B&B + Eve. Meal £31.00-£34.50	

Period mansion house set in own mature grounds on the banks of the River Tay.
Totally peaceful setting in beautiful Perthshire countryside.

CARNOUSTIE Angus	Map 2 D2					
Mrs S M Penman Elm Bank, 3 Camus Street Carnoustie Angus DD7 7PL Tel: (Carnoustie) 01241 852204	COMMENDED Listed	2 Family	1 Pub Bath/Show	B&B per person £14.00-£15.00 Single £14.00-£15.00 Double	Open Jan-Dec	

A warm and friendly welcome. Centrally situated for all amenities and within easy walking distance of golf courses and beach.

Details of Grading and Classification are on page vi.

Key to symbols is on back flap.

CARNOUSTIE continued Mrs E Watson Balhousie Farm Carnoustie Angus DD7 6LG Tel: (Carnoustie) 01241 853533	Map 2 D2	COMMENDED Listed	1 Twin 2 Double	2 Pub Bath/Show	B&B per person from £14.00 Single from £14.00 Double	Open Jan-Dec
			Traditional Victorian family farmhouse on working farm, with sea views. Ideal for golfing and touring, close to local amenities.			
CARRADALE **Argyll** Mrs McCormick The Mains Farm Carradale Argyll PA28 6QG Tel: (Carradale) 01583 431216	Map 1 E7	COMMENDED Listed	1 Single 1 Double 1 Family	1 Pub Bath/Show	B&B per person from £13.50 Single from £13.50 Double	Open Apr-Oct Dinner from 1800 B&B + Eve. Meal from £18.50
			Traditional farmhouse on working farm, on the outskirts of the village and a short walk from the beach. Panoramic views across to the Isle of Arran.			
CARRBRIDGE **Inverness-shire** Craigellachie House Main Street Carrbridge Inverness-shire PH23 3AS Tel: (Carrbridge) 01479 841641	Map 4 C9	COMMENDED 👑 👑	1 Single 2 Twin 2 Double 2 Family	3 En Suite fac 2 Pub Bath/Show	B&B per person £14.00-£20.00 Single £14.00-£17.00 Double	Open Jan-Dec Dinner 1900-2000
			Warm comfortable hospitality assured. Ample parking. Centre of village. Ideal base for holiday activities. Dinners available using fresh Scottish produce.			
M A King Finiskaig, 4 Rowan Park Carrbridge Inverness-shire PH23 3AE Tel: (Aviemore) 01479 841349		COMMENDED Listed	1 Twin 1 Double	1 Pub Bath/Show	B&B per person from £15.00 Single £13.00-£15.00 Double Room only per person £10.00-£11.00	Open Jan-Dec
			Friendly B&B in modern house in picturesque Highland village. Ideal base for touring Strathspey.			
The Mariner Guest House Station Road Carrbridge Inverness-shire PH23 3AN Tel: (Carrbridge) 01479 841331		COMMENDED 👑 👑	2 Twin 2 Double 1 Family	5 En Suite fac 1 Pub Bath/Show	B&B per person £21.00-£23.00 Single £18.00-£20.00 Double	Open Dec-Oct Dinner at 1900 B&B + Eve. Meal £26.00-£31.00
			A modern, purpose-built house in residential area 800m from main street. All ensuite facilities. Ideally situated for touring and skiing.			
CARRONBRIDGE, Denny **Stirlingshire**	Map 2 A4					

Drum Farm

Carronbridge, Stirling, Stirlingshire FK6 5JL
Telephone and Fax: 01324 825518
Beautiful farmhouse situated in unspoilt countryside with views overlooking Carron Dam, just 15 minutes from Stirling and the M9 and M80, where you can start your tours around this beautiful part of Scotland.

Drum Farm Carronbridge Denny Stirlingshire Tel: (Denny) 01324 825518 Fax: 01324 825518		COMMENDED 👑	1 Twin 1 Double	1 Pub Bath/Show	B&B per person £15.00-£18.50 Single £13.50-£16.50 Double	Open Jan-Dec Dinner from 1800
			Modernised 200-year-old farmhouse in quiet location with magnificent views. 7 miles (11kms) from Stirling. Ideal for touring.			

CASTLE DOUGLAS Kirkcudbrightshire Balmaghie House Balmaghie Deer Park Castle Douglas Kirkcudbrightshire DG7 2PB Tel: (Castle Douglas) 01556 670234	Map 2 A10	COMMENDED	2 Family	2 Priv.NOT ensuite	B&B per person £14.00-£16.50 Single £14.00-£16.50 Double	Open Jan-Dec Dinner 1750-2050 B&B + Eve. Meal £20.00-£25.00	

Traditional mansion house in extensive woodland setting.
Shooting by arrangement. Excellent home cooking with local produce.

Mrs S M Brierley Craigvar House 60 St Andrew Street Castle Douglas Kirkcudbrightshire DG7 1EN Tel: (Castle Douglas) 01556 503515		HIGHLY COMMENDED	1 Twin 1 Double	2 En Suite fac	B&B per person £26.00 Single £18.00-£19.00 Double	Open Mar-Oct	

Personally run Georgian town house in quiet residential area. Ideal base
for touring Dumfries and Galloway. Non-smokers only. Both rooms ensuite.

Mrs Margaret Gordon Craig of Balmaghie Farm Laurieston, Castle Douglas Kirkcudbrightshire DG7 2NA Tel: (Laurieston) 01644 450287		COMMENDED	1 Twin 2 Double	1 En Suite fac 1 Pub Bath/Show	B&B per person £17.00-£22.00 Single £14.00-£19.00 Double Room only per person £13.00-£18.00	Open Mar-Nov Dinner 1800-2000 B&B + Eve. Meal £21.00-£26.00	

Warm and friendly working upland farm set in rolling countryside 2 miles (3kms)
north of Laurieston. 8 miles from the market town of Castle Douglas.

Mrs McBride Airds Farm Crossmichael by Castle Douglas Kirkcudbrightshire DG7 3BG Tel: (Crossmichael) 01556 670418		COMMENDED	1 Single 1 Twin 1 Double 1 Family	1 En Suite fac 1 Pub Bath/Show	B&B per person £17.00-£18.00 Single £14.00-£17.00 Double Room only per person £17.00-£18.00	Open Mar-Nov	

On mixed livestock farm in quiet rural location, with excellent views
to Loch Ken. 4 miles (6kms) from Castle Douglas.

CRAIGADAM

CASTLE DOUGLAS, KIRKCUDBRIGHTSHIRE DG7 3HU
Telephone: 01556 650233   Fax: 01556 650233

Eighteenth-century farmhouse with panoramic views of surrounding
countryside. An ideal base for golf, walking, fishing. Come home in
the evening to comfort, super food and good Scottish hospitality.
We specialise in local produce including venison, pheasant, salmon.
All rooms are en-suite.

Mrs C Pickup Craigadam Castle Douglas Kirkcudbrightshire DG7 3HU Tel: (Kirkpatrick Durham) 01556 650233 Fax: 01556 650233		COMMENDED	2 Twin 1 Double	3 En Suite fac	B&B per person £17.00 Single £17.00 Double	Open Jan-Dec Dinner 1800-2030 B&B + Eve. Meal £27.00	

Working farm, with private trout loch and extensive stalking,
driven and rough shooting.

Rose Cottage Guest House Gelston by Castle Douglas Kirkcudbrightshire DG7 1SH Tel: (Castle Douglas) 01556 502513		COMMENDED	3 Twin 2 Double	1 En Suite fac 2 Pub Bath/Show	B&B per person £16.00-£18.50 Single	Open Jan-Dec Dinner at 1830 B&B + Eve. Meal £25.00	

Friendly welcome in personally run guest house situated in quiet village.
Ideal for walkers and birdwatchers. Some accommodation in annexe.

Details of Grading and Classification are on page vi. | Key to symbols is on back flap. | 53

CASTLETOWN, by Thurso Caithness	Map 4 D3

GARTH HOUSE

Castletown, Caithness KW14 8SL   *Tel: 01847 821429*

Garth House is over 250 years old. This comfortable family home has been carefully restored by the present owners. It is situated between Wick and Thurso near Dunnet Bay and Dunnet Head, Britain's most northerly mainland point. There is a large garden for guests' enjoyment, also an outdoor model railway.   *Open January to December.*

Mr & Mrs P Garfield Garth House Castletown Caithness KW14 8SL Tel: (Castletown) 01847 821429	**HIGHLY COMMENDED** 👑👑	1 Twin 1 Double	1 En Suite fac 1 Priv. NOT ensuite	B&B per person from £18.00 Double	Open Jan-Dec	

Large stone-built house dated 1727. Lovingly restored, this "gentleman's seat" welcomes you in comfort and style. Garden railway.

CAWDOR Nairn Mrs Jennifer MacLeod Dallaschyle Cawdor Nairn IV12 5XS Tel: (Croy) 01667 493422	Map 4 C8 **COMMENDED** Listed	1 Double 1 Family	1 Pub Bath/Show	B&B per person from £20.00 Single from £15.00 Double	Open Apr-Nov	

Spacious modern house in peaceful woodland setting with large garden. Close to Cawdor Castle and Culloden Moor.

Mrs Mhairi Munro Limegrove Cawdor Nairn IV12 5RA Tel: (Cawdor) 01667 404307	**COMMENDED** Listed	1 Twin 2 Double	1 Pub Bath/Show	B&B per person from £14.50 Single from £14.50 Double	Open Jan-Dec	

Highland welcome. Comfortable accommodation in picturesque conservation village of Cawdor. Short walk to Cawdor Castle.

CLYDEBANK, Glasgow Dunbartonshire Mrs M Johnston Tudor House, 10 Drumry Road Clydebank, Glasgow G81 Tel: 0141 941 3171	Map 1 H5 **APPROVED** 👑	2 Single 2 Twin 1 Family	2 Limited ensuite 2 Pub Bath/Show	B&B per person £15.00-£17.00 Single from £15.00 Double	Open Jan-Dec	

Family guest house with Cable TV in bedrooms. Situated in residential area. Convenient for the College, train station, shopping centre and business park.

COCKBURNSPATH Berwickshire Mrs B M Russell Townhead Farm Cockburnspath Tel: (Innerwick) 01368 830465	Map 2 E5 **COMMENDED** Listed	2 Double	2 Pub Bath/Show	B&B per person £12.50-£14.00 Single £12.50-£14.00 Double	Open Apr-Oct	

Warm welcome at this family farmhouse set high above the sea. Sandy beaches nearby. Edinburgh only 38 miles (61kms).

WELCOME

Whenever you are in Scotland, you can be sure of a warm welcome at your nearest Tourist Information Centre.

For guide books, maps, souvenirs, our Centres provide a service second to none – many now offer bureau-de-change facilities. And, of course, Tourist Information Centres offer free, expert advice on what to see and do, route-planning and accommodation for everyone – visitors and residents alike!

BY COLDSTREAM Berwickshire Mrs Forrester Homebank House, Nr Birgham Village Coldstream Berwickshire TD12 4ND Tel: (Birgham) 01890 830285	Map 2 E6	COMMENDED 👑👑	1 Twin 1 Double	2 Priv. NOT ensuite 2 Pub Bath/Show	B&B per person from £18.00 Single £18.00-£20.00 Double	Open Apr-Oct Dinner 1800-2000

Elegant country house set in beautiful gardens convenient for touring the Scottish Borders and Northumbria.

COLONSAY, Isle of Argyll — Map 1 C4

SEAVIEW

Isle of Colonsay, Argyll PA61 7YN
Telephone: 01951 200315

Situated in a quiet crofting community by the standing stones at Kilchattan looking out over the Atlantic to Dhu Hertach Lighthouse soon to be designated an environmentally sensitive area. Comfort and good home cooking. A warm welcome assured.

Mr & Mrs Lawson Seaview Colonsay, Isle of Argyll PA61 7YN Tel: (Colonsay) 01951 200315	COMMENDED Listed	2 Twin 1 Double	1 Pub Bath/Show	B&B per person £20.00 Single £20.00 Double Room only per person £15.00	Open Apr-Oct Dinner at 1900

Traditional island hospitality on working croft. Comfortable rooms with interesting touches. Mrs Lawson is a keen cook, and home baker.

COMRIE Perthshire Mossgiel Guest House Burrell Street Comrie Perthshire PH6 2JP Tel: (Comrie) 01764 670567/ 0374 400750 (mobile)	Map 2 A2	COMMENDED 👑	2 Twin 2 Double 1 Family	2 Pub Bath/Show	B&B per person £16.00-£18.00 Single £15.00-£17.00 Double	Open Jan-Dec Dinner 1830-1930 B&B + Eve. Meal £23.50-£26.50

Traditional stone-built house with modern wing on the main road in the village. Near to all amenities. Choice of home-cooked dishes.

CONNEL BY OBAN Argyll — Map 1 E2

KILCHURN

Connel, Oban, Argyll PA37 1PG   Tel: 01631 710581

5 miles from Oban, Kilchurn is situated overlooking Loch Etive and Ben Lora in the picturesque village of Connel. You are assured of a warm welcome with a high standard of accommodation, also ample off-street parking. Ideal base for touring the west Highlands, walking, fishing or boat trips.

Mrs Clark Kilchurn Connel, by Oban Argyll PA37 1PG Tel: (Connel) 01631 710581	COMMENDED 👑👑	1 Twin 2 Double	1 En Suite fac 1 Pub Bath/Show	B&B per person £15.00-£18.00 Single	Open Apr-Oct

Stone-built detached Victorian house on the shores of Loch Etive overlooking Ben Lora, Falls of Lora and the Connel Bridge. Off-street parking.

CONNEL BY OBAN continued	Map 1 E2

ACH-NA-CRAIG
Grosvenor Crescent, Connel, Argyll PA37 1PQ
Telephone: 01631 710588

Ach-na-Craig is situated in a woodland glade with extensive private parking space in the picturesque village of Connel (5 miles from Oban). We offer warm comfortable accommodation with breakfast and evening meal (if required). Ground-floor bedrooms are centrally heated with en-suite shower room, colour TV and tea/coffee facilities.

Mr R Craig Ach-na-Craig Grosvenor Crescent Connel, by Oban Argyll Tel: (Connel) 01631 710588	COMMENDED	2 Twin 1 Double	3 En Suite fac	B&B per person from £17.00 Single	Open Jan-Dec Dinner 1830-2000 B&B + Eve. Meal from £24.50

Newly-built family house in quiet village, 5 miles (8kms) from Oban. Secure off-street parking. All rooms on ground floor and ensuite.

CONON BRIDGE **Ross-shire** Mrs C Morrison Dun Eistein, Alcaig Conon Bridge, by Dingwall Ross-shire IV7 8HS Tel: (Dingwall) 01349 862210	Map 4 A8	COMMENDED	1 Double 1 Family	1 En Suite fac 1 Priv. NOT ensuite	B&B per person £19.00 Single £14.50 Double	Open Apr-Oct

Highland cottage on country road with views of Ben Wyvis from garden. 11 miles (18kms) north of Inverness. Non-smoking.

CONTIN **Ross-shire** Mrs A Dale Larchfield, Craigdarroch Drive Contin Ross-shire IV14 9EL Tel: (Strathpeffer) 01997 421157	Map 4 A8	HIGHLY COMMENDED	1 Twin 1 Double 1 Family	2 En Suite fac 1 Priv. NOT ensuite	B&B per person £16.00-£19.00 Double	Open Jan-Dec

A warm welcome awaits at this modern house set in country surroundings and furnished to a high standard.

CORPACH, by Fort William **Inverness-shire**	Map 3 H12

TRAVEE
CORPACH, FORT WILLIAM, INVERNESS-SHIRE PH33 7LR
Telephone and Fax: 01397 772380

Superbly situated on an elevated site, TRAVEE is a comfortable detached house with breathtaking views over Loch Linnhe, Ben Nevis and Fort William. An ideal base for touring Oban, Mull, Loch Ness. A very warm Scottish welcome awaits you after a day's sightseeing or walking.

R Cumming Travee Corpach, by Fort William Inverness-shire PH33 7LR Tel: (Corpach) 01397 772380 Fax: 01397 772380	COMMENDED	1 Twin 2 Double	1 Pub Bath/Show	B&B per person £18.50 Single £14.50 Double Room only per person £18.50	Open Jan-Dec

Friendly, welcoming, family home, 4 miles (6kms) from Fort William, with super views over Loch Linnhe and Ben Nevis.

Mrs McCallum The Neuk Corpach, by Fort William Inverness-shire PH33 7LR Tel: (Corpach) 01397 772244	COMMENDED	2 Twin 1 Family	3 En Suite fac	B&B per person £22.00-£30.00 Single £16.00-£20.00 Double	Open Jan-Dec Dinner 1730-1900 B&B + Eve. Meal £30.00-£38.00

Detached villa on the Mallaig road (A830). View of Ben Nevis across Loch Linnhe. Evening meal and home cooking.

VAT is shown at 17.5%: changes in this rate may affect prices. Prices shown are for guidance only. Please send SAE with each enquiry.

Mrs MacPhee Tangasdale Corpach, by Fort William Inverness-shire PH33 7LT Tel: (Corpach) 01397 772591		**COMMENDED** 👑	2 Family	1 Pub Bath/Show	B&B per person from £13.50 Single	Open Jan-Dec	
			Modern bungalow with all rooms on the ground floor, close to the canal and Neptune's staircase.				
Mrs Wynne Heston Corpach, by Fort William Inverness-shire PH33 7LT Tel: (Fort William) 01397 772425		**COMMENDED** 👑👑	1 Twin 1 Double	1 En Suite fac 1 Pub Bath/Show	B&B per person £14.00-£16.00 Single £13.00-£17.00 Double	Open Mar-Oct	
			Modern family home with magnificent views across Loch Linnhe. 4 miles (6kms) from Fort William.				
CORRIECRAVIE **Isle of Arran** Mrs Adamson Rosebank, Corriecravie Kilmory Isle of Arran KA27 8PD Tel: (Sliddery) 01770 870228	Map 1 E7	**COMMENDED** 👑👑	1 Single 1 Twin 1 Family	1 En Suite fac 1 Pub Bath/Show	B&B per person £15.00-£17.00 Single from £15.00 Double Room only per person from £15.00	Open Jan-Nov	
			Traditional farmhouse with warm welcome, home baking and open fires. Views over sea to Mull of Kintyre and Ireland.				
COUPAR ANGUS **Perthshire** Mr & Mrs Broadley St Catherine's Croft 14 Union Street Coupar Angus Perthshire PH13 9AE Tel: (Coupar Angus) 01828 627753	Map 2 C1	**APPROVED** 👑	1 Single 1 Twin 1 Family	1 Limited ensuite 1 Pub Bath/Show	B&B per person £15.00-£19.00 Single £15.00-£18.00 Double	Open Jan-Dec	
			Semi-detached stone-built property in centre of Coupar Angus. Ideal for fishing, golfing and all outdoor activities.				
CRAIGNURE **Isle of Mull, Argyll** Pennygate Lodge Craignure Isle of Mull, Argyll PA65 6AY Tel: (Craignure) 01680 812333	Map 1 D2	**COMMENDED** 👑👑👑	2 Twin 3 Double 2 Family Suites avail	4 En Suite fac 2 Pub Bath/Show	B&B per person £15.00-£28.00 Double	Open Jan-Dec Dinner 1800-1930 B&B + Eve. Meal £29.00-£41.00	
			Former Georgian manse set in 4.5 acres of landscaped garden with magnificent views of the Sound of Mull. Ideal base for touring, near main bus route and ferry terminal.				
Redburn Redburn, Lochdon Craignure Isle of Mull, Argyll PA64 6AP Tel: (Craignure) 01680 812370		**COMMENDED** 👑👑	1 Twin 2 Double	3 En Suite fac	B&B per person £18.00 Single £18.00 Double	Open Jan-Dec Dinner at 1800 B&B + Eve. Meal £29.00	
			Converted croft house in quiet location on lochside. 3 miles (4.8kms) Craignure Ferry. Area for natural history enthusiasts. Home cooking.				

OLD MILL COTTAGE GUEST HOUSE AND RESTAURANT

Lochdon Head, by Craignure, Isle of Mull, Argyll PA64 6AP Tel: 01680 812442

Situated on a sheltered sea loch 3 miles from Craignure Ferry. Our intimate restaurant boasts a varied cuisine. A-la-carte menu includes local sea food and Scottish beef. A beautiful location with the loch attracting a wealth of water fowl both summer and winter. **Jim and Jenny Smith offer a warm welcome.**   COMMENDED 👑👑👑

Mrs J Smith Old Mill Guest House & Restaurant Lochdon, Craignure Isle of Mull, Argyll PA64 6AP Tel: (Craignure) 01680 812442		**COMMENDED** 👑👑👑	1 Twin 1 Double	2 En Suite fac	B&B per person £21.00-£25.00 Single £21.00-£23.00 Double	Open Jan-Dec Dinner 1800-2000	
			Centrally situated at the head of Loch Don. Birdwatchers' paradise. A wealth of fresh local seafood and produce just for you. Non-smoking restaurant.				

BY CRAIGNURE
Isle of Mull, Argyll
Helen Wilson
Inverlussa
Craignure
Isle of Mull, Argyll
PA65
Tel: (Craignure) 01680 812436
Fax: 01680 812436

Map 1
D2

HIGHLY
COMMENDED
Listed

1 Twin
1 Double
1 Family

1 En Suite fac
1 Pub Bath/Show

B&B per person
£16.00-£18.00 Single
£16.00-£18.00 Double
Room only per person
£12.00-£14.00

Open Apr-Oct

Personally run modern house in idyllic setting. Ideal base for touring Isle of Mull.

CRAIL
Fife
Hazelton Guest House
29 Marketgate
Crail
Fife
KY10 3TH
Tel: (Crail) 01333 450250

Map 2
D3

COMMENDED
Listed

1 Single
2 Twin
2 Double
2 Family

2 Pub Bath/Show

B&B per person
£16.00-£18.00 Single
£16.00-£18.00 Double

Open Jan-Dec
Dinner 1900-1930
B&B + Eve. Meal
£31.00-£33.00

In the heart of small fishing town, a friendly guest house personally run by
the owners. Fresh local produce used whenever possible. Taste of Scotland.

Selcraig Guest House
47 Nethergate
Crail
Fife
KY10 3TX
Tel: (Crail) 01333 450697

COMMENDED

2 Twin
2 Double
1 Family

2 Pub Bath/Show

B&B per person
£22.00-£24.00 Single
£17.00-£19.00 Double

Open Jan-Dec
Dinner 1800-1900
B&B + Eve. Meal
£29.00-£36.00

200-year-old Listed house in quiet street close to sea shore.
Convenient for touring the East Neuk of Fife. Non-smoking.

CRAOBH HAVEN,
by Lochgilphead
Argyll
Buidhe Lodge
Eilean Buidhe
Craobh Haven
Argyll
PA31 8UA
Tel: (Barbreck) 01852 500291

Map 1
E3

COMMENDED

6 Twin

6 En Suite fac

B&B per person
£26.00-£31.00 Single
£20.00-£25.00 Double

Open Jan-Dec
Dinner 1930-2100
B&B + Eve. Meal
£32.00-£37.00

Architect-designed, timber lodge, on unique island setting connected by
causeway to village.Mountain bikes for hire with detailed route maps available..

CRATHIE
Aberdeenshire
Mrs Webster
Birchwood
Crathie
Aberdeenshire
AB35 5TN
Tel: (Crathie) 013397 42341

Map 4
D11

COMMENDED

1 Twin
1 Double
1 Family

2 En Suite fac
1 Priv. NOT ensuite

B&B per person
£20.00-£21.00 Single
£16.00-£17.00 Double

Open Jan-Dec
Dinner 1830-2030
B&B + Eve. Meal
£30.00-£32.00

Traditional country cottage set in the heart of Royal Deeside.
Adjacent to`Balmoral Castle. Sightseers', hillwalkers' and skiers' paradise.

CRAWFORD
Lanarkshire
Field End Guest House
The Loaning
Crawford
Lanarkshire
ML12 6TN
Tel: (Crawford) 01864 502276

Map 2
B7

APPROVED

1 Single
1 Double
1 Family

1 En Suite fac
2 Priv. NOT ensuite

B&B per person
£17.00-£19.00 Single
£14.00-£17.00 Double

Open Jan-Dec,
exc Xmas/New Year
Dinner 1830-1930
B&B + Eve. Meal
from £20.50

Stone villa overlooking fields, located up the hill opposite the church.
Ideal half-way house and touring centre. No smoking or pets. Families welcome.

CRIANLARICH **Perthshire** Ewich House Crianlarich Perthshire FK20 8RU Tel: (Crianlarich) 01838 300300	**Map 1** G2	COMMENDED 👑👑👑	3 Twin 2 Double	5 En Suite fac 1 Pub Bath/Show	B&B per person £20.00-£25.00 Single £17.00-£25.00 Double	Open Jan-Dec Dinner 1930-2030 B&B + Eve. Meal £32.00-£37.00	

150-year-old stone-built farmhouse, completely renovated stone work, secluded setting with river and mountain views

Glenardran Guest House Crianlarich Perthshire FK20 8QS Tel: (Crianlarich) 01838 300236		COMMENDED Listed	1 Single 2 Twin 3 Double	1 En Suite fac 1 Pub Bath/Show	B&B per person from £17.50 Single from £17.50 Double	Open Jan-Dec Dinner 1915-2000	

Late Victorian house in centre of village.
Excellent base for touring, walking or climbing. Non-smoking.

CRIEFF **Perthshire** Galvelbeg House Perth Road Crieff Perthshire PH7 3EQ Tel: (Crieff) 01764 655061	**Map 2** A2	COMMENDED 👑👑	1 Single 1 Twin 2 Double 1 Family	4 En Suite fac 1 Limited ensuite	B&B per person £19.00-£22.00 Single £19.00-£22.00 Double	Open Jan-Dec	

Situated 500 yards from Crieff town centre and Crieff Golf Club.
A good central base for touring and sightseeing.

MacKenzie Lodge Broich Terrace Crieff Perthshire PH7 3BD Tel: (Crieff) 01764 653721		COMMENDED 👑👑	2 Twin 2 Double 1 Family	2 En Suite fac 2 Pub Bath/Show	B&B per person £16.50-£25.00 Single £16.50-£21.00 Double	Open Jan-Dec	

Elegant Victorian "A" Listed home retaining many original features.
Winner of "Warmest Welcome in Perthshire 1991". Private parking.

Mrs MacLellan Bell House, 1 Broich Terrace Crieff Perthshire PH7 3BD Tel: (Crieff) 01764 654689		COMMENDED Listed	1 Twin 2 Double	1 En Suite fac 1 Pub Bath/Show	B&B per person £14.00-£18.00 Double	Open Jan-Dec	

Detached Victorian villa in quiet residential area. Convenient base for touring.

Mrs Scott Concraig Farm, Muthill Road Crieff Perthshire PH7 4HH Tel: (Crieff) 01764 653237		COMMENDED Listed	1 Twin 2 Double	1 Pub Bath/Show	B&B per person £15.00-£16.00 Double	Open Apr-Oct	

Comfortable farmhouse with spacious rooms. Peacefully situated
just outside Crieff. Ideal location for golfing and touring.

Mrs Katie Sloan Somerton House Crieff Holiday Village Turret Bank, Crieff Perthshire PH7 4JN Tel: (Crieff) 01764 653513		COMMENDED 👑👑	1 Twin 1 Double 1 Family	3 En Suite fac	B&B per person from £18.00 Single from £15.00 Double	Open Jan-Dec	

Friendly bed and breakfast within 15 minutes walk of town. Ideal touring base.
Home of the Turretbank Cavalier King Charles spaniels.

CRINAN Argyll Mrs Mairi Anderson Tigh Na Glaic Crinan, by Lochgilphead Argyll PA31 8SW Tel: (Crinan) 01546 830245	Map 1 E4	COMMENDED	1 Twin 1 Double	2 En Suite fac 1 Pub Bath/Show	B&B per person from £20.00 Single from £20.00 Double Room only per person from £20.00	Open Jan-Dec

Country cottage in peaceful setting, overlooking Loch Crinan to Duntrune Castle. Ideal area for artists, photographers and walkers.

CULLEN Banffshire Mrs Margaret Kirk Homelea, 7 South Castle Street Cullen, Buckie Banffshire AB56 2RT Tel: (Cullen) 01542 841052	Map 4 E7	COMMENDED Listed	1 Single 1 Twin 1 Double	2 Pub Bath/Show	B&B per person £13.00-£14.00 Single £13.00-£14.00 Double	Open Apr-Oct Dinner 1800-1900 B&B + Eve. Meal from £20.00

Small and friendly cottage offering traditional hospitality. Close to all amenities.

Mrs Marian Sleightholm Norwood House, 11 Seafield Place Cullen, Buckie Banffshire AB56 2TE Tel: (Cullen) 01542 840314		APPROVED	1 Single 1 Twin 1 Double	2 En Suite fac 1 Priv. NOT ensuite 1 Pub Bath/Show	B&B per person £13.00-£15.00 Single £13.00-£15.00 Double	Open Apr-Oct Dinner from 1830 B&B + Eve. Meal £21.00-£24.00

Personally run with friendly atmosphere, in quiet residential area, yet with easy access to centre of town and all amenities. Private parking.

Mrs Hazel Taylor Stroma, 4 Seafield Place Cullen, Buckie Banffshire AB56 2TF Tel: (Cullen) 01542 840295		COMMENDED	1 Twin 2 Double	2 Pub Bath/Show	B&B per person £13.00 Single £13.00 Double	Open May-Sep Dinner 1830-1930 B&B + Eve. Meal from £21.00

Traditional Scottish hospitality in friendly family home. Ideal for golfing, bowling and walking holidays.

CULLODEN MOOR Inverness-shire Mrs E M C Alexander Culdoich Farm Culloden Moor, by Inverness Inverness-shire IV1 2EP Tel: (Culloden) 01463 790268	Map 4 B8	COMMENDED	1 Double 1 Family	1 Pub Bath/Show	B&B per person from £15.00 Double	Open May-Oct Dinner from 1900 B&B + Eve. Meal from £24.00

18th-century farmhouse on mixed arable and livestock farm, on hillside near Culloden Battlefield and Clava Stones. Home baking and cooking.

Mrs P Alexander Ballagan Farm Culloden Moor, by Inverness Inverness-shire IV1 2EL Tel: (Culloden) 01463 790213		COMMENDED Listed	1 Twin 1 Family	1 Pub Bath/Show	B&B per person from £15.00 Single from £15.00 Double	Open Apr-Oct Dinner 1830-1930 B&B + Eve. Meal from £23.00

Farmhouse on working cattle farm in rural location 8 miles (13kms) south east of Inverness. Culloden Battlefield and Clava Cairns are nearby.

Mrs M Campbell Bayview, Westhill Culloden Moor Inverness-shire IV1 2BP Tel: (Culloden) 01463 790386		COMMENDED	1 Twin 2 Double	2 En Suite fac 1 Priv. NOT ensuite	B&B per person from £16.00 Single from £16.00 Double	Open Apr-Oct Dinner at 1830 B&B + Eve. Meal £25.00-£27.00

Quiet, comfortable house in pleasant country surroundings with magnificent views over the Moray Firth. Evening meals by arrangement; home cooking.

Mrs M MacLean Woodside of Culloden Westhill, Inverness Inverness-shire IV1 2BP Tel: (Culloden) 01463 790242		**HIGHLY COMMENDED**	2 Twin 1 Double	3 En Suite fac	B&B per person from £17.00 Single	Open Mar-Nov Dinner from 1830 B&B + Eve. Meal from £26.00	

Working farm overlooking Moray Firth, close to Culloden Battlefield and 3 miles (5kms) east of Inverness. Specialist in sheepdog trials.

Mr & Mrs J R Mullen Strathmore, Viewhill Farm Road Culloden Moor Inverness-shire IV1 2EA Tel: (Culloden) 01463 791607		**COMMENDED**	1 Family	1 En Suite fac	B&B per person £14.00-£20.00 Single	Open May-Oct	

Spacious self-contained accommodation with own sitting room and bathroom. One mile from Culloden Battlefield. Inverness 7 miles.

CUMBERNAULD **Dunbartonshire** Mrs M Abercrombie 68 Lammermoor Drive Greenfaulds, Cumbernauld Dunbartonshire G67 4BE Tel: (Cumbernauld) 01236 721307	Map 2 A5	**COMMENDED** **Listed**	3 Twin	1 Pub Bath/Show	B&B per person £16.00 Single £16.00 Double	Open Jan-Dec	

Modern family home, centrally situated with easy access to main roads to Glasgow, Stirling and Edinburgh.

CUPAR **Fife**	Map 2 C3

'EASTERHILLS'

Castlebank Road, Cupar, Fife KY15 4BN
Contact: Mrs Lynda Gibson – Telephone: 01334 654275

A Victorian home of charm and character, set in extensive grounds, offering good food and comfortable accommodation with friendly service. Ideal base for touring, golfing, etc. Ladybank, St Andrews, Carnoustie, Gleneagles, all within easy reach.

Lynda M Gibson Easterhills, Castlebank Road Cupar Fife KY15 4BN Tel: (Cupar) 01334 654275		**COMMENDED**	1 Single 1 Twin 1 Family	1 En Suite fac 2 Pub Bath/Show	B&B per person £25.00-£27.00 Single £21.00-£23.00 Double	Open Mar-Oct	

Victorian house of charm and character, with attractive large gardens. Ideal base for visiting the many historic attractions and numerous golf courses.

BY CUPAR **Fife**	Map 2 C3

TODHALL HOUSE

DAIRSIE, BY CUPAR, FIFE KY15 4RQ
Telephone and Fax: 01334 656344

An attractive listed country house overlooking the rolling farmlands of *North-East Fife*, seven miles from *St Andrews*. Ideally situated for pursuing many varied sporting activities and exploring the historic *Kingdom of Fife*. More than just another B&B! *Come enjoy country comfort at its best. Please call **Gill Donald** for details.*

Mrs Gillian Donald Todhall House Dairsie, by Cupar Fife KY15 4RQ Tel: (Cupar) 01334 656344 Fax: 01334 656344		**HIGHLY COMMENDED**	1 Twin 2 Double	3 En Suite fac	B&B per person £24.00-£26.00 Single £19.00-£24.00 Double	Open Mar-Oct Dinner 1900-1930	

Traditional Scottish country house peacefully located in lovely scenery. Tastefully appointed bedrooms, one with 4-poster bed.

DALBEATTIE **Kirkcudbrightshire** Briardale House Haugh Road Dalbeattie Kirkcudbrightshire DG5 4AR Tel: (Dalbeattie) 01556 611468/ 0850 267251 (mobile)	Map 2 A10 **DELUXE**	1 Twin 2 Double	3 En Suite fac	B&B per person £19.00 Double	Open Jan-Oct Dinner 1800-1900 B&B + Eve. Meal £30.00

Detached Victorian villa retaining many original features in residential area on the outskirts of town. Excellent food; no licence, no corkage.

Mrs M Maddison Broomlands House Haugh Road Dalbeattie Kirkcudbrightshire DG5 4AR Tel: (Dalbeattie) 01556 611463 Fax: 01556 611462	**DELUXE**	1 Twin 2 Double	3 En Suite fac	B&B per person from £22.00 Double	Open Jan-Dec Dinner 1900-2100 B&B + Eve. Meal from £32.00

A magnificent granite house, lavishly refurbished, set in over 3 acres of landscaped grounds – very spacious.

DALCROSS, by Inverness **Inverness-shire**	Map 4 B8

Easter Dalziel Farmhouse

Easter Dalziel Farm, Dalcross, Inverness IV1 2JL
Telephone and Fax: 01667 462213
This Scottish farming family offers true Highland hospitality on 200 acre stock/arable farm 7 miles east of Inverness, between A96 and B9039. Delightful early Victorian farmhouse in superb central location with panoramic views. Many recommendations including Elizabeth Gundrey's S.O.T.B.T. and the Best Bed and Breakfast.
AA QQQ RECOMMENDED

Mrs Pottie Easter Dalziel Farm Dalcross Inverness-shire IV1 2JL Tel: (Ardersier) 01667 462213 Fax: 01667 462213	**HIGHLY COMMENDED**	1 Twin 2 Double	2 Pub Bath/Show	B&B per person £22.00-£24.00 Single £15.00-£17.00 Double	Open Jan-Dec Dinner from 1900 B&B + Eve. Meal £25.00-£27.00

Victorian farmhouse, on stock/arable farm. Friendly atmosphere. Log fire in lounge and home baking. Inverness 7 miles (11kms). Culloden 5 miles (8kms).

Mrs Simpson Woodend House Dalcross Inverness-shire IV1 2JJ Tel: (Croy) 01667 493234	**HIGHLY COMMENDED** Listed	2 Twin 1 Double	2 Pub Bath/Show	B&B per person £20.00 Single £14.50-£15.00 Double Room only per person £12.00	Open Apr-Oct Dinner from 1900 B&B + Eve. Meal £20.00-£22.00

Former Victorian farmhouse in secluded setting, 7 miles (11kms) east of Inverness. Elegantly furnished with accent on comfort. Close to airport.

DALGETY BAY **Fife** Mrs Punler Seal Bay House, 42 The Wynd Dalgety Bay Fife KY11 5SJ Tel: (Dalgety Bay) 01383 822790	Map 2 B4 **COMMENDED** Listed	2 Twin 1 Double	2 Pub Bath/Show	B&B per person from £19.00 Single from £19.00 Double	Open Jan-Dec Dinner from 1800

A large, modern house situated on the sea-front at Dalgety Bay and enjoying its own heated indoor swimming pool, solarium, jacuzzi and sauna.

DALKEITH **Midlothian** Mrs M Blair 'Woodcot' 22 Bonnyrigg Road Eskbank, Dalkeith Midlothian EH22 3EZ Tel: 0131 663 2628	Map 2 C5	APPROVED Listed	2 Family	1 Pub Bath/Show	B&B per person £15.00-£17.00 Single	Open Jan-Dec		

Family home with convenient access to city. Ideal base for touring Lothians. Parking.

Mrs Margaret Jarvis Belmont, 47 Eskbank Road Dalkeith Midlothian EH22 3BH Tel: 0131 663 8676 Fax: 0131 663 8676	COMMENDED Listed	1 Twin 2 Double	1 En Suite fac 1 Pub Bath/Show	B&B per person £16.00-£20.00 Single £16.00-£18.00 Double	Open Jan-Dec		

Large Victorian house, with original features.
Set in extensive landscaped gardens. Off-street parking.

Mrs A Taylor Dalhousie Mains Farmhouse Eskbank Dalkeith Midlothian EH22 3LZ Tel: 0131 663 5182	-APPROVED Listed	1 Twin 1 Double 1 Family	2 En Suite fac 1 Priv. NOT ensuite 1 Pub Bath/Show	B&B per person £15.00-£20.00 Single £15.00-£20.00 Double	Open Jan-Dec		

A lovely 18th-century house 7 miles (11 kms) south of Edinburgh.
Friendly atmosphere, large gardens, some rooms ensuite.

DALMALLY **Argyll**	Map 1 F2

CRUACHAN

DALMALLY, ARGYLL PA33 1AA
Telephone: 01838 200496

Comfortable Edwardian house in quiet Highland village. Offers excellent French and Scottish cooking. Lovely views, walks, fishing, golf, climbing. Two bedrooms are purpose-built for disabled visitors and along with guests' lounge, dining room are totally wheelchair accessible. Ample parking and large garden. Ideal centre for Glencoe, Inveraray, Mull and Iona.

Mrs Borrett Cruachan Dalmally Argyll PA33 1AA Tel: (Dalmally) 01838 200496	COMMENDED 👑👑 ♿	2 Twin 1 Double	3 En Suite fac	B&B per person from £20.00 Single from £15.00 Double	Open Jan-Dec Dinner 1900-2000 B&B + Eve. Meal from £25.00		

Traditional stone villa with purpose-built accommodation for disabled guests.
Multi-lingual proprietors offer friendly, informal atmosphere.

Craig Villa Guest House Dalmally Argyll PA33 1AX Tel: (Dalmally) 01838 200255	COMMENDED 👑👑👑	2 Twin 2 Double 2 Family	5 En Suite fac 1 Priv. NOT ensuite	B&B per person £20.00-£25.00 Single £19.00-£23.00 Double	Open Apr-Oct Dinner from 1900 B&B + Eve. Meal £30.00-£35.00		

Personally run guest house in own grounds amidst breathtaking scenery.
Good touring base. Home cooking.

WELCOME

Whenever you are in Scotland, you can be sure of a warm welcome at your nearest Tourist Information Centre.

For guide books, maps, souvenirs, our Centres provide a service second to none – many now offer bureau-de-change facilities. And, of course, Tourist Information Centres offer free, expert advice on what to see and do, route-planning and accommodation for everyone – visitors and residents alike!

DALMALLY continued Mrs MacDougall Strathorchy Dalmally Argyll Tel: (Dalmally) 01838 200373 Fax: 01838 200373	Map 1 F2	COMMENDED ♛♛	2 Twin 2 Double	2 En Suite fac 1 Pub Bath/Show	B&B per person £14.00-£17.00 Single £14.00-£17.00 Double	Open Jan-Dec

Recently built traditional style house in countryside setting beside 1st tee on golf course. Good base for touring Argyll and the Glenards Islands.

Orchy Bank Guest House Dalmally Argyll PA33 1AS Tel: (Dalmally) 01838 200370		COMMENDED Listed	2 Single 2 Twin 2 Double 2 Family	2 Pub Bath/Show	B&B per person £16.00-£18.00 Single £16.00-£18.00 Double	Open Jan-Dec Dinner 1900-2000 B&B + Eve. Meal £26.00-£28.00

Personally run Victorian former village shop on banks of the River Orchy. 24 miles (38 kms) to Oban, 16 miles (26 kms) to Inveraray. Near Glencoe.

DALMELLINGTON Ayrshire- Mrs Taveren Benbain, Cumnock Road Dalmellington Ayrshire KA6 7PS Tel: (Dalmellington) 01292 550556	Map 1 H8	COMMENDED Listed	1 Single 1 Twin 1 Double	2 Pub Bath/Show	B&B per person £14.00-£16.00 Single £14.00-£16.00 Double	Open Jan-Dec Dinner 1800-2100 B&B + Eve. Meal £22.00-£24.00

17th-century house and converted byre with superb views of Galloway hills. Excellent baking, cooking and personal touches.

DAVIOT Inverness-shire Greystanes B&B Daviot West Inverness-shire IV1 2EP Tel: (Farr) 01808 521381	Map 4 B9	HIGHLY COMMENDED Listed	2 Single 1 Twin 1 Double	1 En Suite fac 1 Pub Bath/Show	B&B per person from £16.00 Single from £16.00 Double	Open Jan-Dec Dinner 1830-2000 B&B + Eve. Meal from £26.00

Spacious modern bungalow in 5.5 acres (1.5 acres woodland). Panoramic views of Strathnairn. Excellent country walks. One en suite room.

M MacLeod Chalna Daviot Inverness-shire IV1 2XQ Tel: (Daviot) 01463 772239		COMMENDED ♛♛	1 Twin 1 Double 1 Family	1 En Suite fac 1 Pub Bath/Show	B&B per person from £15.00 Double	Open Mar-Sep

Modern, detached stone-built villa, in extensive grounds in rural setting. 7 miles (11kms) south of Inverness. Fishing available.

DENHOLM Roxburghshire	Map 2 D7					

The Fox and Hounds Inn
Main Street, Denholm, Roxburghshire TD9 8NU
Telephone: 01450 870247   Fax: 01450 870500

This charming 300-year-old inn overlooks the village green of historic Denholm amidst the rolling Border hills and between Hawick and Jedburgh with riding, golfing and fishing all close by. As well as home-cooked lunches and dinners, guests are well catered for in the adjoining cottage with its family comforts. Enjoy!

Mr Douglas Newlands The Fox and Hounds Inn, Main Street Denholm Roxburghshire TD9 8NU Tel: (Denholm) 01450 870247 Fax: 01450 870500		COMMENDED ♛	1 Single 1 Double 1 Family	3 En Suite fac 2 Pub Bath/Show	B&B per person £18.00-£20.00 Single from £18.00 Double	Open Jan-Dec Dinner 1800-2100 B&B + Eve. Meal £26.00-£30.00

Family run Inn situated in pretty village overlooking the green. Enclosed beer garden and children's play area. A wide selection of Real Ales available.

VAT is shown at 17.5%: changes in this rate may affect prices. Prices shown are for guidance only. Please send SAE with each enquiry.

DERVAIG **Isle of Mull, Argyll** Ardrioch Farm Guest House Dervaig, by Tobermory Isle of Mull, Argyll PA75 6QR Tel: (Dervaig) 01688 400264 Fax: 01688 400264	**Map 1** C1	COMMENDED ♛ ♛	1 Single 2 Twin 2 Double	2 En Suite fac 1 Pub Bath/Show	B&B per person £18.00-£20.50 Single £18.00-£20.50 Double	Open Apr-Oct Dinner 1830-2000 B&B + Eve. Meal £29.50-£32.00	

Attractive cedarwood house with adjoining farm; lovely loch and hill views. Home cooking. Taste of Scotland. Inter-island cruises. Chalet annexe.

Mr C A & Mrs H A Arnold Balmacara Dervaig Isle of Mull Argyll PA75 6QN Tel: (Dervaig) 01688 400363 Fax: 01688 400363		HIGHLY COMMENDED ♛ ♛ ♛	2 Twin 1 Double	2 En Suite fac 1 Priv. NOT ensuite	B&B per person £24.00-£26.00 Single £24.00-£26.00 Double	Open Jan-Dec Dinner 1900-2000 B&B + Eve. Meal £33.50-£35.50	

Brand new property high above Dervaig Village. Overlooking Glen Bellort and Loch Cuin, framed by the hills and forests of North West Mull.

John and Mary Porter Tigh an Allt Dervaig Isle of Mull, Argyll PA75 6QR Tel: (Dervaig) 01688 400247		COMMENDED ♛	1 Twin 1 Double	1 Pub Bath/Show	B&B per person £19.00-£20.00 Single £16.00-£17.00 Double	Open Jan-Dec Dinner to 1900 B&B + Eve. Meal £25.00-£29.50	

Modern family house in quiet secluded setting. Close to Mull Little Theatre. Ideally situated for wildlife and bird observation. Non-smoking.

Mrs Smith Achnacraig Dervaig Isle of Mull, Argyll PA75 6QW Tel: (Dervaig) 01688 400309		COMMENDED ♛	1 Single 1 Twin 1 Family	2 Pub Bath/Show	B&B per person £16.00-£17.50 Single	Open Apr-Oct Dinner from 1930 B&B + Eve. Meal £25.00-£26.00	

Winding river, circling buzzards, stone farmhouse, stupendous views. Home-grown produce, real cooking.

DIABAIG **Ross-shire** Mrs B J Peacock Upper Diabaig Torridon, Achnasheen Ross-shire IV22 2HE Tel: (Diabaig) 01445 790227	**Map 3** F8	COMMENDED Listed	2 Twin 1 Double	1 Pub Bath/Show	B&B per person from £14.00 Double	Open Apr-Sep Dinner from 1900 B&B + Eve. Meal from £25.00	

Dramatic drive by Torridon Hills to modern house on working croft. Traditional Scottish hospitality. Warm and comfortable. Good home cooking.

Miss I A Ross 3 Diabaig Torridon, Achnasheen Ross-shire IV22 2HE Tel: (Diabaig) 01445 790240/790268		COMMENDED Listed	1 Single 1 Twin 1 Double	1 Priv. NOT ensuite 1 Pub Bath/Show	B&B per person £13.00-£13.50 Single £13.00-£13.50 Double Room only per person from £9.00	Open Jan-Dec Dinner 1900-2130 B&B + Eve. Meal £21.50-£22.00	

Modern bungalow in village of Diabaig, looking out over bay to surrounding hills. Ideal for boat and fishing trips, walking and climbing in Torridon Mountains.

DINGWALL **Ross-shire** Mrs M Duffus 18 Millcraig Road Dingwall Ross-shire IV15 9PS Tel: (Dingwall) 01349 862194	**Map 4** A8	COMMENDED ♛	1 Twin 1 Double	2 Pub Bath/Show	B&B per person £11.50-£13.00 Single £11.50-£13.00 Double	Open Apr-Oct	

With a warm welcome, home bakes and a cheerful smile you soon join the ranks of Mabel's extended family.

Details of Grading and Classification are on page vi.

Key to symbols is on back flap.

DINGWALL continued

Map 4 A8

Kirklee B & B
1 Achany Road
Dingwall
IV15 9JB
Tel: (Dingwall) 01349 863439

COMMENDED
Listed

1 Single
1 Twin
2 Double

2 Pub Bath/Show

B&B per person
to £14.00 Single
to £14.00 Double

Open Jan-Dec

Spacious Victorian family run house in own garden, in quiet cul-de-sac, close to town centre, near to rail and bus station.

Mrs J MacLean
Duart, 1 Logan Drive
Dingwall
Ross-shire
IV15 9LN
Tel: (Dingwall) 01349 862387

COMMENDED
Listed

2 Twin

1 Pub Bath/Show

B&B per person
from £14.00 Double

Open Feb-Nov

Comfotable bed and breakfast situated in quiet residential area with private parking. Ideal base for touring the Highlands.

DORES
Inverness-shire

Map 4 B9

Mrs J Morrison
Beinn Dhearg, Torr Gardens
Dores
Inverness-shire
IV1 2TS
Tel: (Dores) 01463 751336

COMMENDED

1 Twin
1 Double
1 Family

3 En Suite fac
1 Pub Bath/Show

B&B per person
£16.00-£18.00 Double

Open Apr-Sep

Modern spacious bungalow in quiet setting 100yds from Loch Ness 8 miles (13kms) south of Inverness. Wonderful views across Loch Ness. All rooms with private facilities.

DORNIE, by Kyle of Lochalsh
Ross-shire

Map 3 G9

Tigh Tasgaidh
Dornie, Kyle of Lochalsh, Ross-shire IV40 8EH
Telephone: 01599 555242

The old bank house, situated in Dornie village. Overlooking Loch Long with views of the Isle of Skye and the Cuillins. Ideal centre for walking or touring. Comfortable non-smoking accommodation, bedrooms with private facilities, central heating, colour TV, tea and coffee-making facilities.

Mrs Clayton
Tigh Tasgaidh
Dornie, by Kyle of Lochalsh
Ross-shire
IV40 8EH
Tel: (Dornie) 01599 555242

COMMENDED

1 Twin
2 Double

3 En Suite fac
1 Pub Bath/Show

B&B per person
£15.00-£18.00 Double

Open Feb-Nov

Detached house standing in its own grounds overlooking Loch Long. In a quiet residential area but near main Inverness-Skye road. Non-smoking.

Mrs Alexina Finlayson
2 Sallachy
Dornie
Ross-shire
IV40 8DZ
Tel: (Kililan) 01599 588238

COMMENDED

1 Twin
1 Double

1 Pub Bath/Show

B&B per person
from £14.00 Double

Open Apr-Oct
Dinner 1900-2000
B&B + Eve. Meal
from £22.00

Modern bungalow on working croft. An elevated position with views across Loch Long.

Mrs Peterkin Sealladh-mara Dornie, by Kyle of Lochalsh Ross-shire IV40 Tel: (Dornie) 01599 555296	**COMMENDED** Listed	1 Twin 1 Double 1 Family	1 Pub Bath/Show	B&B per person £13.00-£14.00 Single £13.00-£14.00 Double	Open Jan-Dec Dinner 1800-2030 B&B + Eve. Meal £23.00-£24.00	
		Modern family home, looking over Loch Duich and Eilean Donan Castle towards Kintail mountains. Handy for touring to Skye and Wester Ross. Ideal for walking.				

DORNOCH Sutherland	Map 4 B6					

Fourpenny Cottage
Skelbo, by Dornoch, Sutherland IV25 3QF
Telephone: 01862 810727 Fax: 01862 810727

Fourpenny Cottage overlooks the nature reserve at Loch Fleet and the Dornoch Firth. Situated in 2½ acres of grounds the cottage has en-suite facilities, colour TV and tea/coffee makers in each bedroom. We specialise in traditional cooking. Close to Dornoch, Golspie, Brora golf courses. Ideal centre for touring holidays.
B&B from £24; DB&B from £35.50   NO SMOKING!

S M Board Fourpenny Cottage Skelbo, by Dornoch Sutherland IV25 3QF Tel: (Dornoch) 01862 810727 Fax: 01862 810727	**HIGHLY COMMENDED** 👑👑👑	2 Twin 1 Double 1 Family	4 En Suite fac	B&B per person from £24.00 Double	Open Feb-Dec Dinner at 1900 B&B + Eve. Meal from £35.50	
		Large detached house in quiet rural position 2 miles (3 kms) from Dornoch. Overlooks Loch Fleet. Friendly atmosphere. Traditional home-cooking. Some annexe accommodation.				

HIGHFIELD
Evelix Road, Dornoch, Sutherland IV25 3HR
Telephone and Fax: 01862 810909

Highfield is a large, comfortable, non-smoking house standing in an acre of ground, with beautiful southerly views, yet only a few hundred yards from the centre of Dornoch. Our renowned hospitality, high standards of service and informal atmosphere ensure guests return year after year to golf, explore or just relax.

Mrs J Dooley Highfield, Evelix Road Dornoch Sutherland IV25 3HR Tel: (Dornoch) 01862 810909 Fax: 01862 810909	**DELUXE** 👑👑	1 Twin 2 Double	3 En Suite fac	B&B per person £28.00-£30.00 Single £21.00-£23.00 Double	Open Jan-Dec	
		A modern house at edge of the picturesque golfing town – a warm welcome assured in this very comfortable family home.				

Mrs E A Dunlop Cluaine, Evelix Dornoch Sutherland IV25 3RD Tel: (Dornoch) 01862 810276	**COMMENDED** 👑👑	1 Twin 1 Family	1 En Suite fac 1 Priv. NOT ensuite	B&B per person £16.00-£20.00 Single £15.00-£18.00 Double	Open May-Oct	
		Personally run B&B with ground-floor rooms, set in 3 acres of woodland and gardens. Ideal base for touring. Beaches and golf courses nearby.				

DORNOCH continued Fearn Guest House High Street Dornoch Sutherland IV25 3SH Tel: (Dornoch) 01862 810249	Map 4 B6	COMMENDED 👑👑	2 Twin 1 Double	2 En Suite fac 1 Limited ensuite 1 Priv. NOT ensuite	B&B per person £20.00-£25.00 Single £17.00-£20.00 Double	Open Jan-Dec

A friendly welcome at stone-built house on quiet street in centre of Dornoch overlooking cathedral.

Mrs B Fraser Khuzistan, 9 Poles Road Dornoch Sutherland IV25 3HP Tel: (Dornoch) 01862 810552		HIGHLY COMMENDED 👑👑	1 Twin 2 Double	1 En Suite fac 2 Priv. NOT ensuite	B&B per person £15.00-£17.50 Double	Open Apr-Oct

Friendly, family run modern home (incl a ground-floor room) with excellent garden area. Off-road parking available.

ACHANDEAN

The Meadows, Off Castle Close, Dornoch, Sutherland IV25 3SF
Telephone: 01862 810413

Comfortable, spacious bungalow of character, situated on *Right-Hand Side of Town Centre*, off Castle Close, very central to shops, beach and championship golf course. Loch Fleet Nature Reserve is nearby. Ideal for touring the Highlands, walks, etc. This picturesque little town has a 13th-century cathedral amongst its attractions.

Mrs Audrey Hellier Achandean, The Meadows off Castle Close Dornoch Sutherland IV25 3SF Tel: (Dornoch) 01862 810413		COMMENDED 👑👑	1 Twin 2 Double	2 En Suite fac 1 Priv. NOT ensuite	B&B per person £28.00-£32.00 Single £18.00-£24.00 Double	Open Jan-Dec Dinner 1830-1930

Bungalow set one road back from cathedral town centre on right-hand side. Ideal touring base with off-road parking in this central quiet location.

PARFOUR

Rowan Crescent, Dornoch IV25 3QP
Telephone: 01862 810955

Modern family home. Situated close to Royal Dornoch Golf Club and miles of sandy beaches. Guest lounge, private parking. Activity holidays, *Golf* tee times arranged for Brora, Tain, Dornoch, Golspie. *Walking* guide available for daily scenic walking.

Mrs S Young Parfour, Rowan Crescent Dornoch Sutherland IV25 3QP Tel: (Dornoch) 01862 810955		HIGHLY COMMENDED 👑👑	2 Double/ Twin/Family 1 Twin	3 En Suite fac	B&B per person £19.00-£27.00 Single £18.50-£20.50 Double	Open Jan-Dec B&B + Eve. Meal from £29.50

Homely, modern bungalow. Convenient for town centre, golf course and beach. Private parking.

DOUGLAS Lanarkshire Mrs E J Scott The Limes Douglas Lanarkshire ML11 0PX Tel: (Douglas) 01555 851388	Map 2 A7	COMMENDED 👑👑	1 Twin 1 Double 1 Family	1 En Suite fac 1 Priv. NOT ensuite 2 Pub Bath/Show	B&B per person £20.00 Single £16.00-£18.00 Double	Open Apr-Oct Dinner 1900-2000 B&B + Eve. Meal £30.00

A former 200-year-old manse set in an acre of woodland, in the heart of Clyde Valley. Ample parking. Homebaking and freshly prepared cooking.

DOUNE **Perthshire** Mrs Joyce Anderson Inverardoch Mains Farm Doune (B824), Dunblane Perthshire FK15 9NZ Tel: (Dunblane) 01786 841268	Map 2 A3	COMMENDED ♔	1 Twin 1 Double 1 Family	1 Limited ensuite 1 Pub Bath/Show	B&B per person £16.00-£18.00 Single £14.50-£15.50 Double	Open Apr-Oct	

Traditional Victorian farmhouse on 200-acre working farm.
Originally main farm of 15th-century. Doune Castle.

Mrs F J R Graham Mackeanston House Doune Perthshire Tel: (Doune) 01786 850213 Fax: 01786 850414		COMMENDED ♔ ♔	1 Twin 1 Double	2 En Suite fac	B&B per person £26.00-£31.00 Single £20.00-£25.00 Double	Open Jan-Dec Dinner from 2000 B&B + Eve. Meal £43.50-£49.50	

Peaceful, comfortable old farmhouse with large garden. Enjoy open fires,
home cooking with free range eggs and home-made bread. Ensuite bathrooms.

DRUMBEG **Sutherland** Mrs M Waud Taigh Druimbeag Drumbeg Sutherland IV27 4NW Tel: (Drumbeg) 01571 833209	Map 3 G4	COMMENDED ♔ ♔ ♔	1 Twin 2 Double	3 En Suite fac	B&B per person from £22.50 Double	Open Easter-Oct Dinner 1800-1900 B&B + Eve. Meal £35.00	

In house-party style, Ron and Margaret provide a warm welcome, convivial company.
Fresh veg, self-indulgent puddings. Wonderfully peaceful situation.

DRUMNADROCHIT **Inverness-shire** Mrs Tina Beet Heatherlea, Balmacaan Road Drumnadrochit Inverness-shire IV3 6UR Tel: (Drumnadrochit) 01456 450561	Map 4 A9	HIGHLY COMMENDED Listed	1 Twin 2 Double	1 En Suite fac 1 Pub Bath/Show	B&B per person from £12.50 Double	Open Jan-Dec	

Modern family home in popular Highland village close to Loch Ness.
Good views to loch and hills. Inverness 14 miles (22 kms).

WOODLANDS

East Lewiston, Drumnadrochit, Inverness-shire IV3 6UL
Telephone: 01456 450356
Relax in our modern, comfortable family home set in
the quiet Highland village of Lewiston, Drumnadrochit.
Close to Loch Ness an ideal centre for touring the Highlands
and only 15 miles from Inverness.
Jim and Janette await to give you a
warm Scottish welcome.

J & J Drysdale Woodlands, East Lewiston Drumnadrochit Inverness-shire IV3 6UL Tel: (Drumnadrochit) 01456 450356		COMMENDED ♔ ♔ ♔	1 Twin 2 Double	2 En Suite fac 1 Priv. NOT ensuite	B&B per person from £14.00 Double	Open Jan-Dec Dinner 1800-1900 B&B + Eve. Meal from £22.00	

Modern house with an acre of garden in quiet situation on edge of
Drumnadrochit close to Loch Ness. Inverness 15 miles (24kms).

Glen Rowan Guest House West Lewiston Drumnadrochit Inverness-shire IV3 6UW Tel: (Drumnadrochit) 01456 450235		COMMENDED ♔ ♔	2 Twin 1 Double	3 En Suite fac	B&B per person £25.00-£35.00 Single £14.50-£18.50 Double	Open Jan-Dec excl Christmas Dinner 1830-1900 B&B + Eve. Meal £24.50-£50.00	

Modern house with garden running down to river in a quiet village by Loch Ness
between Drumnadrochit and Urquhart Castle. Non-smoking.

DRUMNADROCHIT continued	Map 4 A9						

Mrs H MacDonald
Maes Howe, Walled Garden
Balmacaan
Drumnadrochit
Inverness-shire
IV3 6UP
Tel: (Drumnadrochit)
01456 450382

HIGHLY COMMENDED
Listed

1 Single   2 Pub Bath/Show
1 Twin
1 Double

B&B per person
£13.50 Single
£13.50 Double

Open Mar-Oct

Modern house in old walled garden, with panoramic views of hills;
2 miles (3kms) from Loch Ness and 14 miles (22kms) from Inverness.

Borlum Farmhouse

*Borlum Farm Country Holidays, Drumnadrochit,
Inverness IV3 6XN   Telephone and Fax: 01456 450358
This 180-year-old farmhouse has a unique position overlooking
Loch Ness. Borlum is an historic working hill farm dating back to
its service to Urquhart Castle in the 16th century. The farm also has
its own BHS approved riding centre, making it the ideal place to
spend a riding holiday,*

Capt & Mrs A D MacDonald-Haig
Borlum Farm
Drumnadrochit
Inverness-shire
IV3 6XN
Tel: (Drumnadrochit)
01456 450358
Fax: 01456 450358

COMMENDED

1 Twin   2 En Suite fac
3 Double   1 Pub Bath/Show
1 Family

B&B per person
£18.75-£27.00 Double

Open Jan-Dec

Comfortable country house with many period features, welcomes non-smokers.
On working farm with fine views of Loch Ness. Riding available.

Mr R J MacGregor
Riverbank, West Lewiston
Drumnadrochit
Inverness-shire
IV3 6UL
Tel: (Drumnadrochit)
01456 450274

COMMENDED

1 Twin   1 En Suite fac
2 Double   2 Pub Bath/Show

B&B per person
£14.00-£16.00 Single
£12.50-£15.50 Double

Open Mar-Oct

Modern house with ground-floor accommodation peacefully situated.
Ample parking. Riverside and woodland walks.

John & Rosemary MacKenzie
Carrachan House, Milton
Drumnadrochit
Inverness-shire
IV3 6UA
Tel: (Drumnadrochit)
01456 450254

COMMENDED

2 Double   2 Pub Bath/Show
1 Family

B&B per person
£12.50-£13.50 Single

Open Jan-Dec,
exc Xmas

Traditional stone house in peaceful village at entrance to Glen Urquhart
and less than 3 miles (5kms) from Loch Ness. Fishing and golf nearby.

Mrs MacLennan
Benview, Lewiston
Drumnadrochit
Inverness-shire
IV3 6UW
Tel: (Drumnadrochit)
01456 450379

APPROVED
Listed

1 Twin   1 Pub Bath/Show
1 Double

B&B per person
£12.00-£12.50 Single

Open Jan-Dec

19th-century cottage in quiet village. 1.5 miles (800m) walk from Loch Ness.
Near to bus stop by Lewiston Arms Hotel. 14 miles (22kms) from Inverness.

Mrs E Paterson
Allanmore Farm
Drumnadrochit
Inverness-shire
IV3 6XE
Tel: (Drumnadrochit)
01456 450247

COMMENDED
Listed

1 Twin   1 Pub Bath/Show
2 Double

B&B per person
£13.50-£14.00 Double

Open Apr-Oct

16th-century farmhouse on stock and arable farm in peaceful setting.

VAT is shown at 17.5%: changes in this rate may affect prices. Prices shown are for guidance only. Please send SAE with each enquiry.

Sandra & Bill Silke Westwood, Lower Balmacaan Drumnadrochit Inverness-shire IV3 6UL Tel: (Drumnadrochit) 01456 450826		**COMMENDED** Listed	2 Twin 1 Double	1 En Suite fac 1 Pub Bath/Show	B&B per person £13.00-£18.00 Double	Open Jan-Dec Dinner 1800-2030 B&B + Eve. Meal £22.00-£27.00	

Modern centrally heated bungalow. Quiet location in popular Highland village near Loch Ness and Glen Affric.

Mrs Caroline Urquhart Drumbuie Farm, Drumbuie Drumnadrochit Inverness-shire IV3 6XP Tel: (Drumnadrochit) 01456 450634		**HIGHLY COMMENDED**	1 Twin 2 Double	3 En Suite fac	B&B per person from £18.00 Single £14.00-£18.00 Double	Open Jan-Dec Dinner 1900-2000 B&B + Eve. Meal £22.00-£26.00	

Modern farmhouse, with all rooms en-suite, on an elevated site overlooking Loch Ness and surrounding farmland: own herd of Highland cattle.

Mrs M Van Loon Kilmore Farm House Drumnadrochit Inverness-shire IV3 6UH Tel: (Drumnadrochit) 01456 450524		**COMMENDED**	1 Twin 2 Double	3 En Suite fac	B&B per person from £14.00 Double	Open Jan-Dec Dinner 1830-1930 B&B + Eve. Meal from £22.00	

Modern farmhouse peacefully situated with splendid views of surrounding hills. Site of Special Scientific Interest. Highland cattle.

Mr & Mrs Vaughan Gillyflowers Drumnadrochit Inverness-shire IV3 6UW Tel: (Drumnadrochit) 01456 450641		**COMMENDED**	1 Twin 2 Double	1 En Suite fac 2 Pub Bath/Show	B&B per person £15.00-£20.00 Single £12.50-£22.00 Double	Open Jan-Dec	

Renovated farmhouse of character and charm. Countryside location close to Loch Ness. Hospitality assured. Evening meal available.

DRYMEN **Stirlingshire** Mrs Julia Cross Easter Drumquhassle Farm Gartness Road Drymen Stirlingshire G63 0DN Tel: (Drymen) 01360 660893	Map 1 H4	**COMMENDED** Listed	1 Double 1 Family	1 En Suite fac 1 Priv. NOT ensuite	B&B per person £16.00-£19.00 Single £15.00-£17.00 Double	Open Jan-Dec Dinner 1800-2000 B&B + Eve. Meal £23.50-£25.00	

Studio-type bedroom and accommodation in main house. Ideal base for touring Loch Lomond area. Quiet, rural location. Spectacular views. Come and be well fed.

DUFFTOWN **Banffshire** Mrs Lynn Morrison Nashville, 8a Balvenie Street Dufftown, Keith Banffshire AB55 4AB Tel: (Dufftown) 01340 820553	Map 4 E9	**COMMENDED**	1 Twin 1 Double 1 Family	1 Pub Bath/Show	B&B per person £12.00-£14.00 Single £12.00-£14.00 Double	Open Jan-Dec	

Family run home in town centre. Convenient for Whisky Trail. A warm welcome awaits you.

Mrs E MacMillan Davaar, Church Street Dufftown, Keith Banffshire AB55 4AR Tel: (Dufftown) 01340 820464		**COMMENDED** Listed	1 Twin 2 Double	2 En Suite fac 1 Pub Bath/Show	B&B per person from £13.50 Single to £16.00 Double	Open Jan-Dec Dinner 1800-2000 B&B + Eve. Meal £21.50-£24.00	

Comfortable and personally run accommodation. Close to Whisky and Castle Trails. Traditional Scottish home baking.

DUFFTOWN continued

Map 4 E9

Mrs Mary M Robertson
11 Conval Street
Dufftown, Keith
Banffshire
AB55 4AE
Tel: (Dufftown) 01340 820818

COMMENDED

1 Twin   1 Pub Bath/Show
1 Double

B&B per person
from £15.00 Single
£12.00-£14.00 Double

Open Jan-Dec
Dinner 1800-2000
B&B + Eve. Meal
£18.00-£20.00

Warm welcome at quiet modern bungalow, off main street 18 miles (29 kms)
south of Elgin. On Whisky Trail.

Tannochbrae
Guest House & Restaurant
22 Fife Street
Dufftown, Keith
Banffshire
AB55 4AL
Tel: (Dufftown) 01340 820541

COMMENDED

1 Single   5 En Suite fac
1 Twin
1 Double
2 Family

B&B per person
£15.50-£18.00
Single

Open Jan-Dec
Dinner 1700-2100
B&B + Eve. Meal
£25.00-£28.00

Personally run restaurant and guest house in the centre of Dufftown. Scottish
chef specialises in local fayre. Ideal for Speyside Way and the famous Whisky Trail.

DUIRINISH, by Plockton
Ross-shire

Map 3 F9

Mrs MacKenzie
Seann Bhruthach
Duirinish, by Plockton
Ross-shire
IV40
Tel: (Plockton) 01599 544204

COMMENDED
Listed

1 Twin   1 Pub Bath/Show
2 Double

B&B per person
£13.00-£14.00 Single
£13.00-£14.00 Double

Open Jan-Dec
Dinner 1930-2000
B&B + Eve. Meal
£20.00-£22.00

Comfortable modern house in picturesque crofting township
with outstanding views over the Inner Hebrides.

DULNAIN BRIDGE,
by Grantown-on-Spey
Moray

Map 4 C9

Rosegrove Guest House

Skye of Curr, Dulnain Bridge, by Grantown-on-Spey
Inverness-shire PH26 3PA.   Tel: 01479 851335

Ideal centre for exploring Scottish Highlands. Good food, local
salmon, Scotch beef and venison. Bring your own wine. Relax at log
fire with mountain views. Pets welcome. Open festive season.
Weekly terms available. Details from Fiona Watson.

Rosegrove Guest House
Skye of Curr
Dulnain Bridge
by Grantown-on-Spey
Inverness-shire
PH26 3PA
Tel: (Dulnain Bridge)
01479 851335

COMMENDED

2 Single   3 En Suite fac
2 Twin   3 Pub Bath/Show
2 Double
1 Family

B&B per person
£15.50-£18.50 Single
£15.50-£18.50 Double

Open Jan-Dec
Dinner 1830-1930

Modern house, personally run. Home cooking.
A short distance from Dulnain Bridge.

DUMBARTON

Map 1 G5

Mrs A S Robinson
Rayport, 14 Glenpath
Dumbarton
Dunbartonshire
G82 2QL
Tel: (Dumbarton)
01389 761948

COMMENDED

1 Twin   1 Pub Bath/Show
1 Double

B&B per person
£18.00-£20.00 Single
£15.00-£18.00 Double

Open Apr-Oct

Modern family home in quiet residential area, 13 miles from airport.
Ideal for touring Clyde coast and Loch Lomond. Easy access to Glasgow.

| DUMFRIES | Map 2 B9 | COMMENDED Listed | 1 Twin 1 Double | 1 Pub Bath/Show | B&B per person £14.50 Single £14.50 Double | Open Jan-Dec Dinner 1800-2000 B&B + Eve. Meal £22.50 | |

Mrs Burdekin, Shambellie View, Wellgreen, Glencaple Rd, Dumfries, DG1 4TD. Tel: (Dumfries) 01387 269331

Comfortable home with rural outlook, peacefully situated 1.5 miles (2.5kms) from town centre. Good base for touring Dumfries and Galloway.

| Dalston House | | COMMENDED | 3 Single 3 Twin 7 Double 4 Family | 16 En Suite fac 1 Priv. NOT ensuite 1 Pub Bath/Show | B&B per person £30.00-£48.00 Single £25.00-£30.00 Double | Open Jan-Dec Dinner 1800-2100 B&B + Eve. Meal £40.00-£55.00 | |

Laurieknowe, Dumfries, DG2 7AH. Tel: (Dumfries) 01387 254422. Fax: 01387 254422

Family run establishment close to town centre and all amenities. Varied menu with accent on fresh produce. Special breaks off-season. Ground-floor accommodation available.

| Laurelbank Guest House | | COMMENDED | 2 Twin 1 Double 1 Family | 3 Limited ensuite 1 Pub Bath/Show | B&B per person £24.00 Single £17.00-£18.00 Double | Open Feb-Nov | |

7 Laurieknowe, Dumfries, DG2 7AH. Tel: (Dumfries) 01387 269388

Elevated sandstone villa, a short walk to River Nith, town centre and Bus Station. Ice Bowl 3 minutes away. Private car park at rear.

| Mrs C A Murphy | | HIGHLY COMMENDED | 1 Twin 1 Double 1 Family | 3 En Suite fac | B&B per person from £25.00 Single from £18.50 Double | Open Jan-Dec | |

Orchard House, 298 Annan Road, Dumfries, DG1 3JE. Tel: (Dumfries) 01387 255099

On the outskirts of the town, converted stable block offering spacious annexe accommodation with extensive parking.

| BY DUMFRIES | Map 2 B9 | COMMENDED | 1 Twin 1 Double | 2 En Suite fac | B&B per person from £18.00 Single £12.50-£15.00 Double | Open Jan-Dec | |

Mrs Hood, Kirk House Farm, Beeswing, by Dumfries, DG2 8JF. Tel: (Kirkgunzeon) 01387 760209

Working dairy farm in quiet village with fine views. Sauna available for guests' use.

| Mr Ireson | | APPROVED Listed | 1 Twin 1 Double 1 Family | 1 En Suite fac 2 Pub Bath/Show | B&B per person £13.50-£17.50 Double | Open Jan-Dec Dinner 1800-2000 B&B + Eve. Meal £22.00-£26.00 | |

Smithy House, Torthorwald, by Dumfries, Dumfriesshire, DG1 3PT. Tel: (Collin) 01387 750518

Converted village smithy with annexe accommodation available. 3 miles (5km) from busy shopping town of Dumfries and local amenities.

| Mrs C M Schooling | | COMMENDED | 1 Twin 1 Family | 1 En Suite fac 1 Pub Bath/Show | B&B per person £15.00-£18.00 Single £15.00-£18.00 Double Room only per person £13.00-£16.00 | Open Jan-Dec Dinner 1800-2000 B&B + Eve. Meal £22.00-£25.00 | |

Locharthur House, Beeswing, by Dumfries, Dumfriesshire, DG2 8JG. Tel: (Dumfries) 01387 760235

Late Georgian house set in 3 acres of grounds with access off A711. Excellent views of countryside. Home baking and cooking. Good base for touring.

DUNBAR **East Lothian** St Beys Guest House 2 Bayswell Road Dunbar East Lothian EH42 1AB Tel: (Dunbar) 01368 863571	Map 2 E4	**APPROVED** ♕	2 Single 1 Twin 2 Double 2 Family	3 Limited ensuite 1 Pub Bath/Show	B&B per person £17.50-£18.50 Single £17.50-£18.50 Double	Open Jan-Dec Dinner 1830-2000 B&B + Eve. Meal £26.50-£29.00	
			A warm welcome and home cooking, using fresh ingredients, at this Victorian house overlooking the seafront, a few minutes walk from town centre.				
Springfield Guest House Belhaven Road Dunbar East Lothian EH42 1NH Tel: (Dunbar) 01368 862502		**COMMENDED** ♕♕	1 Single 1 Twin 1 Double 2 Family	1 Priv. NOT ensuite 2 Pub Bath/Show	B&B per person £17.50 Single £16.50 Double	Open Jan-Nov Dinner at 1800 B&B + Eve. Meal £26.50	
			An elegant 19th-century villa with attractive garden. Family run with home-cooking. Ideal base for golf and touring.				
DUNBEATH **Caithness** Mrs M MacDonald Tormore Farm Dunbeath Caithness KW6 6EH Tel: (Dunbeath) 01593 731240	Map 4 D4	**COMMENDED** Listed	1 Twin 1 Double 1 Family	1 Pub Bath/Show	B&B per person £12.00-£13.00 Single £12.00-£13.00 Double	Open May-Sep Dinner 1800-2130 B&B + Eve. Meal £17.00-£20.00	
			Warm Highland hospitality on this traditional working farm. Dinner available on request. One ground-floor bedroom.				
DUNBLANE **Perthshire**	Map 2 A3						

MOSSGIEL

DOUNE ROAD, DUNBLANE, PERTHSHIRE FK15 9ND
Telephone: 01786 824325

Situated in a country setting, **Mossgiel** offers guests a warm
welcome, comfortable, well-equipped bedrooms –
two ensuite and one private, large garden with safe
off-road parking and a good Scottish breakfast.
Mossgiel is located near the M9 Motorway and is an ideal
base for touring *Loch Lomond* and *The Trossachs*.

Mrs Judy Bennett Mossgiel, Doune Road Dunblane Perthshire FK15 9ND Tel: (Dunblane) 01786 824325		**COMMENDED** ♕♕ 🚶	2 Twin 1 Double	2 En Suite fac 1 Priv. NOT ensuite	B&B per person £17.00-£18.00 Double	Open Apr-Oct	
			Bungalow in beautiful rural setting, 1 mile (2 km) from Dunblane on A820. Two ground-floor ensuite bedrooms.				
Mrs Isobel Lymburn Schiehallion House, 31 Doune Road Dunblane Perthshire FK15 9AT Tel: (Dunblane) 01786 823141 Fax: 01786 824604		**COMMENDED** ♕♕	2 Twin 1 Double 2 Family	4 En Suite fac 1 Priv. NOT ensuite	B&B per person £28.00-£30.00 Single £17.00-£19.00 Double	Open Apr-Oct Dinner from 1930 B&B + Eve. Meal £27.00-£45.00	
			Personally run, in residential area. Reputation for fine food in dining room with feature Minstrel's gallery. Traditional Scottish menu.				
DUNDEE **Angus** Anderson's Guest House 285 Perth Road Dundee Angus DD2 1JS Tel: (Dundee) 01382 668585	Map 2 C2	**APPROVED** Listed	1 Single 2 Twin 2 Double 2 Family	6 En Suite fac 1 Priv. NOT ensuite	B&B per person £18.00-£25.00 Single £16.00-£20.00 Double	Open Jan-Dec	
			Centrally heated, comfortable, refurbished accommodation on main bus route for city centre, close to University and Ninewells Hospital. Many ensuite rooms and river views.				

Ashgrove, Mrs H Thomson 251 Perth Road Dundee Angus Tel: (Dundee) 01382 566175	COMMENDED	1 Twin 1 Double	1 Pub Bath/Show	B&B per person £14.50-£15.50 Single £14.50-£15.00 Double	Open Jan-Dec Dinner 1700-1900	

Traditional stone-built terraced house (B listed) fifteen minutes walk to city centre and five minutes walk to the seawall.

The Birks 149 Arbroath Road Dundee Angus DD4 6LP Tel: (Dundee) 01382 453393	COMMENDED Listed	2 Family	2 Pub Bath/Show	B&B per person £16.00-£18.00 Single £15.00-£17.00 Double	Open Jan-Dec	

Detached stone-built house in residential area in east end of city.
Guests' car parking; on main bus route Dundee/Broughty Ferry.

Mrs Sheila Charlett The Laurels, 65 Camphill Road Broughty Ferry, Dundee Angus DD5 2LY Tel: (Dundee) 01382 776203	HIGHLY COMMENDED Listed	1 Single 1 Twin	1 Pub Bath/Show	B&B per person £17.50-£20.00 Single £17.50-£20.00 Double	Open Jan-Dec	

Georgian family house in quiet residential area.
Views across River Tay to Fife. Secluded garden

Errolbank Guest House 9 Dalgleish Road Dundee Angus DD4 7JN Tel: (Dundee) 01382 462118	COMMENDED	1 Single 2 Twin 2 Double 1 Family	4 En Suite fac 1 Pub Bath/Show	B&B per person £17.00-£21.00 Single £16.00-£17.50 Double	Open Jan-Dec	

Victorian villa, quiet residential area, centrally situated for touring,
golf and all local amenities.

Mrs M Laing Auchenean 177 Hamilton Street Broughty Ferry, Dundee Angus DD5 2RE Tel: (Dundee) 01382 774782	HIGHLY COMMENDED Listed	1 Single 1 Twin	1 Pub Bath/Show	B&B per person from £14.00 Single from £14.00 Double	Open Mar-Oct Dinner 1800-2000 B&B + Eve. Meal from £21.50	

Detached house in quiet cul-de-sac. Residents' lounge opening onto secluded garden.
Morning tea served free of charge. 5 minutes from seafront.

Mrs E M & Mr A E Lerpiniere 43 Denoon Terrace Dundee Angus DD2 2EB Tel: (Dundee) 01382 668512	COMMENDED Listed	1 Double 1 Family	2 Pub Bath/Show	B&B per person £15.00-£16.00 Single £14.50-£15.50 Double	Open Jan-Dec	

Comfortable family home in quiet residential area of Dundee.
Ground-floor rooms. Close Ninewells Hospital. Ideal sightseeing base.

Mrs Hazel Milne 8 Nelson Terrace Dundee Angus DD1 2PR Tel: (Dundee) 01382 225354	COMMENDED Listed	3 Twin	2 Pub Bath/Show	B&B per person £13.50-£16.50 Single £13.50-£14.50 Double	Open Jan-Dec Dinner 1700-1800	

Family home in residential area, close to the town centre.

Mrs E Park 1 Fyne Road, Broughty Ferry Dundee Angus DD5 3JF Tel: (Dundee) 01382 778980	COMMENDED	1 Single 1 Twin	1 Pub Bath/Show	B&B per person £13.00-£15.00 Single £12.00-£14.00 Double Room only per person £13.00-£15.00	Open Jan-Dec	

Modern semi-detached house in quiet residential area.
Easy travelling distance to town centre and Discovery. Close to bus stop.

Details of Grading and Classification are on page vi. | Key to symbols is on back flap. |

DUNDEE continued

Map 2 C2

Mrs Florence Taylor
Ardmoy, 359 Arbroath Road
Dundee
Angus
DD4 7SQ
Tel: (Dundee) 01382 453249

COMMENDED
Listed

1 Twin 1 Pub Bath/Show
1 Double

B&B per person
£16.00–£21.00 Single
£16.00–£18.00 Double

Open Jan-Dec
Dinner 1700-1900
B&B + Eve. Meal
£22.00–£27.00

Spacious stone-built house in own garden on direct route to centre.
Private parking. Ideal touring base. Close to Discovery and city centre.

Mr & Mrs B Wallace
The Bend, 17a Claypotts Road
Broughty Ferry
Dundee
Angus
DD5 1BS
Tel: (Dundee) 01382 730085

COMMENDED

1 Twin 1 En Suite fac

B&B per person
to £25.00 Single
£17.00–£17.50 Double

Open Jan-Dec

Private suite with secluded garden in quiet area with off-street parking.
Convenient for Dundee, East Coast, and golf courses. Regret no smoking.

DUNDONNELL

Ross-shire
Map 3 G6

Mr & Mrs P Hayball
The Old Schoolhouse, Badcaul
Dundonnell
Ross-shire
IV23 2QY
Tel: (Dundonnell) 01854 633311
Fax: 01854 633311

COMMENDED

1 Twin 1 Pub Bath/Show
1 Double

B&B per person
£15.00–£17.00 Single
£13.00–£15.00 Double

Open Mar-Nov
Dinner 1900-2030
B&B + Eve. Meal
£23.00–£27.00

Traditional stone-built house on Little Loch Broom near An Teallach.
Warm welcome and home cooking.

Mrs A Ross
4 Camusnagaul
Dundonnell
Ross-shire
IV23 2QT
Tel: (Dundonnell)
01854 633237

HIGHLY
COMMENDED

1 Twin 1 Pub Bath/Show
1 Double
1 Family

B&B per person
£13.50–£14.00 Double

Open Jan-Dec

Ideal for walkers and climbers, being close to the An Teallach Mountain Range.

DUNFERMLINE

Fife
Map 2 B4

Clarke Cottage Guest House
139 Halbeath Road
Dunfermline
Fife
KY11 4LA
Tel: (Dunfermline)
01383 735935

COMMENDED

4 Twin 4 En Suite fac

B&B per person
£21.00–£25.00 Single
£19.00–£23.00 Double
Room only per person
£18.00–£22.00

Open Jan-Dec

Ensuite accommodation forming part of original Victorian house near
main road and town centre. Private parking. Ideal for visiting Edinburgh and Fife.

Mrs Dunsire
The Haven, 82 Pilmuir Street
Dunfermline
Fife
KY12 0LN
Tel: (Dunfermline)
01383 729039

COMMENDED
Listed

2 Twin 2 Pub Bath/Show
1 Family

B&B per person
from £16.00 Single
from £14.00 Double
Room only per person
from £15.00

Open Jan-Dec

Family run Victorian guest house in a central location,
with many period features. Warm and friendly welcome.

Mrs E M Fotheringham
Bowleys Farm, Roscobie
Dunfermline
Fife
KY12 0SG
Tel: (Dunfermline)
01383 721056

COMMENDED

1 Twin 1 Pub Bath/Show
1 Family

B&B per person
£18.00–£20.00 Single
£16.00–£18.00 Double

Open Apr-Oct
Dinner 1800-1900
B&B + Eve. Meal
£24.00–£25.00

Quiet, peaceful and relaxing 19th-century working stock farm set in 170 acres.
Warm welcome and homebaking. 5 miles (8kms) north of Dunfermline.

Clive & Elaine Guyton Hopetoun Lodge 141 Halbeath Road Dunfermline Fife, KY11 4LA Tel: (Dunfermline) 01383 620906	COMMENDED	2 Twin 1 Family	1 En Suite fac 2 Priv. NOT ensuite 2 Pub Bath/Show	B&B per person £23.50-£27.50 Single £18.50-£23.50 Double	Open Jan-Dec		

Personally run B&B, conveniently located for M90. Within easy reach of Edinburgh.
Tastefully renovated, good sized rooms. Large Art-deco bathroom.

Mrs Hooper Hillview House 9 Aberdour Road Dunfermline, Fife KY11 4PB Tel: (Dunfermline) 01383 726278	COMMENDED	1 Twin 2 Double	1 Limited ensuite 2 Pub Bath/Show	B&B per person £16.00-£17.00 Single £15.00-£16.00 Double	Open Jan-Dec		

Friendly family home on the outskirts of the town. Comfortable and
well-appointed rooms, some overlooking attractive rear garden.

PITCAIRN HOUSE

82a Halbeath Road, Dunfermline, Fife KY12 7RS
Telephone: 01383 732901

Pitcairn House is a well-established family run bed and breakfast
business, situated within walking distance of the town centre. Facilities
include en-suite, tea and coffee, colour TV, telephone, which are
provided within a very comfortable surrounding. Car parking available.

Mr H Pitcairn Pitcairn House 82a Halbeath Road Dunfermline Fife, KY12 7RS Tel: (Dunfermline) 01383 732901	COMMENDED	2 Twin 1 Double	3 En Suite fac	B&B per person £23.00 Single £20.00 Double	Open Jan-Dec		

Small and friendly. Easy access to M90 and town centre.
12 miles (19 kms) from Edinburgh and good base for touring the Fife coast.
All en-suite ground-floor rooms.

DUNKELD **Perthshire** Mrs Hannah S Crozier Balmore, Perth Road Birnam, by Dunkeld Perthshire PH8 0BH Tel: (Dunkeld) 01350 728885	Map 2 B1	HIGHLY COMMENDED	1 Twin 2 Double	1 En Suite fac 1 Pub Bath/Show	B&B per person from £18.00 Single	Open Mar-Sep Dinner 1900-1930 B&B + Eve. Meal from £29.00	

Friendly welcome at family run house, with well-furnished accommodation
in small village, just off A9. 12 miles (19kms) from Perth. Parking.

The Tap Inn

PERTH ROAD, BIRNAM, BY DUNKELD
PERTHSHIRE PH8 0AA
TELEPHONE: 01350 727699
EN-SUITE TWIN BEDROOMS FROM £18 PER PERSON.
TV AND TEA AND COFFEE FACILITIES.
FOOD AND DRINKS IN OUR VILLAGE PUB AND BEER
GARDEN WITH FRIENDLY ATMOSPHERE.

The Tap Inn Birnam, by Dunkeld Perthshire PH8 0AA Tel: (Dunkeld) 01350 727699	APPROVED	6 Twin	6 En Suite fac	B&B per person £25.00 Single to £18.00 Double	Open Jan-Dec Dinner 1800-2100		

Family run inn situated in the old village of Birnam.
Convenient for fishing, golfing and touring. Annexe bedrooms.

| DUNKELD continued | Map 2 B1 | COMMENDED ♔ | 1 Single
2 Twin
2 Double
1 Family | 2 Pub Bath/Show | B&B per person
£16.00-£17.00 Single
£16.00-£17.00 Double
Room only per person
£14.00-£15.00 | Open Jan-Dec
Dinner 1830-2000
B&B + Eve. Meal
£24.00-£25.00 |

Waterbury Guest House
Birnam, by Dunkeld
Perthshire
PH8 0BG
Tel: (Dunkeld) 01350 727324

Traditional Scottish hospitality in this Listed building in rural village
on Grampian fringe. Ideal for walkers and bird watchers.

| BY DUNKELD
Perthshire | Map 2 B1 | | | | | |

LETTER FARM

Loch of the Lowes, by Dunkeld, Perthshire PH8 0HH
Telephone: 01350 724254

This tastefully renovated farmhouse offers a warm friendly
welcome to all. En-suite facilities, kingsize beds, log fires and good
home baking. The farm is central to Perthshire attractions, but
exudes peace and tranquillity nestled next to Loch of the Lowes
Wildlife Reserve, home of the Osprey.

| Mrs Jo Andrew
Letter Farm, Loch of the Lowes
Dunkeld
Perthshire
PH8 0HH
Tel: (Butterstone)
01350 724254 | | COMMENDED ♔♔ | 1 Twin
1 Double
1 Family | 3 En Suite fac | B&B per person
£18.00-£25.00 Single
£18.00 Double | Open Jan-Dec |

Tastefully renovated farmhouse on working farm 1.5 miles (2.5 kms) from
Scottish Wildfowl Trust Reserve. 3 miles (5kms) from Dunkeld. Peaceful location.

| Mrs Jessie Mathieson
The Coppers
Inchmagrannachan
Dunkeld
Perthshire
PH8 0JS
Tel: (Dunkeld) 01350 727372 | | COMMENDED
Listed | 1 Twin
1 Double | 1 En Suite fac
1 Pub Bath/Show | B&B per person
£13.00-£17.00 Single
£13.00-£17.00 Double | Open Apr-Oct
Dinner from 1830
B&B + Eve. Meal
£21.00-£24.00 |

Typical Highland welcome and home cooking in this bungalow with
one en suite bedroom. Access to fishing and golf, superb walks.

| Mrs Paterson
The Orchard
Dalguise, by Dunkeld
Perthshire
PH8 0JX
Tel: (Dunkeld) 01350 727446 | | COMMENDED ♔♔♔ | 1 Twin
1 Double | 2 En Suite fac | B&B per person
£18.00-£23.50 Single
£16.00-£18.50 Double | Open Jan-Dec
Dinner 1830-1930
B&B + Eve. Meal
£24.00-£26.50 |

Set in over two acres, a detached bungalow in the heart of Beatrix Potter country.
Scottish produce used wherever possible.

| Mrs A W Smith
Stralochy Farm
Spittalfield, by Murthly
Perthshire
PH1 4LQ
Tel: (Caputh) 01738 710447 | | COMMENDED
Listed | 1 Twin
1 Double
1 Family | 2 Pub Bath/Show | B&B per person
£14.00-£18.00 Single
£14.00-£15.00 Double
Room only per person
£10.00 | Open May-Sep
Dinner from 1830
B&B + Eve. Meal
£20.00-£22.00 |

Real farmhouse hospitality on working farm overlooking the Howe of Strathmore,
enjoying superb open views. Evening meals on request.

| DUNLOP
Ayrshire
Struther Farm Guest House
17 Newmill Road
Dunlop
Ayrshire
KA3 4BA
Tel: (Stewarton) 01560 484946 | Map 1 G6 | APPROVED ♔ | 1 Twin
1 Double
2 Family | 2 Pub Bath/Show | B&B per person
£16.00-£20.00 Single
£16.00-£20.00 Double | Open Jan-Dec
Dinner 1830-1930 |

Old Scottish farmhouse with large garden. Fresh seafood and meat in season.
Only 17 miles (27kms) from Glasgow. Good base for touring.

| DUNNET
Caithness
Dianne Thomson
Tigh-Na-Muir, Rattar
Dunnet, Thurso
Caithness
KW14 8LX
Tel: (Barrock) 01847 851760 | Map 4
D2 | HIGHLY
COMMENDED
👑 👑 | 1 Single
1 Double
1 Family | 1 En Suite fac
1 Pub Bath/Show | B&B per person
£13.50-£16.50 Single
£13.50-£16.50 Double
Room only per person
£10.00-£12.00 | |

Modern comfortable bungalow, midway between Thurso and John O'Groats with uninterrupted views to Stroma and Orkney.

DUNOON Argyll	Map 1 F5

The Anchorage

Shore Road, Ardnadam, Sandbank
Dunoon PA23 8QG
Tel: 01369 705108 Fax: 01369 705108

Built around 1870 the Anchorage is a stylish Victorian villa standing in an acre of gardens by the shores of the Holy Loch. Throughout the Anchorage there is an exceptionally high standard of decoration and furnishings all complementing the Victorian country house style. The Anchorage is strictly non-smoking for the comfort of all guests. The bedrooms have luxury en-suite bath or shower rooms, CTV, and complementary tea and coffee-making facilities. The four-poster bedroom is ideal for that honeymoon or other special occasion. Complete your stay at the Anchorage by relaxing and dining each evening in the conservatory "under nature's canopy".

| The Anchorage
Shore Road, Ardnadam
Dunoon
Argyll
PA23 8QG
Tel: (Dunoon) 01369 705108
Fax: 01369 705108 | HIGHLY
COMMENDED
👑 👑 👑 | 1 Twin
4 Double | 5 En Suite fac | B&B per person
£37.00-£42.50 Single
£19.50-£25.00 Double | Open Jan-Dec
Dinner 1800-2200
B&B + Eve. Meal
£32.00-£40.00 | |

Traditional stone villa c.1870 with open views over Holy Loch.
1 mile (2kms) from Western Ferry Terminal.

CLAYMORE

Wellington Street, Dunoon, Argyll PA23 7LA
Telephone: 01369 702658

Sample the warmth and hospitality of superior accommodation. Centrally located. All rooms tastefully furnished with en-suite facilities, tea/coffee, satellite TV, books, hairdryers etc. Renowned for good food, we can guarantee an enjoyable evening meal. Relax in our pleasant garden area or enjoy a leisurely walk along the nearby promenade.

| Mrs Smith
Claymore, Wellington Street
Dunoon
Argylee
PA23 7LA
Tel: (Dunoon) 01369 702658 | COMMENDED
👑 👑 👑 | 1 Twin
1 Double
1 Family | 4 En Suite fac | B&B per person
£15.00-£18.50 Double | Open Jan-Dec
Dinner 1800-2000
B&B + Eve. Meal
£24.00 - £27.50 | |

Comfortable accommodation in family run villa within a few minutes walk of shops, ferry and promenade.

DUNS **Berwickshire** Mrs Hannay St Albans, Clouds Duns Berwickshire TD11 3BB Tel: (Duns) 01361 883285/ 0589 683799 (mobile)	Map 2 E5	COMMENDED	1 Twin 1 Double	1 Priv. NOT ensuite 1 Pub Bath/Show	B&B per person £14.50-£19.00 Double	Open Jan-Dec

Pleasant Georgian house with secluded south-facing garden.
Magnificent view over small town to Cheviot Hills. Close to town centre.

BY DUNS **Berwickshire** Mrs Margaret Millican Herriot Bank, Whitsome Duns Berwickshire TD11 3NB Tel: (Whitsome) 01890 870239	Map 2 E5	COMMENDED Listed	2 Twin 1 Double	1 Pub Bath/Show	B&B per person from £16.00 Single from £16.00 Single Room only per person from £18.00	Open Apr-Oct

Spacious home in quiet village. Handy for all coastal and Borders attractions.
Own plant nursery adjacent.

DUNURE, by Ayr **Ayrshire** Mrs L Wilcox Fisherton Farm Dunure Ayrshire KA7 4LF Tel: (Dunure) 01292 500223	Map 1 G7	COMMENDED	2 Twin	1 Pub Bath/Show	B&B per person from £15.00 Single from £15.00 Double	Open Mar-Nov

Traditional stone-built farmhouse on working mixed farm, with extensive sea
views to Arran. 5 miles (8kms) from Ayr. Ground-floor accommodation available.

DUNVEGAN, **Isle of Skye, Inverness-shire** Mrs A E Gracie Silverdale, 14 Skinidin Dunvegan Isle of Skye, Inverness-shire IV55 8ZS Tel: (Dunvegan) 01470 521251 Fax: 01470 521251	Map 3 D9	HIGHLY COMMENDED	1 Twin 1 Double 1 Family	1 En Suite fac 1 Pub Bath/Show	B&B per person from £15.50 Double	Open Jan-Dec

Modern house with superb views over Loch Dunvegan.
Decor and furnishings to a high standard. Acclaimed restaurant nearby.

Mrs MacDonald Cnoc-Nan-Craobh, Orbost Farm Dunvegan Isle of Skye, Inverness-shire IV55 8ZB Tel: (Dunvegan) 01470 521225		COMMENDED	2 Twin 1 Double	2 Pub Bath/Show	B&B per person from £14.00 Single	Open Jan-Dec

Traditional Highland hospitality on working farm. Highland cattle.

Mrs MacDonald Herebost Dunvegan Isle of Skye, Inverness-shire IV55 8GZ Tel: (Dunvegan) 01470 521255		COMMENDED	1 Twin 2 Double	1 En Suite fac 1 Priv. NOT ensuite 1 Pub Bath/Show	B&B per person £15.00-£18.00 Double	Open Apr-Oct

Modern bungalow on working sheep farm situated just off the Dunvegan Road
with views to the south. Supper in the lounge in the evening.

DUROR OF APPIN, **by Kentallen, Argyll** Mrs F C Worthington Lagnaha Farm Duror of Appin Argyll PA38 4BS Tel: (Duror) 01631 740207 Fax: 01631 740207	Map 1 E1	COMMENDED	1 Single 2 Double	1 En Suite fac 1 Pub Bath/Show	B&B per person £15.00-£20.00 Single £15.00-£20.00 Double	Open Easter-October

Traditional Listed 19th-century farmhouse 6 miles (10 kms) from Glencoe.
An ideal base for touring Appin and the West of Scotland.

EAGLESFIELD, by Lockerbie **Dumfriesshire** Mrs Fletcher Glengower Eaglesfield, by Lockerbie Dumfriesshire DG11 3LT Tel: (Kirtlebridge) 01461 500253	Map 2 C9	COMMENDED	1 Single 1 Twin 1 Double 1 Family	1 Priv. NOT ensuite 2 Pub Bath/Show	B&B per person £13.00-£14.00 Single £13.00-£14.00 Double	Open Apr-Oct

Spacious, modern villa in rural location, yet convenient for A74.
Ground-floor accommodation available. Families welcome.

EARLSTON **Berwickshire** Colin MacDonald Ardross, Melrose Road Earlston Berwickshire Tel: (Earlston) 01896 848007	Map 2 D6	COMMENDED Listed	1 Single 1 Twin 1 Double	1 Priv. NOT ensuite 2 Pub Bath/Show	B&B per person £16.00 Single £16.00 Double	Open Jan-Dec Dinner 1800-2200

Comfortable accommodation in large bungalow. Central heating and log fire. Private parking. Ideal for all Borders attractions. Private bathroom available.

Mrs Susan Sillar Birkhill, Birkenside Earlston Berwickshire TD4 6AR Tel: (Earlston) 01896 849307 Fax: 01896 848206		HIGHLY COMMENDED	2 Twin 1 Double	1 En Suite fac 2 Priv. NOT ensuite 1 Pub Bath/Show	B&B per person £30.00-£32.50 Single £25.00-£28.50 Double	Open Jan-Dec Dinner 1930-2130 B&B + Eve. Meal £40.00-£46.00

Elegant white Georgian house set in 12 acres of woodland and gardens. Good home cooking. Ideal base from which to enjoy the Scottish Borders and Edinburgh. Parking.

Mr and Mrs J Todd Melvaig, Lauder Road Earlston Berwickshire TD4 6EE Tel: (Earlston) 01896 849303 Fax: 01896 849303		COMMENDED	1 Twin 1 Double 1 Family	1 En Suite fac 1 Pub Bath/Show	B&B per person £15.00-£18.00 Single £15.00-£18.00 Double	Open Feb-Dec

A warm welcome at this comfortable personally run Bed and Breakfast. Ideal for touring the Borders. Off-road parking.

EAST CALDER **West Lothian**	Map 2 B5

Near EDINBURGH
OVERSHIEL FARM, EAST CALDER
Telephone: 01506 880469 Fax: 01506 883006

A LOVELY STONE-BUILT FARMHOUSE (6 MILES WEST OF EDINBURGH, 5 MILES FROM EDINBURGH AIRPORT). THE SPACIOUS BEDROOMS LOOK ONTO A LARGE, ATTRACTIVE GARDEN AND ACRES OF FARMLAND. THERE IS A RESIDENTS' LOUNGE WITH A REAL COAL FIRE. GOLF, FISHING AND HORSE-RIDING AVAILABLE NEARBY.

Mrs Jan Dick Overshiel Farm East Calder, Livingston West Lothian EH53 0HT Tel: (Mid Calder) 01506 880469 Fax: 01506 883006	COMMENDED	2 Twin 1 Double	2 En Suite fac 2 Pub Bath/Show	B&B per person £20.00-£25.00 Single £16.00-£18.00 Double	Open Jan-Dec

Stone-built farmhouse set in large garden and surrounded by acres of farmland. 5 miles (8 kms) from Edinburgh Airport. Easy access to M8 and M9.

EAST LINTON **East Lothian**	Map 2 D4

Kiloran House
East Linton, East Lothian EH40 3AY   *Tel: 01620 860410*

Within easy reach of the A1, Kiloran House is stone-built, standing in an acre of ground with tennis court and children's play area. Ample parking, short drive to coastal towns, beaches and golf courses. Always a warm welcome from the owners.

RATES: £16.00 to £21.00.   NO SMOKING THROUGHOUT
Highly Commended 🏵🏵

Mrs M Henderson Kiloran House East Linton East Lothian EH40 3AY Tel: (East Linton) 01620 860410	HIGHLY COMMENDED	2 Double 1 Family	1 En Suite fac 2 Pub Bath/Show	B&B per person £16.00-£25.00 Single Room only per person £16.00-£21.00	Open Jan-Dec

A Victorian house of great character, furnished to a high standard. Relaxed and friendly atmosphere. Non-smoking house.

EAST LINTON continued

Map 2 D4

Miss E Jeffrey
The Red House, 2 The Square
East Linton
East Lothian
EH40 3AD
Tel: (East Linton)
01620 860347

COMMENDED

1 Single	1 En Suite fac	B&B per person
2 Double	1 Priv. NOT ensuite	£18.00-£25.00 Single
	1 Pub Bath	£16.00-£19.00 Double

Open Jan-Dec

Traditional house with private gardens in the centre of this attractive village. Creative interior environment. Bedrooms have own private bathrooms.

ECCLEFECHAN
Dumfriesshire

Map 2 C9

Carlyle House

Main Street, Ecclefechan, Lockerbie DG11 3DG
Telephone: 01576 300322

18th-century house situated in centre of village, ideally placed for exploring Borders and Dumfries and Galloway. Home cooking, ample parking.

Mrs M Martin
Carlyle House
Ecclefechan
Dumfriesshire
DG11 3DG
Tel: (Ecclefechan)
01576 300322

APPROVED
Listed

1 Single	2 Pub Bath/Show	B&B per person
1 Twin		£12.00 Single
1 Family		£12.00 Double

Open Jan-Dec
Dinner 1800-2000
B&B + Eve. Meal
£17.00

Comfortable family accommodation convenient for A74.
Children and pets welcome. Opposite Carlyle's birthplace.

ECCLES, by Kelso
Roxburghshire
Mr & Mrs N Helliker
Eccles House
Eccles, by Kelso
Roxburghshire
TD5 7QS
Tel: (Leitholm) 01890 840205
Fax: 01890 840367

Map 2 E6

COMMENDED
Listed

1 Single	5 En Suite fac	B&B per person
1 Twin		£18.00-£20.00 Single
3 Double		

Open Jan-Dec,
exc Xmas/New Year
Dinner 1900-2000

Large Victorian country house with 20 acre garden.
Warm welcome with a relaxed comfortable atmosphere.

EDINBURGH

Map 2 C5

Aaron Guest House
16 Hartington Gardens
Edinburgh
EH10 4LD
Tel: 0131 229 6459
Fax: 0131 228 5807

COMMENDED
Listed

2 Single	8 En Suite fac	B&B per person
4 Twin	1 Limited ensuite	£16.00-£30.00 Single
2 Double	2 Pub Bath/Show	£16.00-£30.00 Double
2 Family		

Open Jan-Dec

Family run, in quiet residential area, yet close to the west end of city.
Private parking. Many rooms have ensuite facilities.

Abbeylodge Guest House
137 Drum Street
Edinburgh
EH17 8RJ
Tel: 0131 664 9548

COMMENDED

1 Single	5 En Suite fac	B&B per person
2 Twin		£35.00-£50.00 Single
1 Double		£18.50-£25.00 Double
1 Family		

Open Jan-Dec
Dinner 1800-2100

New guest house in Edinburgh all on ground level. Close to city centre,
A1 and City Bypass. All rooms ensuite, Sky TV, telephone. Private parking.

Abbottshead House
40 Minto Street
Edinburgh
EH9 2BR
Tel: 0131 668 1658

COMMENDED

2 Twin	4 Limited ensuite	B&B per person
3 Family	1 Pub Bath/Show	£18.00-£25.00 Single
		£15.00-£22.00 Double

Open Jan-Dec

Personally run guest house. Centrally located to main city routes
and all attractions.

Abcorn Guest House 4 Mayfield Gardens Edinburgh EH9 2BU Tel: 0131 667 6548	COMMENDED 👑👑	1 Single 2 Twin 2 Double 2 Family	7 En Suite fac	B&B per person £20.00-£28.00 Single £20.00-£28.00 Double	Open Jan-Dec	
		Detached house with private parking on main route to city centre.				
Acorn Guest House 70 Pilrig Street Edinburgh EH6 5AS Tel: 0131 554 2187	COMMENDED 👑	1 Twin 1 Double 3 Family	2 Pub Bath/Show	B&B per person £14.00-£16.50 Double	Open Jan-Dec	
		Terraced house on bus route to and from city centre.				

ADAM GUEST HOUSE
2 HARTINGTON GARDENS, EDINBURGH EH10 4LD
Telephone: 0131 229 8664   Fax: 0131 229 9743
ADAM HOUSE is a family run, non-smoking guest house situated in a quiet cul-de-sac only 15 minutes walk from the city centre. We are close to bus routes, shops, theatres and restaurants. Our bedrooms are bright and comfortable with colour television and hot drinks facilities.
We look forward to welcoming you.

Adam Guest House 2 Hartington Gardens Edinburgh EH10 4LD Tel: 0131 229 8664 Fax: 0131 229 9743	COMMENDED Listed	1 Single 1 Twin 1 Double 2 Family	1 En Suite fac 1 Priv. NOT ensuite 2 Pub Bath/Show	B&B per person £18.00-£28.00 Single £20.00-£25.00 Double Room only per person £15.00-£25.00	Open Jan-Dec	
		Family run Victorian terraced house in quiet cul-de-sac. Easy access to city centre by bus. Unrestricted parking. Non-smoking.				
A-Haven in Edinburgh 180 Ferry Road Edinburgh EH6 4NS Tel: 0131 554 6559 Fax: 0131 554 5252	COMMENDED 👑👑👑	2 Single 3 Twin 3 Double 3 Family	9 En Suite fac 2 Priv. NOT ensuite	B&B per person £30.00-£40.00 Single £25.00-£37.50 Double	Open Jan-Dec Dinner 1830-1930	
		Family run city centre guest house with private parking and main bus routes. Scottish welcome and hospitality.				
Airlie Guest House 29 Minto Street Edinburgh EH9 1SB Tel: 0131 667 3562 Fax: 0131 662 1399	COMMENDED 👑👑	2 Single 3 Twin 5 Double 2 Family	7 En Suite fac 1 Priv. NOT ensuite 2 Pub Bath/Show	B&B per person £18.00-£25.00 Single £16.00-£25.00 Double	Open Jan-Dec	
		Formerly two terraced houses, some rooms featuring plaster cornicing. On bus route with easy access to city centre.				
Amaragua Guest House 10 Kilmaurs Terrace Edinburgh EH16 5DR Tel: 0131 667 6775	APPROVED 👑👑	2 Single 2 Twin 1 Double 1 Family	3 En Suite fac 2 Pub Bath/Show	B&B per person £17.00-£25.00 Single £17.00-£25.00 Double Room only per person £15.00-£20.00	Open Jan-Dec	
		Victorian terraced house in residential area, close to Prestonfield Golf Course, Holyrood Park and Commonwealth Pool. Nearby bus routes to centre.				
An Fuaran Guest House 35 Seaview Terrace, Joppa Edinburgh EH15 2HE Tel: 0131 669 8119	COMMENDED 👑👑	2 Twin 1 Double 1 Family	4 En Suite fac	B&B per person £18.00-£25.00 Single £17.50-£23.00 Double	Open Jan-Dec	
		Victorian house overlooking the Firth of Forth, 4 miles (6 kms) from Edinburgh city centre. Regular bus service. Evening meal by arrangement.				

Details of Grading and Classification are on page vi.

Key to symbols is on back flap.

	Map 2 C5						
EDINBURGH continued Ardgarth Guest House 1 St Mary's Place, Portobello Edinburgh EH15 2QF Tel: 0131 669 3021	COMMENDED Listed	3 Single 2 Twin 3 Double 2 Family	2 En Suite fac 3 Pub Bath/Show	B&B per person £15.00-£20.00 Single £15.00-£20.00 Double	Open Jan-Dec Dinner 1800-2000 B&B + Eve. Meal £20.00-£30.00	
Comfortable accommodation in friendly guest house. Close to sea. Special diets catered for, full ensuite disabled facilities. French spoken.							
Ardmor Guest House 74 Pilrig Street Edinburgh EH6 5AS Tel: 0131 554 4944	COMMENDED	3 Twin 1 Double 1 Family	2 Limited ensuite 2 Pub Bath/Show	B&B per person £15.00-£17.00 Single £15.00-£17.00 Double	Open Jan-Dec	
Stone-built house in residential area overlooking Pilrig Park 0.5 miles (1km) from city centre, with convenient bus routes.							
Rachel G Argo 61 Lothian Road Edinburgh EH1 2DJ Tel: 0131 229 4054	COMMENDED Listed	1 Single 1 Twin 1 Double	1 Pub Bath/Show	B&B per person £16.00-£19.00 Single £16.00-£19.00 Double	Open May-Sep	
First-floor Victorian flat. 2 minutes walk from castle and theatres.							
Mrs Armstrong 481 Queensferry Road Edinburgh EH4 7ND Tel: 0131 336 5595	APPROVED Listed	1 Twin 1 Double	2 En Suite fac	B&B per person £30.00-£35.00 Single £20.00-£25.00 Double	Open May-Sep	
Family house on busy road easy access to all routes. Excellent bus service to city centre. Non-smoking house. All ensuite.							

Ashdene House

23 Fountainhall Road, Edinburgh EH9 2LN
Telephone: 0131 667 6026

Short Break or Longer Stay: make *Ashdene House* your base. Situated in high amenity, quiet conservation area, typical Edwardian town house with many original features preserved. *Ashdene House* has been modernised to a high standard and is non-smoking throughout. All centrally heated bedrooms are equipped with private facilities, colour TV, direct-dial telephone, hairdryer, beverage-making facilities, comfort and privacy. City Centre is ten minutes by bus. Unrestricted parking.
Special Breaks: Available **November** to **March** – Tariff (per person): **£18** to **£25** per night including individually cooked breakfast.

AA QQQ   RAC "Acclaimed"   STB Highly Commended

Ashdene House 23 Fountainhall Road Edinburgh EH9 2LN Tel: 0131 667 6026	HIGHLY COMMENDED	1 Twin 2 Double 2 Family	4 En Suite fac 1 Priv. NOT ensuite	B&B per person £18.00-£25.00 Double	Open Jan-Dec	
Edwardian town house retaining many features, in quiet residential conservation area. Convenient for bus route to city centre (10 minutes). Non-smoking establishment.						
Ashgrove House 12 Osborne Terrace Edinburgh EH12 5HG Tel: 0131 337 5014 Fax: 0131 313 5043	HIGHLY COMMENDED	2 Single 2 Twin 2 Double 1 Family	5 En Suite fac 2 Pub Bath/Show	B&B per person £18.00-£26.00 Single £18.00-£28.00 Double	Open Jan-Dec	
Detached Victorian villa centrally located within 1 mile (1.6 kms) of Princes Street with private parking. Convenient bus route to city centre and airport.						

Ashlyn Guest House 42 Inverleith Row Edinburgh EH3 5PY Tel: 0131 552 2954	HIGHLY COMMENDED	2 Single 2 Twin 3 Double 1 Family	5 En Suite fac 1 Priv. NOT ensuite 3 Pub Bath/Show	B&B per person £20.00-£30.00 Single £18.00-£30.00 Double Room only per person £18.00-£28.00	Open Jan-Dec	
		Georgian listed building in residential area of city. Approx. 1.5m (2.5kms) on main bus route to centre with street parking.				
Ashwood Guest House 20 Minto Street Edinburgh EH9 1RQ Tel: 0131 667 8024	COMMENDED Listed	1 Twin 1 Double 2 Family	2 En Suite fac 1 Limited ensuite 1 Pub Bath/Show	B&B per person £20.00-£25.00 Single £18.00-£25.00 Double	Open Jan-Dec	
		Small, friendly guest house, ideally situated close to the city centre and tourist attractions. Private parking, en suite rooms.				
Auld Reekie Guest House 16 Mayfield Gardens Edinburgh EH9 2BZ Tel: 0131 667 6177 Fax: 0131 662 0033	COMMENDED	1 Single 1 Twin 2 Double 3 Family	7 En Suite fac	B&B per person £18.00-£35.00 Single £18.00-£27.50 Double	Open Jan-Dec	
		Family run stone-built house on south side of city centre. On main bus route to Princes Street.				

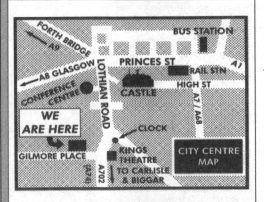

CENTRAL EDINBURGH

AVERON GUEST HOUSE

44 Gilmore Place, Edinburgh EH3 9NQ

Built in 1770 as a farmhouse, charming, centrally situated Georgian period house offers a high standard of accommodation at favourable terms.

- Full cooked breakfast •
- All credit cards accepted •
- 10 minutes walk to Princes Street and Castle •
- STB Approved • AA Listed •
- Private car park •

Tel: 0131-229 9932

Averon Guest House 44 Gilmore Place Edinburgh EH13 9NQ Tel: 0131 229 9932	APPROVED	1 Single 4 Twin 2 Double 3 Family	3 Pub Bath/Show	B&B per person £15.00-£24.00 Single £13.00-£22.00 Double	Open Jan-Dec	
		Central location with private car park to rear. Tea-making facilities in all bedrooms.				

 When you visit a Tourist Information Centre you are guaranteed a welcome by people who really know their country.

For information, maps, holiday reading, accommodation bookings and much more, look for the information *i*

EDINBURGH continued Avondale Guest House 10 South Gray Street Edinburgh EH9 1TE Tel: 0131 667 6779	Map 2 C5	COMMENDED Listed	1 Single 1 Twin 2 Double 1 Family	2 Pub Bath/Show	B&B per person £15.00-£30.00 Single £13.00-£25.00 Double	Open Jan-Dec

Central and quiet location but near main route to the city.
Family run with friendly atmosphere.

Mr P Ayres 21 Mayfield Road, Newington Edinburgh EH9 2NQ Tel: 0131 667 8435	COMMENDED	1 Family	1 Priv. NOT ensuite	B&B per person £17.00-£25.00 Single £17.00-£20.00 Double	Open May-Sep

Warm welcome assured in traditionally furnished Victorian family home.
2 kms to city centre.

Mrs Helen Baird

'Arisaig', 64 Glasgow Road, Edinburgh EH12 8LN
Telephone: 0131 334 2610

Warm Scottish welcome awaits you here at this highly commended
private home with lovely gardens. The bedrooms are kept to a very
high standard with tea/coffee-making facilities and delicious
breakfast. Good local restaurants. Three miles from City Centre.
Parking spaces. Good bus service. All private facilities.
Lounge with TV.

Mrs H Baird 64 Glasgow Road Edinburgh EH12 8LN Tel: 0131 334 2610	HIGHLY COMMENDED	1 Twin 1 Double	2 En Suite fac	B&B per person £21.00-£42.00 Single £20.00-£21.00 Double	Open May-Sep

Personally run comfortable and friendly accommodation in detached dormer bungalow.
Good bus service to town centre, approx 3 miles (5 kms).

Balmoral Guest House 32 Pilrig Street Edinburgh EH6 5AL Tel: 0131 554 1857	COMMENDED	1 Single 3 Twin 1 Double 2 Family	2 Pub Bath/Show	B&B per person £16.00-£19.00 Single £16.00-£19.00 Double	Open Jan-Dec

Situated in residential area of city, convenient for all amenities.
On main bus route and with easy access to city centre.

Balquhidder Guest House 94 Pilrig Street Edinburgh EH6 5AY Tel: 0131 554 3377	COMMENDED	1 Single 2 Twin 2 Double 1 Family	5 En Suite fac 1 Limited ensuite 1 Pub Bath/Show	B&B per person £18.00-£25.00 Single £18.00-£24.00 Double	Open Jan-Dec

Detached house in its own grounds overlooking public park
and on bus routes to the city centre.

Mrs E Banigan Elliston, 5 Viewforth Terrace Edinburgh EH10 4LH Tel: 0131 229 6698	APPROVED Listed	1 Single 1 Twin	1 Pub Bath/Show	B&B per person £16.00-£18.00 Single £16.00-£18.00 Double	Open Apr-Sep

Victorian villa approx 2 miles (3kms) from Princes Street.
In quiet residential location. Close to bus routes.

Mrs Helen Barnie The McDonald 5 McDonald Road Edinburgh EH7 4LX Tel: 0131 557 5935	COMMENDED	2 Twin 1 Double	2 En Suite fac 1 Priv. NOT ensuite	B&B per person £18.00-£24.00 Single £18.00-£24.00 Double	Open May-Sep

Comfortable accommodation 10 minutes walk from Princes Street.
Adjacent to main bus routes.

Barrosa Guest House 21 Pilrig Street Edinburgh EH6 5AN Tel: 0131 554 3700	COMMENDED Listed	1 Twin 2 Double 3 Family	4 En Suite fac 3 Pub Bath/Show	B&B per person £18.50-£27.00 Double	Open Jan-Dec	

Georgian house only ten minutes from city centre on bus route.

Belford Guest House
13 Blacket Avenue, Edinburgh EH9 1RR
Telephone: 0131 667 2422
Small and friendly family run guest house in quiet tree-lined avenue 1 mile from the city centre. Buses run from either end of the avenue to all attractions in the city.
Private parking.

Belford House 13 Blacket Avenue Edinburgh EH9 1RR Tel: 0131 667 2422	COMMENDED ♔	3 Twin 4 Family	2 Pub Bath/Show	B&B per person £20.00-£22.00 Single £18.00-£20.00 Double	Open Jan-Dec	

Family run guest house in quiet road just off main A68/A7.
Conveniently situated for main tourist attractions and town centre.

Bellevue Guest House 8 East Claremont Street Edinburgh EH7 4JP Tel: 0131 556 4862	COMMENDED ♔♔	1 Single 3 Twin 2 Double 2 Family	8 En Suite fac	B&B per person £22.00-£30.00 Single £20.00-£28.00 Double Room only per person £20.00-£28.00	Open Jan-Dec	

Family run Victorian terraced townhouse within walking distance
of city centre and Playhouse Theatre. Car parking, on street.

Ben-Craig House

3 CRAIGMILLAR PARK,
EDINBURGH EH16 5PG
Telephone: 0131 667 2593

Edinburgh's newest guest house, completely refurbished with your comfort in mind.

Walking distance to Princes Street.

Large well-appointed bedrooms all with en-suite facilities.

Bus service to most areas of town.

Private parking.

Ben Craig House 3 Craigmillar Park Edinburgh EH16 5PG Tel: 0131 667 2593	HIGHLY COMMENDED ♔♔	1 Twin 2 Double 1 Family	4 En Suite fac	B&B per person £20.00-£32.00 Single £20.00-£32.00 Double	Open Jan-Dec	

Traditional, detatched, stone Victorian town house with quiet gardens.
On main route for city centre.

Details of Grading and Classification are on page vi.

Key to symbols is on back flap.

EDINBURGH continued	Map 2 C5	COMMENDED ♔	1 Twin 1 Double 2 Family	2 Pub Bath/Show	B&B per person £15.00-£18.00 Single £13.00-£15.00 Double	Open May-Sep	
Mrs P Birnie Casa Buzzo, 8 Kilmaurs Road Edinburgh EH16 5DA Tel: 0131 667 8998							

A terraced property, conveniently situated for bus routes to the city centre and visitor attractions. Unrestricted parking. Non-smoking house.

MRS BARBARA BLOWS
FAIRHOLME
13 Moston Terrace, Edinburgh EH9 2DE
Telephone: 0131-667 8645

Set in a quiet terrace adjoining major bus routes, under the personal supervision of the owners, this spacious family home offers Victorian elegance to your stay.

Mrs B Blows Fairholme, 13 Moston Terrace Edinburgh EH9 2DE Tel: 0131 667 8645	COMMENDED Listed ♔	1 Single 1 Twin 1 Double	2 Pub Bath/Show	B&B per person £12.00-£16.50 Single £11.00-£16.00 Double	Open Apr-Oct Dinner 1800-1900 B&B + Eve. Meal £15.00-£20.50	

Comfortable elegant period home, friendly ambience, convenient for city centre.

BONNINGTON GUEST HOUSE
202 Ferry Road, Edinburgh EH6 4NW
Telephone: 0131 554 7610

A comfortable early Victorian house (built 1840), personally run, where a friendly and warm welcome awaits guests. Situated in residential area of town on main bus routes. Private car parking.
For further details contact Eileen and David Watt, Proprietors.

Bonnington Guest House 202 Ferry Road Edinburgh EH6 4NW Tel: 0131 554 7610	HIGHLY COMMENDED ♔♔	3 Double 3 Family	3 En Suite fac 1 Priv. NOT ensuite 1 Pub Bath/Show	B&B per person £25.00-£30.00 Single £20.00-£28.00 Double	Open Jan-Dec	

Early Victorian Listed building with private parking on the north side of the city; convenient bus routes to centre.

T Borland Arrandale House, 28 Mayfield Gardens Edinburgh EH9 2BZ Tel: 0131 667 6029	COMMENDED ♔♔	1 Twin 1 Double 1 Family	2 En Suite fac	B&B per person £18.00-£25.00 Single £18.00-£26.00 Double	Open May-Sep	

Ideally situated for visiting Edinburgh. On main bus route. Five minutes to city centre. Limited parking.

Mrs F Bowman 15 Davidson Road Edinburgh EH4 2PE Tel: 0131 332 4445	COMMENDED Listed	1 Twin	1 Priv.NOT ensuite	B&B per person £17.00-£18.00 Single £15.00-£18.00 Double	Open May-Sep	

Traditional bungalow (1938) in quiet residential area near Western General Hospital. Within walking distance of city centre.

Mrs Maria Boyle Villa Maria; 6a Mayfield Gardens Edinburgh EH9 2BU Tel: 0131 667 7730	COMMENDED Listed	1 Double 1 Family	1 Pub Bath/Show	B&B per person £25.00-£30.00 Single £15.00-£18.00 Double	Open Apr-Oct	

Victorian house on main road, but with quiet rooms. On bus route to city centre 1 mile (2kms) to Princes Street and all attractions. Parking.

Brae Guest House 119 Willowbrae Road Edinburgh EH8 7HN Tel: 0131 661 0170	COMMENDED	1 Single 1 Twin 1 Double 1 Family	2 En Suite fac 1 Pub Bath/Show	B&B per person £15.00-£25.00 Single £15.00-£28.00 Double	Open Jan-Dec	

Friendly, family run guest house on bus route to city centre.
10 minutes walk from Meadowbank Stadium and Holyrood Palace.

Brig O'Doon Guest House 262 Ferry Road Edinburgh EH5 3AN Tel: 0131 552 3953	COMMENDED Listed	3 Twin 1 Double 2 Family	3 Pub Bath/Show	B&B per person £20.00-£22.00 Single £16.00-£18.00 Double	Open Jan-Dec	

Stone-built terraced house on north side of city centre, overlooking playing fields
with fine views to castle. Bus route to city centre.

Bruntsfield Guest House 55 Leamington Terrace Edinburgh EH10 4JS Tel: 0131 228 6458 Fax: 0131 228 6458	COMMENDED Listed	2 Single 2 Twin 2 Double 1 Family	1 En Suite fac 2 Pub Bath/Show	B&B per person £20.00-£24.00 Single £18.00-£28.00 Double	Open Jan-Dec	

Situated in residential area close to main bus route to city centre.
No residents' lounge but TV in all bedrooms.

Birchtree Cottage

1 BARNTON GROVE, EDINBURGH EH4 6EQ
Telephone: 0131 339 3611

Scottish Tourist Board "Highly Commended" – "Listed"

A warm welcome awaits you at Birchtree Cottage – one of Edinburgh's finest B&B's. Situated in north-west Edinburgh, just 3 miles from city centre and 3 miles from Edinburgh airport. Quiet, residential area close to the sea, with many interesting walks. Opposite one of Scotland's finest golf courses – "The Royal Burgess".

All rooms have central heating, remote control colour TV, radio/alarm, trouser press, tea and coffee-making facilities, etc. Telephone. Full Scottish Breakfast. The nearby Barnton Hotel with three restaurants offers a wide range of cuisine.

Mrs Bryan Birchtree Cottage 1 Barnton Grove Edinburgh EH4 6EQ Tel: 0131 339 3611	HIGHLY COMMENDED Listed	1 Double 1 Family	1 Pub Bath/Show	B&B per person £18.00-£20.00 Single £18.00-£20.00 Double	Open Apr-Oct Dinner 1800-2000	

Detached single storey cottage, 3 miles (7kms) from city centre,
just off Forth Bridge route. Large gardens; friendly atmosphere.
Close to airport.

THE BUCHAN

3 COATES GARDENS, EDINBURGH EH12 5LG
Telephone: 0131 337 1045   Fax: 0131 539 7055

A warm welcome awaits you in this elegant family run *Town House*, quietly but conveniently situated within *The West End*. Only minutes walk to Princes Street and main attractions, some 200 metres from Haymarket Railway Station and on the main Airport bus route. Comfortable refurbished bedrooms with ensuite bathrooms, colour TV and complimentary tray.

Buchan Guest House 3 Coates Gardens Edinburgh EH12 5LG Tel: 0131 337 1045 Fax: 0131 538 7055	COMMENDED	2 Single 1 Twin 2 Double 5 Family	10 En Suite fac 2 Pub Bath/Show	B&B per person £25.00-£35.00 Single £20.00-£30.00 Double	Open Jan-Dec	

Comfortable former merchant's house.
Centrally situated for Princes Street and close to Haymarket Station.

EDINBURGH continued	Map 2 C5

BUCHANAN GUEST HOUSE

97 Joppa Road, Edinburgh EH15 2HB
Telephone: 0131 657 4117

A warm welcome is extended to all visitors by Margaret and Stewart Buchanan at their personally run Victorian guest house with panoramic view overlooking Firth of Forth. The bedrooms are well equipped with every comfort in mind and full Scottish breakfast is provided. Conveniently located. Frequent bus service to city centre and en-route to main golf courses. Businessmen welcome. FREE UNRESTRICTED PARKING. W

Buchanan Guest House 97 Joppa Road Edinburgh EH15 2HB Tel: 0131 657 4117	COMMENDED	2 Twin 1 Double 1 Family	1 En Suite fac 2 Pub Bath/Show	B&B per person £16.00-£22.00 Single £16.00-£22.00 Double	Open Jan-Dec

Comfortable personally run guest house, on major bus route to city centre. Unrestricted parking. Front views overlooking sea.

BURNS B&B

Tel: 0131 229 1669
Fax: 0131 229 9225

67 Gilmore Place, Edinburgh EH3 9NU

Comfortable homely B&B very close to King's Theatre, Princes Street, tourist attractions, restaurants etc. (bus routes 10 & 27). All rooms en-suite shower, toilet WHB. Non-smoking house. Free parking, access at all times with your own keys.

Write, telephone or fax Mrs Burns.

Mrs M Burns 67 Gilmore Place Edinburgh EH3 9NU Tel: 0131 229 1669 Fax: 0131 229 9225	COMMENDED	1 Twin 2 Double	3 En Suite fac	B&B per person £30.00 Single £20.00-£26.00 Double	Open Apr-Oct

Victorian terraced house close to city centre, tourist attractions, King's Theatre and local restaurants. All ensuite. Non-smoking.

Pauline Burns-Strachan Abingdon Lodge, 24 Cammo Crescent Edinburgh EH4 8DZ Tel: 0131 339 4994	HIGHLY COMMENDED	2 Single 1 Twin 1 Double	1 En Suite fac 2 Limited ensuite 2 Pub Bath/Show	B&B per person £18.00-£28.00 Single Room only per person £16.00-£24.00	Open Jan-Dec

Victorian family mansion house designed by Sir Robert Lorimer. Gardens, bililard room, satellite TV. Airport 3 miles. City centre 4 miles.

Mrs Cairns 28 Cammo Road Edinburgh EH4 8AP Tel: 0131 339 3613	HIGHLY COMMENDED Listed	2 Double	1 Pub Bath/Show	B&B per person £18.00 Single £16.00 Double	Open Apr-Oct

Family home in quiet residential area with easy access to Queensferry Road and Airport.Ideal base for touring Edinburgh and surrounding countryside.

VAT is shown at 17.5%: changes in this rate may affect prices. Prices shown are for guidance only. Please send SAE with each enquiry.

CAMERON TOLL GUEST HOUSE

299 DALKEITH ROAD, EDINBURGH EH16 5JX
Telephone: 0131 667 2950   Fax: 0131 662 1987

Our friendly family-run Guest House has 11 bedrooms with own shower and toilet, colour TV and tea/coffee facilities. The spacious lounge offers comfort and plenty of tourist information. We are ideally situated on the A7 (close to the University and Commonwealth Pool) handy for exploring city and countryside. We have private parking and frequent bus services, only 10 minutes drive from the City Centre. We can help arrange activities, local tours and bagpiping from our resident piper. We offer a varied Scottish breakfast and evening meals. Picnic lunches and special diets by arrangement.

Contact Andrew and Mary Deans.

| Cameron Toll Guest House
299 Dalkeith Road
Edinburgh
EH16 5JX
Tel: 0131 667 2950
Fax: 0131 662 1987 | COMMENDED
🏵🏵🏵 | 3 Single
2 Twin
3 Double
3 Family | 10 En Suite fac
1 Priv. NOT ensuite | B&B per person
£22.00-£32.00 Single
£18.00-£30.00 Double | Open Jan-Dec
Dinner 1800-1900
B&B + Eve. Meal
£26.00-£40.00 | |

Family run guest house with some private parking.
Conveniently located on A7 with frequent bus service to city centre.
Close to Commonwealth Pool.

CAMUS HOUSE

4 SEAVIEW TERRACE, EDINBURGH EH15 2HD
Telephone: 0131 657 2003

Overlooking the Firth of Forth, this centrally heated, well-furbished Victorian terraced villa offers very comfortable accommodation in a peaceful seaside location with easy access, by public transport, to Edinburgh's historical, cultural and leisure attractions. **Camus House** is an ideal centre for touring and golfing holidays.

Genuine welcome assured.

| Camus House
4 Seaview Terrace, Joppa
Edinburgh
EH15 2HD
Tel: 0131 657 2003 | HIGHLY
COMMENDED
Listed | 3 Double
1 Family | 1 Priv. NOT ensuite
2 Pub Bath/Show | B&B per person
£14.00-£22.00 Single
£14.00-£22.00 Double
Room only per person
£12.50-£20.00 | Open Jan-Dec | |

Fully refurbished Victorian terraced house with fine sea views.
Relaxed and comfortable atmosphere; easy access to the city.
Ideal touring base.

| Mrs Janie Carter
Upway, 107 Hillhouse Road
Edinburgh
Midlothian
EH4 7AD
Tel: 0131 539 4455 | COMMENDED
Listed | 1 Single
2 Twin | 2 Pub Bath/Show | B&B per person
£15.00-£20.00 Single
£13.00-£20.00 Double | Open Apr-Oct | |

Welcoming family home with easy access to bypass and city centre.
Approx 4 miles (6kms) from airport.

| Castle Park Guest House
75 Gilmore Place
Edinburgh
EH3 9NU
Tel: 0131 229 1215 | APPROVED
Listed | 2 Single
2 Twin
3 Double
1 Family | 3 En Suite fac
1 Limited ensuite
2 Pub Bath/Show | B&B per person
£15.00-£19.00 Single
£15.00-£17.50 Double
Room only per person
£12.00-£14.00 | Open Jan-Dec | |

Family run guest house close to city centre.
Convenient for King's Theatre and bus routes to all amenities.

EDINBURGH continued	Map 2 C5

CARRONVALE

38 Corstorphine Bank Drive, Edinburgh EH12 8RN
Telephone: 0131 334 3291 Fax: 0131 334 3883

Spacious, centrally heated bungalow with unrestricted parking in quiet residential area, three miles from city centre and four miles from airport. Ground-floor bedrooms, en-suite facilities, colour TV, tea and coffee provided. Residents' lounge, own keys. Full Scottish breakfast. Good bus service to city centre.

Mrs E Caven Carronvale, 38 Corstorphine Bank Drive Edinburgh EH12 8RN Tel: 0131 334 3291 Fax: 0131 334 3883	COMMENDED ♛♛	3 Twin	1 En Suite fac 1 Pub Bath/Show	B&B per person £21.00-£28.00 Single £16.00-£23.00 Double	Open Easter-Oct	
		In quiet residential area, a delightful detached home with colourful gardens. 3 miles (5kms) west of the city centre.				

Chalumna Guest House 5 Granville Terrace Edinburgh EH10 4PQ Tel: 0131 229 2086	APPROVED ♛	1 Single 2 Twin 4 Double 1 Family	4 En Suite fac 1 Limited ensuite 1 Pub Bath/Show	B&B per person £25.00-£45.00 Single £16.00-£28.00 Double Room only per person £22.00-£42.00	Open Jan-Dec	
		Family run guest house in quiet residential area, close to King's Theatre and within easy reach of Princes Street.				

Charleston House Guest House 38 Minto Street Edinburgh EH9 2BS Tel: 0131 667 6589	COMMENDED Listed	1 Twin 1 Double 2 Family	2 Pub Bath/Show	B&B per person £15.00-£25.00 Single £15.00-£25.00 Double Room only per person £13.00-£23.00	Open Jan-Dec	
		Traditionally furnished Georgian family home – 1826, 1.5 miles from city centre.				

Mrs Margaret Clark Sakura House, 18 West Preston Street EH8 9PU EH8 9PU Tel: 0131 668 1204	APPROVED Listed	1 Single 3 Family	2 En Suite fac 1 Priv. NOT ensuite 2 Pub Bath/Show	B&B per person £14.00-£20.00 Single £12.00-£18.00 Double Room only per person £12.00-£18.00	Open Apr-Sep	
		Victorian house in central location, close to Castle and shopping centre. Continental breakfast only.				

Classic House

50 Mayfield Road, Edinburgh EH9 2NH
Telephone: 0131 667 5847   Fax: 0131 662 1016

A warm welcome awaits you at this elegant Victorian house. Frequent bus service to all major attractions. All rooms with private/en-suite shower rooms, TV, central heating, hospitality tray. Relaxed and comfortable atmosphere at this totally non-smoking guest house.
STB Highly Commended ♛♛   AA QQQQ

Classic Guest House 50 Mayfield Road Edinburgh EH9 2NH Tel: 0131 667 5847 Fax: 0131 662 1016	HIGHLY COMMENDED ♛♛	1 Single 1 Twin 1 Double 1 Family	3 En Suite fac 1 Priv. NOT ensuite 1 Pub Bath/Show	B&B per person £18.00-£28.00 Single £18.00-£28.00 Double	Open Jan-Dec Dinner 1800-1900	
		Friendly welcome at this family home, recently refurbished to a high standard. Short bus ride from city centre. Non-smoking.				

Claymore Guest House
68 Pilrig Street
Edinburgh
EH6 5AS
Tel: 0131 554 2500
Fax: 0131 554 2500

COMMENDED

2 Twin
2 Double
2 Family

3 En Suite fac
1 Priv. NOT ensuite
1 Pub Bath/Show

B&B per person
£17.00-£23.50 Single
£16.00-£23.50 Double

Open Jan-Dec

Red sandstone Victorian terraced villa, a former manse,
situated close to the city centre and on the main bus routes.

The Hollies

54 Craigmillar Park, Edinburgh EH16 5PS
Telephone and Fax: 0131 668 3408

This elegant Victorian town house offers gracious living in an environment that retains original cornices and architectural artifacts. Three of our former drawing/reception rooms have been tastefully modernised, and guests can relax amid the old and the new. A small reflection of former services is enacted by the provision of a full cooked breakfast, served to your room. All en-suite rooms are on ground level. The Hollies is situated less than 15 minutes from City Centre and adjacent to cheap efficient transport. Your host Margaret Coleman offers you hospitality with a *Scottish Accent*, and will assist with all your enquiries.

Mrs M Coleman
The Hollies, 54 Craigmillar Park
Edinburgh
EH16 5PS
Tel: 0131 668 3408
Fax: 0131 668 3408

HIGHLY
COMMENDED

1 Twin
2 Double

3 En Suite fac

B&B per person
£45.00 Single
£25.00-£27.00 Double

Open May-Sep

Fine town house, many period features. High standard of decor and furnishings.
All rooms ground floor. Excellent bus service. Parking available.

Commonwealth Guest House
96 Dalkeith Road
Edinburgh
Midlothian
EH16 5HA
Tel: 0131 668 1680
Fax: 0131 668 1680

COMMENDED

1 Single
2 Twin
2 Double
1 Family

6 En Suite fac

B&B per person
£25.00 Single
£20.00 Double

Open Jan-Dec

Family run stone-built house, all bedrooms with ensuite facilities situated
on south side of city centre close to Royal Commonwealth Swimming Pool
and Edinburgh University residences.

Braid Hills Cottage

20 Jordan Lane, Edinburgh EH10 4QZ
Telephone: 0131 447 3650

This early 19th-century detached cottage is in a quiet corner near the centre of Edinburgh. There is a large garden, private parking and several bus routes to the City Centre. Appointments can be made for a variety of complementary therapies. Vegetarian breakfasts are a speciality. Families are welcome.

Lynn Cooper
20 Jordan Lane
Edinburgh
EH10 4QZ
Tel: 0131 447 3650

APPROVED
Listed

1 Single
1 Twin
1 Double
1 Family

1 En Suite fac
1 Pub Bath/Show

B&B per person
£20.00-£25.00 Single
£18.00-£20.00 Double
Room only per person
£15.00-£20.00

Open Apr-Oct

Stone-built 19th-century single-storey house with large garden in quiet location.
Convenient bus routes to city centre.

Details of Grading and Classification are on page vi. | Key to symbols is on back flap. |

EDINBURGH continued	Map 2 C5						
Mrs M Coutts Meadowplace House 1 Meadowplace Road Edinburgh EH12 7TZ Tel: 0131 334 8459		APPROVED Listed	1 Single 1 Twin 1 Family	2 Pub Bath/Show	B&B per person £15.00 Single £13.00-£15.00 Double	Open Apr-Oct	
			Comfortable, personally run B+B close to major bus routes to city centre and airport. Own parking. Ideal base for touring.				

Mrs Moira Conway
Crannoch But & Ben
467 QUEENSFERRY RD EDINBURGH EH4 7ND TEL: 0131 336 5688

STB Grade of Highly Commended and Classification of 👑👑 has been awarded to this outstanding family home. This bungalow has private facilities for all rooms and residents' lounge. Near Airport on A90 and three miles from city centre with excellent bus service and car parking.
All guests receive a warm welcome.

Cranноch But & Ben 467 Queensferry Road Edinburgh EH4 7ND Tel: 0131 336 5688		HIGHLY COMMENDED 👑👑	1 Twin 1 Family	2 En Suite fac 1 Pub Bath/Show	B&B per person £20.00-£27.00 Single £20.00-£23.00 Double	Open Jan-Dec	
			Detached bungalow with warm and friendly atmosphere on Forth Road Bridge route, 3 miles (5kms) from city centre. Ensuite bathrooms, parking.				
Cree House 77 Mayfield Road Edinburgh EH9 3AA Tel: 0131 667 2524 Fax: 0131 667 2524		APPROVED Listed	2 Single 3 Twin 1 Double 1 Family	2 Limited ensuite 1 Pub Bath/Show	B&B per person £13.00-£20.00 Single £15.00-£20.00 Double Room only per person £11.00-£18.00	Open Jan-Dec	
			Friendly accommodation close to the university. Convenient for city centre and all tourist attractions.				
Crioch Guest House 23 East Hermitage Place Edinburgh EH6 8AD Tel: 0131 554 5494		APPROVED Listed	2 Single 3 Twin 1 Family	2 Pub Bath/Show	B&B per person £14.00-£22.00 Single £14.00-£22.00 Double	Open Jan-Dec	
			Victorian terraced house overlooking Leith Links. Convenient bus route to city centre.				

Crion Guest House
33 Minto Street, Edinburgh EH9 2BT
Telephone: 0131 667 2708 Fax: 0131 662 1946

A warm friendly welcome awaits you at the family-run guest house. Fully refurbished with your comfort in mind offering outstanding Bed & Breakfast value. 3 en-suite rooms now available. Situated within 1½ miles of city centre on an excellent bus route near most tourist attractions, near University and Commonwealth Pool. For enquiries send SAE or telephone.

| Crion Guest House
33 Minto Street
Edinburgh
EH9 2BT
Tel: 0131 667 2708
Fax: 0131 662 1946 | | COMMENDED
👑👑 | 1 Single
2 Twin
2 Double
1 Family | 3 En Suite fac
3 Pub Bath/Show | B&B per person
£18.00-£23.00 Single
£16.00-£21.00 Double | Open Jan-Dec | |
| | | | Refurbished, friendly family run guest house, close to Commonwealth Pool
and University. On main bus route to city centre. | | | | |

Mrs P Crolla 4 Brunton Place Edinburgh EH7 5EG Tel: 0131 556 3566	COMMENDED Listed	1 Twin 1 Family	1 Pub Bath/Show	B&B per person £20.00-£24.00 Single £18.00-£22.00 Double	Open Apr-Sep	
	Georgian terraced house, 10 minutes walk from Princes Street and main line station. Italian and French spoken.					

Cruachan Guest House 53 Gilmore Place Edinburgh EH3 9NT Tel: 0131 229 6219 Fax: 0131 229 6219	APPROVED	2 Single 1 Twin 1 Double 1 Family	1 En Suite fac 1 Limited ensuite 1 Pub Bath/Show	B&B per person £15.00-£25.00 Single £13.00-£25.00 Double	Open Jan-Dec	
	Comfortable family run accommodation close to city centre and major bus routes.					

Mrs Cumming 3 Drummond Place Edinburgh EH3 6PH Tel: 0131 557 4660	HIGHLY COMMENDED Listed	1 Single 1 Twin	2 En Suite fac	B&B per person from £25.00 Single from £22.50 Double	Open May-Oct, exc Sept	
	Traditional B&B in centre of Edinburgh's New Town. Close to city centre.					

Daisy Park Guest House 41 Abercorn Terrace, Joppa Edinburgh EH15 2DG Tel: 0131 669 2503 Fax: 0131 669 0189	COMMENDED	1 Single 2 Twin 1 Double 2 Family	4 En Suite fac 1 Pub Bath/Show	B&B per person £20.00-£30.00 Single £20.00-£30.00 Double	Open Jan-Dec	
	Family run small guest house with spacious rooms on bus route for city centre. 100 yards from beach. Vegetarians welcome. Single room is compact.					

Dene Guest House 7 Eyre Place Edinburgh EH3 5ES Tel: 0131 556 2700	APPROVED Listed	1 Single 3 Twin 1 Double 2 Family	2 En Suite fac 2 Pub Bath/Show	B&B per person £20.00-£23.00 Single £18.00-£23.00 Double Room only per person £17.00-£20.00	Open Jan-Dec	
	Family run, centrally located guest house, close to Botanic Gardens.					

Devon Guest House 2 Pittville Street, Portobello Edinburgh EH15 2BY Tel: 0131 669 6067	COMMENDED	1 Single 2 Twin 2 Double 2 Family	4 En Suite fac 1 Pub Bath/Show	B&B per person £16.00-£22.50 Single £16.00-£22.50 Double	Open Jan-Dec	
	Victorian villa in quiet residential cul-de-sac. 100 metres from sandy beach. 4 miles (6kms) to Princes Street. Excellent bus service. Unrestricted parking.					

Eileen Dickie – B&B at "No. 22"

22 EAST CLAREMONT STREET, EDINBURGH EH7 4JP
Telephone: 0131-556 4032 Fax: 0131-556 9739

City centre Victorian terraced guest house on cobbled street only 15 minutes walk from Princes Street. Four very comfortable and well-equipped bedrooms (2 en-suite). Excellent breakfast choice including Scottish, vegetarian and fish dishes.
Eileen and John Dickie look forward to welcoming you to our family home.

Dickie Guest House 22 East Claremont Street Edinburgh EH7 4JP Tel: 0131 556 4032 Fax: 0131 556 9739	COMMENDED	1 Single 1 Twin 1 Double 1 Family	2 En Suite fac 1 Pub Bath/Show	B&B per person £22.00-£24.00 Single £21.00-£27.00 Double	Open Jan-Dec	
	Small, friendly and family run; a Victorian town house in a cobbled street only 15 minutes walk from Princes Street. Scottish breakfasts a speciality.					

EDINBURGH continued	Map 2 C5						
Mr & Mrs Divine 116 Greenbank Crescent Edinburgh EH10 5SZ Tel: 0131 447 9454		APPROVED Listed	1 Single 1 Twin	2 Pub Bath/Show	B&B per person £15.00-£17.00 Single £15.00-£17.00 Double	Open Apr-Oct	

Family home in quiet residential area with easy access to city centre and by-pass. Parking. On main bus routes.

INVERMARK

Commended 👑

60 Polwarth Terrace, Edinburgh EH11 1NJ
Telephone: 0131 337 1066

Invermark is situated in quiet suburbs on main bus route into city, 5 minutes by car. Private parking. Accommodation: single, twin, family with wash-hand basins and tea/coffee-making facilities. TV lounge/dining room, toilet, bathroom/shower. Friendly atmosphere, children and pets welcome.

| Mrs H Donaldson
Invermark, 60 Polwarth Terrace
Edinburgh
EH11 1NJ
Tel: 0131 337 1066 | COMMENDED
👑 | 1 Single
1 Twin
1 Family | 1 Pub Bath/Show | B&B per person
£16.00 Single
£16.00 Double | Open Apr-Oct | |

Victorian house situated in quiet residential area a few minutes from city centre. Next to main bus route.

Dukes of Windsor Street

17 WINDSOR STREET, EDINBURGH EH7 5LA
Telephone and Fax: 0131 556 6046

Lovingly restored Georgian townhouse in quiet, central location near stations, principal shopping areas and historic monuments. Restaurants, pubs and theatre close by. Plenty of on-street parking. Breakfast is very high-quality continental served to a dining table in your bedroom.

| Dukes of Windsor Street
17 Windsor Street
Edinburgh
EH7 5LA
Tel: 0131 556 6046
Fax: 0131 556 6046 | COMMENDED
Listed | 1 Single
3 Twin
5 Double
1 Family | 10 En Suite fac | B&B per person
£25.00-£65.00 Single
£20.00-£35.00 Double | Open Jan-Dec | |

Continental breakfast served in your own bedroom in this elegantly refurbished private hotel. Convenient for Princes Street and the theatre.

| Dunard Guest House
16 Hartington Place
Edinburgh
EH10 4LE
Tel: 0131 229 6848 | APPROVED
Listed | 2 Single
2 Twin
1 Family | 2 Pub Bath/Show | B&B per person
£15.00-£22.00 Single
£15.00-£20.00 Double | Open Jan-Dec | |

Friendly guest house in residential area with easy access to city centre. Evening meal by arrangement.

| Dunedin Guest House
8 Priestfield Road
Edinburgh
EH16 5HH
Tel: 0131 668 1949 | COMMENDED
👑 👑 | 1 Single
2 Twin
3 Double
1 Family | 6 En Suite fac
1 Priv. NOT ensuite
1 Pub Bath/Show | B&B per person
£18.00-£35.00 Single
£18.00-£27.50 Double | Open Jan-Dec | |

Friendly family run guest house in residential area, close to Commonwealth Pool and bus route. 1.5 miles (2.5kms) from city centre. Parking available.

Edinburgh Thistle Guest House 10 East Hermitage Place, Leith Links, Edinburgh EH6 8AA Tel: 0131 554 8457/5864	APPROVED Listed	1 Twin 1 Double 3 Family	2 En Suite fac 1 Pub Bath/Show	B&B per person £18.00-£25.00 Single £15.00-£20.00 Double Room only per person £15.00-£25.00	Open Jan-Dec Dinner 1800-1930 B&B + Eve. Meal £20.00-£30.00	
		Victorian, ex-sea merchant's house, overlooking park. Close to local amenities.				
Ellesmere Guest House 11 Glengyle Terrace Edinburgh EH3 9LN Tel: 0131 229 4823 Fax: 0131 229 5285	HIGHLY COMMENDED	1 Single 1 Twin 2 Double 1 Family	6 En Suite fac	B&B per person £19.00-£30.00 Single £19.00-£30.00 Double	Open Jan-Dec	
		Terraced house overlooking the Meadows. Quiet location within walking distance of King's Theatre, Conference Centre and all amenities; bus routes to city centre.				
Mrs A Fairbairn The Knoll, 8 Glenlockhart Bank Edinburgh Midlothian EH14 1BL Tel: 0131 443 1710 Fax: 0131 443 1710	COMMENDED	1 Single 1 Twin 1 Double	1 Pub Bath/Show	B&B per person £20.00-£30.00 Single £20.00-£26.00 Double Room only per person £18.00	Open Apr-Oct	
		Personally run family house in quiet residential location. Approximately 4 miles (6 kms) from city centre.				
Mrs Jane Forno 35 Newington Road Edinburgh EH9 1QR Tel: 0131 667 2839	COMMENDED Listed	1 Twin 1 Family	2 En Suite fac	B&B per person £16.00-£21.00 Single £16.00-£21.00 Double	Open Apr-Oct	
		Full of character, tastefully decorated garden flat. Conveniently located 20 minutes walk from Princes Street.				
Fountainhall Guest House 40 Fountainhall Road Edinburgh EH9 2LW Tel: 0131 667 2544	APPROVED	1 Single 2 Twin 1 Double 3 Family	1 Limited ensuite 3 Pub Bath/Show	B&B per person £20.00-£22.00 Single £18.00-£20.00 Double	Open Jan-Dec	
		Victorian house in quiet residential area, 2 miles (3 kms) from City Centre, with public transport nearby.				
Mrs D R Frackelton 17 Hope Park Terrace Edinburgh EH8 9LZ Tel: 0131 667 7963	APPROVED Listed	1 Single 1 Double	1 Pub Bath/Show	B&B per person £18.00-£20.00 Single £18.00-£20.00 Double	Open Easter-Oct	
		Ground floor flat on regular bus route to city centre. Restaurants nearby.				
Mr & Mrs G Fraser 7 Bellevue Place Edinburgh EH7 4BS Tel: 0131 556 5123 Fax: 0131 556 5123	COMMENDED Listed	1 Twin 1 Double 1 Family	1 Pub Bath/Show	B&B per person £16.00-£23.00 Single £16.00-£23.00 Double Room only per person £15.00-£22.00	Open Apr-Oct, Xmas/New Year	
		Personally run refurbished terraced house Approx 0.5 mile (1km) from east end and Princes Street.				
Galloway Guest House 22 Dean Park Crescent Edinburgh EH4 1PH Tel: 0131 332 3672	COMMENDED	1 Single 3 Twin 3 Double 3 Family	6 En Suite fac 2 Pub Bath/Show	B&B per person £22.00-£40.00 Single £17.00-£25.00 Double	Open Jan-Dec	
		Friendly, family run guest house, beautifully restored and situated in a residential area of the city centre. Free street parking.				

Ellesmere House

11 Glengyle Terrace,
EDINBURGH

Tel: 0131 229 4823   EH3 9LN   Fax: 0131 229 5285

"Your home away from home"

Ellesmere House is situated in an enviable location overlooking "Bruntsfield Links" in the centre of Edinburgh, within easy walking distance of most places of interest. The King's Theatre and various good restaurants situated nearby. All rooms are en-suite and all are furnished and decorated to a very high standard and are fully equipped with every comfort in mind. There is a four-poster bed available. Start the day with our delicious full Scottish breakfast. **Prices from £19, all rooms en-suite.**

Personally run by Cecilia & Tommy Leishman who extend a very warm welcome to all of their guests.

STB Highly Commended ♛♛ AA: QQQQ "Selected"

Mrs M R B Garvie 99 Joppa Road Edinburgh EH15 2HB Tel: 0131 669 8695	COMMENDED Listed	1 Single 2 Twin 1 Double	1 En Suite fac 1 Priv. Bath/Show 1 Pub Bath/Show	B&B per person £18.50 Single £17.50 Double	Open Jan-Dec Dinner 1800-2000

Situated 10 minutes drive from Princes Street on major City Centre route and easy access to city bypass. Seaviews and safe beaches close by.

Gifford House 103 Dalkeith Road Edinburgh EH16 5AJ Tel: 0131 667 4688	COMMENDED	1 Single 2 Twin 1 Double 3 Family	5 En Suite fac 2 Priv. NOT ensuite 1 Pub Bath/Show	B&B per person £18.00-£40.00 Single £18.00-£32.00 Double Room only per person £15.00-£35.00	Open Jan-Dec

Situated on one of the main routes into Edinburgh.
A well-appointed guest house with nearby bus service to city centre.
Commonwealth Pool 300 metres.

Gilmore Guest House 51 Gilmore Place Edinburgh EH3 9NT Tel: 0131 229 5008 Fax: 0131 229 5008	APPROVED	1 Single 1 Twin 3 Double 2 Family	4 En Suite fac 1 Pub Bath/Show	B&B per person £15.00-£22.00 Single £14.00-£25.00 Double	Open Jan-Dec

Family run guest house, close to the city centre and most of the major tourist attractions. Assured of a warm friendly welcome.

Glenalmond Guest House 25 Mayfield Gardens Edinburgh EH9 2BX Tel: 0131 668 2392	COMMENDED	1 Twin 5 Double 1 Family	7 En Suite fac	B&B per person £18.00-£52.00 Single £18.00-£26.00 Double	Open Mar-Oct

Personally run guest house with private parking. On main bus routes to city centre.

Glenerne Guest House 4 Hampton Terrace West Coates Edinburgh EH12 5JD Tel: 0131 337 1210	COMMENDED	1 Twin 2 Double	2 En Suite fac 1 Priv. NOT ensuite	B&B per person £30.00-£65.00 Single £27.50-£35.00 Double	Open Jan-Dec

Comfortable family home with off-street parking within walking distance of city centre. All rooms with private facilities.

Glenesk Guest House 39 Liberton Brae Edinburgh EH16 6AG Tel: 0131 664 1529 Fax: 0131 664 1529	APPROVED Listed	2 Twin 1 Double 1 Family	1 Pub Bath/Show	B&B per person £15.00-£20.00 Double Room only per person £15.00-£20.00	Open Jan-Dec Dinner 1800-2000

Personally run, small guest house. Convenient for bus route to city centre.
Limited car parking available.

The Gorvic Guest House 14 Granville Terrace Edinburgh EH10 4PQ Tel: 0131 229 6565/229 0447	COMMENDED Listed	1 Twin 3 Double 4 Family	2 En Suite fac 3 Limited ensuite 2 Pub Bath/Show	B&B per person £20.00-£30.00 Single £16.00-£25.00 Double	Open Jan-Dec

Traditional terraced house 10 minutes from city centre. On main bus routes.

Mrs Alexia Graham 18 Moston Terrace Edinburgh EH9 2DE Tel: 0131 667 3466	HIGHLY COMMENDED Listed	2 Double	1 Pub Bath/Show	B&B per person £20.00-£35.00 Single £17.00-£20.00 Double Room only per person £18.00-£30.00	Open Apr-Oct

Traditionally furnished, elegant Victorian house in quiet, residential area.
Convenient for main bus routes to city centre. Unrestricted parking.

Details of Grading and Classification are on page vi. | Key to symbols is on back flap. |

EDINBURGH continued	Map 2 C5

The Grange
2 MINTO STREET, EDINBURGH EH9 1RG
Telephone and Fax: 0131 667 2125

Family run guest house with warm eastern hospitality. One mile from Princes Street. Frequent bus services. Comfortable rooms. TV, central heating, H&C, tea/coffee facilities in all rooms. Full ensuite facilities. Three family rooms. Walking distance to Commonwealth Swimming Pool, Holyrood Park and Palace. University and Royal College of Surgeons and Physicians nearby.

The Grange 2 Minto Street Edinburgh EH9 1RG Tel: 0131 667 2125 Fax: 0131 667 2125	APPROVED	3 Twin 2 Double 3 Family	8 En Suite fac	B&B per person £17.00-£25.00 Double	Open Jan-Dec	
		Stone-built Georgian house on main A7 and bus route for the city centre and all amenities.				

Mrs A Hamilton 6 Cambridge Gardens Edinburgh EH6 5DJ Tel: 0131 554 3113	APPROVED Listed	1 Double 1 Family	1 Pub Bath/Show	B&B per person £11.00-£13.00 Single £11.00-£12.50 Double	Open May-Sep	
		Terraced house in residential area next to Pilrig Park on east side of city centre. Spanish and Italian spoken here.				

The Havrist Guest House 33 Straiton Place, The Promenade, Portobello Edinburgh EH15 2BH Tel: 0131 657 3160 Fax: 0131 657 3160	APPROVED	2 Single 1 Twin 2 Double 2 Family	2 En Suite fac 2 Pub Bath/Show	B&B per person £14.00-£24.00 Single £12.00-£20.00 Double	Open Jan-Dec	
		Terraced house overlooking beach and promenade. Some private and street parking. Convenient bus access for city centre.				

Hermitage Guest House 16 East Hermitage Place Leith Links Edinburgh EH6 8AB Tel: 0131 555 4868	COMMENDED	2 Twin 1 Double 2 Family	2 Pub Bath/Show	B&B per person £20.00-£25.00 Single £15.00-£20.00 Double	Open Jan-Dec	
		Victorian terraced villa overlooking park, offering a warm and friendly welcome. Close to main bus route (10 minutes from city centre).				

HIGHLAND PARK GUEST HOUSE
16 KILMAURS TERRACE, EDINBURGH EH16 5DR
Telephone: 0131 667 9204

Comfortable guest house situated in quiet street off Dalkeith Road. Unrestricted parking and easy access to City Centre. Near Holyrood Park, University and Royal College of Surgeons.
All rooms TV, Tea/Coffee, Central Heating and H&C.

Highland Park Guest House 16 Kilmaurs Terrace Edinburgh EH16 5DR Tel: 0131 667 9204	COMMENDED	1 Single 2 Twin 2 Family	2 Pub Bath/Show	B&B per person £14.00-£20.00 Single £14.00-£20.00 Double	Open Jan-Dec	
		Victorian stone-built house retaining many original features in quiet residential area 1.5 miles (3kms) from city centre. On main bus routes.				

ELMVIEW

15 GLENGYLE TERRACE, EDINBURGH EH3 9LN
Telephone and Fax: 0131 228 1973

Quietly situated in a fine Victorian terrace only one kilometre from *Edinburgh Castle* and the *City Centre*. **ELMVIEW** is close to the *International Conference Centre, Theatres* and many of Edinburgh's finest restaurants.

Recently refurbished to a very high standard **ELMVIEW** offers every modern comfort and convenience, yet retains its Victorian elegance, enhanced by Zoffany wallpapers and beautiful fabrics.

There are three spacious ensuite bedrooms each with direct-dial telephone, TV/VCR, fridge, ironing centre and many other features.

Whether your visit is for business or pleasure you will find a welcome oasis here in the *Heart of Edinburgh*.
Totally non-smoking.

Mrs Marny Hill Elmview, 15 Glengyle Terrace Edinburgh EH3 9LN Tel: 0131 228 1973 Fax: 0131 228 1973	**HIGHLY COMMENDED** Listed	2 Twin 1 Double	3 En Suite fac	B&B per person £35.00-£45.00 Single £28.00-£35.00 Double	Open Apr-Oct	

Victorian terraced house in centre of Edinburgh.
0.5 mile (1km) from Princes Street. Non-smoking.

HILLVIEW

22 Hillview, Queensferry Road, Blackhall, Edinburgh EH4 2AF
Telephone: 0131 343 2969

Elegant terraced house with easy access to historic Edinburgh 2 miles. Buses pass door. Establishment is completely non-smoking. Well furnished and good breakfast provided. Airport travel is four miles and city bypass nearby. Good centre for touring central Scotland, Trossachs, Fife, East Lothian and the Borders. Personal Scottish hospitality.

Hillview 22 Hillview, Queensferry Road, Blackhall Edinburgh EH4 2AF Tel: 0131 343 2969	**HIGHLY COMMENDED** 👑👑	1 Double 1 Family	2 En Suite fac	B&B per person £20.00-£25.00 Single £16.00-£23.00 Double	Open Jan-Dec	

Elegant Edwardian terraced family home with easy access to the city centre.

EDINBURGH
Hopetoun Guest House

15 Mayfield Road, Edinburgh EH9 2NG   **Tel: 0131 667 7691**

Stone-built Victorian terraced house on bus route to City Centre. A pleasant 25-minute walk through quiet suburban streets takes you to the Royal Mile and Castle. Parking. TV, Central Heating, Tea/Coffee-making facilities.
COMPLETELY NON-SMOKING
Prices from £16-£22 including breakfast

Hopetoun Guest House 15 Mayfield Road Edinburgh EH9 2NG Tel: 0131 667 7691	**COMMENDED** 👑	1 Double 2 Family	2 Pub Bath/Show	B&B per person £20.00-£25.00 Single £16.00-£22.00 Double	Open Jan-Dec	

Completely non-smoking, small, friendly guest house on the
south side of the city, 1.5 miles (2.5kms) from Princes Street.

Details of Grading and Classification are on page vi.   Key to symbols is on back flap.

EDINBURGH continued	Map 2 C5						
House O'Hill Bed & Breakfast 7 House O'Hill Terrace Blackhall, Edinburgh EH4 2AA Tel: 0131 332 3674		COMMENDED	2 Twin 1 Double	2 En Suite fac 1 Priv. NOT ensuite	B&B per person £20.00-£35.00 Single £15.00-£23.00 Double Room only per person £13.00-£33.00	Open Apr-Oct	

Semi-detached house approx 1.5 miles (2.5kms) from West End.
Convenient access to city, via Queensferry Road. Parking.

| Mrs L Hume
13 Moat Street
Edinburgh
EH14 1PE
Tel: 0131 443 8266 | | COMMENDED
Listed | 1 Twin
1 Family | 1 Pub Bath/Show | B&B per person
£13.00-£15.00 Single
£13.00-£15.00 Double | Open May-Sep | |

Family house in quiet residential street. Close to main city centre bus routes.

| David & Theresa Ingram
24 Northumberland Street
Edinburgh
EH3 6LS
Tel: 0131 556 8140
Fax: 0131 556 4423 | | HIGHLY
COMMENDED
Listed | 3 Twin | 2 En Suite fac
1 Limited ensuite | B&B per person
£45.00 Single
£30.00 Double | Open Jan-Dec | |

Georgian townhouse in heart of Edinburgh's New Town.
Bedrooms with ensuite and private facilities. Fax available; individual telephones.

| International Guest House
37 Mayfield Gardens
Edinburgh
EH9 2BX
Tel: 0131 667 2511/9833
Fax: 0131 667 1109 | | HIGHLY
COMMENDED | 3 Single
2 Twin
2 Double
1 Family | 8 En Suite fac | B&B per person
£23.00-£32.00 Single
£19.00-£32.00 Double | Open Jan-Dec | |

Stone-built Victorian house in residential area with regular bus service
to city centre. All rooms have private facilities. Some private parking.

| Ivy Guest House
7 Mayfield Gardens, Newington
Edinburgh
EH9 2AX
Tel: 0131 667 3411 | | COMMENDED | 2 Twin
3 Double
3 Family | 6 En Suite fac
2 Priv. NOT ensuite | B&B per person
£20.00-£40.00 Single
£17.00-£27.50 Double | Open Jan-Dec | |

Victorian terraced house on convenient bus route for city centre.
Recommended restaurants nearby. Handy for Commonwealth Pool.
Private car park.

| Joppa Turrets Guest House
1 Lower Joppa
Edinburgh
EH15 2ER
Tel: 0131 669 5806
Fax: 0131 669 5190 | | COMMENDED | 1 Twin
4 Double | 3 En Suite fac
1 Pub Bath/Show | B&B per person
£14.00-£25.00 Single
£14.00-£22.00 Double | Open Jan-Dec | |

Quiet and friendly, with fine sea views from every room.
Close to sandy beach. Easy access to city centre. Unrestricted parking.

| Mr Andrew M Kay
30 Arboretum Place
Inverleith
Edinburgh
EH3 5NZ
Tel: 0131 332 7315 | | COMMENDED
Listed | 2 Double | 1 Pub Bath/Show | B&B per person
£20.00-£25.00 Single
£15.00-£22.50 Double | Open Apr-Oct | |

Modern house in quiet, residential area next to Royal Botanic Gardens.
Convenient for city centre. Free street parking available.

VAT is shown at 17.5%: changes in this rate may affect prices. Prices shown are for guidance only. Please send SAE with each enquiry.

International Guest House

37 MAYFIELD GARDENS, EDINBURGH EH9 2BX

Telephone: 0131 667 2511

EDINBURGH

Fax: 0131 667 1109

SCOTTISH TOURIST BOARD. HIGHLY COMMENDED ♛♛. AA. QQQQ

"One of the best Guest Houses in town."

"International reputation for quality – service – comfort"

- Well appointed bedrooms all with en-suite facilities
- Colour TV's tea/coffee making facilities
- Short distance from city centre
- Realistic rates from £18.00 Bed & Breakfast
- Own keys for all day access
- Warm and friendly atmosphere
- Some private parking

"All the comforts of home at a price you can afford"

| EDINBURGH continued | Map 2 C5 | | |

KENVIE GUEST HOUSE

16 Kilmaurs Road, Edinburgh EH16 5DA
Telephone/Fax: 0131 668 1964

Quiet and comfortable house situated in a residential area with easy access to City Centre on an excellent bus route. All rooms have tea and coffee-making facilities and TV. Central heating throughout.
A warm and friendly welcome is guaranteed.

| Kenvie Guest House
16 Kilmaurs Road
Edinburgh
EH16 5DA
Tel: 0131 668 1964
Fax: 0131 668 1964 | COMMENDED 👑👑 | 2 Twin
1 Double
2 Family | 2 En Suite fac
2 Pub Bath/Show | B&B per person
£18.00-£25.00 Single
£18.00-£25.00 Double | Open Jan-Dec | |
| | | **Personally run, situated in quiet residential area close to city centre, and on main bus routes.** | | | | |

| Kew Guest House
1 Kew Terrace, Murrayfield
Edinburgh
EH12 5JE
Tel: 0131 313 0700
Fax: 0131 313 0747 | HIGHLY COMMENDED 👑👑 | 1 Single
1 Twin
2 Double
2 Family | 4 En Suite fac
1 Pub Bath/Show | B&B per person
£27.00-£38.00 Single
£24.00-£32.50 Double | Open Jan-Dec | |
| | | **Victorian terraced house situated on main Glasgow road 1 mile (2kms) from West End with secure parking.** | | | | |

| Kingsley Guest House
30 Craigmillar Park
Edinburgh
EH16 5PS
Tel: 0131 667 8439
Fax: 0131 667 8439 | COMMENDED 👑👑 | 2 Twin
1 Double
3 Family | 4 En Suite fac
1 Priv. NOT ensuite
2 Pub Bath/Show | B&B per person
£16.00-£23.00 Double
Room only per person
£15.00-£22.00 | Open Jan-Dec | |
| | | **Friendly, comfortable and family run Victorian villa with own private car park. Excellent bus service for all major attractions in the city.** | | | | |

Kirkland Bed and Breakfast

6 Dean Park Crescent, Edinburgh EH4 1PN
Telephone: 0131 332 5017

Warm friendly Victorian house on two floors, only 10 minutes walk from West End of Princes Street. Recently refurbished and offering interesting local shops and restaurants. Traditional Scottish breakfast is available and we are happy to cater for any special needs you may have.

| Mrs M Kirkland
Kirkland Bed & Breakfast
6 Dean Park Crescent
Edinburgh
EH4 1PN
Tel: 0131 332 5017 | COMMENDED Listed | 1 Single
1 Twin
2 Double
1 Family | 1 En Suite fac
2 Pub Bath/Show | B&B per person
£15.00-£30.00 Single
£15.00-£24.00 Double | Open Apr-Oct | |
| | | **Centrally situated terraced house with convenient access to city centre, West End and Queensferry Road.** | | | | |

| Kirtle Guest House
8 Minto Street
Edinburgh
EH9 1RG
Tel: 0131 667 2813 (office)/
5353 (guests) | COMMENDED 👑👑 | 3 Double
4 Family | 4 En Suite fac
3 Limited ensuite
2 Pub Bath/Show | B&B per person
£34.00-£40.00 Single
£17.00-£20.00 Double | Open Jan-Dec | |
| | | **On main bus routes for city centre, 1 mile (2kms). Some private car parking available. Close to Commonwealth Pool.** | | | | |

Mr M Klimczyk Ballarat, 14 Gilmore Place Edinburgh EH3 9NQ Tel: 0131 229 7024	**COMMENDED** Listed	2 Twin 2 Double 2 Family	3 Pub Bath/Show	B&B per person £15.00-£20.00 Single £13.00-£18.00 Double	Open Apr-Sep	

Friendly welcome at this family guest house.
Easy access to bus routes and within walking distance of city centre.

The Lairg 11 Coates Gardens Edinburgh EH12 5LG Tel: 0131 337 1050 Fax: 0131 346 2167	**APPROVED** 👑👑	2 Single 3 Twin 2 Double 3 Family	10 En Suite fac	B&B per person £18.00-£30.00 Single £18.00-£30.00 Double	Open Jan-Dec Dinner 1715-1745 B&B + Eve. Meal £25.00-£35.00	

Personally run guest house with large lounge area.
Easy access to city centre and all tourist attractions.

Lauderville Guest House 52 Mayfield Road Edinburgh EH9 2NH Tel: 0131 667 7788/4005 Fax: 0131 667 7788	**HIGHLY** **COMMENDED** 👑👑	1 Twin 2 Double 1 Family	3 En Suite fac 1 Limited ensuite	B&B per person £20.00-£40.00 Single £18.00-£30.00 Double	Open Jan-Dec	

The Marriots warmly welcome visitors to Edinburgh.
Comfortable surroundings, substantial breakfasts, centrally located for attractions.

Mrs Mary Ledingham Averon, 57 Lilyhill Terrace Edinburgh Midlothian EH8 7DR Tel: 0131 661 1417	**COMMENDED** Listed	1 Twin 1 Double	1 Pub Bath/Show	B&B per person £17.00 Single £15.00-£17.00 Double	Open May-Sep	

Terraced villa overlooking Holyrood Park in hilltop position.
Warm welcome guaranteed. Unrestricted street parking. Gaelic spoken.

Mrs Valerie Livingstone Ceol-na-Mara, 50 Paisley Crescent Edinburgh EH8 7JQ Tel: 0131 661 6337	**COMMENDED** Listed	1 Twin 2 Double	1 Limited ensuite 1 Pub Bath/Show	B&B per person £16.00-£19.00 Single £16.00-£18.00 Double	Open Apr-Oct	

Modern terraced villa in quiet area adjacent to Arthur's Seat, with fine views
over Firth of Forth. Near main bus route to city centre. No smoking.

Lorne Villa Guest House 9 East Mayfield Edinburgh EH9 1SD Tel: 0131 667 7159	**COMMENDED** Listed	1 Single 2 Double 4 Family	3 En Suite fac 1 Priv. NOT ensuite 2 Pub Bath/Show	B&B per person £18.00-£25.00 Single £18.00-£25.00 Double	Open Jan-Dec	

Personally run guest house conveniently situated for city centre bus route
with off-street parking.

Lugton's Guest House 29 Leamington Terrace Edinburgh EH10 4JS Tel: 0131 229 7033 Fax: 0131 228 9483	**COMMENDED** Listed	1 Single 1 Twin 1 Double 1 Family	3 En Suite fac 1 Priv. NOT ensuite 1 Pub Bath/Show	B&B per person £18.00-£25.00 Single £18.00-£25.00 Double	Open Jan-Dec	

Personally run terraced house 1 mile (2 kms) from West End.
Ensuite rooms available.

BE SURE TO CHOOSE THE
SCOTTISH TOURIST BOARD'S
SIGN OF QUALITY

EDINBURGH continued	Map 2 C5

Ecosse International — Commended 🏵🏵

15 McDonald Road, Edinburgh EH7 4LX
Telephone: 0131 556 4967   Fax: 0131 556 7394

Central, luxury Guest House. Bedrooms with private bathrooms, one four-poster, TV, centrally heated, tea/coffee served in Lounge, courtesy whisky and parking. Personally run by the owner – warm, friendly atmosphere. Central to Edinburgh Castle, Holyrood Palace, Botanic Gardens, galleries, museums and zoo. An ideal base for day trips to Loch Lomond, Gleneagles and Borders.

A good night's sleep awaits you in our comfortable beds.

Elizabeth McIntyre 15 McDonald Road Edinburgh EH7 4LX Tel: 0131 556 4967 Fax: 0131 556 7394	COMMENDED 🏵🏵🏵	1 Twin 1 Double 1 Family	3 En Suite fac	B&B per person £25.00-£30.00 Single £20.00-£27.50 Double B&B + Eve. Meal £37.00-£40.00	Open Jan-Dec Dinner 1800-2000
		Personally run with friendly atmosphere. Situated in residential area with easy access to city centre and station.			
Dorothy M G McKay 41 Corstorphine Bank Drive Edinburgh EH12 8RH Tel: 0131 334 4100	COMMENDED Listed	1 Twin 1 Double	1 Priv. NOT ensuite 2 Pub Bath/Show	B&B per person £16.00-£18.00 Single £15.00-£17.00 Double	Open Apr-Oct
		Detached house in quiet residential area. About 3 miles (5kms) from city centre and 4 miles (6kms) from airport. 500 yards from bus stop.			
Mrs E M MacKinnon 5 Bangholm Terrace Edinburgh EH3 5QN Tel: 0131 552 3320	COMMENDED Listed	1 Twin 1 Double	1 Pub Bath/Show	B&B per person £16.00-£20.00 Single £16.00-£17.50 Double	Open Apr-Oct Dinner 1800-1930 B&B + Eve. Meal £21.00-£25.50
		Personally run, comfortable family tenement home, close to Botanic Gardens, convenient for city centre.			
Mrs S J McLennan Airdenair, 29 Kilmaurs Road Edinburgh EH16 5DB Tel: 0131 668 2336	APPROVED 🏵	2 Twin 1 Double	1 Pub Bath/Show	B&B per person £16.00-£18.00 Single £15.00-£17.00 Double	Open Apr-Oct
		Double upper flatted villa. Quiet residential area on south side of city. Near Royal Commonwealth Pool, Holyrood Park. Good bus routes to centre.			
Ms A McTavish 9B Scotland Street Edinburgh EH3 6PP Tel: 0131 556 5080 Fax: 0131 556 5080	COMMENDED Listed	1 Single 1 Twin 1 Double	2 Pub Bath/Show	B&B per person £18.00-£20.00 Single £18.00-£20.00 Double	Open May-Sep
		Personally run centrally located house with antique furnishings. Approximately 1/4 mile (1/2km) to Princes Street and city centre. Vegetarians welcome.			
Mrs Eileen McTighe 4 Coinyie House Close Royal Mile Edinburgh EH1 1NL Tel: 0131 556 3399	APPROVED Listed	1 Twin 1 Family	1 Pub Bath/Show	B&B per person £20.00-£25.00 Single £14.00-£18.00 Double	Open Apr-Oct
		Renovated 18th-century ground-floor flat set in courtyard just behind the Royal Mile in the historical heart of Edinburgh.			
Mrs E Manson Doocote House, 15 Moat Street Edinburgh EH14 1PE Tel: 0131 443 5455	COMMENDED Listed	1 Twin 1 Double 1 Family	2 Pub Bath/Show	B&B per person £17.00-£18.00 Single £14.00-£18.00 Double Room only per person £14.00-£18.00	Open Apr-Sep
		Terraced house with attractive garden in quiet street just off main bus route. Approx. 2 miles (3kms) from city centre.			

Maple Leaf Guest House 23 Pilrig Street Edinburgh EH6 5AN Tel: 0131 554 7692	**COMMENDED** 👑👑👑	2 Single 2 Twin 2 Double 3 Family	5 En Suite fac 2 Limited ensuite 1 Priv. NOT ensuite 2 Pub Bath/Show	B&B per person £19.00-£23.00 Single £15.00-£24.00 Double	Open Jan-Dec	
		Georgian, terraced house, conveniently situated 5 minutes from town centre. A good Scottish welcome here. French spoken.				
Marrakech Guest House 30 London Street Edinburgh EH3 6NA Tel: 0131 556 4444/7293 Fax: 0131 557 3615	**COMMENDED** 👑👑👑	2 Single 3 Twin 4 Double 2 Family	9 En Suite fac 2 Pub Bath/Show	B&B per person £20.00-£30.00 Single £20.00-£30.00 Double Room only per person £20.00-£30.00	Open Jan-Dec Dinner 1800-2200	
		Family run in New Town. Close to the city centre with its own restaurant serving North African cuisine and featuring many home-made specialities.				

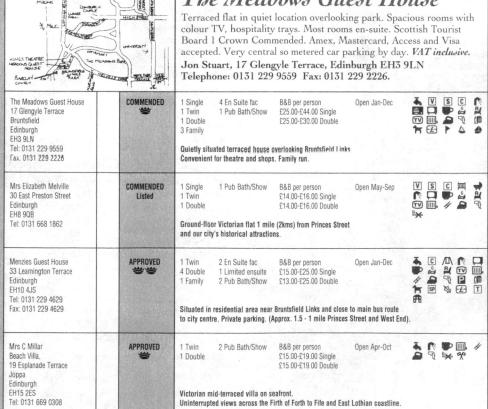

The Meadows Guest House

Terraced flat in quiet location overlooking park. Spacious rooms with colour TV, hospitality trays. Most rooms en-suite. Scottish Tourist Board 1 Crown Commended. Amex, Mastercard, Access and Visa accepted. Very central so metered car parking by day. *VAT inclusive.*

Jon Stuart, 17 Glengyle Terrace, Edinburgh EH3 9LN
Telephone: 0131 229 9559 Fax: 0131 229 2226.

The Meadows Guest House 17 Glengyle Terrace Bruntsfield Edinburgh EH3 9LN Tel: 0131 229 9559 Fax: 0131 229 2226	**COMMENDED** 👑	1 Single 1 Twin 1 Double 3 Family	4 En Suite fac 1 Pub Bath/Show	B&B per person £25.00-£44.00 Single £25.00-£30.00 Double	Open Jan-Dec	
		Quietly situated terraced house overlooking Bruntsfield Links Convenient for theatre and shops. Family run.				
Mrs Elizabeth Melville 30 East Preston Street Edinburgh EH8 9QB Tel: 0131 668 1862	**COMMENDED** Listed	1 Single 1 Twin 1 Double	1 Pub Bath/Show	B&B per person £14.00-£16.00 Single £14.00-£16.00 Double	Open May-Sep	
		Ground-floor Victorian flat 1 mile (2kms) from Princes Street and our city's historical attractions.				
Menzies Guest House 33 Leamington Terrace Edinburgh EH10 4JS Tel: 0131 229 4629 Fax: 0131 229 4629	**APPROVED** 👑👑	1 Twin 4 Double 1 Family	2 En Suite fac 1 Limited ensuite 2 Pub Bath/Show	B&B per person £15.00-£25.00 Single £13.00-£25.00 Double	Open Jan-Dec	
		Situated in residential area near Bruntsfield Links and close to main bus route to city centre. Private parking. (Approx. 1.5 - 1 mile Princes Street and West End).				
Mrs C Millar Beach Villa, 19 Esplanade Terrace Joppa Edinburgh EH15 2ES Tel: 0131 669 0308	**APPROVED** 👑	1 Twin 1 Double	2 Pub Bath/Show	B&B per person £15.00-£19.00 Single £15.00-£19.00 Double	Open Apr-Oct	
		Victorian mid-terraced villa on seafront. Uninterrupted views across the Firth of Forth to Fife and East Lothian coastline.				

EDINBURGH continued	Map 2 C5						
Milton House 24 Duddingston Crescent Edinburgh EH15 3AT Tel: 0131 669 4072		COMMENDED ♛	1 Twin 2 Double	3 Pub Bath/Show	B&B per person £15.00-£18.00 Single £15.00-£18.00 Double Room only per person £15.00-£18.00	Open Jan-Dec	

Friendly family atmosphere with off-street parking and easy access to city centre. Adjacent to 9-hole golf course.

| Mrs N Mitchell 19 Meadowplace Road Edinburgh EH12 7UJ Tel: 0131 334 8483 | | COMMENDED ♛ | 1 Twin 1 Family | 1 Pub Bath/Show | B&B per person £17.00 Single £14.00-£16.00 Double | Open Apr-Oct | |

On the west side of the city, detached bungalow offering ground-floor accommodation and off-street parking.

| Mrs Margaret Moore Moores, 44B Stevenson Drive Edinburgh EH11 3DJ Tel: 0131 443 9370 | | COMMENDED Listed | 1 Single 1 Twin | 2 En Suite fac | B&B per person £16.00-£18.00 Single £16.00-£18.00 Double | Open May-Sep | |

Comfortable well-furnished personally run bed and breakfast. Unrestricted parking. Close to major bus routes to city centre.

| Muffin Guest House 164 Ferry Road Edinburgh EH6 4NS Tel: 0131 554 4162 | | COMMENDED ♛♛ | 2 Single 1 Twin 3 Double 1 Family | 2 En Suite fac 2 Pub Bath/Show | B&B per person £16.00-£25.00 Single £14.00-£30.00 Double | Open Jan-Dec Dinner 1830-1930 | |

Personally run, situated on main bus route with easy access to town centre and all amenities.

| Murrayfield Park Guest House 89 Corstorphine Road Murrayfield Edinburgh EH12 5QE Tel: 0131 337 5370 Fax: 0131 337 3772 | | COMMENDED ♛♛ | 1 Single 4 Twin 1 Double | 5 En Suite fac 1 Pub Bath/Show | B&B per person £22.00-£25.00 Single £22.00-£25.00 Double | Open Jan-Dec | |

10 minutes by bus from the city centre, this location is ideal for enjoying the attractions of Edinburgh. Near to airport. Private parking.

Newington Guest House 18 Newington Road Edinburgh EH9 1QS Tel: 0131 667 3356 Fax: 0131 667 8307	COMMENDED ♛♛	1 Single 2 Twin 3 Double 2 Family	5 En Suite fac 1 Limited ensuite 1 Pub Bath/Show	B&B per person £27.50-£30.00 Single £19.50-£29.50 Double Room only per person £17.50-£23.50	Open Jan-Dec

Interestingly furnished Victorian house on main road into city from South.
Easy access to centre, most rooms double-glazed.

Mrs Helen Olson 20 Esplanade Terrace Edinburgh EH15 2ES Tel: 0131 669 1010	COMMENDED ♛	2 Double	2 Pub Bath/Show	B&B per person £20.00-£22.00 Single £16.00-£17.00 Double	Open May-Sep

Victorian terraced house situated on sea front at east end of Portobello
pedestrian promenade. Fine views across Firth of Forth.

Mrs C Parent 5A Melgund Terrace Edinburgh Midlothian EH7 4BU Tel: 0131 557 9550	COMMENDED Listed	2 Double	1 En Suite fac 1 Pub Bath/Show	B&B per person £18.00-£25.00 Double	Open Apr-Oct

Scottish hospitality in friendly B&B situated in central Edinburgh. French spoken.

Parklands Guest House 20 Mayfield Gardens Edinburgh EH9 2BZ Tel: 0131 667 7184	COMMENDED ♛♛	2 Twin 3 Double 1 Family	5 En Suite fac 1 Priv. NOT ensuite	B&B per person £18.00-£27.00 Double Room only per person £16.00-£25.00	Open Jan-Dec

Look forward to a warm welcome at this late Victorian house with fine woodwork
and ceilings, situated on the south side. On main bus routes to city centre.

Pollock Halls of Residence
University of Edinburgh
18 Holyrood Park Road, Edinburgh EH16 5AY
Tel: 0131 667 0662　　　　　　**Fax: 0131 668 3217**

Great value rooms in our properties within minutes of the Old Town and overlooking Holyrood Park. Excellent quality catering at nearby John McIntyre Centre. New en-suite as well as modern single rooms with wash basins only. *Send for our free colour brochure today.*

Pollock Halls of Residence 18 Holyrood Park Road Edinburgh EH16 5AY Tel: 0131 667 0662 Fax: 0131 668 3217	APPROVED ♛ up to COMMENDED ♛♛♛	853 Single 122 Double	375 En Suite fac 100 Pub Bath/Show	B&B per person £19.50-£38.20 Single £19.50-£31.50 Double	Open Mar-Apr, Jun-Sep Dinner 1800-1900

On Campus in Holyrood Park beside Arthur's Seat. Close to Royal Commonwealth
Pool and well sited for city centre. Conference and meeting facilities.

Mr & Mrs G Pretsell Colligan, 40 Drum Brae North Edinburgh EH4 8AZ Tel: 0131 339 6811	COMMENDED ♛	1 Twin 1 Double	1 Pub Bath/Show	B&B per person £16.00-£18.00 Single £13.00-£15.00 Double Room only per person £14.00-£16.00	Open Apr-Oct

Personally run Bed and Breakfast, close to airport and
main bus route to city centre. Off-road parking.

Mrs M Rooney Edinburgh House 11 McDonald Road Edinburgh EH7 4LX Tel: 0131 556 3434	COMMENDED ♛♛♛	2 Twin 2 Double	2 En Suite fac 2 Pub Bath/Show	B&B per person £20.00-£40.00 Double	Open Apr-Oct Dinner 1800-1900

Personally run tenement house, approx. 0.5 mile from Princes Street.

EDINBURGH continued	Map 2 C5						
Roselea House 11 Mayfield Road Edinburgh EH9 2NG Tel: 0131 667 6115 Fax: 0131 667 3556	HIGHLY COMMENDED 👑👑	1 Single 2 Twin 2 Double 2 Family	5 En Suite fac 2 Priv. NOT ensuite	B&B per person £25.00-£35.00 Single £20.00-£35.00 Double	Open Jan-Dec		
		A warm welcome at personally run guest house close to city centre on main bus route. Ideal touring base.					

ROSEVALE GUEST HOUSE

15 KILMAURS ROAD, EDINBURGH EH16 5DA
Telephone: 0131 667 4781

Quiet residential area, close to city centre and Royal Commonwealth Pool. Unrestricted street parking. Choice of bed and breakfast or room only at reduced prices. Colour televisions and tea/coffee facilities. Full Scottish breakfast or if preferred packed lunches as alternative. Reduced rates during off-peak season.

Rosevale House 15 Kilmaurs Road Edinburgh EH16 5DA Tel: 0131 667 4781	APPROVED Listed	2 Double 3 Family	5 En Suite fac	B&B per person £23.00-£25.00 Single £18.00-£22.00 Double Room only per person £16.00-£19.00	Open Jan-Dec		
		In quiet residential area near Commonwealth Pool, with nearby transport connections to city centre. Most rooms ensuite.					
Angela Ross 3a Clarence Street Edinburgh EH3 5AE Tel: 0131 557 9368	COMMENDED Listed	1 Twin 1 Double	1 Pub Bath/Show	B&B per person £13.00-£16.00 Single £13.00-£16.00 Double Room only per person £12.00-£16.00	Open Apr-Oct		
		Garden flat in Georgian terrace in New Town. Central location yet in quiet area.					
Rowan Guest House 13 Glenorchy Terrace Edinburgh EH9 2DQ Tel: 0131 667 2463	COMMENDED 👑	2 Single 2 Twin 3 Double 2 Family	2 En Suite fac 2 Pub Bath/Show	B&B per person £19.00-£25.00 Single £18.00-£25.00 Double	Open Jan-Dec		
		Victorian town house in quiet residential area with easy access to city centre and all amenities.					
Roxzannah 36 Minto Street Edinburgh EH9 2BS Tel: 0131 667 8933	COMMENDED 👑	1 Twin 1 Double 2 Family	1 En Suite fac 1 Pub Bath/Show	B&B per person £17.00-£25.00 Single £15.00-£25.00 Double	Open Jan-Dec		
		B Listed Georgian villa, situated 5 minutes from city centre. Ideal location for all amenities and attractions. Parking facility.					
St Bernards Guest House 22 St Bernards Crescent Edinburgh EH4 1NS Tel: 0131 332 2339	COMMENDED 👑👑	3 Single 1 Twin 2 Double	4 En Suite fac 2 Pub Bath/Show	B&B per person £25.00-£35.00 Single £25.00-£30.00 Double	Open Jan-Dec		
		Elegant terraced house in Georgian New Town area of the city. Convenient for Princes Street. Many excellent restaurants within walking distance.					

ST MARGARET'S GUEST HOUSE

18 Craigmillar Park, Edinburgh EH16 5PS
Telephone/Fax: 0131 667 2202

St Margaret's is situated on the south side of Edinburgh on the A701/A772. Excellent bus service, city centre 10 mins ride. Individually decorated bedrooms most en-suite, colour TV, tea/coffee facilities. Many extras for guests' comfort. Private car park. Credit cards accepted.

AA QQQ Recommended.

St Margaret's Guest House 18 Craigmillar Park Edinburgh EH16 5PS Tel: 0131 667 2202 Fax: 0131 667 2202	COMMENDED 👑👑	3 Twin 3 Double 2 Family	4 En Suite fac 1 Priv. NOT ensuite 2 Pub Bath/Show	B&B per person £20.00-£25.00 Single £15.00-£24.00 Double	Open Mar-Dec

Well appointed Victorian house with spacious lounge and thoughtfully decorated. bedrooms. Many additional features for guests' comfort. Private car park.

"The Salisbury"

45 SALISBURY ROAD,
EDINBURGH EH16 5AA
TELEPHONE/FAX: 0131 667 1264

Enjoy real Scottish hospitality in the comfort of this Georgian House, quietly situated yet only two minutes walk from main bus routes to City Centre. Comfortable, centrally-heated bedrooms, all with private facilities, colour TV, tea/coffee-making etc. Convenient for bus/railway stations. Private car park.
We will be delighted to assist with arranging local tours and activities.

AA/RAC ACCLAIMED.

***Contact:* Mr and Mrs William Wright.**

Salisbury Guest House 45 Salisbury Road Edinburgh EH16 5AA Tel: 0131 667 1264 Fax: 0131 667 1264	COMMENDED 👑👑	2 Single 4 Twin 3 Double 3 Family	9 En Suite fac 3 Priv. NOT ensuite	B&B per person £24.00-£30.00 Single £20.00-£26.00 Double	Open Jan-Dec

Georgian Listed building in quiet conservation area 1 mile (2kms) from city centre. En suite and private facilities. Private car park.

LOOK FOR THE SIGNS OF THE WELCOME HOSTS

EDINBURGH continued	Map 2 C5

'33 Colinton Road'

33 COLINTON ROAD, EDINBURGH EH10 5DR
Telephone: 0131 447 8080

'33 Colinton Road' is a Victorian terraced, 2 crown commended friendly family home. Conveniently situated for all amenities and within walking distance of the city centre. On major bus routes. All rooms non-smoking with private facilities. Diets catered for. Children welcome. Open March-October, other times by arrangement.

Mrs J Sandeman 33 Colinton Road Edinburgh EH10 5DR Tel: 0131 447 8080	COMMENDED ♛♛	1 Single 1 Twin 1 Double	2 En Suite fac 1 Priv. NOT ensuite	B&B per person £28.00-£35.00 Single £21.00-£25.00 Double Room only per person £25.00-£30.00	Open Mar-Oct

Victorian terraced house within easy reach of city centre.
Warm welcome, relaxed family atmosphere, unrestricted parking, non-smoking.

Sandilands House

25 QUEENSFERRY ROAD, EDINBURGH EH4 3HB
Telephone: 0131 332 2057

Superbly situated only 5 minutes from city centre for exploration of Scotland's capital. Furnished to a high standard with colour TVs, tea-making facilities, hair dryers, all rooms have en-suite facilities. Includes full Scottish breakfast. Special diets and evening meals on request. Near Murrayfield Rugby Stadium. Children under 3 years free, under 12 years ½ price sharing. Car parking on-site. *Contact: Mrs Maureen Sandilands.*

Mrs Sandilands 25 Queensferry Road Edinburgh EH4 3HB Tel: 0131 332 2057	COMMENDED ♛	1 Twin 1 Double 1 Family	3 En Suite fac	B&B per person £22.50-£28.00 Single £16.00-£24.00 Double	Open Apr-Oct

Personally run family house with convenient access to West End and City Centre. Private parking.

Shalimar Guest House 20 Newington Road Edinburgh EH9 1QS Tel: 0131 667 2827/0789	COMMENDED ♛♛	1 Single 3 Twin 2 Double 3 Family	5 En Suite fac 3 Limited ensuite 3 Pub Bath/Show	B&B per person £20.00-£25.00 Single £20.00-£22.00 Double Room only per person £20.00-£22.00	Open Jan-Dec

Family run guest house under 1 mile (2 kms) from city centre. Vegetarian breakfasts available.

Scotland for Golf . . .

Find out more about golf in Scotland. There's more to it than just the championship courses so get in touch with us now for information on the hidden gems of Scotland.

Write to: Information Unit, Scottish Tourist Board, 23 Ravelston Terrace, Edinburgh EH4 3EU or call: 0131-332 2433

Sharon Guest House

**1 KILMAURS TERRACE,
EDINBURGH EH16 5BZ
Tel: 0131 667 2002 Fax: 0131 316 4755**

Quiet, semi-detached Victorian house in residential area just off A7 (pre-1992 A68) and only 5 minutes by public transport to city centre. Close to Commonwealth Swimming Pool and Royal College of Surgeons.
OFF-STREET PARKING with access all day.
House completely refurbished recently to a high standard. H&C, central heating, shaver point, tea/coffee facilities and colour TV in all rooms.
LARGE traditional Scottish breakfast.
Menu available and special diets catered for.
See symbols below for additional facilities.

Sharon Guest House 1 Kilmaurs Terrace Edinburgh EH16 5BZ Tel: 0131 667 2002 Fax: 0131 316 4755	COMMENDED Listed	2 Single 1 Twin 3 Double 3 Family	2 Pub Bath/Show	B&B per person £16.00-£24.00 Single £12.00-£22.00 Double Room only per person £14.00-£22.00	Open Jan-Dec
		Victorian house in residential area but near bus routes for city centre.			
Sheridan Guest House 1 Bonnington Terrace Edinburgh EH6 4BP Tel: 0131 554 4107	COMMENDED ♛♛	6 Twin 1 Family	2 En Suite fac 1 Priv. NOT ensuite 2 Pub Bath/Show	B&B per person £19.00-£28.00 Single £19.00-£28.00 Double Room only per person £16.00-£25.00	Open Jan-Dec
		Situated in residential area of bus route to city centre and its amenities. No parking restrictions.			
Sherwood Guest House 42 Minto Street Edinburgh EH9 2BR Tel: 0131 667 1200	COMMENDED ♛♛	1 Twin 2 Double 3 Family	5 En Suite fac 1 Priv. NOT ensuite	B&B per person £20.00-£34.00 Single £16.00-£28.00 Double	Open Jan-Dec
		Stone-built Georgian terraced house in residential area of city. On main bus route, 1.5 miles (2.5kms) to city centre. Limited parking.			
Mrs Aurora Sibbet Sibbet House, 26 Northumberland Street Edinburgh EH3 6LS Tel: 0131 556 1078 Fax: 0131 557 9445	DELUXE ♛♛♛	1 Twin 1 Double 1 Family	3 En Suite fac	B&B per person £40.00-£50.00 Single £30.00-£35.00 Double	Open Apr-Oct Dinner 1800-1930 B&B + Eve. Meal £50.00-£75.00
		Georgian town house of considerable character built in 1809 and furnished with antiques. Bagpipes played on request. 5 minutes walk from Princes St.			
Mrs E C Simpson 17 Crawfurd Road Edinburgh EH16 5PQ Tel: 0131 667 1191	COMMENDED Listed	1 Twin 1 Double	2 Pub Bath/Show	B&B per person £15.50-£18.00 Single £13.50-£18.00 Double	Open May-Sep
		Friendly welcome in late Victorian family home in quiet residential area, with easy access to city centre. Unrestricted parking.			

EDINBURGH continued	Map 2 C5

LANSDOWNE
Commended ♕♕

1 Wester Coates Road, Edinburgh EH12 5LU
Telephone: 0131 337 5002 *Proprietor:* **Mrs R. Sinclair**

Pleasantly situated villa in attractive garden in a quiet residential area near West End of Princes Street. Very convenient for buses, stations, airport. Private parking. All rooms have wash-hand basins, electric blankets, radio and central heating – one room on ground floor. Spacious and comfortable guests' lounge.
You are assured of a warm welcome.

Mrs R Sinclair Lansdowne, 1 Wester Coates Road Edinburgh EH12 5LU Tel: 0131 337 5002	COMMENDED ♕♕	1 Single 1 Double 1 Family	2 Pub Bath/Show	B&B per person £18.00-£24.00 Single £14.00-£22.00 Double	Open Easter-Oct

Detached villa in pleasant garden in quiet residential area near west end of city. Close to main bus routes, convenient for station and airport.

Six Mary's Place Guest House 6 Mary's Place Edinburgh EH4 1JD Tel: 0131 332 8965	COMMENDED ♕♕	3 Single 2 Twin 3 Double	2 En Suite fac 2 Pub Bath/Show	B&B per person £22.00-£25.00 Single £22.00-£25.00 Double Room only per person £20.00-£22.00	Open 10 Jan-Dec Dinner 1800-2130 B&B + Eve. Meal £29.50-£34.50

Restored Georgian townhouse in central location offering vegetarian cuisine and a restful homely atmosphere.

Mrs J Skidmore 2 Braid Hills Road Edinburgh EH10 6EZ Tel: 0131 447 8848	APPROVED Listed	1 Single 2 Double 1 Family	1 Pub Bath/Show	B&B per person £20.00-£25.00 Single £18.00-£20.00 Double Room only per person £20.00-£25.00	Open May-Sep Dinner 1800-2000

Personally run bed and breakfast close to centre. By main bus routes. Convenient base for touring.

Mrs Elizabeth Smith 14 Lennel Avenue Edinburgh EH12 6DW Tel: 0131 337 1979	HIGHLY COMMENDED Listed	2 Twin 1 Double	2 Pub Bath/Show	B&B per person £25.00-£30.00 Single £18.00-£24.00 Double	Open Apr-Oct

Personally run, beautiful house, quietly situated in residential area. Approx. 1.5 miles (3 kms) to West End and Princes Street. Unrestricted parking.

Sonas Guest House 3 East Mayfield Edinburgh EH9 1SD Tel: 0131 667 2781 Fax: 0131 667 0454	COMMENDED ♕♕	1 Single 2 Twin 4 Double 1 Family	8 En Suite fac	B&B per person £20.00-£40.00 Single £20.00-£32.50 Double	Open Jan-Dec

Terraced house situated on south side of city. With private parking. Convenient bus routes to centre and all amenities.

Southdown Guest House 20 Craigmillar Park Edinburgh EH16 5PS Tel: 0131 667 2410	COMMENDED ♕♕	2 Twin 2 Double 2 Family	4 En Suite fac 2 Limited ensuite 2 Pub Bath/Show	B&B per person £22.50-£35.00 Single £18.00-£25.00 Double	Open Feb-Nov

Victorian terraced house in residential area on main A701 road, with many bus routes to city centre. Friendly and family run. Private car park. Satellite TV.

A Stark 17 McDonald Road Edinburgh Midlothian EH7 4LX Tel: 0131 556 3709	COMMENDED ♕♕	1 Twin 2 Double 1 Family	3 En Suite fac 1 Priv. NOT ensuite	B&B per person £25.00-£35.00 Single £20.00-£25.00 Double	Open Apr-Oct

Centrally located, personally run, terraced house 0.5 mile (1 km) to Princes St. All ensuite. Unrestricted parking.

Strathmohr House 23 Mayfield Gardens Edinburgh EH9 2BX Tel: 0131 667 8475	COMMENDED ♔♔	1 Twin 2 Double 4 Family	7 En Suite fac 2 Pub Bath/Show	B&B per person £25.00-£35.00 Single £18.00-£30.00 Double	Open Jan-Dec
		Welcome to our refurbished Victorian villa. Easy access to city centre. Ensuite facilities. Private parking. Non-smoking.			

Mrs Gloria Stuart 20 London Street Edinburgh EH3 6NA Tel: 0131 557 0216 Fax: 0131 556 6445	HIGHLY COMMENDED ♔♔	1 Twin 1 Double	2 En Suite fac	B&B per person £30.00-£35.00 Double	Open Apr-Oct
		Centrally located in the heart of Georgian Edinburgh. Beautifully appointed house. Bedrooms containing many thoughtful accessories.			

Stuart House

12 East Claremont Street, Edinburgh EH7 4JP
Telephone: 0131 557 9030 Fax: 0131 557 0563

Come and experience hospitality and a warm welcome. Traditional old town house in city centre beautifully renovated and decorated. 7 comfortable bedrooms with private facilities equipped with CTV, telephone, hospitality tray and hairdryers. Home cooked breakfast served in elegant dining room. *Strictly no smoking.* A stay to remember.

Stuart House 12 East Claremont Street Edinburgh EH7 4JP Tel: 0131 557 9030 Fax: 0131 557 0563	HIGHLY COMMENDED ♔♔	1 Single 2 Twin 3 Double 1 Family	6 En Suite fac 1 Priv.NOT ensuite	B&B per person £32.00 Single £35.00-£37.00 Double	Open Jan-Dec
		Comfortable, Georgian style house (c1860) situated in the historic New Town. Close to the city centre and Princes Street.			

Sylvern Guest House 22 West Mayfield Edinburgh EH9 1TQ Tel: 0131 667 1241	APPROVED Listed	2 Twin 1 Double 3 Family	4 En Suite fac 2 Pub Bath/Show	B&B per person £20.00-£30.00 Single £17.00-£22.00 Double	Open Jan-Dec
		Detached Victorian house in residential area. Private parking and convenient for main bus routes. Four rooms ensuite.			

Tania Guest House 19 Minto Street Edinburgh EH9 1RQ Tel: 0131 667 4144	APPROVED Listed	1 Single 1 Twin 1 Double 3 Family	1 En Suite fac 1 Pub Bath/Show	B&B per person £15.00-£24.00 Single £15.00-£22.50 Double	Open Jan-Dec
		Situated on main bus route, 10 minutes from city centre. Private parking.			

Tankard Guest House 40 East Claremont Street Edinburgh EH7 4JR Tel: 0131 556 4218 Fax: 0131 452 8630	APPROVED Listed	2 Twin 1 Double 3 Family	2 Pub Bath/Show	B&B per person £17.00-£21.00 Single £17.00-£21.00 Double	Open Jan-Dec
		Town house convenient for bus route to city centre and within walking distance of Playhouse Theatre.			

Andrea Targett-Adams 27 Heriot Row Edinburgh Midlothian EH3 6EN Tel: 0131 225 9474/220 1699 Fax: 0131 557 4535	DELUXE ♔♔♔	1 Single 1 Twin 1 Double	3 En Suite fac	B&B per person £40.00-£45.00 Single £35.00 Double Room only per person £40.00-£45.00	Open Apr-Oct Dinner 1800-1900 B&B + Eve. Meal £65.00-£70.00
		An elegant Georgian house, a stone's throw from Princes Street. All rooms are luxuriously furnished with bathrooms ensuite.			

Details of Grading and Classification are on page vi. | Key to symbols is on back flap. |

EDINBURGH continued	Map 2 C5

The Thirty-Nine Steps Guest House
62 South Trinity Road, Edinburgh EH5 3NX
Telephone: 0131 552 1349   Fax: 0131 552 7282

Victorian house quietly situated, close to city-centre and Royal Botanic Gardens. All rooms tastefully decorated with colour TV, tea/coffee facilities and full central heating. Traditional Scottish breakfast served. Easy access to main A9 road north. Bed and Breakfast ensuite from £17.50. Easy parking. A warm and friendly welcome is assured from resident proprietors Shirley and Derek Mowat.

The Thirty-Nine Steps Guest House
62 South Trinity Road
Edinburgh
EH5 3NX
Tel: 0131 552 1349
Fax: 0131 552 7282

COMMENDED

1 Single
2 Twin
1 Double
3 Family

3 Pub Bath/Show

B&B per person
£18.00-£22.00 Single
£14.50-£19.50 Double

Open Jan-Dec

Victorian terraced house in quiet residential area.
Convenient bus route for city centre. Unrestricted parking.

Mrs M Thom
Cruachan, 6 Pittville Street
Edinburgh
EH15 2BY
Tel: 0131 669 2195

COMMENDED
Listed

2 Single
1 Twin
1 Double

1 Limited ensuite
2 Pub Bath/Show

B&B per person
£15.00-£18.00 Single
£15.00-£18.00 Double
Room only per person
£12.00-£14.00

Open Apr-Oct

Georgian house close to the beach with Adam room used as guests' lounge.
Good bus service to town centre.

Torivane Guest House
1 Morton Street
Edinburgh
EH15 2EW
Tel: 0131 669 1648

COMMENDED

1 Single
1 Twin
1 Double

1 En Suite fac
1 Pub Bath/Show

B&B per person
£14.00-£18.00 Single
£14.00-£18.00 Double

Open Jan-Nov

Stone-built house on main bus route to city centre.
A one minute walk to beach and seafront promenade.

The Town House
65 Gilmore Place
Edinburgh
EH3 9NU
Tel: 0131 229 1985

HIGHLY COMMENDED

1 Single
2 Twin
1 Double
1 Family

4 En Suite fac
1 Priv. NOT ensuite

B&B per person
£22.00-£30.00 Single
£22.00-£30.00 Double

Open Jan-Dec

A Victorian terraced family house c.1876 in a residential area.
Easy walking distance of West End, Princes Street and King's Theatre.

J Toynbee
21 Dean Park Crescent
Edinburgh
EH4 1PH
Tel: 0131 332 3096

COMMENDED

1 Single
1 Double
1 Family

1 Limited ensuite
1 Priv. NOT ensuite
1 Pub Bath/Show

B&B per person
£17.00-£19.00 Single
£16.50-£18.50 Double
Room only per person
£17.00-£19.00

Open May-Sep

Terraced Georgian house close to city centre. Within walking distance of shops, restaurants and cultural attractions. Refrigerator and microwave in each room.

Mrs June Tulloch
Da Homin
24 Summerside Street
Edinburgh
EH6 4NU
Tel: 0131 554 8652
Fax: 0131 554 8652

COMMENDED
Listed

1 Twin
2 Double

2 Pub Bath/Show

B&B per person
£13.00-£16.00 Single
£10.00-£16.00 Double
Room only per person
£10.00-£16.00

Open Apr-Oct

Victorian house, north of city centre on excellent bus route.
Parking. Friendly atmosphere. All welcome.

| Turret Guest House
8 Kilmaurs Terrace
Edinburgh
EH16 5DR
Tel: 0131 667 6704 | **HIGHLY COMMENDED** | 1 Single
2 Twin
2 Double
1 Family | 4 En Suite fac
2 Pub Bath/Show | B&B per person
£18.00-£26.00 Single
£18.00-£26.00 Double | Open Jan-Dec |

Recently refurbished Victorian house in quiet residential area. Convenient for buses to city centre. Commonwealth Pool nearby.

Villa Nina House
39 LEAMINGTON TERRACE, EDINBURGH EH10 4JS
Telephone and Fax: 0131 229 2644
Very comfortable Victorian terraced house situated in a quiet residential part of the city yet only ten minutes walk to Princes Street, Edinburgh Castle, theatres, shops and major attractions. Some rooms with private showers. TV in all rooms. Full cooked breakfast. Member of STB, GHA & AA.
Bed and Breakfast from £15 per person.

| Villa Nina Guest House
39 Leamington Terrace
Edinburgh
EH10 4JS
Tel: 0131 229 2644
Fax: 0131 229 2644 | **APPROVED**
Listed | 1 Twin
2 Double
1 Family | 3 Limited ensuite
2 Pub Bath/Show | B&B per person
£18.00-£20.00 Single
£15.00-£19.00 Double | Open Jan-Dec |

Terraced house. Approximately 1 mile (2 kms) from city centre. Near King's Theatre, the Castle and shops. Showers in bedrooms.

| Mrs J Williamson
Hopebank,
33 Hope Lane, Portobello
Edinburgh
EH15 2PZ
Tel: 0131 657 1149 | **COMMENDED** | 1 Twin
2 Double | 3 Limited ensuite
1 Pub Bath/Show | B&B per person
£18.00 Single
£18.00 Double | Open Jul-Sep |

19th-century terraced villa in quiet residential area with ample parking. Traditional Scottish hospitality. Good bus service for city centre. Close to beach.

Albion House
6 Templeland Road, Corstorphine, Edinburgh EH12 8RP
Telephone: 0131 539 0840
A friendly welcome along with daily complimentary home baking and biscuits awaits at our comfortable Edwardian family home. Non-smoking, situated three miles west of city centre with fast frequent bus service to town. Three miles from airport with easy access to main touring routes.

| Mrs Wilson
6 Templeland Road
Edinburgh
EH12 8RP
Tel: 0131 539 0840 | **HIGHLY COMMENDED**
Listed | 1 Single
1 Twin
1 Double | 1 En Suite fac
2 Priv. NOT ensuite
1 Pub Bath/Show | B&B per person
£16.00-£20.00 Single
£16.00-£20.00 Double | Open Apr-Oct |

Semi-detached Edwardian sandstone house in peaceful location in west of city. 3 miles (5kms) from airport. Non-smoking house.

| Mr and Mrs R J R Wright
40 Moray Place
Edinburgh
EH3 6BT
Tel: 0131 225 1966
Fax: 0131 220 3966 | **DELUXE** | 1 Twin
2 Double | 2 En Suite fac
1 Priv. NOT ensuite | B&B per person
£45.00-£50.00 Single
£30.00-£35.00 Double | Open Apr-Oct |

Elegant Georgian townhouse peacefully situated overlooking private gardens in central, historic area of the city.

EDZELL **Angus** Mrs J Myles The Gorse, Dunlappie Road Edzell Angus DD9 7UB Tel: (Edzell) 01356 648207 Fax: 01356 648265	**Map 4** F12	**COMMENDED**	1 Single 2 Twin	2 Pub Bath/Show	B&B per person from £14.00 Single from £13.50 Double	Open Jan-Dec	**Quietly situated opposite golf course with open views of hills to rear.** **Home baking and a warm welcome. A non-smoking house.**
ELGIN **Moray** Blackfriars Guest House 8 Trinity Place Elgin Moray IV30 1UL Tel: (Elgin) 01343 541092	**Map 4** D8	**COMMENDED** **Listed**	2 Single 4 Family	4 En Suite fac 2 Priv. NOT ensuite	B&B per person from £18.00 Single from £18.00 Double Room only per person from £18.00	Open Jan-Dec	**Traditional Scottish hospitality in friendly guest house. Ideal for golfing holidays.**
The Lodge Guest House 20 Duff Avenue Elgin Moray IV30 1QS Tel: (Elgin) 01343 549981		**COMMENDED**	4 Single 2 Twin 1 Double 1 Family	8 En Suite fac	B&B per person £17.00-£19.00 Single £16.00-£18.00 Double	Open Jan-Dec	**Recently refurbished Listed villa in extensive grounds with private parking.** **Quietly situated but convenient for all amenities.**
Mr & Mrs H McMillan Belleville 14 South College Street Elgin Moray IV30 1EP Tel: (Elgin) 01343 541515/ 0374 866068 (mobile) Fax: 01343 540033		**COMMENDED** **Listed**	1 Twin 1 Double	2 En Suite fac	B&B per person £17.00-£20.00 Single £16.00-£18.00 Double	Open Jan-Dec	**Personally run pre-war detached villa, with off-street parking.** **A few minutes walk from the town centre and Cathedral. No smoking.**
The Piñes Guest House East Road Elgin Moray IV30 1XG Tel: (Elgin) 01343 542766		**HIGHLY COMMENDED**	2 Double 2 Family	3 En Suite fac 1 Pub Bath/Show	B&B per person £16.00-£25.00 Single £16.00-£20.00 Double	Dinner 1800-1900 B&B + Eve. Meal £24.00-£40.00	**Victorian elegance with modern comforts. Friendly atmosphere.** **Freshly prepared food. Convenient for golf, fishing, Whisky and Castle Trails.**
Mr W G Ross The Bungalow 7 New Elgin Road Elgin Moray IV30 3BE Tel: (Elgin) 01343 542035		**COMMENDED**	1 Single 1 Twin 1 Double	2 Pub Bath/Show	B&B per person £12.50-£15.00 Single £12.50-£15.00 Double	Open Jan-Dec	**Comfortable accommodation in friendly family home on outskirts of city.** **5 minutes from city centre.**
Southbank Guest House 36 Academy Street Elgin Moray IV30 1LP Tel: (Elgin) 01343 547132		**COMMENDED**	2 Single 2 Twin 3 Double 4 Family	2 En Suite fac 3 Pub Bath/Show	B&B per person from £17.00 Single £15.00-£19.00 Double	Open Jan-Dec Dinner from 1800 B&B + Eve. Meal £20.00-£25.00	**Family run, Georgian detached house in quiet residential street.** **5 minutes walk from railway station and town centre.**

 VAT is shown at 17.5%: changes in this rate may affect prices. Prices shown are for guidance only. Please send SAE with each enquiry.

BY ELGIN Moray	Map 4 D8

ARDGYE HOUSE
Elgin, Moray IV30 3UP   Tel/Fax: 01343 850618

ARDGYE HOUSE is a spacious mansion house set in 150 acres, situated close to main Aberdeen to Inverness Road (3.5 miles west of Elgin). Superb accommodation in quiet surroundings. Central position ideal for beaches, golf, riding, fishing, castles and distilleries.

For full details contact Carol and Alistair McInnes.

Ardgye House Elgin Moray IV30 3UP Tel: (Alves) 01343 850618 Fax: 01343 850618	**HIGHLY COMMENDED** 👑👑	1 Single 2 Twin 3 Double 3 Family	3 En Suite fac 3 Limited ensuite 3 Priv. NOT ensuite	B&B per person £16.00-£18.00 Single £16.00-£18.00 Double	Open Jan-Dec

Gracious Edwardian mansion in own extensive grounds easily accessible from A96. 3 miles (5kms) from Elgin. Private facilities available.

Mrs J Goodwin Foresters House, Newton Elgin Moray IV30 3XW Tel: (Elgin) 01343 552862	**COMMENDED** 👑	2 Family	2 Limited ensuite 1 Pub Bath/Show	B&B per person £14.00-£16.00 Double	Open Jan-Dec

Traditional stone-built house in the middle of open countryside. 3 miles (5kms) from Elgin. A Scottish welcome awaits you.

BY ELGOL Isle of Skye, Inverness-shire Strathaird House by Elgol Isle of Skye, Inverness-shire IV49 9AX Tel: (Loch Scavaig) 01471 866269/ 01444 452990 (off season)	Map 3 E10 **APPROVED** Listed	2 Single 1 Double 4 Family	4 Pub Bath/Show	B&B per person £16.20-£25.00 Single £14.40-£23.00 Double	Open Apr-Sep Dinner 1900-2000 B&B + Eve. Meal £27.00-£37.50

Family run guest house in own extensive grounds with views of sea and Cuillins. 10 miles (16 kms) west of Broadford.

ELIE Fife The Elms 14 Park Place Elie Fife KY9 1DH Tel: (Elie) 01333 330404	Map 2 D3 **COMMENDED** 👑👑👑	1 Single 3 Twin 1 Double 2 Family	4 En Suite fac 2 Pub Bath/Show	B&B per person £23.50-£45.00 Single £18.00-£24.50 Double	Open May-Sep Dinner from 1900 B&B + Eve. Meal £28.50-£55.00

Victorian House with walled garden in picturesque coastal village with safe sandy beaches. Ideal base for East Neuk, St Andrews, golf and the many local attractions.

ELLON Aberdeenshire Ashlea House 58 Station Road Ellon Aberdeenshire AB41 9AL Tel: (Ellon) 01358 720263	Map 4 G9 **COMMENDED** 👑	2 Twin	1 Pub Bath/Show	B&B per person £15.00-£17.00 Single £13.50-£15.00 Double Room only per person £12.50-£14.50	Open Jan-Dec

Delightful family run Victorian house, close to local amenities. Handy for Castle and Whisky Trails.

ELLON continued Mr Deans 77 Ness Circle Ellon Aberdeenshire AB41 9BU Tel: (Ellon) 01358 724145	Map 4 G9	COMMENDED Listed	1 Single 1 Twin	1 Pub Bath/Show	B&B per person £14.00-£16.00 Single £14.00-£16.00 Double Room only per person £12.00-£14.00	Open Jan-Dec

In quiet residential area, 5 minutes from town centre, restaurants and shops.
Ideally situated for golf, fishing and riding. Continental breakfast only.

EMBO, by Dornoch **Sutherland** Mrs D Fraser Corven, Station Road Embo, by Dornoch Sutherland IV25 3PT Tel: (Dornoch) 01862 810128	Map 4 B6	APPROVED Listed	1 Double 1 Family	1 Pub Bath/Show	B&B per person £14.00-£16.00 Single to £12.00 Double Room only per person £12.00-£14.00	Open Feb-Nov

Small detached bungalow with fine views across the bay to hills beyond.
Sandy beaches and golf courses nearby.

ETTRICKBRIDGE **Selkirkshire** Mrs S Nixon Oakwood Farm Ettrickbridge, Selkirk Selkirkshire TD7 5HJ Tel: (Selkirk) 01750 52245	Map 2 D7	COMMENDED Listed	1 Twin 1 Double	1 Pub Bath/Show	B&B per person £13.00 Single	Open Jan-Dec

Large spacious farmhouse in quiet rural location on mixed farm 4 miles
(5kms) from Selkirk.

EVIE **Orkney** Woodwick House Evie Orkney KW17 2PQ Tel: (Evie) 01856 751330 Fax: 01856 751383	Map 5 B10	COMMENDED	1 Single 1 Twin 2 Double 1 Family Suites avail	3 En Suite fac 2 Pub Bath/Show	B&B per person £20.00-£33.00 Single £20.00-£33.00 Double	Open Jan-Dec Dinner 1900-2030 B&B + Eve. Meal £33.00-£50.00

Peace and seclusion in idyllic surroundings. 12 acres of wooded grounds
with views to the islands. Imaginative fresh food.

EYEMOUTH **Berwickshire** Mrs McGovern Ebba House, Upper Houndlaw Eyemouth Berwickshire TD14 5BU Tel: (Eyemouth) 018907 50350	Map 2 F5	COMMENDED Listed	2 Single 1 Twin 1 Double	2 Pub Bath/Show	B&B per person £15.00-£16.00 Single £15.00-£16.00 Double	Open Jan-Dec Dinner 1730-1830 B&B + Eve. Meal £23.00-£25.00

Centrally located terraced house in quiet street. Short walk to beach,
harbour and shops. Friendly welcome, home cooking.

Mrs J MacKay Hillcrest, Coldingham Road Eyemouth Berwickshire TD14 5AN Tel: (Eyemouth) 018907 50463		COMMENDED Listed	1 Twin 1 Double	1 Pub Bath/Show	B&B per person £15.00-£16.00 Single £15.00-£16.00 Double	Open Jan-Dec

Pleasantly situated with own garden in residential area of coastal town.
Ideal for touring.

FAIRLIE **Ayrshire** Mrs Gardner Mon Abri, 12 Main Road Fairlie Ayrshire KA29 0DP Tel: (Fairlie) 01475 568241	Map 1 F6	COMMENDED	1 Single 1 Twin 1 Family	1 Pub Bath/Show	B&B per person £16.00 Single to £16.00 Double Room only per person to £16.00	Open Jan-Dec Dinner from 1800 B&B + Eve. Meal £23.50

Detached bungalow on main tourist route, overlooking the Firth of Clyde.
45 minutes by road from Glasgow. Personally run, evening meals available.

FALKIRK	Map 2
Stirlingshire	A4

Darroch House
Camelon Road, Falkirk, Stirlingshire FK1 5SQ
Telephone: (01324) 623041 Fax: (01324) 626288

Darroch House is a small well proportioned Victorian Manor House set in nine acres of garden and woodland. This family home offers friendly relaxed and exceptionally comfortable accommodation in large well appointed guest rooms. Scottish breakfast is served in the original dining room overlooking the tennis lawn and donkey pasture.

Mrs Mitchell	**HIGHLY**	1 Twin	3 En Suite fac	B&B per person	Open Jan-Dec
Darroch House, Camelon Road	**COMMENDED**	2 Double		£40.00-£50.00 Single	Dinner 1900-2100
Falkirk				£25.00-£30.00 Double	B&B + Eve. Meal
Stirlingshire					£55.00-£65.00
FK1 5SG					
Tel: (Falkirk) 01324 623041					
Fax: 01324 626288					

Built in 1838. Family home. Well-proportioned, Victorian manor house, set in 9 acres of garden and woodland in the heart of Falkirk.

Mrs S Taylor	**COMMENDED**	2 Twin	2 Pub Bath/Show	B&B per person	Open Jan-Oct
Wester Carmuirs Farm		1 Double		from £18.00 Single	
Larbert, by Falkirk				from £16.00 Double	
Stirlingshire					
FK5 3NW					
Tel: (Bonnybridge)					
01324 812459					

Family house on working arable and beef farm.
Falkirk leisure centre, 0.5miles (1 km). Bonnybridge 1.5 miles (3kms).
Good base for touring.

FALKLAND	Map 2
Fife	C3

Mrs A Heather	**COMMENDED**	1 Twin	2 En Suite fac	B&B per person	Open Jan-Dec
Ladieburn Cottage, High Street		1 Family		£19.00-£21.00 Single	Dinner 1800-2000
Falkland				£16.00-£18.00 Double	
Fife					
KY15 7BZ					
Tel: (Falkland) 01337 857016					

19th-century house in centre of village opposite the historic Falkland Palace.
Both bedrooms overlook the palace and have ensuite facilities. Dinner available.

Mrs Sarah G McGregor	**COMMENDED**	1 Double	2 Pub Bath/Show	B&B per person	Open Apr-Oct
Templelands Farm		1 Family		from £17.00 Single	Dinner from 1900
Falkland				£15.50-£16.00 Double	B&B + Eve. Meal
Fife					£22.00-£23.00
KY15 7DE					
Tel: (Falkland) 01337 857383					

Farmhouse on side of Lomond Hills with superb views over Howe of Fife.
Home cooking using fresh local produce. 20 miles (32 kms) from St Andrews.

FEARNAN, by Kenmore	Map 2
Perthshire	A1

LETTERELLAN
Fearnan, by Aberfeldy PH15 2NY
Telephone: 01887 830221

Situated in the heart of Scotland with spectacular views over Loch Tay and Ben Lawers, this rose-fronted (non-smoking) house, standing in wooded and rhododendroned grounds, offers tranquillity and a high degree of comfort to visitors. Tourist attractions and a wide range of sporting activities exist within easy reach.

Mr G A MacKay	**COMMENDED**	2 Twin	3 Priv. NOT ensuite	B&B per person	Open Mar-Oct
Letterellan		1 Double		£18.50-£20.00 Double	
Fearnan, by Aberfeldy					
Perthshire					
PH15 2NY					
Tel: (Kenmore) 01887 830221					

Rose-covered house tastefully restored, all bedrooms with private bathrooms.
Superb views over Loch Tay.

FINDHORN
Moray

Mrs E Cowie
Heath House
Findhorn
Moray
IV36 0YY
Tel: (Findhorn) 01309 691082
Fax: 01309 691082

Map 4
C7

HIGHLY COMMENDED
Listed

1 Twin   1 En Suite fac
2 Double   1 Pub Bath/Show

B&B per person
£17.50-£20.00 Single
£16.00-£18.00 Double

Open Feb-Oct
Dinner 1800-1900
B&B + Eve. Meal
£24.00-£32.00

Modern house in secluded setting on outskirts of Findhorn close to beach.
Warm and friendly welcome.

FIONNPHORT
Isle of Mull, Argyll

Map 1
C2

DINNER, BED AND BREAKFAST
SEAVIEW

Fionnphort, Isle of Mull PA66 6BL   Tel: 01681 700235

Traditional Scottish granite house with spectacular 'seaviews' overlooking Iona
Sound. Two minutes walk from Iona and Staffa ferries. Warm and comfortable.
Sitting room with log fire. Well-appointed rooms. Home cooking, friendly
welcome. Pub and shop nearby.

B & B £12-£15 per person. Private facilities available. Private parking.

Mrs Noddings
Seaview
Fionnphort
Isle of Mull, Argyll
PA66 6BL
Tel: (Fionnphort) 01681 700235

COMMENDED

2 Twin   1 En Suite fac
2 Double   2 Pub Bath/Show

B&B per person
£17.00-£20.00 Single
£12.00-£15.00 Double

Open Jan-Dec
Dinner 1830-1930
B&B + Eve. Meal
£22.00-£30.00

Granite-built house with views over the Sound of Iona and only 3 minutes
walk to Iona and Staffa ferries. Friendly atmosphere. Private facilities.

Dungrianach Bed & Breakfast

Fionnphort, Isle of Mull, Argyll, PA66 6BL   Tel: 01681 700417

*Dungrianach offers comfortable accommodation and a relaxed
friendly atmosphere. Cosy guest sittingroom with open fire,
reference books and guides. Good breakfast, idyllic location.
An ideal base for exploring beautiful unspoilt Mull and
historic Iona. Good pub food nearby. Boat trips to Staffa,
Treshnish Isles, Iona from village pier.*

Ms A Rimell
Dungrianach
Fionnphort
Isle of Mull, Argyll
PA66 6BL
Tel: (Fionnphort) 01681 700417

COMMENDED

2 Twin   2 En Suite fac

B&B per person
£18.00-£20.00 Single
£16.00 Double

Open Jan-Dec

Comfortable, friendly cottage. Enviable location above sandy beach
with views to Iona. Ferry 3 minutes walk away.

BY FOCHABERS
Moray

Mrs Mary K Shand
Castlehill Cottage, Blackdam
Fochabers
Moray
IV32 7LJ
Tel: (Fochabers) 01343 820761

Map 4
E8

COMMENDED

1 Twin   2 Pub Bath/Show
1 Family

B&B per person
from £14.00 Single
from £12.00 Double
Room only per person
from £9.00

Open Jan-Dec

Family cottage set back from A96, with own flower garden
and ample parking 6 miles (10kms) east of Elgin.

FORFAR
Angus

Mrs M Graham
Cosy Neuk, 41 Westfield Loan
Forfar
Angus DD8 1EJ
Tel: (Forfar) 01307 464553

Map 2
D1

COMMENDED
Listed

2 Twin   2 En Suite fac
1 Family   1 Pub Bath/Show

B&B per person
£20.00-£25.00 Single
£15.00-£18.00 Double

Open Jan-Dec

"Cosy Neuk" describes it all. With excellent facilities, will haste ye back to Forfar.

Farmhouse Bed & Breakfast

WEST MAINS OF TURIN, FORFAR DD8 2TE
Telephone: 01307 830229 Fax: 01307 830229

Family run stock farm has a panoramic view over Rescobie Loch. Warm welcome awaits you. Good home cooking and baking ensures guests have an enjoyable stay. Ideal area for golfing (20 mins from Carnoustie), hillwalking, horse-riding, visiting Castles, National Trust properties and gardens. Snooker for evening entertainment.

Mrs C Jolly West Mains of Turin Rescobie, Forfar Angus DD8 2TE Tel: (Aberlemno) 01307 830229	**COMMENDED** 👑👑	1 Single 1 Double 1 Family	1 En Suite fac 1 Priv. NOT ensuite 1 Pub Bath/Show	B&B per person £14.00-£17.00 Single £14.00-£17.00 Double	Open Mar-Oct Dinner 1800-1830 B&B + Eve. Meal £22.00-£25.00

Farmhouse on working stock farm 4 miles (6kms) east of Forfar.
In elevated position with fine views southwards over Rescobie Loch.

WEMYSS FARM

Montrose Road, Forfar DD8 2TB   Tel/Fax: Forfar 01307 462887

Situated 2¹/₂ miles along the B9113, our 190-acre farm has a wide variety of animals. Glamis Castle nearby. Many other castles etc. within easy reach. Ideal touring base for Glens, Dundee, Perth, St Andrews, Aberdeen, Edinburgh, Balmoral, Deeside and East Coast resorts. Hillwalking, shooting, golf and fishing nearby. Children welcome.

A warm welcome awaits!

Mrs D Lindsay Wemyss Farm, Montrose Road Forfar Angus DD8 2TB Tel: (Forfar) 01307 462887 Fax: 01307 462887	**COMMENDED** **Listed**	1 Double 1 Family	2 Pub Bath/Show	B&B per person £17.00-£18.00 Single £14.00-£15.00 Double	Open Jan-Dec Dinner 1800-1930 B&B + Eve. Meal from £22.50

Family farmhouse on working farm. Centrally situated for touring Angus
and east coast. Home cooking and baking. Children welcome.

BY FORFAR **Angus** Mrs J McKenzie Quarrybank Cottage Balgavies, by Forfar Angus DD8 2TF Tel: (Aberlemmo) 01307 830303	Map 2 D1	**HIGHLY COMMENDED** 👑👑👑	3 Double	2 En Suite fac 1 Priv. NOT ensuite	B&B per person £20.00-£25.00 Single £18.00-£20.00 Double	Open Mar-Oct, Xmas/New Year Dinner 1900-2100 B&B + Eve. Meal £27.00-£29.00

Family home in peaceful rural location, 4.5 miles (7km) east of Forfar.
Woodland garden. Private parking. Home cooking using local produce.

Mrs P M Powell Broadlands, Loanhead by Forfar Angus DD8 1XF Tel: (Forfar) 01307 462059	**COMMENDED** 👑	1 Single 1 Twin	1 En Suite fac 1 Priv. NOT ensuite	B&B per person £15.00-£18.00 Single £15.00-£18.00 Double	Open Jan-Dec Dinner 1900-1930 B&B + Eve. Meal £23.00-£26.00

Comfortable modern house in peaceful rural situation with lovely views
over countryside and hills.

BY FORFAR continued	Map 2 D1

FINAVON FARMHOUSE

Finavon, by Forfar, Angus DD8 3PX
Telephone: 01307 850269

A warm welcome awaits friends both old and new, in comfort and ease let the Romes cosset you, with good food to tempt taste buds and a large garden to view.
Let our Finavon Farmhouse be your next holiday venue.

Mrs L Rome Finavon Farmhouse Finavon, by Forfar Angus DD8 3PX Tel: (Finavon) 01307 850269	HIGHLY COMMENDED ♛♛♛	2 Twin 1 Double	3 En Suite fac	B&B per person £15.50-£21.00 Single £15.50-£16.50 Double	Open Feb-Nov Dinner 1830-2000 B&B + Eve. Meal £24.00-£29.50	

Warm welcome assured in this modern house in extensive secluded grounds at foot of Finavon Hill. Offers excellent facilities. Good base for touring.

FORRES **Moray**	Map 4 C8				
Mr Brian Atkiss Clifton House, Caroline Street Forres IV36 0AQ Tel: (Forres) 01309 673440 Fax: 01309 673440	COMMENDED Listed	1 Twin 1 Double 1 Family	1 En Suite fac 2 Pub Bath/Show	B&B per person £13.50-£15.50 Double	Open Jan-Dec	

Large house in central Forres. Family run and convenient for all local amenities.

Mrs Catherine M Bain Springfield, Croft Road Forres Moray IV36 0JS Tel: (Forres) 01309 676965 Fax: 01309 673376	HIGHLY COMMENDED ♛♛	1 Double 1 Family	1 En Suite fac 1 Priv. NOT ensuite 1 Pub Bath/Show	B&B per person £18.00-£22.00 Single £15.00-£17.50 Double	Open Jan-Dec	

Large comfortable modern home set in own grounds. Non-smoking house.

Mrs Jacqueline S Banks April Rise, 16 Forbes Road Forres Moray IV36 0HP Tel: (Forres) 01309 674066	COMMENDED Listed	1 Single 1 Twin 1 Family	2 En Suite fac 1 Pub Bath/Show	B&B per person £15.00-£16.50 Single £14.00-£16.50 Double	Open Jan-Dec Dinner 1800-1900 B&B + Eve. Meal £19.00-£21.50	

Traditional Scottish hospitality in friendly family home. Ideal touring base.

Russell House

RUSSELL PLACE, FORRES, MORAY IV36 0BL
Telephone: 01309 672455

Visit our unique home and relish the wide choice of delicious breakfasts. Stroll to award-winning parks and restaurants, or enjoy the superb coastline, castles and nearby golf courses. Our spacious heated bedrooms all have electric blankets, drinks, colour TVs and luxurious bathrooms. *Discounts available.* **Ring now for details.**

Judith Binney Russell House, Russell Place Forres Moray IV36 0BL Tel: (Forres) 01309 672455	COMMENDED ♛♛	1 Twin 1 Double	1 En Suite fac 1 Priv. NOT ensuit	B&B per person £16.00-£19.00 Double	Open Jan-Dec	

Lovely old family home quietly situated only yards from beautiful Grant Park and Forres High Street. Ensuite bathroom available.

Mr and Mrs B MacDonald The Pines, Victoria Road Forres Moray IV36 0BN Tel: (Forres) 01309 673810		**COMMENDED** Listed	1 Twin 1 Family	1 En Suite fac 1 Priv. NOT ensuite	B&B per person £15.00-£17.50 Double	Open Jan-Dec
			Traditional Victorian terraced house. Original features throughout. Convenient for town amenities.			
Mrs L Ross 11 High Street Forres Moray IV36 0BU Tel: (Forres) 01309 673837		**COMMENDED** 👑👑	1 Twin 2 Double	1 En Suite fac 2 Pub Bath/Show	B&B per person £20.00-£25.00 Single £14.00-£20.00 Double	Open Apr-Oct
			Relax in pleasant comfortable surroundings overlooking prize-winning gardens. Friendly service and full Scottish breakfast.			
BY FORRES **Moray** Mrs Flora Barclay Moss-Side Farm, Rafford Forres Moray IV36 0SL Tel: (Forres) 01309 672954	Map 4 C8	**COMMENDED** Listed	1 Twin 1 Double 1 Family	1 Pub Bath/Show	B&B per person £12.00-£13.00 Single £12.00-£13.00 Double	Open May-Sep Dinner from 1900 B&B + Eve. Meal £22.00-£23.00
			Traditional farmhouse with modern extension set in 28 acres on the outskirts of Forres. Ideal for golf, fishing and walking.			
Mrs Angela Fowler Invercairn House, Brodie Forres Moray IV36 0TD Tel: (Brodie) 01309 641261		**COMMENDED** 👑	2 Single 2 Twin 1 Family	2 Pub Bath/Show	B&B per person £12.00-£16.00 Single £12.00-£16.00 Double	Open Jan-Dec Dinner 1800-2100 B&B + Eve. Meal from £18.00
			Intriguing former Victorian railway station adjacent to Brodie Castle. Excellent touring base. Local produce, deliciously prepared. Warm, comfortable and friendly atmosphere.			
Mrs Elizabeth J Masson Gateside Farm Alves, Forres Moray IV36 0RB Tel: (Alves) 01343 850246		**HIGHLY** **COMMENDED** 👑👑	1 Twin 1 Double 1 Family	1 Priv. NOT ensuite 2 Pub Bath/Show	B&B per person £20.00-£25.00 Single £16.00-£20.00 Double	Open Apr-Oct
			A friendly welcome, home baking and personal attention await our guests. Well-appointed comfortable accommodation. Conveniently situated.			
FORT AUGUSTUS **Inverness-shire** Mairi MacIver Fort Augustus Abbey Fort Augustus Inverness-shire PH32 4BD Tel: (Fort Augustus) 01320 366233 Fax: 01320 366228	Map 4 A10	**APPROVED** Listed	12 Single 16 Twin 1 Family	8 Pub Bath/Show	B&B per person £11.50-£15.00 Single £8.00-£11.00 Double Room only per person £8.00-£11.00	Open Jan-Dec Dinner 1730-2000 B&B + Eve. Meal £17.50-£21.50
			A unique experience staying in a former Benedictine public school. Fascinating historical tour open to the public.			
Mrs J MacKenzie The Old Pier Fort Augustus Inverness-shire PH32 4BX Tel: (Fort Augustus) 01320 366418 Fax: 01320 366770		**COMMENDED** 👑👑👑	1 Twin 1 Double 1 Family	3 En Suite fac	B&B per person £25.00-£40.00 Single £20.00-£25.00 Double	Open Apr-Oct Dinner 1800-2000 B&B + Eve. Meal £32.50-£53.50
			50-acre farm by Loch Ness with panoramic views. Highland cattle; riding, boating and fishing available. No smoking.			

FORT AUGUSTUS continued — Map 4 A10

J G Nairn
Appin, Inverness Road
Fort Augustus
Inverness-shire
PH32 4DH
Tel: (Fort Augustus)
01320 366541

COMMENDED

1 Twin / 2 Double — 1 En Suite fac / 1 Pub Bath/Show — B&B per person £13.00-£18.00 Double — Open Apr-Oct

Detached modern bungalow on the edge of a small village.
Ideal base for touring the Highlands.

Mrs L H Service
Sonas
Fort Augustus
Inverness-shire
PH32 4DH
Tel: (Fort Augustus)
01320 366291

HIGHLY COMMENDED

1 Twin / 1 Double / 1 Family — 2 En Suite fac / 1 Priv. NOT ensuite — B&B per person £13.00-£17.00 Double — Open Jan-Dec

Modern house in elevated position on the northern edge of the village,
with excellent views of surrounding hills.

Mr Chris Stephenson
Greystones, Station Road
Fort Augustus
Inverness-shire
PH32 4AY
Tel: (Fort Augustus)
01320 366390

APPROVED Listed

1 Twin / 2 Double — 2 Pub Bath/Show — B&B per person £10.00-£12.50 Single £10.00-£12.50 Double — Open Jan-Dec

Economical Bed and Breakfast by Loch Ness.
Centrally situated for touring the Highlands.

FORTINGALL — Perthshire — Map 2 A1

Mrs Tulloch
Fendoch
Fortingall
Perthshire
PH15 2LL
Tel: (Kenmore) 01887 830322

COMMENDED

1 Twin / 1 Double / 1 Family — 2 En Suite fac / 1 Priv. NOT ensuite / 1 Pub Bath/Show — B&B per person £15.00-£17.00 Single £15.00-£17.00 Double — Open Jan-Dec, Dinner 1800-2200, B&B + Eve. Meal £26.00-£30.00

A warm welcome and home cooking at this house in quiet attractive village
at foot of Glen Lyon. An ideal base for touring and outdoor activities.

FORT WILLIAM — Inverness-shire — Map 3 H12

Achintee Farm Guest House
Glen Nevis
Fort William
Inverness-shire
PH33 6TE
Tel: (Fort William)
01397 702240/705899
Fax: 01397 702240

COMMENDED

1 Single / 1 Twin / 3 Double — 2 En Suite fac / 1 Pub Bath/Show — B&B per person £16.00-£20.00 Single — Open Jan-Dec, Dinner from 1900, B&B + Eve. Meal to £28.00

Farmhouse in Glen Nevis, at the start of the path to Ben Nevis and the
end of the West Highland Way. About 2 miles (3 kms) from town centre.

Mrs E Brady
24 Henderson Row
Fort William
Inverness-shire
PH33 6HT
Tel: (Fort William)
01397 702711

COMMENDED Listed

1 Single / 2 Twin — 1 Pub Bath/Show — B&B per person £13.00-£15.00 Single — Open Jan-Dec, Dinner 1800-1900, B&B + Eve. Meal £16.00-£18.00

In quite cul-de-sac, ten minutes from town.
Good food plus both rooms with colour TV and tea-making.

Mrs B Cameron
Rodane, Badabrie
Banavie, Fort William
Inverness-shire
PH33 7LX
Tel: (Corpach) 01397 772603

COMMENDED

1 Single / 2 Family — 1 Priv. NOT ensuite / 2 Pub Bath/Show — B&B per person from £15.00 Single from £15.00 Double — Open Jan-Dec, Dinner from 1800, B&B + Eve. Meal from £22.00

Modern house in quiet residential area 3 miles (5kms) from Fort William.
Fine views to Ben Nevis and Loch Linnhe.

Mrs N Cameron Bardnaclavan, 17 Sutherland Avenue Fort William Inverness-shire PH33 6JS Tel: (Fort William) 01397 704678	COMMENDED Listed	1 Single 1 Twin 1 Family	1 Pub Bath/Show	B&B per person £14.00-£16.00 Single £13.00-£14.00 Double	Open Easter-Oct	
		Family home affording splendid views over Loch Linnhe. 1 mile (2kms) from town centre. Non-smoking.				
Mrs Fiona Campbell Leasona Torlundy, Fort William Inverness-shire PH33 6SW Tel: (Fort William) 01397 704661	COMMENDED	1 Twin 2 Double	1 Pub Bath/Show	B&B per person £13.50 Single £13.50 Double Room only per person £16.00	Open Jan-Dec	
		Modern family home in super glen setting, views to Ben Nevis. Ideal base for hillwalking, birdwatching, ponytrekking and Aonach Mor.				

THE GRANGE

**Grange Road, Fort William
Inverness-shire PH33 6JF
Telephone: 01397 705516**

A charming house dating back to 1884, sympathetically refurbished to a very high standard yet still retaining many of its original features. Situated in its own grounds overlooking Loch Linnhe, yet only 10 mins walk from the town centre, it offers a warm and friendly atmosphere and is a peaceful retreat in which to relax. All rooms have private facilities and the lounge, which is filled with books and fresh flowers, offers fine views of the loch and hills. A large varied breakfast menu is served and vegetarians are catered for.

A colour brochure is available on request.

Mrs J Campbell The Grange, Grange Road Fort William Inverness-shire PH33 6JF Tel: (Fort William) 01397 705516	DELUXE	3 Double	3 En Suite fac	B&B per person £25.00-£32.00 Double	Open Apr-Oct	
		Late Victorian house sympathetically renovated within easy walking distance of Fort William (10 minutes). Views over Loch Linnhe.				
Mrs F A Cook Melantee, Achintore Road Fort William Inverness-shire PH33 6RW Tel: (Fort William) 01397 705329	COMMENDED	1 Single 1 Twin 1 Double 1 Family	2 Pub Bath/Show	B&B per person £13.00-£15.00 Single £13.00-£15.00 Double Room only per person £10.00-£12.00	Open Jan-Dec	
		Bungalow 1.5 miles (3kms) from town centre, overlooking the shores of Loch Linnhe and the Ardgour hills and on the main A82 road.				
Craig Nevis Guest House Belford Road Fort William Inverness-shire PH33 6BU Tel: (Fort William) 01397 702023	COMMENDED	1 Twin 3 Double 2 Family	2 Pub Bath/Show	B&B per person from £13.00 Single	Open Jan-Dec	
		Personally run guest house. Short distance from town centre, swimming pool and all amenities.				

FORT WILLIAM continued	Map 3 H12						

Crolinnhe Grange Road Fort William Inverness-shire PH33 6JF Tel: (Fort William) 01397 702709	DELUXE 👑👑	1 Twin 4 Double	3 En Suite fac 1 Priv. NOT ensuite 1 Pub Bath/Show	B&B per person £25.00-£32.00 Double	Open Mar-Nov	

Family run detached Victorian villa c1880, refurbished to a high standard. Friendly and welcoming atmosphere. Large colourful garden. Superb views.

VORINGFOSS

5 Stirling Place, Fort William PH33 6UW   Tel: 01397 704062

Highland hospitality at its best for those who prefer a quiet situation within one mile of the town centre. Landscaped garden affords panoramic views to surrounding hills. An ideal centre from which to explore the West Highlands. Private parking and easy access to local bus route. Special diets catered for.

Mr & Mrs Fraser Voringfoss, 5 Stirling Place Fort William Inverness-shire PH33 6UW Tel: (Fort William) 01397 704062	HIGHLY COMMENDED 👑👑	1 Single 1 Twin 1 Double	2 En Suite fac 2 Pub Bath/Show	B&B per person £14.00-£30.00 Single £14.00-£24.00 Double	Open Jan-Dec	

Modern family home in quiet residential area 1 mile (2kms) from town centre. On main bus route.

Glenlochy Guest House

Nevis Bridge, Fort William
Inverness-shire PH33 6PF
Telephone: 01397 702909

This comfortable, family-run guest house is situated in its own spacious grounds, overlooking the River Nevis close to Ben Nevis, 3/4 mile from town centre. It is an ideal base for touring. Eight of the 10 rooms are en-suite. Colour TV and tea/coffee facilities in all rooms. Private parking.

For brochure and details contact Mrs MacBeth.

Glenlochy Guest House Nevis Bridge Fort William Inverness-shire PH33 6PF Tel: (Fort William) 01397 702909	COMMENDED 👑👑	4 Twin 4 Double 2 Family	8 En Suite fac 1 Pub Bath/Show	B&B per person £16.00-£22.00 Single £15.00-£22.00 Double Room only per person £16.00-£22.00	Open Jan-Dec	

Detached house with garden situated at Nevis Bridge, midway between Ben Nevis and the town centre. 0.5 miles (1km) to railway station. 2 annexe rooms.

Glen Shiel Guest House Achintore Road Fort William Inverness-shire PH33 6RW Tel: (Fort William) 01397 702271	COMMENDED 👑👑	1 Twin 3 Double 1 Family	2 En Suite fac 1 Priv. NOT ensuite 2 Pub Bath/Show	B&B per person £15.00-£18.00 Double	Open Apr-Oct	

Modern house on the outskirts of the town with excellent views over Loch Linnhe. Good touring base.

Guisachan House Alma Road Fort William Inverness-shire PH33 6HA Tel: (Fort William) 01397 703797/704447	COMMENDED 👑👑👑	2 Single 5 Twin 6 Double 3 Family	15 En Suite fac 1 Priv. NOT ensuite	B&B per person £17.00-£25.00 Single £17.00-£25.00 Double	Open Jan-Dec Dinner from 1830 B&B + Eve. Meal £25.00-£34.00	

Family run establishment within easy walking distance of town centre, rail and bus stations. Home cooking. Some annexe accommodation.

Westhaven

Achintore Road, Fort William PH33 6RW
Telephone: 01397 705500

Magnificent situation overlooking Loch Linnhe and surrounding hills.
All bedrooms are tastefully decorated with private facilities, colour TV and
hospitality tray. There is a comfortable residents' lounge, pleasant garden
and ample parking. Perfect base for touring.

Open all year   **HIGHLY COMMENDED** 👑👑

Mrs E Hamill Westhaven, Achintore Road Fort William Inverness-shire PH33 6RW Tel: (Fort William) 01397 705500	HIGHLY COMMENDED 👑👑	1 Twin 2 Double	3 En Suite fac	B&B per person £18.00-£22.00 Single £17.50-£21.00 Double	Open Jan-Dec	

Modern detached house overlooking Loch Linnhe with all facilities
and ample parking. Town centre 1.5 miles (2.4kms).

Mrs Ann Hearmon Balcarres, Seafield Gardens Fort William Inverness-shire PH33 6RJ Tel: (Fort William) 01397 702377	COMMENDED 👑👑	1 Twin 1 Double 1 Family	3 En Suite fac	B&B per person £16.00-£20.00 Single £15.00-£18.00 Double	Open Jan-Oct	

Modern newly-built family home in quiet area.
Excellent views across the loch. Close to the town centre.

ASHBURN HOUSE

Achintore Road, Fort William PH33 6RQ
Tel: 01397 706000 Fax: 01397 706000

Enjoy the comfortable luxury of a unique no-
smoking private hotel specialising in B&B. Set in
private grounds yet only 5 mins. from town centre.
Full central heating, private facilities, tea-making
hospitality tray, TV. Free private parking. This is
an excellent base for touring the Highlands
(Oban, Mallaig, Inverness all nearby) or leave your
car and day trip to Mallaig by steam train
(summer only) or take coach tours, boat trips or
mountain gondola.

AA QQQQQ RAC Highly acclaimed.

Deluxe 👑👑
Contact: A W Henderson for brochure.
B&B £25 to £33 – weekly from £130.

T B Henderson, Ashburn House Achintore Road Fort William Inverness-shire PH33 6RQ Tel: (Fort William) 01397 706000 Fax: 01397 706000	DELUXE 👑👑	2 Single 1 Twin 3 Double 1 Family	7 En Suite fac	B&B per person £25.00-£33.00 Single £25.00-£33.00 Double	Open Feb-Nov	

Family run totally refurbished Victorian villa in its own grounds,
with magnificent views across the loch. Near to town centre.

Details of Grading and Classification are on page vi.   Key to symbols is on back flap.

FORT WILLIAM continued	Map 3 H12				

Hillview Guest House
Achintore Road
Fort William
Inverness-shire
PH33 6RW
Tel: (Fort William)
01397 704349

COMMENDED

1 Single
2 Twin
4 Double
1 Family

4 En Suite fac
2 Pub Bath/Show

B&B per person
£15.00-£18.00 Single
£15.00-£18.00 Double

Open Jan-Dec

Family run guest house overlooking Loch Linnhe and about 1.5 miles (2.5kms) from Fort William.

Mrs A R Lee
Leesholme, Cameron Road
Fort William
Inverness-shire
PH33 6LH
Tel: (Fort William)
01397 704204

COMMENDED Listed

1 Twin
2 Double

1 Pub Bath/Show

B&B per person
£14.00-£15.00 Single
£13.00-£14.00 Double

Open May-Sep

Modern family home in quiet residential area above the town. Short walk from town centre. Off-street parking. Non-smoking.

Lochan Cottage Guest House
Lochyside, by Fort William
Inverness-shire
PH33
Tel: (Fort William)
01397 702695

COMMENDED

1 Twin
5 Double

4 En Suite fac
2 Priv. NOT ensuite
1 Pub Bath/Show

B&B per person
£12.00-£19.00 Single

Open Jan-Dec
Dinner from 1800
B&B + Eve. Meal
£21.00-£28.00

Friendly guest house in quiet location; Fort William 2 miles (3kms). Large garden with views of Ben Nevis and Aonach Mor. German, Dutch and French spoken.

Lochiel Villa Guest House
Achintore Road
Fort William
Inverness-shire
PH33 6RQ
Tel: (Fort William)
01397 703616

COMMENDED

1 Twin
6 Double
1 Family

3 En Suite fac
3 Pub Bath/Show

B&B per person
£15.00-£25.00 Double

Open Feb-Nov

Granite semi-villa with open views over Loch Linnhe. 500 yards (450m) from town centre.

LOCHVIEW GUEST HOUSE
Heathercroft Road, Fort William PH33 6RE
Telephone/Fax: 01397 703149
Lochview is situated on the hillside above the town in a quiet location with panoramic views over Loch Linnhe and the Ardgour Hills. All bedrooms are tastefully decorated and have private facilities, colour TV and tea/coffee facilities. There is a large garden and private parking.

Lochview Guest House
Heathercroft, off Argyll Terrace
Fort William
Inverness-shire
PH33 6RE
Tel: (Fort William)
01397 703149
Fax: 01397 703149

COMMENDED

1 Single
2 Twin
5 Double

8 En Suite fac

B&B per person
£23.00-£28.00 Single
£18.00-£21.00 Double

Open Apr-Oct

Situated on a hillside above the town giving panoramic views over Loch Linnhe and the Ardgour Hills. Non-smoking house.

Mrs T MacDonald
Dorlin, Cameron Road
Fort William
Inverness-shire
PH33 6LJ
Tel: (Fort William)
01397 702016

COMMENDED

2 Double

2 En Suite fac

B&B per person
£16.00-£19.00 Double

Open Jan-Dec

Modern bungalow in elevated position in quiet residential area close to town centre. Fine views over Loch Linnhe.

Mrs Mary MacLean
Innishfree
Lochyside, by Fort William
Inverness-shire
PH33 7NX
Tel: (Fort William)
01397 705471

COMMENDED

1 Double
1 Family

2 En Suite fac

B&B per person
£15.00-£18.00 Single

Open Jan-Nov

Modern family home, with open outlook towards Ben Nevis and Aonach Mor. Open all year; private parking.

VAT is shown at 17.5%: changes in this rate may affect prices. Prices shown are for guidance only. Please send SAE with each enquiry.

| Mrs J MacLeod
Rustic View
Lochyside, by Fort William
Inverness-shire
PH33 7NX
Tel: (Fort William)
01397 704709 | **HIGHLY COMMENDED** 👑👑 | 2 Double | 2 En Suite fac | B&B per person
£16.00-£19.00 Double | Open Apr-Oct | |

Modern family home in large garden. Short way from town centre and all amenities. Panoramic mountain views.

| Mrs Mooney
Ben Nevis View
Corpach, by Fort William
Inverness-shire
PH33 7JH
Tel: (Corpach) 01397 772131 | **COMMENDED** 👑👑 | 1 Double
1 Family | 2 En Suite fac | B&B per person
£13.00-£17.00 Double | Open Mar-Oct | |

Modern house near to Fort William and Caledonian Canal, on Road to the Isles. Beautiful view of Ben Nevis.

| Heather & Charles Moore
Abrach House
4 Caithness Place
Fort William
Inverness-shire
PH33 6JP
Tel: (Fort William)
01397 702535 | **COMMENDED** 👑 | 1 Single
1 Double
1 Family | 2 Pub Bath/Show | B&B per person
£13.00-£16.00 Single
£13.00-£16.00 Double | Open Jan-Oct | |

Modern house in elevated position with excellent views over Fort William and surrounding hills and loch.

| V Moreland
Dalbreac, Mallaig Road
Corpach, by Fort William
Inverness-shire
PH33 7JR
Tel: (Corpach) 01397 772309 | **COMMENDED** 👑👑 | 1 Twin
2 Double | 2 En Suite fac
1 Priv. NOT ensuite | B&B per person
£18.00-£20.00 Single
£15.00-£18.00 Double | Open Apr-Oct | |

Bungalow on the Road to the Isles. Homely atmosphere. Evening meal on request. Home cooking and baking.

| Orchy Villa Guest House
Alma Road
Fort William
Inverness-shire
PH33 6HA
Tel: (Fort William)
01397 702445 | **COMMENDED** 👑 | 1 Twin
2 Double
1 Family | 4 Pub Bath/Show | B&B per person
£12.00-£15.00 Single
£12.00-£15.00 Double
Room only per person
£12.00-£15.00 | Open Jan-Dec | |

Personally run quiet house close to town centre, swimming pool and leisure centre. Short distance to bus and railway station. Panoramic views.

| Rhu Mhor Guest House
Alma Road
Fort William
Inverness-shire
PH33 6BP
Tel: (Fort William)
01397 702213 | **COMMENDED** Listed | 3 Twin
3 Double
1 Family | 2 Pub Bath/Show | B&B per person
£16.50-£17.00 Single
£16.50-£17.00 Double | Open Apr-Oct
Dinner from 1900
B&B + Eve. Meal
£26.00-£27.00 | |

Large family house with extensive wild garden in quiet area above town. Short distance from town centre and all amenities.

| Mrs Sweeney
Kintail, Seafield Gardens
Fort William
Inverness-shire
PH33 6RJ
Tel: (Fort William)
01397 702942
Fax: 01397 700344 | **COMMENDED** 👑👑 | 1 Twin
2 Double | 3 En Suite fac | B&B per person
£14.00-£18.00 Single
£14.00-£18.00 Double
Room only per person
£12.00-£14.00 | Open Mar-Oct | |

Modern family house in quiet, residential street, 1 mile (2 kms) from town centre. Extensive views across loch to hills beyond.

| Mrs Turner
Corrie View
Lochyside, by Fort William
Inverness-shire
PH33 7NX
Tel: (Fort William)
01397 703608 | **COMMENDED** 👑👑 | 1 Twin
2 Double | 2 En Suite fac
1 Priv. NOT ensuite | B&B per person
from £15.00 Single | Open Jan-Dec | |

Detached family home in quiet residential area 2 miles (3kms) from Fort William. Convenient for touring West Coast.

FORT WILLIAM continued	Map 3 H12

Ardmory

VICTORIA ROAD, FORT WILLIAM PH33 6BH
Telephone: 01397 705943

Ardmory is open all year with one twin, two double and three with private facilities. Modern house in quiet, residential area only 3 minutes walk from Town Centre. Fine views over Loch Linnhe and surrounding hills.

SINGLE: £16 - £24   TWIN and DOUBLE: £16 - £22

Mrs Varley
Ardmory, Victoria Road
Fort William
Inverness-shire
PH33 6BH
Tel: (Fort William)
01397 705943

COMMENDED 🏵️🏵️

1 Twin
2 Double

2 En Suite fac
1 Priv. NOT ensuite
1 Pub Bath/Show

B&B per person
£16.00-£24.00 Single
£16.00-£22.00 Double
Room only per person
£16.00-£22.00

Open Jan-Dec

Modern family home in quiet residential street.
Short walk from town centre and all amenities.

Mrs Walker
Viewfield House, Alma Road
Fort William
Inverness-shire
PH33 6HD
Tel: (Fort William)
01397 704763

COMMENDED 🏵️

3 Family

2 Pub Bath/Show

B&B per person
£15.00-£18.00 Single
£12.00-£16.00 Double
Room only per person
£13.00-£16.00

Open Jan-Dec

Family house in elevated location set above Fort William yet within
walking distance of town centre. Private parking available.

Mrs Wiseman
17 Mossfield Drive, Lochyside
Fort William
Inverness-shire
PH33 7PE
Tel: (Fort William)
01397 703502

COMMENDED
Listed

1 Single
1 Twin
1 Double

1 En Suite fac
1 Pub Bath/Show

B&B per person
£16.00-£17.00 Single
Room only per person
£16.00-£17.00

Open Apr-Oct

Modern bungalow set in quiet residential area 2.5 miles (4kms)
outside Fort William. Restaurants and hotels nearby.

Mrs R Wynne
St Andrews East, Fassfern Road
Fort William
Inverness-shire
PH33 6BD
Tel: (Fort William)
01397 702337

COMMENDED 🏵️🏵️

1 Twin
2 Double

2 Pub Bath/Show

B&B per person
£16.00-£17.00 Single

Open May-Oct

Scottish, Baronial-style house dating from 1880.
In centre of town – convenient for all amenities. Private parking.

BY FORT WILLIAM Inverness-shire	Map 3 H12

Mrs Cameron
Strone Farm, by Muirshearlich
Banavie, Fort William
Inverness-shire
PH33 7PB
Tel: (Spean Bridge)
01397 712773

COMMENDED 🏵️🏵️🏵️

2 Double

2 En Suite fac

B&B per person
£22.00 Single
£17.00 Double

Open Jan-Sep
Dinner from 1900
B&B + Eve. Meal
£27.00-£32.00

Farmhouse situated on working farm overlooking the Caledonian Canal
with magnificent view towards Ben Nevis. 7 miles (12kms) north of Fort William.

Mrs Davie
Carinbrook
Banavie, by Fort William
Inverness-shire
PH33 7LX
Tel: (Corpach) 01397 772318

COMMENDED 🏵️🏵️🏵️

1 Twin
2 Double

2 En Suite fac
2 Pub Bath/Show

B&B per person
from £20.00 Single
from £17.00 Double

Open Jan-Nov
Dinner 1830-1930
B&B + Eve. Meal
£23.00-£25.00

Modern family house, 4 miles (6 kms) from Fort William.
Excellent views of Ben Nevis, Fort William and Loch Linnhe.

Mrs B Grieve Nevis View, 14 Farrow Drive Corpach, by Fort William Inverness-shire PH33 7JW Tel: (Corpach) 01397 772447/ 0589 535036 (mobile) Fax: 01397 772800	COMMENDED Listed	1 Single 1 Pub Bath/Show 1 Family	B&B per person £16.50-£17.50 Single £13.50-£14.50 Double Room only per person £14.00-£15.00	Open Jan-Dec Dinner 1800-1900 B&B + Eve. Meal £25.00-£26.50

Family home in quiet residential estate. Views of Ben Nevis and Loch Eil. Home cooking. No-smoking house. Vegetarian and vegan diets catered for.

Taormina
Banavie, Fort William PH33 7LY
Telephone: 01397 772217

Taormina is in a quiet situation in Banavie village close to Neptune's Staircase on the Caledonian Canal. From the large garden can be seen Ben Nevis and Aonach Mor. Banavie Scotrail station and bus halt are five minutes walk away.
Above all is our aim to make guests feel welcome.

Mrs McInnes Taormina Banavie, by Fort William Inverness-shire PH33 7LY Tel: (Corpach) 01397 772217	COMMENDED ♛	1 Single 2 Pub Bath/Show 1 Twin 1 Double	B&B per person £14.00 Single £13.50-£14.00 Double	Open Mar-Oct

Modern bungalow quietly situated off "Road to the Isles". Restaurant and railway nearby. Caledonian Canal 50 metres, Fort William 3 miles (5kms).

Algarve
Badabrie, Banavie, Fort William PH33 7LX
Telephone: 01397 772461

This modern comfortable family home is situated in quiet residential area just five minutes from Fort William. Beautiful views of Ben Nevis and neighbouring mountains. Ideal centre for touring the Highlands. Only a few minutes walk from hotels and restaurants. Ample car parking. Personal attention of proprietor.   **Price £16 min.**

Mrs Margaret MacIntyre Algarve, Badabrie Banavie, by Fort William Inverness-shire PH33 7LX Tel: (Corpach) 01397 772461	HIGHLY COMMENDED ♛♛	1 Twin 1 Priv. NOT ensuite 2 Double 2 Pub Bath/Show	B&B per person to £16.00 Single £15.50-£16.50 Double	Open Jan-Dec

Detached modern villa in an elevated position overlooking Fort William, Loch Linnhe and the Ben Nevis range.

Mrs Mary Maclachlan 10 Guisach Terrace Corpach, Fort William Inverness-shire PH33 7JN Tel: (Corpach) 01397 772785	COMMENDED Listed	1 Twin 1 Pub Bath/Show 2 Double	B&B per person £15.00-£17.50 Single £15.00-£17.50 Double	Open Jan-Dec

Family home in quiet village, 5 miles (8 kms) from Fort William on Mallaig road. Good base for touring.

Mrs I MacLean Grianan, 4 Lochiel Crescent Banavie, Fort William Inverness-shire PH33 7LZ Tel: (Corpach) 01397 772659	COMMENDED ♛	3 Double 1 Pub Bath/Show	B&B per person £13.00-£14.50 Double	Open Apr-Oct

Modern detached bungalow in a quiet residential area near to Neptune's Staircase on the Caledonian Canal. Fine views towards Ben Nevis.

BY FORT WILLIAM continued	Map 3 H12

CLINTWOOD

23 HILLVIEW DRIVE, CORPACH, FORT WILLIAM PH33 7LS
TELEPHONE: 01397 772680

Let us welcome you to our home, a modern villa situated 4 miles from town. We enjoy magnificent views of Ben Nevis and surrounding mountains. All bedrooms are tastefully furnished and have private facilities, central heating, TV, welcome tray. The breakfast room looks onto a pleasant garden as does the guests' lounge.

Mrs McLeod Clintwood, 23 Hillview Drive Corpach, by Fort William Inverness-shire PH33 7LS Tel: (Corpach) 01397 772680	HIGHLY COMMENDED	1 Twin 2 Double	2 En Suite fac 1 Priv. NOT ensuite	B&B per person from £19.00 Double	Open Apr-Oct	
		A warm Highland welcome in this attractively appointed modern villa in village of Corpach. Fort William 4 miles (6kms).				
Mansfield Guest House Corpach, by Fort William Inverness-shire PH33 7LT Tel: (Corpach) 01397 772262	COMMENDED	1 Twin 2 Double 2 Family	1 En Suite fac 2 Pub Bath/Show	B&B per person £15.00-£18.50 Double	Open Jan-Dec Dinner from 1900 B&B + Eve. Meal £25.00-£28.50	
		Victorian house with its own garden. 3 miles (5kms) from Fort William, on the Road to the Isles. Home cooking and preserves, fresh produce.				
Mrs Nisbet Dailanna House Kinlocheil, Fort William Inverness-shire PH33 7NP Tel: (Kinlocheil) 01397 772253	COMMENDED	1 Twin 2 Double	3 En Suite fac 1 Pub Bath/Show	B&B per person £17.50-£22.50 Single £35.00-£45.00 Double	Open Apr-Nov Dinner 1900-2000 B&B + Eve. Meal £27.50-£30.00	
		Detached bungalow with large garden in elevated, peaceful position with fine views southwards over Loch Eil to the hills of Ardgour.				

TORBEAG HOUSE

Muirshearlich, Banavie, By Fort William PH33 7PB
Telephone: 01397 772412

This elegant country house must surely occupy one of the most stunning locations in Scotland with magnificent views of *Ben Nevis* and the *Great Glen*. Here you will find a warm welcome, peace and tranquillity, luxurious accommodation and good food, including home-made bread and preserves etc, all in beautiful surroundings.

TAIGH TORBEAG COMHAIR BEINN NIMHEIS
(House on the little hill opposite the Hill of Heaven)

Further details from
GLADYS or KEN WHYTE

Torbeag House Muirshearlich, Banavie Fort William Inverness-shire PH33 7PB Tel: (Corpach) 01397 772412	DELUXE	1 Twin 1 Double	2 En Suite fac	B&B per person £18.00-£25.00 Double	Open Jan-Oct Dinner from 1930	
		Spacious modern country home in secluded setting. 5.5 miles (9km) from Fort William. Magnificent views of Ben Nevis. Warm welcome, log fire, home baking.				

Mrs Williamson Aonach View, Hillview Croft Banavie, by Fort William Inverness-shire PH33 7PB Tel: (Corpach) 01397 772794		COMMENDED	1 Twin 2 Double	2 Pub Bath/Show	B&B per person £13.50-£16.00 Single £12.50-£15.00 Double	Open Jan-Dec
			Modern family home in secluded rural location with superb views of Ben Nevis and Aonach Mor. 4 miles (6kms) from Fort William.			
FOYERS **Inverness-shire** Foyers Bay House Lower Foyers Inverness-shire IV1 2YB Tel: (Gorthleck) 01456 486624 Fax: 01456 486337	Map 4 A10	COMMENDED	2 Twin 1 Double	3 En Suite fac	B&B per person £20.50-£28.00 Single £18.00-£23.00 Double	Open Jan-Dec Dinner 1900-2000 B&B + Eve. Meal £24.00-£30.00
			Friendly welcome at modernised Victorian house overlooking Loch Ness and set in 4 acres of ground. 500 yards from Falls of Foyers.			
FRASERBURGH **Aberdeenshire** Mrs M Greig Clifton House 131 Charlotte Street Fraserburgh Aberdeenshire AB43 5LS Tel: (Fraserburgh) 01346 518365	Map 4 G7	COMMENDED	2 Single 1 Double 1 Family	1 En Suite fac 1 Limited ensuite 2 Pub Bath/Show	B&B per person from £15.00 Single from £15.00 Double	Open Jan-Dec
			Family run Guest House in centre of Fraserburgh. Near shopping facilities and all amenities. On main bus routes.			
FREUCHIE **Fife** Mrs J Duncan Little Freuchie Farm Freuchie, by Falkland Fife KY15 7HU Tel: (Falkland) 01337 857372	Map 2 C3	COMMENDED	1 Twin 1 Family	2 Pub Bath/Show	B&B per person £17.00-£18.00 Single from £16.00 Double	Open Mar-Nov
			Spacious, comfortable farmhouse in own gardens. Panoramic views. Centrally situated for walking, golf & historic Falkland. St Andrews only 20 mins away.			
GAIRLOCH **Ross-shire** Lynn Bennett-MacKenzie Croit Mo Sheanair, 29 Strath Gairloch Ross-shire IV21 2DA Tel: (Gairloch) 01445 712389	Map 3 F7	COMMENDED	1 Twin 1 Double	1 Pub Bath/Show	B&B per person £14.50-£18.00 Single £14.50-£18.00 Double	Open Jan-Dec Dinner 1800-1830 B&B + Eve. Meal £23.50-£29.00
			Modern house on edge of Gairloch village, looking out over bay towards Skye. Evening meals – home cooking.			
Birchwood Guest House Gairloch Ross-shire IV21 2AH Tel: (Gairloch) 01445 712011		COMMENDED	3 Twin 2 Double 1 Family	6 En Suite fac 1 Pub Bath/Show	B&B per person £18.00-£23.00 Single	Open Apr-Oct
			Personally run, completely refurbished house in elevated position affording excellent views over harbour. All rooms with ensuite facilities.			
Charleston Guest House Gairloch Ross-shire IV21 2AH Tel: (Gairloch) 01445 712497		COMMENDED	2 Single 2 Twin 2 Double 3 Family	2 Pub Bath/Show	B&B per person from £16.50 Single from £16.50 Double	Open Apr-Oct Dinner from 1900 B&B + Eve. Meal from £23.50
			Large 18th-century house, situated on sea-loch overlooking Gairloch harbour. Personally run, all home cooking. Children and pets welcome.			

GAIRLOCH continued — Map 3 F7

Horisdale House
Strath
Gairloch
Ross-shire
IV21 2DA
Tel: (Gairloch) 01445 712151

HIGHLY COMMENDED

2 Single / 1 Twin / 1 Double
2 Priv. NOT ensuite
1 Pub Bath/Show

B&B per person
to £19.00 Single
to £18.00 Double

Open May-Sep
Dinner from 1900
B&B + Eve. Meal
to £29.00

Modern detached house with attractive garden and excellent views.
Home cooking with emphasis on fresh produce. Regret no pets allowed.

Kerrysdale House

Gairloch, Ross-shire IV21 2AL
Telephone: 01445 712292

This tastefully decorated farmhouse, built for the MacKenzies of Gairloch in 1793, is centrally located in Wester Ross and just one mile from Gairloch. Make Kerrysdale House your base from which you spend your days unwinding in the splendid beauty that surrounds. Contact Mrs Marie Macrae.

Kerrysdale House
Gairloch
Ross-shire
IV21 2AL
Tel: (Gairloch) 01445 712292

COMMENDED

1 Twin / 2 Double
2 En Suite fac
1 Priv. NOT ensuite

B&B per person
£18.00-£20.00 Single
£18.00-£20.00 Double

Open Feb-Nov
Dinner from 1900
B&B + Eve. Meal
£28.00-£30.00

18th-century farmhouse recently refurbished and tastefully decorated.
Modern comforts in a peaceful setting. 1 mile (2kms) south of Gairloch.

Miss I MacKenzie
Duisary, 24 Strath
Gairloch
Ross-shire
IV21 2DA
Tel: (Gairloch) 01445 712252

COMMENDED

1 Twin / 1 Double / 1 Family
1 En Suite fac
2 Pub Bath/Show

B&B per person
from £15.00 Single
from £15.00 Double

Open Apr-Oct

Traditional stone-built croft house on edge of village, with fine views
across Gairloch to the hills of Torridon.

The Mountain Restaurant & Lodge
Strath Square
Gairloch
Ross-shire
IV21 2BX
Tel: (Gairloch) 01445 712316

COMMENDED

1 Twin / 2 Double
2 En Suite fac
1 Priv. NOT ensuite

B&B per person
from £19.95 Single
£19.95-£24.50 Double

Open Apr-Oct
Dinner 1830-2100

In Gairloch's main square, with views across the bay.
Day time coffee shop, dinners by candlelight in an informal atmosphere.

Whindley Guest House
Auchtercairn
Gairloch
Ross-shire
IV21 2BN
Tel: (Gairloch) 01445 712340
Fax: 01445 712340

COMMENDED

1 Twin / 2 Double / 2 Family
5 En Suite fac

B&B per person
£14.00-£34.00 Single
£14.00-£20.00 Double

Open Jan-Dec
Dinner 1850-2000
B&B + Eve. Meal
£23.50-£29.50

Modern bungalow with large garden in elevated position, with fine views
overlooking Gairloch Bay. Some annexe accommodation with steep access.

GALASHIELS
Selkirkshire — Map 2 D6

Mrs S Field
Ettrickvale, 33 Abbotsford Road
Galashiels
Selkirkshire
TD1 3HW
Tel: (Galashiels) 01896 755224

COMMENDED

1 Single / 2 Twin
2 Pub Bath/Show

B&B per person
from £16.00 Single
from £13.00 Double

Open Jan-Dec

Comfortable semi-detached bungalow with garden on A7 on outskirts of town
but only a short walk from local amenities. All accommodation on ground floor.

Mrs Murray
Binniemyre House,
Abbotsford Road
Galashiels
Tel: (Galashiels) 01896 757137
Fax: 01896 757137

COMMENDED

1 Single / 1 Double / 3 Family
3 En Suite fac
2 Priv. NOT ensuite

B&B per person
£17.50-£25.00 Single
£17.50-£25.00 Double
Room only per person
£17.50-£25.00

Open Jan-Dec
Dinner 1800-2000
B&B + Eve. Meal
£26.00-£34.00

A Victorian detached house recently refurbished
set in its own grounds on the edge of town.

Mrs A M Platt Wakefield Bank, 9 Abbotsford Road Galashiels Selkirkshire TD1 3DP Tel: (Galashiels) 01896 752641		HIGHLY COMMENDED 👑👑	1 Twin 2 Double	1 Priv. NOT ensuite 2 Pub Bath/Show	B&B per person from £16.00 Double	Open Apr-Oct Dinner from 1800 B&B + Eve. Meal from £26.00

Elegant house c.1840, retaining fine original features.
Private garaging, easy access to town centre. A non-smoking house.
Awarded top B&B by "Discover Britain".

Mr & Mrs W Warner Monorene, 23 Stirling Street Galashiels Selkirkshire TD1 1BY Tel: (Galashiels) 01896 3073		COMMENDED 👑	2 Single 3 Twin 1 Double 1 Family	2 Pub Bath/Show	B&B per person from £15.00 Single from £15.00 Double	Open Jan-Dec Dinner 1800-1900 B&B + Eve. Meal from £20.00

Stone-built house situated near to town centre,
especially convenient for bus station.

BY GALASHIELS Selkirkshire Mrs Sheila Bergius Over Langshaw Farm Langshaw, by Galashiels Selkirkshire TD1 2PE Tel: (Blainslie) 01896 860244	Map 2 D6	COMMENDED 👑	1 Double 1 Family	1 En Suite fac 1 Priv. NOT ensuite	B&B per person £16.00-£19.00 Double	Open Jan-Dec

Traditional farmhouse on mixed working farm of 500 acres. 4 miles (6kms)
from Galashiels with spectacular views of surrounding countryside.

GALSTON Ayrshire Mrs J Bone Auchencloigh Farm Galston Ayrshire KA4 8NP Tel: (Galston) 01563 820567	Map 1 H6	COMMENDED Listed	2 Twin 1 Double	1 Pub Bath/Show	B&B per person from £15.00 Single from £15.00 Double	Open Apr-Nov Dinner from 1830 B&B + Eve. Meal £23.00-£26.00

Spacious 18th-century farmhouse amidst large gardens on 240-acre farm.
Non-smokers only please.

GAMRIE Banffshire Lucy R Smith Bankhead Croft Gamrie Banffshire Tel: (Gardenstown) 01261 851584	Map 4 G7	COMMENDED 👑👑👑	1 Twin 1 Double 1 Family	2 En Suite fac 1 Priv. NOT ensuite	B&B per person £14.50-£16.00 Single £14.50-£16.00 Double	Open Jan-Dec Dinner 1800-2000 B&B + Eve. Meal from £22.00

Modern country cottage in peaceful surroundings. 2 miles (3 kms) from coast.
6 miles (10 kms) east of Banff. Home cooking. Large caravan available.

GARDENSTOWN, by Banff Banffshire Mrs P Duncan Palace Farm Gamrie, by Banff Banffshire AB45 3HS Tel: (Gardenstown) 01261 851261	Map 4 G7	COMMENDED 👑👑👑	1 Twin 1 Double 1 Family	2 En Suite fac 1 Pub Bath/Show	B&B per person £17.00-£19.00 Single £16.00-£18.00 Double Room only per person £14.00-£18.00	Open Mar-Nov Dinner 1830-2100

Warm welcome in family farmhouse only 2 miles (3kms) from the sea.
Excellent home cooking.

BY GARMOUTH Moray Mrs Lorna Smith Gladhill Farm Garmouth, Fochabers Moray IV32 7NN Tel: (Spey Bay) 01343 870331	Map 4 E7	COMMENDED 👑	1 Twin 1 Double 1 Family	2 Pub Bath/Show	B&B per person £15.00 Double	Open May-Sep Dinner from 1830 B&B + Eve. Meal £21.00

Traditional Scottish hospitality in friendly farmhouse. Ideal touring base.

| GARTOCHARN | Map 1 |
| Dunbartonshire | G4 |

THE OLD SCHOOL HOUSE

GARTOCHARN, BY LOCH LOMOND G83 8SB
Telephone and Fax: 01389 830373
Winner of the 1994 Award for the Best Bed and Breakfast.
Built late 18th Century THE OLD SCHOOL HOUSE has been converted to provide comfortable ensuite bedrooms. Restricted hotel licence complements excellent cooking in a warm friendly atmosphere. *Wonderful views towards Loch Lomond.*

Mrs Judith L Harbour
The Old School House
Gartocharn, by Loch Lomond
Dunbartonshire
G83 8SB
Tel: (Gartocharn)
01389 830373

COMMENDED

1 Single   3 En Suite fac
1 Twin
1 Double

B&B per person
£21.00-£23.00 Single
£21.00-£23.00 Double

Open Jan-Dec
Dinner 1900-2030
B&B + Eve. Meal
£35.50-£37.50

18th-century school house tastefully converted and providing comfortable accommodation. Well situated for touring Loch Lomond. Home cooking and baking.

| GARVE | Map 4 |
| Ross-shire | A8 |

MRS HAZEL HAYTON

Birch Cottage, Station Road, Garve, Ross-shire IV23 2PS
Telephone: 01997 414237
Comfortable, friendly accommodation. Ideal base for touring and walking. All rooms en-suite, TV, tea-making. Guest lounge, garden, patio, parking. *Open all year.*

Mrs Hayton
Birch Cottage, Station Road
Garve
Ross-shire
IV23 2PS
Tel: (Garve) 01997 414237

HIGHLY
COMMENDED

1 Twin   3 En Suite fac
1 Double   1 Pub Bath/Show
1 Family

B&B per person
£15.00 Single
£13.50 Double

Open Jan-Dec

Traditional Highland cottage en route to Gairloch/Ullapool. Refurbished to a high standard. Garve railway station 50 metres. 2 annexe bedrooms.

| GATEHOUSE OF FLEET | Map 1 |
| Kirkcudbrightshire | H10 |

Crab Cottage

Sandgreen, Gatehouse of Fleet, Kirkcudbrightshire DG7 2DU
Telephone: 01557 814461
Uniquely situated with lawns leading onto a quiet sandy beach and beautiful views of the sea and hills. Lovely walks along the unspoilt coastline with an abundance of birds and wild flowers. Ideally central for touring Galloway and South West Scotland. Excellent for golf with reduced fees at the local course.

Mrs Sheard
Crab Cottage, Sandgreen
Gatehouse of Fleet
Kirkcudbrightshire
DG7 2DU
Tel: (Gatehouse of Fleet)
01557 814461

HIGHLY
COMMENDED

1 Twin   1 En Suite fac
1 Family   1 Priv. NOT ensuite

B&B per person
£30.00-£35.00 Single
£17.50-£20.00 Double
Room only per person
£25.00-£30.00

Open Jan-Dec

Situated on the shore, overlooking the sea and the hills. Easy access to conservation village and major routes.

BY GATEHOUSE OF FLEET **Kirkcudbrightshire** Girthon Kirk Guest House Sandgreen Road by Gatehouse of Fleet Kirkcudbrightshire DG7 2DW Tel: (Gatehouse) 01557 814352	Map 1 H10	COMMENDED ♛♛♛	1 Twin 2 Double	2 En Suite fac 1 Priv. NOT ensuite	B&B per person £19.00-£22.00 Double	Open Mar-Sep Dinner from 1830 B&B + Eve. Meal £28.50-£31.50

Lovely country house in idyllic rural setting. Fine home cooking. All rooms with private facilities. 0.5 miles (1 km) off A75 on Sandgreen road.

GIFFORD **East Lothian** Mrs M B Whiteford Rowan Park Longnewton Farm Gifford East Lothian EH41 4JW Tel: (Gifford) 01620 810327	Map 2 D5	HIGHLY COMMENDED Listed	1 Twin 1 Double	1 Priv. NOT ensuite 1 Pub Bath/Show	B&B per person from £16.00 Double	Open Mar-Nov

Modern house furnished to a high standard. Quiet, comfortable and relaxing. Close to Lammermuir hills.

GIGHA, Isle of **Argyll** Post Office House Gigha, Isle of Argyll PA41 7AA Tel: (Gigha) 01583 505251	Map 1 D6	COMMENDED Listed	1 Single 1 Twin 1 Double 1 Family	1 Pub Bath/Show	B&B per person £16.00-£17.00 Single £15.00-£16.00 Double	Open Jan-Dec Dinner from 1800 B&B + Eve. Meal £25.00-£26.00

House, c.1850, with steep access to top floor, on lovely island with famous garden and sandy beaches. Cycles for hire. Home-cooking.

GIRVAN **Ayrshire** Glendrissaig Guest House Newton Stewart Road by Girvan Ayrshire KA26 0HJ Tel: (Girvan) 01465 714631	Map 1 F8	HIGHLY COMMENDED ♛♛♛	1 Twin 1 Double 1 Family	2 En Suite fac 1 Priv. NOT ensuite 1 Pub Bath/Show	B&B per person £19.00-£25.00 Single £18.00-£22.00 Double	Open Apr-Oct Dinner 1800-1900 B&B + Eve. Meal £26.00-£32.00

Modern detached house in elevated position with excellent outlook towards Mull of Kintyre. Organic produce when available used in vegetarian meals.

Mrs L Hogarth St Oswalds 5 Golf Course Road Girvan Ayrshire KA26 9HW Tel: (Girvan) 01465 713786		COMMENDED ♛♛	1 Twin 1 Double	1 En Suite fac 1 Priv. NOT ensuite	B&B per person £16.00-£20.00 Double	Open Jan-Dec

Semi-detached Victorian seaside villa. Close to beach and harbour and short walk to municipal golf course.

Mrs Isobel Kyle Hawkhill Farm Old Dailly, by Girvan Ayrshire KA26 9RD Tel: (Old Dailly) 01465 871232		HIGHLY COMMENDED ♛♛	1 Twin 2 Double	1 En Suite fac 1 Priv. NOT ensuite 1 Pub Bath/Show	B&B per person from £17.50 Double	Open Mar-Oct Dinner from 1900 B&B + Eve. Meal from £25.50

Large traditional farmhouse on mixed farm, 3 miles (5 kms) from Girvan. Friendly, informal atmosphere, home-baking and cooking using fresh produce.

J & G Mulholland Appin Cottage 29 Ailsa Street West Girvan Ayrshire KA26 9AD Tel: (Girvan) 01465 713214		COMMENDED ♛♛♛	1 Twin 1 Double	2 En Suite fac 1 Pub Bath/Show	B&B per person £16.00-£18.00 Double	Open mid Apr-Sep

Converted fishermen's cottages set between shore and town.

Details of Grading and Classification are on page vi.　　　　Key to symbols is on back flap.　　139

GIRVAN continued
Map 1 F8

Thistleneuk Guest House
19 Louisa Drive
Girvan
Ayrshire
KA26 9AH
Tel: (Girvan) 01465 712137

COMMENDED 👑👑

1 Single	6 En Suite fac
2 Twin	1 Pub Bath/Show
2 Double	
2 Family	

B&B per person
£18.50-£19.00 Single
£18.50-£19.00 Double

Open Jan-Dec
Dinner from 1800

19th-century terraced house on seafront overlooking Ailsa Craig.
Within easy walking distance of town centre.

BY GIRVAN
Ayrshire
Map 1 F8

Glengennet Farm

Barr, by Girvan, Ayrshire KA26 9TY
Telephone: 01465 861220

Victorian shooting lodge on hill farm, lovely views over Stinchar Valley and neighbouring Galloway forest park. Has en-suite bedrooms with tea trays. Near conservation village with 2 hotels for evening meals. Good base for Glentrool, Burns Country, Culzean Castle, Ayrshire coast.
Contact Mrs V. Dunlop for a brochure.

Mrs V Dunlop
Glengennet Farm
Barr, by Girvan
Ayrshire
KA26 9TY
Tel: (Barr) 01465 861220

COMMENDED 👑👑

1 Twin	2 En Suite fac
1 Double	

B&B per person
from £17.50 Single

Open Apr-Oct

Former shooting lodge set on hillside overlooking Stinchar Valley,
1.5 miles (3kms) from Barr, a conservation village.

Mrs S Fergusson
The Yett, 4 Manse Road
Colmonell
Ayrshire
KA26 0SA
Tel: (Colmonell) 01465 881223

COMMENDED
Listed

2 Twin	2 Pub Bath/Show
1 Double	

B&B per person
from £11.50 Single
from £11.50 Double

Open Easter-Oct

In quiet country location with excellent views over Stinchar Valley.
Ideal for touring, fishing and birdwatching.

Mrs M Whiteford
Maxwelston Farm
Dailly, by Girvan
Ayrshire
KA26 9RH
Tel: (Dailly) 01465 811210

HIGHLY
COMMENDED 👑👑

1 Double	2 En Suite fac
1 Family	

B&B per person
from £18.00 Double

Open Mar-Oct
Dinner 1830-1930

18th-century Listed farmhouse on working sheep and beef farm,
5 miles (8kms) inland from Girvan. New golf course adjacent to farm.

GLAMIS
Angus
Map 2 C1

Mrs G Jarron
Hatton of Ogilvy
Glamis, Forfar
Angus
DD8 1UH
Tel: (Glamis) 01307 840229
Fax: 01307 840229

HIGHLY
COMMENDED 👑👑

1 Twin	1 En Suite fac

B&B per person
£18.00 Single
£16.00 Double

Open Apr-Oct

Ideal base for touring Angus and Glamis Castle.
A warm welcome awaits at this traditional farmhouse on mixed farm.
Ideal base for the Angus glens, folk museum and many castles.

GLASGOW
Map 1 H5

Mrs I Adey
4 Holyrood Crescent
Glasgow
G20 6HJ
Tel: 0141 334 8390

COMMENDED 👑

1 Twin	3 Limited ensuite
1 Double	2 Pub Bath/Show
1 Family	

B&B per person
£18.00-£20.00 Single
£14.00-£15.00 Double

Open Apr-Sep

Early Victorian townhouse ideally situated with easy access to
city centre, M8 and Loch Lomond.

Alamo Guest House 46 Gray Street Glasgow G3 7SE Tel: 0141 339 2395	APPROVED	2 Single 1 Twin 1 Double 5 Family	2 En Suite fac 3 Pub Bath/Show	B&B per person from £17.00 Single from £15.00 Double	Open Jan-Dec Dinner 1800-1930 B&B + Eve. Meal from £22.00	
		Friendly family run, in quiet location overlooking park. Easy access to centre and within walking distance of SECC, galleries and Transport Museum.				
Belle Vue Guest House 163 Hamilton Road, Mount Vernon Glasgow G32 9QT Tel: 0141 778 1077	APPROVED Listed	3 Single 3 Twin 2 Double 2 Family	1 En Suite fac 2 Pub Bath/Show	B&B per person £18.00-£20.00 Single to £16.00 Double	Open Jan-Dec	
		Personally run long-established guest house in residential area on main route into city. Convenient for M8 and M74.				
Mrs A Bennett 107 Dowanhill Street Glasgow G12 9EQ Tel: 0141 337 1307	COMMENDED Listed	2 Twin	1 En Suite fac 1 Pub Bath/Show	B&B per person £18.00-£22.00 Single £16.00-£18.50 Double	Open Jan-Dec	
		Early Edwardian terraced townhouse in the West End. Convenient for buses and underground to city centre.				
John G Bristow 56 Dumbreck Road Glasgow G41 5NP Tel: 0141 427 0129	COMMENDED	1 Twin 1 Double	2 En Suite fac	B&B per person £20.00-£25.00 Single £17.00-£20.00 Double	Open Jan-Dec	
		Traditional Victorian semi-villa with full disabled facilities. Easy access to M8. Convenient for Burrell Collection, city and touring.				
Browns Guest House 2 Onslow Drive Glasgow G31 5LX Tel: 0141 554 6797	APPROVED Listed	7 Single 3 Twin 2 Double 2 Family	4 Pub Bath/Show	B&B per person £15.00 Single £13.00-£15.00 Double	Open Jan-Dec	
		Victorian semi-villa in the East End, approximately 1 mile (2kms) from city centre. Convenient access to motorway network.				
Margaret Bruce 24 Greenock Avenue Glasgow G44 5TS Tel: 0141 637 0608	HIGHLY COMMENDED	1 Single 2 Twin 1 Double	2 En Suite fac 2 Pub Bath/Show	B&B per person £17.50-£20.00 Single £17.50-£20.00 Double	Open Jan-Dec	
		Modern, architect-designed villa, peacefully situated in residential area, 5 minutes from train station. Private parking.				
Chez Nous Guest House 33 Hillhead Street Glasgow G12 Tel: 0141 334 2977	COMMENDED	13 Single 4 Twin 8 Double 7 Family	14 En Suite fac 4 Limited ensuite 6 Pub Bath/Show	B&B per person £18.50-£25.00 Single £18.50-£25.00 Double	Open Jan-Dec	
		Situated in West End of city, close to University and Art Gallery. Within easy reach of M8 and all amenities. Private parking.				
Craigielea House 35 Westercraigs Glasgow G31 2HY Tel: 0141 554 3446	APPROVED Listed	2 Twin 1 Double 1 Family	1 Limited ensuite 1 Pub Bath/Show	B&B per person £16.50-£18.00 Single £14.00-£15.00 Double	Open Jan-Dec	
		Victorian semi-villa in East End of city, yet close to centre and all amenities.				
Craigpark Guest House 33 Circus Drive Glasgow G31 2JG Tel: 0141 554 4160	COMMENDED Listed	1 Single 2 Twin 1 Double 1 Family	1 Limited ensuite 3 Pub Bath/Show	B&B per person from £16.00 Single £14.00-£15.00 Double	Open Jan-Dec	
		In quiet residential area in East End of city near Cathedral. Easy access to M8.				

Map 1
H5

HOLLY HOUSE
54 IBROX TERRACE, GLASGOW G51 2TB
Telephone: 0141 427 5609

Holly House, family owned, offers spacious rooms,
ensuite, situated in an early Victorian tree-lined terrace in
city centre south. Convenient amenities: *Burrell Gallery,
Rennie Macintosh House, Ibrox Stadium, SECC* and five
minutes to *Glasgow International Airport* makes your stay
comfortable and warm welcome assured by resident owner.

Mr Peter Divers Holly House 54 Ibrox Terrace Glasgow G51 2TB Tel: 0141 427 5609	COMMENDED Listed	1 Double 1 Family	2 En Suite fac	B&B per person £20.00-£25.00 Single £18.00-£25.00 Double	Open Apr-Dec

Holly House offers spacious en-suite rooms within early Victorian,
tree-lined terrace in city centre south. Convenient for all city centre amenities.

Kirkland House

42 St Vincent Crescent, Glasgow G3 8NG
Telephone and Fax: 0141 248 3458

City-centre guest house in *Glasgow's Little Chelsea* in
the area known as Finnieston offers excellent rooms,
most with ensuite facilities, full central heating,
colour TV, tea and coffee makers.
The house is located within walking distance of the
Scottish Exhibition Centre, Museum, Art Gallery and
Kelvingrove Park. We are very convenient to all City
Centre and West End facilities, also only ten minutes
from Glasgow International Airport.
Our house is featured in the *Frommers Tour Guide*.
Being family owned you can be assured of a
friendly welcome.
Contact Carole Divers for details.

Mrs C Divers Kirkland House, 42 St Vincent Crescent Glasgow G3 8NG Tel: 0141 248 3458 Fax: 0141 248 3458	COMMENDED Listed	2 Single 1 Twin 1 Double 1 Family	3 En Suite fac 2 Limited ensuite	B&B per person £25.00-£35.00 Single £23.00-£27.00 Double	Open Mar-Oct

Ideally situated for city centre, S.E.C.C., University and Museums.
Easy access to M8. Continental breakfast served in bedrooms.

Mrs R Easton 148 Queen's Drive Glasgow G42 8QN Tel: 0141 423 3143	COMMENDED	1 Twin 1 Family	1 Pub Bath/Show	B&B per person from £18.00 Single from £16.00 Double	Open Apr-Sep

1st floor flat in B Listed Victorian tenement overlooking Queens Park.
Convenient for Burrell Collection; city centre. Unrestricted street parking.

Glades Guest House 142 Albert Road Glasgow G42 8UF Tel: 0141 423 4911	APPROVED	1 Single 3 Double 2 Double 2 Family	2 En Suite fac 2 Pub Bath/Show	B&B per person £18.00-£21.00 Single £18.00-£21.00 Double	Open Jan-Dec

Grey sandstone house in quiet cul de sac of residential area.
7 minutes by train to the city centre.

Mrs D Hallam Park House, 13 Victoria Park Gardens South Glasgow G11 7BX Tel: 0141 339 1559 Fax: 0141 339 1559	**HIGHLY COMMENDED**	1 Twin 1 Double	1 En Suite fac 1 Priv. NOT ensuite	B&B per person £25.00-£30.00 Single £20.00-£25.00 Double	Open Apr-Sep Dinner 1800-2030 B&B + Eve. Meal £30.00-£40.00

Large Victorian town house in quiet residential area.
Convenient for Clydeside Expressway to city centre. Ideal base for touring.

| Mrs M Hendry
Redtops, 248 Wedderlea Drive
Glasgow
G52 2SB
Tel: 0141 883 7186 | **COMMENDED**
Listed | 1 Twin
1 Double | 1 Pub Bath/Show | B&B per person
from £18.00 Single
£15.00-£16.00 Double | Open Apr-Sep |

Detached bungalow in quiet residential area short drive from Glasgow Airport.
Convenient public transport to both Glasgow and Paisley.

| Number Thirty Six
36 St Vincent Crescent
Glasgow
G3 8NG
Tel: 0141 248 2086 | **COMMENDED**
Listed | 1 Twin
1 Double | 2 En Suite fac | B&B per person
£25.00-£35.00 Single
£23.00-£27.00 Double | Open Apr-Sep |

Situated in Victorian terrace, convenient for the Exhibition Centre.
Continental breakfast served in the comfort of your bedroom.

| Mrs Margaret Ogilvie
Lochgilvie, 117 Randolph Road
Glasgow
G11 7DS
Tel: 0141 357 1593/
0831 379732 | **COMMENDED**
Listed | 1 Single
2 Twin | 2 Limited ensuite
2 Pub Bath/Show | B&B per person
£20.00-£25.00 Single
£18.00-£22.00 Double | Open Jan-Dec |

Victorian townhouse in popular West End with bus and rail connections nearby.
Easy access to A82 for Loch Lomond and Trossachs.

| Mrs A Paterson
16 Bogton Avenue
Glasgow
G44 3JJ
Tel: 0141 637 4402/
0589 534965 | **COMMENDED** | 1 Single
1 Double | 1 Priv. NOT ensuite
2 Pub Bath/Show | B&B per person
£18.00 Single
£17.00 Double
Room only per person
£16.00 | Open Jan-Dec
Dinner 1800-1900
B&B + Eve. Meal
£25.00 |

Family home in quiet residential area, 200 yds from railway station
with direct access to city centre by train or bus.

| Regent Guest House
44 Regent Park Square
Glasgow
G41 2AG
Tel: 0141 422 1199
Fax: 0141 423 7531 | **APPROVED** | 3 Single
1 Twin
1 Double
2 Family | 2 En Suite fac
2 Pub Bath/Show | B&B per person
£20.00-£26.00 Single
£20.00-£24.00 Double | Open Jan-Dec |

1860 terraced house in quiet, residential area. Ideal for city centre and
under 2 miles (3kms) from the Burrell Collection. Warm welcome.

| Rosewood Guest House
4 Seton Terrace
Glasgow
G31 2HU
Tel: 0141 550 1500/556 2478 | **COMMENDED**
Listed | 1 Single
4 Twin
1 Double
2 Family | 3 Pub Bath/Show | B&B per person
from £16.50 Single
from £14.50 Double | Open Jan-Dec |

Refurbished guest house in quiet residential area. Convenient for transport
to city centre, cathedral and Royal Infirmary.

| Mrs M Ross
3 Beech Avenue
Glasgow
G41 5DE
Tel: 0141 427 0194 | **COMMENDED** | 2 Twin
1 Double | 2 En Suite fac
1 Priv. NOT ensuite | B&B per person
£25.00-£28.00 Single
£18.00-£20.00 Double | Open Jan-Dec |

Traditional villa on the south side of the Clyde.
Well placed for central Glasgow and the airport yet convenient for Ayrshire.

| Mrs J Sinclair
23 Dumbreck Road
Glasgow
G41 5LJ
Tel: 0141 427 1006 | **COMMENDED**
Listed | 1 Single
1 Twin
1 Double | 2 Pub Bath/Show | B&B per person
£20.00-£22.00 Single
to £18.00 Double | Open Apr-Sep
Dinner 1800-2100
B&B + Eve. Meal
£24.00-£27.00 |

Spacious Victorian house close to Bellahouston Park and local amenities.
On bus route to Burrell Collection.

GLASGOW continued	Map 1 H5						
The Town House 4 Hughenden Terrace Glasgow G12 9XR Tel: 0141 357 0862 Fax: 0141 339 9605	HIGHLY COMMENDED 👑👑👑	3 Twin 5 Double 2 Family	10 En Suite fac	B&B per person £48.00-£52.00 Single £29.50-£31.00 Double	Open Jan-Dec Dinner 1830-2000		
		Elegantly refurbished Victorian town house in quiet conservation area in Glasgow's West End.					
Mrs P Wells 21 West Avenue Stepps Glasgow G33 6ES Tel: 0141 779 1990 Fax: 0141 779 1990	COMMENDED 👑	1 Double 1 Family	2 En Suite fac	B&B per person £20.00-£24.00 Single £18.00-£22.00 Double	Open Jan-Dec		
		Family home in quiet residential area with easy access to motorway network and city centre.					
GLENCOE Argyll	Map 1 F1						

DORRINGTON LODGE GUEST HOUSE

Tighphuirst, Glencoe PA39 4HN   Tel: 01855 811653

Ideally situated overlooking Loch Leven and the Mamore Hills at the end of this famous Highland Glen. This is an excellent base to explore the Highlands. We offer our guests a warm welcome, comfortable accommodation and excellent cuisine, including vegetarian.

Further details or reservations contact: Joy or Stewart Hilton.

Dorrington Lodge 6 Tighphuirst Glencoe Argyll PA39 4HN Tel: (Ballachulish) 01855 811653	COMMENDED 👑	1 Twin 3 Double 1 Family	3 En Suite fac 3 Pub Bath/Show	B&B per person from £16.50 Single £13.50-£15.50 Double	Open Feb-Oct, Xmas/New Year Dinner from 1900 B&B + Eve. Meal £23.50-£25.00		
		Comfortable, modern house just off main road, with excellent views over Loch Leven. Home-cooked meals using quality local produce. No smoking.					
Dunire Guest House Glencoe Argyll PA39 4HS Tel: (Ballachulish) 01855 811305	COMMENDED 👑👑	2 Twin 3 Double	4 En Suite fac 2 Pub Bath/Show	B&B per person £13.00-£18.00 Double	Open 28th Dec-Oct		
		Modern bungalow in centre of Glencoe Village. Ideal base for touring, climbing and hill walking.					

SCORRYBREAC GUEST HOUSE

GLENCOE, ARGYLL PA39 4HT
Telephone: 01855 811354

Scorrybreac is a comfortable well-appointed guest house in beautiful woodland surroundings managed by the resident owners. We are a no-smoking establishment. It is an ideal base for exploring the Glencoe and Ben Nevis area or for a shorter stay on a more extended tour of the Highlands.

Scorrybreac Guest House Glencoe Argyll PA39 4HT Tel: (Ballachulish) 01855 811354	COMMENDED 👑👑	3 Twin 3 Double	5 En Suite fac 1 Priv. NOT ensuite	B&B per person £15.00-£20.00 Single £13.00-£18.00 Double	Open Dec-Oct Dinner 1800-1830 B&B + Eve. Meal £24.50-£29.50		
		Modern single storey house with large garden overlooking Loch Leven. In a quiet secluded situation on the edge of the village with local forest walks.					

GLENCOE
STRATHLACHLAN – THE GLENCOE GUEST HOUSE
Upper Carnoch, Glencoe PA39 4HT   Tel: 01855 811244

A family run guest house in a quiet, peaceful, riverside setting. Spectacular mountain views. Comfortable en-suite rooms. Tea and coffee-making facilities. Central heating. Pleasant residents' lounge. Drying room.
An ideal location for touring and sightseeing the beautiful West Coast or local walking, climbing and skiing.

Strathlachlan The Glencoe Guest House Glencoe Argyll PA39 4HT Tel: (Ballachulish) 01855 811244 Fax: 01855 811244		COMMENDED 👑👑	2 Twin 2 Double 2 Family	4 En Suite fac 1 Pub Bath/Show	B&B per person £14.00-£18.00 Double	Open Jan-Dec Dinner 1900-2000
			Quiet peaceful riverside setting on edge of village. Magnificent views. Ideal base for touring and for mountain sports. Family run.			
GLENDALE **Isle of Skye, Inverness-shire** Mrs Kernachan 4 Lephin Glendale Isle of Skye, Inverness-shire IV55 8WJ Tel: (Glendale) 01470 511376	Map 3 C8	COMMENDED Listed	2 Twin 1 Double	1 Pub Bath/Show	B&B per person from £18.50 Single from £13.50 Double	Open Jan-Dec Dinner 1830-2000 B&B + Eve. Meal from £21.00
			Situated with views across Glendale Valley this is a quiet and beautiful part of N W Skye. Evening meal available.			
GLENHINNISDALE **Isle of Skye, Inverness-shire** Mrs I Nicolson Glenhinnisdale, Snizort Isle of Skye, Inverness-shire IV51 Tel: (Uig) 01470 542406	Map 3 D8	COMMENDED 👑	1 Twin 1 Double 1 Family	3 Pub Bath/Show	B&B per person to £15.00 Single to £13.00 Double	Open Apr-Oct Dinner 1830-1930 B&B + Eve. Meal to £22.00
			Farmhouse in quiet elevated position overlooking Glenhinnisdale. 6 miles (9.6kms) from Uig Ferry. 100-acre croft. Home cooking.			
GLENISLA, by Kirriemuir **Angus** Mrs M Clark Purgavie Farm Glenisla, by Kirriemuir Angus DD8 5HZ Tel: (Lintrathen) 01575 560213/ 0860 392794 (mobile) Fax: 01575 560213	Map 4 D12	HIGHLY COMMENDED 👑👑👑	1 Twin 2 Family	2 En Suite fac 1 Priv. NOT ensuite	B&B per person £16.00-£21.00 Single £16.00-£18.00 Double	Open Jan-Dec Dinner from 1800 B&B + Eve. Meal from £24.00
			19th-century house on working farm, with views over Strathmore Valley. Glamis Castle 7 miles (11kms), Kirriemuir 6 miles (11kms). Scottish cooking.			

Scotland for Golf . . .
Find out more about golf in Scotland. There's more to it than just the championship courses so get in touch with us now for information on the hidden gems of Scotland.
Write to: **Information Unit, Scottish Tourist Board, 23 Ravelston Terrace, Edinburgh EH4 3EU**
or call: 0131-332 2433

GLENLIVET
Banffshire

Map 4
D9

Roadside Cottage

Tomnavoulin, Glenlivet, Ballindalloch, Banffshire AB37 9JL
Telephone: 01807 590486

Peace, quiet and comfort in the Rainbow Glen. Excellent touring centre but it's fun to stay put, too. Walk the moors and hills, see the wildlife, fish the rivers, drink the malt, visit distilleries, castles, gardens, battlefields and ski-slopes. Savour fine food.
Enjoy friendly personal service.

Mrs Rita Marks Roadside Cottage, Tomnavoulin Glenlivet, Ballindalloch Banffshire AB37 9JL Tel: (Glenlivet) 01807 590486	COMMENDED Listed	1 Single 1 Double 1 Family	1 Pub Bath/Show	B&B per person £12.00-£15.00 Single £12.00-£15.00 Double	Open Jan-Dec, exc Xmas Dinner 1800-2200 B&B + Eve. Meal £18.00-£21.00

Traditional stone-built Highland cottage tastefully restored to modern standards.
Children and pets welcome.

GLENLUCE **Wigtownshire** Mrs C Marshall Grayhill Farm Glenluce Wigtownshire DG8 0NS Tel: (Glenluce) 01581 300400	Map 1 G10 COMMENDED Listed	1 Twin 1 Double	1 Pub Bath/Show	B&B per person £15.00-£16.00 Single £14.00-£15.00 Double	Open Apr-Oct

Friendly, family welcome on a traditional farm (with shooting rights)
on outskirts of village. Centrally situated for touring and leisure pursuits.
Convenient for Irish ferries.

Mrs M Stewart Bankfield Farm Glenluce Wigtownshire DG8 0JF Tel: (Glenluce) 01581 300281	COMMENDED	1 Twin 1 Double 1 Family	1 Pub Bath/Show	B&B per person from £15.00 Single	Open Apr-Oct

Farmhouse on 370-acre working farm conveniently situated between
the village and the main A75 tourist route. 5 minutes walk into village.

GLENROTHES **Fife** Jean F Baxter New Inn House Markinch Fife KY7 6LR Tel: (Glenrothes) 01592 752623	Map 2 C3 COMMENDED Listed	1 Single 1 Twin 1 Double	1 Pub Bath/Show	B&B per person £14.00-£16.00 Single £14.00-£16.00 Double Room only per person £14.00-£16.00	Open Jan-Dec

Family home in rural location, set back from main A92, giving excellent access
to Falkland, Perth, St Andrews and the East Neuk. All ground-floor bedrooms.

WELCOME

Whenever you are in Scotland, you can be sure of a warm welcome at your nearest Tourist Information Centre.

For guide books, maps, souvenirs, our Centres provide a service second to none – many now offer bureau-de-change facilities. And, of course, Tourist Information Centres offer free, expert advice on what to see and do, route-planning and accommodation for everyone – visitors and residents alike!

| GLENSHIEL | Map 3 |
| Ross-shire | G10 |

GLOMACH HOUSE
Glenshiel, by Kyle IV40 8HN
Telephone: 01599 511222 Fax: 01599 511382

Barrier free bungalow overlooking Loch Duich. Here are castles, historical brochs, battlesites, mountains, lochs, rivers, wildlife, flora all in abundance. Glomach House is a spacious comfortable place to stop and enjoy a leisurely breakfast watching the seals and porpoises. Large garden, quiet walking space.

Mrs Munro
Glomach House
Glenshiel, by Kyle of Lochalsh
Ross-shire
Tel: (Glenshiel) 01599 511222
Fax: 01599 511382

COMMENDED

1 Twin 3 Priv. NOT ensuite
2 Double 2 Pub Bath/Show

B&B per person
£15.00-£25.00 Single
£15.00-£20.00 Double

Open Jan-Dec

Modern house overlooking Loch Duich, near junction to Glenelg ferry road and on main route to Skye, on National Trust for Scotland estate.

GLENURQUHART
Inverness-shire
Mrs Patricia Moir
Cragaig
Glenurquhart
Inverness-shire
IV3 6TN
Tel: (Glenurquhart)
01456 476246

Map 4
A9

COMMENDED

1 Twin 2 Pub Bath/Show
2 Double

B&B per person
£14.00-£16.00 Single
£14.00-£16.00 Double

Open Apr-Sep

Set in its own attractive gardens, 5.5m (9km) from Drumnadrochit. Cragaig overlooks Loch Meiklie and is convenient for Glen Affric, Strathglass and Loch Ness.

GOLSPIE
Sutherland
Mrs N Grant
Deo Greine Farm, Backies
Golspie
Sutherland
KW10 6SE
Tel: (Golspie) 01408 633106

Map 4
B6

COMMENDED

2 Twin 3 En Suite fac
1 Double 1 Priv. NOT ensuite
1 Family

B&B per person
from £17.00 Single
from £16.50 Double

Open Apr-Oct
Dinner from 1800
B&B + Eve. Meal
from £26.50

Crofting farmhouse, situated in hills behind Golspie, in an elevated position overlooking surrounding countryside.

GOREBRIDGE
Midlothian
Mrs Cathie Nelson
18 Bellmains
Gorebridge
EH23 4QD
Tel: (Gorebridge)
01875 820252

Map 2
C5

COMMENDED

1 Twin 2 Pub Bath/Show
1 Double

B&B per person
£17.00-£20.00 Single
from £17.00 Double

Open Apr-Oct

Private bungalow, well appointed inside and out. Quiet residential area 10 miles South of Edinburgh on the A7. Five minutes from Borthwick Castle and 5 mins from Dalhousie Castle.

GRANGEMOUTH
Stirlingshire
Bill & Doreen Robertson
Kylie House, 55 Bo'ness Road
Grangemouth
Stirlingshire
FK3 9BJ
Tel: (Grangemouth)
01324 471301

Map 2
B4

COMMENDED
Listed

1 Twin 2 Pub Bath/Show
1 Double
1 Family

B&B per person
£16.00-£18.00 Single
£16.00-£18.00 Double

Open Jan-Dec

Victorian house with parking on main road equidistant between Edinburgh and Glasgow. Convenient for town centre, motorway and sports complex.

Details of Grading and Classification are on page vi. | Key to symbols is on back flap. | 147

GRANTOWN-ON-SPEY Moray	Map 4 C9

Ardconnel House ⚓

Woodlands Terrace, Grantown-on-Spey,
Moray PH26 3JU   Tel/Fax: 01479 872104
DELUXE ♛♛♛   AA QQQQQ PREMIER SELECTED

Ardconnel House is situated at the southern fringe of
Grantown-on-Spey opposite Lochan, Forest and Hills;
the charming town centre and world-famous River Spey
are just a short walk. The house is beautifully furnished
throughout; there is a spacious sitting room with log fire
and all bedrooms have ensuite private facilities and are
extremely comfortable being equipped with quality
beds, colour televisions, welcome trays and hairdryers.
Excellent home cooking using fresh local produce is
complemented by an interesting selection of modestly
priced wines.
Deluxe accommodation at a realistic price.
Colour brochure available on request –
please call 01479 872104.

Ardconnel House Woodlands Terrace Grantown-on-Spey Moray PH26 3JU Tel: (Grantown-on-Spey) 01479 872104 Fax: 01479 872104	DELUXE ♛♛♛	1 Twin 4 Double 1 Family	6 En Suite fac	B&B per person £30.00-£32.00 Single £24.00-£32.00 Double	Open Mar-Oct Dinner from 1900 B&B + Eve. Meal £39.00-£47.00	

Splendid Victorian villa with ample private car parking,
all rooms ensuite; no smoking throughout; superb 4-poster room;
Taste of Scotland selected member.

The Ardlarig

Woodlands Terrace, Grantown on Spey PH26 3JU
Telephone: 01479 873245

An imposing Victorian villa with superb views of surrounding countryside.
Service is friendly and informal and Mike and Sue make every effort to
make your visit enjoyable. Breaks are available throughout the year. Please
contact us for brochure details.
YOU CAN'T AFFORD NOT TO STAY WITH US.

The Ardlarig Woodlands Terrace Grantown-on-Spey Moray PH26 3JU Tel: (Grantown-on-Spey) 01479 873245	COMMENDED ♛♛	1 Single 2 Twin 3 Double 1 Family	2 Priv. NOT ensuite 3 Pub Bath/Show	B&B per person £15.00-£17.50 Single £15.00-£17.50 Double	Open Jan-Dec Dinner at 1900 B&B + Eve. Meal £25.00-£28.00	

Comfortable Victorian home, many original features, set in 3/4 acre garden,
Views of Cromdale Hills and pine woodlands. Emphasis on Scottish fayre.

Brooklynn Grant Road Grantown-on-Spey Moray PH26 3LA Tel: (Grantown-on-Spey) 01479 873113	COMMENDED ♛♛	1 Single 1 Twin 4 Double	2 En Suite fac 1 Pub Bath/Show	B&B per person £16.50-£19.50 Single £16.50-£19.50 Double	Open Jan-Dec Dinner 1830-1930 B&B + Eve. Meal £25.50-£38.50	

Attractive villa and garden in quiet area within easy walking distance of town,
woods and river. Many personal touches; evening meal by arrangement.

Crann Tara Guest House High Street Grantown-on-Spey Moray PH26 3EN Tel: (Grantown-on-Spey) 01479 872197	COMMENDED ♛	1 Single 1 Twin 3 Family	2 Pub Bath/Show	B&B per person £15.00-£16.00 Single £15.00-£16.00 Double	Open Jan-Dec Dinner from 1830 B&B + Eve. Meal £23.00-£25.00	

19th-century town house, recently modernised and personally run. Near River Spey,
with rod storage and drying room. Cycle hire and repair. Off-street car parking.
Dinner available.

Culdearn House

WOODLANDS TERRACE
GRANTOWN-ON-SPEY PH26 3JU
TEL: 01479 872106   FAX: 01479 873641

Elegant Country House offering house party atmosphere and warm welcome from the Scottish hosts Isobel and Alasdair Little who provide freshly prepared food and modestly priced wines. All guest rooms have ensuite private facilities with colour TV, radio, hairdryer and welcome tray. Culdearn House has been modernised and decorated with sympathy to offer a high standard of comfort. Ideal location for fishing, golf, riding, walking, birdwatching and visiting castles and historic sites. Log fires in season. 3 and 7 day breaks available from £120 all rates include dinner.

AA Premier selected RAC Highly Acclaimed.
Taste of Scotland selected members.
"AA Guest House of the Year" 1995
Please contact Isobel and Alasdair Little for reservations.

Culdearn House Woodlands Terrace Grantown-on-Spey Moray PH26 3JU Tel: (Grantown-on-Spey) 01479 872106 Fax: 01479 873641	DELUXE 👑👑👑	1 Single 3 Twin 5 Double	9 En Suite fac	Open Mar-Oct Dinner 1845-1930 B&B + Eve. Meal £43.00-£49.50	

Elegant Victorian house, retaining many original features.
Warm and friendly atmosphere. All rooms ensuite facilities.
Taste of Scotland member.

Garden Park Guest House

Woodside Avenue, Grantown-on-Spey, Moray PH26 3JN
Telephone: 01479 873235

Near golf course and pine forest walks, charming Victorian house set in lovely gardens. No steps, parking in grounds. Five en-suite bedrooms (one ground floor). Peat/wood fires. Excellent home cooking. AA selected RAC acclaimed. Licensed. Attractive golf package.

From £20.50 BB and £30.50 DB&B

Garden Park Guest House Woodside Avenue Grantown-on-Spey Moray PH26 3JN Tel: (Grantown-on-Spey) 01479 873235	COMMENDED 👑👑👑	3 Twin 2 Double	5 En Suite fac	B&B per person £20.50-£23.00 Single £20.50-£23.00 Double	Open Mar-Oct Dinner 1830-1900 B&B + Eve. Meal £30.50-£33.50	

Victorian, stone-built house set in own grounds. Home cooking, peat fires.
No steps and ground-floor accommodation.

Bank House

1 The Square, Grantown-on-Spey, Moray PH26 3HG
Telephone: 01479 873256

Centrally situated for Inverness, Elgin, Forres, Nairn and Aviemore. Large comfortable heated rooms with colour TV, tea/coffee facilities and armchairs. Full Scottish breakfast. Private bathroom available at extra charge. Five minutes walk from the renowned River Spey and golf course.

Mrs Helen Hunter Bank House, 1 The Square Grantown-on-Spey Moray PH26 3HG Tel: (Grantown-on-Spey) 01479 873256	COMMENDED Listed	1 Single 1 Twin 1 Double 1 Family	1 Priv. NOT ensuite 1 Pub Bath/Show	B&B per person £14.00-£16.00 Single £14.00-£16.00 Double	Open Jan-Dec	

Former Bank Manager's flat offering very spacious comfortable accommodation.
Ideal touring base.

Details of Grading and Classification are on page vi. | Key to symbols is on back flap. |

GRANTOWN-ON-SPEY cont	Map 4 C9

KINROSS HOUSE

Woodside Avenue, Grantown-on-Spey PH26 3JR
Tel: 01479 872042 Fax: 01479 873504

Kinross House sits on a quiet and pretty avenue an easy stroll from pinewoods and river, and from the centre of this delightful country town.

David and Katherine Elder provide Highland hospitality and comfort at its very best in their smoke-free house.

- Bedrooms are bright, warm and restful. All have welcome tray and colour TV.
- Five bedrooms have en-suite facilities. One of these is suitable for ambulant disabled guests.
- Children from 7 years.
- Delicious traditional Dinner freshly prepared with quality ingredients and served by David wearing his McIntosh kilt.

Kinross Guest House Woodside Avenue Grantown-on-Spey Moray PH26 3JR Tel: (Grantown-on-Spey) 01479 872042 Fax: 01479 873504	HIGHLY COMMENDED ⚜⚜⚜	2 Single 2 Twin 1 Double 1 Family	5 En Suite fac 2 Pub Bath/Show	B&B per person £20.00-£28.00 Single £22.00-£25.00 Double	Open Apr-Oct Dinner from 1900 B&B + Eve. Meal £32.00-£40.00	
		Victorian villa with original features in peaceful residential area. Friendly, informal atmosphere with Scottish hosts. No-smoking house.				
Miss Fenella Palmer Fearna House, Old Spey Bridge Grantown-on-Spey Moray PH26 3NQ Tel: (Grantown-on-Spey) 01479 872016	COMMENDED ⚜⚜	2 Twin 1 Double	2 En Suite fac 1 Priv. NOT ensuite	B&B per person £17.00-£27.00 Single £17.00 Double	Open Jan-Dec Dinner 1830-2000 B&B + Eve. Meal £27.00-£37.00	
		19th-century country house situated 1 mile (2kms) from town, overlooking the River Spey to the hills beyond.				
Parkburn Guest House High Street Grantown-on-Spey Moray PH26 3EN Tel: (Grantown-on-Spey) 01479 873116	COMMENDED ⚜⚜	1 Single 2 Twin 2 Double	2 En Suite fac 1 Pub Bath/Show	B&B per person from £16.00 Single from £15.00 Double	Open Jan-Dec Dinner at 1900 B&B + Eve. Meal from £25.00	
		Semi-detached Victorian villa standing back from main road with ample parking available. Fishing and fishing tuition can be arranged.				
The Pines Woodside Avenue Grantown-on-Spey Moray PH26 3JR Tel: (Grantown-on-Spey) 01479 872092 Fax: 01479 872092	COMMENDED ⚜⚜⚜	1 Single 3 Twin 2 Double 3 Family	5 En Suite fac 2 Pub Bath/Show	B&B per person £17.00-£22.00 Single £17.00-£22.00 Double	Open Jan-Dec Dinner from 1830 B&B + Eve. Meal £26.00-£31.00	
		Family run, situated on edge of pine wood, only 0.5 miles (1km) from town centre. All home cooking. Dogs welcome.				
Rossmor Guest House Woodlands Terrace Grantown-on-Spey Moray PH26 3JU Tel: (Grantown-on-Spey) 01479 872201 Fax: 01479 872201	COMMENDED ⚜⚜⚜	2 Twin 2 Double 1 Family	5 En Suite fac	B&B per person £20.00-£25.00 Single £20.00 Double	Open Jan-Dec Dinner at 1830 B&B + Eve. Meal £33.00	
		Spacious Victorian detached house with original features and large garden. Magnificent views of countryside. Home cooking; a warm welcome. Parking.				

GRETNA
Dumfriesshire
Mrs Donabie
The Beeches, Loanwath Road
off Sarkfoot Road
Gretna
Dumfriesshire
DG16 5EP
Tel: (Gretna) 01461 337448

Map 2
C10

COMMENDED
👑 👑

| 1 Twin | 2 En Suite fac | B&B per person | Open Feb-Nov |
| 1 Family | | £17.00-£18.00 Double | |

Former farmhouse overlooking the Solway and Lakeland hills.
A non-smoking house with homely and peaceful atmosphere, ensuite facilities.

Mrs V Greenhow
164-166 Central Avenue
Gretna
Dumfriesshire
DG16 5AF
Tel: (Gretna) 01461
337533/337307

COMMENDED
Listed

1 Twin	1 Pub Bath/Show	B&B per person	Open Mar-Oct
2 Double		£13.00-£14.00 Single	
		£13.00-£14.00 Double	
		Room only per person	
		£13.00	

Terraced house 100 yards to registrar's office in centre of village.
Close to all local amenities.

GRETNA GREEN
Dumfriesshire
Mrs O Crosbie
Alexander House
Gretna Green
Dumfriesshire
DG16 5DU
Tel: (Gretna) 01461 337597

Map 2
C10

COMMENDED
Listed

| 1 Twin | 2 En Suite fac | B&B per person | Open Jan-Dec |
| 3 Double | 1 Pub Bath/Show | £15.00-£18.00 Double | |

Modern bungalow, easy access to the M74. Close to amenities in Gretna Green.
All ground-floor accommodation.

Kathleen M Smith
The Mill, Grahamshill
Kirkpatrick Fleming
Gretna Green
Dumfriesshire
DG11 3BQ
Tel: (Kirkpatrick Fleming)
01461 800344/800603

COMMENDED
Listed

3 Twin	9 En Suite fac	B&B per person	Open Jan-Dec
1 Double		£20.00-£25.00 Single	Dinner 1800-2200
5 Family		£16.50-£17.50 Double	
		Room only per person	
		£18.00-£20.00	

Converted farm steading. Stone-built chalet accommodation just off the M74.
Fully licensed bar restaurant. Continental breakfast only.

GRIMSAY
North Uist, Western Isles
Mrs C MacLeod
Glendale, 7 Kallin
Grimsay
North Uist, Western Isles
HS6 5HY
Tel: (Benbecula)
01870 602029

Map 3
B8

COMMENDED
👑 👑

2 Twin	2 En Suite fac	B&B per person	Open Jan-Dec
1 Double	1 Priv. NOT ensuite	from £15.00 Single	Dinner 1900-2000
		from £15.00 Double	B&B + Eve. Meal
			from £25.00

Modern house in quiet position overlooking the harbour.
Views over the Minch and to the hills of South Uist.
All rooms with private facilities.

GULLANE
East Lothian
Mrs I Knight
Hopefield House, Main Street
Gullane
East Lothian
EH31 2DP
Tel: (North Berwick)
01620 842191

Map 2
D4

COMMENDED
👑 👑

🚶

3 Twin	3 En Suite fac	B&B per person	Open Apr-Sep
1 Double	1 Priv. NOT ensuite	£19.00-£20.00 Single	
		£19.00-£20.00 Double	

Traditional 19th-century stone-built farmhouse in centre of Gullane
and golfing countryside. 0.25 miles (0.5kms) from sandy beach and dunes.

Mr & Mrs G Nisbet
Faussett Hill House
Main Street
Gullane
East Lothian
EH31 2DR
Tel: (Gullane) 01620 842396

COMMENDED
👑 👑

2 Twin	2 En Suite fac	B&B per person	Open Mar-Dec
1 Double	1 Priv. NOT ensuite	from £20.00 Double	
	1 Pub Bath/Show		

Detached Edwardian house with pleasant garden. Edinburgh 30 minutes.
Sandy beaches and several golf courses nearby. Private parking.

HADDINGTON **East Lothian** Mrs Avril E Clark The Farmhouse, Upper Bolton Haddington East Lothian EH41 4HW Tel: (Gifford) 01620 810476	Map 2 D4	COMMENDED Listed	1 Twin 1 Double	1 Pub Bath/Show	B&B per person £17.00-£19.00 Single £16.00-£18.00 Double Room only per person £15.00-£17.00	Open Jan-Dec Dinner from 1830 B&B + Eve. Meal £26.00-£28.00
A warm welcome awaits you at this traditional farmhouse on working farm. Ideal for exploring E Lothian, Borders and Edinburgh.						
Mrs S A Clark Fieldfare, Upper Bolton Farm Haddington East Lothian EH41 4HW Tel: (Gifford) 01620 810346		COMMENDED 👑👑	1 Twin 1 Double 1 Family	1 Priv. NOT ensuite 2 Pub Bath/Show	B&B per person £17.00-£19.00 Single £16.00-£18.00 Double Room only per person £15.00-£17.00	Open Jan-Dec Dinner from 1800 B&B + Eve. Meal £26.00-£28.00
Modernised Victorian farm cottage in peaceful rural situation yet only half an hour's drive from Edinburgh. Local produce when available.						
Mrs C M D Gibson Carfrae, Garvald Haddington East Lothian EH41 4LP Tel: (Haddington) 01620 830242		HIGHLY COMMENDED 👑👑	1 Twin 2 Double	1 En Suite fac 1 Pub Bath/Show	B&B per person £18.00-£22.00 Double	Open May-Oct
19th-century listed farmhouse with open aspect overlooking own walled garden. Furnished to a high standard. Edinburgh, the Borders and many golf courses within easy reach.						
Mrs M Horsburgh Hillview, 10 Abbots View Haddington East Lothian EH41 3QG Tel: (Haddington) 01620 822987		COMMENDED Listed	1 Twin 1 Double	1 Pub Bath/Show	B&B per person £13.50 Single	Open Jan-Dec
Warm and comfortable modern house only half an hour's drive from Edinburgh.						
Mrs K Kerr Barney Mains Farm House Haddington East Lothian EH41 3SA Tel: (Athelstaneford) 01620 880310 Fax: 01620 880639		COMMENDED Listed	2 Twin 1 Double	1 Priv. NOT ensuite 2 Pub Bath/Show	B&B per person £17.00-£23.00 Single £15.00-£20.00 Double	Open Mar-Nov
Peaceful and comfortable farmhouse with superb views of surrounding countryside. Half an hour's drive from Edinburgh.						

HERE'S THE DIFFERENCE

STB's scheme has two distinct elements, grading and classification.

GRADING:

Measures the quality and condition of the facilities and services offered, eg, the warmth of welcome, quality of food and its presentation, condition of decor and furnishings, appearance of buildings, tidiness of grounds and gardens, condition of lighting and heating and so on.

Grading awards are: **Approved, Commended, Highly Commended, Deluxe.**

CLASSIFICATION:

Measures the range of physical facilities and services offered, eg, rooms with private bath, heating, reception, lounges, telephones and so on.

Classification awards are: **Listed to five crowns or one to five crowns.**

The Plough Tavern Hotel

11 Court Street, Haddington, East Lothian EH41 3DS
Telephone: 01620 823326   Fax: 01875 852240

The Plough Tavern Hotel has been owned and managed by Allan and Alison Inglis since 1990 and has been completely refurbished during this period. The bedrooms are warm and comfortable with ensuite facilities, TV and tea/coffee tray. The Plough has an excellent reputation for its friendly atmosphere and good food both with locals and returning visitors. Located thirty minutes drive from Edinburgh, in the centre of Haddington, county town of beautiful East Lothian, which hosts a variety of shops, sports facilities, golf courses and historic buildings. The Plough is an ideal base for all age groups.

The Plough Tavern 11 Court Street Haddington East Lothian EH41 3DS Tel: (Haddington) 01620 823326 Fax: 01875 852240	COMMENDED	2 Twin 2 Family	4 En Suite fac	B&B per person £20.00-£25.00 Single £20.00-£22.50 Double	Open Jan-Dec Dinner 1900-2100	
		19th-century traditional family run Inn. Comfortably furnished, with good home cooking. Ideal base for Golf. Edinburgh 17 miles (27kms).				
Catherine Richards Schiehallion, 19 Church Street Haddington East Lothian EH41 3EX Tel: (Haddington) 01620 825663/ 0378 841931(mobile)	COMMENDED	1 Twin 1 Double	1 Pub Bath/Show	B&B per person £17.00-£20.00 Single £17.00-£20.00 Double	Open Jan-Dec Dinner 1900-2100 B&B + Eve. Meal £23.00-£26.00	
		Victorian terraced family home in historic county town. Central location, 2 Old English sheepdogs in residence.				
Mrs N D Steven Under Bolton Farmhouse Under Bolton Haddington EH41 4HL Tel: (Gifford) 01620 810318 Fax: 01620 810379	COMMENDED	2 Twin	2 En Suite fac 2 Pub Bath/Show	B&B per person from £18.00 Single from £14.00 Double Room only per person from £12.00	Open Apr-Oct	
		Elegantly furnished farmhouse, peacefully situated 3 miles (5 kms) from Haddington. Within easy reach of East Coast golfing resorts. Some annexe accommodation.				
Mrs B Williams Eaglescairnie Mains Gifford, Haddington East Lothian EH41 4HN Tel: (Gifford) 01620 810491 Fax: 01620 810491	COMMENDED	2 Single 1 Twin 1 Double	1 En Suite fac 1 Priv. NOT ensuite 2 Pub Bath/Show	B&B per person £16.00-£20.00 Single	Open Jan-Dec	
		In quiet rural situation, on working mixed farm, large family house with magnificent views of Fife and Lammermuirs, 4 miles (6kms) from Haddington.				
HALKIRK **Caithness** Mrs M Banks Glenlivet, Fairview Halkirk Caithness KW12 6XF Tel: (Halkirk) 01847 831302	Map 4 D3 COMMENDED	1 Single 2 Twin 1 Double	2 Pub Bath/Show	B&B per person £13.00 Single £13.00 Double Room only per person £13.00	Open Jan-Dec	
		Modern house on outskirts of the village, close to river and 6 miles (10kms) south of Thurso.				

HALKIRK continued

Sandy & Jessie Waters
The Bungalow,
Banachmore Farm
Harpsdale, Halkirk
Caithness
KW12 6UN
Tel: (Westerdale) 01847 841216

Map 4
D3

HIGHLY COMMENDED

1 Twin
1 Double
1 Family

3 En Suite fac
1 Pub Bath/Show

B&B per person
from £16.00 Double

Open Jan-Dec
Dinner 1830-2000

Modern detached house on a working farm in a quiet rural setting,
3/4 mile(1.5kms) from salmon fishing on River Thurso.

HAWICK
Roxburghshire
Mrs Sandra Allan
Hillview, 4 Weensland Road
Hawick
Roxburghshire
TD9 9NP
Tel: (Hawick) 01450 374100

Map 2
D7

COMMENDED
Listed

1 Single
1 Twin
1 Double

1 Pub Bath/Show

B&B per person
from £16.00 Single
from £14.00 Double

Open Jan-Dec
Dinner 1700-1800
B&B + Eve. Meal
£18.00-£20.00

Comfortable, terraced house on main tourist route near town centre.
Public car park opposite. Near leisure centre.

Mr & Mrs Borthwick
Hopehill House
Hawick
Roxburghshire
TD9 7EH
Tel: (Hawick) 01450 375042

COMMENDED

1 Twin
1 Double
1 Family

2 En Suite fac
1 Limited ensuite
1 Priv. NOT ensuite

B&B per person
£15.00-£25.00 Single
£15.00-£25.00 Double
Room only per person
£15.00-£20.00

Open Jan-Dec
Dinner 1830-2100
B&B + Eve. Meal
£32.00-£35.00

Detached Victorian house in large secluded gardens.
Near centre of town, with panoramic views of hills from bedrooms.

Ellistrin
6 Fenwick Park, Hawick, Borders TD9 9PA
Telephone: (01450) 374216

Situated on the outskirts of the knitwear town of Hawick this family house enjoys an elevated position with a lovely view. All local amenities within easy walking distance. An attractive base for touring the lovely Borders countryside or walking in the Borders hills.

Mrs E Smith
Ellistrin, 6 Fenwick Park
Hawick
Roxburghshire
TD9 9PA
Tel: (Hawick) 01450 374216

COMMENDED

1 Twin
2 Double

2 En Suite fac
1 Pub Bath/Show

B&B per person
£14.00-£17.00 Single
£14.00-£17.00 Double

Open Apr-Oct
Dinner 1830-1930
B&B + Eve. Meal
£22.00-£25.00

Comfortable Victorian villa within spacious grounds in an elevated position
overlooking Hawick. 2 rooms ensuite. Meals available. Private parking.

Mrs Telfer
Craig-Ian, 6 Weensland Road
Hawick
Roxburghshire
TD9 9NP
Tel: (Hawick) 01450 373506

COMMENDED

1 Twin
2 Double

2 Pub Bath/Show

B&B per person
from £14.00 Double

Open Apr-Oct

Large Victorian terraced house, set above main A698 tourist route
and close to centre of historic Borders town.

BY HAWICK
Roxburghshire
Mrs A Bell
Kirkton Farmhouse
Hawick
Roxburghshire
TD9 8OJ
Tel: (Hawick) 01450 372421

Map 2
D7

COMMENDED
Listed

1 Twin
2 Double

1 Pub Bath/Show

B&B per person
£16.00 Single
£14.00 Double

Open Mar-Nov
Dinner 1800-2100
B&B + Eve. Meal
£21.00-£23.00

Spacious Border farmhouse with friendly family welcome.
Private loch fishing. Golf packages.

VAT is shown at 17.5%: changes in this rate may affect prices. Prices shown are for guidance only. Please send SAE with each enquiry.

Mrs M Jackson Colterscleugh, Teviothead Hawick Roxburghshire TD9 0LF Tel: (Teviotdale) 01450 850247		APPROVED ♛	1 Single 1 Twin 1 Family	1 Limited ensuite 1 Pub Bath/Show	B&B per person from £15.00 Single Room only per person from £14.00	Open Jan-Dec Dinner from 1900

Country house conveniently situated on the A7, with grounds and garden for guests to enjoy. Peaceful riverside setting. Evening meal available.

Mrs S Shell Wiltonburn Farm Hawick Roxburghshire TD9 7LL Tel: (Hawick) 01450 372414/ 0374 192551 (mobile)		COMMENDED Listed	1 Single 1 Double 1 Family	1 Limited ensuite 1 Pub Bath/Show	B&B per person £16.00-£17.00 Single £16.00-£17.00 Double Room only per person £16.00-£17.00	Open Jan-Dec

A friendly welcome at this comfortable farmhouse, in a sheltered valley, under 2 miles (3kms) from Hawick.

Mrs Margaret Young Flex Farm Hawick Roxburghshire TD9 0PB Tel: (Hawick) 01450 75064		COMMENDED Listed	1 Twin 1 Family	1 Pub Bath/Show	B&B per person £13.00-£15.00 Single £13.00-£15.00 Double	Open May-Oct

19th-century Borders farmhouse set in quiet countryside, 2 miles (3km) from Hawick. Fishing, shooting and golf nearby.

HELENSBURGH **Dunbartonshire** Bellfield Guest House 199 East Clyde Street Helensburgh Dunbartonshire G84 7AJ Tel: (Helensburgh) 01436 671628 Fax: 01436 671628	Map 1 G4	COMMENDED ♛♛♛	1 Single 1 Twin 1 Double 1 Family	2 En Suite fac 2 Pub Bath/Show	B&B per person £16.00-£20.00 Single £21.00-£30.00 Double Room only per person £14.50-£20.00	Open Jan-Dec Dinner 1800-1900

A family run guest house. Friendly accommodation in "The Garden City of the Firth of Clyde". Ideal for touring.

Mrs E Blackwell Longleat, 39 East Argyle Street Helensburgh Dunbartonshire G84 7EN Tel: (Helensburgh) 01436 672465		COMMENDED ♛	1 Twin 2 Double	1 Pub Bath/Show	B&B per person £17.00-£18.00 Single £17.00-£18.00 Double	Open Jan-Dec

Magnificently situated family house in quiet residential area overlooking Firth of Clyde. Non-smoking.

Mrs Johnston Lethamhill 20 West Dhuhill Drive Helensburgh Dunbartonshire G84 Tel: (Helensburgh) 01436 676016		COMMENDED ♛♛♛	1 Single 1 Double 1 Family	1 En Suite fac 1 Priv. NOT ensuite 1 Pub Bath/Show	B&B per person £19.00-£30.00 Single from £19.00 Double	Open Jan-Dec Dinner 1800-1900 B&B + Eve. Meal £31.00-£42.00

'B' listed Edwardian Mock Tudor house with extensive garden in quiet residential area.

BE SURE TO CHOOSE THE SCOTTISH TOURIST BOARD'S SIGN OF QUALITY

Middledrift

85 James Street, Helensburgh, Dunbartonshire G84 9LE
Telephone: 01436 674867 Fax: 01436 679000

Detached 19th-century villa in central location. Large garden, 5 minutes walk from sea front, 45 minutes from Glasgow and Stirling. 5 miles to Loch Lomond. Ideal touring base, off-street parking, friendly and comfortable, everyone welcome.

Mrs M K Paul Middledrift, 85 James Street Helensburgh Dunbartonshire G84 9LE Tel: (Helensburgh) 01436 674867	COMMENDED	1 Single 1 Twin 1 Family	1 En Suite fac 1 Priv. NOT ensuite 1 Pub Bath/Show	B&B per person £20.00-£22.00 Single £18.00-£20.00 Double	Open Jan-Dec	
		1860 sandstone family home of character with large established garden. Children and pets welcome.				
Mrs M Richards Ravenswood, 32 Suffolk Street Helensburgh Dunbartonshire G84 9PA Tel: (Helensburgh) 01436 672112 Fax: 01436 672112	COMMENDED	2 Single 1 Twin 1 Double	2 En Suite fac 2 Priv. NOT ensuite 1 Pub Bath/Show	B&B per person £22.50-£40.00 Single £19.00-£25.00 Double	Open Jan-Dec Dinner from 1830 B&B + Eve. Meal £34.00-£50.00	
		Victorian family home. Quiet location with mature gardens, close to Hill House, town centre and Loch Lomond.				
Mrs Dorothy Ross Eastbank, 10 Hanover Street Helensburgh Dunbartonshire G84 7AW Tel: (Helensburgh) 01436 673665	APPROVED Listed	1 Single 1 Twin 1 Family	1 Pub Bath/Show	B&B per person £20.00-£25.00 Single £15.00-£17.00 Double	Open Jan-Dec	
		1st floor flat conversion with all accommodation on same level. Fine views from lounge across the Clyde to Greenock. Knitting instruction available.				
Mrs D M Smith Hapland East Abercromby Street Helensburgh Dunbartonshire G84 7SD Tel: (Helensburgh) 01436 674042/679243	COMMENDED	2 Twin 1 Double	3 En Suite fac	B&B per person £21.00-£25.00 Single £18.50-£21.00 Double	Open Jan-Dec	
		Large Victorian family home in extensive grounds. 10 minutes from Loch Lomond. Short walk from the Upper Station and golf course. Warm friendly atmosphere.				

Thorndean House

64 COLQUHOUN ST.
HELENSBURGH
G84 9JP
Tel: 01436 674922
Fax: 01436 679913

Warm Scottish welcome, good food, spacious comfort, modern amenities and private facilities. Large gardens with off-street parking. No smoking.

Excellent touring centre for Loch Lomond, Trossachs, Clyde Coast. Glasgow airport only 40 mins.

Mrs Urquhart Thorndean 64 Colquhoun Street Helensburgh Dunbartonshire G84 9JP Tel: (Helensburgh) 01436 674922 Fax: 01436 679913	COMMENDED	1 Twin 1 Double 1 Family	2 En Suite fac 1 Pub Bath/Show	B&B per person £17.00-£30.00 Single £17.00-£21.00 Double	Open Jan-Dec	
		Spacious family home in quiet residential area within easy walking distance of a fine selection of shops and quality restaurants.				

HELMSDALE Sutherland	Map 4 C5

Broomhill House
Helmsdale, Sutherland KW8 6JS
Telephone: 01431 821259

This family run house lies just beyond the 30 mile limit on the north side of the village. An ideal base for touring the north and west and as a stopover en route to Orkney.

Mrs S Blance
Broomhill House
Helmsdale
Sutherland KW8 6JS
Tel: (Helmsdale) 01431 821259
Fax: 01431 821259

COMMENDED ♕♕♕

1 Twin
1 Double

2 En Suite fac
1 Pub Bath/Show

B&B per person
£17.00-£21.00 Single
£15.00-£19.00 Double

Open Apr-Oct
Dinner 1700-1900
B&B + Eve. Meal
£25.00-£29.00

Victorian, stone-built house with turret.
Magnificent panoramic view over Helmsdale to the sea.

Mrs H Clegg
Alderwood
157 West Helmsdale
Helmsdale
Sutherland KW8 6HH
Tel: (Helmsdale) 01431 821538
Fax: 01431 821538

COMMENDED ♕♕

1 Twin
1 Double
1 Family

2 Priv. NOT ensuite

B&B per person
£14.50-£17.00 Single
£14.50-£17.00 Double

Open Jan-Dec

Family home in detached house on the edge of Helmsdale in a quiet
crofting area. Convenient touring centre. Cycle hire available.

Mrs E McAngus
Glebe House
Sutherland Street, Helmsdale
Sutherland KW8 6LQ
Tel: (Helmsdale) 01431 821682

COMMENDED ♕

1 Twin
1 Double

2 En Suite fac
2 Pub Bath/Show

B&B per person
£15.00 Double

Open Jan-Dec

Detached traditional stone-built house, in quiet cul-de-sac with parking at rear.

Mrs M C Polson
Torbuie, Navidale
Helmsdale
Sutherland
KW8 6JS
Tel: (Helmsdale) 01431 821424

HIGHLY COMMENDED ♕♕

2 Double

2 En Suite fac

B&B per person
£15.00-£17.00 Single
£15.00-£17.00 Double
Room only per person
£15.00-£17.00

Open Apr-Oct

Well-appointed house with superb views overlooking sea. Good base for touring.

HUNTLY Aberdeenshire	Map 4 F9

Mrs B Barclay
Elmbank, Richmond Road
Huntly
Aberdeenshire AB54 5BA
Tel: (Huntly) 01466 792809

HIGHLY COMMENDED ♕

3 Double

2 En Suite fac
1 Priv. NOT ensuite

B&B per person
to £26.00 Single
£18.00-£20.00 Double

Open Jan-Dec
Dinner from 2000
B&B + Eve. Meal
£25.95-£47.50

Gracious Victorian townhouse, newly refurbished.
Providing cosy en suite bedrooms. Peaceful location, friendly atmosphere.
Private garden and parking.

"BRAESIDE"
Provost Street, Huntly, Aberdeenshire AB54 5BB
Telephone: 01466 793825

Modern detached chalet bungalow situated in a quiet residential conservation area, close to town centre and railway station. Local amenities within walking distance. Many country pursuits and sporting activities available locally. Ideal centre for touring. On Castle Trail and within easy reach of Whisky Trail and Moray Coast.

Mr & Mrs D Calcraft
Braeside, Provost Street
Huntly
Aberdeenshire
AB54 5BB
Tel: (Huntly) 01466 793825

COMMENDED

1 Single
1 Twin
1 Double

1 En Suite fac
1 Pub Bath/Show

B&B per person
from £14.00 Single
£14.00-£17.00 Double

Open Jan-Dec

Modern detached house with private parking in quiet location.
Close to town centre, railway station and all amenities.

HUNTLY continued

Map 4 F9

Mrs Manson
Greenmount, 43 Gordon Street
Huntly
Aberdeenshire
AB54 5EQ
Tel: (Huntly) 01466 792482

COMMENDED

2 Single	4 En Suite fac	B&B per person
4 Twin	1 Priv. NOT ensuite	£14.00-£20.00 Single
2 Family	1 Pub Bath/Show	£14.00-£18.00 Double

Open Jan-Dec,
ex Xmas/New Year
Dinner 1800-1900

c1854 town house with annexe. Friendly personal attention; laundry room; private parking. In town centre but quiet. On Castle and Whisky Trails.

Mrs R M Thomson
Southview, Victoria Road
Huntly
Aberdeenshire
AB54 5AH
Tel: (Huntly) 01466 792456

COMMENDED

2 Twin	2 Pub Bath/Show	B&B per person
1 Double		£14.00 Single
1 Family		£14.00 Double

Open Jan-Dec
Dinner 1700-1800
B&B + Eve. Meal
£20.00

Detached Victorian house in quiet residential area close to town centre. Overlooking the bowling green.

BY HUNTLY
Aberdeenshire

Map 4 F9

Mrs A J Morrison
Haddoch Farm
Huntly
Aberdeenshire
AB54 4SL
Tel: (Rothiemay)
01466 711217

COMMENDED
Listed

1 Double	2 Pub Bath/Show	B&B per person
1 Family		£13.00-£15.00 Single
		£12.00-£15.00 Double
		Room only per person
		£13.00-£15.00

Open Apr-Sep
Dinner 1800-2000
B&B + Eve. Meal
£18.00-£20.00

Mixed stock/arable farm near River Deveron, 3 miles (5kms) and 15 miles (24kms) from coast. Fine views of countryside. Home cooking.

Paula Ross
Yonder Bognie
Forgue, by Huntly
Aberdeenshire
AB54 6BR
Tel: (Forgue) 01466 730375

COMMENDED

2 Double	1 Pub Bath/Show	B&B per person
		from £13.00 Single
		from £12.50 Double
		Room only per person
		from £13.00

Open Jan-Dec
Dinner at 1800
B&B + Eve. Meal
from £18.50

Traditional family farmhouse on mixed 152 acre farm.
7 miles (11 kms) from Huntly, 12 miles (19 kms) from Banff; on A97.
French and Italian spoken.

INNERLEITHEN
Peeblesshire
Caddon View Guest House
14 Pirn Road
Innerleithen
Peeblesshire
EH44 6HH
Tel: (Innerleithen)
01896 830208

Map 2 C6

COMMENDED

1 Single	2 En Suite fac	B&B per person
2 Twin	1 Priv. NOT ensuite	£17.00-£18.00 Single
1 Double	1 Pub Bath/Show	£15.00-£18.00 Double
1 Family		

Open Jan-Dec
Dinner 1830-1900
B&B + Eve. Meal
£25.00-£28.00

A warm welcome and home cooking at this substantial Victorian house, with many period features. Ideal for touring the Borders.

BY INSCH
Aberdeenshire

Map 4 F9

Mrs Grant
Earlsfield Farm
Kennethmont, by Insch
Aberdeenshire
AB52 6YQ
Tel: (Kennethmont)
01464 831473
Fax: 01464 831473

COMMENDED

1 Single	1 En Suite fac	B&B per person
1 Double	1 Priv. NOT ensuite	£16.00 Single
1 Family	2 Pub Bath/Show	£14.00-£16.00 Double

Open Jan-Dec
Dinner at 1900
B&B + Eve. Meal
from £20.00

Arable farm within 1 mile (2kms) of Leith Hall (NTS) and close to Castle and Whisky Trails. Beautiful countryside, ideal hillwalking.

INSH, Kincraig
Inverness-shire

Map 4 B10

Ian & Pamela Grant
Greenfield Croft
Insh
Inverness-shire
PH21 1NT
Tel: (Kingussie) 01540 661010

HIGHLY
COMMENDED

1 Twin	3 En Suite fac	B&B per person
2 Double		from £16.00 Single
		from £15.00 Double

Open Jan-Dec
Dinner from 1900
B&B + Eve. Meal
from £25.00

Newly built house on a working croft in quiet Highland village with superb views. Home cooking; log fire; all rooms with ensuite facilities.

INVERARAY Argyll	Map 1 F3

CREAG DHUBH
INVERARAY, ARGYLL PA32 8XT
Telephone: 01499 302430
Situated in own grounds and gardens with views of Loch Fyne and the Cowal Hills.
Scenic and historic area ideal for touring.

Mrs MacLugash Creag Dhubh Inveraray Argyll PA32 8XT Tel: (Inveraray) 01499 302430		COMMENDED ✿✿	1 Twin 2 Double 1 Family	1 En Suite fac 2 Pub Bath/Show	B&B per person £14.00-£18.00 Double	Open Mar-Nov

Large stone-built house with extensive garden and excellent views over Loch Fyne.

INVERGARRY Inverness-shire Mr & Mrs Buswell Nursery Cottages Invergarry Inverness-shire PH35 4HL Tel: (Invergarry) 01809 501297	Map 3 H11 COMMENDED ✿	1 Single 1 Double 1 Family	1 Priv. NOT ensuite 2 Pub Bath/Show	B&B per person £14.00-£15.00 Single £13.00-£16.00 Double	Open Jan-Dec Dinner 1800-1900

Mid 19th-century homely cottage. 7 miles (11kms) south of Fort Augustus.
Centrally located for touring the Highlands.

FOREST LODGE
South Laggan, Invergarry, by Spean Bridge
Inverness-shire PH34 4EA. Telephone: 01809 501219

Staying one night or more, Ian and Janet Shearer's comfortable home offers pleasant en-suite accommodation, relaxed surroundings and home cooking served with friendly attention. Forest Lodge is conveniently situated in the centre of the Great Glen and is ideal for touring or participating in out-door pursuits.

Forest Lodge Guest House South Laggan Invergarry, by Spean Bridge Inverness-shire PH34 4EA Tel: (Invergarry) 01809 501219		COMMENDED ✿✿✿	2 Twin 3 Double 2 Family	6 En Suite fac 1 Priv. NOT ensuite	B&B per person £15.00-£18.00 Double	Open Jan-Dec Dinner from 1930 B&B + Eve. Meal £25.00-£28.00

Family run guest house in the heart of the Great Glen where Caledonian Canal joins Lochs Lochy and Oich. Ideal centre for outdoor activities.

Drynachan Cottage
INVERGARRY, INVERNESS-SHIRE PH35 4HL
Telephone: 01809 501225
Seventeeth-century Highland cottage, visited by *Bonnie Prince Charlie* in 1746, idyllically situated on the shores of Loch Oich. Comfortable accommodation with open fire and home cooking. Large garden with many birds. Access to Great Glen Cycle Track. Ideal for hillwalking, ski-ing, cycling and touring. Cycle store and drying area.

Ms Caroline Francis Drynachan Cottage Invergarry Inverness-shire PH35 4HL Tel: (Invergarry) 01809 501225		COMMENDED ✿✿	1 Twin 1 Double 1 Family	1 En Suite fac 1 Pub Bath/Show	B&B per person £14.00-£19.00 Single £13.00-£18.00 Double	Open Jan-Dec Dinner 1900-1930 B&B + Eve. Meal £20.00-£26.00

Historic Highland cottage, recently renovated, centrally situated in the Great Glen, 25 miles north of Fort William. Log fire, home cooking.

	Map 3 H11						
INVERGARRY continued Mrs H Fraser Ardfriseal, Mandally Road Invergarry Inverness-shire PH35 4HR Tel: (Invergarry) 01809 501281		COMMENDED ♛	1 Twin 2 Double	1 Pub Bath/Show	B&B per person from £14.00 Single	Open May-Oct	

Modern family home in secluded area with magnificent views of surrounding hills.
1 mile (2kms) from Invergarry.

| Mrs F I Jamieson
Lilac Cottage, South Laggan
Spean Bridge
Inverness-shire
PH34 4EA
Tel: (Invergarry) 01809 501410 | COMMENDED Listed | 1 Twin
1 Double
1 Family | 1 Pub Bath/Show | B&B per person
£14.00-£16.00 Single
£14.00-£16.00 Double | Open Jan-Dec
Dinner 1900-2000 | |

Modernised 100-year-old croft house convenient for touring West of Scotland.
Evening meal and home cooking.

North Laggan Farmhouse
by Spean Bridge, Inverness PH34 4EB
Telephone: 01809 501335

Overlooking the Caledonian Canal and Loch Oich, set ½ mile off A82, 2 miles south of Invergarry amidst sheep farming country. A completely modernised croft house which retains much of its original character. Two comfortable bed/sitting rooms. Home-made bread, good food and individual attention guaranteed.

| Mrs Waugh
North Laggan Farmhouse
by Invergarry
Inverness-shire
PH34 4EB
Tel: (Invergarry) 01809 501335 | COMMENDED Listed | 1 Twin
1 Family | 1 Pub Bath/Show | B&B per person
£18.50 Single
£14.50 Double | Open May-Sep
Dinner from 1900
B&B + Eve. Meal
£24.00-£28.00 | |

In peaceful open countryside overlooking the Caledonian Canal and Loch Oich.
Warm welcome, home-made bread and good home cooking. Non-smoking home.

INVERGLOY Inverness-shire	Map 3 H11

RIVERSIDE
INVERGLOY, SPEAN BRIDGE, INVERNESS-SHIRE PH34 4DY
Telephone and Fax: 01397 712684

Guests return year after year to this warm and comfortable bungalow set in spectacular gardens overlooking *Loch Lochy*. There are five restaurants within five miles and **Invergloy** is ideally placed for a wide range of day tours encompassing the very best of the *West Highlands*.

| Mrs D Bennet
Riverside
Invergloy, by Spean Bridge
Inverness-shire
PH34 4DY
Tel: (Spean Bridge)
01397 712684
Fax: 01397 712684 | HIGHLY COMMENDED ♛♛ | 1 Double
1 Family | 1 En Suite fac
1 Priv. NOT ensuite | B&B per person
£22.00-£24.00 Single
£17.00-£19.00 Double | Open Jan-Dec | |

Cosy bungalow in secluded lochside setting. Extensive grounds with over
200 varieties of rhododendron. Ideal base for Great Glen and West Coast.

| **INVERGORDON**
Ross-shire
Craigaron Guest House
17 Saltburn
Invergordon
Ross-shire
IV18 0JX
Tel: (Invergordon)
01349 853640 | Map 4 B7 | COMMENDED ♛♛ | 1 Single
3 Twin
1 Double | 3 En Suite fac
1 Pub Bath/Show | B&B per person
from £17.00 Single
from £16.00 Double
Room only per person
from £14.00 | Open Jan-Dec
Dinner 1900-1930
B&B + Eve. Meal
£26.00-£35.00 | |

19th-century converted fisherman's cottage overlooking the sea.
Five minute drive from town centre.

VAT is shown at 17.5%: changes in this rate may affect prices. Prices shown are for guidance only. Please send SAE with each enquiry.

INVERKEITHING Fife	Map 2 B4

The Roods Guest House
16 Bannerman Avenue, Inverkeithing, Fife KY11 1NG
Telephone and Fax: 01383 415049

Family run and set in quiet secluded gardens yet with rail and bus links nearby. Ony a few minutes drive from the Forth Bridges and fifteen minutes from Edinburgh make for an ideal touring base. We offer a high standard of accommodation with 1st class facilities.

Mrs Marley
The Roods
16 Bannerman Avenue
Inverkeithing
Fife
KY11 1NG
Tel: (Inverkeithing)
01383 415049
Fax: 01383 415049

COMMENDED

1 Twin   2 En Suite fac
1 Double

B&B per person
£18.00-£23.00 Single
£17.00-£22.00 Double

Open Jan-Dec
Dinner 1900-2000
B&B + Eve. Meal
£28.00-£35.00

Modern house with quiet garden close to Forth Bridges, near town centre and railway station. Conveniently situated for touring Forth Valley and Fife

---

INVERKIP Renfrewshire	Map 1 F5

Mrs Russell
Ellenbank
Inverkip
Renfrewshire
PA16 0AX
Tel: (Wemyss Bay)
01475 521209

COMMENDED

2 Twin   1 En Suite fac
        2 Pub Bath/Show

B&B per person
£24.00-£28.00 Single
£17.00-£19.00 Double
Room only per person
£20.00-£24.00

Open Apr-Sep

Late Georgian 'B' Listed house retaining many original features situated above village overlooking Firth of Clyde and Inverkip marina.

Mrs Wallace
The Foresters, Station Road
Inverkip
Renfrewshire
PA16
Tel: (Wemyss Bay)
01475 521433
Fax: 01475 522000

APPROVED

1 Twin   1 Pub Bath/Show
2 Family

B&B per person
£20.00-£25.00 Single
£17.50-£20.00 Double

Open Jan-Dec

Original forester's house c1890 in conservation village, near marina. Transport connections 2 minutes walk.

INVERMORISTON Inverness-shire	Map 4 A10

Mr & Mrs M Douglas
Burnside, Dalcataig
Glenmoriston
Inverness-shire
IV3 6YG
Tel: (Glenmoriston)
01320 351262

COMMENDED

1 Single   2 En Suite fac
1 Twin   1 Priv. NOT ensuite
1 Double

B&B per person
£15.00-£18.00 Single
£15.00-£18.00 Double

Open Apr-Oct
Dinner at 1900
B&B + Eve. Meal
£25.00-£28.00

Warm Highland hospitality at this modern bungalow 1 mile (2kms) from Invermoriston and near Loch Ness. Peace and tranquillity with birdsong.

Mrs I Greig
Georgeston
Invermoriston
Inverness-shire
IV3 6YA
Tel: (Glenmoriston)
01320 351264

A10

COMMENDED

1 Twin   1 Pub Bath/Show
2 Double

B&B per person
£13.00-£16.00 Single
£13.00-£16.00 Double
Room only per person
£13.00-£16.00

Open Jan-Dec

Detached bungalow on outskirts of village and just off main road. Ample parking and nice views.

INVERNESS	Map 4 B8					

Abbey House
Bruce Gardens
Inverness
IV3 5ED
Tel: (Inverness) 01463 242448
Fax: 01463 714236

COMMENDED 👑👑

2 Double
3 Family
5 En Suite fac

B&B per person
£16.50-£22.50 Single
£16.50-£22.50 Double

Open Jan-Dec
Dinner 1830-2000
B&B + Eve. Meal
£22.00-£28.00

Abbey House has ensuites of a good standard and a guests' lounge.
Dining room in adjoining Alban House.

Aberfeldy Lodge Guest House
11 Southside Road
Inverness
IV2 3BG
Tel: (Inverness) 01463 231120

COMMENDED 👑👑👑

3 Twin
3 Double
3 Family
9 En Suite fac

B&B per person
£25.00-£35.00 Single
£19.00-£25.00 Double

Open Jan-Dec
Dinner 1800-1830
B&B + Eve. Meal
£37.50-£47.50

Substantial detached house with large garden in quiet residential area.
Close to town centre and convenient for bus and railway stations. Private parking.

Abermar Guest House
25 Fairfield Road
Inverness
IV3 5QD
Tel: (Inverness) 01463 239019

APPROVED 👑👑

5 Single
2 Twin
2 Double
2 Family
3 En Suite fac
2 Limited ensuite
3 Pub Bath/Show

B&B per person
£15.00-£16.00 Single
£15.00-£16.00 Double

Open Jan-Dec

Detached house situated in a residential area. 5 minutes walk from the
town centre. Convenient base for touring the Highlands. Private parking.

Ach Aluinn Guest House
27 Fairfield Road
Inverness
IV3 5QD
Tel: (Inverness) 01463 230127

COMMENDED 👑👑

1 Single
2 Twin
2 Family
4 En Suite fac
1 Priv. NOT ensuite

B&B per person
£18.00-£20.00 Single
£18.00-£20.00 Double
Room only per person
£18.00-£20.00

Open Jan-Dec

Newly refurbished, detached, Victorian house with private parking in quiet
residential road. 10 minutes walk from town centre. All rooms ensuite.

Mrs C D Aird
Pitfarrane, 57 Crown Street
Inverness
IV2 3AY
Tel: (Inverness) 01463 239338

COMMENDED 👑

1 Single
2 Twin
2 Double
4 Limited ensuite
1 Pub Bath/Show

B&B per person
£14.00-£16.00 Single
£14.00-£15.00 Double
Room only per person
from £12.00

Open Jan-Dec

End terraced house in quiet residential area within 10 minutes walk of
town centre. Some private parking.

Alban House
Bruce Gardens
Inverness
IV3 5ED
Tel: (Inverness) 01463 714301
Fax: 01463 714236

COMMENDED 👑👑👑
♿

3 Family
3 En Suite fac

B&B per person
£16.50-£22.50 Single
£16.50-£22.50 Double

Open Jan-Dec
Dinner 1800-2100

Alban House has been refurbished to a high standard. In partnership with
adjoining Abbey House, it contains the shared dining room.

Amulree
40 Fairfield Road, Inverness IV3 5QD
Telephone: 01463 224822

Convenient accommodation with comfortable rooms at
affordable prices. Excellent facilities and breakfast menu. Eight
minutes walk from town centre. This homely bed and breakfast
incorporates a small holistic centre offering aromatherapy,
reflexology, chiropody etc. *A relaxing place to stop over!*

Amulree
40 Fairfield Road
Inverness
IV3 5QD
Tel: (Inverness) 01463 224822

COMMENDED 👑👑

2 Single
1 Twin
1 Double
2 En Suite fac
1 Limited ensuite

B&B per person
£13.00-£18.00 Single
£13.00-£18.00 Double
Room only per person
£11.00-£16.00

Open Jan-Dec
Dinner 1800-2000
B&B + Eve. Meal
£18.00-£24.00

Warm and friendly welcome in Victorian house within easy walking distance
of station and all facilities.

Mrs Pamela Angus-Wood Number One, 1 Gordonville Road Inverness IV2 4SU Tel: (Inverness) 01463 712434	HIGHLY COMMENDED	1 Twin 1 Double	1 En Suite fac 1 Priv. NOT ensuite	B&B per person £15.00-£17.00 Single £15.00-£17.00 Double	Open Jan-Dec Dinner 1800-1945 B&B + Eve. Meal £15.00-£17.00	

Quiet residential location, next to park, river and gardens.
Walking distance from town centre and theatre. Off-road parking.

Ardnacoille Guest House 1a Annfield Road Inverness IV2 3HP Tel: (Inverness) 01463 233451	COMMENDED	1 Twin 1 Double 1 Family	1 Priv. NOT ensuite 2 Pub Bath/Show	B&B per person £15.00-£17.00 Double	Open Mar-Oct	

1865 red sandstone house in residential area. Spacious bedrooms.
10 minute walk from town centre. Ample parking.

ATHERSTONE

42 Fairfield Road, Inverness IV3 5QD
Telephone: 01463 240240

A warm Highland welcome awaits you at this Victorian home –
minutes from Inverness town centre. Atherstone offers en-suite rooms,
central heating, TV, tea/coffee trays and parking. The friendly
atmosphere and personal attention make Atherstone the ideal place to
relax after a day touring Loch Ness and the Highlands.

Atherstone Guest House 42 Fairfield Road Inverness IV3 5QD Tel: (Inverness) 01463 240240	COMMENDED	1 Single 1 Double 1 Family	3 En Suite fac	B&B per person £16.00-£18.00 Single	Open Jan-Dec	

Attractively decorated and comfortably furnished with a homely atmosphere.
All rooms ensuite. Private parking.

Mrs Boynton 12 Annfield Road Inverness IV2 3HX Tel: (Inverness) 01463 233188	COMMENDED	1 Double 1 Family	2 Pub Bath/Show	B&B per person £13.50 Single	Open Jan-Dec	

Family run house in quiet residential area within easy walking distance
of town centre. Home baking and preserves.

Mrs L Cameron Tay Villa, 40 Harrowden Road Inverness IV3 5QN Tel: (Inverness) 01463 232984	COMMENDED	1 Twin 1 Double	2 En Suite fac 1 Pub Bath/Show	B&B per person £15.00-£16.00 Single £15.00-£16.00 Double	Open Feb-mid Dec	

Stone-built house, in quiet residential area, yet with easy access
to town centre. All bedrooms with private facilities.

Mr & Mrs J Campbell St Vincents 12A Diriebught Road Inverness IV2 3QW Tel: (Inverness) 01463 224717	COMMENDED	1 Twin 1 Double 1 Family	2 En Suite fac 1 Priv. NOT ensuite	B&B per person £14.00-£17.50 Single	Open Jan-Dec	

Newly built modern spacious family house in quiet residential area.
Close to town centre and all amenities. Private parking.

Welcome Host

LOOK FOR
THE SIGNS OF
THE WELCOME HOSTS

INVERNESS continued	Map 4 B8					

Mrs Carson-Duff
Cambeth Lodge
49 Fairfield Road
Inverness
IV3 5QP
Tel: (Inverness) 01463 231764

COMMENDED

2 Twin   1 En Suite fac
1 Family   1 Pub Bath/Show

B&B per person
£13.50-£17.00 Double

Open Jan-Dec
Dinner from 1800
B&B + Eve. Meal
£25.00-£28.00

Victorian, stone building with private parking in quiet residential area.
10 minutes walk to town centre.

Cedar Villa
33 Kenneth Street
Inverness
IV3 5DH
Tel: (Inverness) 01463 230477
Fax: 01463 230477

COMMENDED

1 Single   4 En Suite fac
1 Twin   1 Pub Bath/Show
1 Double
3 Family

B&B per person
£13.00-£20.00 Single

Open Jan-Dec

Centrally situated with easy access to theatre, bus and railway station.

Mrs Elizabeth Chisholm
Carbisdale, 43 Charles Street
Inverness
IV2 3AH
Tel: (Inverness) 01463 225689
Fax: 01463 225689

HIGHLY COMMENDED

1 Twin   2 Pub Bath/Show
2 Double

B&B per person
from £13.00 Single
from £13.00 Double

Open Jan-Dec

Terraced family home furnished to high standard. Warm welcome.
Close to town centre, and easy walk from rail station.

Clisham House
43 Fairfield Road
Inverness
IV3 5QP
Tel: (Inverness) 01463 239965
Fax: 01463 239965

COMMENDED

2 Double   4 En Suite fac
2 Family

B&B per person
from £20.00 Double

Open Jan-Dec

Large detached town house with interior woodwork of character.
Ample parking. Within walking distance of town centre.

Craigside Lodge
4 Gordon Terrace
Inverness
IV2 3HD
Tel: (Inverness) 01463 231576
Fax: 01463 713409

COMMENDED

3 Twin   6 En Suite fac
3 Double   1 Priv. NOT ensuite

B&B per person
£16.00-£18.00 Single
Room only per person
£16.00-£18.00

Open Jan-Dec

Detached Victorian house set in quiet elevated position.
Outstanding views of Castle, river and town.

Dionard Guest House
39 Old Edinburgh Road
Inverness
IV2 3HJ
Tel: (Inverness) 01463 233557

HIGHLY COMMENDED

1 Twin   3 En Suite fac
2 Double

B&B per person
£20.00-£30.00 Single
£18.00-£22.00 Double

Open Jan-Dec

Victorian house with modern extension, 1/2 mile (1 km) from town centre.
Car parking available.

Mrs I Donald
Kerrisdale, 4 Muirfield Road
Inverness
IV2 4AY
Tel: (Inverness) 01463 235489

HIGHLY COMMENDED

1 Twin   1 En Suite fac
1 Double   1 Pub Bath/Show
1 Family

B&B per person
£15.00-£18.00 Single
£15.00-£18.00 Double

Open Jan-Dec
Dinner at 1800
B&B + Eve. Meal
£23.00-£26.00

Spacious Victorian house with large garden, situated in quiet residential area
within walking distance of the town centre. Home cooking.

East Dene Guest House
6 Ballifeary Road
Inverness
IV3 5PJ
Tel: (Inverness) 01463 232976

HIGHLY COMMENDED

1 Twin   3 En Suite fac
3 Double   1 Priv. NOT ensuite

B&B per person
£23.00-£30.00 Single
£16.00-£21.00 Double

Open Jan-Dec
Dinner 1815-1900
B&B + Eve. Meal
£30.00-£44.00

Detached house in quiet residential area, 3 minutes from Eden Court Theatre
and riverside walks. 10 minutes from town centre.

Mrs Margaret Edwards
St Kilda, 28 Rangemore Road
Inverness
IV3 5EA
Tel: (Inverness) 01463 235200

COMMENDED

1 Single   2 Pub Bath/Show
1 Double
1 Family

B&B per person
£15.00 Single
£14.00 Double

Open Jan-Dec

Victorian house in quiet residential area and close to city centre and all amenities.

Clach Mhuilinn

**7 HARRIS ROAD
INVERNESS
IV2 3LS
TEL: 01463 237059**

Let us welcome you to our no-smoking detached house in a quiet, residential area 20 minutes stroll from Inverness centre. Stay a while and unwind, enjoying delicious breakfasts overlooking the lovely garden. Explore the beautiful Highlands, returning nightly to your comfortable room. Bar meals available nearby.
Contact: Mrs Jacqi Elmslie.

Mrs J R Elmslie
Clach Mhuilinn, 7 Harris Road
Inverness
IV2 3LS
Tel. (Inverness) 01463 237059	HIGHLY COMMENDED 👑👑	1 Single
1 Twin
1 Double	1 En Suite fac
1 Priv. NOT ensuite
1 Pub Bath/Show	B&B per person
£18.00-£21.00 Single
£18.00-£21.00 Double	Open Mar-Nov
Modern non-smoking family house in residential area with attractive garden; off-street parking.					
Mrs June Fiddes
The Tilt, Old Perth Road
Inverness
IV2 3UT
Tel: (Inverness) 01463 225352	COMMENDED Listed	1 Single
1 Twin
1 Family	1 Pub Bath/Show	B&B per person
from £13.00 Single
from £13.00 Double	Open Jan-Dec
Family home within short distance of A9, town centre and all amenities. Convenient for Raigmore Hospital. Strictly non-smoking. Vegetarian menus.					
Mrs L Fraser
Edenview, 26 Ness Bank
Inverness
IV2 4SF
Tel: (Inverness) 01463 234397	COMMENDED 👑👑	2 Twin
1 Double	2 En Suite fac
2 Pub Bath/Show	B&B per person
£18.00-£20.00 Single	Open Jan-Dec
A large and spacious house on the riverside close to the town centre. Friendly and homely atmosphere. Private parking.					
Furan Cottage
100 Old Edinburgh Road
Inverness
IV2 3HT
Tel: (Inverness) 01463 712094	COMMENDED Listed	1 Single
1 Double
1 Family	2 Limited ensuite
2 Pub Bath/Show	B&B per person
£14.00-£17.00 Single
£14.00-£17.00 Double	Open Jan-Dec
Dinner 1800-2000
B&B + Eve. Meal
£22.00-£27.00
Family home on main road: 1 mile (2kms) from town centre. Home cooked evening meals provided. Private parking.					
Mrs D Gander
Canmore, 3 Heathcote Gdns
Muirfield Road
Inverness
IV2 4AZ
Tel: (Inverness) 01463 230228	HIGHLY COMMENDED 👑👑	1 Single
1 Twin
1 Double	1 En Suite fac
1 Priv. NOT ensuite
1 Pub Bath/Show	B&B per person
£18.00-£20.00 Single
£18.00-£20.00 Double	Open Apr-Sep
Detached family house situated in secluded cul-de-sac with private parking. Within walking distance of town centre.					

Sunnyholm

**12 MAYFIELD ROAD, INVERNESS IV2 4AE
Telephone: 01463 231336**
This well-appointed, traditionally built Scottish bungalow of the early 1930s is situated in a large, mature, secluded garden in a very pleasant, residential area and has ample private parking. It is within 6-7 minutes walking distance of the Town Centre, Castle, Tourist Information Centre Office and other essential holiday amenities.

Mrs Agnes Gordon
Sunnyholm, 12 Mayfield Road
Inverness
IV2 4AE
Tel: (Inverness) 01463 231336	COMMENDED 👑👑	2 Twin
2 Double	4 En Suite fac	B&B per person
£20.00-£25.00 Single
£16.00-£18.00 Double	Open Jan-Dec
Bungalow situated in quiet residential area close to town centre and Castle. All bedrooms ensuite. Private car park.					

INVERNESS continued	Map 4 B8					
Neil & Margaret Hart Melrose Villa 35 Kenneth Street Inverness IV3 5DH Tel: (Inverness) 01463 233745	COMMENDED Listed	3 Single 3 Double 3 Family	6 En Suite fac 1 Pub Bath/Show	B&B per person £15.00-£20.00 Single £13.00-£20.00 Double	Open Jan-Dec	

Family run guest house within a few minutes walk of the town centre. Warm and friendly atmosphere.

| Mrs Maureen Hutcheson
Mardon, 37 Kenneth Street
Inverness
IV3 5DH
Tel: (Inverness) 01463 231005
Fax: 01463 240501 | COMMENDED | 1 Single
2 Twin
3 Double
1 Family | 3 En Suite fac
1 Pub Bath/Show | B&B per person
from £12.00 Single
from £12.00 Double | Open Jan-Dec | |

Detached town house in close proximity to town centre and Loch Ness. Friendly atmosphere, special diets catered for.

| Ivybank Guest House
28 Old Edinburgh Road
Inverness
IV2 3HJ
Tel: (Inverness) 01463 232796 | HIGHLY COMMENDED | 3 Double | 2 En Suite fac
1 Pub Bath/Show | B&B per person
£15.00-£30.00 Single
£18.00-£25.00 Double | Open Jan-Dec | |

Georgian villa, retaining many original features, with walled and landscaped garden, ample parking, about half a mile (1 km) walk from the town centre.

| Mrs F Kennedy
7 Broadstone Park
Inverness
IV2 3JZ
Tel: (Inverness) 01463 236807 | COMMENDED
Listed | 3 Twin | 1 Pub Bath/Show | B&B per person
£15.00-£17.00 Single | Open Jan-Dec | |

Detached family house in a quiet residential area near town centre and railway station.

| Mrs Helen Kennedy
Kendon, 9 Old Mill Lane
Inverness
IV2 3XP
Tel: (Inverness) 01463 238215 | COMMENDED | 1 Twin
2 Double | 3 En Suite fac | B&B per person
£17.00-£20.00 Double | Open Mar-Nov | |

Modern bungalow. A family home in quiet residential area. 1 mile (2kms) from town centre. Easy access off A9. All bedrooms ensuite.

Kinkell House

11 Old Edinburgh Road, Inverness IV2 3HF
Telephone: 01463 235243

This beautiful Victorian family home offers a warm welcome with typical Highland hospitality. Situated in a quiet area very close to the Town Centre, the spacious bedrooms and magnificent lounge ensure a comfortable stay. Kinkell House has a secluded setting offering private parking.

| Kinkell House
11 Old Edinburgh Road
Inverness
IV2 3HF
Tel: (Inverness) 01463 235243 | COMMENDED
Listed | 1 Twin
2 Double
3 Family | 2 Pub Bath/Show | B&B per person
£15.00-£23.00 Single
£15.00-£18.00 Double | Open Jan-Dec
Dinner 1830-2000
B&B + Eve. Meal
£23.00-£32.00 | |

Large Victorian house close to city centre; warm welcome; off-street parking.

| Larchfield House
14/15 Ness Bank
Inverness
IV2 4SF
Tel: (Inverness) 01463 233874
Fax: 01463 711600 | APPROVED | 3 Single
6 Twin
5 Double
3 Family | 8 En Suite fac
3 Limited ensuite
3 Priv. NOT ensuite
3 Pub Bath/Show | B&B per person
£20.00-£25.00 Single
£22.50-£25.00 Double | Open Jan-Dec | |

Personally run, on east bank of River Ness. Close to town centre. Open fire in lounge.

| Mrs Gillian Lee
Millwood House,
36 Old Mill Road
Inverness IV2 3HR
Tel: (Inverness)
01463 237254 | DELUXE | 1 Twin
1 Double | 1 Priv. NOT ensuite
1 Pub Bath/Show | B&B per person
from £18.00 Double | Open Jan-Dec | |

A warm friendly welcome in comfortable family home. Large secluded garden, in pleasant residential area close to town centre.

Name & Address	Grading	Rooms	Bathrooms	Prices	Open
Isabella & Allan McColl, Heathfield, 2 Kenneth Street, Inverness, IV2 5NR, Tel: (Inverness) 01463 230547	COMMENDED	1 Twin, 2 Double	1 En Suite fac, 1 Pub Bath/Show	B&B per person £13.00-£17.00 Double	Open Jan-Dec
Semi-detached stone house. Close to town centre, Eden Court Theatre and all amenities.					
Mrs MacCuish, 1 Caulfield Park, Inverness, IV1 2GB, Tel: (Inverness) 01463 792882	HIGHLY COMMENDED	1 Twin, 1 Double	1 En Suite fac, 1 Pub Bath/Show	B&B per person to £18.00 Single to £16.00 Double	Open May-Sep
Modern detached house with large garden on eastern outskirts of Inverness. 3 miles (5kms) from Culloden Battlefield. Private parking.					
Mrs MacCuish, 50 Argyle Street, Inverness, IV2 3BB, Tel: (Inverness) 01463 235150	APPROVED Listed	1 Double, 1 Family	1 Pub Bath/Show	B&B per person £13.00 Single £13.00 Double	Open Apr-Oct
Terraced house within 10 minutes walk of the town centre.					
Mrs C MacDonald, An Airidh, 65 Fairfield Road, Inverness, IV3 5LH, Tel: (Inverness) 01463 240673	COMMENDED Listed	1 Twin, 1 Double, 1 Family	1 Priv. NOT ensuite, 2 Pub Bath/Show	B&B per person £13.00-£16.00 Single £12.00-£15.00 Double	Open Nov-Sep Dinner 1830-2000 B&B + Eve. Meal £21.00-£23.00
Family home in quiet residential area. Short walking distance from town centre and all amenities.					
Mrs L M MacDonald, Baemore, 48 Fairfield Road, Inverness, IV3 5QD, Tel: (Inverness) 01463 234095	COMMENDED	1 Twin, 1 Family	1 Pub Bath/Show	B&B per person £12.00-£14.00 Double	Open Apr-Sep
Highland hospitality in friendly family home. Short walk to town centre.					
Mrs Zandra MacDonald, 5 Muirfield Gardens, Inverness, IV2 4HF, Tel: (Inverness) 01463 238114	COMMENDED	1 Twin, 2 Double	2 Pub Bath/Show	B&B per person £14.00-£16.00 Single	Open Jan-Dec
Family home in quiet residential area, 15 minutes stroll from the town centre. All accommodation on the ground floor.					
Ms H M M MacGregor, Abbotsford, 7 Fairfield Road, Inverness, Inverness-shire, IV3 5QA, Tel: (Inverness) 01463 238412	COMMENDED	1 Twin, 1 Double	2 En Suite fac	B&B per person £17.00-£20.00 Single £17.00-£20.00 Double Room only per person £12.00-£15.00	Open Jan-Dec
Small and friendly guest house within easy walking distance of city centre.					
Mrs Margaret MacGruer, 62 Old Edinburgh Road, Inverness, Inverness-shire, IV2 3PG, Tel: (Inverness) 01463 238892	HIGHLY COMMENDED	1 Double, 1 Family	1 Pub Bath/Show	B&B per person £15.00-£16.00 Double	Open Feb-Nov
Detached house standing in its own grounds in a quiet residential area but only 0.5 miles (1km) from the town centre.					
Mr & Mrs MacKay, 50 Fairfield Road, Inverness, IV3 5QW, Tel: (Inverness) 01463 712623	COMMENDED	1 Twin, 1 Double, 1 Family	2 En Suite fac, 1 Pub Bath/Show	B&B per person £15.00-£18.00 Double	Open Jan-Dec
Victorian, corner terraced house in residential area. Convenient for town centre, 0.5 miles (1km) away.					
A MacKenzie, Ardconnel House, 21 Ardconnel Street, Inverness, IV2 3EU, Tel: (Inverness) 01463 240455	HIGHLY COMMENDED	1 Twin, 1 Double, 3 Family	2 Pub Bath/Show	B&B per person from £16.00 Single from £16.00 Double	Open Jan-Dec
Listed, Victorian, terraced house in residential area. Convenient for town centre and railway station.					

Details of Grading and Classification are on page vi.

Key to symbols is on back flap.

INVERNESS continued	Map 4 B8						
Mr & Mrs McKenzie Trafford Bank, 96 Fairfield Road Inverness IV3 5LL Tel: (Inverness) 01463 241414		COMMENDED Listed	1 Twin 2 Double 2 Family	4 En Suite fac 1 Priv. NOT ensuite 1 Pub Bath/Show	B&B per person from £16.00 Single from £16.00 Double	Open Jan-Dec Dinner 1900-2000 B&B + Eve. Meal from £27.50	

Spacious Victorian house convenient for the town centre. Traditional comfort and hospitality. Good food.

| Mrs A MacKenzie Braehead, 5 Crown Circus Inverness IV2 3NH Tel: (Inverness) 01463 224222 | | COMMENDED | 1 Single 1 Double 1 Family | 2 Pub Bath/Show | B&B per person from £14.50 Double | Open Jan-Dec | |

Traditional stone-built Victorian villa in residential area of Inverness with easy access to town centre and all amenities. Non-smoking.

| Mrs A MacKinnon 6 Broadstone Park Inverness IV2 3LA Tel: (Inverness) 01463 221506 | | COMMENDED | 1 Single 1 Twin 1 Family | 3 En Suite fac 1 Pub Bath/Show | B&B per person from £18.00 Single from £17.00 Double | Open Jan-Dec | |

Semi-detached house in quiet residential road, 5 minutes walk from town centre, bus and railway stations.

| Mr D MacLennan The Bungalow, 21 Planefield Road Inverness IV3 5DL Tel: (Inverness) 01463 230337 | | COMMENDED | 1 Twin 2 Double | 3 En Suite fac | B&B per person £15.50-£17.00 Single £15.50-£17.00 Double | Open Jan-Dec | |

Modern detached bungalow in quiet residential area. Own parking. Short walk from town centre and all amenities. All rooms en-suite, non-smoking.

| Mrs Mactaggart 1 Ross Avenue Inverness IV3 5QJ Tel: (Inverness) 01463 236356 | | COMMENDED | 2 Twin 1 Double | 2 En Suite fac 1 Pub Bath/Show | B&B per person £16.00-£18.00 Single £15.00-£18.00 Double | Open Jan-Dec | |

Terraced house in quiet residential area, close to town centre, bus and railway stations.

| Mrs U Moffat Lorne House, 40 Crown Drive Inverness IV2 3QG Tel: (Inverness) 01463 236271 | | HIGHLY COMMENDED | 1 Double 1 Family | 1 En Suite fac 1 Priv. NOT ensuite 1 Pub Bath/Show | B&B per person £16.00-£22.50 Double | Open Jan-Dec | |

Victorian detached house in quiet residential area, close to town centre and railway station. Guest car parking. Private and en-suite facilities.

HERE'S THE DIFFERENCE

STB's scheme has two distinct elements, grading and classification.

GRADING:

Measures the quality and condition of the facilities and services offered, eg, the warmth of welcome, quality of food and its presentation, condition of decor and furnishings, appearance of buildings, tidiness of grounds and gardens, condition of lighting and heating and so on.

Grading awards are: **Approved, Commended, Highly Commended, Deluxe.**

CLASSIFICATION:

Measures the range of physical facilities and services offered, eg, rooms with private bath, heating, reception, lounges, telephones and so on.

Classification awards are: **Listed to five crowns or one to five crowns.**

'Bonnieview'

Towerbrae (North), Westhill
Inverness IV1 2BW   Tel: 01463 792468

At 'Bonnieview' experience a special warmth and hospitality rare in its sincerity – look out from the dining room with marvellous views stretching over the Beauly and Moray Firths, whilst enjoying highly acclaimed home cooking and baking. Excellent as a touring base for day trips around the Highlands. Complete en-suite in all rooms. You can relax with tea and conversation in the lounge beside a soothing coal fire on those chilly days.
A fine welcome awaits you all.
B&B £18 per person, £10 dinner.
OPEN ALL YEAR.

Details from *Marjory O'Connor.*

Marjory O'Connor Bonnieview, Tower Brae North, Westhill Inverness IV1 2BW Tel: (Inverness) 01463 792468	COMMENDED 👑👑	1 Single 1 Double 1 Family	3 En Suite fac	B&B per person £18.00 Single £18.00 Double Room only per person £18.00	Open Jan-Dec Dinner from 1800 B&B + Eve. Meal £28.00

Friendly welcome at this modern house quietly located overlooking the Moray Firth. 2 miles (3kms) from Culloden Moor, 4 miles (6kms) from Inverness.

Oakfield Guest House 1 Darnaway Road, Kingsmills Inverness IV2 3LF Tel: (Inverness) 01463 237926	COMMENDED 👑👑	1 Single 2 Twin 3 Double	5 En Suite fac 1 Priv. NOT ensuite	B&B per person £20.00-£24.00 Single £18.00-£24.00 Double	Open Jan-Dec Dinner 1800-1900 B&B + Eve. Meal £28.00-£34.00

Detached house with private parking in peaceful residential area within easy walking distance of town centre. Home cooking. Credit cards accepted.

The Old Rectory Guest House 9 Southside Road Inverness IV2 3BG Tel: (Inverness) 01463 220969	HIGHLY COMMENDED 👑👑	1 Twin 2 Double 1 Family	4 En Suite fac	B&B per person £17.00-£24.00 Single £17.00-£20.00 Double	Open Jan-Dec

Privately owned former Victorian manse with large garden situated in residential area close to town centre. Good car parking. Non-smoking.

The Old Royal Guest House 10 Union Street Inverness IV1 1PL Tel: (Inverness) 01463 230551 Fax: 01463 230551	COMMENDED 👑👑	2 Single 2 Twin 4 Double 2 Family	5 En Suite fac 3 Pub Bath/Show	B&B per person £21.00-£24.00 Single £18.50-£24.00 Double	Open Feb-Nov

Four-storey terraced guest house in the heart of the town centre and a few hundred yards from the railway station.

Mrs Reid 101 Kenneth Street Inverness IV3 5QQ Tel: (Inverness) 01463 237224	COMMENDED Listed	2 Single 1 Twin 1 Double 2 Family	3 Pub Bath/Show	B&B per person £15.00 Single £13.00 Double	Open Jan-Dec

Comfortable family run guest house close to the centre of Inverness and all facilities. Private parking.

INVERNESS continued

Map 4 B8

Roseneath Guest House
39 Greig Street
Inverness
IV3 5PX
Tel: (Inverness) 01463 220201

COMMENDED 👑

1 Twin	5 En Suite fac	B&B per person	Open Jan-Dec
2 Double	1 Priv. NOT ensuite	£13.00-£18.00 Single	
3 Family		£13.00-£18.00 Double	

Family run guest house, quiet area, short distance from the town centre.
Off-street parking; 5 minutes walk from Eden Court Theatre.

Mrs M Shields
Ardgowan, 45 Fairfield Road
Inverness
IV3 5QP
Tel: (Inverness) 01463 236489

COMMENDED 👑👑

1 Twin	1 En Suite fac	B&B per person	Open Jan-Dec
1 Family	1 Pub Bath/Show	from £14.50 Double	
		Room only per person	
		from £13.50	

A large semi-detached house with spacious rooms within
a few minutes walk of the town centre.

Mrs Sinclair
7 Broadstone Avenue
Inverness
IV2 3LE
Tel: (Inverness) 01463 225728

COMMENDED 👑👑

2 Double	3 En Suite fac	B&B per person	
1 Family	2 Pub Bath/Show	£15.00-£25.00 Single	
		£15.00-£20.00 Double	

Friendly family guest house in a residential area of the town,
close to all amenities.

Jacqueline Stewart
Bridge House, 19 Harris Road
Inverness
IV2 3LS
Tel: (Inverness) 01463 714770

COMMENDED Listed

2 Single	1 Pub Bath/Show	B&B per person	Open Jan-Dec
1 Twin		£15.00-£17.00 Single	
		£15.00-£17.00 Double	
		Room only per person	
		£15.00	

Family home in modern bungalow situated in quiet residential area.

Mr & Mrs D Taylor
Carsaig, 7 Cawdor Road
Inverness
IV2 3NR
Tel: (Inverness) 01463 238662

COMMENDED Listed

1 Single	1 En Suite fac	B&B per person	Open Jan-Dec
2 Double	1 Pub Bath/Show	£15.00-£20.00 Single	

Comfortable accommodation in late Victorian house.
In quiet residential street in centre of town.

Mrs Wallace
1 Broadstone Park
Inverness
IV2 3JZ
Tel: (Inverness) 01463 231822

APPROVED 👑

2 Single	2 Pub Bath/Show	B&B per person	Open Jan-Dec
3 Twin		£15.00-£16.00 Single	
1 Double		£14.00-£15.00 Double	

Detached villa in quiet residential area but near the centre of town.
Scots Pine is a feature of the house.

Mrs J Wilson
Cairnsmore, 41 Charles Street
Inverness
IV2 3AH
Tel: (Inverness) 01463 233485

HIGHLY COMMENDED Listed

1 Twin	1 Pub Bath/Show	B&B per person	Open Jan-Dec
2 Double		from £15.00 Double	

Terraced house in quiet residential area, renovated to a high standard,
close to shops, town centre, rail and bus stations.

BY INVERNESS

Map 4 B8

Mrs T M Honnor
Westhill House, Westhill
by Inverness
IV1 2BP
Tel: (Inverness) 01463 793225
Fax: 01463 792503

COMMENDED 👑

2 Twin	2 En Suite fac	B&B per person	Open Mar-Oct
		to £16.00 Single	

Modern family home, own grounds, open countryside.
1 mile (2kms) Culloden Battlefield. 4 miles (6kms) Inverness.
Two rooms one annexe. Warm welcome.

Mrs M Mansfield
3a Resaurie
Smithton, by Inverness
Inverness-shire
IV1 2NH
Tel: (Inverness) 01463 791714

COMMENDED 👑👑

1 Twin	1 En Suite fac	B&B per person	Open Jan-Dec
2 Double	1 Pub Bath/Show	£22.00-£25.00 Single	Dinner 1800-2000
		£15.00-£19.00 Double	B&B + Eve. Meal
			£27.00-£31.00

Modern house set in quiet residential area 4 miles (6kms) from Inverness
with panoramic views across the Moray Firth. Warm and friendly stay assured.

| Mrs Effie Rowan
Laimrig, Upper Myrtlefield,
Nairnside
Inverness
IV1 2BX
Tel: (Inverness) 01463 793464 | | HIGHLY
COMMENDED
👑👑 | 1 Twin
2 Double | 3 En Suite fac | B&B per person
from £16.00 Single
from £17.00 Double | Open Jan-Dec | |

Modern family house with large garden 4 miles (6kms) from Inverness town centre.
Extensive views over Moray Firth to Black Isle. Private parking.

LAGGAN VIEW

Ness Castle Fishings, Dores Road, Inverness IV1 2DH
Telephone: 01463 235996 Fax: 01463 711552

Attractive centrally heated spacious house in rural setting with scenic
views of Ness Valley yet only 3 miles from town centre on B862.
Walks nearby through woods and by the river. Full facilities with all
bedrooms including colour television. Evening meals served at time to
suit individual requirements.

| Mrs E S Saggers
Laggan View,
Ness Castle Fishings
Dores Road, by Inverness
Inverness-shire
IV1 2DH
Tel: (Inverness) 01463 235996
Fax: 01463 711552 | COMMENDED
👑👑👑 | 1 Twin
1 Double
1 Family | 2 En Suite fac
1 Priv. NOT ensuite | B&B per person
from £18.00 Single
from £16.00 Double | Open Jan-Dec
Dinner 1800-2100
B&B + Eve. Meal
from £25.00 | |

Quiet secluded house in countryside with magnificent views.
Close to Inverness; ideal base for touring the Highlands.

| Sky House
Upper Cullernie
Balloch, by Inverness
Inverness-shire
IV1 2HU
Tel: (Inverness) 01463 792582 | COMMENDED
👑👑👑 | 3 Twin | 3 En Suite fac | B&B per person
£18.00-£24.00 Double | Open Jan-Dec
Dinner from 1930
B&B + Eve. Meal
£28.00-£34.00 | |

A friendly and relaxed welcome at this modern house with superb views
over Moray Firth to Black Isle. 4 miles (6kms) from Inverness.

| **INVERURIE**
Aberdeenshire
Mrs Black
Breaslann, Old Chapel Road
Inverurie
Aberdeenshire
AB51 4QN
Tel: (Inverurie) 01467 621608
Fax: 01467 621608 | Map 4
G9 | COMMENDED
👑 | 3 Twin | 3 En Suite fac
1 Pub Bath/Show | B&B per person
£20.00-£22.00 Single
£15.00-£18.00 Double | Open Jan-Dec | |

Modern comfortable bungalow with attractive gardens and off-street parking.
10 minutes walk from town centre.

✳ MILL CROFT GUEST HOUSE

Lawrence Road, Old Rayne, Aberdeenshire AB52 6RY
Telephone: 01464 851210

Comfortable cottage with attractive garden on edge of small village
under personal management of Dorothy and Peter Thomson. Home
baking, two ground floor bedrooms. Fire certificate. Holiday care
awards 1990 and 1993. Ideal for walking, hill climbing, fishing, golf etc.

| Mill Croft Guest House
Old Rayne, by Inverurie
Aberdeenshire
AB52 6RY
Tel: (Old Rayne)
01464 851210 | HIGHLY
COMMENDED
👑👑👑
♿ | 1 Twin
1 Double
1 Family | 2 En Suite fac
1 Priv. NOT ensuite | B&B per person
£16.00-£18.00 Single
£16.00-£18.00 Double | Open Jan-Dec
Dinner 1830-1930
B&B + Eve. Meal
£22.00-£24.00 | |

Friendly welcome at working croft with excellent views over Grampian countryside,
on Castle Trail. Residential wood craft courses.

BY INVERURIE
Aberdeenshire — Map 4 G9

Mrs G Adam Boatleys Farm Kemnay Aberdeenshire AB51 9NA Tel: (Kemnay) 01467 642533	COMMENDED Listed	1 Twin 1 Double	2 Pub Bath/Show	B&B per person to £20.00 Single to £18.50 Double	Open Jan-Dec

Recently completed spacious bungalow on mixed working farm.
Friendly atmosphere with home baking. On Castle and Whisky Trails.

Mrs Wilma Crosland Homefarm of Logie Pitcaple, by Inverurie Aberdeenshire AB51 5EE Tel: (Pitcaple) 01467 681481	HIGHLY COMMENDED Listed	2 Twin 1 Double	1 Pub Bath/Show	B&B per person £20.00-£25.00 Single £17.00-£20.00 Double	Open Jan-Nov

Delightful traditional house, in pleasant countryside convenient to A96.
Close to Bennachie. Haven for walkers. Castle and archaeological trails.

IONA, Isle of
Argyll — Map 1 B2

Miss A M Wagstaff Finlay, Ross Limited Iona, Isle of Argyll PA76 Tel: (Iona) 01681 700357/700365 Fax: 01681 700357	APPROVED Listed	1 Single 8 Twin 2 Double 2 Family	3 En Suite fac 1 Priv. NOT ensuite 2 Pub Bath/Show	B&B per person from £18.00 Single from £15.00 Double	Open Jan-Dec

Purpose-built rooms all on one level and convenient for the ferry.
Continental breakfast only provided in bedrooms. Also cottage annexe with lounge.

IRVINE
Ayrshire — Map 1 G6

Mr J Daunt The Conifers 40 Kilwinning Road Irvine Ayrshire KA12 8RY Tel: (Irvine) 01294 278070	APPROVED	3 Single 1 Twin 1 Double 1 Family	2 En Suite fac 1 Priv. NOT ensuite	B&B per person £15.00-£20.00 Single £15.00-£18.00 Double	Open Jan-Dec

Bungalow with large well-maintained garden, convenient for town centre.
Ample off-street parking in safe location. All rooms can be let as singles.

Mr & Mrs J Ferguson Laurelbank Guest House, 3 Kilwinning Road Irvine Ayrshire KA12 8RR Tel: (Irvine) 01294 277153	COMMENDED	2 Single 1 Twin 1 Double 1 Family	2 Pub Bath/Show	B&B per person £15.00-£18.00 Single £14.00-£15.00 Double	Open Jan-Dec Dinner 1700-1900

Traditional Scottish hospitality afforded to all guests and
golfers visiting the Ayrshire coast and the Magnum Centre.

ISLEORNSAY
Isle of Skye, Inverness-shire — Map 3 F10

Tawny Croft

Isleornsay, Sleat, Isle of Skye IV43 8QS
Telephone/Fax: 01471 833325

Overlooking Isleornsay harbour our non-smoking home Tawny Croft provides a high level of accommodation with bedrooms having en-suite facilities. A spacious lounge with an enamelled multi-fuel stove allows you to relax and enjoy the wildlife library and paintings. Complemented by excellent home cooking served in the separate dining room. Guided walks with experienced naturalist provide opportunities to view wildlife for longer stay guests. Associated video or slides shown during evening; opportunities also for photography and sketching.

Mr R Cottis Tawny Croft Isleornsay, Sleat Isle of Skye, Inverness-shire Tel: (Isleornsay) 01471 833325 Fax: 01471 833325	COMMENDED	2 Family	2 En Suite fac	B&B per person £20.00-£24.00 Double	Open Jan-Dec Dinner from 19.30 B&B + Eve Meal £30.00-£34.00

Modernised croft house specialising in wildlife interest holidays.
Field trips available. Tranquil setting overlooking Isleornsay Harbour.

Mrs MacDonald 6 Duisdale Beag Isleornsay, Sleat Isle of Skye, Inverness-shire Tel: (Isleornsay) 01471 833230		COMMENDED 👑👑	1 Twin 2 Double	2 En Suite fac 2 Pub Bath/Show	B&B per person £14.00-£18.00 Single £14.00-£17.00 Double	Open Mar-Sep	
			Modern bungalow in elevated position in small country village overlooking the sea. Home baking in lounge in evening.				
JEDBURGH **Roxburghshire** Mrs I Balderston Nisbet Mill Farm Jedburgh Roxburghshire TD8 6TT Tel: (Crailing) 01835 850228 Fax: 01835 850766	Map 2 E7	COMMENDED 👑👑	2 Double	1 En Suite fac 1 Priv. NOT ensuite	B&B per person £16.00-£18.50 Single £16.00-£18.50 Double	Open Apr-Sep	
			Spacious farmhouse overlooking River Teviot on working mixed farm. Central situation for touring. Woodland walks. Home baking and cooking, open fires.				
Mrs Clark Strowan, Oxnam Road Jedburgh Roxburghshire TD8 6QJ Tel: (Jedburgh) 01835 862248		COMMENDED Listed	2 Single 1 Twin 1 Double	1 Limited ensuite 1 Pub Bath/Show	B&B per person to £17.00 Single £17.00-£18.00 Double	Open Apr-Oct	
			Old manse house of character on the edge of the town, set in its own grounds of nearly 2 acres. One room with own shower.				
Mrs M Crone 15 Hartrigge Crescent Jedburgh Roxburghshire TD8 6HT Tel: (Jedburgh) 01835 862738		COMMENDED Listed	1 Twin 1 Double	1 Pub Bath/Show	B&B per person £13.00-£13.50 Single £13.00-£13.50 Double	Open Jan-Dec	
			Friendly family house in quiet residential area within walking distance of the town.				

FROYLEHURST
The Friars, Jedburgh TD8 6BN
Telephone: 01835 862477

An impressive Grade 'B' Listed Victorian Town-house dated 1894, retaining original fireplaces, stained glass windows, cornices and tiled vestibule. Offering spacious and comfortable guest rooms and residents' lounge. Enjoying an elevated position in a large secluded garden in a quiet residential area with ample private off-street parking, yet only 2 minutes from town centre. All bedrooms have wash basins, shaver points, tea/coffee-making facilities, colour TV and radio. Full Scottish breakfast. This is a family home, and guests are made welcome by the owner.
Further details are available from Mrs H Irvine.
AA Selected QQQQ

Froylehurst Guest House Mrs H Irvine, Friars Jedburgh Roxburghshire TD8 6BN Tel: (Jedburgh) 01835 862477 Fax: 01835 862477	HIGHLY COMMENDED 👑	1 Twin 2 Double 1 Family	2 Pub Bath/Show	B&B per person £15.00-£16.50 Double	Open Mar-Nov	
		Detached Victorian house with large garden and private parking. Spacious rooms. Overlooking town, 2 minutes walk from the centre.				

JEDBURGH continued	Map 4 E7

KENMORE BANK

Oxnam Road, Jedburgh TD8 6JJ
Telephone: 01835 862369

A charming Victorian villa with residential licence just off
the A68. Situated beside the River Jed with panoramic
views of the Abbey and ancient town of Jedburgh yet just
five minutes walk from shops, restaurants and pubs. Almost
adjacent to the leisure centre with heated pool, sauna, gym
and solarium. Choice of menu, wines and snacks.
All bedrooms en-suite with colour TV. Central heating.
Private parking.
Package golf holidays available on 17 courses.
Short breaks from £29 D,B&B
overnight from £18 B&B
Proprietors Charles and Joanne Muller.

COMMENDED 👑👑👑

Kenmore Bank Guest House Oxnam Road Jedburgh Roxburghshire TD8 6JJ Tel: (Jedburgh) 01835 862369	COMMENDED 👑👑👑	2 Twin 2 Double 2 Family	6 En Suite fac	B&B per person £25.00-£42.00 Single £18.00-£22.00 Double Room only per person £25.00-£40.00	Open Jan-Dec Dinner 1830-1930

Friendly, relaxing family run hotel with residential licence and good home cooking.
Splendid views of the Abbey. Excellent base for touring the Borders.

Mrs Pat McNab The Broch, Lanton Road Jedburgh Roxburghshire TD8 6SY Tel: (Jedburgh) 01835 863542	COMMENDED 👑👑	1 Twin 2 Double	3 En Suite fac	B&B per person £20.00 Single £19.00 Double	Open Jan-Dec

Family home approximately 1 mile (2kms) from Jedburgh.
Breathtaking views over beautiful Borders countryside.

THE SPINNEY GUEST HOUSE

Langlee, Jedburgh, Roxburghshire TD8 6PB
Telephone: 01835 863525 Fax: 01835 863525

*Attractive house set in extensive garden with quality
accommodation and friendly welcome. Private bathrooms and
ample parking. Two miles south of Jedburgh on A68.*

Spinney Guest House The Spinney, Langlee Jedburgh Roxburghshire TD8 6PB Tel: (Jedburgh) 01835 863525 Fax: 01835 863525	DELUXE 👑👑	1 Twin 2 Double	2 En Suite fac 1 Priv. NOT ensuite	B&B per person £25.00-£30.00 Single £18.00-£20.00 Double	Open Mar-Nov

A warm welcome at this attractive house with large pleasant garden
lying just off main A68. All rooms have private facilities. Ample parking.

WILLOW COURT

The Friars, Jedburgh, Roxburghshire TD8 6BN
Tel: 01835 863702   Fax: 01835 864601

Willow Court in a peaceful setting overlooking historic Jedburgh is only two minutes walk from the Town Centre. The two acres of garden provide most of the fruit and vegetables needed in the kitchen and fill the house with flowers. Breakfast and dinner are served in the bright conservatory, which enjoys panoramic views to the wooded hillsides. The outlook is shared by the sitting rooms and some of the fresh, warm ensuite bedrooms, most located on the gound floor.

Children welcome. Private parking.
Member of the Taste of Scotland Scheme.
AA QQQQ 'SELECTED'

Willow Court The Friars Jedburgh Roxburghshire TD8 6BN Tel: (Jedburgh) 01835 863702 Fax: 01835 864601		HIGHLY COMMENDED ♛♛♛	1 Twin 2 Double 1 Family	3 En Suite fac 1 Priv. NOT ensuite	B&B per person £20.00-£32.00 Single £14.00-£19.00 Double	Open Jan-Dec Dinner 1800-1830 B&B + Eve. Meal £24.50-£35.00

Set in 2 acres above the town; excellent views. Family run with home cooking, home-grown produce in season. Ground-floor accommodation available. "Taste of Scotland".

BY JEDBURGH Roxburghshire Mrs J S Butt Lethem Farm, Camptown Jedburgh Roxburghshire Tel: (Camptown) 01835 840255	Map 2 E7	COMMENDED ♛♛	1 Twin 1 Double 1 Family	3 En Suite fac	B&B per person £18.00-£22.00 Single £16.00-£18.00 Double	Open Jan-Dec

Comfortable farmhouse in secluded setting, in the hills on the Scottish Border. 1 mile from A68.

Sally Jane Henman Sharplaw Farm Cottage Jedburgh Roxburghshire TD8 6SQ Tel: (Jedburgh) 01835 863747		COMMENDED ♛♛	1 Twin	1 En Suite fac	B&B per person to £17.50 Single to £17.50 Double Room only per person to £17.50	Open Jan-Dec Dinner 1830-2000 B&B + Eve. Meal £20.00-£28.50

Lovingly refurbished cottage of character, peacefully set in fields less than 1/2 mile to Jedburgh. Stunning views over the town.

Ancrum Craig

ANCRUM, JEDBURGH, ROXBURGHSHIRE TD8 6UN
Telephone: 01835 830280

ANCRUM CRAIG is a comfortable country home two miles from Ancrum Village, surrounded by farmland and enjoying beautiful views to the south. All rooms have charm and guests are welcome to enjoy the elegant lounge. We serve our own fresh eggs for breakfast.

DUTCH AND GERMAN ARE SPOKEN.

Mrs Hensens Ancrum Craig Ancrum, Jedburgh Roxburghshire TD8 6UN Tel: (Ancrum) 01835 830280		COMMENDED ♛♛	1 Twin 2 Double	3 En Suite fac	B&B per person £18.00-£21.00 Double	Open Mar-Oct

Country house with many authentic 19th-century features. Large garden and magnificent views of surrounding countryside. Open fire. All rooms ensuite.

	Map 2 E7						
EBY JEDBURGH continued Mrs McNeill Millheugh Jedburgh Roxburghshire TD8 6RA Tel: (Jedburgh) 01835 862208		**HIGHLY COMMENDED** Listed	1 Single 1 Twin 1 Double	1 Pub Bath/Show	B&B per person £15.00-£16.00 Single £15.00-£16.00 Double Room only per person £12.00-£13.00	Open May-Oct	

Non-smokers welcomed to this charming farmhouse to which guests regularly return. Jedburgh 3.5 miles (6kms), Kelso 10 miles (16 kms).

| Mr and Mrs M R Taylor Southdean House, Chesters Hawick Roxburghshire TD9 8TN Tel: (Bonchester Bridge) 01450 860686 | **HIGHLY COMMENDED** ♛ | 2 Double | 1 En Suite fac 1 Priv. NOT ensuite | B&B per person to £24.00 Single to £20.00 Double | Open Jan-Dec Dinner from 1900 B&B + Eve. Meal £32.50-£36.50 |

Secluded, well-furnished country house on the Jed Water. Well situated for touring and country pursuits. Warm welcome. Excellent home-cooking.

| Mrs Whittaker Hundalee House Jedburgh Roxburghshire TD8 6PA Tel: (Jedburgh) 01835 863011 | **DELUXE** ♛♛ | 1 Twin 2 Double 1 Family | 3 En Suite fac 1 Pub Bath/Show | B&B per person £20.00-£30.00 Single £16.50-£20.00 Double | Open Mar-Oct |

Extensively refurbished country house 1 mile (2 kms) south of Jedburgh. Excellent views of Cheviot Hills. One bedroom with a 4-poster bed. Ideal touring base.

	Map 4 E2						
JOHN O'GROATS Caithness Mrs Barton Bencorragh House Upper Gills, Canisbay Caithness KW1 4YB Tel: (John O'Groats) 01955 611449		**APPROVED** ♛♛	1 Twin 2 Double 1 Family	4 En Suite fac	B&B per person £17.00-£21.00 Single £17.00-£19.00 Double	Open Apr-Oct Dinner 1800-2030 B&B + Eve. Meal from £25.50	

A working croft in grounds of ten acres. All rooms en-suite. Large conservatory and comfortable lounge. Angling holidays a speciality.

| Caber Feidh Guest House John O'Groats Caithness KW1 4YR Tel: (John O'Groats) 01955 611219 | **APPROVED** Listed | 4 Single 3 Twin 2 Double 3 Family | 3 En Suite fac 3 Pub Bath/Show | B&B per person £14.00-£15.00 Single £13.00-£14.00 Double | Open Jan-Dec Dinner 1830-2000 B&B + Eve. Meal £18.00-£19.00 |

Centrally situated in John O'Groats and 2 miles (3kms) from Duncansby Head it is well situated for exploring the north.

| Mrs J Sinclair Swona View John O'Groats Caithness KW1 4YS Tel: (John O'Groats) 01955 611297 | **COMMENDED** ♛ | 1 Twin 2 Double | 1 En Suite fac 2 Pub Bath/Show | B&B per person £13.00-£16.00 Double | Open Apr-Oct |

Comfortable modern bungalow with fine views across Pentland Firth to Orkney.

| Mrs Wilkins The Farmhouse, Midtown Freswick KW1 4XX Tel: (John O'Groats) 01955 611254 | **COMMENDED** Listed | 1 Single 1 Twin 1 Double 2 Family | 2 Pub Bath/Show | B&B per person £16.50-£17.50 Single £13.00-£14.00 Double | Open Jan-Dec Dinner 1830-1930 B&B + Eve. Meal £18.00-£21.50 |

Farmhouse in rural location, modernised, views over the North Sea.

BY JOHN O'GROATS
Caithness
Mrs C G Manson
Post Office
Canisbay
Caithness
KW1 4YH
Tel: (John O'Groats)
01955 611213

Map 4
E2

COMMENDED
👑👑

1 Twin	1 En Suite fac	B&B per person	Open Apr-Sep
2 Double	2 Limited ensuite	£16.50-£18.50 Single	
	1 Pub Bath/Show	Room only per person	
		£18.00-£20.00	

100-year-old Post Office house. Panoramic views of Pentland Firth close to John O'Groats and Orkney Ferries. Personally run. Extensive breakfast menu.

JOHNSHAVEN
Kincardineshire
Mrs Margaret Gibson
Ellington, Station Place
Johnshaven
Kincardineshire
DD10 0JD
Tel: (Johnshaven)
01561 362756

Map 4
G12

COMMENDED
👑

1 Twin	2 En Suite fac	B&B per person	Open Jan-Dec
1 Double		to £16.00 Single	
		£16.00-£18.00 Double	

New family home, quietly situated in fishing village of Johnshaven. Bedrooms ensuite and one ground-floor bedroom.

JOHNSTONE
Renfrewshire
Mrs C Capper
Auchans Farm
Johnstone
Renfrewshire
PA6 7EE
Tel: (Johnstone)
01505 320131

Map 1
G5

COMMENDED
Listed

1 Twin	3 Priv. NOT ensuite	B&B per person	Open Jan-Dec
1 Double	2 Pub Bath/Show	£15.00-£18.00 Single	
1 Family		£15.00-£18.00 Double	

Friendly welcome awaits on working farm, a few minutes away from motorway link and Glasgow Airport. Easy access to tourist routes.

BY KEITH
Banffshire
Mrs Eileen Fleming
Chapelhill Croft, Grange
Keith
Banffshire
AB55 3LQ
Tel: (Grange) 01542 870302

Map 4
E8

COMMENDED
Listed

1 Twin	1 En Suite fac	B&B per person	Open Jan-Dec
1 Double	1 Pub Bath/Show	£13.00-£16.00 Double	Dinner 1730-2000
			B&B + Eve. Meal
			£21.50-£24.50

Warm, friendly welcome on working croft. Guests welcome to participate in running of the croft. Home cooking.

Mrs Jean Jackson
The Haughs
Keith
Banffshire
AB55 3QN
Tel: (Keith) 01542 882238

COMMENDED
👑👑👑

| 2 Twin | 3 En Suite fac | B&B per person | Open Apr-Oct |
| 2 Double | 1 Priv. NOT ensuite | £15.00-£18.00 Double | Dinner 1800-1900 |

Traditional farmhouse on 165-acre farm near town just off main road. On Whisky Trail; many local sports; golf available at numerous courses.

KELSO
Roxburghshire
Bellevue House
Bowmont Street
Kelso
Roxburghshire
TD5 7DZ
Tel: (Kelso) 01573 224588

Map 2
E6

COMMENDED
👑👑👑

2 Single	5 En Suite fac	B&B per person	Open Jan-Dec
1 Twin	1 Pub Bath/Show	£19.00-£28.00 Single	Dinner 1900-2000
3 Double		£20.00-£24.00 Double	
1 Family		Room only per person	
		£19.00-£22.50	

Family run hotel, situated in residential area, close to town centre and entrance to Floors Castle. Car parking.

KELSO continued	Map 2 E6					

"MO DHACHAIGH"
11 Kings Croft, Kelso TD5 7NU
Telephone: 01573 225480

Comfortable welcoming family home with outstanding panoramic view over Kelso within walking distance of town centre. Bedrooms: 1 double, 1 twin. Bath/shower rooms: 1 public. **Price per person £15.00. Open April-October.**

| Mrs M Ferguson Mo Dhachaigh, 11 Kings Croft Kelso Roxburghshire TD5 7NU Tel: (Kelso) 01573 225480 | **HIGHLY COMMENDED** Listed | 1 Twin 1 Double | 1 Pub Bath/Show | B&B per person £15.00 Double | Open Apr-Oct | |

Comfortable welcoming family home with panoramic view over Kelso, within walking distance of centre.

| Ms Hawkins Wester House, 155 Roxburgh Street Kelso Roxburghshire Tel: (Kelso) 01573 225479 | **COMMENDED** Listed | 1 Single 1 Double 1 Family | 1 En Suite fac 1 Pub Bath/Show | B&B per person £18.00-£22.00 Single £18.00-£22.00 Double | Open Jan-Dec | |

Comfortably furnished 16th-century town house. Warm welcome and friendly atmosphere. A few minutes walk from town centre and Floors Castle.

| Miss W Hess Abbey Bank, The Knowes Kelso Roxburghshire TD5 7BH Tel: (Kelso) 01573 226550 Fax: 01573 226550 | **HIGHLY COMMENDED** Listed | 2 Single 1 Twin 3 Double | 3 En Suite fac 1 Priv. NOT ensuite 1 Pub Bath/Show | B&B per person £17.50-£35.00 Single £17.50-£25.00 Double | Open Jan-Dec | |

Elegant town house with character c1820, providing comfortable accommodation and a friendly welcome. Close to centre of Kelso. Ideal touring base.

| Mrs Jan McDonald Craignethan House, Jedburgh Road Kelso Roxburghshire TD5 8BZ Tel: (Kelso) 01573 224818 | **COMMENDED** Listed | 1 Twin 2 Double | 2 Pub Bath/Show | B&B per person from £16.50 Single from £16.50 Double | Open Jan-Dec | |

Delightful detached house overlooking the town centre with panoramic views of Floors Castle and surrounding countryside. Ground-floor bedroom.

| Mrs J M Middlemas Charlesfield, Edenside Road Kelso Roxburghshire TD5 7BS Tel: (Kelso) 01573 224583 | **HIGHLY COMMENDED** Listed | 1 Twin 1 Double | 1 Pub Bath/Show | B&B per person from £16.50 Single from £16.50 Double | Open Jan-Dec | |

Delightful Victorian house most tastefully decorated with large secluded garden. Situated within a few minutes walk of the historic town centre.

| Mr D Watson Clashdale, 26 Inchmead Drive Kelso Roxburghshire TD5 7LW Tel: (Kelso) 01573 223405 | **COMMENDED** Listed | 1 Single 1 Double | 1 Pub Bath/Show | B&B per person £13.00 Single £13.00 Double | Open Jan-Dec | |

Comfortable, double-glazed, centrally heated accommodation in quiet cul-de-sac. 5 minutes from town centre. Tea on arrival and evening cuppa.

| **BY KELSO** Roxburghshire Mrs McCririck Whitmuirhaugh, Sprouston Kelso Roxburghshire TD5 8HP Tel: (Kelso) 01573 224615 | Map 2 E6 **COMMENDED** | 1 Twin 1 Double | 2 En Suite fac | B&B per person from £20.00 Single from £16.00 Double | Open Apr-Oct Dinner 1900-2030 B&B + Eve. Meal from £30.00 | |

18th-century farmhouse, 3 miles (5kms) from Kelso (B6350) on 600-acre farm with views of River Tweed. Trout fishing available.

Barn Owl Lodge
Smailholm, Kelso, Roxburghshire TD5 7PH
Telephone and Fax: 01573 460373

Unique timber house, all rooms ensuite, set in the beautiful Borders countryside with magnificent views of the Eildon Hills. Historical Smailholm Tower is nearby.

Mrs Ruth McGrath Barn Owl Lodge Smailholm, Kelso Roxburghshire TD5 7PH Tel: (Smailholm) 01573 460373 Fax: 01573 460373	COMMENDED	2 Twin 1 Double	3 En Suite fac	B&B per person £20.00-£25.00 Single £16.00-£20.00 Double	Open Jan-Dec
Enjoy spectacular views of the Eildons in this unique timber-frame house peacefully situated in glorious Borders countryside. Ensuite ground-floor rooms.					
Mrs D M Playfair Morebattle Tofts Kelso Roxburghshire TD5 8AD Tel: (Morebattle) 01573 440364 Fax: 01573 420227	COMMENDED	1 Twin 2 Double	2 En Suite fac 1 Priv. NOT ensuite	B&B per person £15.00-£17.00 Single £15.00-£17.00 Double Room only per person £15.00-£17.00	Open Apr-Oct Dinner 1900-2000 B&B + Eve. Meal £26.00-£38.00
Elegant 18th-century farmhouse set in idyllic location beside the Kalewater. Ideal base for touring, walking, fishing, golf.					
Mrs B Smith Whitehill Farm Nenthorn, by Kelso Roxburghshire TD5 7RZ Tel: (Stichill) 01573 470203 Fax: 01573 470203	HIGHLY COMMENDED	2 Single 2 Twin	1 En Suite fac 1 Pub Bath/Show	B&B per person £16.50-£17.50 Single £16.50-£17.50 Double Room only per person from £16.50	Open Jan-Dec Dinner 1900-2000 B&B + Eve. Meal £20.00-£29.00
18th-century farmhouse with superb views on mixed farm. Ideally placed for touring the Borders region and just off the Kelso/Edinburgh road. Real cooking; fresh food.					
Mr & Mrs Archie Stewart Cliftonhill Farm Kelso Roxburghshire TD5 7QE Tel: (Kelso) 01573 226416 Fax: 01573 226416	COMMENDED	1 Twin 1 Family	2 En Suite fac	B&B per person from £25.00 Single £18.50-£20.00 Double Room only per person from £25.00	Open Jan-Dec
On working farm, large detached farmhouse with extensive garden, 2 miles (3 kms) from Kelso.					
BY KENMORE **Perthshire** Mr & Mrs Jolly Lower Duallin Croft Lawers, Loch Tayside Perthshire PH15 2NZ Tel: (Killin) 01567 820353	Map 2 A1 COMMENDED Listed	1 Single 1 Twin 1 Double	2 En Suite fac 1 Priv. NOT ensuite 1 Pub Bath/Show	B&B per person £14.00 Single £14.00 Double	Open Jan-Dec Dinner 1700-2000
Custom-built whitewashed croft. Fantastic views over Loch Tay and Ben Lawers. Ideal for fishing, hillwalking, wild flowers and birdwatching.					

KENSALEYRE, by Portree
Isle of Skye, Inverness-shire
Corran Guest House
Eyre
Kensaleyre, by Portree
Isle of Skye, Inverness-shire
IV51 9XE
Tel: (Skeabost Bridge)
01470 532311

Map 3 D8

COMMENDED

1 Single | 3 Priv. NOT ensuite | B&B per person | Open Jan-Dec
1 Double | 3 Pub Bath/Show | to £18.00 Single | Dinner at 1900
2 Family | | to £18.00 Double

In a small country village overlooking Loch Snizort, 6 miles (10kms) from Portree and from Uig ferry terminal. Extensive gardens with lovely views.

KILBARCHAN
Renfrewshire
Mrs Douglas
Gladstone Farmhouse
Kilbarchan, by Johnstone
Renfrewshire
PA10 2PB
Tel: (Kilbarchan) 01505 702579

Map 1 G5

COMMENDED
Listed

1 Twin | 1 En Suite fac | B&B per person | Open Jan-Dec
1 Double | 1 Pub Bath/Show | from £15.00 Single | Dinner 1800-1900
1 Family | | from £15.00 Double
| | Room only per person
| | from £12.00

300-year-old farmhouse on working farm. 7 miles (11kms) from Airport. Convenient for touring Ayrshire and Loch Lomond.

KILCHOAN, by Ardnamurchan
Argyll
Mrs Catriona MacMillan
Doirlin House
Kilchoan, by Ardnamurchan
Argyll
PH36 4LH
Tel: (Kilchoan) 01972 510209
Fax: 01972 510209

Map 3 E12

COMMENDED

1 Twin | 2 En Suite fac | B&B per person | Open Mar-Nov
1 Double | 1 Pub Bath/Show | £16.00-£24.00 Single
1 Family | | £16.00-£18.50 Double

In the heart of this quiet village with pleasant views across the bay to Mull.

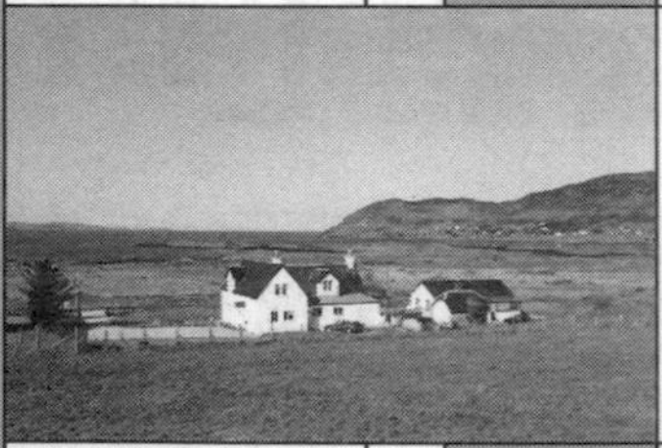

Far View Cottage

Mingary Pier Road, Kilchoan, Ardnamurchan, Argyll PH36 4LH
Telephone: 01972 510357

One of nature's last, accessible, unspoilt havens, Ardnamurchan's mountains, moorlands, oak forests, white sands and crystal waters abound with rare wildlife. This extended keeper's cottage offers panoramic sea views, beautifully furnished comfort and friendly, informal hospitality, bringing Rob & Joan Thompson many regular visitors. Ring for area/house leaflets, sample menus.

Mr and Mrs R Thompson
Far View Cottage
Mingary Pier Road
Kilchoan, Acharacle
Argyll
PH36 4LH
Tel: (Kilchoan) 01972 510357

HIGHLY COMMENDED

1 Twin | 2 En Suite fac | B&B per person | Open Mar-Nov
2 Double | 1 Priv. NOT ensuite | £24.00-£27.00 Single | Dinner at 1930
| | £21.00-£31.00 Double | B&B + Eve. Meal
| | | £29.00-£39.00

Residents' lounge with open fire; private suite available; imaginative home cooking; table licence; near Mull ferry.

KILCHRENAN
Argyll
Mrs K Lambie
Thistle-Doo
Kilchrenan, by Taynuilt
Argyll
PA35 1HF
Tel: (Kilchrenan) 018663 339

Map 1 F2

COMMENDED

1 Twin | 3 En Suite fac | B&B per person | Open Jan-Dec
2 Double | | £15.00-£18.00 Single | Dinner 1800-2100
| | | B&B + Eve. Meal
| | | £25.00-£30.00

Modern family bungalow in idyllic secluded setting overlooking Loch Awe. Home cooking.

VAT is shown at 17.5%: changes in this rate may affect prices. Prices shown are for guidance only. Please send SAE with each enquiry.

KILLIECRANKIE Perthshire Mrs E Goodfellow Tighdornie, Aldclune Killiecrankie Perthshire PH16 5LR Tel: (Pitlochry) 01796 473276	Map 4 C12	COMMENDED	1 Twin 1 Double 1 Family	2 En Suite fac 1 Priv. NOT ensuite	B&B per person £18.00-£19.00 Double	Open Jan-Dec

Modern house on outskirts of Killiecrankie, ideal location for outdoor pursuits.
Ample parking. Lovely scenery.

KILLIN Perthshire	Map 1 H2

Fairview House
MAIN STREET, KILLIN, PERTHSHIRE FK21 8UT
Telephone: 01567 820667

Muriel and *Roger Bedwell* extend a very warm Scottish welcome
to their guest house in the *Heart of Scotland* where they specialise
in good food in relaxing and comfortable surroundings.
The picturesque village set amidst the mountains of the *Central
Highlands* makes an ideal centre for touring or hill walking.

Fairview House Main Street Killin Perthshire FK21 8UT Tel: (Killin) 01567 820667		COMMENDED	1 Single 2 Twin 4 Double	3 En Suite fac 2 Pub Bath/Show	B&B per person £15.00-£17.00 Single £15.00-£17.00 Double	Open Jan-Dec Dinner from 1930 B&B + Eve. Meal £23.00-£25.00

Small family run guest house specialising in home cooking.
Excellent touring centre, good walking and climbing area.

Invertay House Killin Perthshire FK21 8TN Tel: (Killin) 01567 820492		COMMENDED	2 Twin 2 Double 2 Family	3 En Suite fac 1 Priv. NOT ensuite 1 Pub Bath/Show	B&B per person £15.00-£18.00 Single £15.00-£18.00 Double	Open Jan-Dec Dinner from 1900 B&B + Eve. Meal £25.00-£28.00

Traditional stone-built Listed house in extensive garden,
on edge of village overlooking River Lochy.

KILLMARNOCK Ayrshire Dean Park Guest House 27 Wellington Street Kilmarnock Ayrshire KA3 1DW Tel: (Kilmarnock) 01563 572794/532061	Map 1 G6	COMMENDED	1 Single 2 Twin 2 Double 1 Family	2 En Suite fac 2 Pub Bath/Show	B&B per person £15.00-£20.00 Single £15.00-£18.00 Double	Open Jan-Dec

Semi-detached villa, 5 minutes walk from town centre and station.
Private off-street parking.

Eriskay Guest House 2 Dean Terrace Kilmarnock Ayrshire KA3 1RJ Tel: (Kilmarnock) 01563 532061/05851 09971		COMMENDED	2 Single 1 Twin 3 Double 1 Family	3 En Suite fac 2 Pub Bath/Show	B&B per person £15.00-£20.00 Single £15.00-£18.00 Double	Open Jan-Dec

Detached villa conveniently situated on main bus route and close to
Dean Park and Castle. Enclosed secure car park.

Mrs A Grant 177 Dundonald Road Kilmarnock Ayrshire KA2 0AB Tel: (Kilmarnock) 01563 522733		APPROVED	2 Twin 1 Double	1 En Suite fac 1 Pub Bath/Show	B&B per person from £18.00 Single from £14.00 Double	Open Apr-Oct

Modern detached home with attractive enclosed patio and garden on town outskirts.
Golf and good touring base. Under 30 miles (48kms) from Glasgow.

KILMARNOCK continued

Map 3 G6

Mrs Mary Howie
Hillhouse Farm
Grassyards Road
Kilmarnock
Ayrshire
KA3 6HG
Tel: (Kilmarnock)
01563 523370

COMMENDED

1 Twin   1 En Suite fac
2 Family   2 Pub Bath/Show

B&B per person
£14.00-£17.00 Single
£13.00-£17.00 Double

Open Jan-Dec

Working dairy farm (500 acres) with fine views of Ayrshire countryside situated about 2 miles (4 kms) east of Kilmarnock.

Mrs M Love
Muirhouse Farm
Gatehead, by Kilmarnock
Ayrshire
KA2 0BT
Tel: (Kilmarnock)
01563 523975

COMMENDED

1 Twin   2 En Suite fac
1 Double   1 Priv. NOT ensuite
1 Family

B&B per person
£15.00-£18.00 Single
£14.00-£17.00 Double
Room only per person
£12.00-£16.00

Open Jan-Dec
Dinner 1800-1900

Large family farmhouse on 170-acre dairy farm 2 miles (3kms) from Kilmarnock. Quiet rural position.

"Tamarind"
24 Arran Avenue, Kilmarnock KA3 1TP
Telephone and Fax: 01563 571788

The accommodation at 'Tamarind' was created with the International visitor in mind. Rooms are equipped with remote control TV and all are en-suite. A heated swimming pool (in season) is also available for your enjoyment.
Discerning travellers will feel at home here.

Mrs C Turner
Tamarind, 24 Arran Avenue
Kilmarnock
Ayrshire
KA3 1TP
Tel: (Kilmarnock)
01563 571788
Fax: 01563 571788

COMMENDED

2 Single   5 En Suite fac
1 Twin
1 Double
1 Family

B&B per person
£22.50-£30.00 Single
£17.50-£22.50 Double
Room only per person
£17.50-£25.00

Open Jan-Dec
Dinner at 1900
B&B + Eve. Meal
£35.00-£42.50

Ranch-style bungalow with small heated swimming pool in residential area. Convenient base for touring.

BY KILMARNOCK
Ayrshire

Map 1 G6

Mrs L Howie
Muirhouse Farm
Symington, by Kilmarnock
Ayrshire
KA1 5PA
Tel: (Symington) 01563 830218

COMMENDED

1 Twin   1 Pub Bath/Show
1 Double

B&B per person
from £18.00 Single
from £16.00 Double

Open Jan-Dec

Traditional farmhouse peacefully situated and convenient for A77. Provides good base for touring Ayrshire coast, golfing, fishing, walking etc.

KILMORE, by Oban
Argyll

Map 1 E2

Braeside Guest House
Kilmore, by Oban
Argyll
PA34 4QR
Tel: (Kilmore) 01631 770243

COMMENDED

1 Twin   4 En Suite fac
3 Double   1 Priv. NOT ensuite
1 Family

B&B per person
£16.50-£22.50 Single
£16.50-£22.50 Double

Open Feb-Nov
Dinner 1830-1900
B&B + Eve. Meal
£25.50-£32.50

Modern guest house 3 miles (5kms) south of Oban. Car parking. Roadside position with superb views. Evening meal. Fine wines. Vegetarian food. Non-smoking.

KILMORE, Sleat
Isle of Skye, Inverness-shire

Map 3 F10

Mrs Julia MacDonald
3 Kilmore
Sleat
Isle of Skye, Inverness-shire
IV44 8RG
Tel: (Ardvasar) 01471 844272

COMMENDED

2 Single   1 En Suite fac
1 Twin   1 Pub Bath/Show
1 Double

B&B per person
£15.00 Single
£14.00-£16.00 Double

Open Apr-Oct

Modern bungalow in elevated position. On working croft with panoramic views towards Knoydart hills. 2.5 miles (4 kms) from Armadale ferry.

KILMUIR, Uig Isle of Skye, Inverness-shire	Map 3 D7

Kilmuir House

**Kilmuir
Near Uig
Isle of Skye
IV51 9YN
Tel: 01470 542262**

Lovely old manse in large walled garden overlooking Loch Snizort and Outer Hebrides. Furnished with antiques and centrally heated throughout, we offer excellent home cooking using local produce and our own free range eggs. Kilmuir is steeped in history and Gaelic culture and tradition is still much in evidence here.

Mrs S Phelps Kilmuir House Kilmuir, by Uig Isle of Skye, Inverness-shire IV51 9YN Tel: (Uig) 01470 542262	COMMENDED Listed	1 Twin 1 Double 1 Family	2 Pub Bath/Show	B&B per person £14.00-£15.00 Double	Open Jan-Dec Dinner 1900-2000 B&B + Eve. Meal from £23.00	

Former manse in superb situation overlooking loch to Outer Isles.
Warm hospitality and high standard of home cooking using fresh local produce.

KILSYTH **Stirlingshire** Mrs E MacGregor Allanfauld Farm Kilsyth Stirlingshire G65 9DF Tel: (Kilsyth) 01236 822155	Map 2 A4 COMMENDED Listed	1 Twin 1 Family	1 Pub Bath/Show	B&B per person £15.00 Single £15.00 Double	Open Jan-Dec	

Working stock farm on Kilsyth Hills with large south-facing garden.
12 miles (19kms) north of Glasgow.

KILTARLITY Inverness-shire	Map 4 A9

BROOMHILL

**Kiltarlity, Beauly, Inverness-shire IV4 7JH
Telephone: 01463 741447**

Former Edwardian manse retaining its original character, set in peaceful countryside 11 miles from Inverness and 8 miles from Loch Ness. Large, warm, comfortable rooms. Traditional home cooking with dinners and packed lunches if required. Pleasant walks in all directions through farmland, woodland and forest.

Mrs Eunice Ramsden Broomhill Kiltarlity, Beauly Inverness-shire IV4 7JH Tel: (Kiltarlity) 01463 741447	COMMENDED Listed	1 Twin 1 Double	1 Pub Bath/Show	B&B per person £11.00-£12.50 Single £11.00-£12.50 Double	Open Jan-Dec Dinner 1800-1900 B&B + Eve. Meal £16.00-£17.50	

Large country house set in own grounds amongst open countryside.
11 miles (18kms) from Inverness. Totally non-smoking.
Packed lunches and evening meals available.

KILWINNING **Ayrshire** Mrs C Harris Woodburn Cottage Woodwynd Kilwinning Ayrshire Tel: (Kilwinning) 01294 551657/ 0589 494567 (mobile) Fax: 01294 558297	Map 1 G6 COMMENDED Listed	1 Single 2 Twin	1 Pub Bath/Show	B&B per person £15.00-£17.00 Single £15.00-£17.00 Double	Open Jan-Dec	

Attractive cottage in its own grounds – a little bit of countryside
in the centre of Kilwinning.

KINCRAIG Inverness-shire	Map 4 C10

Braeriach Guest House
Kincraig, By Kingussie, Inverness-shire PH21 1QA
Telephone: 01540 651369

Braeriach Guest House sits on the banks of the River Spey with superb views of the Cairngorm Mountains beyond. Ideal base for walking, birdwatching, fishing, golf and exploring. Comfy en-suite rooms with river views. Imaginative freshly prepared 3-course dinners. Peaceful surroundings and a warm welcome.

Braeriach Guest House Kincraig, by Kingussie Inverness-shire PH21 1QA Tel: (Kincraig) 01540 651369	COMMENDED 👑👑👑	1 Twin 2 Double	3 En Suite fac	B&B per person £18.00-£22.00 Single £16.00-£18.00 Double	Open Jan-Dec Dinner from 1900 B&B + Eve. Meal £28.00-£30.00	
		Former manse situated on the banks of the River Spey with picturesque garden extending to private jetty.				

Grampian View Kincraig Inverness-shire PH21 1NA Tel: (Kincraig) 01540 651383	COMMENDED 👑👑	1 Single 2 Twin 2 Double	4 En Suite fac 1 Priv. NOT ensuite	B&B per person from £17.00 Single from £17.00 Double	Open Jan-Dec Dinner 1845-1930 B&B + Eve. Meal from £26.50	
		Family run Victorian house, with original fireplaces and woodwork, offering bed and breakfast with a touch of elegance. Ideal touring base.				

Insh Hall Lodge
KINCRAIG, INVERNESS-SHIRE PH21 1NU
Telephone: 01540 651272 Fax: 01540 651208

Welcoming family-run Lodge in 14-acre woodland setting, bordering scenic Loch Insh with a backdrop of the Cairngorm Mountains. *Ensuite B&B from £14.50. Family of four: B&B ensuite from £42.* Full board available. TV Lounges, games, sauna, minigym, laundry. Free watersports hire (set times) for guests staying minimum two nights. Licensed, log and stone-built Lochside Restaurant, recommended by *Les Routiers*, with balcony overlooking windsurfing, sailing, canoeing, salmon and trout fishing. Watersports hire and instruction by the hour, day and week. Dry ski slope, mountain bike hire, rowing, fitness and interpretation trail, adventure park, BBQ, picnic sites. Central for many visitor attractions, golf, riding, RSPB Reserve.

Insh Hall Lodge Kincraig Kingussie Inverness-shire PH21 1NU Tel: (Kincraig) 01540 651272 Fax: 01540 651208	COMMENDED Listed	7 Twin 8 Family	13 En Suite fac 2 Pub Bath/Show	B&B per person £11.50-£20.00 Single £11.50-£15.00 Double Room only per person £9.00-£11.50	Open Jan-Dec Dinner 1800-2200 B&B + Eve. Meal £26.00-£27.00	
		Comfortable ensuite accommodation 100 yards from Loch Insch. Sauna, mini-gym, TV lounge. Central for visitor attractions. Licensed restaurant. Water sports and winter skiing.				

Insh House Guest House Kincraig Inverness-shire PH21 1NU Tel: (Kincraig) 01540 651377	COMMENDED 👑	2 Single 1 Twin 1 Double 1 Family	2 Pub Bath/Show	B&B per person £15.00-£16.00 Single £15.00-£16.00 Double	Open Jan-Dec Dinner at 1900 B&B + Eve. Meal £23.00-£25.00	
		Fine example of a Telford house in 2 acres of secluded grounds. Close to Loch Insh, 10 minutes to Aviemore. Skiing, watersports, riding, gliding.				

Mrs V MacLeod Carn Ban, by Loch Insh Kincraig Inverness-shire PH21 1NU Tel: (Kincraig) 01540 651313	COMMENDED 👑	1 Twin 1 Family	1 Pub Bath/Show	B&B per person £16.00 Single £14.00-£15.00 Double	Open Jan-Dec

Traditional Scottish hospitality in modern house on shores of Loch Insh.

Commended
👑👑👑

March House

Lagganlia, Feshiebridge, Kincraig PH21 1NG
Telephone and Fax: 01540 651388

Uniquely situated in Glen Feshie with beautiful views and peaceful surroundings. Imaginative evening meals, recommended by the **Taste of Scotland**, are served in our new conservatory/dining-room and prepared using fresh local produce and herbs from our garden. Individually decorated bedrooms with en-suite facilities and other home comforts. A warm relaxing atmosphere.

March House Guest House Feshiebridge Kincraig Inverness-shire PH21 1NG Tel: (Kincraig) 01540 651388 Fax: 01540 651388	COMMENDED 👑👑👑	3 Twin 2 Double 1 Family	5 En Suite fac 1 Priv. NOT ensuite	B&B per person £16.00-£20.00 Single £16.00-£20.00 Double	Open Dec-Oct Dinner from 1900 B&B + Eve. Meal £28.00-£32.00

Peaceful location in beautiful Glenfeshie. Personally run with relaxing atmosphere. Emphasis on fresh food served in our new spacious conservatory overlooking the mountains. Taste of Scotland.

Kirkbeag

KINCRAIG, KINGUSSIE, INVERNESS-SHIRE PH21 1ND
Telephone: 01540 651298

Enjoy a Highland Welcome and home cooking in our comfortable family home, located on the B9152, 1 mile north of Kincraig Village. Ideal for watersports, walking, touring, bird-watching, skiing, or learning to woodturn, carve or silversmith. Children welcome. Regret no pets.
B&B from £15 per person per night. Dinners by arrangement.
Full details from Sheila Paisley.

Mr & Mrs J Paisley Kirkbeag, Milehead Kincraig Inverness-shire PH21 1ND Tel: (Kincraig) 01540 651298	COMMENDED Listed	1 Twin 1 Double	2 Pub Bath/Show	B&B per person £15.00-£19.00 Single £15.00-£17.00 Double	Open Jan-Dec Dinner 1800-2000 B&B + Eve. Meal £24.00-£26.00

19th-century church, converted to family home. Spiral staircase and craft workshop. Craft courses available. Aviemore 5 miles. Smokers welcome.

KINGSBARNS Fife Mrs Farida Hay Kingsbarns Bed & Breakfast, 3 Main Street, Kingsbarns Fife KY16 8SL Tel: (Boarhills) 01334 880234	Map 2 D3 COMMENDED 👑👑	2 Twin 2 Double	3 En Suite fac 1 Priv. NOT ensuite	B&B per person £17.00-£18.00 Single	Open Mar-Oct

Family run, 6 miles (10kms) from St Andrews. Off-street parking and only 0.5 mile (1km) from the beach. Wide choice of golf courses.

Scotland for Golf . . .

Find out more about golf in Scotland. There's more to it than just the championship courses so get in touch with us now for information on the hidden gems of Scotland.

Write to: **Information Unit, Scottish Tourist Board, 23 Ravelston Terrace, Edinburgh EH4 3EU or call: 0131-332 2433**

KINGUSSIE Inverness-shire Avondale Guest House Newtonmore Road Kingussie Inverness-shire PH21 1HF Tel: (Kingussie) 01540 661731	Map 4 B11	HIGHLY COMMENDED ♕♕♕ 🚶	1 Single 3 Twin 2 Double 1 Family	5 En Suite fac 2 Pub Bath/Show	B&B per person £17.00-£20.00 Single £17.00-£20.00 Double	Open Jan-Dec Dinner 1900-1930 B&B + Eve. Meal £25.50-£28.50

Stone-built house with own large garden near centre of village.
Friendly atmosphere, ample parking. Skiing and fishing can be arranged.

Mr and Mrs R W Dawkins The Auld Poor Hoose Laggan Cottage Kingussie Inverness-shire PH21 1LS Tel: (Kingussie) 01540 661558	COMMENDED Listed	3 Twin	1 Pub Bath/Show	B&B per person from £16.00 Double	Open Jan-Dec Dinner 1800-2000 B&B + Eve. Meal £23.00-£25.00

A home from home providing a warm welcome amid mountains and wild walks.
We always knew we'd end up in the poor hoose. Why not join us and leave your diet at home.

J Gibson Bhuna Monadh 85 High Street Kingussie Inverness-shire PH21 1HX Tel: (Kingussie) 01540 661186	COMMENDED ♕♕	1 Twin 1 Double	2 En Suite fac	B&B per person £16.00-£19.00 Single £16.00-£19.00 Double	Open Jan-Dec Dinner from 1900 B&B + Eve. Meal from £24.50

This recently refurbished Listed building offers comfortable accommodation
in spacious bedrooms with en-suite bathrooms, TV and hot drink facilities.

HOMEWOOD LODGE
Newtonmore Road, Kingussie, Inverness-shire PH21 1HD
Telephone: 01540 661507

This 19th-century villa on outskirts of village enjoys panoramic views to surrounding hills and Cairngorm Mountains and is ideally situated for exploring the many activities in the area. Home comforts can be enjoyed including good Scottish home cooking; therefore evening meals must be booked in advance!

Homewood Lodge Newtonmore Road Kingussie Inverness-shire PH21 1HD Tel: (Kingussie) 01540 661507	COMMENDED ♕♕	1 Twin 1 Double 1 Family	3 En Suite fac	B&B per person from £19.50 Single from £19.50 Double	Open Jan-Dec Dinner from 1900 B&B + Eve. Meal from £30.00

Friendly guest house on edge of village. Views to Cairngorm Mountains.
Ideal base for touring area.

Mrs Jarratt St Helens Ardbroilach Road Kingussie Inverness-shire PH21 1JX Tel: (Kingussie) 01540 661430	HIGHLY COMMENDED ♕♕♕	1 Twin 2 Double	2 En Suite fac 1 Priv. NOT ensuite	B&B per person £18.00-£20.00 Single £18.00-£20.00 Double	Open Jan-Dec

Elegant stone-built house c1895 in elevated position with large secluded gardens
and excellent views over village and Cairngorm Mountains beyond.

GLENGARRY

Highly Commended
♥♥

East Terrace, Kingussie, Inverness-shire PH21 1JS
Telephone: 01540 661386

Beautifully situated in its own grounds, this high-quality establishment, with an enviable reputation, is ideally suited to the discerning visitor. The perfect base for summer and winter pursuits. Well-appointed bedrooms, private off-road parking and a tranquil setting.
For brochure and details contact: Mel and Ann Short, Proprietors.

Mr & Mrs M B Short Glengarry, East Terrace Kingussie Inverness-shire PH21 1JS Tel: (Kingussie) 01540 661386	HIGHLY COMMENDED ♥♥	2 Single 2 Double	1 Priv. NOT ensuite 1 Pub Bath/Show	B&B per person £16.00-£18.00 Single £16.00-£18.00 Double	Open Jan-Dec Dinner at 1900 B&B + Eve. Meal £24.50-£26.50	

Stone-built house c1900 with large garden and summer house, in quiet residential area, only a few minutes walk from centre of Kingussie. No smoking throughout.

Sonnhalde Guest House East Terrace Kingussie Inverness-shire PH21 1JS Tel: (Kingussie) 01540 661266 Fax: 01540 661266	COMMENDED ♥♥	2 Twin 3 Double 2 Family	4 En Suite fac 2 Pub Bath/Show	B&B per person £22.00-£26.00 Single £17.00-£21.00 Double	Open Jan-Oct Dinner from 1830 B&B + Eve. Meal £9.00-£10.00	

Warm welcome at Victorian villa overlooking Cairngorms. Home cooking. Natural history and photographic holidays. Fly-fishing and walking courses.

KINLOCHEWE Ross-shire	Map 3 G8

Cromasaig

Kinlochewe, Wester Ross IV22 2PE
Telephone and Fax: 01445 760234

Warm welcome, homely atmosphere, comfortable accommodation and good food. Drying facilities available, guided walks and transport locally. Explore rugged mountains, deserted beaches and ancient woodland. Watch golden eagle and deer from our windows. Have dinner interrupted to see pine marten on our bird table. *Bring plenty of camera film!*

Mrs E Forrest Cromasaig, Torridon Road Kinlochewe Ross-shire Tel: (Kinlochewe) 01445 760234 Fax: 01445 760234	COMMENDED Listed	1 Twin 1 Double 1 Family	1 Pub Bath/Show	B&B per person £15.00-£16.00 Single £15.00-£16.00 Double	Open Jan-Dec Dinner 1800-2000 B&B + Eve. Meal £23.00-£25.00	

Warm hospitality from climbing hosts. Re-furbished croft cottage with log fire, drying facilities. At foot of Beinn Eighe – transport available.

Hillhaven

KINLOCHEWE, WESTER ROSS IV22 2PA
Telephone: 01445 760204

Modern bungalow close to *Torridon Mountains*
and *Loch Maree*.
Guest sitting and dining rooms,
with all bedrooms ensuite.
Home cooking and baking.

Hillhaven Kinlochewe Ross-shire IV22 2PA Tel: (Kinlochewe) 01445 760204	COMMENDED ♥♥	1 Twin 2 Double	3 En Suite fac	B&B per person £15.00-£17.00 Single £15.00-£17.00 Double	Open Jan-Dec Dinner 1830-1930 B&B + Eve. Meal £24.00-£26.00	

Small guest house close to Torridon Mountains and Loch Maree. All rooms ensuite. Home cooking. Non-smoking.

Details of Grading and Classification are on page vi.

Key to symbols is on back flap.

KINLOCHLEVEN **Argyll** Mrs Robertson Edencoille, Garbhien Road Kinlochleven Argyll PA40 4SE Tel: (Kinlochleven) 01855 831358	Map 3 H12	COMMENDED	3 Twin	2 Pub Bath/Show	B&B per person £13.00-£20.00 Single £13.00-£15.00 Double	Open Jan-Dec Dinner 1800-2100 B&B + Eve. Meal £21.00-£23.00	

Family home on scenic road from Glencoe.
Central for walking, climbing and skiing in the Lochaber area.

KINLOCH RANNOCH **Perthshire**	Map 1 H1

BUNRANNOCH HOUSE

Kinloch Rannoch, Perthshire PH16 5QB
Tel: 01882 632407

Lovely Victorian house set in 2 acres of grounds on the outskirts of Kinloch Rannoch. A warm welcome awaits you, together with a complimentary tea tray of home cooking on arrival. Comfortable accommodation includes 3 double, 2 twin and 2 family rooms, most en-suite. All rooms have uninterrupted Highland views and tea/coffee-making facilities. Fire Certificate.

Fishing, walking, cycling, birdwatching, boating and horse-riding provide ample choice. Log fires and good cooking.

B&B FROM £16.00.

Mrs J Skeaping Bunrannoch House Kinloch Rannoch Perthshire PH16 5QB Tel: (Kinloch Rannoch) 01882 632407		COMMENDED	1 Single 1 Twin 3 Double 2 Family	5 En Suite fac 2 Pub Bath/Show	B&B per person £16.00-£18.00 Single £16.00-£18.00 Double	Open Jan-Dec, exc Xmas/New Year Dinner 1900-2130 B&B + Eve. Meal £30.00-£32.00	

With supreme hospitality Jenny welcomes you into her warm, friendly home, a former shooting lodge. Taste of Scotland home cooking with local produce.

Mrs Steffen Cuilmore Cottage Kinloch Rannoch Perthshire PH16 5QB Tel: (Kinloch Rannoch) 01882 632218 Fax: 01882 632218		DELUXE	1 Twin 1 Double	2 Priv. NOT ensuite	B&B per person £20.00-£25.00 Single	Open Feb-Nov Dinner 1900-2100 B&B + Eve. Meal £45.50-£50.00	

Traditional, cosy 18th-century croft. Best of local produce, own fruit and vegetables, home baking. Taste of Scotland special award winner.

KINLOCHSPELVE **Isle of Mull, Argyll** Mrs Railton-Edwards Barrachandroman Kinlochspelve Loch Buie Isle of Mull, Argyll PA62 6AA Tel: (Kinlochspelve) 01680 814220 Fax: 01680 814220	Map 1 D2	HIGHLY COMMENDED	2 Double	1 En Suite fac 1 Priv. NOT ensuite	B&B per person from £20.00 Single Room only per person from £20.00	Open Jan-Dec Dinner 1800-2200 B&B + Eve. Meal £32.00-£34.00	

Luxuriously converted barn in secluded lochside location, both rooms with private facilities. Accent on fresh fish and seafood.

KINROSS	Map 2						
Kinross-shire	B3	COMMENDED	1 Twin	1 En Suite fac	B&B per person	Open Mar-Nov	
Mrs A Bell		Listed	2 Double	2 Pub Bath/Show	£18.00-£20.00 Single		
Hillview House, Gairneybank					£15.00-£18.00 Double		
Kinross							
Tel: (Kinross) 01577 863802							

Modern detached house with large garden overlooking open countryside, yet close to the motorway and only 2 miles (3kms) from Kinross. Home-made bread and jams.

The Grouse & Claret		COMMENDED	1 Twin	3 En Suite fac	B&B per person	Open Jan-Dec	
Heatheryford		♛♛♛	2 Double		£24.50-£29.50 Single	Dinner 1900-2100	
Kinross					£22.50-£24.50 Double	B&B + Eve. Meal	
KY13 7NQ						£35.00-£42.00	
Tel: (Kinross) 01577 864212							
Fax: 01557 864920							

Restaurant with separate accommodation, both overlooking the trout lochans to the Ochil Hills beyond. Conveniently situated for the M90 motorway.

The Innkeeper's Cottage

32 MUIRS, KINROSS KY13 7AS
Telephone and Fax: 01577 862270

Commended
Listed

This cottage dates back to the *Battle of Waterloo* and is the home of the *Keeper of the Inn*. It has been welcoming guests for many years by offering good, clean, comfortable accommodation in small but cosy country-style rooms. This is complemented by fresh homecooked country fayre provided at the inn opposite.

The Innkeeper		COMMENDED	1 Twin	1 Pub Bath/Show	B&B per person	Open Jan-Dec	
Innkeeper's Cottage		Listed	2 Double		£25.00-£30.00 Single	Dinner 1700-2100	
32 Muirs, Kinross					£12.00-£17.50 Double	B&B + Eve. Meal	
Kinross-shire						£22.00-£40.00	
KY13 7AS							
Tel: (Kinross) 01577 862270							
Fax: 01577 862270							

This idyllic cottage is the home of the Keeper of the Inn opposite and has been welcoming guests for years.

THE MUIRS INN

49 MUIRS, KINROSS KY13 7AU
Telephone: 01577 862270
Commended ♛♛♛

A quaint Scottish Country Inn – at its best. Offering traditional en-suite bedroom comfort and value for money with award nominated home-cooked country cuisine served at sensible prices in its popular "Maltings" restaurant plus a connoisseur's choice of Scottish Wines, Real Ales and Malt Whiskies in addition to the Inn's own branded beers and ciders.

Situated in the Historical Town of Kinross, this well-appointed Inn is great for sporting and touring holidays with all Scotland's cities and 120 golf courses within driving distance plus local trout fishing on Loch Leven or walking and pony trekking in the surrounding hills. It's ideal for leisure or pleasure and The Inn is *Really* – Simply Something Special.

The Muirs Inn Kinross		COMMENDED	2 Twin	5 En Suite fac	B&B per person	Open Jan-Dec	
49 Muirs		♛♛♛	3 Double		£35.00-£40.00 Single	Dinner 1700-2100	
Kinross					£25.00-£30.00 Double	B&B + Eve. Meal	
KY13 7AU						£45.00-£50.00	
Tel: (Kinross) 01577 862270							
Fax: 01577 862270							

Scottish country Inn. Award nominated restaurant. Simply something special.

	Map 2 B3					
BY KINROSS **Kinross-shire** Agnes Shand Schiehallion Crook of Devon, by Kinross Kinross-shire KY13 7UL Tel: (Fossoway) 01577 840356		COMMENDED	1 Twin 1 Double 1 Family	1 En Suite fac 1 Priv. NOT ensuite 2 Bath/Show	B&B per person £15.00-£16.00 Single £15.00-£17.00 Double	Open Jan-Dec

On the outskirts of the village, a peaceful situation, family home with comfortable rooms. Non-smokers preferred.

	Map 1 H4					
KIPPEN **Stirlingshire** Mrs M M Adam Hill of Arnmore Farm, Arnprior Kippen Stirlingshire Tel: (Kippen) 01786 870225		COMMENDED Listed	1 Double 1 Family	1 Pub Bath/Show	B&B per person £15.00-£16.00 Double	Open Jan-Dec

Farmhouse situated in 300-acre arable farm with open views of the Trossachs hills. Good touring base.

Mrs A McCallum Sealladh Ard, Station Brae Kippen Stirlingshire Tel: (Stirling) 01786 870291		HIGHLY COMMENDED Listed	2 Twin 1 Double	1 Pub Bath/Show	B&B per person £17.50-£19.00 Single from £17.50 Double	Open Jan-Dec, exe Xmas/New Year

Detached house on edge of village with panoramic views across the valley to the Trossachs Hills.

	Map 2 A10					
KIPPFORD, by Dalbeattie **Kirkcudbrightshire** Janet M McKinnon Brookside Kippford, by Dalbeattie Kirkcudbrightshire DG5 4LL Tel: (Kippford) 01556 620240		COMMENDED	1 Twin 1 Double	1 En Suite fac 1 Priv. NOT ensuite	Room only per person from £17.50	Open Mar-Oct

Comfortable family home. Quiet location set in large garden overlooking Urr Estuary. Private parking. Ideal base for touring.

Mrs J Muir Rosemount, On the Sea Front Kippford, by Dalbeattie Kirkcudbrightshire DG5 4LN Tel: (Kippford) 01556 620214		COMMENDED	2 Twin 2 Double 1 Family	3 En Suite fac 2 Priv. NOT ensuite 2 Pub Bath/Show	B&B per person from £20.00 Single £17.50-£20.00 Double	Open Feb-Nov Dinner from 1900

Small friendly guest house on the Urr Estuary offering a superb view and spectacular sunsets. Smoking and non-smoking lounges.

	Map 2 B10					
KIRKBEAN **Dumfriesshire** Mrs J I Ballard Drumpagan Cottage Kirkbean Dumfriesshire DG2 8DW Tel: (Kirkbean) 01387 880203 Fax: 01387 880657		HIGHLY COMMENDED	2 Twin	1 Pub Bath/Show	B&B per person from £25.00 Single from £17.50 Double	Open Jan-Dec

Recently refurbished and modernised cottage in tranquil setting. Traditional Scottish breakfast imaginatively presented. Golfing, fishing, bird-watching.

	Map 2 C4					
KIRKCALDY **Fife** Mrs Elizabeth Duncan Bennochy Bank 26A Carlyle Road Kirkcaldy Fife KY1 1DB Tel: (Kirkcaldy) 01592 200733/ 0831 150607 (mobile)		COMMENDED	1 Twin 1 Double 1 Family	1 En Suite fac 1 Pub Bath/Show	B&B per person £17.00-£18.50 Single £15.00-£20.00 Double	Open Jan-Dec

Comfortable accommodation on upper floors of large Victorian house in residential area, close to town centre and railway station. Private parking.

VAT is shown at 17.5%: changes in this rate may affect prices. Prices shown are for guidance only. Please send SAE with each enquiry.

Mrs B Linton Norview, 59 Normand Road Dysart, Kirkcaldy Fife KY1 2XP Tel: (Kirkcaldy) 01592 652804		APPROVED Listed	2 Twin 1 Double	1 Pub Bath/Show	B&B per person £12.00-£14.00 Single £12.00-£14.00 Double Room only per person £10.00-£12.00	Open Jan-Dec	

Personally run bed and breakfast on main tourist route.
Ideal for touring Fife. Golf courses and other amenities close by.

Mrs Nicol Cherrydene, 44 Bennochy Road Kirkcaldy Fife KY2 5RB Tel: (Kirkcaldy) 01592 202147/644618		COMMENDED	1 Single 1 Double 1 Family	2 En Suite fac 1 Pub Bath/Show	B&B per person £17.00-£20.00 Single £15.00-£18.00 Double Room only per person £17.00-£20.00	Open Jan-Dec Dinner 1800-2000 B&B + Eve. Meal £21.00-£25.00	

Victorian end terraced house in quiet residential area,
yet within easy reach of all amenities. Private parking.

KIRKCOWAN **Wigtownshire** Church End B&B 6 Main Street Kirkcowan Wigtownshire DG8 0HG Tel: (Kirkcowan) 01671 830246	Map 1 G10	COMMENDED	1 Twin 1 Double 1 Family	3 En Suite fac	B&B per person £16.00-£18.00 Single £14.00-£16.00 Double Room only per person £12.00-£14.00	Open Jan-Dec Dinner 1800-1900	

Converted 18th-century farmworkers' cottages with full ensuite rooms.
Home cooking with fresh produce.

KIRKCUDBRIGHT Gladstone House 48 High Street Kirkcudbright DG6 4JX Tel: (Kirkcudbright) 01557 331734	Map 2 A10	HIGHLY COMMENDED	3 Double	3 En Suite fac	B&B per person £32.00-£34.00 Single £25.00-£28.00 Double	Open Jan-Dec	

Elegance and comfort in sympathetically restored Georgian town house
in a quiet corner of the old town. Secret garden.

MILLBURN HOUSE
Millburn Street, Kirkcudbright DG6 4ED
Telephone: 01557 330926

A warm friendly welcome awaits you at this small, non-smoking house. Stone-built, white-painted with delightful conservatory breakfast room. Much praised breakfast menu caters for most tastes and diets. Three charming bedrooms, all with hospitality trays. Two en-suite, one with own shower room and toilet.

Len Rutter Millburn House, Millburn Street Kirkcudbright DG6 4ED Tel: (Kirkcudbright) 01557 330926		COMMENDED	2 Twin 1 Double	2 En Suite fac 1 Priv. NOT ensuite	B&B per person £22.50-£45.00 Single £22.50 Double	Open Jan-Dec	

A warm, friendly welcome awaits you at this small guest house.
Listed building, situated in a quiet area close to the centre of the town.

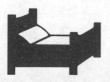

Book your accommodation anywhere in
Scotland the easy way – through your nearest
Tourist Information Centre.

A booking fee of £2.75 is charged, and you will be asked for
a small deposit.

Local bookings are usually free, or a small fee will be charged.

KIRKMICHAEL **Perthshire** Mr & Mrs Mills Ardlebrig Kirkmichael Perthshire PH10 7NY Tel: (Strathardle) 01250 881350	**Map 4** D12	COMMENDED	1 Single 1 Twin 1 Family	1 Pub Bath/Show	B&B per person £13.50 Single £13.50 Double	Open Jan-Dec Dinner 1800-2100 B&B + Eve. Meal £19.50

Family run B&B, set among the scenic splendour of Perthshire, offering quality home cooking.

Mr and Mrs A Van der Veldt Curran House Kirkmichael, Blairgowrie Perthshire PH10 7NA Tel: (Strathardle) 01250 881229		COMMENDED	1 Twin 2 Double	1 En Suite fac 2 Pub Bath/Show	B&B per person £14.00-£16.00 Single £14.00-£16.00 Double	Open Jan-Nov

19th-century house with large garden in peaceful rural setting, yet only 0.5 miles (1km) from the centre of the village.

KIRKMUIRHILL, Lesmahagow **Lanarkshire** Mrs I H McInally Dykecroft Farm Kirkmuirhill, by Lesmahagow Lanarkshire ML11 0JQ Tel: (Lesmahagow) 01555 892226	**Map 2** A6	COMMENDED Listed	1 Twin 2 Double	1 Pub Bath/Show	B&B per person £17.00-£18.00 Single £15.50-£16.50 Double	Open Jan-Dec

Modern farmhouse bungalow in rural situation 20 miles (32kms) south of Glasgow.

KIRKWALL **Orkney** Mrs M Bain 6 Frasers Close Kirkwall Orkney KW15 1DT Tel: (Kirkwall) 01856 872862	**Map 5** B11	COMMENDED	1 Twin 2 Double	1 En Suite fac 3 Pub Bath/Show	B&B per person £12.00-£14.00 Single £12.00-£14.00 Double	Open Jan-Dec

House of character, situated in quiet lane in the centre of town. Car park adjacent.

Mrs Braun Shearwood, Muddisdale, Pickaquoy Road Kirkwall Orkney KW15 1RR Tel: (Kirkwall) 01856 873494		COMMENDED	1 Twin 1 Double	1 Pub Bath/Show	B&B per person £13.00-£14.00 Single £13.00-£14.00 Double	Open Jan-Dec

Bungalow situated in quiet residential area, 10 minutes walk from the town centre with own enclosed garden.

Mrs M Flett Briar Lea, 10 Dundas Crescent Kirkwall Orkney KW15 1JQ Tel: (Kirkwall) 01856 872747		COMMENDED Listed	2 Single 2 Twin	2 Pub Bath/Show	B&B per person £15.00-£16.00 Single £15.00-£16.00 Double	Open Jan-Dec

19th-century stone-built house retaining many original features with large walled garden. Residential area with easy access to town centre.

Mrs Golding Kemuel, Bignold Park Road Kirkwall Orkney KW15 1PT Tel: (Kirkwall) 01856 873092		COMMENDED	1 Single 1 Twin 1 Double	1 Pub Bath/Show	B&B per person £14.00-£15.00 Single £14.00-£15.00 Double	Open Apr-Sep Dinner 1900-2130 B&B + Eve. Meal £19.00-£20.00

Detached house on main road 10 minutes walk from town centre, close to creamery and distillery.

Mr & Mrs E Linklater Craigwood, Cromwell Road Kirkwall Orkney KW15 1LN Tel: (Kirkwall) 01856 872006		COMMENDED Listed	1 Twin 1 Double	2 Pub Bath/Show	B&B per person £12.00-£15.00 Single £11.00-£14.00 Double	Open Jan-Dec

Warm hospitality. Set in easy walking distance of town centre. Off-street parking.

Sanderlay Guest House 2 Viewfield Drive Kirkwall Orkney KW15 1RB Tel: (Kirkwall) 01856 872343 Fax: 01856 876350	COMMENDED 👑👑	1 Single 1 Twin 2 Double 2 Family	4 En Suite fac 1 Pub Bath/Show	B&B per person £13.00-£21.00 Single £13.00-£19.00 Double Room only per person £10.00-£18.00	Open Jan-Dec

Comfortable modern house in quiet residential area on outskirts of town.
Some en suite and 2 self-contained family units.

KIRRIEMUIR — Map 2 C1
Angus

Mrs B Ewart Middlefield House, Knowehead Kirriemuir Angus DD8 5AA Tel: (Kirriemuir) 01575 572924	COMMENDED Listed	1 Single 1 Twin 1 Double	1 Pub Bath/Show	B&B per person £13.50-£15.00 Single £13.50-£15.00 Double	Open Jan-Dec

Situated in own grounds, stone-built house offers comfortable
accommodation, town centre nearby. Gateway to Angus Glens.

Mrs J Lindsay Crepto, Kinnordy Place Kirriemuir Angus DD8 4JW Tel: (Kirriemuir) 01575 572746	COMMENDED Listed	1 Single 1 Twin 1 Double	1 Pub Bath/Show	B&B per person £14.50-£15.50 Single £14.50 Double	Open Jan-Dec

Modern house in quiet cul-de-sac. 10 minutes walk from centre of town.
Gateway to Angus Glens.

Mrs M Marchant The Welton of Kingoldrum Kirriemuir Angus DD8 5HY Tel: (Kirriemuir) 01575 574743	COMMENDED 👑👑👑	1 Twin 2 Double	3 En Suite fac	B&B per person £18.00-£21.00 Single £15.00-£18.00 Double Room only per person £10.00	Open Jan-Dec Dinner 1830-2130 B&B + Eve. Meal £23.00-£27.50

Self-contained flat on working hill farm. Situated in an Angus Glen
with panoramic views. Access to local hills.

BY KIRRIEMUIR — Map 2 C1
Angus

Mrs D Grimmond Lismore Airlie, by Kirriemuir Angus DD8 5NP Tel: (Craigton) 01575 530213	COMMENDED Listed	1 Twin 1 Double	1 Pub Bath/Show	B&B per person from £12.00 Single from £12.00 Double	Open Apr-Oct Dinner 1900-2100 B&B + Eve. Meal from £17.00

Detached bungalow, in the heart of the country, but within easy reach of Perth,
Dundee and Angus Glens. Warm welcome. Home baking.

KISHORN — Map 3 F9
Ross-shire

The Croft House
Achintraid, Kishorn, Ross-shire IV54 8XB Tel: 01520 733212

Situated in a tranquil setting on the south shore of Loch Kishorn, with magnificent views of the Applecross Mountains, The Croft House offers en-suite accommodation throughout, log fires and excellent cuisine, largely based on fresh local game and seafood from our own boat. The perfect touring centre for Wester Ross.

Mrs M Beaton The Croft House, Achintraid Kishorn Ross-shire IV54 8XB Tel: (Kishorn) 01520 733212	COMMENDED 👑👑👑	4 Twin 2 Double	6 En Suite fac	B&B per person £15.00-£18.00 Single £15.00-£18.00 Double	Open Jan-Dec Dinner 1900-2030 B&B + Eve. Meal from £25.00

Purpose-built guest house in peaceful location.
Superb views over Loch Kishorn to Applecross Hills.

KISHORN continued	Map 3 F9		

'An Dail'

Kishorn, Strathcarron, Ross-shire IV54 8XB
Telephone: 01520 733455

Modern family home in peaceful lochside location. Splendid views of Applecross hills and Cuillins of Skye. Ideal for walking, climbing and touring. TV lounge, tea/coffee-making. Local seafood dinners. 6 miles north of Lochcarron on A896 to Kishorn stores. Approx 0.5 miles past store, turn left to Achintraid.

| Mrs A Finlayson
An Dail
Kishorn
Ross-shire
IV54 8XB
Tel: (Kishorn) 01520 733455 | COMMENDED
Listed | 2 Twin
1 Double | 1 En Suite fac
2 Pub Bath/Show | B&B per person
from £15.00 Double | Open Jan-Dec
Dinner 1800-2000 | |

Secluded family home. Spectacular views of hills and over Loch Kishorn to Cuillin range on Skye. Evening meals include local seafood as available.

M. Moyes

1 Achintraid, Kishorn, Ross-shire IV54 8XB
Telephone: 01520 733224 Fax: 01520 733232

Very comfortable family home on edge of Loch Kishorn, ideal base for walking or touring, large upstairs residents' lounge with patio overlooking 'Bealach na bo' and the Cuillins of Skye. We provide a full Scottish breakfast and good home cooking using the best of fine Highland produce.
Ample parking. Central heating.

| Mrs M Moyes
1 Achintraid
Kishorn
Ross-shire
IV54 8XB
Tel: (Kishorn) 01520 733224
Fax: 01520 733232 | COMMENDED | 1 Twin
1 Double | 2 En Suite fac | B&B per person
£18.00-£20.00 Single
£15.00-£18.00 Double | Open Jan-Dec
Dinner 1800-2000
B&B + Eve. Meal
£25.00-£28.00 | |

Friendly, comfortable, en-suite accommodation. Large upstairs lounge with patio, looking towards Bealach Na Bo. Ideal base for walks and touring.

| Mrs P Van Hinsbergh
Craigellachie, Achintraid
Kishorn
Ross-shire
IV54 8XB
Tel: (Kishorn) 01520 733253 | COMMENDED | 1 Twin
1 Double | 2 En Suite fac | B&B per person
£15.00-£18.00 Single
from £15.00 Double | Open Apr-Sep
Dinner 1800-2000
B&B + Eve. Meal
£24.00-£27.00 | |

Situated on the shore of Loch Kishorn with superb views towards the Applecross Mountains.

KYLE OF LOCHALSH Ross-shire	Map 3 F9		

Old Schoolhouse Licensed Restaurant

Tigh Fasgaidh, Erbusaig, By Kyle, Ross-shire IV40 8BB
Telephone and Fax: 01599 534369

Idyllically situated on the outskirts of Erbusaig, this former schoolhouse offers high standards of comfort in accommodation with its spacious ensuite bedrooms. The charming restaurant provides a relaxed atmosphere for fine dining from the à la carte menu. Taste of Scotland recommended. Three miles from Kyle, four miles from Plockton.

| Mr & Mrs Cumine
The Old Schoolhouse
Licensed Restaurant
Erbusaig, Kyle of Lochalsh
Ross-shire, IV40 8BB
Tel: (Kyle) 01599 534369
Fax: 01599 534369 | COMMENDED | 1 Twin
1 Double | 2 En Suite fac | B&B per person
£25.00-£30.00 Single
£18.00-£25.00 Double | Open Apr-Oct
Dinner 1900-2230 | |

Restaurant with en-suite accommodation, 3 miles (5kms) from Skye ferry at Kyle of Lochalsh, 4 miles (6kms) from Plockton.

Castle View

Upper Ardelve, By Dornie, Kyle of Lochalsh IV40 8EY
Telephone: 01599 555453

The countryside surrounding Eilean Donan is of exceptional beauty and grandeur with magnificent mountain, loch and forest scenery. Rich in wildlife, the area offers fascinating rewards for observant nature lovers. There are otters, seals, wildgoats and deer, whilst overhead may be seen ravens, buzzards, falcons and the magnificent Golden Eagle.

Rosemary McClelland Castleview, Upper Ardelve Dornie, By Kyle of Lochalsh Ross-shire IV40 8EY Tel: (Dornie) 01599 555453	COMMENDED	1 Twin 1 Double 1 Family	3 En Suite fac	B&B per person £16.00-£18.00 Double	Open Jan-Dec Dinner 1900-2000 B&B + Eve. Meal £23.00-£25.00

Warm welcome assured in new croft house with breathtaking views to Eilean Donan Castle, Loch Duich and the Sisters of Kintail.

	Map 3 H4					
KYLESKU **Sutherland** Mrs C Evans The Ridge, Unapool Croft Road Kylesku, by Lairg Sutherland IV27 4HW Tel: (Scourie) 01971 502226		HIGHLY COMMENDED	1 Twin 1 Double	1 Pub Bath/Show	B&B per person to £15.00 Single to £15.00 Double	Open Jan-Dec Dinner 1900-1930 B&B + Eve. Meal to £25.00

Tranquillity, superb views and home cooking in this small and friendly house. Ideal centre for walking and sightseeing.

Non-Smokers' Sanctuary

"Linne Mhuirich", Unapool Croft Road, KYLESKU via Lairg,
Sutherland IV27 4HW   Tel: 01971 502227

Fiona and Diarmid MacAulay welcome non-smokers to their modern crofthouse, "Taste of Scotland" recommended. Their guests return year after year for the peace, comfort and attention, wonderful views and excellent food. Varied and interesting menus: local fish, seafood, pâtés, soups, casseroles, vegetarian dishes, delicious home baking. 1 twin has private bathroom.   **EARLY BOOKING ESSENTIAL**

Mrs F MacAulay Linne Mhuirich, Unapool Croft Road Kylesku, via Lairg Sutherland IV27 4HW Tel: (Scourie) 01971 502227	COMMENDED	1 Twin 1 Double	1 Priv. NOT ensuite 1 Pub Bath/Show	B&B per person to £22.50 Single £17.50-£20.50 Double	Open May-Oct Dinner at 1930 B&B + Eve. Meal £28.00-£31.00

Friendly and attentive Taste of Scotland recommended croft house. Peacefully situated near Kylesku Bridge. Directions for walks provided.

Newton Lodge Newton Kylesku Sutherland IV27 4HW Tel: (Scourie) 01971 502070	HIGHLY COMMENDED	3 Twin 4 Double	7 En Suite fac	B&B per person £24.50 Double	Open Apr-Oct Dinner 1830-1930 B&B + Eve. Meal £36.00

A large, purpose-built guest house surrounded by an inspiring panorama of mountains and lochs.

SCOTTISH TOURIST BOARD
QUALITY COMMENDATIONS ARE:

Deluxe – An EXCELLENT quality standard
Highly Commended – A VERY GOOD quality standard
Commended – A GOOD quality standard
Approved – An ACCEPTABLE quality standard

| LAIDE | Map 3 |
| Ross-shire | F6 |

'CUL NA MARA'

Sand Passage, Laide, Ross-shire IV22 2ND
Telephone: 01445 731295

Highly Commended

A stay at "Cul Na Mara" (*Gaelic – Song of the sea*) is an enjoyable experience. Superior bed and breakfast accommodation. Guest rooms fully en-suite and fitted with colour television. Private dining room – dinner a speciality – fully laid out garden overlooking the Minch. Private parking. *Early booking advisable.*

Bill and Mavis Hart Cul na Mara, Sand Passage Laide Ross-shire IV22 2ND Tel: (Aultbea) 01445 731295	HIGHLY COMMENDED	1 Double 2 En Suite fac 1 Family	B&B per person from £18.00 Double	Open Jan-Dec Dinner from 1900 B&B + Eve. Meal from £30.00

Modern Highland home in quiet crofting area. Excellent sandy beaches nearby. Home cooking, with emphasis on fresh produce.

The Old Smiddy

LAIDE, WESTER ROSS IV22 2NB
Telephone and Fax: 01445 731425

HIGHLY COMMENDED

Steve and Kate Macdonald offer you a relaxed friendly atmosphere with personal attention. **Taste of Scotland** recommendation guarantees quality fayre from breakfast to evening dinners. Ensuite accommodation, guest lounge and dining room, garden, patio. Ideally situated for hill, coastal walks on beautiful clean sandy beaches. Inverewe Gardens eight miles.

Old Smiddy Guest House Laide Ross-shire Tel: (Aultbea) 01445 731425 Fax: 01445 731425	HIGHLY COMMENDED	1 Double 1 En Suite fac 1 Family 1 Priv. NOT ensuit	B&B per person £16.50-£22.00 single £16.50-£22.00 Double	Open Feb-Nov Dinner 1900-1930 B&B + Eve. Meal £30.00-£36.00

Enjoy a west Highland experience with your Highland hosts in their delightful cottage. Private fishing on 18 lochs.

| LAIRG | Map 4 |
| Sutherland | A6 |

Mrs M K Fraser Ambleside, Lochside Lairg Sutherland IV27 4EG Tel: (Lairg) 01549 402130	COMMENDED	1 Twin 3 En Suite fac 2 Double	B&B per person £15.00-£15.50 Double	Open Apr-Oct

Modern personally run bed and breakfast, comfortable and well furnished, centrally situated in quiet location with private parking.

Margaret Walker Park House Lairg Sutherland IV27 4AU Tel: (Lairg) 01549 402208 Fax: 01549 402208	COMMENDED	1 Twin 3 En Suite fac 1 Double 1 Family	B&B per person £18.00-£31.00 Single £18.00-£21.00 Double	Open Jan-Dec Dinner from 1900

A warm welcome awaits you in this Victorian-style house overlooking Loch Shin. Friendly and relaxed atmosphere. Emphasis on home-cooking.

When you visit a Tourist Information Centre you are guaranteed a welcome by people who really know their country.

For information, maps, holiday reading, accommodation bookings and much more, look for the information *i*

LANARK	Map 2 A6					

Jerviswood Mains Farm
LANARK ML11 7RL   Telephone: 01555 663987

Good hospitality is offered in this early 19th-century traditional farmhouse, 1 mile from Lanark on the A706, heading northwards. We are near a trout and deer farm and provide good food in a relaxed atmosphere. We combine old world charm with modern amenities.
The unique 1758 industrial village of New Lanark, now a world heritage site, and many places of historical interest are nearby, equidistant between Glasgow and Edinburgh. This is an excellent touring base.

Mrs M Findlater Jerviswood Mains Farm Lanark ML11 7RL Tel: (Lanark) 01555 663987	COMMENDED ♛	1 Twin 2 Double	2 Pub Bath/Show	B&B per person £20.00-£25.00 Single £16.00-£19.00 Double	Open Jan-Dec
		19th-century stone-built farmhouse of considerable character, 1 mile (2 kms) from historic market town.			
Mrs Faye Hamilton Corehouse Home Farm by Lanark ML11 9TQ Tel: (Lanark) 01555 661377	COMMENDED ♛♛	1 Double 2 Family	2 En Suite fac 1 Priv. NOT ensuite	B&B per person £12.00-£18.00 Single £12.00-£15.00 Double	Open Jan-Dec
		Warm family welcome on traditional mixed farm close to Falls of Clyde and nature reserve. 3 miles (5km) from Lanark and Heritage Centre.			

LARGS **Ayrshire**	Map 1 F5					

Lilac Holm Guest House 14 Noddleburn Road, Off Barr Crescent Largs Ayrshire KA30 8PY Tel: (Largs) 01475 672020	COMMENDED ♛	2 Single 2 Twin 3 Double 1 Family	2 Pub Bath/Show	B&B per person from £15.00 Single from £15.00 Double	Open Jan-Dec Dinner from 1800
		Built in 1935; in quiet residential area overlooking the Noddle Burn. Evening meals available. Personal attention of owners.			
Mrs M L Russell Rutland Guest House, 22 Charles Street Largs Ayrshire KA30 8HJ Tel: (Largs) 01475 675642	COMMENDED ♛♛	1 Single 1 Twin 1 Family	3 Priv. NOT ensuite 2 Pub Bath/Show	B&B per person £15.00-£16.00 Single £14.00-£15.00 Double	Open Jan-Dec
		1930s terraced house in quiet residential area near the promenade. An easy 5 minutes walk to the town centre.			
Tigh-na-Ligh Guest House 104 Brisbane Road Largs Ayrshire KA30 8NN Tel: (Largs) 01475 673975	COMMENDED ♛♛♛	2 Twin 2 Double 1 Family	4 En Suite fac 1 Priv. NOT ensuite	B&B per person £21.00-£23.00 Double	Open Jan-Dec Dinner from 1800
		Red sandstone house in quiet residential area, close to local amenities and convenient for touring Firth of Clyde area and Burns Country.			

South Whittlieburn Farm
Brisbane Glen, Largs, Ayrshire KA30 8SN
Telephone: 01475 675881

Welcome Host
AA QQQ rated
Commended ♛♛

Why not try our superb farm house accommodation? With lovely peaceful panoramic country views, ample parking, five minutes drive from the popular tourist resort of Largs and near the ferries for Islands of Arran, Bute, Cumbrae and Dunoon. (45 minutes from Glasgow or Prestwick Airports). Warm friendly hospitality. Enormous breakfasts – highly recommended.
A warm welcome from Mary Watson

Mrs M Watson South Whittlieburn Farm Brisbane Glen Largs Ayrshire KA30 8SN Tel: (Largs) 01475 675881	COMMENDED ♛♛	1 Twin 1 Double 1 Family	1 En Suite fac 2 Pub Bath/Show	B&B per person from £16.00 Single from £15.50 Double	Open Jan-Dec
		Working 150-acre sheep farm, warm friendly atmosphere, comfortable rooms. Beautiful quiet location only 5 minutes by car from the centre of Largs.			

	Map	Grade	Rooms	Facilities	Prices	Opening
LASSODIE, by Dunfermline Fife Mr N. Woolley Loch Fitty Cottage Lassodie, by Dunfermline Fife KY12 0SP Tel: (Kelty) 01383 831081	Map 2 B4	COMMENDED Listed	1 Twin 1 Double 1 Family	1 En Suite fac 1 Priv. NOT ensuite 1 Pub Bath/Show	B&B per person £15.00-£20.00 Single £14.00-£17.00 Double	Open Jan-Dec

Rural roadside location with large natural garden, yet close to all local amenities and major attractions. Children welcome.

	Map	Grade	Rooms	Facilities	Prices	Opening
LASSWADE Midlothian Mrs M R Denton 5 Elm Row Lasswade Midlothian EH18 1AG Tel: 0131 663 1741	Map 2 C5	COMMENDED Listed	1 Twin 1 Double	1 Pub Bath/Show	B&B per person from £18.00 Single from £18.00 Double Room only per person from £18.00	Open Jan-Dec Dinner 1700-1800 B&B + Eve. Meal £23.00-£28.00

Terraced family home with garden offering comfortable accommodation, ideally situated for touring. 5 miles (8kms) from Edinburgh.

Mrs Ann O'Brien Droman House Lasswade Midlothian EH18 1HA Tel: 0131 663 9239		COMMENDED Listed	1 Single 2 Twin 1 Family	2 Pub Bath/Show	B&B per person £15.00 Single £15.00 Double Room only per person £15.00	Open May-Oct

Former Georgian Manse in secluded setting. Informal and warm welcome assured. Ample private parking.

	Map	Grade	Rooms	Facilities	Prices	Opening
LATHERON Caithness Mrs C Sinclair Upper Latheron Farm Latheron Caithness KW5 6DT Tel: (Latheron) 01593 741224	Map 4 D4	HIGHLY COMMENDED Listed	1 Twin 1 Double 1 Family	1 Pub Bath/Show	B&B per person £18.00 Single £15.00 Double	Open May-Sep

Comfortable farmhouse bed and breakfast, furnished to a high standard, home baking. Fine views of this dramatic coastline.

	Map	Grade	Rooms	Facilities	Prices	Opening
LAUDER Berwickshire Mr P Gilardi The Grange, 6 Edinburgh Road Lauder Berwickshire TD2 6TW Tel: (Lauder) 01578 722649	Map 2 D6	COMMENDED	2 Twin 1 Double	1 Pub Bath/Show	B&B per person £14.00-£18.00 Single £14.00-£16.00 Double	Open Jan-Dec

Detached house standing in large garden with lovely views of surrounding countryside. Good home cooking and a warm welcome. A non-smoking house.

	Map	Grade	Rooms	Facilities	Prices	Opening
LEITHOLM, by Coldstream Berwickshire Mrs Sally Myers Stainrigg Mansion Leitholm, by Coldstream Berwickshire TD12 4JE Tel: (Leitholm) 01890 840308/840595 Fax: 01890 840505	Map 2 E6	HIGHLY COMMENDED	2 Twin 2 Double	2 En Suite fac 2 Priv. NOT ensuite	B&B per person to £20.00 Single to £20.00 Double	Open 3 Jan-23 Dec Dinner from 1930 B&B + Eve. Meal to £32.00

Elegant country house, c1880 with log fire in hall, set amongst mature trees and grounds extending to 14 acres. 6 miles (10kms) from Coldstream and Kelso.

	Map	Grade	Rooms	Facilities	Prices	Opening
LEVERBURGH Harris, Western Isles Mrs MacKenzie Caberfeidh House Leverburgh Harris, Western Isles PA83 3TL Tel: (Leverburgh) 01859 520276	Map 3 C7	COMMENDED Listed	1 Twin 1 Double 1 Family	1 Pub Bath/Show	B&B per person from £15.00 Single from £15.00 Double Room only per person from £15.00	Open Jan-Dec Dinner 1800-2000 B&B + Eve. Meal from £24.00

Detached family house with own garden, in centre of village overlooking the Millpool.

LINICLATE **Benbecula, Western Isles** Inchyra Guest House Liniclate Benbecula, Western Isles HS7 5PY Tel: (Benbecula) 01870 602176	Map 3 B8	COMMENDED ♔♔♔	2 Single 5 Twin 1 Double	8 En Suite fac	B&B per person £26.00 Single £20.00 Double	Open Jan-Dec Dinner 1800-2000

Family run guest house, on working croft on main Lochmaddy to Lochboisdale road, about 6 miles (10 kms) from Benbecula airport. Annexe accommodation.

LINLITHGOW **West Lothian**	Map 2 B4

Woodcockdale Farm
Lanark Road, Linlithgow, West Lothian EH49 6QE
Telephone: 01506 842088 Fax: 01506 842088

Look no further – be among the many guests who return regularly to Woodcockdale – a busy dairy and sheep farm with easy access to all tourist and business attractions in central Scotland. Edinburgh 17 miles, Glasgow 33 miles, Stirling 17 miles. Four-poster bed. *Phone now!*

Mrs W Erskine Woodcockdale Farm Lanark Road West Lothian EH49 6QE Tel: (Linlithgow) 01506 842088	APPROVED Listed	1 Single 1 Twin 1 Family	1 En Suite fac 2 Pub Bath/Show	B&B per person from £18.00 Single from £16.00 Double	Open Jan-Dec

Modern farmhouse on working farm in rural area yet with easy access to Edinburgh, Glasgow and the Lothians.

Thornton
Edinburgh Road, Linlithgow, West Lothian EH49 6AA
Telephone: 01506 844216

An elegantly furnished, listed Victorian villa which is our family home. Thornton is situated in historical Linlithgow five minutes from town centre and railway station. Ample private parking. Rooms have en-suite facilities and colour TV. Personal attention and cuisine are to the highest standard. Excellent touring base for Central Scotland.

Mrs M J Inglis Thornton, Edinburgh Road Linlithgow West Lothian EH49 6AA Tel: (Linlithgow) 01506 844216	HIGHLY COMMENDED ♔♔	1 Twin 1 Double	2 En Suite fac	B&B per person from £25.00 Single from £20.00 Double	Open Jan-Dec

Comfortable, elegant non-smoking family-run Victorian villa. Large garden, ample private parking. 0.5 mile (1km) from rail station. Personal attention assured.

Mrs Moyra Mitchell Monthouse, Parkhead Road Linlithgow West Lothian EH49 7BS Tel: (Linlithgow) 01506 842234	HIGHLY COMMENDED ♔♔	2 Twin 1 Double	2 En Suite fac 1 Priv. NOT ensuite	B&B per person £20.00 Single £18.00-£20.00 Double	Open Jan-Nov

Modern detached house in quiet location with south-facing garden overlooking Linlithgow Loch and Palace. Non-smoking house.

BY LINLITHGOW **West Lothian** Carol Jones The Kennels, Threemiletown by Linlithgow West Lothian EH49 6NF Tel: (Philipstoun) 01506 834200	Map 2 B4 COMMENDED Listed	2 Twin 1 Double	1 En Suite fac 2 Pub Bath/Show	B&B per person £20.00-£25.00 Single £16.00-£20.00 Double	Open Jan-Dec

Traditional farmhouse with dogs, cats, pigs and goat. Home baking. Delightful breakfast using home-reared organic bacon and free range eggs.

LIVINGSTON
West Lothian

Map 2
B5

ASHCROFT FARMHOUSE
EAST CALDER, NR EDINBURGH, EH53 0ET
Tel: 01506 881810 Fax: 01506 884327

New, tastefully furnished house. All rooms on ground floor. All bedrooms have tea-making facilities plus colour TV. Ashcroft is surrounded by farmland yet only 10m city centre, 6m airport, 5m city bypass and M8/M9. Ideal base for touring, golfing or sightseeing. Early morning tea is provided for guests before they are tempted with a full Scottish breakfast with home-made sausage, local produce and even whisky marmalade. Four-poster bedroom. All bedrooms en-suite.

Derek and Elizabeth Scott extend a warm Scottish welcome to all guests.

★ *Fire Certificate.* ★ *AA Selected QQQQ* ★
SORRY NO SMOKING

Derek and Elizabeth Scott Ashcroft Farmhouse East Calder, Livingston West Lothian EH53 0ET Tel: (Mid Calder) 01506 881810 Fax: 01506 884327	HIGHLY COMMENDED	3 Twin 1 Double 2 Family	6 En Suite fac	B&B per person £22.00-£24.00 Single £22.00-£24.00 Double	Open Jan-Dec	

Large, modern family run bungalow in own grounds with private parking. All rooms ensuite. Totally non-smoking.

LOANHEAD
Midlothian

Map 2
D5

Aaron Glen Guest House
7 Nivensknowe Road, Loanhead EH20 9AU
Telephone: 0131 440 1293   Fax: 0131 440 2155

Newly built family run guest house conveniently situated just of city bypass and minutes from city centre on main bus route. Tastefully decorated with all rooms en-suite, Sky TV, tea/coffee facilities, hairdryers, beautiful Scottish breakfast. Drinks served in licensed lounge with evening meals served on request. Monitored car park. Disabled facilities.

Aaron Glen Guest House 7 Nivensknowe Road Loanhead Midlothian EH20 9QQ Tel: 0131 440 1293 Fax: 0131 440 2155	COMMENDED	1 Twin 1 Double 3 Family	5 En Suite fac	B&B per person £20.00-£30.00 Single £17.50-£25.00 Double Room only per person £20.00-£30.00	Open Jan-Dec Dinner 1700-2100	

Modern purpose-built guest house with all rooms ensuite. Convenient for Edinburgh city centre. On main bus route.

LOCHBOISDALE
South Uist, Western Isles
Mrs C MacLeod
Innis Ghorm, 422 Lochboisdale
Lochboisdale
South Uist, Western Isles
PA81 5TH
Tel: (Lochboisdale)
01878 700232

Map 3
B10

COMMENDED	1 Twin 1 Double	1 Pub Bath/Show	B&B per person £15.00-£16.00 Single	Open Jan-Dec	

Croft house situated close to bus route and 0.5 miles (1km) from ferry terminal. Washbasins in all bedrooms.

VAT is shown at 17.5%: changes in this rate may affect prices. Prices shown are for guidance only. Please send SAE with each enquiry.

Mrs Murray Brae Lea House Lochboisdale South Uist, Western Isles PA81 5TH Tel: (Lochboisdale) 01878 700497	COMMENDED 👑👑	1 Single 1 Double 1 Family	3 En Suite fac	B&B per person £18.00-£25.00 Single £18.00-£25.00 Double Room only per person £15.00-£18.00	Open Jan-Dec Dinner 1800-2100

Modern bungalow with full en-suite facilities. Quietly situated at edge of village. Well situated for ferry.

LOCHCARRON **Ross-shire** Mrs Flora Catto The Creagan Lochcarron Ross-shire IV54 8YH Tel: (Lochcarron) 01520 722430	Map 3 G9 COMMENDED 👑	1 Double 1 Family	1 Pub Bath/Show	B&B per person £15.00 Single £14.00-£15.00 Double	Open Apr-Oct

Modern bungalow, peacefully situated, with magnificent views over Loch Carron and the hills beyond.

Kinloch House
Lochcarron, Ross-shire IV54 8YS
Telephone: 01520 722417

This lovely former manse allows us to offer the best in comfort as a base for exploring our spectacularly beautiful and varied region, including Skye, Glenelg, Torridon and the Applecross Peninsula. Fine walks and numerous restaurants nearby.
Come for a night and wish you had booked for a week.

Susan Duncan Kinloch House Lochcarron Ross-shire IV54 8YS Tel: (Lochcarron) 01520 722417	COMMENDED 👑👑	1 Double 1 Family	2 En Suite fac	B&B per person from £30.00 Single £20.00-£23.00 Double	Open Apr-Oct

Spacious Victorian house by golf course, near sea loch and village. All rooms ensuite. Breakfasts to suit your taste.

Ms M F Innes Aultsigh, Croft Road Lochcarron Ross-shire IV54 8YA Tel: (Lochcarron) 01520 722558	COMMENDED Listed	1 Twin 2 Double	2 Pub Bath/Show	B&B per person £15.00-£16.00 Single £14.00-£16.00 Double	Open Jan-Dec

Detached modern bungalow in elevated position, with magnificent panoramic views of Loch Carron and hills.

Mrs L Leckie Clisham, Main Street Lochcarron Ross-shire IV54 8YA Tel: (Lochcarron) 01520 722610	COMMENDED 👑	1 Twin 2 Double	2 Pub Bath/Show	B&B per person from £16.00 Single from £14.00 Double	Open Jan-Dec Dinner 1830-1930 B&B + Eve. Meal £22.00-£24.00

Friendly, family run guest house with views over Loch Carron. Tea Room available with home baking. Parking opposite

Mrs A MacKenzie Chuillinn, Croft Road Lochcarron Ross-shire IV54 8YA Tel: (Lochcarron) 01520 722460	COMMENDED 👑👑	1 Twin 1 Family	1 En Suite fac 1 Pub Bath/Show	B&B per person £14.00-£17.00 Single £14.00-£17.00 Double Room only per person £14.00-£17.00	Open Apr-Oct

New bungalow in quiet location overlooking the village, with fine views across Loch Carron.

Mrs C Michael Castle Cottage, Main Street Lochcarron Ross-shire IV54 8YB Tel: (Lochcarron) 01520 722564	COMMENDED 👑👑	1 Twin 2 Double	1 En Suite fac 1 Pub Bath/Show	B&B per person £15.00-£18.00 Single £15.00-£18.00 Double	Open Jan-Dec

Modernised detached house in village centre with fine views across Loch Carron from all rooms.

Details of Grading and Classification are on page vi.　　　Key to symbols is on back flap.

LOCHCARRON continued	Map 3 G9

GLAISBHEINN

Lochcarron, Ross-shire IV54 8YB
Telephone: 01520 722367

Lochside traditional cottage. All rooms Hot and Cold, Central Heating, tea and coffee. Electric blankets. Comfortable lounge with open fire when appropriate. Near good restaurants. Ideally situated for touring, walking, sailing, bird watching, golf. Wildlife includes red deer, roe deer, pine martens, seals, otters, eagles. **And Lochcarron is so friendly!**

Mr R Pillinger Glaisbheinn Lochcarron Ross-shire IV54 8YB Tel: (Lochcarron) 01520 722367	COMMENDED ♛	2 Twin 1 Double	2 Pub Bath/Show	B&B per person £14.00-£15.00 Single £14.00-£15.00 Double	Open Apr-Oct

Comfortable house overlooking the loch. Traditionally furnished.
Centrally heated house with open fire in lounge. TV on request.

BY LOCHGILPHEAD	Map 1 E4
Argyll	

Tigh-Na-Glaic

By Lochgilphead, Argyllshire PA31 8SW
Telephone: 01546 830245

Superbly situated in its own grounds with beautiful views over Loch Crinan and Duntrune Castle. An ideal base for touring, walking, fishing, boating and golfing. All rooms en-suite. T.V., Tea/Coffee facilities. There is ample car parking and a large garden for guests to enjoy.

Mrs Mairi Anderson Tigh Na Glaic Crinan, by Lochgilphead Argyll PA31 8SW Tel: (Crinan) 01546 830245	COMMENDED ♛♛♛	1 Twin 1 Double	2 En Suite fac 1 Pub Bath/Show	B&B per person from £20.00 Single from £20.00 Double Room only per person from £20.00	Open Jan-Dec

Country cottage in peaceful setting, overlooking Loch Crinan to Duntrune Castle. Ideal area for artists, photographers and walkers.

LOCHGOILHEAD Argyll Shore House Inn Lochgoilhead Argyll Tel: (Lochgoilhead) 01301 703340/703580	Map 1 F3	APPROVED Listed	1 Single 3 Twin 1 Double 2 Family	2 En Suite fac 1 Pub Bath/Show	B&B per person from £15.00 Single £13.00-£18.00 Double	Open Jan-Dec Dinner 1730-2100

Peacefully situated on the shore of Loch Goil, with open views down the loch. Informal and friendly. Pets welcome. Bar and Restaurant.

LOCHINVER Sutherland Ann H Brown Suilven, Badnaban Lochinver Sutherland IV27 4LR Tel: (Lochinver) 01571 844358	Map 3 G5	COMMENDED ♛	1 Twin 1 Double	1 Pub Bath/Show	B&B per person from £20.00 Single from £15.00 Double	Open Jan-Dec Dinner 1830-2000 B&B + Eve. Meal from £26.00

Bungalow with superb views across Loch Inver.
Mrs Brown prides herself on her home cooking. Boat trips and sea angling.

Mrs M Garner Veyatie, 66 Baddidarroch Lochinver Sutherland IV27 4LP Tel: (Lochinver) 01571 844424	HIGHLY COMMENDED ♛♛♛	2 Twin 1 Double	2 En Suite fac 1 Priv. NOT ensuite	B&B per person £20.00-£23.00 Double	Open Apr-Oct

Spacious modern bungalow in secluded situation. Facing south with magnificent views across the harbour to Suilven. Private parking on site.

Mrs J Matheson Polcraig Lochinver Sutherland IV27 4LD Tel: (Lochinver) 01571 844429	COMMENDED	2 Twin 2 En Suite fac 1 Double 1 Pub Bath/Show B&B per person £14.00-£18.00 Double Open Apr-Oct

Modern family run home in quiet situation, with views to Lochinver Bay.
Ample car parking on site.

Mrs J McBain Davar Lochinver Sutherland IV27 4LJ Tel: (Lochinver) 01571 844501	HIGHLY COMMENDED	1 Twin 3 En Suite fac 2 Double B&B per person from £18.00 Single from £18.00 Double Open Apr-Sep

Modern family run house overlooking Lochinver Bay, with range of
comfortable facilities. Private parking on site.

Mr & Mrs A Munro Ardglas Lochinver Sutherland IV27 4LJ Tel: (Lochinver) 01571 844257 Fax: 01571 844360	COMMENDED	1 Single 3 Pub Bath/Show 1 Twin 4 Double 2 Family B&B per person £13.00-£15.00 Single £13.00-£15.00 Double Open Jan-Dec

Set above this popular fishing village with spectacular harbour,
sea and mountain views. Homely atmosphere. Private parking.

LOCH MAREE, by Achnasheen
Ross-shire   Map 3 F7

Mrs I Grant Garbhaig House Loch Maree, by Achnasheen Ross-shire IV22 2HW Tel: (Gairloch) 01445 712412	COMMENDED	1 Double 2 Pub Bath/Show 2 Family B&B per person £13.50-£14.00 Single £13.50-£14.00 Double Room only per person £13.50-£14.00 Open Jan-Dec Dinner 1830-1900 B&B + Eve. Meal £21.50-£22.00

Modernised, detached bungalow on working croft with fine views over
Loch Maree to hills beyond. Warm welcome with simple plain home cooking.

The Old Mill Highland Lodge Talladale Loch Maree, by Achnasheen Ross-shire IV22 2HL Tel: (Kinlochewe) 01445 760271	HIGHLY COMMENDED	4 Twin 5 En Suite fac 2 Double 1 Priv. NOT ensuite B&B per person £32.00 Single £32.00 Double Open Jan-Dec Dinner from 1930 B&B + Eve. Meal from £48.50

Beside a mountain stream sits this imaginative conversion of an old horsemill.
Comfortable house with an accent on good food, wine and tranquillity.

LOCHRANZA
Isle of Arran   Map 1 E6

Kincardine Lodge Guest House Lochranza Isle of Arran KA27 8HL Tel: (Lochranza) 01770 830267	APPROVED	2 Twin 3 En Suite fac 2 Double 1 Pub Bath/Show 2 Family B&B per person £17.00-£19.00 Single £17.00-£19.00 Double Open Mar-Oct Dinner 1830-1900

Facing a sea loch, with panoramic views of the castle,
its mountain backdrop and the coasts of Kintyre and Bute.

BY LOCHWINNOCH
Renfrewshire   Map 1 G5

Mrs D Rothney Springfield Kerse, by Lochwinnoch Renfrewshire PA12 4DT Tel: (Beith) 01505 503690	COMMENDED Listed	1 Single 1 Pub Bath/Show 1 Twin 1 Double B&B per person £16.00 Single £16.00 Double/Twin Room only per person £12.00-£13.00 Open Jan-Dec Dinner 1700-1930

Detached house in rural setting, convenient for RSPB reserve,
golf-course and watersports centre on local loch. Airport 15 mins.

LOCKERBIE
Dumfriesshire   Map 2 C9

Mrs C Hislop Carik Cottage Waterbeck, Lockerbie Dumfriesshire DG11 3EU Tel: (Waterbeck) 01461 600652	HIGHLY COMMENDED Listed	1 Twin 1 En Suite fac 2 Double 1 Pub Bath/Show B&B per person £15.00-£23.00 Single £14.00-£18.00 Double Open Mar-Oct

Tastefully converted cottage in peaceful rural setting yet only 3 miles (5kms)
from the A74. Ideal for touring the Border countryside.

LOCKERBIE continued	Map 2 C9

NETHER BORELAND FARM
BORELAND, LOCKERBIE, DUMFRIESSHIRE DG11 2LL
Telephone/Fax: 01576 610248

Sample Scottish hospitality. Peaceful, friendly surroundings, hearty breakfasts with our free range eggs and home-made preserves. The spacious comfortable farmhouse has two en-suite bedrooms and one with private bathroom, tea/coffee trays, hairdryers, clock radios and TV. Ideal base for touring, golfing, walking or simply relaxing. *Brochure available.*

Mrs M Rae
Nether Boreland Farm
Boreland
Lockerbie
Dumfriesshire DG11 2LL
Tel: (Boreland) 01576 610248
Fax: 01576 610248

HIGHLY COMMENDED

1 Twin / 2 Double — 1 En Suite fac / 1 Priv. NOT ensuite — B&B per person £19.00-£21.00 Double — Open Mar-Nov

Stone-built farmhouse situated beside B783, in centre of small village. Excellent views of surrounding hill country.

Rosehill Guest House
Mr & Mrs R A Callander
Carlisle Road
Lockerbie
Dumfriesshire
DG11 2DR
Tel: (Lockerbie) 01576 202378

COMMENDED

1 Single / 1 Twin / 1 Double / 2 Family — 1 En Suite fac / 3 Pub Bath/Show — B&B per person £18.00-£20.00 Single £18.00-£20.00 Double — Open Jan-Dec

Family guest house in residential area, 5 minutes walk from town centre. Ample car parking.

LONGNIDDRY
East Lothian
Map 2 D4

Mrs M Anderson
5 Stevenson Way
Longniddry
East Lothian EH32 0PF
Tel: (Longniddry)
01875 853395

COMMENDED Listed

2 Double — 1 Pub Bath/Show — B&B per person from £15.00 Single from £15.00 Double — Open May-Sep

Bungalow with small attractive garden in quiet residential area, yet with easy access to Edinburgh and East Lothian Golf Courses.

Mr & Mrs George Playfair
The Spinney, Old School Lane
Longniddry
East Lothian
EH32 0NQ
Tel: (Longniddry)
01875 853325

COMMENDED

1 Twin / 2 Family — 1 En Suite fac / 1 Pub Bath/Show — B&B per person £16.00-£18.00 Single £14.00-£16.00 Double — Open Feb-Nov

Traditional farmhouse breakfast in secluded bungalow in village. Train, bus, beach, golf courses and hills within easy reach.

LOSSIEMOUTH
Moray
Map 4 D7

Mrs M Jean D Cox
Mormond, Prospect Terrace
Lossiemouth
Moray
IV31 6JS
Tel: (Lossiemouth)
01343 813143

HIGHLY COMMENDED

1 Twin / 2 Double — 2 Pub Bath/Show — B&B per person £13.50-£18.00 Single £13.50-£14.50 Double — Open Jan-Nov

Traditional villa in quiet residential area with outstanding view across Moray Firth. Close to all amenities. Friendly, happy atmosphere.

Mrs Marjorie MacKenzie
Moray View, 1 Seatown Road
Lossiemouth
Moray IV31 6JL
Tel: (Lossiemouth)
01343 813915

COMMENDED

1 Twin / 2 Double — 2 Pub Bath/Show — B&B per person to £18.00 Single £14.00-£15.00 Double — Open Jan-Dec

350-year-old house of character immediately on sea front, overlooking harbour and beach. Convenient for town centre and all amenities.

Mrs Anne Main
Letchworth Lodge
Dunbar Street
Lossiemouth
Moray IV31 6AN
Tel: (Lossiemouth)
01343 812132

COMMENDED Listed

2 Twin / 1 Double — 1 Pub Bath/Show — B&B per person £13.50-£15.50 Double — Open Jan-Dec

Traditional family run guest house with friendly atmosphere. Convenient for championship golf course, beach and town.

Mrs Jean R McPherson Skerry Lodge, Stotfield Road Lossiemouth Moray IV31 6QR Tel: (Lossiemouth) 01343 814981	COMMENDED Listed	1 Twin 2 Double	1 Priv. NOT ensuite 1 Pub Bath/Show	B&B per person £15.00-£16.00 Single £13.00-£16.00 Double	Open Jan-Dec	

Traditional, family run establishment, with friendly atmosphere. Situated on sea front with magnificent views of Moray Firth. No smoking. Residents' lounge.

Mrs Frances Reddy Lossiemouth House, 33 Clifton Road Lossiemouth Moray IV31 6DP Tel: (Lossiemouth) 01343 813397	COMMENDED	1 Single 1 Double 1 Family	1 En Suite fac 2 Pub Bath/Show	B&B per person £15.00-£16.00 Single £15.00-£16.00 Double Room only per person £13.00	Open Jan-Dec	

200-year-old former Dower House, situated in its own grounds in the residential area of the town, a mere 2 minute walk from the seafront.

Mrs Jennifer I Toye 45 St Gerardines Road Lossiemouth Moray IV31 6JX Tel: (Lossiemouth) 01343 812276	COMMENDED	1 Twin 1 Double	1 Pub Bath/Show	B&B per person £13.00-£15.00 Double	Open Apr-Oct	

Modern detached bungalow with large garden in residential area on south side of town centre, within walking distance of beach, golf and bowling.

LUNAN, by Montrose Angus	Map 2 E1						
Mrs A MacKintosh Lunan Lodge Lunan, by Montrose Angus DD10 9TG Tel: (Inverkeilor) 01241 830267 Fax: 01241 830435		COMMENDED	2 Twin 1 Family	2 Pub Bath/Show	B&B per person from £20.00 Single from £16.00 Double	Open Apr-Oct	

Warm welcome at modernised 18th-century manse in quiet countryside overlooking Lunan Bay. 15 mins walk from sea. 4 miles (5kms) Montrose and Bird Sanctuary.

LUNCARTY, by Perth Perthshire	Map 2 B2						
Mrs Haddow Ordie House Luncarty, Perth Perthshire PH1 4PR Tel: (Stanley) 01738 828471		COMMENDED	1 Twin 2 Double	2 En Suite fac 1 Limited ensuite 1 Pub Bath/Show	B&B per person £17.00 Single £16.00 Double	Open Jan-Dec Dinner 1700-1830	

Traditional Scottish hospitality in friendly family home. Ideal touring base.

LUSS, by Alexandria Dunbartonshire	Map 1 G4

Shantron Farm Cottage

Shantron Farm, Luss, Alexandria G83 8RH
Telephone: 01389 850231 Fax: 01389 850231

Enjoy a relaxing break in a spacious bungalow with outstanding views of Loch Lomond. Our 5000-acre hill farm is the setting for Morag's croft in "Take the High Road" 30 minutes from Glasgow airport. An ideal touring base and for hillwalking, fishing, watersports, golf. Large garden for guests' enjoyment.

Mrs A Lennox Shantron Farm Cottage Shantron Farm Luss, by Alexandria Dunbartonshire Tel: (Arden) 01389 850231 Fax: 01389 850231	COMMENDED Listed	2 Double 1 Family	1 En Suite fac 1 Pub Bath/Show	B&B per person £25.00-£30.00 Single £14.00-£20.00 Double	Open Easter-Oct	

Cottage, in elevated position with superb views over Loch Lomond. Farm is used regularly for film of "Take the High Road".

Mrs Robertson Doune of Glen Douglas Farm Luss Dunbartonshire G83 8PD Tel: (Arrochar) 01301 702312	HIGHLY COMMENDED	1 Double 1 Family	1 En Suite fac 1 Pub Bath/Show	B&B per person £16.00-£22.00 Double	Open Mar-Oct	

18th-century farmhouse on working hill sheep farm in Glen Douglas. 2 miles (3kms) from A82. Ideal for hill walking.

LUSS continued

Map 1 G4

Mrs J T K Short
Ardallie House
Luss, by Alexandria
Dunbartonshire
G83 8NU
Tel: (Luss) 01436 860272

COMMENDED

2 Twin	1 Priv. NOT ensuite	B&B per person	Open Apr-Oct
1 Double	1 Pub Bath/Show	£21.00-£23.00 Single	
		£16.00-£18.00 Double	

Charming country house on hillside off A82 in woodland garden.
Magnificent views over Loch Lomond.

---

per Mrs K R Wragg
Glenmollochan Farm
Luss
Dunbartonshire
G83 8PB
Tel: (Luss) 01436 860246
Fax: 01436 860246

COMMENDED

| 1 Twin | 2 En Suite fac | B&B per person | Open Easter-Oct |
| 1 Double | | £15.00-£19.50 Double | |

Situated on working sheep farm, 2 miles (3 kms) from Luss.
Ensuite bedrooms both with superb views of Loch Lomond.

MACDUFF
Banffshire

Map 4 F7

Mrs Kathleen Greig
11 Gellymill Street
Macduff
Banffshire
AB44 1TN
Tel: (Macduff) 01261 833314

COMMENDED
Listed

1 Twin	1 Pub Bath/Show	B&B per person	Open Jan-Dec
1 Double		from £13.00 Single	Dinner 1930-2000
		from £12.00 Double	B&B + Eve. Meal
			£18.00-£19.00

Comfortable family home in quiet street near to harbour in small fishing town.
Home cooking and baking.

Monica & Martin`s B & B
21 Gellymill Street
Macduff
Banffshire
Tel: (Macduff) 01261 832336

COMMENDED
Listed

1 Twin	2 En Suite fac	B&B per person	Open Jan-Dec
1 Double	1 Pub Bath/Show	£12.50-£16.00 Single	
1 Family		£12.50-£16.00 Double	

Detached house in centre of Macduff, close to shops and harbour.
Evening meals available.

MALLAIG
Inverness-shire

Map 3 F11

Western Isles Guest House
East Bay
Mallaig
Inverness-shire
PH41 4QG
Tel: (Mallaig) 01687 2320

COMMENDED

1 Single	3 Pub Bath/Show	B&B per person	Open Jan-Nov
1 Double		£15.00-£17.00 Single	Dinner 1800-1930
1 Family		£15.00-£17.00 Double	

Modern house overlooking the harbour and fishing boats, well situated for
ferries to the islands. 4 miles (6kms) from renowned Morar sands.

MARKINCH
Fife

Map 2 C3

Mrs C Craig
Shythrum Farm
Markinch, by Glenrothes
Fife
KY7 6HB
Tel: (Glenrothes) 01592 758372

COMMENDED
Listed

1 Twin	1 Pub Bath/Show	B&B per person	Open Jan-Dec
1 Family		£15.00-£18.00 Single	Dinner from 1800
		from £15.00 Double	
		Room only per person	
		from £12.00	

Working farm adjacent to coaching route used by Mary Queen of Scots.
Balgonie Castle 0.5 miles (1km), Falkland Palace 5 miles (8kms),
Glenrothes 2 miles (3kms).

MAUCHLINE
Ayrshire

Map 1 H7

Mrs Smith
Dykefield Farm
Mauchline
Ayrshire
KA5 6EY
Tel: (Mauchline) 01290 550328

APPROVED
Listed

1 Double	1 Pub Bath/Show	B&B per person	Open Jan-Dec
1 Family		from £10.00 Single	Dinner 1800-2200
		from £10.00 Double	B&B + Eve. Meal
		Room only per person	from £14.00
		from £10.00	

Working dairy farm, 2 miles (3kms) from Mauchline in the centre of Burns Country.
Evening meal and home baking.

VAT is shown at 17.5%: changes in this rate may affect prices. Prices shown are for guidance only. Please send SAE with each enquiry.

MAYBOLE Ayrshire	Map 1 G8		

HOMELEA

62 Culzean Road, Maybole, Ayrshire KA19 8AH
Tel: 01655 882736   Fax: 01655 883557

Attractive Victorian family home. Large walled garden,
tea/coffee, home baking on arrival. Burns Country,
Galloway Forest, Turnberry, near by.
Culzean Castle four miles.
No smoking.

Mrs J McKellar
Homelea, 62 Culzean Road
Maybole
Ayrshire
KA19 8AH
Tel: (Maybole) 01655 882736
Fax: 01655 883557

COMMENDED
Listed

1 Double   2 Pub Bath/Show
1 Family

B&B per person
from £16.00 Single
from £14.50 Double

Open Mar-Oct

Victorian family villa on B7023, 4 miles (6kms) north of Culzean Castle.
Ideal centre for touring Burns Country.

MEIGLE
Perthshire
Ray & May Eskdale
Stripside, Longleys
Meigle
Perthshire
PH12 8QX
Tel: (Meigle) 01828 640388

Map 2
C1

HIGHLY
COMMENDED

1 Twin   3 En Suite fac
2 Double

B&B per person
£20.00 Single
£16.50 Double

Open Jan-Dec
Dinner 1830-2000
B&B + Eve. Meal
£24.50-£28.00

Renovated farmhouse with a ground-floor bedroom, set back from the A94.
Open rural views. Registered cattery.

MELROSE
Roxburghshire
Mrs M Aitken
The Gables, Darnick
Melrose
Roxburghchiro
TD6 9AL
Tel: (Melrose) 01896 822479

Map 2
D6

COMMENDED

1 Single   1 Pub Bath/Show
1 Twin
1 Double

B&B per person
£14.00-£16.00 Single
£14.00-£16.00 Double

Open Jan-Dec
Dinner 1800-1930
B&B + Eve. Meal
£22.00-£24.00

Georgian villa in centre of quiet village, 1 mile (2kms) from Melrose.
Ideal base for touring the Borders. Good home cooking.

Mrs J Bennet
Collingwood
Waverly Road
Melrose
Roxburghshire
TD6 9AA
Tel: (Melrose) 01896 822670

COMMENDED

1 Single   1 Pub Bath/Show
1 Twin
1 Double

B&B per person
£14.00-£16.00 Single
£14.00-£16.00 Double

Open Jan-Dec
Dinner 1800-1930
B&B + Eve. Meal
£22.00-£24.00

Detached Victorian house on outskirts of Melrose with
enclosed garden and good parking.

Mrs Christine Dalgetty
Little Fordel, Abbey Street
Melrose
Roxburghshire
TD6 9PX
Tel: (Melrose) 01896 822206

HIGHLY
COMMENDED

1 Twin   2 En Suite fac
1 Double

B&B per person
£20.00-£25.00 Single
from £21.00 Double

Open Jan-Dec

Former school house, quietly situated near the centre of town,
own car parking in rear courtyard.

Dunfermline House
  Guest House
Buccleuch Street
Melrose
Roxburghshire
TD6 9LB
Tel: (Melrose) 01896 822148
Fax: 01896 822148

HIGHLY
COMMENDED

1 Single   4 En Suite fac
2 Twin   1 Priv. NOT ensuite
2 Double

B&B per person
£21.00-£22.00 Single
£21.00-£22.00 Double

Open Jan-Dec

Comfortable family home overlooking Melrose Abbey.
Ideal base for touring Scott Country and Edinburgh. No smoking.

Mrs M Graham
Braidwood, Buccleuch Street
Melrose
Roxburghshire
TD6 9LD
Tel: (Melrose) 01896 822488

HIGHLY
COMMENDED

1 Single   1 En Suite fac
1 Twin   1 Pub Bath/Show
1 Double

B&B per person
£17.00-£20.00 Single

Open Jan-Dec

Friendly welcome in attractive Listed town house only a stone's throw
from Melrose Abbey and Priorwood Gardens. Home baking.

Details of Grading and Classification are on page vi.

Key to symbols is on back flap.

MELROSE continued	**Map 2** **D6**					
Mrs M Martin Little Broadmeadows, Waverly Road Melrose Roxburghshire TD6 9AA Tel: (Melrose) 01896 822739		COMMENDED Listed	1 Single 1 Double	1 Pub Bath/Show	B&B per person £15.00-£18.00 Single £15.00-£18.00 Double Room only per person £15.00-£18.00	Open Jan-Dec

Comfortable lodge house on outskirts of Melrose. Good base for touring the Borders. Approximately 1 hour's drive from Edinburgh.

Mrs L A Paterson Fiorlin, Abbey Street Melrose Roxburghshire TD6 9PX Tel: (Melrose) 01896 822984	COMMENDED	1 Double 1 Family	2 En Suite fac	B&B per person from £20.00 Double	Open Jan-Dec

Detached house of character set in quiet residential area with private parking. Convenient for town centre and restaurants, ideal touring base.

Mrs P Schofield Torwood Lodge, High Cross Avenue Melrose Roxburghshire TD6 9SU Tel: (Melrose) 01896 822220	COMMENDED	1 Twin 2 Double	3 En Suite fac	B&B per person £26.00-£27.00 Single £21.00-£22.00 Double	Open Jan-Dec

Large comfortable Victorian family house in attractive location. Easy walking distance to town, River Tweed and Eildon Hills. All en suite facilities.

MELVICH **Sutherland**	**Map 4** **C3**

The Shieling Guest House
MELVICH, SUTHERLAND, KW14 7YJ
Telephone: 01641 531256   Fax: 01641 531356

Guests return annually to this high-quality accommodation with emphasis on comfort, huge choice breakfast and Taste-of-Scotland dinners by arrangement. Two beautifully furnished lounges and separate dining room exclusively for guests' use, ensure privacy or company. Born in Sutherland, Joan and Hugh guarantee genuine native hospitality. Spectacular views! Perfect peace!

Shieling Guest House Melvich Sutherland KW14 7YJ Tel: (Melvich) 01641 531256 Fax: 01641 531356	HIGHLY COMMENDED	1 Twin 2 Double	2 En Suite fac 1 Priv. NOT ensuite	B&B per person £21.00-£23.00 Double	Open Apr-Oct Dinner at 1830 B&B + Eve. Meal £33.00-£35.00

Genuine Highland hospitality, home-cooked meals, choice of menu. Spectacular views over bay. Picture window in coffee lounge; separate TV lounge. Taste of Scotland.

Tigh-na-Clash Guest House (Mrs Joan Ritchie) Melvich Sutherland KW14 7YJ Tel: (Melvich) 01641 531262 Fax: 01641 531262	COMMENDED	2 Single 2 Twin 4 Double	4 En Suite fac 2 Pub Bath/Show	B&B per person £17.00-£21.00 Single £17.00-£21.00 Double	Open Apr-Oct Dinner 1700-2030

Personally run Guest House, pub and restaurant complex. Ideal for touring north coast and overnight stop for Orkney Isles.

METHLICK **Aberdeenshire**	**Map 4** **G9**				
Mrs C Staff Sunnybrae Farm, Gight Methlick, Ellon Aberdeenshire AB41 0JA Tel: (Methlick) 01651 806456	APPROVED	1 Single 1 Twin 1 Double	2 En Suite fac 1 Pub Bath/Show	B&B per person £17.00-£20.00 Single £17.00-£20.00 Double	Open Jan-Dec

Comfortable accommodation on a working farm, in a quiet peaceful location with superb views. Close to Castle and Whisky trails.

MILNATHORT, by Kinross **Kinross-shire** Mr & Mrs Cameron Warroch Lodge Milnathort Kinross-shire KY13 7RS Tel: (Kinross) 01577 863779	Map 2 B3	COMMENDED 👑👑	2 Twin	1 En Suite fac 1 Priv. NOT ensuite 1 Pub Bath/Show	B&B per person £14.00-£16.00 Single £14.00-£16.00 Double	Open Jan-Dec

Period lodge house set in attractive countryside. Located 4 miles (6 kms) from Junction 6 of M90, with easy access to major towns.

MILNGAVIE, Glasgow Mrs G Groves 58 Keystone Quadrant Milngavie, Glasgow G62 6LP Tel: 0141 956 5615	Map 1 H5	COMMENDED Listed	1 Single 1 Twin	1 Pub Bath/Show	B&B per person £15.00-£16.00 Single £15.00-£16.00 Double	Open Jan-Dec Dinner 1700-1900 B&B + Eve. Meal from £21.00

Detached bungalow in quiet residential area, yet only a few minutes walk from main road. Walkers welcome. Evening meal by arrangement.

J M & J G McColl Westview 1 Dougalston Gardens South Milngavie, Glasgow G62 6HS Tel: 0141 956 5973		COMMENDED 👑👑	1 Twin 1 Double 1 Family	3 En Suite fac	B&B per person from £18.00 Single from £16.00 Double	Open Jan-Dec

Detached house in cul-de-sac, with private parking. Families welcome.

MINARD, by Inveraray **Argyll**	Map 1 F4

Victoria House
Minard, by Inveraray PA32 8YB
Telephone: 01546 886224

Granite-faced house overlooking Loch Fyne ideal for walking, sailing and climbing. Close to Crarae Gardens situated on A83 midway between Inveraray and Lochgilphead. Ideal overnight stop for Islay and Arran ferries.

Mrs J MacVicar Victoria House Minard, by Inveraray Argyll PA32 8YB Tel: (Minard) 01546 886224		COMMENDED 👑	1 Single 1 Twin 1 Double	1 Pub Bath/Show	B&B per person from £14.00 Single	Open Apr-Oct

Stone-built villa in centre of village with uninterrupted views over Loch Fyne.

MOFFAT **Dumfriesshire** Mr & Mrs D A Armstrong Boleskine, 4 Well Road Moffat Dumfriesshire DG10 9AS Tel: (Moffat) 01683 220601	Map 2 B8	COMMENDED 👑👑	1 Single 1 Twin 2 Double	2 En Suite fac 1 Pub Bath/Show	B&B per person £16.00-£18.00 Single £16.00-£18.00 Double	Open Jan-Dec Dinner 1900-2000 B&B + Eve. Meal £24.00-£26.00

A large Victorian house, built in 1886. Close to the town centre it offers comfortable spacious accommodation.

WELCOME

Whenever you are in Scotland, you can be sure of a warm welcome at your nearest Tourist Information Centre.
For guide books, maps, souvenirs, our Centres provide a service second to none – many now offer bureau-de-change facilities. And, of course, Tourist Information Centres offer free, expert advice on what to see and do, route-planning and accommodation for everyone – visitors and residents alike!

Details of Grading and Classification are on page vi. | Key to symbols is on back flap. |

MOFFAT continued	Map 2 B8

Burnock Water
Haywood Road, Moffat DG10 9BU
Telephone: 01683 221329

Comfortable Victorian house in peaceful scenic location, yet only ½ mile from town centre. En-suite facilities. Ground floor bedroom. All bedrooms have central heating, colour TV, tea/coffee tray. Secluded garden and ample parking. Cycles for hire. Evening meal by prior arrangement. Fire certificate. Less mobile grading. Warm welcome.

David Barclay
Burnock Water, Haywood Road
Moffat
Dumfriesshire
DG10 9BU
Tel: (Moffat) 01683 221329

COMMENDED 👑👑

1 Twin	3 En Suite fac	B&B per person
2 Double	1 Pub Bath/Show	£17.00-£19.00 Single
2 Family		£15.00-£17.00 Double

Open Jan-Dec
Dinner 1800-2000
B&B + Eve. Meal
£23.00-£25.00

Personally run c.1845 large house, in own grounds and secluded garden. Approx. 1/2 mile (1 km) to High Street. Private parking.

Barnhill Springs Country Guest House
Moffat
Dumfriesshire
DG10 9QS
Tel: (Moffat) 01683 220580

COMMENDED 👑👑

2 Twin	1 Priv. NOT ensuite	B&B per person
2 Double	2 Pub Bath/Show	£19.00-£20.00 Single
1 Family		£19.00-£20.00 Double

Open Jan-Dec
Dinner from 1830
B&B + Eve. Meal
£31.50-£32.50

Early Victorian country house, ideally situated for walking the Southern Upland Way. Access from A74 via south-bound slip road at Moffat junction.

Mrs Eileen Baty
Thai-Ville, 3 Dundanion Place
Moffat
Dumfriesshire
DG10 9GD
Tel: (Moffat) 01683 220922

DELUXE 👑👑

2 Twin	2 En Suite fac	B&B per person
		£25.00 Single
		£17.00 Double
		Room only per person
		£25.00

Open Mar-Nov

Modern bungalow with individual style, in quiet residential area, close to town centre. Warm and friendly welcome, ensuite rooms. Ground-floor accommodation.

Buchan Guest House
Beechgrove
Moffat
Dumfriesshire
DG10 9RS
Tel: (Moffat) 01683 220378

COMMENDED 👑👑

1 Single	4 En Suite fac	B&B per person
2 Twin	2 Priv. NOT ensuite	£22.00-£25.00 Single
3 Double	2 Pub Bath/Show	£18.00-£20.00 Double
2 Family		

Open Jan-Dec
Dinner from 1830
B&B + Eve. Meal
£25.00-£27.00

Victorian house in quiet residential area, close to centre of Moffat. Ideal base for touring.

Gilbert House
Beechgrove
Moffat
Dumfriesshire
DG10 9RS
Tel: (Moffat) 01683 220050

HIGHLY COMMENDED 👑👑👑

1 Single	4 En Suite fac	B&B per person
1 Twin	2 Limited ensuite	£17.00-£19.50 Single
2 Double	1 Pub Bath/Show	£17.00-£19.50 Double
2 Family		

Open Jan-Dec
Dinner from 1830
B&B + Eve. Meal
£27.50-£30.00

Spacious family run guest house in residential area, 5 minutes walk from the centre of Moffat. Emphasis on good food. Ideal base for touring.

Mrs Gourlay
Fernhill, Grange Road
Moffat
Dumfriesshire
DG10 9HT
Tel: (Moffat) 01683 220077

DELUXE 👑👑

1 Twin	1 En Suite fac	B&B per person
1 Double	1 Priv.NOT ensuite	£15.00-£20.00 Single
	2 Pub Bath/Show	£15.00-£16.50 Double

Open Apr-Sep

A warm welcome assured with lots of care, attention and personal touches in this quietly situated house. Delightful garden. A few minutes walk from town centre.

Woodhead Farm
Old Carlisle Road, Moffat DG10 9LU
Telephone: 01683 220225

Luxuriously appointed farmhouse just two miles from centre of Moffat. Breakfast is served in beautiful garden room, overlooking mature garden. All rooms are en-suite and have views of surrounding hills. Murray and Sylvia extend a warm welcome to all their guests. Ample safe parking.

Mrs Jackson Woodhead Farm Moffat Dumfriesshire DG10 9LU Tel: (Moffat) 01683 220225	**HIGHLY COMMENDED**	2 Twin 1 Double	3 En Suite fac	B&B per person £24.00 Single £22.00-£24.00 Double	Open Jan-Dec Dinner 1900-2000 B&B + Eve. Meal £34.00-£36.00	

Luxuriously furnished farmhouse situated on 220-acre working stock farm with commanding panoramic views of the surrounding countryside. All ensuite.

Craigie Lodge
Craigie Lodge, Ballplay Road, Moffat DG10 9JU
Telephone: 01683 221037

A true Scottish welcome awaits you in this beautiful Victorian Home offering quality food and accommodation. Situated on outskirts of Moffat yet only 10 minutes walk from centre. Off-road parking and large garden for guests' enjoyment. Ground floor en-suite room available, also separate self-catering cottage.

Mrs Jappy Craigie Lodge, Ballplay Road Moffat Dumfriesshire DG10 9JU Tel: (Moffat) 01683 221037	**COMMENDED**	1 Twin 1 Double 1 Family	3 En Suite fac	B&B per person £22.00 Single £15.00-£16.50 Double	Open Jan-Dec, ex Xmas/New Year Dinner from 1830 B&B + Eve. Meal £24.00-£25.50	

Large Victorian family house set in mature 0.5 acre garden. All rooms private facilities. Ground-floor accommodation available. Reduced rates for 3 days.

Evelyn Lindsay Alba House, 20 Beechgrove Moffat Dumfriesshire DG10 9RS Tel: (Moffat) 01683 220418	**DELUXE**	1 Twin 1 Double 1 Family	3 En Suite fac	B&B per person £18.50-£20.00 Double	Open Apr-Oct	

A delightful old house c.1730 with beamed dining room, inglenook, colourful garden. Warm and friendly welcome. Quietly set within walking distance of town.

Mrs S Long Coxhill Farm, Old Carlisle Road Moffat Dumfriesshire DG10 9QN Tel: (Moffat) 01683 220471	**COMMENDED**	1 Twin 2 Double	3 Pub Bath/Show	B&B per person £18.00-£20.00 Single £16.00 Double	Open Mar-Oct	

Attractive modern farmhouse in peaceful setting.
Fine views over open countryside, 1 mile (2kms) from Moffat.

Joan & John Marchington Seamore House Academy Road Moffat Dumfriesshire DG10 9HW Tel: (Moffat) 01683 220404	**COMMENDED**	1 Single 1 Twin 2 Double 2 Family	2 En Suite fac 2 Pub Bath/Show	B&B per person £13.00-£16.00 Single £14.00-£16.50 Double	Open Jan-Dec Dinner 1830-1930 B&B + Eve. Meal £19.00-£22.50	

Comfortable family run guest house in centre of Moffat.
Children and pets welcome. Good centre for touring.

Mrs K Miller Broomlands Farm Beattock, Moffat Dumfriesshire DG10 9PQ Tel: (Beattock) 01683 300320 Fax: 01683 300320	**HIGHLY COMMENDED**	1 Single 1 Twin 1 Double	3 En Suite fac	B&B per person from £20.00 Single £17.00-£19.00 Double	Open Apr-Oct	

Farmhouse on a working 200-acre mixed farm. Convenient to A74 and 2 miles (3kms) from Moffat. Self-catering cottage available.

Details of Grading and Classification are on page vi. | Key to symbols is on back flap. | 211

| MOFFAT continued | Map 2 B8 | | |

Queensberry House

12 Beechgrove, Moffat, Dumfriesshire DG10 9RS
Telephone: 01683 220538

Moffat has proven itself as an ideal touring base. Explore its own beautiful countryside, drive around the Solway Coast or visit the cities of Edinburgh or Glasgow, just one hour's drive away.
Stay 3 nights at Queensberry House for £15 per person per night.
All facilities ground floor.

| Mrs Vivienne Murray
Queensberry House
12 Beechgrove
Moffat
Dumfriesshire
DG10 9RS
Tel: (Moffat) 01683 220538 | HIGHLY COMMENDED 👑👑 | 3 Double | 3 En Suite fac | B&B per person
£16.50-£20.00 Single
£16.50 Double | Open Mar-Oct | |
| | | Recently refurbished Victorian house in quiet area opposite park and bowling green and within a few minutes walk of the town centre. | | | | |

| Mrs P Pirie
Annavah, 23 Beechgrove
Moffat
Dumfriesshire
DG10 9RS
Tel: (Moffat) 01683 220550 | HIGHLY COMMENDED 👑 | 2 Twin
1 Double | 1 Pub Bath/Show | B&B per person
£15.50-£16.00 Double | Open Easter-Oct
Dinner 1800-1900
B&B + Eve. Meal
£25.50-£26.00 | |
| | | Attractive and quietly situated opposite the park, 5 minutes walk from the centre. Home cooking using fresh local produce when available. Private parking. | | | | |

| Rockhill Guest House
14 Beechgrove
Moffat
Dumfriesshire
DG10 9RS
Tel: (Moffat) 01683 220283 | COMMENDED 👑👑👑 | 2 Single
1 Twin
3 Double
4 Family | 5 En Suite fac
2 Pub Bath/Show | B&B per person
£16.00-£19.50 Single
£16.00-£19.50 Double | Open Jan-Nov
Dinner from 1830
B&B + Eve. Meal
£23.50-£27.00 | |
| | | Victorian house overlooking bowling green and park, in quiet area close to town centre. Open outlook to hills. Own private car park, ensuite rooms. | | | | |

Merkland House

Buccleuch Place, Moffat, Dumfriesshire DG10 9AN
Telephone: 01683 220957

An elegant Victorian house situated in 2½ acres of quiet woodland gardens, close to Moffat Town Centre, offering ensuite accommodation. A comfortable residents' lounge with open fire, ample parking and a varied breakfast menu also catering for vegetarians.
Relaxing aromatherapy sessions can also be arranged to enhance your stay.

| Mr A Tavener
Merkland House
Buccleuch Place
Moffat
Dumfriesshire
DG10 9AN
Tel: (Moffat) 01683 220957 | COMMENDED 👑👑 | 1 Single
2 Double
2 Family | 3 En Suite fac
1 Priv. NOT ensuite
1 Pub Bath/Show | B&B per person
£15.00-£18.00 Single | Open Jan-Dec | |
| | | 19th-century detached villa in 2.5 acres of gardens situated in quiet residential area, yet only 5 minutes walk from town centre. | | | | |

CARRADALE
Beechgrove, Moffat DG10 9RU
Telephone: 01683 221274

A warm welcome awaits you at Carradale where recently en-suites have been installed to this lovely cedar bungalow with its uninterrupted views over Annan Water Valley. ½ mile from Moffat town centre 1½ miles from A74/ M74. There is ample parking and a large garden for guests' enjoyment.

Mr & Mrs R Tennant Carradale, Beechgrove Moffat DG10 9RU Tel: (Moffat) 01683 221274	HIGHLY COMMENDED	1 Double 1 Family	2 En Suite fac	B&B per person £18.00-£20.00 Single £16.00-£18.50 Double Room only per person £15.00-£18.00	Open Jan-Dec	

Attractive cedarwood bungalow on outskirts of town with open views over the Annan Water. Both rooms ensuite.

Mrs G T Walker Springbank, Beechgrove Moffat Dumfriesshire DG10 9RS Tel: (Moffat) 01683 220070	HIGHLY COMMENDED	1 Twin 1 Double	1 Priv. NOT ensuite 2 Pub Bath/Show	B&B per person £14.00-£15.00 Double	Open Mar-Nov	

Early 19th-century detached house in quiet residential area. Home baking a speciality. Private parking and colourful garden.

Mrs Ruth Watson Hazel Bank, Academy Road Moffat Dumfriesshire DG10 9HP Tel: (Moffat) 01683 220294	COMMENDED	1 Single 1 Twin 1 Double	1 En Suite fac 2 Pub Bath/Show	B&B per person £18.00-£20.00 Single £15.00-£17.00 Double	Open Jan-Dec	

Family home, centrally situated 2 minutes from town centre. Good base for touring. Ground floor ensuite available.

Mrs Wells Morlich House, Ballplay Road Moffat Dumfriesshire DG10 9JU Tel: (Moffat) 01683 220589	COMMENDED	1 Twin 2 Double 2 Family	4 En Suite fac 1 Priv.NOT ensuite	B&B per person £20.00-£25.00 Single to £15.00 Double	Open Feb-Nov Dinner 1830-2030 B&B + Eve. Meal to £23.50	

Small family run guest house set in 1/2 acre. Ideal base for touring, hillwalking, riding and bird-watching. Warm friendly atmosphere.

MONTROSE **Angus** The Limes Guest House 15 King Street Montrose Angus DD10 8NL Tel: (Montrose) 01674 677236 Fax: 01674 677236	Map 4 F12 COMMENDED	2 Single 4 Twin 4 Double 2 Family	4 En Suite fac 4 Limited ensuite 2 Priv. NOT ensuite 3 Pub Bath/Show	B&B per person from £18.00 Single from £16.50 Double Room only per person from £16.50	Open Jan-Dec Dinner from 1800	

Family run, centrally situated in quiet, residential part of town. A few minutes walk from the centre, railway station and beach. Private parking.

Mrs P H Massuch The Station House Farnell, by Brechin Angus DD9 6UH Tel: (Farnell) 01674 820208	COMMENDED	3 Twin	1 En Suite fac 2 Pub Bath/Show	B&B per person from £16.00 Single from £14.50 Double	Open Jan-Dec Dinner 1700-2000 B&B + Eve. Meal from £24.00	

Pleasant rural setting in large grounds. Minutes from numerous activities. Spacious accommodation. Large car park. Dog kennels.

MONTROSE continued

Oaklands Guest House
10 Rossie Island Road
Montrose
Angus
DD10 9NN
Tel: (Montrose) 01674 672018
Fax: 01674 672018

Map 4 F12

COMMENDED

1 Single — 7 En Suite fac
3 Twin
2 Double
1 Family

B&B per person
from £20.00 Single
from £16.50 Double

Open Jan-Dec

Ensuite facilities available at this comfortable family house within walking distance of Montrose town centre. Parking. Boat fishing available.

Mrs H Robertson
Stone of Morphie
Montrose
Angus
DD10 0AA
Tel: (Hillside) 01674 830388

COMMENDED Listed

1 Twin — 2 Pub Bath/Show
1 Double
1 Family

B&B per person
to £15.00 Single
to £15.00 Double

Open Jan-Dec

Friendly working farm, with large garden overlooking Montrose. Nearby beaches and Nature Reserve. Children and pets welcome.

Mrs A Ruxton
Muirshade of Gallery Farm
Montrose
Angus
DD10 9JU
Tel: (Northwaterbridge)
01674 840209

COMMENDED

1 Twin — 2 En Suite fac
2 Double — 1 Priv. NOT ensuite
— 1 Pub Bath/Show

B&B per person
to £16.00 Single
to £16.00 Double

Open Apr-Oct
Dinner 1800-1930
B&B + Eve. Meal
from £24.00

Farmhouse on working stock and cereal farm 5 miles (8kms) from Montrose and sandy beaches. Ideal for touring coast and Angus glens. Home baking.

Mrs M Scott
Fairfield, 24 The Mall
Montrose
Angus
DD10 8NW
Tel: (Montrose) 01674 676386

COMMENDED Listed

2 Twin — 1 Pub Bath/Show
1 Double

B&B per person
from £16.00 Single
from £14.00 Double

Open Jan-Dec

Detached Georgian house, centrally situated in residential area, with ample street parking. Secure cycle parking. All rooms with washbasin, TV and tea-making facilities.

MORAR, by Mallaig
Inverness-shire

Sunset
Morar, by Mallaig
Inverness-shire
PH40 4PA
Tel: (Mallaig) 01687 462259

Map 3 F11

APPROVED

1 Twin — 1 Pub Bath/Show
1 Double
2 Family

B&B per person
£12.50-£16.00 Single
£12.50-£15.00 Double

Open Jan-Dec
Dinner 1900-2100
B&B + Eve. Meal
£18.00-£22.00

Small family house in West Highland village, very close to the renowned Morar Sands. Mallaig 3 miles (5km) with ferries to Skye and Small Isles.

MOREBATTLE
Roxburghshire

Mrs Marie-France Taylor
Kaleview, Main Street
Morebattle
Roxburghshire
TD5 8QQ
Tel: (Morebattle) 01573 440345

Map 2 E7

COMMENDED Listed

1 Single — 1 Priv. NOT ensuite
2 Twin — 2 Pub Bath/Show

B&B per person
£15.00-£17.00 Single
£14.00-£17.00 Double

Open Jan-Dec
Dinner 1800-2000
B&B + Eve. Meal
£22.00-£25.00

Friendly and comfortable. Good home cooking. Walkers drying facilities, village inn, fishing available. French and Italian spoken.

MUASDALE
Argyll

Mrs MacMillan
Seafield
Muasdale, by Tayinloan
Argyll
PA29 6XD
Tel: (Glenbarr) 01583 421240

Map 1 D6

COMMENDED Listed

2 Double — 1 Pub Bath/Show
1 Family

B&B per person
to £16.00 Single
to £15.00 Double

Open Mar-Oct

House standing in its own grounds under 1 mile (2kms) from small village on west coast of Kintyre. Lovely seascapes towards Gigha, Islay and Jura.

VAT is shown at 17.5%: changes in this rate may affect prices. Prices shown are for guidance only. Please send SAE with each enquiry.

MUIR OF ORD **Ross-shire** Mrs E Brown Hawthorn Bank Black Isle Road Muir-of-Ord Ross-shire IV6 7RR Tel: (Muir of Ord) 01463 870188	Map 4 A8	COMMENDED Listed	1 Double 1 Family	1 Pub Bath/Show	B&B per person £15.00 Single £13.50 Double	Open Apr-Oct

Traditional Scottish hospitality in friendly family home.
Ideal base for touring this beautiful part of Scotland.

Mrs W A Keir Monadh Liath, Ord Wood Muir-of-Ord Ross-shire IV6 7XS Tel: (Muir of Ord) 01463 870587		COMMENDED	2 Twin 1 Double	1 Pub Bath/Show	B&B per person from £13.50 Double	Open Jan-Dec

In quiet residential area, on the outskirts of the town,
large modern house set in extensive gardens.

Mrs C MacKenzie Dungrianach, Corry Road Muir of Ord Ross-shire IV6 7TN Tel: (Muir of Ord) 01463 870316		COMMENDED Listed	1 Twin 1 Double	1 Pub Bath/Show	B&B per person £14.00 Single £14.00 Double	Open May-Oct

Modern farmhouse with own garden, situated in secluded rural position,
1.5miles (3kms) from Muir of Ord. Ideal location for touring Ross-shire.

MUSSELBURGH **East Lothian**	Map 2 C5

Mrs Elizabeth Aitken

COMMENDED

18 WOODSIDE GARDENS, MUSSELBURGH, EAST LOTHIAN EH21 7LJ
Telephone: 0131 665 3170/3344
Well-appointed bungalow within 6 miles of Edinburgh in quiet suburb with
private parking. Excellent bus/train service to city. 2 minutes from oldest
golf course in world and race course. Easy access to beaches and beautiful
countryside.

All rooms hot and cold, colour TV and tea/coffee.   *Private parking.*

Mrs E Aitken 18 Woodside Gardens Musselburgh East Lothian EH21 7LJ Tel: 0131 665 3170/3344		COMMENDED	1 Single 1 Twin 1 Family	2 Pub Bath/Show	B&B per person from £15.00 Single from £15.00 Double	Open Jan-Dec

Detached bungalow in quiet residential area, close to Musselburgh Racecourse
and golf course. Private parking.

Craigesk Guest House 10 Albert Terrace Musselburgh East Lothian EH21 7LR Tel: 0131 665 3344/3170		APPROVED	2 Twin 2 Family	2 Pub Bath/Show	B&B per person from £15.00 Single from £15.00 Double	Open Jan-Dec

Victorian terraced house with private parking, overlooking golf and racecourse.
Convenient bus route to city centre (20 minutes).

Mrs C Douglas 5 Craighall Terrace Musselburgh East Lothian EH21 7PL Tel: 0131 665 4294		APPROVED Listed	1 Double 1 Family	1 Pub Bath/Show	B&B per person from £18.00 Single from £15.00 Double	Open May-Oct

Family bungalow with private parking in quiet residential area,
close to seashore, golf course and race course.

Mr W Wilson 17 Windsor Park Musselburgh East Lothian EH21 7QL Tel: 0131 665 2194		COMMENDED Listed	1 Single 1 Twin 1 Double	1 En Suite fac 2 Priv. NOT ensuite 1 Pub Bath/Show	B&B per person £16.00-£20.00 Single	Open Jan-Dec Dinner 1700-1900 B&B + Eve. Meal £24.00-£28.00

Personally run Bed and Breakfast. Comfortable accommodation in quiet residential
area with unrestricted parking. Close to main bus route to Edinburgh city centre.

NAIRN Mrs P Hudson & Mr Maxwell Durham House, 4 Academy Street Nairn Inverness-shire IV12 4RJ Tel: (Nairn) 01667 452345	**Map 4** C8	COMMENDED	1 Twin 1 Double 1 Family	1 En Suite fac 2 Pub Bath/Show	B&B per person £16.00-£19.00 Double	Open Jan-Dec Dinner 1800-1930 B&B + Eve. Meal £25.00-£28.00	
			19th-century elegant villa, set in its own grounds, with off-street parking. Extensive home baking and cooking.				
BY NAIRN Mr & Mrs G Pearson Brightmony Farm House Auldearn Nairn IV12 5PP Tel: (Nairn) 01667 455550	**Map 4** C8	COMMENDED Listed	1 Twin 2 Double	1 Pub Bath/Show	B&B per person £12.50-£15.00 Single £12.50-£15.00 Double	Open Mar-Nov	
			A listed, Georgian farmhouse, large bedrooms, log fire, peaceful and relaxed, superb views over Moray Firth.				
NETHY BRIDGE **Inverness-shire** Linda Renton Aspen Lodge Nethy Bridge Inverness-shire PH25 3DA Tel: (Nethy Bridge) 01479 821042 Fax: 01479 821042	**Map 4** C9	COMMENDED Listed	1 Twin 1 Double	1 En Suite fac 1 Priv. NOT ensuite	B&B per person from £18.50 Single from £18.50 Double	Open Jan-Dec	
			Situated in the heart of picturesque Nethybridge. Ideal base for touring beautiful Strathspey.				
NEWBURGH **Fife** Mrs Barbara Baird Ninewells Farm Woodriffe Road Newburgh Fife KY14 6EY Tel: (Newburgh) 01337 840307	**Map 2** C2	HIGHLY COMMENDED Listed	2 Twin	1 Priv. NOT ensuite 2 Pub Bath/Show	B&B per person from £20.00 Single £16.00-£20.00 Double	Open Apr-Oct	
			Traditional farmhouse on operational arable/stock farm. Elevated position with panoramic views of Tay Valley. Convenient for Edinburgh, Perth and many golf courses.				
Mrs A Duff Hillview, 46 Scotland Terrace Newburgh Fife KY14 6AR Tel: (Newburgh) 01337 840570		COMMENDED Listed	1 Twin 1 Double	1 Pub Bath/Show	B&B per person £13.00-£15.00 Single £13.00-£15.00 Double	Open Apr-Sep	
			Family home in quiet residential area of Fife village. Ideal centre for touring. 12 miles (19kms) from Perth, 20 miles (32kms) from Dundee.				
NEWCASTLETON **Roxburghshire** Mrs Linda Stenhouse Borders Honey Farm Newcastleton Roxburghshire TD9 0SG Tel: (Liddlesdale) 013873 76737 Fax: 013873 76737	**Map 2** D9	COMMENDED	1 Single 1 Twin 1 Double	1 En Suite fac 1 Priv. NOT ensuite	B&B per person £20.00 Single £20.00 Double	Open Jan-Dec Dinner 1930-2030 B&B + Eve. Meal £30.00-£35.00	
			Peaceful house of real character nestling at the foot of the forest and Harriston Fells. Lovely walking country.				
NEW GALLOWAY **Kirkcudbrightshire** Mr & Mrs R Walker Carrick New Galloway Kirkcudbrightshire DG7 3RZ Tel: (New Galloway) 01644 420747	**Map 1** H9	COMMENDED Listed	1 Twin 1 Family	1 Pub Bath/Show	B&B per person from £14.00 Double	Open Apr-Oct	
			Modern property, adjacent to Galloway Forest, one mile from village. Ideal base for walking, fishing, bird-watching, golf and water-sports.				

BY NEW GALLOWAY Kirkcudbrightshire	Map 1 H9

HIGH PARK FARM

Balmaclellan, New Galloway, Castle Douglas DG7 3PT
Telephone: 01644 420298

HIGH PARK is a comfortable stone-built farmhouse built in 1838. The 171-acre dairy, sheep and stock rearing farm is situated by Loch Ken on the A713 amidst Galloway's beautiful scenery within easy reach of hills and coast. Good food guaranteed. All bedrooms have washbasins, shaver points, tea/coffee facilities. Pets welcome.

Commended ♛   Brochure: Mrs Jessie E. Shaw at above address

Mrs J Shaw High Park Balmaclellan Kirkcudbrightshire DG7 3PT Tel: (New Galloway) 01644 420298	COMMENDED ♛	1 Twin 2 Double	1 Pub Bath/Show	B&B per person £14.00-£15.00 Single £14.00-£15.00 Double	Open Apr-Oct Dinner from 1900 B&B + Eve. Meal £21.50-£22.50	

Early 19th-century farmhouse on working dairy and sheep farm, situated by Loch Ken off A713, amidst beautiful Galloway scenery.

KALMAR

Balmaclellan, Nr New Galloway, Castle Douglas DG7 3QE
Telephone: 01644 420685   Fax: 01644 420244

New, purpose-built, centrally heated, all rooms ensuite.
Set amidst beautiful Galloway countryside with mountain views – central for all activities of the area.
After dinner, enjoy the ambience of our large residents' lounge with leather furniture and log burning stove.
One suite on the ground floor.   *Off-road parking.*

Wallace & Doreen Wood 'Kalmar' Balmaclellan Kirkcudbrightshire DG7 3QE Tel: (Balmaclellan) 01644 420685 Fax: 01644 420244	HIGHLY COMMENDED ♛	1 Twin 1 Family	2 En Suite fac	B&B per person to £22.50 Single to £17.50 Double	Open Jan-Dec Dinner 1830-2000 B&B + Eve. Meal £25.50-£30.50	

Recently built, village home, set amidst beautiful Galloway countryside. Full office facilities available. Home-cooking. Ground-floor accommodation.

NEWMILLS Fife Mrs P McFarlane Langlees Farm Newmills, by Culross Fife KY12 8HA Tel: (Newmills) 01383 881152	Map 2 B4 COMMENDED Listed	1 Single 1 Twin	1 Pub Bath/Show	B&B per person from £14.00 Single from £14.00 Double Room only per person from £12.00	Open Jan-Dec Dinner 1700-2000	

Family B&B on working farm. Large garden. Lovely local walks. Children welcome. Ideal touring base for central Scotland.

BY NEWPORT-ON-TAY Fife Forgan House Forgan Newport-on-Tay Fife DD6 8RB Tel: (Newport-on-Tay) 01382 542760 Fax: 01382 542760	Map 2 D2 HIGHLY COMMENDED ♛♛♛	2 Twin 2 Double	3 En Suite fac 1 Priv. NOT ensuite	B&B per person £25.00-£35.00 Single £22.50-£30.00 Double Room only per person £25.00-£35.00	Open Jan-Dec Dinner 1900-2000 B&B + Eve. Meal £37.50-£47.50	

Georgian country house set in 5 acres of grounds and gardens located between Dundee and St Andrews.

NEWTONHILL **Kincardineshire** Patricia A Allen 3 Greystone Place Newtonhill Kincardineshire AB3 2PW Tel: (Newtonhill) 01569 730391	Map 4 G11	**APPROVED** Listed	1 Twin 1 Double	2 Pub Bath/Show	B&B per person £14.00-£20.00 Single £14.00-£15.00 Double	Open Jan-Dec Dinner 1830-2000 B&B + Eve. Meal £20.00

A friendly welcome awaits at this comfortable semi-detached house set in coastal village 10 miles from Aberdeen. Evening meals by arrangement.

NEWTONMORE **Inverness-shire**	Map 4 B11

BEN-Y-GLOE
Fort William Road, Newtonmore, Inverness-shire PH20 1DG
Telephone and Fax: 01540 673633
Celia and John would like to welcome you to their family home.
An attractive spacious house set in its own grounds, centrally situated
for all amenities and ideal for touring the Highlands. Ground-floor
bedrooms with private facilities, tea-coffee, colour TV, own keys,
TV lounge and delicious cooked breakfasts.

Celia Ferrie Ben-y-Gloe, Fort William Road Newtonmore Inverness-shire PH20 1DG Tel: (Newtonmore) 01540 673633 Fax: 01540 673633		**COMMENDED**	1 Twin 2 Double	3 En Suite fac	B&B per person from £15.00 Single from £15.00 Double	Open Jan-Dec

Traditional Scottish hospitality in friendly Bed & Breakfast. Within walking distance of all village amenities and ideal touring base for Spey Valley.

Mrs M Johnston Ardnabruach, Glen Road Newtonmore Inverness-shire PH20 1DZ Tel: (Newtonmore) 01540 673339		**COMMENDED** Listed	1 Single 1 Twin 1 Double	1 Pub Bath/Show	B&B per person from £12.50 Single from £12.50 Double	Open Jan-Dec

Set in own grounds, our friendly relaxed Victorian home offers you Highland hospitality and personal attention. Beautiful location overlooking village.

Mrs K Main Craigellachie House Main Street Newtonmore Inverness-shire PH20 1DA Tel: (Newtonmore) 01540 673360		**COMMENDED**	1 Double 1 Family	1 Pub Bath/Show	B&B per person £16.00-£18.00 Single £15.00-£17.00 Double	Open Jan-Dec, exc Xmas Dinner 1830-2000 B&B + Eve. Meal from £23.00

Oldest house in Newtonmore offering comfortable accommodation in family home. Vegetarians catered for.

Mrs A Morrison Woodcliffe, Laggan Road Newtonmore Inverness-shire PH20 1DG Tel: (Newtonmore) 01540 673839		**COMMENDED** Listed	1 Double 1 Family	1 Pub Bath/Show	B&B per person £12.50-£14.00 Single £12.50-£14.00 Double	Open Jan-Dec

Stone-built house on edge of quiet Highland village. Comfortable stay assured in this welcoming family home. Garden nursery business in grounds.

Dorothy Muir Greenways, Golf Course Road Newtonmore Inverness-shire PH20 1AT Tel: (Newtonmore) 01540 673325		**COMMENDED**	1 Single 1 Twin 1 Double	1 Pub Bath/Show	B&B per person from £12.50 Single from £12.50 Double	Open Jan-Dec

Personally run friendly bed and breakfast overlooking golf course in centre of village. Ideal touring base.

Valerie Tonkin Eagle View, Perth Road Newtonmore Inverness-shire PH20 1AP Tel: (Newtonmore) 01540 673675	COMMENDED	2 Twin 2 Double	3 En Suite fac 1 Priv. NOT ensuite	B&B per person £17.00-£19.00 Single £15.00-£16.00 Double	Open Jan-Dec Dinner from 1900 B&B + Eve. Meal £23.00-£35.00

Traditional stone built house with large garden and ample parking.
Warm and friendly atmosphere, situated near centre of village.

NEWTON STEWART **Wigtownshire** Mrs P Adams Clugston Farm Newton Stewart Wigtownshire DG8 9BH Tel: (Kirkcowan) 01671 830338	Map 1 G10 COMMENDED	1 Twin 2 Double	2 Pub Bath/Show	B&B per person £14.00-£16.00 Single £14.00-£16.00 Double	Open Apr-Oct Dinner from 1800

About 5 miles (8kms) off the A75. Near the sea, hill walking and
easy access to 3 golf courses. Two ground-floor rooms.

Flower Bank Guest House Minnigaff Newton Stewart Wigtownshire DG8 6PJ Tel: (Newton Stewart) 01671 402629	COMMENDED	1 Twin 4 Double 1 Family	3 En Suite fac 1 Priv. NOT ensuite 2 Pub Bath/Show	B&B per person £15.50-£17.50 Single £15.50-£16.50 Double	Open Jan-Dec Dinner from 1830 B&B + Eve. Meal £23.50-£25.50

Detached 18th-century house set in 1 acre of grounds on banks of River Cree.
Quiet peaceful location 0.5 miles (1km) from town centre.

Mrs J Gustafson Lynwood, Corvisel Road Newton Stewart Wigtownshire DG8 6LN Tel: (Newton Stewart) 01671 402074	COMMENDED	1 Twin 1 Double 1 Family	2 Pub Bath/Show	B&B per person £14.00-£15.00 Single	Open Jan-Dec Dinner from 1830 B&B + Eve. Meal £22.00-£23.00

Spacious Victorian house in quiet residential area, close to the town centre.
Ideal for families and young children. Vegetarians catered for.

AUCHENLECK FARM

NEWTON STEWART, WIGTOWNSHIRE DG8 7AA
Telephone: 01671 402035

*Original hunting lodge now comfortable, homely, well-equipped farmhouse in
Glentrool Forest Park. Ideal for hill forest walking, cycling, fishing, golf,
birdwatching, red roe and fallow deer abound. All bedrooms private bathrooms.
Tea/coffee facilities with home baking and radio/alarms. Visitors' lounge with
Teletext TV, board games and well-stocked book shelves.*
Prices: Daily £18.50 pp; Weekly £126 pp.   Packed lunches available.

Mrs M Hewitson Auchenleck Farm Newton Stewart Wigtownshire DG8 7AA Tel: (Newton Stewart) 01671 402035	COMMENDED	1 Twin 2 Double	1 En Suite fac 2 Priv. NOT ensuite	B&B per person £18.00-£18.50 Double	Open Easter-Oct

Turretted former shooting lodge on working sheep-farm. Set within
Glen Trool National Park. Ideally situated for fishing, cycling, walking and touring.

NEWTOWN ST BOSWELLS **Roxburghshire** Mrs Margaret Clyde West Mount, Langlands Place Newtown St Boswells Roxburghshire TD6 0RY Tel: (Newtown St Boswells) 01835 822077	Map 2 D6 APPROVED Listed	1 Single 1 Double	1 Pub Bath/Show	B&B per person £12.50 Single £12.50 Double Room only per person £10.00	Open Jan-Dec exc Xmas Dinner 1700-2000

Victorian town-house, just off A68. Centrally situated for touring the
Borders Abbeys and all attractions.

Details of Grading and Classification are on page vi. | Key to symbols is on back flap. |

NORTH BERWICK East Lothian Mrs Fife Beehive Cottage, Kingston North Berwick East Lothian EH39 5JE Tel: (North Berwick) 01620 894785	Map 2 D4 COMMENDED	1 Double	1 En Suite fac	B&B per person £18.00-£20.00 Single £16.00-£18.00 Double Room only per person £16.00-£18.00	Open Feb-Sep	
		200-year-old cottage with pantiled roof and garden with extensive views. 2 miles (3kms) drive to the sea. Home-produced honey. Ground-floor accommodation available.				
Mrs S Gray Seabank, 12 Marine Parade North Berwick East Lothian EH39 4LD Tel: (North Berwick) 01620 892884 Fax: 01620 895561	COMMENDED Listed	1 Twin 4 Family	2 Pub Bath/Show	B&B per person from £16.50 Single £14.50-£17.50 Double	Open Jan-Dec	
		Stone-built house with seaviews and adjoining sandy beach. Tennis courts behind. Off-road parking.				

The Studio

Grange Road, North Berwick EH39 4QT
Telephone: 01620 895150 Fax: 01620 895120

Newly refurbished and extended historic building, tastefully decorated and furnished, situated within a walled garden. Guests can enjoy a high degree of privacy in quiet rural surroundings yet convenient for North Berwick and railway station. Private sittingroom with television with French doors to garden. Regret no smoking. Parking available.

Mrs M Ramsay The Studio, Grange Road North Berwick East Lothian EH39 4QT Tel: (North Berwick) 01620 895150 Fax: 01620 895120	HIGHLY COMMENDED	1 Double	1 Priv. NOT ensuite	B&B per person £25.00 Single £20.00 Double Room only per person £20.00	Open Jan-Dec	
		Attractive listed building set in walled garden. Quiet peaceful location, private parking. Close to all amenities and local golf courses.				
Mrs G Scott The Glebe House, Law Road North Berwick East Lothian EH39 4PL Tel: (North Berwick) 01620 892608	HIGHLY COMMENDED Listed	2 Twin 1 Double	2 En Suite fac 1 Priv. NOT ensuite 1 Pub Bath/Show	B&B per person £16.50-£20.00 Double	Open Jan-Dec	
		Former Georgian Manse (1780) furnished in period style and set in own grounds above North Berwick with views of the sea and Berwick Law.				
Mrs P Swanston Chestnut Lodge, 2A Ware Road North Berwick East Lothian EH39 4BN Tel: (North Berwick) 01620 894256 Fax: 01620 894256	COMMENDED	2 Twin 1 Double	3 En Suite fac	B&B per person £14.00-£17.00 Double	Open Jan-Dec, ex Xmas/New Year	
		Modern well-appointed house in quiet location. Public transport nearby. Ideal base for golfing and other sporting activities. Private parking.				
NORTH KESSOCK Ross-shire Mrs Jane Clark Kinellan North Kessock Tel: (Kessock) 01463 731459	Map 4 B8 HIGHLY COMMENDED	2 Double	1 En Suite fac 1 Priv. NOT ensuite	B&B per person £14.00-£15.00 Double	Open Apr-Sep	
		Modern bungalow on shore edge with all rooms overlooking the Moray Firth.				

VAT is shown at 17.5%: changes in this rate may affect prices. Prices shown are for guidance only. Please send SAE with each enquiry.

Mrs Grigor Redfield Farm North Kessock Ross-shire IV1 1XD Tel: (Munlochy) 01463 811228	COMMENDED 👑👑👑	1 Twin 1 Double	1 En Suite fac 1 Priv. NOT ensuite 2 Pub Bath/Show	B&B per person from £16.00 Single from £16.00 Double Room only per person from £13.00	Open Jan-Dec Dinner 1900-2000 B&B + Eve. Meal £23.00-£24.00	

On mixed working farm, 4 miles (7kms) north of Inverness,
large family farmhouse. Home baking.

Mrs D Hewlett Drumlochy, Drumsmittal North Kessock Ross-shire IV1 1XF Tel: (North Kessock) 01463 731427	APPROVED 👑👑	2 Family	2 En Suite fac	B&B per person £14.00-£16.00 Double	Open Jan-Dec	

Modern bungalow set in beautiful farming country just 4 miles (6kms)
from Inverness. Family atmosphere with prize-winning ponies and floppy rabbit.

Mr & Mrs R S Prentice Kilda, 3 Bellfield Drive North Kessock Ross-shire IV1 IXT Tel: (Kessock) 01463 731567	COMMENDED Listed	1 Twin 1 Double	1 Pub Bath/Show	B&B per person £15.00 Single £13.50 Double	Open May-Sep	

Situated right on the seafront with uninterrupted views across the Beauly Firth.
Dolphin viewing from the property.

OBAN Argyll	Map 1 E2

Ardblair
Dalriach Road, Oban, Argyll PA34 5JD
Tel: 01631 562668

Oban's Leading Guest House

We're the third generation of this family-run business. We specialise in home-cooking and good old-fashioned friendly welcome and comfort. Our spacious sun-lounge and our garden have magnificent views over Oban Bay, and yet we're very central – only 3 minutes' walk from the town centre. Our safe car park takes 10 cars. We're very easy to find: just turn left half way down the hill coming into Oban, up past the tennis courts, swimming pool and there we are! We'll gladly send you a brochure, or why not phone **Ian and Monika Smyth**.

AA QQQ and RAC Acclaimed

Ardblair Guest House Dalriach Road Oban Argyll PA34 5JD Tel: (Oban) 01631 562668	COMMENDED 👑👑👑	3 Single 3 Twin 6 Double 3 Family Suite avail	12 En Suite fac 1 Limited ensuite 2 Pub Bath/Show	B&B per person £18.00-£21.00 Single £27.00-£31.00 Double Room only per person £18.00-£21.00	Dinner from 1830	

Personally run guest house close to town centre, swimming pool and
all amenities. Off-street parking.

Beechgrove Guest House Croft Road Oban Argyll PA34 5JL Tel: (Oban) 01631 566111	COMMENDED 👑👑👑	1 Twin 1 Double 1 Family	3 En Suite fac	B&B per person from £17.50 Double	Open Mar-Oct Dinner from 1800 B&B + Eve. Meal from £28.00	

Family run guest house a short walk from the harbour and shops,
with pleasant views of Oban Bay and the Sound of Kerrera.

OBAN continued	Map 1 E2						
Braehead Guest House Albert Road Oban Argyll PA34 5EJ Tel: (Oban) 01631 563341	COMMENDED ♔	2 Twin 3 Double 1 Family	1 En Suite fac 2 Pub Bath/Show	B&B per person £18.00-£20.00 Single	Open Jan-Dec	

Attractive house convenient for town centre. Ground-floor ensuite.
Private parking area.

| Mrs Calderwood
The Torrans, Drummore Road
Oban
Argyll
Tel: (Oban) 01631 565342 | COMMENDED ♔♔ | 1 Twin
2 Double | 2 En Suite fac
1 Priv. NOT ensuite | B&B per person
£17.00-£20.00 Single
£14.00-£17.00 Double | Open Jan-Dec | |

Comfortable family home in quiet residential cul-de-sac.
1 mile (2kms) from town centre and all amenities.

Glenara Guest House

ROCKFIELD ROAD, OBAN, ARGYLL PA34 5DQ
Telephone: 01631 563172

We offer to our guests a quality of room and breakfast (vegetarians catered for) which will ensure your return. *Glenara Guest House* is centrally situated with off-street parking. The house is individually furnished reflecting Dorothy's enthusiasm for objets d'art.
For the comfort of our guests we are a no-smoking house.

| Glenara Guest House
Rockfield Road
Oban
Argyll
PA34 5DQ
Tel: (Oban) 01631 563172 | COMMENDED ♔♔ | 1 Single
1 Twin
3 Double
1 Family | 4 En Suite fac
1 Limited ensuite
1 Priv. NOT ensuite
1 Pub Bath/Show | B&B per person
£16.00-£20.00 Single
£16.00-£20.00 Double | Open Jan-Dec | |

Family run guest house close to the town centre and all amenities.
Private parking. Non-smoking house.

| Glenroy Guest House
Rockfield Road
Oban
Argyll
PA34 5DQ
Tel: (Oban) 01631 562585 | COMMENDED ♔♔ | 1 Single
1 Twin
5 Double | 4 En Suite fac
3 Pub Bath/Show | B&B per person
£16.00-£17.00 Single
£15.00-£17.50 Double | Open Jan-Dec | |

Family run guest house overlooking Oban Bay.
Centrally situated and convenient for all amenities. Private parking.

| Mrs Harrold
Latheron, Longsdale Road
Oban
Argyll
PA34 5JU
Tel: (Oban) 01631 564974 | HIGHLY COMMENDED ♔♔ | 1 Twin
1 Double | 2 En Suite fac | B&B per person
£20.00-£25.00 Single
£17.00-£20.00 Double | Open Apr-Sep | |

Family home in quiet residential area of Oban. Close to town centre,
swimming pool, harbour and all amenities.

OAKBANK

BENVOULIN ROAD, OBAN, ARGYLL PA34 5EF
Telephone: 01631 563482

A family home situated overlooking Oban Bay with panoramic views across to the Hills of Mull. Only a five-minute walk to the Town Centre and all amenities including bus, train and ferry terminals (pick-up can be arranged). A friendly welcome is guaranteed as well as helpful holiday advice.

Sadie & Tam Hobbs Oakbank, Benvoulin Road Oban Argyll Tel: (Oban) 01631 563482	COMMENDED 👑	1 Twin 2 Double	1 Limited ensuite 1 Pub Bath/Show	B&B per person £12.00-£16.00 Single £12.00-£16.00 Double	Open Jan-Dec

Small family run bed and breakfast with fine views across Kerrera to the Isle of Mull, yet only 4 minutes walk from town centre, harbour and promenade.

Mrs Hopkin Ardview, Ardconnel Road Oban Argyll PA34 5DP Tel: (Oban) 01631 565112	COMMENDED Listed	1 Twin 1 Double	1 Pub Bath/Show	B&B per person £16.00-£17.00 Single	Open Jan-Dec

In an elevated position with views to Oban Bay and backing onto famous McCaig's Tower. Only 5 minutes walk from the town.

Drumriggend

DRUMRIGGEND, DRUMMORE ROAD, OBAN PA34 4JL
Telephone: 01631 563330

Drumriggend is situated in a quiet residential setting although only 10 - 15 minutes walk from the Town Centre. Private parking. All bedrooms ensuite. Colour TV, central heating, welcome tray, radio alarm, cots available. Morning call for early departure. Dinner available by request.

AA QQQQ   RAC Acclaimed   Highly Commended 👑👑👑

J & D Ledwidge Drumriggend, Drummore Road Oban Argyll PA34 4JL Tel: (Oban) 01631 563330	HIGHLY COMMENDED 👑👑👑	1 Twin 1 Double 1 Family	3 En Suite fac	B&B per person £16.00-£17.00 Single £15.00-£16.00 Double Room only per person £10.00	Open Jan-Dec Dinner 1800-1900 B&B + Eve. Meal £20.00-£24.00

Detached house in quiet residential area. Situated on the south side of town about 1 mile (2kms) from the centre.

Mrs B MacColl Glengorm, Dunollie Road Oban Argyll PA34 5PH Tel: (Oban) 01631 565361	COMMENDED 👑	1 Twin 3 Double	2 Pub Bath/Show	B&B per person £13.00-£16.00 Double	Open Apr-Oct

Attractively decorated, Victorian terraced house on level ground near town centre, convenient for restaurants, entertainments, shops and ferries.

WELCOME

Whenever you are in Scotland, you can be sure of a warm welcome at your nearest Tourist Information Centre.

For guide books, maps, souvenirs, our Centres provide a service second to none – many now offer bureau-de-change facilities. And, of course, Tourist Information Centres offer free, expert advice on what to see and do, route-planning and accommodation for everyone – visitors and residents alike!

OBAN continued	Map 1 E2

BRACKER

Polvinister Road, Oban, Argyll PA34 5TN
Telephone/Fax: 01631 564302

Modern bungalow situated in beautiful quiet residential area within walking distance of town (approx. 8-10 mins.) and the golf course. All bedrooms have private facilities, TV and tea/coffee-making. TV lounge, private parking.

Mrs C MacDonald Bracker, Polvinister Road Oban Argyll PA34 5TN Tel: (Oban) 01631 564302	COMMENDED	1 Twin 2 Double	3 En Suite fac	B&B per person to £18.00 Single £16.00-£17.00 Double	Open Mar-Nov	
		Modern family bungalow in secluded residential area. Short distance from town centre and all amenities. Private parking.				

Mrs MacDougall Harbour View, Shore Street Oban Argyll PA34 4LQ Tel: (Oban) 01631 563462	APPROVED	2 Twin 3 Family	2 Pub Bath/Show	B&B per person £13.00-£15.50 Double	Open Jan-Dec	
		Centrally situated and convenient for a level stroll to ferry, railway station and shops.				

ARGYLL VILLA

Albert Road, entrance on Dalriach Road, Oban PA34 5EJ
Telephone: 01631 566897

A comfortably furnished Victorian House retaining many original features. *Argyll Villa* is a no-smoking establishment. Centrally, yet privately, situated on *Oban Hill* and close to all amenities. All rooms have colour TV, hospitality trays and panoramic views over *Oban Bay* to the *Bens of Mull*. There is a pleasant secluded garden for guests' use.

Mrs McGill Argyll Villa, Albert Road via Dalriach Road Oban Argyll PA34 5EJ Tel: (Oban) 01631 566897	COMMENDED	1 Twin 2 Double	1 En Suite fac 1 Pub Bath/Show	B&B per person £15.00-£22.00 Double	Open Jan-Dec	
		Victorian house. Terraced gardens with pleasant seating areas. All rooms have panoramic views to the Bens of Mull and beyond.				

Mrs E M MacLean Lorne View, Ardconnel Road Oban Argyll PA34 5DW Tel: (Oban) 01631 565500	COMMENDED	1 Twin 2 Double	3 Limited ensuite 2 Pub Bath/Show	B&B per person £15.50-£16.50 Double	Open Mar-Oct Dinner at 1815 B&B + Eve. Meal £26.50-£44.00	
		Quiet location overlooking Oban Bay. Convenient for local sports amenities and town centre. Evening meals with advance notice except Sundays.				

The Old Manse Guest House Dalriach Road Oban Argyll PA34 5JE Tel: (Oban) 01631 564886	COMMENDED	1 Twin 2 Double	3 En Suite fac	B&B per person £18.00-£21.00 Single £18.00-£21.00 Double	Open Feb-Nov Dinner from 1830 B&B + Eve. Meal £26.00-£30.00	
		Victorian house set high above the town with fine views. Private parking and all rooms with private facilities. Real home-cooked food.				

"Dungrianach"

Deluxe
👑👑

(Gaelic – 'the sunny house on the hill')

Although only a few minutes walk from Oban ferry piers and town centre, Dungrianach sits in private woodland, right above the yacht moorings and enjoys unsurpassed views of sea and islands. Accommodation 1 twin and 1 double room, each with private facilities. ***Contact:* Mrs Elaine Robertson, 'Dungrianach', Pulpit Hill, Oban, Argyll PA34 4LX. Telephone: 01631 562840.**

Mrs E Robertson Dungrianach, Pulpit Hill Oban Argyll PA34 4LX Tel: (Oban) 01631 562840	DELUXE 👑👑	1 Twin 1 Double	2 En Suite fac	B&B per person £18.00-£20.00 Double	Open Apr-Sep	
		Secluded, in 4 acres of wooded garden on top of Pulpit Hill. Magnificent views over Oban Bay and the Islands.				

Mrs P Robertson Don-Muir, Pulpit Hill Oban Argyll PA34 4LX Tel: (Oban) 01631 564536 Fax: 01631 563739	COMMENDED 👑👑👑	1 Single 1 Twin 3 Double	3 En Suite fac 2 Pub Bath/Show	B&B per person £15.00-£17.00 Single £15.00-£17.00 Double Room only per person £12.00-£14.00	Open Feb-Oct Dinner 1830-1930 B&B + Eve. Meal £25.50-£27.50	
		Set in quiet residential area, high up on Pulpit Hill and close to public transport terminals. Parking available.				

PINMACHER

Polvinister Road, Oban, Argyll PA34 5TN
Telephone: 01631 563553

Comfortable bungalow in quiet part of Oban, ten minutes walk from bus and rail stations with spacious attractive gardens and ample private parking. Rooms: two double and one twin, all en-suite.
Evening Meal optional.
Prices from £16 B&B.
Brochure and details contact: Ruth Rodaway.

Mrs R Rodaway Pinmacher, Polvinister Road Oban Argyll PA34 5TN Tel: (Oban) 01631 563553	COMMENDED 👑👑👑	1 Twin 2 Double	3 En Suite fac	B&B per person £16.00-£18.00 Single £16.00-£18.00 Double	Open Mar-Oct Dinner 1900-2100 B&B + Eve. Meal £24.00-£28.00	
		Comfortable modern bungalow quietly situated only 10 minutes walk from town centre. Private parking.				

Roseneath Guest House

DALRIACH ROAD, OBAN PA34 5EQ
Telephone: 01631 562929

Victorian house with warm and friendly atmosphere, eight minutes walk from ferries, buses and trains, three minutes from town centre. *Roseneath* is situated in a quiet location close to swimming pool, bowling green, squash and tennis courts. Lovely views over *Oban Bay* to *Mull*. Non-smoking. Private car park.

Roseneath Guest House Dalriach Road Oban Argyll PA34 5EQ Tel: (Oban) 01631 562929	COMMENDED 👑👑	2 Single 2 Twin 6 Double	5 En Suite fac 3 Limited ensuite 2 Pub Bath/Show	B&B per person £14.00-£18.00 Single £14.00-£20.00 Double	Open Jan-Dec	
		Personally run Victorian house in quiet area overlooking town and bay. Near seafront and shops. Private parking.				

OBAN continued	Map 1 E2						
Mrs Russell Torlin House, Glencruitten Road Oban Argyll PA34 4EP Tel: (Oban) 01631 564339	COMMENDED	1 Twin 1 Double 1 Family	3 En Suite fac	B&B per person £14.50-£20.00 Double	Open Jan-Dec Dinner 1800-1900 B&B + Eve. Meal from £25.00		

Stone-built Victorian house in elevated position with off-street parking.
Close to town centre, convenient for restaurants, shops and all activities.

| Sgeir Mhaol Guest House
Soroba Road
Oban
Argyll
PA34 4JF
Tel: (Oban) 01631 62650 | COMMENDED | 1 Twin
2 Double
3 Family | 5 En Suite fac
1 Priv. NOT ensuite
1 Pub Bath/Show | B&B per person
£16.00-£24.00 Single
£16.00-£21.00 Double | Open Jan-Dec
Dinner from 1830
B&B + Eve. Meal
£24.00-£29.00 | | |

Bungalow style, with ample private car parking and only a short walk from
the town centre. All rooms and facilities on the ground floor.

THORNLOE GUEST HOUSE
ALBERT ROAD, OBAN, ARGYLL PA34 5JD
Telephone: 01631 562879

THORNLOE is very central to all local amenities. Large cosy home-
from-home Victorian house. Tea, coffee, television, ensuite for your
comfort in rooms. Substantial breakfast in our dining-room which has
magnificent views over to the *Islands of Kerrera and Mull*. For
something special – 4-poster bedrooms available. Parking Available.

AA QQQ   COMMENDED

| Thornloe Guest House
Albert Road
Oban
Argyll
PA34 5JD
Tel: (Oban) 01631 562879 | COMMENDED | 1 Single
2 Twin
4 Double
1 Family | 6 En Suite fac
2 Pub Bath/Show | B&B per person
£15.00-£20.00 Single
£15.00-£20.00 Double
Room only per person
£15.00-£20.00 | Open Feb-Dec | | |

Completely modernised Victorian semi-detached house in centrally situated
residential area with fine views over Oban Bay towards the Isle of Mull.

| BY OBAN
Argyll
Mrs Margaret MacPherson
Invercairn, Musdale Road
Kilmore, by Oban
Argyll
PA34 4XX
Tel: (Oban) 01631 770301 | Map 1 E2

HIGHLY COMMENDED | 1 Twin
2 Double | 3 En Suite fac | B&B per person
£16.00-£20.00 Double | Open Apr-Sep | | |

Modern bungalow in unspoilt countryside, with superb views.
4 miles (6kms) from Oban.

| OLD DEER, by Peterhead
Aberdeenshire
Mrs Rhind
Old Deer Bank House
6 Abbey Street
Old Deer
Aberdeenshire
AB42 8LN
Tel: (Mintlaw) 01771 623463 | Map 4 G8

COMMENDED | 1 Twin
1 Double | 2 En Suite fac | B&B per person
£17.00-£18.00 Single
£16.00-£17.00 Double | Open Jan-Dec | | |

Originally village bank, now comfortable family home; tastefully refurbished,
in centre of quiet historic village, close to Aden Country Park.

OLDMELDRUM Aberdeenshire	Map 4 G9

CROMLET HILL

SOUTH ROAD, OLDMELDRUM, ABERDEENSHIRE AB51 0AB
Telephone: 01651 872315   Fax: 01651 872164

A superb listed building overlooking *Bennachie* and the *Grampian Hills* beyond. Recently restored, the original features are retained inside and out and the house is furnished in sympathetic and luxurious style. Set in beautiful secluded gardens including a large Victorian conservatory. Private parking. Aberdeen City Centre 30 minutes.

John Page Cromlet Hill, South Road Oldmeldrum Aberdeenshire AB51 0AB Tel: (Oldmeldrum) 01651 872315 Fax: 01651 872164	DELUXE ♛♛♛	1 Twin 3 En Suite fac 1 Double 1 Family	B&B per person £24.00-£40.00 Single £20.00-£35.00 Double	Open Jan-Dec Dinner from 1930 B&B + Eve. Meal £25.00-£50.00

Spacious, elegant listed Georgian mansion in large secluded gardens within conservation area. Airport 20 minutes.

ONICH Inverness-shire	Map 3 G12

Camus House Lochside Lodge

Onich, by Fort William, Inverness-shire PH33 6RY
Telephone: 01855 821200

In extensive lochside gardens, midway between Ben Nevis and Glencoe. Ideal base for touring, walking, climbing and ski-ing. Open from January to November. Most rooms are en-suite with central heating and teasmaid. We provide excellent cooking, friendly service and are licensed.

DB&B £31-£41. Weekly £196 - £273. Brochure available.

Camus House Lochside Lodge Onich Inverness-shire PH33 6RY Tel: (Onich) 01855 821200	COMMENDED ♛♛♛	2 Twin 6 En Suite fac 3 Double 1 Pub Bath/Show 2 Family	B&B per person £17.00-£27.00 Single £17.00-£27.00 Double Room only per person £17.00-£27.00	Open Jan-Nov Dinner to 1915 B&B + Eve. Meal £33.00-£41.00

Large well-appointed house, comfortably furnished, superb views of the sea loch and hills. Fort William 10 miles (16kms), Glencoe 5 miles (8kms).

Mr Collins Tom-na-Creige, North Ballachulish Onich Inverness-shire PH33 6RY Tel: (Onich) 01855 821405	COMMENDED ♛♛	1 Twin 2 En Suite fac 1 Double	B&B per person £15.00-£18.00 Single	Open Jan-Dec

Modern comfortable ensuite accommodation with inspiring views over Loch Linnhe.

Mrs M MacLean Janika, Bunree Onich Inverness-shire PH33 6SE Tel: (Onich) 01855 821359	COMMENDED ♛	1 Twin 1 Pub Bath/Show 1 Double	B&B per person from £15.00 Double	Open Apr-Oct

Family house on five-acre croft, running down to the shores of Loch Linnhe at the Corran Narrows. 8 miles (13 kms) from Fort William.

Tigh-an-Righ House Onich Inverness-shire PH33 6SE Tel: (Onich) 01855 821255/821501	APPROVED ♛♛	1 Single 2 En Suite fac 2 Double 2 Pub Bath/Show 3 Family	B&B per person £14.00-£15.50 Single £14.00-£15.50 Double	Open Jan-Dec Dinner 1845-2050 B&B + Eve. Meal £25.50-£26.50

Personally run guest house on the main A82 tourist route and convenient for the Corran Ferry. Home cooking using fresh produce. One annexe bedroom.

Details of Grading and Classification are on page vi.   Key to symbols is on back flap.

ORD, Sleat **Isle of Skye, Inverness-shire** Mrs B La Trobe Fiordhem Ord Isle of Skye, Inverness-shire IV44 8RN Tel: (Tarskavaig) 01471 855226	Map 3 E10	COMMENDED	1 Twin 3 Double	3 En Suite fac 1 Pub Bath/Show	B&B per person £20.00-£25.00 Single £20.00-£25.00 Double	Open Apr-Oct Dinner 1830-1930 B&B + Eve. Meal £30.00-£35.00	
Unique stone cottage, 20 feet from lochside. Breathtaking views of Cuillins and the Small Isles. Location of distinction.							
OUT SKERRIES **Shetland** Mrs K Johnson Rocklea, East Isle Out Skerries Shetland ZE2 9AS Tel: (Out Skerries) 01806 515228	Map 5 H3	COMMENDED	1 Single 1 Twin 1 Double	2 Pub Bath/Show	B&B per person £13.50 Single £13.50 Double Room only per person £8.00	Open Jan-Dec Dinner 1800-2100 B&B + Eve. Meal £20.00	
Family run, fully modernised house close to the pier. Bird watching, seal watching and sea fishing available.							
PAISLEY **Renfrewshire** Dryfesdale Guest House 37 Inchinnan Road Paisley Renfrewshire PA3 2PR Tel: 0141 889 7178	Map 1 H5	APPROVED Listed	1 Single 1 Twin 1 Family	2 Pub Bath/Show	B&B per person £18.00-£20.00 Single £15.00-£17.00 Double	Open Jan-Dec Dinner 1800-2000	
Privately owned guest house 0.5 mile (1km) from Glasgow Airport and M8 access. Close to Paisley and all facilities.							
Myfarrclan Guest House 146 Corsebar Road Paisley Renfrewshire PA2 9NA Tel: 0141 884 8285 Fax: 0141 884 8285		DELUXE	1 Twin 2 Double	2 En Suite fac 1 Priv. NOT ensuite	B&B per person £30.00-£35.00 Single £25.00-£30.00 Double	Open Jan-Dec Dinner 1900-2030 B&B + Eve. Meal £40.00-£45.00	
Detached bungalow in residential area, convenient for Glasgow Airport. Non-smoking house.							
BY PAISLEY **Renfrewshire** Ashburn Guest House Milliken Park Road Kilbarchan, by Paisley Renfrewshire PA10 2DB Tel: (Kilbarchan) 01505 705477 Fax: 01505 705477	Map 1 H5	APPROVED	1 Single 3 Twin 2 Family	2 En Suite fac 2 Pub Bath/Show	B&B per person £18.00-£30.00 Single £18.00-£26.50 Double Room only per person £16.00-£28.00	Open Jan-Dec Dinner 1800-2000	
19th-century house in an acre of garden, 5 minutes from Glasgow Airport. 20 minutes to Glasgow city centre. 400 yds from railway station.							
PATHHEAD **Midlothian** Mrs Lothian Fala Hall Farm Fala, Pathhead Midlothian EH37 5SZ Tel: (Humbie) 01875 833249	Map 2 D5	COMMENDED Listed	1 Double 1 Family	2 Pub Bath/Show	B&B per person £14.00-£16.00 Double	Open Jan-Dec	
Picturesque 17th-century farmhouse on working farm peacefully set in rolling countryside, yet only 17 miles (27kms) from Edinburgh.							
PEAT INN **Fife** Mrs I Grant West Mains Farm Peat Inn Fife KY15 5LF Tel: (Peat Inn) 01334 840313	Map 2 D3	COMMENDED Listed	1 Twin 1 Double	1 Pub Bath/Show	B&B per person £13.00-£15.00 Double	Open Apr-Oct	
Home baking on mixed farm with open views of countryside. Good base for touring Fife fishing villages. 7 miles (11kms) from St Andrews.							

PEEBLES	Map 2 C6						
Mr K Bowie Minniebank Guest House Greenside Peebles EH45 8JA Tel: (Peebles) 01721 722093		COMMENDED ♛♛	2 Twin 1 Double	2 En Suite fac 1 Pub Bath/Show	B&B per person £20.00-£25.00 Single £18.00-£25.00 Double	Open Jan-Dec Dinner 1900-1930 B&B + Eve. Meal £30.50-£37.50	
			Family run Victorian house c.1895 in quiet residential area overlooking River Tweed. Private parking. Evening meals available.				
Mrs D Davidson Hillside, 44 Edinburgh Road Peebles EH45 8EB Tel: (Peebles) 01721 729817		COMMENDED Listed	1 Double 1 Family	1 En Suite fac 1 Pub Bath/Show	B&B per person £14.00-£16.00 Double	Open Jan-Dec exc Xmas/New Year	
			Detached house with delightful gardens situated on the outskirts of the town - ideal as a touring base.				
Mrs Sheila Goldstraw Venlaw Farm Peebles EH45 8QG Tel: (Peebles) 01721 722040		COMMENDED ♛♛	1 Twin 2 Double 1 Family	2 En Suite fac 1 Priv. NOT ensuite 1 Pub Bath/Show	B&B per person £20.00-£24.00 Single £15.00-£17.50 Double Room only per person £20.00	Open Apr-Oct	
			Personally run modern farmhouse near Peebles. Ideal for walking, fishing and golfing. Good base for touring.				
Mrs Haydock Winkston Farmhouse Peebles EH45 8PH Tel: (Peebles) 01721 721264		HIGHLY COMMENDED ♛♛	1 Twin 2 Double	1 En Suite fac 2 Pub Bath/Show	B&B per person £15.00-£16.00 Double	Open Apr-Oct	
			'B' Listed Georgian farmhouse of historical interest, in own grounds. Friendly family atmosphere. On main bus route, 21 miles (34kms) from Edinburgh.				
Evelyn Inglis Robingarth, 46 Edinburgh Road Peebles EH45 8EB Tel: (Peebles) 01721 720226		COMMENDED Listed	2 Twin 1 Double	1 En Suite fac 1 Pub Bath/Show	B&B per person from £15.00 Double	Open Jan-Dec	
			Personally run, stone-built bungalow offering comfortable accommodation. 0.5 miles (1 km) to town facilities. Ideal touring base.				
Susan Isherwood Grey Gables, Springwood Road Peebles EH45 9HB Tel: (Peebles) 01721 721252		COMMENDED Listed	1 Twin 1 Double	1 Pub Bath/Show	B&B per person £15.00 Single £15.00 Double	Open May-Sep Dinner 1800-1900 B&B + Eve. Meal £20.00	
			Former coachhouse of character in quiet residential area. Vegetarian food a speciality, evening meal on request.				

LINDORES

60 Old Town, Peebles EH45 8JE
Telephone: 01721 720441

Stone-built late Victorian house on edge of town, situated on main A72 tourist route; convenient for touring the Borders and Edinburgh. Secure parking. All bedrooms have central heating, colour TV and tea/coffee-making facilities.

| Mr & Mrs C Lane
Lindores
60 Old Town
Peebles
EH45 8JE
Tel: (Peebles) 01721 720441 | | COMMENDED ♛♛ | 1 Twin
1 Double
3 Family | 2 En Suite fac
2 Pub Bath/Show | B&B per person
£15.00-£20.00 Single
£14.00-£18.00 Double | Open Jan-Dec | |
| | | | Stone-built late Victorian town house near edge of town, situated on main A72 tourist route. Convenient for touring the Borders and Edinburgh. | | | | |

Details of Grading and Classification are on page vi.

Key to symbols is on back flap.

PEEBLES continued	Map 2 C6						

Mrs E McTeir
Colliedean, 4 Elibank Road,
Eddleston
Peebles
EH45 8QL
Tel: (Eddleston) 01721 730281

COMMENDED
Listed

1 Twin 1 Pub Bath/Show
1 Double

B&B per person
to £17.50 Single
to £15.00 Double

Open Apr-Oct

Quietly situated in small village on main bus route to Edinburgh and Borders towns.
Homely and friendly atmosphere. Good restaurant within walking distance.

Mrs Morrison
9 Witchwood Crescent
Peebles
EH45 9AJ
Tel: (Peebles) 01721 721206

COMMENDED
Listed

1 Single 1 Pub Bath/Show
1 Double

B&B per person
from £16.00 Single
from £15.50 Double

Open Apr-Oct

Quiet, comfortable, modern house in pleasant surroundings.
Ideal base for touring and walking.

Mrs Muir
Whitestone House,
Innerleithen Road
Peebles
EH45 8BD
Tel: (Peebles) 01721 720337

COMMENDED

1 Twin 2 Pub Bath/Show
1 Double
1 Family

B&B per person
£15.00-£15.50 Double

Open Jan-Dec

Personally run Victorian house with fine views to surrounding hills.
Ideal touring base for fishing and walking. Parking.

Mrs Jean Kenyon Phillips
Drummore, Venlaw High Road
Peebles
EH45 8RL
Tel: (Peebles) 01721 720336
Fax: 01721 723004

COMMENDED

1 Twin 1 Pub Bath/Show
1 Double

B&B per person
from £16.00 Double

Open Apr-Sep

Hillside house in quiet cul-de-sac off the A703.
Ideally situated for visiting Edinburgh and the Borders.

Mrs M Teasdale
4 Langside Drive
Peebles
Tel: (Peebles) 01721 721931

HIGHLY
COMMENDED

2 Double 1 En Suite fac
1 Priv. NOT ensuite

B&B per person
£17.00-£18.00 Single

Open Apr-Sep

Large attractive bungalow and garden with extensive hill views, situated
on rural outskirts. Ideal for visiting the beautiful Borders and Edinburgh.

BY PEEBLES	Map 2 C6						

Mrs A Campbell
Langhaugh Farmhouse
Kirkton Manor, by Peebles
Peeblesshire
EH45 6JF
Tel: (Kirkton Manor)
01721 740226

COMMENDED

2 Double 2 En Suite fac
2 Family 1 Priv. NOT ensuite
1 Pub Bath/Show

B&B per person
£20.00-£22.00 Single
£20.00-£22.00 Double
Room only per person
£20.00-£22.00

Open Jan-Dec
Dinner 1700-2200
B&B + Eve. Meal
£30.00-£35.00

Large, modernised farmhouse, situated on 2000-acre hill-farm in the
picturesque Manor Valley, 8 miles from Peebles. Excellent base for hill-walkers.

Mrs R Smith
Chapel Hill Farm
Peebles
EH45 8PQ
Tel: (Peebles) 01721 720188

COMMENDED

1 Twin 3 En Suite fac
2 Double 1 Pub Bath/Show

B&B per person
£17.50-£20.00 Single
Room only per person
£22.00

Open May-Sep

Farmhouse c.1695 on working farm offering warm welcome.
Peaceful rural setting yet only 1 mile (2kms) from Peebles.
23 miles (38kms) Edinburgh.

Mrs A Waddell
Lyne Farmhouse, Lyne Farm
Peebles
EH45 8NR
Tel: (Kirkton Manor)
01721 740255

COMMENDED
Listed

1 Twin 2 Priv. NOT ensuite
2 Double 2 Pub Bath/Show

B&B per person
£15.00-£18.00 Single
£15.00-£18.00 Double

Open Mar-Nov

Victorian farmhouse on mixed farm with magnificent views over Stobo Valley.
4 miles (6kms) west of Peebles on A72. 23 miles (32kms) from Edinburgh.

VAT is shown at 17.5%: changes in this rate may affect prices. Prices shown are for guidance only. Please send SAE with each enquiry.

PENICUIK Midlothian	Map 2 C5

Woodhouselee Stables

Easter Howgate, Midlothian EH26 0PF
Telephone: 0131 445 3020

Built in 1809 this traditional stable block with cobbled courtyard is set in 5 acres nestling at the foot of the Pentland Hills in quiet countryside yet only 7 miles from the centre of Edinburgh. We offer comfortable accommodation, hearty breakfast and the company of our family pets.

Mrs Irene Allan Woodhouselee Stables Easter Howgate Midlothian EH26 0PF Tel: 0131 445 3020	COMMENDED Listed	1 Twin 2 Double	1 En Suite fac 1 Pub Bath/Show	B&B per person £18.00-£19.00 Double	Open May-Sep

Traditional, stone-built (1809) stables with cobblestone courtyard.
Set at the foot of the Pentland Hills.

BY PENICUIK Midlothian	Map 2 C5

Patieshill Farm

CARLOPS, PENICUIK EH26 9ND
Telephone: 01968 660551

This is a working hill sheep and cattle farm. Set in the midst of the Pentland Hills with panoramic views of the surrounding countryside yet only 20 minutes drive from the City of Edinburgh. A perfect centre for touring Central Scotland.

A very warm and friendly welcome awaits visitors.

Mrs Janet Burke Patieshill Farm Carlops, by Penicuik Midlothian EH26 9ND Tel: (West Linton) 01968 660551	COMMENDED	1 Twin 2 Double	3 En Suite fac	B&B per person to £20.00 Single to £18.00 Double	Open Jan-Dec

Panoramic views from this hill farm just off A702 13 miles (21 kms)
from Edinburgh. New guest wing all on one level.

M & R Marwick Walltower Farm Howgate, by Penicuik Midlothian EH26 8PY Tel: (Penicuik) 01968 672277	COMMENDED	1 Twin 1 Double 1 Family	1 En Suite fac 1 Pub Bath/Show	B&B per person £12.00-£26.00 Single £13.00-£22.00 Double Room only per person £10.00-£18.00	Open Jan-Dec

Traditional farmhouse, with conservatory, set in mature garden. 10 miles (16 kms)
from Edinburgh and airport. Access to Borders. Non-smoking bedrooms.

BE SURE TO CHOOSE THE SCOTTISH TOURIST BOARD'S SIGN OF QUALITY

| PERTH
Perthshire | Map 2
B2 | | |

"Abercrombie"
85 Glasgow Road, Perth PH2 0PQ
Telephone/Fax: 01738 444728
This beautiful Victorian town house has just been completely refurbished to a very high standard. We are only five minutes walk from the town centre and two minutes from leisure pool, ice rink and bowling rink etc. Ample parking, all rooms en-suite.
IDEAL BASE FOR TOURING OR GOLFING!

| Abercrombie Guest House
85 Glasgow Road
Perth
PH2 0PQ
Tel: (Perth) 01738 444728 | HIGHLY
COMMENDED
Listed | 2 Single
1 Twin
1 Double | 3 En Suite fac
1 Priv. NOT ensuite | B&B per person
£18.00-£25.00 Single
£15.00-£25.00 Double
Room only per person
£13.00-£23.00 | Open Jan-Dec | |
| | | | | | | |

Family-run, Victorian town house, five minutes from town centre.
Ample parking. Ideal for all outdoor activities.

| Achnacarry Guest House
3 Pitcullen Crescent
Perth
PH2 7HT
Tel: (Perth) 01738 621421
Fax: 01738 444110 | HIGHLY
COMMENDED | 1 Twin
1 Double
2 Family | 3 En Suite fac
1 Priv. NOT ensuite | B&B per person
£18.00-£25.00 Single
£18.00-£20.00 Double | Open Jan-Dec
Dinner 1830-1930
B&B + Eve. Meal
£26.00-£34.50 | |

Friendly, family run guest house with off-street parking in an ideal touring area.
One ensuite room on ground floor.

| Adam Guest House
6 Pitcullen Crescent
Perth
PH2 7HT
Tel: (Perth) 01738 627179 | COMMENDED | 1 Single
1 Twin
2 Double
1 Family | 2 En Suite fac
1 Priv. NOT ensuite
1 Pub Bath/Show | B&B per person
£16.00-£18.50 Single
£16.00-£18.50 Double
Room only per person
£14.00-£16.50 | Open Jan-Dec
Dinner 1830-1930
B&B + Eve. Meal
£24.50-£27.00 | |

Small and friendly guest house beside A94, with private off-road parking.
Good home cooking.

| Albert Villa Guest House
63 Dunkeld Road
Perth
PH1 5RP
Tel: (Perth) 01738 622730 | COMMENDED | 3 Single
2 Twin
2 Double
2 Family | 6 En Suite fac
1 Pub Bath/Show | B&B per person
£16.00-£20.00 Single
£17.00-£18.00 Double | Open Jan-Dec | |

Family guest house with ample car parking, close to sports centre and
swimming pool. Ground-floor bedrooms each have their own entrance.

| Almond Villa Guest House
51 Dunkeld Road
Perth
PH1 5RP
Tel: (Perth) 01738 629356 | COMMENDED | 1 Single
1 Twin
1 Double
2 Family | 3 En Suite fac
1 Pub Bath/Show | B&B per person
£14.00-£18.00 Single
£14.00-£18.00 Double
Room only per person
£14.00-£18.00 | Open Jan-Dec
Dinner from 1830
B&B + Eve. Meal
£21.00-£27.50 | |

Semi-detached Victorian villa, close to town centre, Gannochy Trust Sports Complex,
the North Inch and River Tay. NON-SMOKING HOUSE.

| Arisaig Guest House
4 Pitcullen Crescent
Perth
PH2 7HT
Tel: (Perth) 01738 628240
Fax: 01738 628240 | HIGHLY
COMMENDED | 1 Single
1 Twin
1 Double
2 Family | 4 En Suite fac
1 Priv. NOT ensuite | B&B per person
£17.00-£19.00 Single
£17.00-£19.00 Double
Room only per person
from £15.00 | Open Jan-Dec | |

Comfortable family run guest house, with off-street parking.
Close to city's many facilities; local touring base. Ground-floor bedroom.

Auld Manse Guest House Pitcullen Crescent Perth PH2 7HT Tel: (Perth) 01738 629187	COMMENDED	1 Single 1 Twin 2 Double 1 Family	2 En Suite fac 1 Pub Bath/Show	B&B per person £16.00-£18.00 Single £16.00-£18.00 Double	Open Jan-Dec Dinner from 1830 B&B + Eve. Meal £23.00-£25.00	

Former church manse, now family run guest house. On main A94, 10 minutes walk to city centre, 1 mile (2kms) from Scone Palace. Private parking.

Beechgrove Guest House Dundee Road Perth PH2 7AD Tel: (Perth) 01738 636147	HIGHLY COMMENDED	1 Single 2 Twin 2 Double 1 Family	6 En Suite fac	B&B per person £25.00-£45.00 Single £20.00-£25.00 Double	Open Jan-Dec	

Listed building and former manse set in extensive grounds. Peaceful and quiet, yet only a few minutes walk from the city centre. 1 annexe room.

Mrs Anne Campbell St Leonard's House, 4 St Leonard's Bank Perth Perthshire PH2 8EB Tel: (Perth) 01738 627874 Fax: 01738 627874	COMMENDED	1 Twin 4 Family	4 En Suite fac 1 Priv. NOT ensuite	B&B per person £17.50-£20.00 Single £15.00-£17.50 Double	Open Jan-Dec Dinner 1800-1930 B&B + Eve. Meal to £25.50	

Traditional stone house in quiet central location. Two minutes walk from railway station. Ideal touring centre. Private parking.

Clark Kimberley

57-59 Dunkeld Road, Perth PH1 5RP
Tel: 01738 637406   Fax: 01738 643983

Clark Kimberley is a small bed and breakfast establishment, ideally situated for exploring beautiful Perthshire and its many attractions. Personally run by Ian and Kathryn Sayer, the proprietors, it offers comfortable, well-equipped accommodation, with most rooms having en-suite facilities. A warm and friendly welcome awaits.

Clark Kimberley 57-59 Dunkeld Road Perth PH1 5RP Tel: (Perth) 01738 637406 Fax: 01738 643983	COMMENDED	2 Single 2 Double 4 Family	6 En Suite fac 1 Pub Bath/Show	B&B per person £17.00-£25.00 Single £16.00-£19.00 Double	Open Jan-Dec	

Detached house on main Inverness road out of the city. City centre within walking distance. Private parking.

Clunie Guest House 12 Pitcullen Crescent Perth PH2 7HT Tel: (Perth) 01738 623625	COMMENDED	1 Single 1 Twin 2 Double 3 Family	7 En Suite fac	B&B per person from £18.00 Single from £18.00 Double	Open Jan-Dec Dinner from 1800 B&B + Eve. Meal from £27.00	

Personally run in residential part of town. Easy access to town centre and on main bus route.

The Darroch Guest House 9 Pitcullen Crescent Perth PH2 7HT Tel: (Perth) 01738 636893	COMMENDED	2 Single 1 Twin 1 Double 2 Family	3 En Suite fac 1 Pub Bath/Show	B&B per person £14.00-£16.50 Single £14.00-£18.50 Double	Open Jan-Dec Dinner at 1830 B&B + Eve. Meal £21.50-£26.00	

Semi-detached, Victorian villa, easily found on main A94 tourist route. Double-glazed throughout. Extensive breakfast menu. Off-street parking.

Details of Grading and Classification are on page vi. | Key to symbols is on back flap. | 233

PERTH continued	Map 2 B2						

The Gables Guest House
24 Dunkeld Road
Perth
PH1 5RW
Tel: (Perth) 01738 624717
Fax: 01738 624717

COMMENDED 👑

4 Single | 2 Pub Bath/Show
1 Twin
1 Double
2 Family

B&B per person
£18.00-£20.00 Single
£17.00-£19.00 Double

Open Jan-Dec
Dinner 1800-1900
B&B + Eve. Meal
£26.00-£28.00

Stone-built house on main road 1/2 mile (1km) north of city centre.
Close to sports centre, swimming pool and local golf course. Parking.

Mrs V Harding
Rhodes Villa, 75 Dunkeld Road
Perth
PH1 5RP
Tel: (Perth) 01738 628466

COMMENDED 👑👑👑

1 Single | 4 En Suite fac
2 Twin
1 Double

B&B per person
£16.00-£18.50 Single
£16.00-£18.50 Double

Open Jan-Dec
Dinner 1700-1930
B&B + Eve. Meal
£22.00-£24.00

Personal attention and a friendly welcome. Close to amenities with
private parking. En route to the north; ideally situated for touring.

Hazeldene Guest House
Pitcullen Crescent
Perth
PH2 7HT
Tel: (Perth) 01738 623550

COMMENDED 👑👑

1 Single | 5 En Suite fac
1 Twin
2 Double
1 Family

B&B per person
from £18.00 Single
from £16.00 Double

Open Jan-Dec

Family run guest house, on main tourist route to north east but near to
city centre. Private car parking available.

Iona Guest House
2 Pitcullen Crescent
Perth
PH2 7HT
Tel: (Perth) 01738 627261

COMMENDED 👑👑

2 Single | 2 En Suite fac
1 Twin | 2 Pub Bath/Show
1 Double
1 Family

B&B per person
£15.00-£19.00 Single
£15.00-£19.00 Double

Open Jan-Dec
Dinner 1800-1930
B&B + Eve. Meal
£22.00-£27.00

In residential area, 10 minutes from the town centre with private parking.
Over 30 golf courses within 30 miles (48kms) radius.

Kinnaird Guest House
5 Marshall Place
Perth
PH2 8AH
Tel: (Perth) 01738
628021/630685
Fax: 01738 444056

HIGHLY
COMMENDED 👑👑👑

1 Single | 7 En Suite fac
4 Twin
2 Double

B&B per person
from £19.00 Single
from £19.00 Double

Open Jan-Dec
Dinner from 1800

Georgian house, centrally situated overlooking park. Private parking.
Short walk to town centre and convenient for railway and bus stations.

Kinnoull Guest House
5 Pitcullen Crescent
Perth
PH2 7HT
Tel: (Perth) 01738 634165

COMMENDED 👑👑👑

1 Twin | 4 En Suite fac
2 Double
1 Family

B&B per person
from £15.00 Single
£15.00-£20.00 Double
Room only per person
from £12.00

Open Jan-Dec
Dinner 1800-1900
B&B + Eve. Meal
£24.00-£28.00

Family run guest house on main tourist route north (A94),
within easy reach of city centre. Private facilities for all bedrooms.

Lochiel House
Pitcullen Crescent
Perth
PH2 7HT
Tel: (Perth) 01738 633183

COMMENDED 👑👑

1 Twin | 1 Priv. NOT ensuite
2 Double | 1 Pub Bath/Show

B&B per person
£15.00-£20.00 Single
£15.00-£20.00 Double

Open Jan-Dec
Dinner from 1800
B&B + Eve. Meal
£23.00-£29.00

Delightful, comfortable Victorian terraced house, own parking close to town
centre. One room with private bathroom. Exceptional breakfast selection.

Mr & Mrs McNicol
Abbotsford, 23 James Street
Perth
PH2 8LX
Tel: (Perth) 01738 635219

COMMENDED
Listed

1 Single | 6 Limited ensuite
2 Twin
3 Family

B&B per person
£16.00 Single
£14.00-£16.00 Double

Open Jan-Dec

Victorian villa, in quiet residential area, a few minutes walk from the town centre,
station and bus station. All rooms have shower and colour TV.

Clifton House

36 Glasgow Road, Perth PH2 0PB

Telephone: 01738 621997

A delightful Victorian house situated on the outskirts of the city centre, in an elevated position affording views across the city from all rooms. Accommodation is very tastefully furnished and your hosts Colin and Margaret assure you of a very warm welcome and a very comfortable stay.

Mr & Mrs Moreland Clifton House 36 Glasgow Road Perth Perthshire PH2 0PB Tel: (Perth) 01738 621997	COMMENDED	1 Single 1 Double 1 Family	2 En Suite fac 1 Priv. NOT ensuite	B&B per person £15.00-£17.50 Single £15.00-£17.50 Double	Open Jan-Dec

Delightful Victorian house, within easy walking distance of town centre. Ample private parking. Ideal location for all leisure facilities.

Park Lane Guest House 17 Marshall Place Perth PH2 8AG Tel: (Perth) 01738 637218 Fax: 01738 643519	HIGHLY COMMENDED	1 Single 2 Twin 2 Double 1 Family	6 En Suite fac	B&B per person £18.00-£22.00 Single £18.00-£22.00 Double Room only per person £18.00-£22.00	Open Jan-Dec

Georgian house overlooking Perth South Inch but next to city centre. All ensuite rooms, private car park. Walking distance to golf course.

Mr & Mrs Reid Ballabeg, 14 Keir Street, Bridgend Perth PH2 7HJ Tel: (Perth) 01738 620434	COMMENDED	1 Single 1 Double 1 Family	1 Pub Bath/Show	B&B per person £16.00-£18.00 Single £16.00-£18.00 Double	Open Jan-Dec

Friendly, family run house in quiet street off A94. Evening snacks available in rooms. 10 minutes from the city centre.

Mrs P Smith Beeches, 2 Comely Bank Perth PH2 7HU Tel: (Perth) 01738 624486	COMMENDED	2 Single 1 Twin 1 Double	3 En Suite fac 2 Pub Bath/Show	B&B per person £16.00-£20.00 Single £16.00-£20.00 Double	Open Jan-Dec Dinner 1800-1900 B&B + Eve. Meal from £24.00

Semi-detached villa with ample car parking, conveniently situated on A94 tourist route.

STRATHCONA

45 Dunkeld Road, Perth PH1 5RP

Tel: 01738 628773/626701   Fax: 01738 628773

A warm comfortable spacious house (1876) situated in Perth – a beautiful floral city and the ideal centre for touring. There is so much to see and do in this scenic area and the Mortons will be happy to help you plan your days out and arrange holiday activities.

Strathcona 45 Dunkeld Road Perth PH1 5RP Tel: (Perth) 01738 628773/626701 Fax: 01738 628773	COMMENDED	1 Twin 1 Double 1 Family	2 En Suite fac 1 Priv. NOT ensuite	B&B per person £18.00-£25.00 Single £18.00-£19.00 Double	Open Jan-Dec

Semi-detached Victorian villa on main road into Perth. Comfortable and welcoming. Rooms ensuite or with private facilities. Golfing can be arranged.

Tigh Mhorag Guest House 69 Dunkeld Road Perth PH1 5RP Tel: (Perth) 01738 622902	COMMENDED	2 Single 2 Twin 2 Double	3 En Suite fac 1 Pub Bath/Show	B&B per person £15.00-£16.00 Single £30.00-£32.00 Double	Open Jan-Dec Dinner from 1800

Family run guest house with well-kept garden to rear, and convenient for town centre.

PERTH continued

Map 2
B2

Mrs Angela Young
Inchview, 25 Marshall Place
Perth
PH2 8AG
Tel: (Perth) 01738 629610

APPROVED
Listed

1 Single	2 En Suite fac
1 Double	1 Limited ensuite
1 Family	2 Pub Bath/Show

B&B per person
£17.00-£18.00 Single
£16.00-£18.00 Double

Open Jan-Dec

Centrally situated overlooking South Inch Park.
Winner of Perth's Best Floral Display 1991.

BY PERTH

Map 2
B2

Mr and Mrs Iain Comrie
Lismore, 1 Rorrie Terrace
Methven, by Perth
PH1 3PL
Tel: (Methven) 01738 840441

COMMENDED
Listed

| 1 Twin | 1 Pub Bath/Show |
| 1 Double | |

B&B per person
£12.50-£16.50 Single
£12.50-£13.50 Double

Open Dec-Oct

Comfortable home in quiet residential area of village,
6 miles (10kms) from Perth. Good base for touring.

TOPHEAD FARM

· TULLYBELTON, STANLEY, BY PERTH PH1 4PT
Telephone and Fax: 01738 828259

Enjoy the panoramic views from the verandah of this farmhouse which
is tastefully furnished. Superking beds in two of the three comfortable
bedrooms. Guests can relax in the lounge and enjoy breakfasts with a
difference. A good centre for touring, fishing and walking. Glasgow,
Edinburgh and St. Andrews *1 hour away* with Dundee, Pitlochry and
Crief *30 minutes away*. **Come on and spoil yourselves!**

Mrs Dorothy Dow
Tophead Farm, Tullybelton
Stanley, by Perth
Perthshire
PH1 4PT
Tel: (Stanley) 01738 828259
Fax: 01738 828259

HIGHLY
COMMENDED
♛♛♛

1 Twin	1 En Suite fac
1 Double	1 Priv. NOT ensuite
1 Family	1 Pub Bath/Show

B&B per person
£14.00-£18.00 Single
£16.00-£22.00 Double

Open Jan-Dec

A very warm Scottish welcome in this traditional farmhouse on 200-acre
dairy farm. Perth 4 miles (6kms). Extensive views over rural Perthshire.

Mrs A Guthrie
Newmill Farm
Stanley, Perth
Perthshire
PH1 4QD
Tel: (Stanley) 01738 828281

COMMENDED
♛♛♛

| 1 Twin | 3 En Suite fac |
| 2 Double | 2 Pub Bath/Show |

B&B per person
£16.00-£20.00 Single
£16.00-£20.00 Double

Open Feb-Oct
Dinner 1800-1900
B&B + Eve. Meal
£26.00-£30.00

Traditional farm house on 330-acre arable farm. Convenient for the A9
6 miles (10kms) from Perth. Suitable for fishing and other outdoor pursuits.

Mrs Howden
Stanley Farm
Stanley
Perthshire
PH1 4QQ
Tel: (Stanley) 01738 828334

COMMENDED
Listed

| 1 Double | 2 Pub Bath/Show |
| 1 Family | |

B&B per person
£15.00-£19.00 Single
£13.00-£15.00 Double

Open Apr-Oct
Dinner 1900-2030
B&B + Eve. Meal
£21.00-£24.00

Friendly family farmhouse central for touring Perthshire.
Home cooking and baking. Children especially welcome.

HUNTINGTOWER HOUSE

Crieff Road, Perth PH1 3JJ   Tel: 01738 624681

*This is a charming country house with a large secluded garden, near
Perth. There is easy access to main routes throughout Scotland,
and so is an excellent stop for touring holidays or business.
There is ample parking for cars and a friendly welcome is assured.*

Mrs H Lindsay
Huntingtower House
Crieff Road, by Perth
Perthshire
PH1 3JJ
Tel: (Perth) 01738 624681

COMMENDED
♛

| 2 Twin | 1 Pub Bath/Show |
| 1 Double | |

B&B per person
£14.00-£16.00 Single
£14.00-£16.00 Double

Open Jan-Dec

Detached Victorian house with 3/4 acre secluded garden.
Convenient for touring with easy access to the A85 and A9.

VAT is shown at 17.5%: changes in this rate may affect prices. Prices shown are for guidance only. Please send SAE with each enquiry.

Mrs D McFarlane Letham Farm Bankfoot Perthshire PH1 4EF Tel: (Bankfoot) 01738 787322	COMMENDED	1 Twin 1 Double 1 Family	2 Pub Bath/Show	B&B per person £15.00-£17.00 Single £14.00-£15.00 Double	Open Mar-Oct Dinner from 1830 B&B + Eve. Meal £22.00-£23.00

300-acre arable and raspberry farm in beautiful countryside, yet only 10 minutes from Perth. Warm welcome and home cooking.

Mrs Irene Millar Blackcraigs Farmhouse Balbeggie, by Perth Perthshire PH2 7PJ Tel: (Balbeggie) 01821 640254	COMMENDED Listed	2 Twin 1 Double	1 En Suite fac 1 Pub Bath/Show	B&B per person £15.00-£18.00 Single £15.00-£18.00 Double Room only per person £12.00-£15.00	Open Jan-Dec

A warm welcome at this comfortable farmhouse peacefully situated on 260-acre mixed farm, 4 miles (6kms) from Perth.

Pitmurthly

REDGORTON, NEAR LUNCARTY, BY PERTH PH1 3HX
Telephone: 01738 828363   Fax: 01738 828053

Comfortable farmhouse with peaceful garden 4 miles north of Perth (off A9). Bedrooms tastefully furnished, comfortable beds and lovely views. Spacious lounge and dining room for guests. An ideal location for touring Perthshire or for relaxing. Walking, golf, fishing, and good restaurants nearby. River Tay 2 miles.
En-suite available. Ample safe parking. Open all year.
Highly commended. Contact Mrs C Smith.

Mrs C Smith Pitmurthly Farm, Redgorton by Luncarty, by Perth Perthshire PH1 3HX Tel: (Perth) 01738 828363	HIGHLY COMMENDED Listed	1 Single 1 Twin 1 Double	1 En Suite fac 1 Pub Bath/Show	B&B per person £15.00-£18.00 Single £15.00-£18.00 Double	Open Jan-Dec

Traditional Scottish hospitality at this comfortable farmhouse set in peaceful countryside 5 minutes from historic Perth. Ideal for touring, golf and walking.

Mrs Stirrat Fingask Farm Rhynd, by Perth Perthshire PH2 8QF Tel: (Perth) 01738 812220	COMMENDED Listed	1 Single 1 Twin 1 Double	2 Pub Bath/Show	B&B per person from £15.00 Single	Open Feb-Nov Dinner from 1830 B&B + Eve. Meal from £22.50

Enjoy the lovely garden and home cooking at this traditional farmhouse on mixed working farm, approximately 5 miles (8kms) south east of Perth.

Waterybutts Lodge Grange Errol Perthshire PH2 7SZ Tel: (Errol) 01821 642894 Fax: 01821 642523	COMMENDED	3 Twin 5 Double	8 En Suite fac	B&B per person £32.50-£35.00 Single £27.50-£30.00 Double Room only per person £25.00-£27.50	Open Jan-Dec Dinner 1900-2200 B&B + Eve. Meal £47.50-£50.00

Beautiful Georgian Lodge with fine grounds, shrubs and trees and a unique herb garden. Set in the gentle climatic region of the Carse of Gowrie.

PETERHEAD **Aberdeenshire**	Map 4 H8					
Carrick Guest House 16 Merchant Street Peterhead Aberdeenshire AB42 6DU Tel: (Peterhead) 01779 470610 Fax: 01779 470610		COMMENDED	2 Single 3 Twin 2 Family	7 En Suite fac	B&B per person £16.00-£20.00 Single £16.00-£20.00 Double	Open Jan-Dec

Comfortable accommodation, centrally situated for all amenities. Two minutes walk from main shopping centre, harbour and beach.

PITLOCHRY **Perthshire**	Map 2 A1					
Mrs S A Anderson Silver Howe, Perth Road Pitlochry Perthshire PH16 5LY Tel: (Pitlochry) 01796 472181		HIGHLY COMMENDED	2 Twin 2 Double	4 En Suite fac	B&B per person £20.00 Single	Open Jan-Dec

Detached modern bungalow on town outskirts with large south-facing garden and open outlook to Tummel Valley.

	Map 2 A1						
PITLOCHRY continued Mrs Beattie Cresta, 15 Lettoch Terrace Pitlochry Perthshire PH16 5BA Tel: (Pitlochry) 01796 472204		COMMENDED Listed	1 Single 1 Twin 1 Double	1 Pub Bath/Show	B&B per person £14.50-£15.00 Single	Open Apr-Oct	

A friendly welcome in this B&B in a quiet central part of Pitlochry.
Ideal location for touring Perthshire.

Carra-Beag Guest House

16 Toberargan Road, Pitlochry, Perthshire PH16 5HG
Telephone: 01796 472835

Centrally situated in its own grounds with commanding views and ample parking. All rooms have tea/coffee making facilities, colour TV as well as telephones to let someone know you have arrived. Central heating throughout. Nine bedrooms with en-suite facilities. Relax during dinner in our dining room, overlooking the hills. We offer a four course dinner, with a choice of menu. Table license. Patio and putting green. *For colour brochure and tariff please contact the resident proprietor Archie McGhie.*

Carra Beag Guest House 16 Toberargan Road Pitlochry Perthshire PH16 5HG Tel: (Pitlochry) 01796 472835		APPROVED ♚♚♚	3 Single 3 Twin 4 Double 2 Family	9 En Suite fac 1 Pub Bath/Show	B&B per person £18.00-£27.50 Single £18.00-£27.50 Double Room only per person £15.00-£27.00	Open Jan-Dec Dinner 1800-1830 B&B + Eve. Meal £27.00-£40.00	

Quiet and relaxing, centrally situated with commanding views and ample parking.
Patio and putting green. One ensuite annexe.

Craigroyston House

2 LOWER OAKFIELD, PITLOCHRY PH16 5HQ
Telephone: 01796 472053

A Victorian Country House set in own grounds with views of the surrounding hills. Centrally situated, there is direct pedestrian access to the town centre.

★ All rooms have private facilities and are equipped to a high standard.
★ Colour TV, welcome tray, central heating.
★ Residents' lounge.
★ Dining room with separate tables.
★ Safe private parking.
★ Dinner available.
★ Table licence.

AA SELECTED QQQQ

Bed & Breakfast from £18 per person.

Craigroyston House 2 Lower Oakfield Pitlochry Perthshire PH16 5HQ Tel: (Pitlochry) 01796 472053		HIGHLY COMMENDED ♚♚♚	3 Twin 3 Double 2 Family	8 En Suite fac	B&B per person £18.00-£25.00 Single £18.00-£25.00 Double	Open Jan-Dec Dinner 1815-1900 B&B + Eve. Meal £30.00-£37.00	

Family run Victorian villa near town centre with large garden overlooking
wooded hills. 10 minutes walk from theatre.

Derrybeg Guest House

18 Lower Oakfield, Pitlochry PH16 5DS
Telephone: 01796 472070

DERRYBEG is set in a quiet location only a few minutes walk from the town centre, enjoying magnificent views of the Vale of Atholl. The resident proprietors, Derek and Marion Stephenson, ensure only the finest hospitality, comfort, and good home cooking.

- Open all year for B&B or DB&B. Unlicensed, but guests welcome to supply own table wine.
- Full central heating throughout.
- Colour television and welcome tea/coffee tray in all bedrooms.
- All bedrooms with private facilities.
- Comfortable lounge and dining room.
- Food Hygiene Excellent Award.
- Ample parking in the grounds.
- Leisure activities can easily be arranged, i.e. theatre bookings, golf, fishing, pony-trekking, etc.

Colour brochure/tariff and details of weekly reductions available on request.

HIGHLY COMMENDED

Derrybeg Guest House 18 Lower Oakfield Pitlochry Perthshire PH16 5DS Tel: (Pitlochry) 01796 472070	**HIGHLY COMMENDED** 👑👑👑	2 Single 2 Twin 6 Double 1 Family	11 En Suite fac	B&B per person £16.00-£22.00 Single £16.00-£22.00 Double Room only per person from £12.00	Open Jan-Nov Dinner 1815-1845 B&B + Eve. Meal £27.00-£34.00	

Privately owned detached house with large south-facing garden in quiet, but central location. Elevated position overlooking Tummel Valley. 3 annexe rooms.

DUNDARAVE HOUSE

Situated in one of the most enviable areas of Pitlochry, in its own grounds of approx. $\frac{1}{2}$ acre. Dundarave offers the tourist of the 1990s every comfort and amenity required.

- *All rooms, colour TV and tea/coffee-making facilities.*
- *All double/twin-bedded rooms with bathrooms en-suite.*
- *Fully heated.*
- *Residents' lounge – open all day.*

For your overnight stay or longer please contact your hosts: Mae and Bob Collier.

**SPECIAL AA QUALITY AWARD
STB COMMENDED** 👑👑👑

STRATHVIEW TERRACE, PITLOCHRY
Telephone: 01796 473109

Dundarave House Strathview Terrace Pitlochry Perthshire PH16 5AT Tel: (Pitlochry) 01796 473109	**COMMENDED** 👑👑👑	2 Single 2 Twin 2 Double 1 Family	5 En Suite fac 2 Pub Bath/Show	B&B per person £22.00-£28.00 Single £22.00-£28.00 Double	Open Mar-Oct Dinner 1800-1900 B&B + Eve. Meal from £36.00	

Charming Victorian house, quiet location and stunning views close to centre of Pitlochry. Ground-floor room; personal, attentive service.

	Map 2 A1						
PITLOCHRY continued Mrs Miller Dunreen, 8 Lettoch Terrace Pitlochry Perthshire PH16 5BA Tel: (Pitlochry) 01796 472974		COMMENDED Listed	2 Double	1 Pub Bath/Show	B&B per person £14.00 Single £14.00 Double	Open Mar-Oct	

A warm welcome awaits in a comfortable house in a quiet residential area. Private parking. Convenient for town centre. Ideal location for touring.

KINNAIRD HOUSE

Kirkmichael Road, Pitlochry, Perthshire PH16 5JL
Telephone: 01796 472843

Our spacious elegant home is freshly decorated and furnished to a very high standard with your comfort in mind. All bedrooms have new private bath/shower rooms, colour television, radio alarm, beverage trays and duvets and electric blankets on all beds.
We are recommended for our healthy hearty breakfasts!

Mr & Mrs A Norris Kinnaird House Kirkmichael Road Pitlochry Perthshire PH16 5JL Tel: (Pitlochry) 01796 472843	HIGHLY COMMENDED	1 Twin 2 Double	3 En Suite fac	B&B per person £20.00-£25.00 Double	Open Jan-Dec	

Detached Victorian villa in rural setting 1.5 miles (2.5 kms) from the town. Superb views of the surrounding countryside.

The Poplars 27 Lower Oakfield Pitlochry Perthshire PH16 5DS Tel: (Pitlochry) 01796 472129/472554	COMMENDED	2 Twin 3 Double 3 Family	7 En Suite fac 1 Priv. NOT ensuite 1 Pub Bath/Show	B&B per person £19.00-£21.00 Single £17.00-£20.00 Double	Open Apr-Oct Dinner 1830-1900 B&B + Eve. Meal £26.00-£30.00	

Personally run, with large garden in elevated position overlooking town. Quiet location. Home cooking.

Mrs Spaven Wester Knockfarrie Knockfarrie Road Pitlochry Perthshire PH16 5DN Tel: (Pitlochry) 01796 472020	HIGHLY COMMENDED	1 Twin 2 Double	3 En Suite fac	B&B per person £16.00-£22.00 Single	Open Apr-Nov	

Victorian house, elegantly furnished, in quiet location. Open views across Strathtummel and the hills beyond.

COMAR HOUSE

Strathview Terrace, Pitlochry PH16 5AT
Tel: 01796 473531 Fax: 01796 473811

COMAR HOUSE enjoys panoramic views of Pitlochry and the Tummel Valley. It is the ideal base for the discerning traveller.

Perthshire has many varied attractions and Pitlochry with the famous Festival Theatre and Salmon Ladder attracts visitors from all corners of the world.

A warm welcome awaits you from *Isabel and Bill Watson.*

Mr & Mrs W Watson Comar House, Strathview Terrace Pitlochry Perthshire PH16 5AT Tel: (Pitlochry) 01796 473531 Fax: 01796 473811	COMMENDED	1 Single 3 Twin 1 Double 1 Family	3 En Suite fac 1 Pub Bath/Show	B&B per person £16.00-£20.00 Single £16.00-£22.00 Double	Open Apr-Oct	

A friendly welcome in this elegant turreted period house standing high above town with panoramic views.

| Wellwood House
West Moulin Road
Pitlochry
Perthshire
PH16 5EA
Tel: (Pitlochry) 01796 474288/
Fax: 01796 474288 | COMMENDED ♛♛ | 1 Single
4 Twin
4 Double
1 Family | 8 En Suite fac
2 Limited ensuite
2 Pub Bath/Show | B&B per person
£21.50-£25.00 Single
£21.50-£25.00 Double | Open Mar-Nov |
| | | | | | |

Victorian villa, fine views over town yet only 200 yards to town centre. Ideal location for touring Perthshire.

| Mrs Ann Williamson
Lynedoch, 9 Lettoch Terrace
Pitlochry
Perthshire
PH16 5BA
Tel: (Pitlochry) 01796 472119 | COMMENDED
Listed | 1 Twin
2 Double | 2 Pub Bath/Show | B&B per person
£14.00-£15.00 Single
£14.00-£15.00 Double | Open Mar-Oct |
| | | | | | |

Accommodation in adjoining annexe to house in quiet residential area. Convenient for all amenities near the centre of Pitlochry.

| **PLOCKTON**
Ross-shire | Map 3
F9 |

SYBIL CAMERON

2 Frithard Road, Plockton, Ross-shire IV52 8TQ
Telephone: 01599 544226

Bed and Breakfast comfortable family home situated in the village of Plockton looking on to the Applecross Hills. An ideal centre for touring the Highlands. One mile from railway station and six miles from the ferry to Skye.
2 Double and 1 Family – £14-£15 per person. OPEN ALL YEAR.

| Mrs Cameron
2 Frithard Road
Plockton
Ross-shire
IV52 8TQ
Tel: (Plockton) 01599 544226 | COMMENDED ♛♛ | 3 Double | 1 Priv. NOT ensuite
2 Pub Bath/Show | B&B per person
£14.00-£15.00 Single
£14.00-£15.00 Double | Open Jan-Dec |
| | | | | | |

Semi-detached house, comfortable warm and quiet. Ideal for all ages. Situated near village and loch. Ground-floor rooms.

THE SHIELING

THE SHIELING, PLOCKTON, ROSS-SHIRE IV52 8TL
Telephone: 01599 544282

Comfortable, family home centrally situated in Plockton, *1994 Winner of the Tourist Village of the Year* and featured in BBC's *Hamish MacBeth*. Panoramic views over Loch Carron from our spacious residents' lounge, within walking distance of hotels. Ideal base for touring and walking.

| Mrs Jane MacDonald
The Shieling
Plockton
Ross-shire
IV52 8TL
Tel: (Plockton) 01599 544282 | COMMENDED ♛♛ | 2 Double
1 Family | 1 En Suite fac
1 Pub Bath/Show | B&B per person
from £14.00 Double | Open Apr-Oct |
| | | | | | |

Family home with a beautiful view over Loch Carron. Short walk to shops and hotels. Ideal centre for touring and walking.

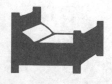

Book your accommodation anywhere in Scotland the easy way – through your nearest Tourist Information Centre.

A booking fee of £2.75 is charged, and you will be asked for a small deposit.

Local bookings are usually free, or a small fee will be charged.

PLOCKTON continued	Map 3 F9

TOMACS
FRITHARD, PLOCKTON, ROSS-SHIRE IV52 8TQ
Telephone: 01599 544321

We are situated at the far end of Plockton, five minutes walk from the hotels and shops. Our comfortable family home has spectacular views of *Loch Carron* and the *Applecross Hills*. Plockton is renowned for its scenery and won the Scottish Tourism Oscar for *Best Village for Tourism 1994.*

Mrs Janet Mackenzie Jones Tomacs, Frithard Plockton Ross-shire IV52 8TQ Tel: (Plockton) 01599 544321	F9	COMMENDED Listed	1 Twin 1 Double 1 Family	1 En Suite fac 1 Priv. NOT ensuite 1 Pub Bath/Show	B&B per person from £15.00 Single from £15.00 Double	Open Jan-Dec	

Comfortable family home in quiet location in village of Plockton.

An-Caladh
25 Harbour Street, Plockton, Ross-shire IV52 8TN
Telephone: 01599 544356

Traditional white-washed Highland cottage overlooking Plockton Bay. Centrally heated throughout. Relax and enjoy the breathtaking views from our garden opening onto the shore. Ideal base for hillwalking, this year we are offering evening wildlife or sea angling trips in our own D.O.T. licensed vessel. Special rates for residents.

Mrs MacAulay Rowe An Caladh, 25 Harbour Street Plockton Ross-shire IV52 8TN Tel: (Plockton) 01599 544356		COMMENDED ♛♛	1 Twin 2 Double	2 En Suite fac 1 Priv. NOT ensuite	B&B per person £15.00-£22.00 Double	Open Jan-Dec	

Traditional cottage, family run, overlooking the bay in peaceful conservation village.

POOLEWE Ross-shire Mrs K MacDonald Benlair, Near Cove Poolewe Ross-shire IV22 2LS Tel: (Poolewe) 01445 781354	Map 3 F7	COMMENDED ♛	2 Twin	2 En Suite fac	B&B per person from £19.00 Double	Open Apr-Oct Dinner from 1800	

Family run cottage in tranquil setting with superb views over the sea, 200 yards from sandy beach, near village of Cove. Occasional evening meals.

Mrs R MacIver Creagard, 2 Naast Poolewe Ross-shire Tel: (Poolewe) 01445 781389		COMMENDED Listed	1 Single 1 Twin 2 Double	1 Pub Bath/Show	B&B per person £11.50-£12.00 Single £12.50-£13.00 Double Room only per person £11.50-£12.00	Open Apr-Oct Dinner 1800-1900 B&B + Eve. Meal £19.50-£20.50	

Modern croft house overlooking Loch Ewe and the Munros beyond. 6 miles (10kms) from Inverewe Gardens.

When you visit a Tourist Information Centre you are guaranteed a welcome by people who really know their country.

For information, maps, holiday reading, accommodation bookings and much more, look for the information [i]

PORT CHARLOTTE Isle of Islay, Argyll	Map 1 B6

NERABUS
Port Charlotte, Isle of Islay PA48 7UE
Telephone and Fax: 01496 850431

House by sea, stunning views of Paps of Jura and Loch Indaal. Peaceful fields 2 miles outside Port Charlotte. Spa bath, all bedrooms ensuite, local produce for meals. Peat fires. Ground floor rooms.

| Mrs P Halsall
Nerabus
Port Charlotte
Isle of Islay, Argyll
PA48 7IIF
Tel: (Port Charlotte)
01496 850431
Fax: 01496 850431 | COMMENDED
👑 | 3 Twin | 3 En Suite fac
1 Pub Bath/Show | B&B per person
to £16.50 Single
from £16.50 Double | Open Jan-Dec
Dinner 1830-2030 | |

Detached house in idyllic setting, overlooking Loch Indaal to the south of the island. Ground-floor bedroom with ensuite spa bath.

PORT ELLEN Isle of Islay, Argyll	Map 1 C6

Glenmachrie Farmhouse
Mrs Rachel Whyte, Port Ellen, Isle of Islay, Argyll PA42 7AW
Tel/Fax: 01496 302560

Glenmachrie is a large traditional farmhouse set in a stone-walled garden by the river and surrounded by 450 acres which support Scottish Blackface Sheep, Highland ponies and Highland cattle. Furnished to a high standard Glenmachrie offers total comfort, friendly welcomes and excellent local and farm-produced food. All bedrooms, tastefully decorated, have full en-suite facilities. The dining room, set with crystal and silverware, provides the ideal setting for our delicious food which has been awarded membership to the "Taste of Scotland". Glenmachrie offers you true Highland hospitality, delicious local food and wonderful memories of an unforgettable Hebridean Holiday!

Highly Commended 👑👑👑

| Glenmachrie Guest House
(Mrs R Whyte)
Glenmachrie Farmhouse
Port Ellen
Isle of Islay, Argyll
PA42 7AW
Tel: (Port Ellen) 01496 302560 | HIGHLY
COMMENDED
👑👑👑 | 3 Twin
2 Double | 5 En Suite fac
1 Pub Bath/Show | B&B per person
£30.00-£40.00 Single
£25.00-£30.00 Double | Open Jan-Dec
Dinner 1900-2000
B&B + Eve. Meal
£40.00-£45.00 | |

Farmhouse in quiet location, fine views westwards across Laggan Bay towards the Rhinns. Family-run farm using the best of Islay's larder. Private fishing for wild brown trout.

| Mrs MacTaggart
Kintra Farmhouse
Kintra Beach, Port Ellen
Isle of Islay, Argyll
PA42 7AT
Tel: (Port Ellen) 01496 302051 | COMMENDED
Listed | 1 Twin
1 Double
1 Family | 2 Pub Bath/Show | B&B per person
£18.00-£20.00 Single
£16.00-£18.00 Double | Open Jan-Dec
Dinner 1700-2100 | |

Traditional farmhouse on 1000-acre hill farm situated beside miles of beach and moorland with walks, birdlife and historical sites. Gaelic spoken.

| The Trout-Fly
Restaurant & Guest House
Port Ellen
Isle of Islay, Argyll
PA42 7DF
Tel: (Port Ellen) 01496 302204 | COMMENDED
Listed | 2 Twin
1 Double | 2 Limited ensuite
2 Pub Bath/Show | B&B per person
from £15.00 Single
from £15.00 Double | Open Jan-Dec
Dinner 1700-2100 | |

Guest house and restaurant in town centre. Convenient for ferry terminal, airport and golf course.

Details of Grading and Classification are on page vi. | Key to symbols is on back flap. | 243

PORTNAHAVEN Isle of Islay, Argyll Mrs MacLean Glenview House Portnahaven Isle of Islay, Argyll PA47 7SL Tel: (Portnahaven) 01496 860303	Map 1 B6	COMMENDED Listed	1 Twin 1 Double 1 Family	1 Pub Bath/Show	B&B per person £14.50-£15.50 Double	Open Jan-Dec Dinner 1800-1930	
			Traditional house, sympathetically converted into a family Bed and Breakfast. Situated in picturesque village. Evening meal – choice of courses.				

PORT OF MENTEITH Perthshire Mrs Norma Erskine Inchie Farm Port of Menteith Perthshire FK8 3JZ Tel: (Port of Menteith) 01877 385233	Map 1 H3	COMMENDED	1 Twin 1 Family	1 Pub Bath/Show	B&B per person £13.00-£14.00 Single £13.00-£14.00 Double	Open Apr-Oct Dinner from 1800 B&B + Eve. Meal £21.00-£22.00	
			Family farm on the shores of Lake of Menteith. Traditional, comfortable farmhouse. Home baking and hospitality a priority.				

Mrs C Tough Collymoon Pendicle Port of Menteith Perthshire FK8 3JY Tel: (Buchlyvie) 01360 850222		COMMENDED	1 Double 1 Family	1 Pub Bath/Show	B&B per person £18.00-£19.00 Single £13.00-£14.00 Double	Open Apr-Oct Dinner 1800-1900 B&B + Eve. Meal from £21.00	
			Family run modern bungalow in country setting surrounded by panoramic views. Home cooking a speciality. Salmon and trout fishing available.				

PORT OF NESS Lewis, Western Isles Kate & Anthony Barber Harbour View Port of Ness Lewis, Western Isles HS2 0XA Tel: (Port of Ness) 01851 810735	Map 3 E3	COMMENDED	1 Twin 1 Double	1 Pub Bath/Show	B&B per person £15.00-£18.00 Single £15.00-£18.00 Double	Open Jan-Dec Dinner to 1930 B&B + Eve. Meal £24.50-£28.00	
			Originally a boat builder's house c.1880, now sympathetically converted. Tea room with home baking and cooking; vegetarians welcome. No smoking.				

PORTPATRICK Wigtownshire Mrs A Moffat Braefield House Portpatrick Wigtownshire DG9 8TA Tel: (Portpatrick) 01776 810255	Map 1 F10	COMMENDED	1 Single 2 Twin 3 Double 1 Family	4 En Suite fac 1 Pub Bath/Show	B&B per person £16.00-£21.00 Single £15.00-£17.00 Double	Open Jan-Dec	
			Family run guest house in excellent position overlooking the harbour, with extensive sea views. Short walk from centre of village.				

PORTREE Isle of Skye, Inverness-shire	Map 3 E9						

AN-AIRIDH

6 FISHERFIELD, PORTREE, ISLE OF SKYE IV51 9EU
Telephone: 01478 612250

The house is situated off the main road within 10 minutes walking distance from Portree overlooking the bay. Accommodation comprises 2 single rooms with H/C facilities, one double with en-suite facilities, one twin with en-suite facilities, also two family rooms with en-suite facilities. Open all year.

Mrs MacLeod An Airidh, 6 Fisherfield Portree Isle of Skye, Inverness-shire IV51 9EU Tel: (Portree) 01478 612250		APPROVED	2 Single 1 Twin 1 Double 2 Family	4 En Suite fac 2 Priv. NOT ensuite 1 Pub Bath/Show	B&B per person to £16.00 Single £19.00-£20.00 Double	Open Jan-Dec Dinner from 1800	
			Modern guest house on edge of Portree overlooking the bay towards Ben Tianavaig and Raasay. Excellent base for exploring Skye.				

		Grading	Rooms	Facilities	B&B	Opening	

Mrs McPhie
Balloch, Viewfield Road
Portree
Isle of Skye, Inverness-shire
IV51 9ES
Tel: (Portree) 01478 612093

COMMENDED

1 Single — 4 En Suite fac
1 Twin
2 Double

B&B per person
from £18.00 Single
from £18.00 Double

Open Mar-Dec

Large comfortable house in own garden on edge of Portree. All rooms ensuite.

Mrs E Nicolson
Almondbank, Viewfield Road
Portree
Isle of Skye, Inverness-shire
JV51 9EU
Tel: (Portree) 01478 612696
Fax: 01478 613114

HIGHLY COMMENDED

2 Twin — 3 En Suite fac
2 Double — 1 Priv. NOT ensuite

B&B per person
£18.50-£25.00 Single
£18.50-£25.00 Double

Open Jan-Dec
Dinner from 1800
B&B + Eve. Meal
£31.00-£37.50

Modern house on the outskirts of Portree.
Well-appointed lounge and dining room with panoramic views of Portree Bay.

The Shielings Guest House
Torvaig
Portree
Isle of Skye, Inverness-shire
IV51 9HU
Tel: (Portree) 01478 613024

COMMENDED

1 Twin — 3 En Suite fac
2 Double — 1 Limited ensuite
1 Family — 1 Priv. NOT ensuite

B&B per person
£16.00-£22.00 Double

Open Jan-Dec
Dinner at 1900
B&B + Eve. Meal
£24.00-£31.00

Converted croft cottage with superb views. Situated just 2 miles (3kms)
outside Portree. Home cooking and a warm homely atmosphere.

Mrs P M Thorpe
Jacamar, Achachork Road
Portree
Isle of Skye, Inverness-shire
IV51 9HT
Tel: (Portree) 01478 612274

COMMENDED

1 Double — 1 En Suite fac
1 Family — 1 Pub Bath/Show

B&B per person
£15.00-£16.00 Single
£12.00-£18.00 Double

Open Jan-Dec
Dinner 1830-1930
B&B + Eve. Meal
£20.00-£26.00

Modern bungalow, with open outlook beyond Portree towards the Cuillins.
Portree 2.5 miles (4 kms).

BY PORTREE
Isle of Skye, Inverness-shire — Map 3 E9
Nevelee Corry
Tianavaig, 1/7 Camastianavaig
Braes, by Portree
Isle of Skye, Inverness-shire
IV51 9LQ
Tel: (Sligachan) 01478 650325

COMMENDED Listed

2 Double — 1 En Suite fac
1 Family — 1 Pub Bath/Show

B&B per person
from £15.00 Single
£14.00-£15.00 Double

Open Feb-Nov

A pretty rural location by the seashore, magnificent sea and mountain views.
Guest lounge with log fire. Portree 5 miles (8kms).

PORT WILLIAM
Wigtownshire — Map 1 G11
Mrs M McMuldroch
Jacob's Ladder
Mochrum, by Port William
Wigtownshire
DG8 9BD
Tel: (Mochrum) 01988 860227

COMMENDED

1 Twin — 2 En Suite fac
2 Double — 1 Pub Bath/Show

B&B per person
£14.00-£18.00 Single
£14.00-£18.00 Double
Room only per person
£14.00-£18.00

Open Jan-Dec
Dinner from 1800
B&B + Eve. Meal
£22.00-£27.00

Farmhouse in a peaceful location. Excellent centre for touring, golf, fishing
and birdwatching. Friendly atmosphere and all home cooking.

PRESTWICK
Ayrshire — Map 1 G7
Fernbank Guest House
213 Main Street
Prestwick
Ayrshire
KA9 1LH
Tel: (Prestwick) 01292 475027

COMMENDED

2 Single — 4 En Suite fac
2 Twin — 1 Priv. NOT ensuite
2 Double — 3 Pub Bath/Show
1 Family

B&B per person
£14.00-£16.00 Single
£16.00-£18.00 Double

Open Jan-Dec

Modernised Edwardian villa near beach and local sports.
1 mile (2kms) from Prestwick Airport.

Mrs Reeve
28 Monkton Road
Prestwick
Ayrshire
KA9 1AR
Tel: (Prestwick) 01292 478816

COMMENDED

1 Single — 1 En Suite fac
2 Double — 1 Pub Bath/Show

B&B per person
£14.00-£18.00 Single
£14.00-£18.00 Double

Open Jan-Dec

Semi-detached, Victorian villa in residential area, with easy access
to airport, railway station and local amenities.

RATHO
Midlothian
Mrs J Small
Ratho Hall, 51 Baird Road
Ratho
Midlothian
EH28 3QY
Tel: 0131 335 3333
Fax: 0131 335 3035

Map 2
B5

HIGHLY
COMMENDED

1 Twin
1 Double

2 En Suite fac

B&B per person
£30.00-£40.00 Single
to £20.00 Double
Room only per person
to £50.00

Open Apr-Oct
Dinner 1900-2300
B&B + Eve. Meal
£40.00-£50.00

A warm welcome awaits you at this classical Georgian House in extensive grounds
with walks, tennis and croquet. Close to Ratho and 1 mile from airport.

RENDALL
Orkney
Mrs I Sinclair
Riff
Rendall
Orkney
KW17 2PB
Tel: (Finstown) 01856 761 541

Map 5
B11

COMMENDED

1 Twin
1 Double

2 Pub Bath/Show

B&B per person
£12.00-£13.00 Single
£11.00 Double

Open Jan-Dec
Dinner 1900-2000
B&B + Eve. Meal
£18.00-£19.00

A fine example of Orcadian hospitality. Mrs Sinclair, in her farmhouse
by the shore, treats you as one of the family. Close to Rousay ferry.

RENFREW

Renfrew Guest House
4 West Avenue
Renfrew
PA4 0SZ
Tel: 0141 886 4350

Map 1
H5

APPROVED
Listed

1 Twin
1 Family

1 Pub Bath/Show

B&B per person
£19.00-£23.00 Single
£15.00-£17.00 Double
Room only per person
£17.00-£21.00

Open Jan-Dec

Family home in quiet residential street. Conveniently situated for airport,
M8 and rail transport. On bus route to Glasgow.

RESTON, by Eyemouth
Berwickshire
Chris & Sheila Olley
Stoneshiel Hall
Reston, by Eyemouth
Berwickshire
TD14 5LU
Tel: (Eyemouth) 018907 61267

Map 2
F5

COMMENDED

1 Twin
1 Double

1 Pub Bath/Show

B&B per person
to £20.00 Single
to £20.00 Double

Open Jan-Dec
Dinner 1800-2100
B&B + Eve. Meal
to £35.00

A warm welcome awaits at this tranquil and historic mansion house,
where home cooking is of particular interest and enjoyment.

ROCKCLIFFE, by Dalbeattie
Kirkcudbrightshire
Millbrae House
Rockcliffe, by Dalbeattie
Kirkcudbrightshire
DG5 4QG
Tel: (Rockcliffe) 01556
630217/0850 038947

Map 2
A10

HIGHLY
COMMENDED

3 Twin
2 Double

4 En Suite fac
1 Priv. NOT ensuite

B&B per person
£15.00-£17.00 Double

Open Jan-Oct
Dinner from 1900
B&B + Eve. Meal
£24.00-£26.00

19th-century guest house close to beach and forest; an ideal base for walkers and
nature lovers. Emphasis on home cooking using fresh local produce.

Torbay Guest House,
Mrs B J Taylor
Torbay Farmhouse
Rockcliffe, by Dalbeattie
Kirkcudbrightshire
DG5 4QE
Tel: (Rockcliffe) 01556 630403
Fax: 01556 630403

DELUXE

1 Twin
2 Double

2 En Suite fac
1 Priv. NOT ensuite

B&B per person
£21.00-£23.00 Single
£17.00-£18.00 Double

Open Mar-Oct
Dinner 1830-1930
B&B + Eve. Meal
£26.00-£28.00

Family house in former farmhouse peacefully situated 0.5 miles (1km) from
picturesque village of Rockcliffe. French and German spoken. Pets welcome.

ROGART **Sutherland** Rovie Farm Guest House Rogart Sutherland 1V28 3YZ Tel: (Rogart) 01408 641209 Fax: 01408 641209	Map 4 B6	COMMENDED ♛	1 Twin 2 Double	2 Pub Bath/Show	B&B per person £16.00-£18.00 Single £16.00-£18.00 Double	Open Apr-Oct Dinner from 1830 B&B + Eve. Meal £29.00-£31.00

Granite farmhouse dating from mid 18th-century with superb views of surrounding hills. Fishing on River Fleet. Parking available.

ROSEMARKIE **Ross-shire** Hillockhead Farmhouse Eathie Road Rosemarkie Ross-shire IV10 8SL Tel: (Fortrose) 01381 621184 Fax: 01381 621184	Map 4 B8	APPROVED ♛♛	1 Twin 1 Double	1 En Suite fac 1 Priv. NOT ensuite	B&B per person £15.00-£17.50 Single £13.50-£15.00 Double Room only per person £13.50-£15.00	Open Jan-Dec Dinner 1800-2000 B&B + Eve. Meal £19.50-£23.50

Comfortable accommodation in a natural setting. This stone-built farmhouse with 164-acre woodland and meadow has magnificent views across the Moray Firth to Fort George and the hills.

ROTHESAY Isle of Bute	Map 1 F5

GLENARCH

21 Craigmore Road, Rothesay, Isle of Bute PA20 9LB
Telephone: 01700 502033

An attractive Victorian family house standing on the shore road with fine views across the Clyde Estuary. Our STB Award assures you of a warm welcome and excellent service. Private parking in our large garden. Attractive guest's lounge, full central heating. En-suite and private facilities available.

Mr & Mrs Clegg Glenarch, 21 Craigmore Road Rothesay Isle of Bute PA20 9LB Tel: (Rothesay) 01700 502033	HIGHLY COMMENDED ♛♛	1 Twin 2 Double	1 En Suite fac 1 Priv. NOT ensuite 1 Pub Bath/Show	B&B per person £27.50-£31.50 Single £17.50-£21.50 Double	Open Jan-Dec

Large family house in quiet residential area. Town centre 1.5 miles (3kms). On main bus route. On seafront with extensive views across Clyde estuary.

ST ABBS **Berwickshire** Castle Rock Guest House Murrayfield St Abbs Berwickshire TD14 5PP Tel: (Coldingham) 01890 771715 Fax: 01890 771520	Map 2 F5	COMMENDED ♛♛♛	1 Single 1 Twin 1 Double 1 Family	4 En Suite fac 1 Pub Bath/Show	B&B per person from £22.00 Single from £22.00 Double	Open Easter-Oct Dinner 1900-1930 B&B + Eve. Meal from £36.00

Good food and comfort plus sea views from all rooms are features of this attractive clifftop house. Close to nature reserve and 3 miles (5kms) from A1.

Wilma Wilson 7 Murrayfield St Abbs Berwickshire TD14 5PP Tel: (Coldingham) 01890 771468	HIGHLY COMMENDED Listed	1 Twin 1 Family	1 Pub Bath/Show	B&B per person £14.00 Single £14.00 Double	Open Jan-Dec

Former fisherman's cottage, in quiet village, close to beach, harbour and nature reserve. Home baking.

BY ST ABBS
Berwickshire
Old Coaching Inn
Westwood House, Houndwood
Eyemouth
Berwickshire
TD14 5TP
Tel: (Grantshouse)
01361 850232
Fax: 01361 850333

Map 2
F5

COMMENDED

1 Single	6 En Suite fac	B&B per person	Open Jan-Dec
2 Twin		£18.00-£27.50 Single	Dinner 1830-2030
1 Double		£18.00-£22.50 Double	B&B + Eve. Meal
2 Family			£27.50-£37.00

Old coaching inn set back from A1. Local Eyemouth seafood a speciality.
Flower arranging, computing and art courses available.

ST ANDREWS
Fife
Mrs M Allan
2 King Street
St Andrews
Fife
KY16 8JQ
Tel: (St Andrews)
01334 476326

Map 2
D2

APPROVED
Listed

1 Twin	2 Priv. NOT ensuite	B&B per person	Open Jan-Dec
1 Double	1 Pub Bath/Show	from £18.00 Single	
		£13.00-£18.00 Double	

Friendly welcome awaits. Quiet. Fairly central.
Within walking distance of town centre and its many amenities.

Argyle House
127 North Street
St Andrews
Fife
KY16 9AG
Tel: (St Andrews)
01334 473387
Fax: 01334 474664

COMMENDED

2 Single	19 En Suite fac	B&B per person	Open Jan-Dec
8 Twin		£20.00-£30.00 Single	
4 Double		£20.00-£30.00 Double	
5 Family		Room only per person	
		£18.00-£28.00	

Family run, late Victorian stone-faced building.
In the town centre 400 yards from famous Old Course and beaches.

Aslar Guest House
120 North Street
St Andrews
Fife
KY16 9AF
Tel: (St Andrews)
01334 473460
Fax: 01334 473460

HIGHLY
COMMENDED

1 Single	5 En Suite fac	B&B per person	Open Jan-Dec
1 Twin		£24.00-£26.00 Single	
2 Double		£24.00-£26.00 Double	
1 Family			

Victorian, family run terraced house furnished to a high standard and centrally
situated for shops, golf courses, restaurants and cultural pursuits. All rooms ensuite.

Brownlees Guest House
7 Murray Place
St Andrews
Fife
KY16 9AP
Tel: (St Andrews)
01334 473868

COMMENDED

2 Single	4 En Suite fac	B&B per person	Open Jan-Dec
1 Twin	2 Pub Bath/Show	£15.00-£22.00 Single	
1 Double		£15.00-£22.00 Double	
2 Family			

Centrally located, personally run Victorian terraced house.
Ideal base for golf, beach and touring.

Cleveden House
3 Murray Place
St Andrews
Fife
KY16 9AP
Tel: (St Andrews)
01334 474212

COMMENDED

2 Single	4 En Suite fac	B&B per person	Open Jan-Dec
2 Twin	1 Priv. NOT ensuite	£17.00-£25.00 Single	
1 Double	1 Pub Bath/Show	Room only per person	
1 Family		£17.00-£25.00	

Personally run guest house, five minutes walk from the Old Course, beaches
and town centre. Large lounge where tea, coffee and home baking served.

Craigmore Guest House
3 Murray Park
St Andrews
Fife
KY16 9AW
Tel: (St Andrews)
01334 472142
Fax: 01334 477963

COMMENDED

1 Twin	6 En Suite fac	B&B per person	Open Jan-Dec
3 Double		£19.00-£35.00 Single	
2 Family		Room only per person	
		£17.00-£25.00	

Long-established very well-appointed traditional stone Guest House in centre
of St Andrews, only minutes from town centre, beaches and "Old Course".

Doune House
5 Murray Place
St Andrews
Fife
KY16 9AP
Tel: (St Andrews) 01334 475195
Fax: 01334 475195

HIGHLY
COMMENDED

1 Single	4 En Suite fac	B&B per person	Open Jan-Dec
1 Twin	1 Priv. NOT ensuite	£17.00-£27.00 Single	
2 Double			
1 Family			

A warm welcome awaits you at this Victorian Town House recently modernised
and beautifully refurbished. Close to town centre, golf courses and historical sites.

Glenderran Guest House 9 Murray Park St Andrews Fife KY16 9AW Tel: (St Andrews) 01334 477951 Fax: 01334 477908	**HIGHLY COMMENDED**	2 Single 1 Twin 2 Double	3 En Suite fac 2 Priv. NOT ensuite	B&B per person £20.00-£26.00 Single £20.00-£26.00 Double	Open Jan-Dec	

Tastefully refurbished Victorian town house retaining some original features. Warm and comfortable atmosphere. Non-smoking throughout.

Lorimer House 19 Murray Park St Andrews Fife KY16 9AW Tel: (St Andrews) 01334 476599 Fax: 01334 476599	**COMMENDED**	1 Single 1 Twin 2 Double 2 Family	4 En Suite fac 1 Limited ensuite 1 Priv. NOT ensuite	B&B per person £17.00-£25.00 Single £17.00-£25.00 Double	Open Jan-Dec	

Carefully restored Victorian town house combining original splendour with modern comfort. 5 minutes walk from town centre and the Old Course.

4 Cairnsden Gardens
St Andrews KY16 8SQ
Telephone: 01334 472433

Spacious modern bungalow in very quiet area.
Good home cooking. Comfortable lounge with TV.
Lots of parking space.

Mrs Lily Mason 4 Cairnsden Gardens St Andrews Fife KY16 8SQ Tel: (St Andrews) 01334 472433	**COMMENDED Listed**	1 Twin 1 Double	2 Pub Bath/Show	B&B per person £16.00-£20.00 Single £14.00-£16.00 Double Room only per person from £14.00	Open Jan-Dec Dinner 1700-2000	

Comfortable personally run bed and breakfast in quiet residential area with private parking. Ideal base for touring Fife and its many golf courses.

Mrs I Methven Ardmore 1 Drumcarrow Road St Andrews Fife KY16 8SE Tel: (St Andrews) 01334 474574	**COMMENDED Listed**	2 Twin	1 Pub Bath/Show	B&B per person £12.00-£14.00 Double	Open Jan-Dec	

Family house in quiet residential area within walking distance of town centre. Convenient for all amenities.

Mrs J Pumford Linton, 16 Hepburn Gardens St Andrews Fife KY16 9DD Tel: (St Andrews) 01334 474673	**HIGHLY COMMENDED**	1 Twin 1 Double	1 En Suite fac 1 Priv. NOT ensuite	B&B per person £18.00-£20.00 Double	Open Apr-Oct	

Spacious Edwardian house, with open views to parkland and beyond. Within a short walk of the town and golf courses. Private parking.

Mrs V Rhind Hazlehead 16 Lindsay Gardens St Andrews Fife KY16 8XB Tel: (St Andrews) 01334 475677	**COMMENDED Listed**	1 Double 1 Family	1 Pub Bath/Show	B&B per person £17.00-£23.00 Single £13.50-£16.00 Double B&B + Eve. Meal £21.00-£24.00	Open Jan-Dec Dinner 1800-2000	

Modern detached villa in quiet residential area 1 mile (2kms) from town centre. Easy parking. Home cooking.

ST ANDREWS	Map 2 D2

Stravithie Country Estate

STRAVITHIE, ST ANDREWS, FIFE KY16 8LT
Tel: 01334 880251 Fax: 01334 880297

Bed and Breakfast on a beautiful old Scottish Country Estate with 30 acres of wooded grounds and gardens. Rooms within east wing of Castle. Facilities within the grounds include horse-riding, trout-fishing, open-air badminton, table-tennis, putting, golf-net, nature trail, launderette and telephone.
How to find us – 3 miles from St Andrews on the Anstruther road. Signpost on right (near Dunino).
B&B FROM £25 per person per night.

Stravithie House Stravithie Country Estate St Andrews Fife KY16 8LT Tel: (St Andrews) 01334 880251 Fax: 01334 880297	COMMENDED 👑👑👑	2 Twin 2 Double	4 En Suite fac	B&B per person £25.00-£30.00 Single £25.00-£28.50 Double Room only per person £15.50-£18.50	Open Mar-Dec Dinner 1800-2000 B&B + Eve. Meal £32.50-£40.00

19th-century mansion house in 30 acres of peaceful grounds with nature walks, trout stream, riding, badminton, putting etc. St Andrews 3 miles (5kms).

West Park House 5 St Mary's Place St Andrews Fife KY16 9UY Tel: (St Andrews) 01334 475933	COMMENDED 👑👑	1 Twin 2 Double 1 Family	3 En Suite fac 1 Pub Bath/Show	B&B per person £18.00-£22.00 Single £16.50-£22.00 Double	Open Jan-Nov

Beautiful, Listed Georgian house c.1830 in heart of historic town. Close to Old Course and all amenities.

BY ST ANDREWS Fife	Map 2 D2

EDENSIDE HOUSE

EDENSIDE, ST ANDREWS, FIFE KY16 9SQ
Telephone: 01334 838108 Fax: 01334 838493

Edenside House enjoys a superb waterfront setting with fine views of the estuary bird sanctuary and nature reserve, yet is within 2¹/₂ miles of St Andrews town (five minutes by car on A91). A listed former Scottish farmhouse predating 1775 now tastefully modernised, **Edenside House** offers a high standard of comfort and is *non-smoking throughout*. All nine double/twin rooms, some ground floor, have ensuite facilities, colour TV and beverage tray. Each room has its own parking space. Our extensive traditional breakfast menu includes fish dishes. There are riding stables nearby. Jim is a keen golfer and is happy to advise our guests on their golfing arrangements.
AA Selected QQQQ

Edenside House Edenside St Andrews Fife KY16 9SQ Tel: (Leuchars) 01334 838108 Fax: 01334 838493	COMMENDED 👑👑	6 Twin 3 Double	9 En Suite fac	B&B per person £20.00-£26.00 Double	Open Mar-Nov

Visible from A91 on approach to St Andrews just over 2 miles (4 kms). Superb setting on Eden estuary waterfront. All rooms ensuite and non-smoking. Own parking.

Mr Peter Erskine Cambo House Kingsbarns, by St Andrews Fife KY16 8QD Tel: (Crail) 01333 450313 Fax: 01333 450987	COMMENDED 👑👑👑	1 Twin 2 Double	2 En Suite fac 2 Priv. NOT ensuite	B&B per person £35.00-£55.00 Single £35.00-£55.00 Double	Open Jan-Dec Dinner 1800-2000	
		Elegant Victorian mansion on wooded coastal estate, close to St Andrews with handsome four-poster bed in principal guest bedroom.				
Feddinch Mansion House Feddinch by St Andrews Fife KY16 8NR Tel: (St Andrews) 01334 477220 Fax: 01334 477220	COMMENDED 👑👑	3 Twin 1 Double 2 Family Suite avail	4 En Suite fac 1 Pub Bath/Show	B&B per person £20.00-£25.00 Single £17.00-£23.00 Double	Open Apr-Oct	
		Fully restored country house in secluded setting 0.5 miles from St Andrews. Swimming Pool, Tennis, Putting Green. Inclusive chauffeur service into town.				

"The Larches"
7 River Terrace, Guardbridge, by St Andrews KY16 0XA
Telephone: 01334 838008 Fax: 01334 838008
Guardbridge is situated on the A919 between St Andrews (3 miles) and Dundee (6 miles). Convenient for golf, riding, beautiful countryside and beaches. All rooms have H&C, Colour TV, tea/coffee facilities. Centrally heated throughout. Residents' lounge always available. VCR with large selection of films plus satellite TV. Early breakfast on request with comprehensive menu *Every home comfort.*

| The Larches
7 River Terrace
Guardbridge, by St Andrews
Fife
KY16 0XA
Tel: (Guardbridge)
01334 838008
Fax: 01334 838008 | COMMENDED 👑 | 1 Twin
1 Double
1 Family | 2 Pub Bath/Show | B&B per person
£17.00-£23.00 Single
£17.00-£18.50 Double | Open Jan-Dec | |
| | | **A former memorial hall, now converted into a family home, near centre of Guardbridge and R.A.F. Leuchars. 4 miles (6kms) from St Andrews.** | | | | |

Pat and Barry Poll
8 ST. ANDREWS ROAD, LARGOWARD, FIFE KY9 1HZ
Telephone: 01334 840523
A warm welcome awaits you at our family home situated in the village of Largoward, seven miles south of St Andrews. An ideal centre for numerous golf courses, visiting many local attractions or just relaxing in our garden. All bedrooms are on the ground floor. Private car parking.

B L Poll 8 St Andrews Road Largoward Fife KY9 1HZ Tel: (Peat Inn) 01334 840523	COMMENDED Listed	1 Twin 1 Double	1 Pub Bath/Show	B&B per person £17.00-£19.00 Single £14.00-£16.00 Double	Open Feb-Dec	
		Comfortable accommodation in small village. Garden and parking. Just 7 miles (11kms) from St Andrews and close to the attractive East Neuk fishing villages.				
Romar Guest House 45 Main Street Strathkinness Fife KY16 9RZ Tel: (Strathkinness) 01334 850308 Fax: 01334 850308	COMMENDED 👑	2 Single 1 Twin 1 Double	2 En Suite fac 2 Pub Bath/Show	B&B per person £16.00-£20.00 Single £16.00-£20.00 Double	Open Jan-Dec	
		Spacious modern house in pleasant rural surroundings, 3 miles (5kms) from St Andrews. Private parking.				

BY ST ANDREWS continued	Map 2 D2

Easter Craigfoodie

Dairsie, Cupar, Fife KY15 4SW
Telephone: 01334 870286

Comfortable farmhouse with wonderful views over bay only 6 miles from St Andrews. Residents' lounge with TV. Ample parking. Ideal golf or touring base.

Mrs C Scott Easter Craigfoodie Dairsie, by Cupar Fife KY15 4SW Tel: (Cupar) 01334 870286	HIGHLY COMMENDED Listed	1 Twin 1 Double 1 Family	1 Pub Bath/Show	B&B per person £16.00-£19.00 Single £15.00-£16.50 Double	Open Jan-Dec

Traditional, Victorian farmhouse with panoramic views across Fife to Firth of Tay and Angus coast. 7 miles (11kms) from St Andrews. Ideal golf base.

Seggie House Cupar Road Guardbridge, by St Andrews Fife KY16 0UP Tel: (Leuchars) 01334 839209	COMMENDED	2 Twin 3 Family	1 En Suite fac 1 Limited ensuite 3 Priv. NOT ensuite	B&B per person £20.00-£25.00 Single £15.00-£22.00 Double Room only per person £15.00-£20.00	Open May-Sept

Gracious Victorian mansion in 5 acres of wooded ground with walled garden. 4 miles (6kms) from St Andrews and its golf courses. Ample parking.

DRUMRACK FARM

By St Andrews KY16 8QQ
Telephone: 01333 310520

Drumrack is a family run farm in Fife, where you are welcome to stay in the comfort of our farmhouse. Only six miles from St Andrews, we are centrally situated for many East Neuk attractions – golf, beaches, historical buildings and quaint villages dotted around the coast.

Mrs H Watson Drumrack Farm by St Andrews Fife KY16 8QQ Tel: (Anstruther) 01333 310520	APPROVED Listed	1 Single 1 Twin 1 Double	2 Pub Bath/Show	B&B per person £15.50-£16.00 Single £15.50-£16.00 Double Room only per person £10.00-£10.50	Open Jan-Nov Dinner 2000-2100 B&B + Eve. Meal £21.50-£22.00

A warm welcome awaits at this family run working farm, 6 miles (10 kms) from St Andrews. Convenient for golf, beaches, fishing villages and historical buildings.

ST CYRUS Kincardineshire	Map 4 G12

BURNMOUTH HOUSE

Burnmouth House, St Cyrus, Nr Montrose DD10 0DL
Telephone: 01674 850430

We are a country seaside B&B 32 miles south of Aberdeen, 8 miles north of Montrose off A92. Ideal base for touring this lovely part of Scotland. 200-year-old house well-appointed, relaxed, friendly atmosphere. Open March to Oct. 1 single, 1 twin en-suite, 1 family en-suite, 2 doubles wash basin, 1 private bathroom, 1 public shower.

Mrs A Coates Burnmouth House St Cyrus Kincardineshire DD10 0DL Tel: (St Cyrus) 01674 850430	COMMENDED Listed	1 Single 1 Twin 2 Double 1 Family	2 En Suite fac 1 Priv. NOT ensuite 2 Pub Bath/Show	B&B per person £14.00-£16.50 Single £14.00-£16.50 Double	Open Mar-Oct Dinner 1800-2000 B&B + Eve. Meal £20.00-£22.00

In small hamlet overlooking the sea, 7 miles (11 kms) north of Montrose. Fishing can be arranged, good base for touring.

Mrs Alison Williamson Kirkside Bothy St Cyrus Nature Reserve St Cyrus Kincardineshire DD10 0AQ Tel: (Montrose) 01674 830780		**COMMENDED** Listed -	3 Twin 1 Family	4 En Suite fac	B&B per person £17.00 Single £17.00 Double	Open Jan-Dec

Stonebuilt 19th-century former fishing station converted to provide ensuite bedroom accommodation in peaceful location overlooking St Cyrus Nature Reserve and sandy beach.

ST FILLANS Perthshire Mrs Spearing Ardsheean St Fillans Perthshire PH6 2ND Tel: (St Fillans) 01764 685245	Map 1 H2	**COMMENDED**	1 Twin 1 Double 1 Family	2 En Suite fac 1 Priv. NOT ensuite	B&B per person £15.00-£20.00 Single £15.00-£16.00 Double	Open Jan-Dec

Spacious Edwardian house with tennis court in grounds of 3.5 acres, close to village centre and Loch Earn. Ensuite bathroom with sauna.

ST MARGARET'S HOPE Orkney Mrs M Norquay Windbreck St Margaret's Hope Orkney Tel: (St Margaret's Hope) 01856 831370	Map 5 B12	**COMMENDED**	1 Single 1 Twin 2 Double	2 En Suite fac 2 Limited ensuite 1 Pub Bath/Show	B&B per person £18.00-£20.00 Single £18.00-£20.00 Double	Open Jan-Dec Dinner 1800-1930 B&B + Eve. Meal £26.00-£28.00

Farmhouse with warm, friendly Orcadian hospitality. Fine panoramic views over St Margaret's Hope and out to Hoy.

ST MONANS Fife Miss M Aitken Inverforth, 20 Braehead St Monans Fife KY10 2AN Tel: (St Monans) 01333 730205	Map 2 D3	**COMMENDED** Listed	2 Twin 1 Double	1 Pub Bath/Show	B&B per person £16.00-£17.50 Single £16.00-£17.50 Double	Open mid May-mid Oct

Overlooking the harbour in this attractive small fishing village, a Victorian house with spacious bedrooms. Home baking.

NEWARK HOUSE
St Monans, Fife KY10 2DB   Tel: 01333 730027
Newark House is a traditional Fife farmhouse in a secluded coastal location enjoying splendid sea views. It is ideally situated for the golfer with St Andrews only 20 mins drive, and for the non-golfer with an abundance of local heritage, walks, bird-watching and local amenities.

Mrs Carol Thomson Newark House St Monans Fife KY10 2DB Tel: (St Monans) 01333 730027		**COMMENDED** Listed	1 Single 1 Double 1 Family	2 En Suite fac 1 Pub Bath/Show	B&B per person £16.00-£20.00 Single £14.00-£16.00 Double	Open Apr-Oct Dinner 1800-1930 B&B + Eve. Meal £20.00-£27.50

Traditional Fife farmhouse in secluded location beside the sea and ruins of Newark Castle. Golf, walks, bird-watching and an abundance of local heritage.

SALINE, by Dunfermline Fife Mrs J Cousar Lynn Farm Saline, by Dunfermline Fife KY12 9LR Tel: (New Oakley) 01383 852261	Map 2 B4	COMMENDED	1 Twin 1 Family	2 Priv. NOT ensuite	B&B per person £16.00-£18.00 Single £15.00-£16.00 Double	Open Mar-Oct
			Peaceful location on a working farm, with views of countryside from private lounge. Rooms with private bath or shower. Convenient M90 and Edinburgh. Non-smoking.			
SANDWICK Orkney Mrs M Grieve Dencraigon Sandwick, by Stromness Orkney KW16 3JB Tel: (Sandwick) 01856 841647	Map 5 A11	COMMENDED	1 Twin 1 Double	1 Pub Bath/Show	B&B per person £11.50-£14.00 Double	Open Apr-Oct
			Bungalow on A967 overlooking Loch Harray, 6 miles (10kms) from Stromness and 3 miles (5kms) from Skara Brae. Washbasins in bedrooms.			
SANQUHAR Dumfriesshire Mrs Norma Turnbull 28 High Street Sanquhar Dumfriesshire DG4 6BL Tel: (Sanquhar) 01659 58143	Map 2 A8	APPROVED Listed	1 Twin 1 Double	1 Pub Bath/Show	B&B per person from £12.50 Single from £12.50 Double	Open Jan-Dec Dinner 1830-1930 B&B + Eve. Meal £17.00-£18.00
			First-floor family flat in main street of Sanquhar. Convenient for shops and all amenities. Ideal stop-over for hill-walkers.			
SCADABAY Harris, Western Isles Mrs I MacLeod Hillhead Scadabay Harris, Western Isles PA85 3ED Tel: (Drinishader) 01859 511226	Map 3 C6	COMMENDED	1 Twin 1 Double 1 Family	1 En Suite fac 2 Pub Bath/Show	B&B per person £14.00-£15.00 Single £14.00-£15.00 Double Room only per person £9.00-£10.00	Open Apr-Oct Dinner from 1900 B&B + Eve. Meal £22.00-£24.00
			Modernised house on working croft where Harris tweed is also woven. One bedroom with ensuite facilities.			
SCALLOWAY Shetland	Map 5 F5					

Broch House Guest House Upper Scalloway Scalloway Shetland ZE1 0UP Tel: (Scalloway) 01595 880767 Fax: 01595 880731		COMMENDED	3 Twin	3 En Suite fac	B&B per person to £19.00 Single Room only per person to £17.00	Open Jan-Dec
			Modern house in elevated position with excellent views over Scalloway. All rooms ensuite facilities.			

SCANIPORT **Inverness-shire** Mrs C M Fraser Borlum House Scaniport Inverness-shire IV1 2DL Tel: (Dores) 01463 751306	Map 4 B9	COMMENDED ♛	1 Twin 2 Double	2 Pub Bath/Show	B&B per person from £14.00 Double	Open Jan-Dec

18th-century farmhouse built on castle ruins in quiet countryside overlooking
River Ness and Caledonian Canal. 3 miles (5kms) from both Dores and Inverness.

SCONE, by Perth
Perthshire — Map 2 B2

"ACUSHLA"

80 Angus Road, Scone, Perth PH2 6RB
Telephone: 01738 552885 Fax: 01738 552010

Detached comfortable friendly family home 2 miles north from Perth in quiet
historic country village close to all Highland amenities including Scone Palace.
Restaurant 5 minutes walk away. Ample parking space. Dundee and
St Andrews ¹/₂ hour, Edinburgh, Glasgow 1 hour, Aberdeen 1¹/₂ hours,
Inverness 2 hours' drive away. The gateway to the Highlands.

Mrs Sue White Acushla, 80 Angus Road Scone, by Perth Perthshire PH2 6RB Tel: (Scone) 01738 552885 Fax: 01738 552010	COMMENDED ♛♛	1 Twin 1 Family	2 Priv. NOT ensuite 2 Pub Bath/Show	B&B per person £15.00-£17.00 Single £15.00-£17.00 Double	Open Jan-Dec

Detached house with warm and friendly atmosphere. On main bus route.
2 miles (3kms) from Perth. Plenty of parking available.

SCOTLANDWELL
Kinross-shire — Map 2 C3

The Grange

SCOTLANDWELL, KINROSS KY13 7JE
Telephone and Fax: 01592 840220

Scotlandwell is an ideal touring base, with St Andrews, Perth, Stirling
and Edinburgh all within 30 miles. The Grange has large gardens, ample
parking and has been extended to provide superb accommodation for
six guests. Meals are served in the original 19th century dining room
and a warm welcome is assured.

Mrs Hodder The Grange Scotlandwell Kinross-shire KY13 7JE Tel: (Scotlandwell) 01592 840220 Fax: 01592 840220	COMMENDED ♛♛	2 Twin 1 Double	1 En Suite fac 1 Pub Bath/Show	B&B per person £20.00-£25.00 Single £14.00-£17.00 Double	Open Apr-Oct Dinner 1800-1930 B&B + Eve. Meal £21.00-£28.00

Friendly family home with well-kept garden. Centrally placed for touring,
golf, gliding, fishing on Loch Leven. Bird sanctuary. Private parking.

SCOTTISH TOURIST BOARD
QUALITY COMMENDATIONS ARE:

Deluxe – An EXCELLENT quality standard
Highly Commended – A VERY GOOD quality standard
Commended – A GOOD quality standard
Approved – An ACCEPTABLE quality standard

Details of Grading and Classification are on page vi. | Key to symbols is on back flap. |

SCOTLANDWELL continued

Mrs S M Wardell
6 Bankfoot Park
Scotlandwell, by Kinross
Kinross-shire
KY13 7JP
Tel: (Scotlandwell)
01592 840515

Map 2 E3

COMMENDED

2 Twin — 1 Priv. NOT ensuite / 1 Pub Bath/Show

B&B per person
£16.00 Single
£15.00 Double

Open Jan-Dec

Family home near Loch Leven. Easy access to Lomond Hills and Fife Coast.
Bee keeping, gliding, fishing, bird watching, country parks.

SCOURIE
Sutherland

Mrs Jana MacDonald
Cnoc Alvinn
Scourie, Sutherland
IV27 4TG
Tel: (Scourie) 01971 502024
Tel: 01971 502024

Map 3 H4

HIGHLY COMMENDED
Listed

2 Double / 1 Family — 3 En Suite fac / 1 Pub Bath/Show

B&B per person
£18.00-£25.00 Double

Open mid Jan
Dinner 1900-2000
B&B + Eve.Meal
£30.00-£37.00

Modern purpose-built guest house with superb views over the Minch.
All home cooking.

Scourie Lodge
Scourie
Sutherland
IV27 4SX
Tel: (Scourie) 01971 502248

HIGHLY COMMENDED
Listed

1 Twin / 2 Double — 2 Pub Bath/Show

B&B per person
£18.50-£23.50 Single
£17.50-£18.50 Double

Open Mar-Oct
Dinner 1800-1930

Beautifully situated on Scourie Bay. Ideal for the north west of Scotland.
Comfortable accommodation. We welcome children. No smoking.

Mrs Sarah Thomson
Braeval, Scourie More
Scourie
Sutherland
IV27 4TG
Tel: (Scourie) 01971 502076

COMMENDED
Listed

1 Twin / 2 Double — 2 Pub Bath/Show

B&B per person
£13.00-£16.00 Single
£13.00-£16.00 Double
Room only per person
£13.00-£16.00

Open May-Sep

Modern bungalow set up above this typical west coast Highland village.
Fine views of Scourie Bay and Handa Island in the distance.

SEAMILL
Ayrshire

Spottiswoode
Sandy Road
Seamill
Ayrshire
KA23 9NN
Tel: (Seamill) 01294 823131
Fax: 01294 823179

Map 1 F6

DELUXE

1 Twin / 2 Double — 1 En Suite fac / 2 Priv. NOT ensuite

B&B per person
£35.00-£47.00 Single
£22.00-£28.00 Double

Open Jan-Dec
Dinner at 1930
B&B + Eve. Meal
£40.00-£50.00

Victorian shore-side home. Tea in garden, island views, imaginative menus,
flowers, music, books. Base for golf, Ayrshire coast, being pampered.

SELKIRK

Mrs P Dickson
Sunnybrae House,
75 Tower Street
Selkirk
TD7 4LS
Tel: (Selkirk) 01750 21156

Map 2 D7

COMMENDED

1 Twin / 1 Double — 2 En Suite fac

B&B per person
to £19.00 Single
to £19.00 Double

Open Jan-Dec
Dinner 1800-2000
B&B + Eve. Meal
to £32.00

Two suites (own private bathroom and sitting room). Home cooking using
local produce. Ideal for touring the Borders and Edinburgh. Private parking.

Mrs T Donaldson
Alwyn, Russell Place
Selkirk
TD7 4NF
Tel: (Selkirk) 01750 22044

COMMENDED

1 Twin / 1 Double — 1 En Suite fac / 1 Pub Bath/Show

B&B per person
£17.00-£20.00 Single
£15.00-£18.00 Double

Open Apr-Oct

Large bungalow quietly situated on outskirts of historic town.
Ideal centre for exploring lovely surrounding countryside.

Mrs D J Hannah
Hillholm, 36 Hillside Terrace
Selkirk
TD7 4ND
Tel: (Selkirk) 01750 21293

COMMENDED

2 Twin / 1 Double — 2 En Suite fac / 1 Priv. NOT ensuite / 1 Pub Bath/Show

B&B per person
from £20.00 Single
from £15.00 Double

Open Mar-Dec
Dinner from 1800

Elegant semi-detached Victorian house on outskirts of Selkirk.
Small interesting garden with rockery and Alpine plants. Ideal base for touring.

VAT is shown at 17.5%: changes in this rate may affect prices. Prices shown are for guidance only. Please send SAE with each enquiry.

Mrs Lindores Dinsburn, 1 Shawpark Road Selkirk TD7 4DS Tel: (Selkirk) 01750 20375	COMMENDED	1 Twin 1 Double 1 Family	2 En Suite fac 1 Priv. NOT ensuite 1 Pub Bath/Show	B&B per person from £14.00 Single from £14.00 Double	Open Jan-Dec Dinner from 1800	

Semi-detached, sandstone Victorian house in residential area
on east side of town centre. Next to bowling green.

Mrs J F MacKenzie Ivybank, Hillside Terrace Selkirk TD7 Tel: (Selkirk) 01750 21270	COMMENDED	1 Twin 1 Double	1 Pub Bath/Show	B&B per person £16.00 Single £15.00 Double	Open Feb-Nov	

Set back from A7 with fine views over the hills beyond.
Private off-street parking.

Mr Eric Paterson Queen's Head Inn 28 West Port Selkirk TD7 4DG Tel: (Selkirk) 01750 21782	APPROVED	1 Double 1 Family	1 Pub Bath/Show	B&B per person £10.00-£17.00 Single Room only per person £8.00-£15.00	Open Jan-Dec Dinner 1700-2100 B&B + Eve. Meal £18.00-£23.00	

Self-contained accommodation in house adjoining popular town-centre pub.
Breakfast in lounge bar.

Mrs S M Todd 34 Hillside Terrace Selkirk TD7 4ND Tel: (Selkirk) 01750 20792	COMMENDED	2 Twin 1 Double	1 Priv. NOT ensuite 2 Pub Bath/Show	B&B per person £13.50-£14.00 Double	Open Mar-Oct	

Family run house in a small, historic border town.
An ideal centre for touring and hillwalking.

SHIELDAIG **Ross-shire** Mrs M C Calcott Tigh Fada, 117 Doireaonar Shieldaig, Strathcarron Ross-shire IV54 8XH Tel: (Shieldaig) 01520 755248	Map 3 F8 COMMENDED Listed	1 Twin 1 Double 1 Family	2 Pub Bath/Show	B&B per person from £13.50 Single from £13.50 Double	Open Jan-Dec Dinner from 1900 B&B + Eve. Meal from £18.50	

Centrally heated accommodation on working croft, specialising in
Hebridean and Angora wool. Evening meal and home baking.

INNIS MHOR

Ardheslaig, Nr Shieldaig, Strathcarron
Ross-shire IV54 8XH Tel/Fax: 01520 755339

COMMENDED

This comfortable, family home is located near Shieldaig on the
scenic coastal road round the Applecross Peninsula and next to
the shore of Loch Torridon. Ideally situated for touring the
West Coast, climbing, walking, fishing, nature watching or just
relaxing amid the breathtaking scenery.
Details from Chris and Erica Sermon.

Mr C Sermon Innis Mhor, Ardheslaig Shieldaig Ross-shire IV54 8XH Tel: (Sheildaig) 01520 755339 Fax: 01520 755339	COMMENDED	2 Single 1 Twin 2 Double	2 Pub Bath/Show	B&B per person £15.50-£22.00 Single £13.50-£14.50 Double	Open Jan-Dec exc Xmas Dinner 1900-2000 B&B + Eve. Meal £22.00-£30.50	

Comfortable family home peacefully located overlooking Loch Torridon and
the Applecross Peninsula. Private parking. Ideal for fishing, walking and climbing.

SOLLAS **North Uist, Western Isles** Mrs Lexy Pillans Creagan Fois, Claddach Vallay Malaclate North Uist, Western Isles HS6 5BX Tel: (Sollas) 01876 560204	Map 3 B7 COMMENDED	1 Twin 1 Double 1 Family	3 En Suite fac	B&B per person from £16.00 Single from £16.00 Double	Open Jan-Dec Dinner 1900-2000 B&B + Eve. Meal from £26.00	

Recently built bungalow with panoramic view overlooking Tidal Strand to Vallay.
Peaceful location which is near RSPB reserve.

SOUTHEND, by Campbeltown **Argyll** Mrs M Ronald Ormsary Farm Southend, by Campbeltown Argyll PA28 6RN Tel: (Southend) 01586 830665	Map 1 D8	COMMENDED 👑👑	2 Double 1 Family	2 En Suite fac 1 Pub Bath/Show	B&B per person £16.00-£18.00 Single £16.00-£18.00 Double	Open Apr-Sep Dinner from 1800 B&B + Eve. Meal £23.00-£24.00

Beautifully situated family farm only 2 miles (3kms) from beach and 18-hole golf course. Children especially welcome. Traditional home cooking and baking.

SOUTH QUEENSFERRY **West Lothian** Priory Guest House 8 The Loan South Queensferry West Lothian EH30 9NS Tel: 0131 331 4345	Map 2 B4	COMMENDED Listed	1 Twin 1 Double 1 Family	2 En Suite fac 1 Pub Bath/Show	B&B per person £20.00-£25.00 Single £15.00-£19.00 Double	Open Jan-Dec

Traditional Scottish hospitality in friendly B & B, located in picturesque village of South Queensferry. Within easy walking distance of Forth Bridges.

SOUTH SHAWBOST **Lewis, Western Isles** Mrs E MacLean Airigh, 1 Teachers House South Shawbost Lewis, Western Isles HS2 9BJ Tel: (Shawbost) 01851 710478	Map 3 D4	COMMENDED 👑👑	1 Twin 2 Double	2 En Suite fac 1 Priv. NOT ensuite 1 Pub Bath/Show	B&B per person £16.00-£20.00 Single £16.00-£20.00 Double	Open Jan-Dec Dinner 1900-2000 B&B + Eve. Meal £26.00-£30.00

Comfortable, home cooking. Situated in rural village, close to sandy beaches, convenient for west side attractions, Tweed weaving demonstrations.

SPEAN BRIDGE **Inverness-shire**	Map 3 H12					

Barbagianni Guest House Tirindrish Spean Bridge Inverness-shire PH34 4EU Tel: (Spean Bridge) 01397 712437		HIGHLY COMMENDED 👑👑👑	1 Single 1 Twin 5 Double	6 En Suite fac 1 Priv. NOT ensuite	B&B per person £15.50-£17.00 Single	Open Mar- 20th Oct Dinner is at 1930 B&B + Eve. Meal £28.00

Detached modern house of interesting design, in its own grounds with excellent views over Ben Nevis and beyond. Friendly atmosphere, home baking. Dinner is at 7.30 pm.

Old Pines

Restaurant with Rooms, Spean Bridge, Inverness-shire PH34 4EG
Telephone: 01397 712324 Fax: 01397 712433

Quiet situation. Breathtaking views of Aonach Mor and Ben Nevis. Ideal base for touring the West Highlands. Happy family home with a relaxing, informal atmosphere, pretty en-suite bedrooms, flowers, books and log fires. Awards-winning dinner by crystal and candlelight.
Contact: Bill and Sukie Barber   *"A Very Special Place"*

Dr & Mrs W J Barber Old Pines, Restaurant with rooms Spean Bridge Inverness-shire PH34 4EG Tel: (Spean Bridge) 01397 712324 Fax: 01397 712433	**HIGHLY COMMENDED**	2 Single 2 Twin 2 Double 2 Family	7 En Suite fac 1 Priv. NOT ensuite 1 Pub Bath/Show	B&B per person £20.00-£40.00 Single £20.00-£35.00 Double	Open Jan-Dec Dinner from 2000 B&B + Eve. Meal £40.00-£60.00	
		"Best Small Hotel in Britain 1994" – Judith Chalmers Holiday Care Award. Winner of the 1995 "Taste of Scotland Classic Scotch Lamb Challenge".				
Mrs E E Bradburn Cabernish Spean Bridge Inverness-shire PH34 4EP Tel: (Spean Bridge) 01397 712020	**APPROVED**	2 Double 1 Family	1 En Suite fac 1 Pub Bath/Show	B&B per person £15.00-£18.00 Single £11.00-£20.00 Double	Open Jan-Dec Dinner 1900-2100 B&B + Eve. Meal £18.00-£26.00	
		Detached bungalow with ample parking conveniently situated 2 miles north of the Aonach Mhor turn-off. Super views of the surrounding mountains.				

INVERGLOY HOUSE

Telephone:
01397 712681

Spean Bridge, Inverness-shire PH34 4DY

100-year-old coach house offering three twin-bedded rooms with ensuite/private bathroom facilities. Overlooking Loch Lochy in 50 acres of rhododendron woodland. 5 miles north of Spean Bridge on A82 to Inverness, signposted on left along wooded drive. Fishing, rowing boats. Youngsters over 8 years. "Non-smoking" house.
S.A.E. for brochure to Mrs M H Cairns.
B&B from £17.00. Evening meal on request £10.00.

HIGHLY COMMENDED

Mrs M Cairns Invergloy House, Invergloy Spean Bridge Inverness-shire PH34 4DY Tel: (Spean Bridge) 01397 712681	**HIGHLY COMMENDED**	3 Twin	2 Pub Bath/Show	B&B per person £17.00-£22.00 Single £17.00 Double	Open Jan-Dec Dinner from 1930 B&B + Eve. Meal from £27.00	
		A warm welcome is offered in our peaceful country home in 50 acres of woodland estate. Access to lochside.				
Coinachan Spean Bridge Inverness-shire Tel: (Spean Bridge) 01397 712417	**COMMENDED**	1 Twin 2 Double	3 En Suite fac	B&B per person £15.00-£17.50 Double	Open Jan-Dec Dinner 1930-2030	
		A warm welcome at this comfortable, tastefully renovated cottage in peaceful location yet convenient for the A82. Excellent views of the Commando Memorial.				
Coire Glas Guest House Roy Bridge Road Spean Bridge Inverness-shire PH34 4EU Tel: (Spean Bridge) 01397 712272	**COMMENDED**	1 Single 5 Twin 5 Double 2 Family	9 En Suite fac 2 Pub Bath/Show	B&B per person £14.00-£17.50 Single £14.00-£17.50 Double	Open Jan-Oct Dinner 1900-2000 B&B + Eve. Meal £24.00-£30.00	
		Family run guest house set back from A86 tourist route, only 8 miles (13kms) from Aonach Mor gondola station. Views of the Ben Nevis mountain range.				

Details of Grading and Classification are on page vi.   Key to symbols is on back flap.

SPEAN BRIDGE continued	Map 3 H12

DISTANT HILLS

Spean Bridge, Inverness-shire PH34 4EU
Telephone: 01397 712452

A comfortable guest house situated on the edge of a quiet Highland village close to all facilities. All rooms en-suite, with coloured television, tea tray etc. Spacious residents' lounge overlooking Nevis Range. Laundry facilities available. Accommodation suitable for assisted disabled. Dogs welcome.

Distant Hills Guest House Spean Bridge Inverness-shire PH34 4EU Tel: (Spean Bridge) 01397 712452	HIGHLY COMMENDED	4 Twin 3 Double	7 En Suite fac 1 Pub Bath/Show	B&B per person £21.00 Single £16.00 Double	Open Feb-Oct Dinner 1700-2030 B&B + Eve. Meal £25.00	

Modern bungalow at edge of quiet village. Friendly and personal attention. Excellent views of Aonach Mor; ideally situated for touring and skiing.

Mrs D Horner Highbridge Spean Bridge Inverness-shire PH34 4EX Tel: (Fort William) 01397 712493	COMMENDED	1 Twin 1 Double	1 En Suite fac 1 Limited ensuite 1 Pub Bath/Show	B&B per person £14.00-£15.00 Single £14.00-£15.00 Double	Open Apr-Oct	

Secluded cedarwood, family home. Excellent views of Ben Nevis and Aonach Mor. Fort William 9 miles (14kms), Spean Bridge 1.5 miles (2kms).

Inverour Guest House

Spean Bridge, Inverness-shire PH34 4EU
Telephone: 01397 712218

Small friendly guest house in pretty Lochaber village. Central touring location. Children welcome. Ample off-road private parking. Evening meals for residents. TV, H&C all rooms. Only 5 miles to Aonach Mor ski area.

Inverour Guest House Spean Bridge Inverness-shire PH34 4EU Tel: (Spean Bridge) 01397 712218	COMMENDED	2 Single 2 Twin 2 Double 1 Family	3 En Suite fac 2 Pub Bath/Show	B&B per person £15.00-£18.00 Single	Open Jan-Dec Dinner 1900-2000 B&B + Eve. Meal £27.00-£30.00	

Comfortable, homely atmosphere. Situated in an ideal centre for touring the West of Scotland.

Springburn Farm House Stronaba Spean Bridge Inverness-shire PH34 4DX Tel: (Spean Bridge) 01397 712707	COMMENDED	1 Twin 2 Double	3 En Suite fac	B&B per person £17.00-£20.00 Double	Open Jan-Dec	

Bungalow-style farmhouse with spacious bedrooms situated 2 miles from Spean Bridge. Ample carparking in large grounds.

Peter & Jean Wilson Tirindrish House Spean Bridge Inverness-shire PH34 4EU Tel: (Spean Bridge) 01397 712520 Fax: 01397 712398	COMMENDED	1 Twin 1 Double 1 Family	1 En Suite fac 2 Priv. NOT ensuite	B&B per person £15.00-£25.00 Single £15.00-£16.00 Double	Open Apr-Oct Dinner 1900-2000 B&B + Eve. Meal to £28.00	

Historic Highland house, dating from Jacobite times, in extensive grounds. 10 miles (16 kms) from Fort William.

STEVENSTON Ayrshire Mrs J Thomson Lochraigs Farm Stevenston Ayrshire KA20 4LB Tel: (Stevenston) 01294 465288	Map 1 G6	COMMENDED Listed	1 Single 1 Twin 1 Double	1 Pub Bath/Show	B&B per person £14.00-£15.00 Single £14.00-£15.00 Double	Open Jan-Dec Dinner from 1830 B&B + Eve. Meal £20.00-£22.00	
			Working beef and cattle farm on outskirts of town. Some views. Central for the north and south Ayrshire coast.				

STIRLING Bannockburn Guest Lodge 24/32 Main Street Bannockburn, Stirling Stirlingshire FK7 8LY Tel: (Bannockburn) 01786 812121/816501 Fax: 01786 817628	Map 2 A4	COMMENDED Lodge	3 Twin 2 Double 1 Family	6 En Suite fac	B&B per person £24.00-£26.00 Single £19.00-£22.00 Double	Open Jan-Dec Dinner at 1800 B&B + Eve. Meal £25.00-£32.00	
			Purpose built 1990s facilities in a 1760s building! Ideal touring centre 1 mile (2kms) from motorway.				
Mrs C Campbell Shaw of Touch Farm Stirling FK8 3AE Tel: (Stirling) 01786 471147		COMMENDED	1 Twin 2 Double	2 Pub Bath/Show	B&B per person £16.00-£20.00 Single £16.00-£18.00 Double	Open Mar-Dec Dinner 1800-2000 B&B + Eve. Meal £24.95-£27.00	
			Turreted farmhouse in 265-acre arable and livestock farm conveniently situated 4 miles (6 kms) from Stirling. Distant views of Ben Lomond and Castle				
Castlecroft Ballengeich Road Stirling FK8 1TN Tel: (Stirling) 01786 474933		HIGHLY COMMENDED	2 Twin 3 Double 1 Family	6 En Suite fac 1 Pub Bath/Show	B&B per person £30.00-£37.00 Single £17.50-£21.00 Double	Open Jan-Dec	
			Nestling on elevated site under Stirling Castle, this comfortable, modern house offers warm welcome. Private facilities, some suitable for disabled.				
Forth Guest House 23 Forth Place, Riverside Stirling FK8 1UD Tel: (Stirling) 01786 471020/ 0850 868501 (mobile) Fax: 01786 447220		HIGHLY COMMENDED	2 Twin 2 Double 1 Family	5 En Suite fac	B&B per person £25.00-£35.00 Single £18.00-£20.00 Double	Open Jan-Dec Dinner 1800-1900 B&B + Eve. Meal £28.00-£30.00	
			Terraced house within easy walking distance of railway station, town centre and swimming pool. Good location for touring.				

Mrs R Johnson Shalom, Manse Crescent Stirling FK7 9AJ Tel: (Stirling) 01786 471092		COMMENDED	1 Single 1 Twin	1 Pub Bath/Show	B&B per person £16.00-£17.00 Single £16.00-£17.00 Double	Open Jan-Dec	
			Bungalow with character in quiet cul-de-sac, 3 minutes walk to frequent bus service, 15 minutes walk to town centre. Off-street parking.				

Details of Grading and Classification are on page vi. | Key to symbols is on back flap. | 261

STIRLING continued — Map 2 A4

Mrs M Johnston
West Plean House, Denny Road
Stirling
FK7 8HA
Tel: (Stirling) 01786 812208

COMMENDED

1 Single / 2 En Suite fac
1 Double / 1 Priv. NOT ensuite
1 Family

B&B per person
£22.00-£30.00 Single
£18.00-£22.00 Double

Open Feb-Nov

200-year-old country house on working farm with extensive grounds and woodlands. Spacious comfort; warm Scottish farming hospitality.

Mrs D Mailer
Ashgrove, 2 Park Avenue
Stirling
Tel: (Stirling) 01786 472640

HIGHLY COMMENDED

1 Twin / 2 En Suite fac
1 Double

B&B per person
from £27.50 Single
from £20.00 Double

Open Jan-Dec

Listed Victorian farmhouse by renowned local architect. Short walk from castle, town centre and all amenities.

Mrs Agnes Thomson
Tiroran, 45 Douglas Terrace
Stirling
FK7 9LW
Tel: (Stirling) 01786 464655

HIGHLY COMMENDED Listed

1 Twin / 1 Pub Bath/Show
1 Double

B&B per person
£15.00-£15.50 Double

Open Apr-Oct

A warm welcome in this modern house, with easy access to the town centre.

STONEHAVEN
Kincardineshire — Map 4 G11
Mrs V Craib
Car-Lyn-Vale
Rickarton, by Stonehaven
Kincardineshire
AB3 2TD
Tel: (Stonehaven)
01569 762406

HIGHLY COMMENDED

1 Twin / 3 En Suite fac
2 Double

B&B per person
£20.00 Single
£16.50-£18.00 Double

Open Jan-Dec

Friendly B & B. Non-smoking. 10 minutes from Stonehaven in rural setting at gateway to Royal Deeside. Ensuite facilities. Ample, safe parking.

Windsor Grove Guest House
Fetteresso
Stonehaven
Kincardine
AB3 2UT
Tel: (Stonehaven) 01569
766299/764257
Fax: 01569 766221

COMMENDED

1 Twin / 3 En Suite fac
1 Double
1 Family

B&B per person
£19.00-£21.00 Single
£17.50-£18.50 Double

Open Jan-Dec

Family run modern house 1.5 miles (2.5kms) from Stonehaven in quiet country location. Easy access to A94. Safe off-road parking.

Woodside of Grasslaw
Stonehaven
Kincardineshire
AB3 2XQ
Tel: (Stonehaven)
01569 763799

COMMENDED

2 Twin / 4 En Suite fac
1 Double
1 Family

B&B per person
£18.00-£22.00 Single
£16.00-£20.00 Double

Open Jan-Dec

Extended, modern bungalow in rural setting, yet within easy access to main routes and Deeside. All rooms ensuite. Warm welcome assured.

BY STONEHAVEN
Kincardineshire — Map 4 G11
Mrs Elizabeth C Farquhar
Tewel Farm
Stonehaven
Kincardineshire
Tel: (Stonehaven)
01569 762306

COMMENDED Listed

1 Twin / 1 En Suite fac
1 Double / 1 Pub Bath/Show

B&B per person
£16.00-£18.00 Single
£14.00-£16.00 Double
Room only per person
£16.00-£18.00

Open Jan-Dec

Traditional farmhouse in quiet location, on outskirts of Stonehaven, with lovely views of surrounding countryside.

STORNOWAY
Lewis, Western Isles — Map 3 D4
Mrs A C MacLeod
Ravenswood
12 Matheson Road
Stornoway
Lewis, Western Isles
HS87 2LR
Tel: (Stornoway) 01851 702673

HIGHLY COMMENDED

1 Single / 2 En Suite fac
1 Twin / 1 Pub Bath/Show
1 Double

B&B per person
£18.00-£20.00 Single

Open Jan-Dec

Turn-of-the-century villa in a quiet area of Stornoway yet a short stroll to the harbour and town centre. Private parking.

STRAITON **Ayrshire** H R Henry Three Thorns Farm Straiton Ayrshire Tel: (Straiton) 01655 770221	Map 1 G8	COMMENDED 👑 👑	1 Twin 1 Double 1 Family	1 En Suite fac 2 Limited ensuite 2 Priv. NOT ensuite	B&B per person from £20.00 Single from £18.00 Double Room only per person from £15.00	Open Jan-Dec	

Farm house on working farm in rural area, 1 mile (2kms) from Conservation Village of Straiton. Trout pond on the farm; fishing and golf available.

STRANRAER **Wigtownshire** Balyett Farmhouse Cairnryan Road Stranraer Wigtownshire DG9 8QL Tel: (Stranraer) 01776 703395	Map 1 F10	COMMENDED 👑 👑 👑	1 Twin 1 Double 1 Family	2 En Suite fac 1 Priv. NOT ensuite 1 Pub Bath/Show	B&B per person £15.00-£19.00 Single £15.00-£19.00 Double	Open Jan-Dec Dinner 1800-1900 B&B + Eve. Meal £22.00-£26.00	

Working farm on edge of town. Convenient for all Irish ferries. Ample secure parking. Home cooking imaginatively presented using farm produce. Children very welcome.

Mrs Black Glen Otter, Leswalt Road Stranraer Wigtownshire DG9 0EP Tel: (Stranraer) 01776 703199		COMMENDED 👑 👑	1 Single 1 Double 1 Family	2 En Suite fac 1 Pub Bath/Show	B&B per person £15.00-£18.00 Single £15.00-£19.00 Double	Open Jan-Dec	

Personally run B&B with private parking in residential area. Within easy access to ferry terminals.

Mrs M Downes Rankins Close, 25/27 Dalrymple Street Stranraer Wigtownshire DG9 7ET Tel: (Stranraer) 01776 702632		COMMENDED Listed	1 Twin 1 Double 1 Family	1 Pub Bath/Show	B&B per person £14.00-£16.00 Single	Open Jan-Dec	

Terraced house, family run, central location. Close to ferry terminals.

Mrs N Farroll Hawthorn Cottage Stoneykirk Road Stranraer Wigtownshire DG9 7BT Tel: (Stranraer) 01776 702032		COMMENDED 👑 👑	1 Twin 2 Double	1 En Suite fac 1 Pub Bath/Show	B&B per person £14.00-£18.00 Single £14.00-£18.00 Double	Open Jan-Dec	

Renovated two-storey cottage, 1 mile from ferry terminals. On main road to Portpatrick, private parking.

Fernlea Guest House Fernlea, Lewis Street Stranraer Wigtownshire DG9 7AQ Tel: (Stranraer) 01776 703037		COMMENDED 👑 👑 👑	1 Twin 2 Double	2 En Suite fac 1 Pub Bath/Show	B&B per person £15.00-£19.00 Single	Open Jan-Dec Dinner 1800-1900 B&B + Eve. Meal £22.50-£26.50	

Personally run, with friendly atmosphere. Close to town centre, Stranraer and Cairnryan ferries. Fully double-glazed and private parking. Non-smoking.

Jan Da Mar Guest House 1 Ivy Place, London Road Stranraer Wigtownshire DG9 8ER Tel: (Stranraer) 01776 706194		COMMENDED 👑 👑	2 Single 3 Twin 3 Family	2 En Suite fac 2 Pub Bath/Show	B&B per person from £16.00 Single £14.00-£18.00 Double	Open Jan-Dec	

Early 19th-century townhouse, modernised yet retaining some original features. Conveniently situated for town centre and ferry terminal.

STRANRAER continued

	Map 1 F10						
Mrs McDonald Auld Ayre, 4 Park Lane Stranraer Wigtownshire DG9 0DS Tel: (Stranraer) 01776 704500		COMMENDED 👑👑👑	1 Twin 1 Double 1 Family	3 En Suite fac	B&B per person £18.00-£25.00 Single £15.00-£17.00 Double	Open Jan-Dec Dinner 1700-1830	

Large detached house in quiet residential area close to seafront, ferry and town centre. Own parking.

| Mr & Mrs Whitworth Kildrochet House Stranraer Wigtownshire DG9 9BB Tel: (Lochans) 01776 820216 | | HIGHLY COMMENDED 👑👑👑 | 2 Twin 1 Double | 2 En Suite fac 1 Priv. NOT ensuite | B&B per person £25.00-£26.00 Single £22.00-£23.00 Double | Open Jan-Dec Dinner at 1930 B&B + Eve. Meal £34.00-£40.00 | |

18th-century Adam Dower House set in peaceful 6 acres of gardens, pasture and woodlands with open views over Rhinns of Galloway. Non-smoking. Home cooking.

BY STRATHAVEN
Lanarkshire

| Mrs Anderson Kypemhor, West Kype Farm by Strathaven Lanarkshire ML10 6PR Tel: (Strathaven) 01357 29831 | Map 2 A6 | COMMENDED Listed | 1 Twin 1 Double | 1 Pub Bath/Show | B&B per person £14.00-£17.00 Single £13.00-£15.00 Double Room only per person £13.00-£16.00 | Open Jan-Dec Dinner 1700-2000 | |

Modern bungalow set in open countryside, with fine views and easy access to Clyde Valley. Good walking country.

STRATHCARRON
Ross-shire — Map 3 G9

"THE SHIELING"

Achintee, Strathcarron, Ross-shire IV54 8YX
Telephone: 01520 722364

Only minutes from a railway station, surrounded by spectacular scenery, a comfortable base for many leisure activities, particularly hill-walking and climbing. Central for day trips to such places as Skye and Inverewe Gardens.

| Mrs J Levy The Shieling, Achintee Strathcarron Ross-shire IV54 8YX Tel: (Lochcarron) 01520 722364 | | COMMENDED Listed | 1 Single 2 Twin | 1 En Suite fac 1 Pub Bath/Show | B&B per person £14.00-£17.00 Single £14.00-£17.00 Double | Open Jan-Dec | |

Welcoming, family home in beautiful West Highland area. Close to station on Kyle line. 2 twins and small single. Evening meal by arrangement. Non-smoking.

STRATHDON
Aberdeenshire

| Mrs Denise Jones The Smiddy House Glenkindie Aberdeenshire AB33 8RX Tel: (Glenkindie) 019756 41216 | Map 4 E10 | COMMENDED Listed | 1 Single 1 Twin 1 Double | 1 Pub Bath/Show | B&B per person £13.00 Single £13.00 Double Room only per person £13.00 | Open Jan-Dec Dinner 1800-1900 B&B + Eve. Meal £20.00 | |

Friendly bed and breakfast on Highland Route and Castle Trail. Set in pleasant surroundings.

| Mrs E Ogg Farmhouse Bed & Breakfast Buchaam Holiday Properties Buchaam Farm Strathdon Aberdeenshire AB36 8TN Tel: (Strathdon) 019756 51238 | | COMMENDED Listed | 1 Twin 1 Double 1 Family | 2 Pub Bath/Show | B&B per person to £14.00 Single to £14.00 Double | Open May-Oct Dinner 1800-1930 B&B + Eve. Meal to £22.00 | |

Large farmhouse on 600-acre mixed farm with sporting facilities including badminton, table tennis and putting green. Free river fishing.

STRATHPEFFER Ross-shire Mrs G P Cameron White Lodge Strathpeffer Ross-shire IV14 9AL Tel: (Strathpeffer) 01997 421730	Map 4 A8 HIGHLY COMMENDED ♛♛♛	1 Twin 1 Double	2 En Suite fac	B&B per person £25.00 Single £17.50-£18.00 Double	Open Apr-Sep Dinner 1830-1930

'B' Listed 18th-century lodge overlooking charming Square of small Highland spa village.

INVER LODGE
STRATHPEFFER, ROSS-SHIRE IV14 9DL
Telephone: 01997 421392
A WARM WELCOME AWAITS YOU AT INVER LODGE.
LOG FIRES, HOME BAKING, GOOD FOOD.
A FRIENDLY RELAXED ATMOSPHERE.
BED & BREAKFAST FROM £14.50.
DINNER AND PACKED LUNCHES AVAILABLE.

Mrs Derbyshire Inver Lodge Strathpeffer Ross-shire IV14 9DL Tel: (Strathpeffer) 01997 421392	COMMENDED ♛	1 Twin 1 Family	2 Pub Bath/Show	B&B per person £18.00-£21.00 Single £14.50-£15.50 Double	Open Mar-Dec Dinner 1930-2030 B&B + Eve. Meal £24.50-£25.50

Stone-built family home in lovely Highland spa town.
Dinner available using quality local produce. Open wood fire.

Gardenside Guest House
STRATHPEFFER, ROSS-SHIRE IV14 9BJ
Telephone: 01997 421242
The Guest House is located on the south-west side of the
village of Strathpeffer surrounded by woodland and fields.
The accommodation consists of six letting rooms, four with ensuite
facilities. All bedrooms are equipped with tea and coffee-making
facilities. A guests' lounge with TV is available to residents.

Gardenside Guest House Strathpeffer Ross-shire IV14 9BJ Tel: (Strathpeffer) 01997 421242	COMMENDED ♛♛♛	2 Twin 4 Double	4 En Suite fac 1 Pub Bath/Show	B&B per person £25.00-£27.00 Single £15.00-£17.00 Double	Open Apr-Nov Dinner 1830-2000 B&B + Eve. Meal £25.00-£27.00

Friendly welcome at family run guest house in spa village.
Good walking country and touring base. 18 miles (27kms) from Inverness.

Mrs J MacDonald Scoraig, 8 Kinnettas Square Strathpeffer Ross-shire IV14 9BD Tel: (Strathpeffer) 01997 421847	COMMENDED Listed	1 Single 1 Twin 1 Double 1 Family	1 En Suite fac 1 Priv. NOT ensuite 2 Pub Bath/Show	B&B per person £12.00-£15.00 Single £12.00-£15.00 Double Room only per person £12.00-£15.00	Open Jan-Dec Dinner 1800-2000 B&B + Eve. Meal £19.00-£22.00

Comfortable personally run B & B, situated in quiet residential area
close to village centre. Ideal touring base, home cooking, private parking.

Mrs M MacKenzie Francisville Strathpeffer Ross-shire IV14 9AX Tel: (Strathpeffer) 01997 421345	COMMENDED ♛	2 Family	1 Pub Bath/Show	B&B per person £13.50-£16.00 Single £13.50-£14.00 Double	Open Apr-Oct

Small cottage located on a quiet road above Strathpeffer with
views across the valley, but 5 minutes walk from the centre.

STRATHPEFFER continued	Map 4 A8

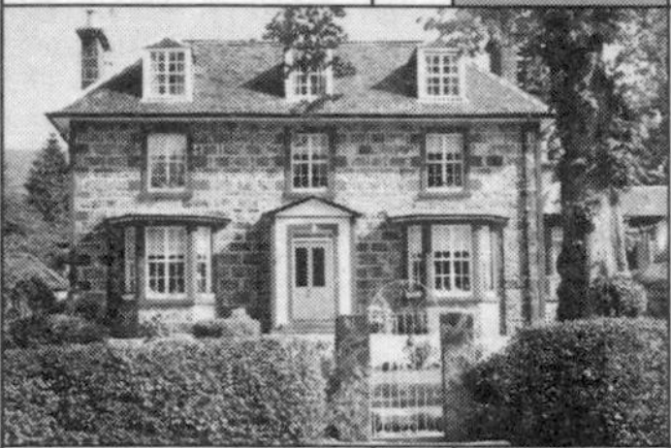

CRAIGVAR

THE SQUARE, STRATHPEFFER IV14 9DL   Tel: 01997 421622

Beautifully situated overlooking the square in this charming Victorian spa village. This distinctive Georgian House offers superb luxury facilities.

★ All rooms have colour TV, tea/coffee facilities, direct-dial telephone.
★ All bedrooms with attractive en-suite bathrooms.
★ Four-poster bedroom/open fires.
★ Excellent parking.
★ Ideal touring base.

Mrs M Scott
Craigvar, The Square
Strathpeffer
Ross-shire
IV14 9DL
Tel: (Strathpeffer)
01997 421622

HIGHLY COMMENDED

1 Single
1 Twin
1 Double

3 En Suite fac

B&B per person
from £20.00 Single
£16.00-£20.00 Double

Open Apr-Oct

Beautifully situated overlooking the square in charming spa village, this distinctive Georgian house offers attractive ensuite rooms. 4-poster bed.

STRATHYRE
Perthshire
Mr & Mrs Ffinch
Dochfour
Strathyre
Perthshire
FK18 8NA
Tel: (Strathyre) 01877 384256
Fax: 01877 384256

Map 1 H3

COMMENDED

2 Double
1 Family

2 En Suite fac
1 Priv. NOT ensuite

B&B per person
£20.00-£24.00 Single
£15.00-£18.00 Double

Open Jan-Dec
Dinner 1800-2000
B&B + Eve. Meal
£20.50-£28.00

Traditional stone-built semi-detached villa in centre of village.
Excellent views to surrounding hills. Home cooking with fresh produce.

Mr & Mrs Reid
Coire Buidhe
Strathyre
Perthshire
FK18 8NA
Tel: (Strathyre) 01877 384288

APPROVED
Listed

2 Single
2 Twin
2 Double
2 Family

1 En Suite fac
3 Pub Bath/Show

B&B per person
£14.00-£17.00 Single
£14.00-£17.00 Double

Open Jan-Dec
Dinner from 1900
B&B + Eve. Meal
£23.50-£26.50

Personally run guest house in centre of small village offering
traditional comfort. Ideal centre for touring the West Highlands.

Rosebank House
Strathyre
Perthshire
FK18 8NA
Tel: (Strathyre) 01877 384208

COMMENDED

1 Single
1 Twin
1 Double
1 Family

1 En Suite fac
1 Pub Bath/Show

B&B per person
£15.00-£17.00 Single
£13.00-£17.00 Double

Open Jan-Dec

A warm welcome awaits you at this comfortable home in Trossachs village
with scenic mountain and river views. Home baking. Coal fire in lounge.

STROMEFERRY
Ross-shire
Mrs P Davey
Soluis Mu Thuath,
Braeintra, Achmore
Stromeferry
Ross-shire
IV53 8UN
Tel: (Stromeferry)
01599 577219

Map 3 F9

COMMENDED

2 Twin
1 Double
1 Family

4 En Suite fac

B&B per person
£15.00-£18.00 Double

Open Feb-Nov

Purpose-built by owners, set amidst quiet countryside.
Excellent centre for Skye, Applecross and Torridon. No smoking.

STROMNESS
Orkney
Mrs C Hourston
15 John Street
Stromness
Orkney
KW16 3AD
Tel: (Stromness)
01856 850642

Map 5 B11

COMMENDED
Listed

2 Single
1 Twin
1 Double

1 Pub Bath/Show

B&B per person
£14.00-£15.00 Single
£14.00-£15.00 Double

Open Jan-Dec

In quiet situation above harbour, convenient for ferry terminal and shops.
Wide choice at breakfast. Rooms with colour TV, tea and coffee and
many accessories.

Mrs S Thomas Stenigar, Ness Road Stromness Orkney KW16 3DW Tel: (Stromness) 01856 850438		COMMENDED 👑👑	2 Twin 1 Double	2 En Suite fac 1 Priv. NOT ensuite	B&B per person £25.00 Single £18.00-£22.00 Double Room only per person £20.00	Open Apr-Oct Dinner 1800-2100 B&B + Eve. Meal £30.00-£34.00

Rambling historic house with bags of character. Comfortable lounge with sea views to Hoy. Golf course and yacht club nearby.

Mrs M Tulloch Olnadale, Innertown Stromness Orkney KW16 3JW Tel: (Stromness) 01856 850418		COMMENDED Listed	1 Twin 2 Double	1 En Suite fac 2 Pub Bath/Show	B&B per person from £16.00 Single £14.00-£16.00 Double	Open Mar-Sep

Modern house in quiet road on edge of town, with panoramic views of Hoy Sound. 5-10 minutes walk to town and harbour. Good base for touring Orkney.

STRUAN **Isle of Skye, Inverness-shire** Mrs Beaton 3 Balmeanach Struan Isle of Skye, Inverness-shire Tel: (Struan) 01470 572300	Map 3 D9	COMMENDED Listed	1 Twin 2 Double	3 En Suite fac	B&B per person £14.00-£17.00 Single £15.00-£15.50 Double	Open Apr-Oct

Comfortable modern house, with outlook over Loch Bracadale towards MacLeod's Tables. Dunvegan 5 miles (8kms).

Mrs Moira Campbell The Anchorage, 9 Ebost West Struan Isle of Skye, Inverness-shire IV56 8FE Tel: (Struan) 01470 572206		COMMENDED 👑👑	1 Twin 2 Double	1 En Suite fac 2 Pub Bath/Show	B&B per person £13.00-£16.00 Double	Open Jan-Dec Dinner 1800-1930 B&B + Eve. Meal £23.00-£26.00

Modern bungalow standing in its own grounds with views over Loch Bracadale. Home cooking and family atmosphere.

TAIN **Ross-shire** Mrs Anderson Rosslyn, 2 Moss Road Tain Ross-shire IV19 1HQ Tel: (Tain) 01862 892697	Map 4 B7	COMMENDED 👑👑	1 Twin 1 Family	2 En Suite fac 1 Pub Bath/Show	B&B per person from £15.00 Single from £13.00 Double Room only per person from £15.00	Open Jan-Dec

Comfortable, personally run B & B close to town centre. Ideal base for touring the Highlands. Private parking.

Mrs M MacLean 23 Moss Road Tain Ross-shire IV19 1HH Tel: (Tain) 01862 894087		COMMENDED 👑	1 Single 1 Twin 1 Double	2 Pub Bath/Show	B&B per person £18.00 Single £14.00-£15.00 Double	Open Jan-Dec

Comfortable family-run home in quiet location. Log-burning stove in lounge and a warm welcome assured.

Mrs K M Roberts Carringtons, Morangie Road Tain Ross-shire IV19 1PY Tel: (Tain) 01862 892635		COMMENDED 👑👑	1 Double 2 Family	1 En Suite fac 1 Limited ensuite 2 Pub Bath/Show	B&B per person from £15.00 Single from £13.00 Double Room only per person from £15.00	Open Jan-Dec

Detached family home on the outskirts of Tain overlooking the sea.

BY TAIN Ross-shire	Map 4 B7

ALDIE HOUSE
ALDIE HOUSE, TAIN, ROSS-SHIRE IV19 1LZ
Telephone and Fax: 01862 893787

Beautiful Victorian mansion house situated in its own six acres of superb garden and woodland. Come and enjoy our excellent kitchen and friendly hospitality. All rooms have central heating and are delightfully decorated. The luxury bedrooms have all ensuite facilities and TV. Ideal place for touring in the Highlands.

Mr & Mrs De Decker Aldie House, Aldie Farm by Tain Ross-shire IV19 1LZ Tel: (Tain) 01862 893787 Fax: 01862 893787	COMMENDED	1 Double 2 Family	3 En Suite fac	B&B per person £22.00 Single £22.00 Double Room only per person £22.00	Open Jan-Dec Dinner 1800-2100

Set in a large mature garden with surrounding woods, this delightful country house has been sensitively renovated to a high standard by its Belgian owners.

Mrs C Paterson Croma, Hilton Fearn Ross-shire IV20 1UZ Tel: (Fearn) 01862 832282	HIGHLY COMMENDED Listed	1 Single 1 Twin 1 Double	2 Pub Bath/Show	B&B per person £13.50-£16.50 Single £13.50-£16.50 Double Room only per person £13.00-£14.00	Open Jan-Dec Dinner 1730-2030 B&B + Eve. Meal £18.50-£25.00

Mr and Mrs Paterson, with their love of antiques, have created a warm and stylish home for holidaymakers and travellers.

TARBERT Harris, Western Isles	Map 3 C6

Allan Cottage Guest House Tarbert Harris, Western Isles PA85 3DJ Tel: (Harris) 01859 502146	HIGHLY COMMENDED	1 Twin 2 Double	2 En Suite fac 1 Priv. NOT ensuite	B&B per person £25.00 Single £25.00 Double	Open Apr-Sep Dinner from 1900 B&B + Eve. Meal £41.00

Recently converted Old Harris Telephone Exchange, offering very high standard of comfort and cuisine.

Flora Morrison Tigh na Mara Tarbert Harris, Western Isles Tel: (Harris) 01859 502270	COMMENDED	1 Single 1 Twin 1 Family	1 Pub Bath/Show	B&B per person £14.00-£15.00 Single £14.00-£15.00 Double	Open Jan-Dec Dinner from 1830

Detached house with scenic views over East Loch Tarbert.
Only about 500 metres from ferry terminal. Ideal centre for touring Harris.

Mrs A Morrison Hillcrest West Tarbert Harris, Western Isles HS3 3AH Tel: (Harris) 01859 502119	HIGHLY COMMENDED	1 Twin 1 Double 1 Family	1 En Suite fac 2 Pub Bath/Show	B&B per person £14.00-£17.00 Single £14.00-£17.00 Double	Open Apr-Nov Dinner from 1900 B&B + Eve. Meal £24.00-£28.00

Modern croft house in elevated position with fine view over West Loch Tarbert. About 1 mile (2kms) from ferry terminal.

TARBERT, Loch Fyne Argyll Mrs Peden The Hollies Tarbert, Loch Fyne Argyll PA29 6YF Tel: (Tarbert) 01880 820742	Map 1 E5	**COMMENDED** ♛	2 Twin 1 Double	2 Pub Bath/Show	B&B per person from £16.00 Double	Open Jan-Dec	

Comfortable accommodation in modern bungalow with open views towards West Loch Tarbert. Convenient for ferries to Islay, Jura, Gigha, Arran, and the Cowal Peninsula.

TARBET, by Arrochar Dunbartonshire Mrs E Fairfield Lochview Tarbet, by Arrochar Dunbartonshire G83 7DD Tel: (Arrochar) 01301 702200	Map 1 G3	**APPROVED** Listed	1 Twin 2 Double	1 Pub Bath/Show	B&B per person £15.00-£18.00 Single £14.00-£16.00 Double	Open Jan-Dec

Georgian house on main road to west coast. Short distance from shore of Loch Lomond. Ideal base for touring.

Mrs Kelly Bon-Etive Tarbet, by Arrochar Dunbartonshire G83 Tel: (Arrochar) 01301 702219		**COMMENDED** Listed	1 Twin 1 Double	1 Pub Bath/Show	B&B per person £15.00-£15.50 Single	Open Apr-Oct

Conveniently situated in quiet cul-de-sac close to the A82, with fine views of Loch Lomond and 'The Ben'.

Tarbet House Tarbet, Loch Lomond Dunbartonshire G83 7DE Tel: (Arrochar) 01301 702349		**COMMENDED** ♛♛	1 Twin 2 Double	1 En Suite fac 2 Pub Bath/Show	B&B per person £20.00-£25.00 Single £16.00-£25.00 Double	Open Jan-Oct

Modern country house in 7 acres. Panoramic view south across Loch Lomond. Dinner by arrangement. Sailing, walking and other activities.

TEANGUE, Sleat Isle of Skye, Inverness-shire B & J Shaw Alltan House Ferindonald, Sleat Isle of Skye, Inverness-shire IV44 8RQ Tel: (Ardvasar) 01471 844342	Map 3 F10	**COMMENDED** Listed	1 Twin 2 Double	2 Pub Bath/Show	B&B per person £15.00-£17.00 Double Dinner from 1900 B&B + Eve. Meal £27.00-£29.00	Open Mar-Nov

Modern house in elevated position offering panoramic views over the Sound of Sleat to the mountains of Knoydart, 4 miles (6kms) from Armadale ferry.

THORNHILL Dumfriesshire Mrs Hill Drumcruilton Thornhill Dumfriesshire DG3 5BG Tel: (Thornhill) 01848 500210	Map 2 A8	**HIGHLY COMMENDED** ♛♛	1 Twin 2 Double	1 En Suite fac 1 Priv.NOT ensuite 2 Pub Bath/Show	B&B per person from £20.00 Single £18.00-£20.00 Double Dinner 1830-1930 B&B + Eve. Meal £30.00-£32.00	Open May-Nov

Refurbished country farmhouse set on working stock farm with excellent views of Lowther Hills. Fishing, shooting, deer stalking can be arranged.

Mrs Maxwell Druidhall Farm Thornhill Dumfriesshire DG3 4NE Tel: (Marrburn) 01848 600271		**APPROVED** Listed	1 Twin 2 Double	2 Pub Bath/Show	B&B per person from £13.00 Single from £13.00 Double Dinner 1800-1900	Open Mar-Dec

Traditional farmhouse set in unspoilt countryside. Ideal base for fishing and touring.

Details of Grading and Classification are on page vi.   Key to symbols is on back flap.   269

THORNHILL Perthshire	Map 2 A4		

Corshill Cottage
BY THORNHILL, STIRLING FK8 3QD
Telephone: 01786 850270

An attractive, former blacksmiths' home and smiddy situated at The Gateway to the Trossachs within easy reach of major cities, many golf courses, unrivalled scenery and historic sites. Offering exceptional accommodation the house is set in well-maintained, mature gardens with ample parking. Our aim is your comfort and satisfaction.

K Fitches Corshill Cottage Thornhill Perthshire FK8 3QD Tel: (Stirling) 01786 850270	**DELUXE** ♛♛♛	1 Twin 3 En Suite fac 2 Double	B&B per person £19.00-£22.00 Single £19.00-£22.00 Double	Open May-Sep Dinner 1900-2000

Tastefully appointed cottage in peaceful, rural setting, with 1 acre of cottage garden, yet only 8 miles (13kms) from Callander, the "Gateway to the Highlands".

THURSO Caithness Mrs J Falconer, Murray House 1 Campbell Street Thurso Caithness KW14 7HD Tel: (Thurso) 01847 895759	Map 4 D3 **HIGHLY COMMENDED** ♛♛	1 Single 2 En Suite fac 1 Twin 2 Pub Bath/Show 1 Double 1 Family	B&B per person £14.00-£20.00 Single	Open Jan-Dec

Set in the centre of the town, a warm welcome and comfortable stay are assured in this refurbished 19th-century town house. Private parking.

Mrs M Fisher Carlingwark, 5 Mears Place Thurso Caithness KW14 7EW Tel: (Thurso) 01847 894124	**HIGHLY COMMENDED** ♛	1 Single 2 Pub Bath/Show 1 Twin 1 Double	B&B per person £14.00-£14.50 Single £14.00-£14.50 Double	Open Jun-Sep

Modern detached bungalow with enclosed landscaped garden in quiet cul-de-sac. Well furnished and comfortable, friendly family home. Evening cup of tea and home baking.

Mrs Henderson Kerrera, 12 Rose Street Thurso Caithness KW14 7HJ Tel: (Thurso) 01847 895127	**COMMENDED** ♛	2 Twin 1 Pub Bath/Show	B&B per person £15.00-£16.00 Single £13.00-£15.00 Double	Open Feb-Nov

A warm welcome awaits you in this comfortable family home; quiet location in centre of town, convenient for railway station.

Mrs McDonald Seaview Farm, Hill of Forss Thurso Caithness KW14 7XQ Tel: (Thurso) 01847 892315	**COMMENDED** Listed	1 Twin 1 Pub Bath/Show 2 Double	B&B per person £14.00-£15.00 Single	Open Jan-Dec

Working farm, warm welcome and home bakes; display of Highland Dancing and trophies. Two miles from Orkney ferry.

Mrs Murray 1 Granville Crescent Thurso Caithness KW14 7NP Tel: (Thurso) 01847 892993	**COMMENDED** ♛♛	2 Twin 1 En Suite fac 1 Pub Bath/Show	B&B per person £15.00-£17.00 Single £15.00-£16.50 Double	Open Jan-Dec

Quietly situated, yet within easy reach of station and all facilities. All ground-floor rooms, one ensuite, one with private bathroom.

Mrs M Sinclair Shinval, Glengolly Thurso Caithness KW14 7XN Tel: (Thurso) 01847 894306	COMMENDED	1 Twin 1 Double 1 Family	1 En Suite fac 1 Priv. NOT ensuite 2 Pub Bath/Show	B&B per person £14.00-£16.00 Single £14.00-£16.00 Double Room only per person £11.50-£13.50	Open Jan-Dec	

Family home in quiet rural setting. 2 miles (3kms) from Thurso. Extensive countryside views.

Mrs E Taylor Oldfield Park Thurso Caithness KW14 8RE Tel: (Thurso) 01847 893637	COMMENDED Listed	1 Twin 2 Double	1 En Suite fac 1 Pub Bath/Show	B&B per person £16.00-£22.00 Single	Open May-Sep	

Comfortable B & B set back from main road, large garden, ample private parking, short walk from town centre.

Mrs D Thomson Annandale 2 Rendel Govan Road Thurso Caithness KW14 7EP Tel: (Thurso) 01847 893942	COMMENDED	2 Twin 1 Double	2 Pub Bath/Show	B&B per person £16.00-£16.50 Single £14.00-£15.00 Double	Open May-Sep	

Comfortable B & B situated in quiet residential area. Ideal base for touring north coast and convenient for Orkney ferry.

Mrs B Tuck Seaview, Dixonfield Thurso Caithness KW14 8YN Tel: (Thurso) 01847 894511	DELUXE	1 Twin 2 Double	2 Pub Bath/Show	B&B per person from £15.00 Single from £15.00 Double	Open Jan-Dec	

Modern bungalow with panoramic views over Thurso harbour and across the sea to Orkney. A warm welcome and most comfortable stay assured.

TILLICOULTRY **Clackmannanshire** Mrs Goddard Wyvis, 70 Stirling Street Tillicoultry Clackmannanshire FK13 6EA Tel: (Tillicoultry) 01259 751513	Map 2 A3 COMMENDED	1 Twin	1 En Suite fac	B&B per person £17.00-£19.00 Single £18.00-£20.00 Double	Open Jan-Dec Dinner 1900-2030	

Cottage in conservation area overlooking the Ochil Hills and ideally situated for hillwalking. Friendly atmosphere, home cooking and baking.

WESTBOURNE
10 Dollar Road, Tillicoultry FK13 6PA. Tel: 01259 750314

Victorian Mill Owner's Mansion set in wooded grounds beneath Ochil Hills. Warm, friendly atmosphere with unusual collection of arts and curios from around the world. Delicious home cooking using local produce. Vegetarian food a speciality. Log fires. Centrally situated for Edinburgh, Glasgow, Perth, Stirling – motorways 15 minutes. Secure off-street parking.

Mrs J O'Dell Westbourne, 10 Dollar Road Tillicoultry Clackmannanshire FK13 6PA Tel: (Tillicoultry) 01259 750314 Fax: 01324 826677	COMMENDED	1 Twin 2 Double	1 En Suite fac 1 Pub Bath/Show	B&B per person £19.00-£23.00 Single £16.00-£20.00 Double	Open Jan-Dec Dinner 1830-2030 B&B + Eve. Meal £29.00-£36.00	

Victorian mansion, full of character, on the Mill Trail below Ochil Hills. Home baking and cooking. Log fire. Secure off-road parking.

TIREE, Isle of **Argyll** Mrs Cameron The Sheiling, Crossapol Isle of Tiree Argyll PA77 6UP Tel: (Scarinish) 01879 220503	Map 1 A2	COMMENDED Listed	1 Single 1 Pub Bath/Show 1 Twin	B&B per person from £15.00 Single from £15.00 Double	Open Apr-Oct Dinner 1800-2000 B&B + Eve. Meal £20.00-£23.00	

Former croft house in its own field with one of the few gardens on Tiree. Gorgeous views across Crossapol Bay. Home cooking with own vegetables.

TOBERMORY **Isle of Mull, Argyll** Baliscate Guest House Tobermory Isle of Mull, Argyll PA75 6QA Tel: (Tobermory) 01688 302048	Map 1 C1	COMMENDED	1 Twin 3 En Suite fac 3 Double 1 Pub Bath/Show 1 Family	B&B per person £17.00-£21.00 Double	Open Jan-Dec	

Set in 1.5 acres of garden and woodland with magnificent views over the Sound of Mull.

Copeland House Jubilee Terrace Tobermory Isle of Mull, Argyll PA75 6PZ Tel: (Tobermory) 01688 302049	COMMENDED	1 Twin 3 En Suite fac 1 Double 1 Family	B&B per person £23.00-£27.00 Single £23.00-£25.00 Double	Open Jan-Dec	

Designed and built in 1993 for use as a small guest house with beautiful views over the Sound of Mull and Tobermory Bay. Close to Tobermory Harbour.

Failte Guest House Main Street Tobermory Isle of Mull, Argyll PA75 6NU Tel: (Tobermory) 01688 302495 Fax: 01688 302232	COMMENDED Listed	3 Twin 7 En Suite fac 3 Double 2 Pub Bath/Show 1 Family	B&B per person from £20.00 Double	Open Mar-Oct	

Scottish hospitality in comfortable guest house in prime position overlooking beautiful Tobermory Bay.

D E McAdam Fairways Lodge Tobermory Isle of Mull, Argyll PA75 6PS Tel: (Tobermory) 01688 302238 Fax: 01688 302238	HIGHLY COMMENDED	1 Single 5 En Suite fac 2 Twin 1 Double 1 Family	B&B per person £29.50 Single £29.50 Double	Open Jan-Dec	

Situated between 3rd and 4th fairways on golf course. Commanding view across Tobermory Bay and Sound of Mull.

Staffa Cottages Guest House Tobermory Isle of Mull, Argyll PA75 6PL Tel: (Tobermory) 01688 302464 Fax: 01688 302464	COMMENDED	2 Twin 4 En Suite fac 2 Double	B&B per person from £25.00 Single from £20.00 Double	Open Jan-Dec Dinner from 1900 B&B + Eve. Meal £28.00-£32.00	

In quiet residential area on slopes above Tobermory with large garden. Fine views over bay to Sound of Mull and Morvern Hills.

Strongarbh House Tobermory Isle of Mull, Argyll PA75 6PR Tel: (Tobermory) 01688 302328 Fax: 01688 302238	HIGHLY COMMENDED	2 Twin 4 En Suite fac 2 Double	B&B per person £45.00-£57.50 Double Room only per person £30.00-£37.50	Open Jan-Dec Dinner 1900-2130 B&B + Eve. Meal £45.00-£55.00	

Stone-built Victorian country house, refurbished throughout. All rooms ensuite; à la carte menu; superb views over bay. Taste of Scotland.

BY TOMINTOUL **Banffshire** Irene Duffus Auchriachan Farmhouse Mains of Auchriachan Tomintoul Ballindalloch, Banffshire AB37 9EQ Tel: (Tomintoul) 01807 580416	Map 4 D10	COMMENDED	1 Twin 2 En Suite fac 1 Double	B&B per person £13.00-£15.00 Double	Open Jan-Dec	

Traditional farmhouse 1 mile (2kms) from Tomintoul centre. Ideal for skiing holidays.

Mrs M C McIntosh Milton Farm Tomintoul, Ballindalloch Banffshire AB37 9EQ Tel: (Tomintoul) 01807 580288		COMMENDED Listed	1 Double 1 Family	1 Pub Bath/Show	B&B per person £13.00-£15.00 Double	Open Jan-Dec	
			Warm welcome at 18th-century farmhouse with panoramic views over hills. Tomintoul 0 .5 miles (1km). Good base for walking, touring. Ground-floor accommodation.				
Mrs Anne Shearer Croughly Farm Tomintoul, Ballindalloch Banffshire AB37 9EN Tel: (Tomintoul) 01807 580476		COMMENDED	1 Double 1 Family	1 En Suite fac 1 Priv. NOT ensuite	B&B per person £15.00-£16.00 Double	Open Apr-Oct	
			18th-century listed farmhouse, overlooking the River Conglass with stunning views of the Cairngorms. 2 miles (3kms) from Tomintoul.				
Mrs Elma Turner Findron Farm, Braemar Road Tomintoul Banffshire AB37 9ER Tel: (Tomintoul) 01807 580382		COMMENDED	2 Double 1 Family	2 En Suite fac 1 Priv. NOT ensuite	B&B per person £13.00-£16.00 Single £13.00-£16.00 Double	Open Jan-Dec Dinner 1800-1930 B&B + Eve. Meal £19.00-£22.00	
			Comfortable farmhouse with a warm and friendly welcome situated 1 mile (2 kms) from Tomintoul. Ensuite and private bathrooms.				
TONGUE **Sutherland** Rhian Guest House Mrs S Mackay Tongue Sutherland IV27 4XJ Tel: (Tongue) 01847 611257	Map 4 A3	COMMENDED	1 Twin 1 Double 1 Family	2 En Suite fac 1 Priv. NOT ensuite	B&B per person £20.00-£25.00 Single £17.00-£19.00 Double	Open Jan-Dec Dinner 1800-1900	
			Charming modernised croft cottage, with peacocks, 0.5 miles (1km) outside village. Dramatic views of Ben Loyal. Owner's painting gallery next door. Annexe outwith scheme.				
TORRIDON **Ross-shire**	Map 3 G8						

BEN DAMPH LODGE
TORRIDON, ROSS-SHIRE IV22 2EY
Telephone: 01445 791251   Fax: 01445 791296
BEN DAMPH LODGE is a former stable block to the
Loch Torridon Hotel.
New spacious, budget accommodation with all
modern facilities.
New Bistro open all day plus bar.
Petrol and Craft Shop.

Ben Damph Lodge Torridon Ross-shire IV22 2EY Tel: (Torridon) 01445 791251/791242 Fax: 01445 791296		COMMENDED Lodge	14 Family	14 En Suite fac	Room only per person £30.00-£40.00	Open Jan-Dec Dinner 1830-2030	
			Comfortable lodge accommodation in the midst of Torridon Mountains. Restaurant and bar close by.				
Mrs M MacDonald Grianan, Inveralligin Torridon, Achnasheen Ross-shire IV22 2HB Tel: (Torridon) 01445 791264		COMMENDED Listed	1 Twin 1 Double	1 Pub Bath/Show	B&B per person from £14.50 Double	Open Apr-Sep	
			Modern bungalow with panoramic views over Loch Torridon to the mountains beyond. Ideal for walking.				

TRANENT **East Lothian** Mrs R Harrison Rosebank House, 161 High Street Tranent East Lothian EH33 1LP Tel: (Tranent) 01875 610967	Map 2 D5	COMMENDED	1 Twin 3 Double 1 Family	2 Pub Bath/Show	B&B per person £15.00-£17.00 Single £14.00-£15.00 Double	Open Jan-Dec

Stone built house near centre of Tranent. 10 miles (16kms) to Edinburgh city centre. Ideal base for golfing and touring East Lothian.

Mrs H C Harvey North Elphinstone Farm Tranent East Lothian EH33 2ND Tel: (Tranent) 01875 610329		COMMENDED Listed	1 Twin 1 Double 1 Family	2 Pub Bath/Show	B&B per person £16.00-£17.00 Single £15.00-£17.00 Double	Open Jun-Sep

Large farmhouse in quiet rural area. 10 miles (16kms) from Edinburgh and convenient for numerous golf courses. Non-smoking. Good touring base.

TREASLANE **Isle of Skye, Inverness-shire** Auchendinny Guest House Treaslane Skeabost Bridge Isle of Skye, Inverness-shire IV51 9NX Tel: (Skeabost Bridge) 01470 532470	Map 3 D8	HIGHLY COMMENDED	2 Twin 4 Double 1 Family	7 En Suite fac	B&B per person £18.00-£19.00 Single £18.00-£19.00 Double	Open Jan-Dec Dinner from 1830 B&B + Eve. Meal £28.00-£30.00

On A850 Dunvegan Road 8.5 miles from Portree. Peaceful lochside setting, beautiful views.

Mrs M Cameron Hillcroft, 2 Treaslane by Portree Isle of Skye, Inverness-shire IV51 9NX Tel: (Edinbane) 01470 582304		HIGHLY COMMENDED	2 Double	1 En Suite fac 1 Priv. NOT ensuite	B&B per person £15.00-£20.00 Double	Open Jan-Dec

Friendly welcome at modernised house on working croft overlooking Loch Snizort. On A850 9 miles (14 kms) north of Portree.

TROON **Ayrshire**	Map 1 G7					

Advie Lodge
2 BENTINCK DRIVE, TROON KA10 6HX
Telephone: 01292 313635

*Welcome to Advie Lodge, where a warm, friendly atmosphere awaits you. This 19th-century listed building is centrally situated close to the beach, shops, marina and golf courses. Our spacious bedrooms are superbly decorated, centrally heated and provided with colour televisions and tea/coffee makers. Private en-suite facilities are available. There is a comfortable lounge and a secluded garden for the use of guests. Private off-road parking is provided. Troon is close to the beautiful island of Arran, historic Ayrshire, its villages, Robert Burns cottage and heritage trail. **Brochure and further details from your hostess, Alison Dickson.***

Advie Lodge 2 Bentinck Drive Troon Ayrshire KA10 6HX Tel: (Troon) 01292 313635		COMMENDED	1 Single 1 Twin 2 Double	2 En Suite fac 2 Priv. NOT ensuite 1 Pub Bath/Show	B&B per person £17.50-£22.50 Single £17.50-£22.50 Double	Open Jan-Dec

A warm welcome awaits you in this 19th-century house. Centrally situated for beach, shops, marina and golf courses. Private parking. Ground-floor accommodation.

Mrs L Devine 5 St Meddans Street Troon Ayrshire KA10 6JU Tel: (Troon) 01292 311423		COMMENDED	2 Twin 1 Double	2 En Suite fac 1 Priv. NOT ensuite	B&B per person from £16.00 Single from £16.00 Double Room only per person from £16.00	Open Jan-Dec	

Stone-built house, centrally located near to beach and golf courses.
All rooms with private facilities.

Tigh Dearg 31 Victoria Drive Troon Ayrshire KA10 6JF Tel: (Troon) 01292 311552		APPROVED	1 Single 1 Twin 1 Family	2 Pub Bath/Show	B&B per person from £13.00 Single from £13.00 Double	Open Jan-Dec	

Red sandstone villa, handy for beach, golf and train.

Mrs M Tweedie The Cherries, 50 Ottoline Drive Troon Ayrshire KA10 7AW Tel: (Troon) 01292 313312		COMMENDED	1 Single 1 Twin 1 Family	1 En Suite fac 2 Pub Bath/Show	B&B per person from £17.00 Single from £17.00 Double Room only per person from £15.00	Open Jan-Dec	

Warm welcome in family home. Quiet residential area backing onto golf course.

TUMMEL BRIDGE **Perthshire** Mrs Sheena Forsythe Heatherbank Tummel Bridge Perthshire PH16 5NX Tel: (Tummel Bridge) 01882 634324	Map 2 A1	COMMENDED Listed	1 Single 1 Twin 1 Double	1 En Suite fac 1 Pub Bath/Show	B&B per person from £13.00 Single £14.00-£16.00 Double	Open Jan-Dec	

Modern detached bungalow in village in area renowned for its
mountain and loch views. One ensuite bedroom. Good touring area.

BY TURRIFF **Aberdeenshire** Mrs C R M Roebuck Lendrum Farm, Birkenhills by Turriff Aberdeenshire AB53 8HA Tel: (Cuminestown) 01888 544285	Map 4 F8	COMMENDED	1 Twin 1 Family	1 En Suite fac 1 Pub Bath/Show	B&B per person £17.00 Single £17.00 Double	Open Jan-Dec	

Historic working farm in Buchan countryside. Near picturesque coast, castles,
gardens, distilleries. Warm welcome, comfortable, good food, peaceful.

TWYNHOLM **Kirkcudbrightshire** Mrs M McMorran Miefield Farm Twynholm Kirkcudbrightshire DG6 4PS Tel: (Twynholm) 01557 860254	Map 2 A10	APPROVED Listed	2 Family	1 Pub Bath/Show	B&B per person £12.50-£13.00 Single £12.50-£13.00 Double Room only per person £12.50-£13.00	Open Apr-Oct Dinner from 1730 B&B + Eve. Meal £17.50-£18.50	

Working sheep and beef farm at the head of a quiet glen.
See sheep dogs and shepherds at work.

Mrs L Robson Glencroft Twynholm Kirkcudbrightshire DG6 4NT Tel: (Twynholm) 01557 860252		COMMENDED	1 Single 1 Double 1 Family	2 Pub Bath/Show	B&B per person £13.50-£14.50 Single £13.50-£14.50 Double	Open Apr-Oct Dinner from 1730 B&B + Eve. Meal £18.50-£19.50	

Modernised, 18th-century former farmhouse with extensive garden and fine
countryside views. 0.25 mile (0.5km) from A75. A non-smoking home.

UIG Isle of Skye, Inverness-shire Mrs R MacKinnon Braigh-Uige Uig Isle of Skye, Inverness-shire Tel: (Uig) 01470 542228	Map 3 D8	HIGHLY COMMENDED	1 Twin	1 Priv. NOT ensuite 1 Pub Bath/Show	B&B per person from £15.00 Double	Open Apr-Oct

Small and personally run, situated in magnificent position overlooking Uig Bay to the Waternish Peninsula.

Idrigill House

1 IDRIGILL, UIG, BY PORTREE, ISLE OF SKYE IV51 9XU
TELEPHONE: 01470 542398

This comfortable modern house is centrally heated and situated in a quiet location at the end of Uig Bay close to the Outer Isles ferry. Ideal retreat for walkers, nature lovers, bird watchers etc with magnificent views across the bay to the distant Cuillin Hills. Ample parking.

Mr and Mrs Watkins Idrigill House, Idrigill Uig Isle of Skye, Inverness-shire Tel: (Uig) 01470 542398	COMMENDED	2 Single 1 Twin 1 Double	2 Pub Bath/Show	B&B per person £15.00-£18.00 Single £15.00-£18.00 Double	Open Jan-Dec

Quiet location with magnificent views. Convenient for ferry to Outer Isles.

ULLAPOOL Ross-shire	Map 3 G6

Ardvreck Guest House

Morefield Brae, Ullapool IV26 2TH
Telephone and Fax: 01854 612028

Spacious and well-appointed accommodation. All rooms ensuite with television and tea/coffee facilities, rural setting with spectacular views of sea, mountains, and Ullapool. Durness on the North Coast (75 miles) can be reached in a day as can the famous Inverewe Gardens (55 miles south)

B&B from £18.00   *Contact Mrs Stockall*

Ardvreck Guest House Morefield Brae Ullapool Ross-shire IV26 2TH Tel: (Ullapool) 01854 612028/612561 Fax: 01854 612028	HIGHLY COMMENDED	2 Single 2 Twin 4 Double 2 Family	10 En Suite fac	B&B per person £18.00-£23.00 Single £18.00-£23.00 Double Room only per person £16.00-£21.00	Open Jan-Dec

Quiet secluded guest house with spectacular views over Loch Broom.
All rooms ensuite. Ullapool 1.5 miles (2.5 kms).

Mrs I Boa Ardale, Market Street Ullapool Ross-shire EH52 6PA Tel: (Ullapool) 01854 612220	COMMENDED	1 Twin 2 Double	1 En Suite fac 1 Pub Bath/Show	B&B per person from £14.00 Single from £14.00 Double	Open Mar-Oct

Modern bungalow in tree-lined avenue. Close to town centre and all amenities.
Car parking available. Gaelic spoken.

Mrs E Campbell Clisham, 56 Rhue Ullapool Ross-shire IV26 2TJ Tel: (Ullapool) 01854 612498 (except Sunday)	COMMENDED	2 Family	1 Pub Bath/Show	B&B per person £13.50-£14.00 Single £13.50-£14.00 Double	Open May-Oct

Small working croft peacefully situated in elevated position,
giving superb views over Loch Broom. 3 miles (5kms) north of Ullapool.

Mrs F Campbell Corrieshalloch House Fasnagrianach Loch Broom, by Ullapool Ross-shire IV23 2RU Tel: (Lochbroom) 01854 655204 Fax: 01854 655204	COMMENDED 👑👑	1 Twin 2 Double	1 En Suite fac 1 Pub Bath/Show	B&B per person £14.00-£16.00 Single £14.00-£16.00 Double	Open Jan-Dec Dinner 1830-1930 B&B + Eve. Meal £23.00-£25.00

New house on a small working croft in attractive countryside setting.
Home cooking using quality local produce and home-grown vegetables.

DROMNAN GUEST HOUSE

Garve Road, Ullapool IV26 2SX   Tel/Fax: 01854 612333

This modern family run guest house is ideally situated on the outskirts of Ullapool. All our rooms are furnished to a high standard with private facilities, colour TVs, hairdryers and courtesy trays. Our open plan lounge and dining room have beautiful views overlooking Loch Broom. Easy access to Summer Isles and Outer Hebrides.

Dromnan Guest House Garve Road Ullapool Ross-shire IV26 2SX Tel: (Ullapool) 01854 612333 Fax: 01854 612333	HIGHLY COMMENDED 👑👑👑 	2 Twin 3 Double 2 Family	7 En Suite fac	B&B per person £17.00-£20.00 Single £17.00-£20.00 Double	Open Jan-Dec

Family run guest house on outskirts of the west coast fishing village of Ullapool,
overlooking Loch Broom. 5 minutes from ferry to the Outer Isles.

Four Seasons
Travel Lodge

GARVE ROAD, ULLAPOOL IV26 2SX
Telephone: 01854 612905 Fax: 01854 612674

Quiet, comfortable accommodation in spectacular scenery. The lodge is situated on the shore of Loch Broom five minutes walk from the village centre. The modern building is set in 1½ acres with lawns leading to the pebble beach at the rear and a large car park at the front. The 16 bright, comfortable bedrooms are divided between ground and first floor and have ensuite facilities, TV and courtesy tray. The breakfast room has unsurpassed views of the loch and harbour. Large, comfortable lounge with access to the garden. *Vegetarians welcome.*
Bed and full Scottish breakfast from £22 per person.

Four Seasons Travel Lodge Garve Road Ullapool Ross-shire IV26 2SX Tel: (Ullapool) 01854 612905 Fax: 01854 612674	COMMENDED Lodge	1 Single 7 Twin 7 Double 1 Family	16 En Suite fac	B&B per person £22.00-£25.00 Single £22.00-£25.00 Double Room only per person £15.00-£20.00	Open Mar-Oct

Modern family run lodge overlooking Loch Broom. Under 1 mile (2 kms) from
Ullapool and the ferry terminal.

Mrs H MacDonald Broomvale, 26 Market Street Ullapool Ross-shire IV26 2XE Tel: (Ullapool) 01854 612559	COMMENDED 👑	1 Twin 2 Double	1 Pub Bath/Show	B&B per person from £13.50 Double	Open Mar-Nov

Comfortable accommodation in quiet location in fishing port of Ullapool.
Excellent touring base, and handy for ferry to Stornoway.

ULLAPOOL continued	Map 3 G6						

ULLAPOOL continued — Map 3 G6

Mrs C Mackenzie
25 Ladysmith Street
Ullapool
Ross-shire
Tel: (Ullapool) 01854 612123

COMMENDED Listed — 2 Double | 1 Pub Bath/Show | B&B per person £13.00-£13.50 Double | Open May-Oct

Comfortable family home in quiet residential street; warm welcome.

Mrs I MacRae
18 Pulteney Street
Ullapool
Ross-shire
IV26 2UP
Tel: (Ullapool) 01854 612397

COMMENDED Listed — 1 Twin, 1 Double, 1 Family | 1 Pub Bath/Show | B&B per person from £14.50 Single £13.00-£14.00 Double | Open Jan-Dec

18th-century stone-built cottage in centre of village. Lounge with open fire.

NO SMOKING HOUSEHOLD

Clachan Farmhouse

Lochbroom, Ullapool, Ross-shire IV23 2RZ
Telephone: 01854 655209

Excellent accommodation is provided in this modern farmhouse seven miles south of Ullapool. Under one hour from Inverness; two minutes off the A835. Electric blankets on beds. Three-course breakfast. Lounge is available all day. The exotic Inverewe Gardens, Corrieshalloch Gorge, and many Munros within easy reach.
No Sunday enquiries please.

Mrs I Renwick
Clachan Farmhouse
Lochbroom, by Ullapool
Ross-shire
IV23 2RZ
Tel: (Lochbroom)
01854 655209

COMMENDED — 1 Single, 1 Twin, 1 Double | 1 Pub Bath/Show | B&B per person to £15.00 Single to £15.00 Double | Open Apr-Nov

Peacefully situated on a working farm 7 miles (11kms) south of Ullapool, 2 minutes off A835. Home baking. Log fire in the lounge.

The Sheiling Guest House
Garve Road
Ullapool
Ross-shire
IV26 2SX
Tel: (Ullapool) 01854 612947

HIGHLY COMMENDED — 3 Twin, 4 Double | 7 En Suite fac | B&B per person £18.00-£25.00 Single £18.00-£21.00 Double | Open Jan-Dec

Modern house with large garden in peaceful location on shore of Loch Broom at the edge of the village. Trout fishing on various local lochs.

Strathmore House
Morefield
Ullapool
Ross-shire
IV26 2TH
Tel: (Ullapool) 01854 612423

COMMENDED — 1 Single, 1 Twin, 4 Double | 4 En Suite fac, 1 Pub Bath/Show | B&B per person £14.00-£20.00 Single £14.00-£20.00 Double Room only per person £10.00-£15.00 | Open Apr-Oct

Guest house enjoying panoramic views over Loch Broom and Ullapool. Some bedrooms have separate front terrace.

The Bungalow

Garve Road, Ullapool, Ross-shire IV26 2SX
Telephone: 01854 612233

Family home overlooking Loch Broom and surrounding hills. 1/4 mile from village. Excellent base for exploring the area. The only two-storey bungalow in Ullapool set back from the main road with fine views of harbour and village. Ample parking available.

Mrs C Sykes
The Bungalow, Garve Road
Ullapool
Ross-shire
IV26 2SX
Tel: (Ullapool) 01854 612233

COMMENDED — 1 Twin, 1 Double | 2 Pub Bath/Show | B&B per person £13.50 Double | Open Apr-Sep

The only two-storey "Bungalow" in Ullapool, set back from the main road, with fine views of the harbour and town. 1/4 mile to centre. Parking available.

Ardlair

MOREFIELD BRAE, ULLAPOOL, ROSS-SHIRE IV26 2TH
Telephone: 01854 612087

Modern bungalow situated on an elevated site overlooking Ullapool and Loch Broom. Ideal for walking, climbing, sailing, bird-watching or touring. One hour to the famous Inverewe Gardens; ferry terminal to Western Isles. There is ample parking and a large garden.

Mrs J Urquhart Ardlair, Morefield Ullapool Ross-shire IV26 2TH Tel: (Ullapool) 01854 612087	COMMENDED 👑👑	2 Double 2 Family	2 En Suite fac 2 Pub Bath/Show	B&B per person £13.00-£16.00 Double	Open May-Oct

Purpose-built modern house in elevated position, giving excellent views over Loch Broom. Under 2 miles (3kms) north of Ullapool.

BY ULLAPOOL **Ross-shire**	Map 3 G6

TORRAN

Loggie, Lochbroom, Ullapool, Ross-shire IV23 2SG
Telephone: 01854 655227

Torran is an attractive family home set in a peaceful location overlooking the beautiful Lochbroom. Ideal for walking, boat trips to the Summer Isles or day trips to the Outer Isles. Ideally located to use as a base for touring Skye, Durness, Gairloch or Inverewe.

Mrs M Mackenzie Torran, Loggie Lochbroom, Ullapool Ross-shire IV23 2SG Tel: (Lochbroom) 01854 655227	COMMENDED 👑	1 Single 1 Twin 1 Double	2 Pub Bath/Show	B&B per person £16.00-£18.00 Single £14.00-£15.00 Double	Open Mar-Nov

New bungalow in peaceful lochside setting. Ideal base for touring, walking, bird-watching and fishing.

UPHALL	Map 1 G6

Coille-Mhor House

20 Houston Mains Holdings, Uphall, West Lothian EH52 6PA
Telephone: 01506 854044   Fax: 01506 855118

Relax in our family run converted small-holding where everyone including children and the disabled are made very welcome. All bedrooms on ground floor with en-suite, house speciality is good honest porridge laced with liqueur, herbal teas, seasonal fruit, Scottish breakfast, private parking. Central for Edinburgh, airport, motorways. Free Brochure.

Coille-Mhor House 20 Houston Mains Holdings Uphall West Lothian EH52 6PA Tel: (Broxburn) 01506 854044 Fax: 01506 855118	COMMENDED 👑👑	1 Twin 4 Double 1 Family	6 En Suite fac	B&B per person from £25.00 Single from £20.00 Double	Open Jan-Dec

Characterful conversion of small holding furnished to a high standard. Close to Edinburgh, Airport and Glasgow motorway. Private parking.

UPLAWMOOR **Renfrewshire** Mrs J MacLeod East Uplaw Farm Uplawmoor Renfrewshire G78 4DA Tel: (Uplawmoor) 01505 850383/850594 Fax: 01505 850383	Map 1 G6	**COMMENDED** Listed	1 Twin 1 Double 1 Family	1 En Suite fac 2 Pub Bath/Show	B&B per person from £14.00 Single £14.00–£16.00 Double Room only per person from £12.00	Open Jan-Dec Dinner 1800-2200 B&B + Eve. Meal £20.00–£24.00

Modern comfortable accommodation, convenient for Burns Country on 320-acre beef farm. Good farmhouse cooking, mainly fresh produce. Children welcome.

WALKERBURN **Peeblesshire** Mrs A Barbour Willowbank, 13 High Cottages Walkerburn Peeblesshire EH43 6AZ Tel: (Walkerburn) 01896 870252	Map 2 C6	**COMMENDED** Listed	2 Twin 1 Double	2 Pub Bath/Show	B&B per person £16.00–£17.00 Single £15.00–£16.00 Double	Open Jan-Dec Dinner 1900-1930 B&B + Eve. Meal £24.00–£25.00

Personally run, stone-built semi-detached villa, situated on main tourist route through the Borders. Outstanding views of surrounding countryside.

WEST LINTON **Peeblesshire** Mrs Cottam Rowallan, Mountain Cross West Linton Peeblesshire EH46 7DF Tel: (West Linton) 01968 660329	Map 2 B6	**COMMENDED**	1 Double 1 Family	2 Pub Bath/Show	B&B per person from £15.00 Double	Open May-Oct

A warm welcome at modern house on A701, about half an hour's drive from Edinburgh. Fine views over the valley. Well situated for touring Borders and Peebles.

Mrs McCallum Lynehurst, Carlops Road West Linton Peeblesshire EH46 7DS Tel: (West Linton) 01968 660795 Fax: 01968 660993		**HIGHLY** **COMMENDED**	1 Twin 2 Double	2 En Suite fac 1 Priv. NOT ensuite 1 Pub Bath/Show	B&B per person £41.00–£46.00 Single £31.00–£36.00 Double	Open Mar-Oct Dinner 1930-2000 B&B + Eve. Meal £52.00–£57.00

Detached Tudor-style house set in 2.5 acres in conservation village. On A702, 20 minutes from Edinburgh by-pass.

WHITEKIRK **East Lothian** Mrs J M Tuer Whitekirk Mains Whitekirk East Lothian EH42 1XS Tel: (Whitekirk) 01620 870245 Fax: 01620 870330	Map 2 D4	**HIGHLY** **COMMENDED**	1 Twin 1 Double 1 Family	2 En Suite fac 1 Priv. NOT ensuite	B&B per person £20.00 Single £17.00–£18.00 Double	Open Mar-Oct

Georgian farmhouse on 600-acre mixed farm at edge of historic village close to new Whitekirk golf course. Oak-panelled dining/drawing rooms. Log fires.

Scotland for Golf . . .

Find out more about golf in Scotland. There's more to it than just the championship courses so get in touch with us now for information on the hidden gems of Scotland.

Write to: Information Unit, Scottish Tourist Board, 23 Ravelston Terrace, Edinburgh EH4 3EU or call: 0131-332 2433

WHITING BAY Isle of Arran	Map 1 F7	

NORWOOD

Smiddy Brae, Whiting Bay, Isle of Arran KA27 8PR
Telephone: 01770 700536

Norwood is centrally situated in Whiting Bay, in well-kept grounds. Bedrooms have wash-hand basin, tea/coffee-making facilities, radio alarm, electric heating and lovely sea views. Drying/ironing facilities and hairdryer are available. There is a comfortable TV lounge overlooking the sea. Private parking.

Mrs E K McCormack
Norwood, Smiddy Brae
Whiting Bay
Isle of Arran
KA27 8PR
Tel: (Whiting Bay)
01770 700536

COMMENDED ♛

1 Twin
1 Double

2 Pub Bath/Show

B&B per person
£14.00-£16.00 Double

Open Jan-Dec

Family home overlooking the Bay.
Centrally situated for craft shops and restaurants.

View Bank
Golf Course Road
Whiting Bay
Isle of Arran
KA27 8QT
Tel: (Whiting Bay)
01770 700326

COMMENDED ♛ ♛

1 Single
1 Twin
3 Double
2 Family

4 En Suite fac
2 Pub Bath/Show

B&B per person
£16.00-£19.50 Single
£16.00-£19.50 Double

Open Jan-Nov
Dinner from 1800
B&B + Eve. Meal
£24.00-£27.50

Converted farmhouse with warm, friendly welcome and home cooking.
Lovely sea views and a large lawned garden. Private parking.

WICK **Caithness**	Map 4 E3	

Mrs Bremner
The Clachan, South Road
Wick
Caithness
KW1 5NH
Tel: (Wick) 01955 605384

HIGHLY
COMMENDED ♛ ♛

1 Twin
2 Double

3 En Suite fac

B&B per person
£20.00-£25.00 Single
£18.00-£20.00 Double

Open Jan-Dec

Family run recently refurbished, detached house dating back to 1938
on quiet main street with off-street parking.

Mrs Coghill
Dunelm, 7 Sinclair Terrace
Wick
Caithness
KW1 5AD
Tel: (Wick) 01955
602120/605791

APPROVED ♛ ♛

1 Single
1 Twin
1 Double
1 Family

1 En Suite fac
3 Limited ensuite
2 Pub Bath/Show

B&B per person
from £15.00 Single
from £14.00 Double
Room only per person
from £11.00

Open Jan-Dec

Stone terraced listed building, 5 minutes walk from town centre and harbour.
Large, comfortable lounge and separate breakfast room.

Mrs C Gunn
Hebron,
25 Beaufoy Street
Wick
Caithness
KW1 5QG
Tel: (Wick) 01955 603515

COMMENDED
Listed

1 Twin
1 Family

1 Limited ensuite
2 Pub Bath/Show

B&B per person
from £15.00 Single
from £15.00 Double

Open Mar-Oct
Dinner 1700-2000
B&B + Eve. Meal
from £21.00

Stone-built house in quiet residential area within easy walking distance of town centre.

Mrs S Gunn
Papigoe Cottage, Papigoe
Wick
Caithness
KW1 4RD
Tel: (Wick) 01955 603363

APPROVED
Listed

1 Twin
1 Double
1 Family

2 Pub Bath/Show

B&B per person
from £13.50 Double

Open Jan-Dec
Dinner 1900-2030
B&B + Eve. Meal
from £16.50

A warm welcome is assured as you are treated as one of the family in
this modest bungalow. Mrs Gunn is knowledgeable on this historic area.

Details of Grading and Classification are on page vi.

Key to symbols is on back flap.

WICK continued	Map 4 E3

GREENVOE

George Street, Wick, Caithness KW1 4DE
Telephone: 01955 603942

Detached house in peaceful situation in large garden close to town centre with panoramic views over Wick River. Supper of sandwiches and home baking provided in evening at no extra charge, bath robes also provided. Private parking, convenient for bus and railway station. 30 minutes to Orkney Ferry.

Mr & Mrs J Johnston Greenvoe, George Street Wick Caithness KW1 4DE Tel: (Wick) 01955 603942	HIGHLY COMMENDED Listed	1 Single 1 Twin 1 Double	2 Pub Bath/Show	B&B per person £13.50 Single £13.50 Double	Open Jan-Dec

A large modern comfortable house, 0.5 miles (1km) from town centre. A non-smoking establishment. Private parking.

BILBSTER HOUSE

5 miles from Wick, Phone Watten 01955 621212

An attractive country house situated in about 5 acres of garden and woodland.

Leave Wick on A882 (Wick-Watten-Thurso). After 5 miles see line of trees on right and signboard. Turn right down lane. Gates face you after 450 yards. (Bilbster House is shown on Ordnance Survey Map. Reference 282533.)

Mr A Stewart Bilbster House Wick Caithness KW1 5TB Tel: (Watten) 01955 621212	COMMENDED	1 Twin 2 Double	2 En Suite fac 1 Pub Bath/Show	B&B per person £14.00-£15.00 Double	Open May-Sep

Listed country house dating from late 1700s set in 5 acres of grounds. Traditionally furnished.

Mrs P Weir Warrington, Thurso Road Wick KW1 5LE Tel: (Wick) 01955 604138	COMMENDED Listed	1 Single 2 Double	1 Pub Bath/Show	B&B per person from £15.00 Single from £15.00 Double	Open Jan-Dec

A warm welcome awaits you at this detached Edwardian villa. Convenient for bus and train stations. Ideal base for exploring Caithness and beyond.

WIGTOWN Mr & Mrs W B Cairns Glaisnock House 20 South Main Street Wigtown DG8 9EH Tel: (Wigtown) 01988 402249	Map 1 H10 COMMENDED	1 Single 1 Twin 1 Family	1 En Suite fac 1 Limited ensuite 2 Pub Bath/Show	B&B per person £14.50-£15.50 Single £14.50-£15.50 Double	Open Jan-Dec Dinner 1800-2030 B&B + Eve. Meal £22.00-£23.00

Family run guest house with restaurant in the heart of the town.

YELL, Island of Shetland Pinewood Guest House South Aywick, East Yell Shetland ZE2 9AX Tel: (Mid Yell) 01957 702427	Map 5 G2 COMMENDED	2 Twin 1 Double	2 En Suite fac 1 Limited ensuite 1 Pub Bath/Show	B&B per person £23.00-£28.00 Single £19.00-£24.00 Double	Open Jan-Dec Dinner from 1900 B&B + Eve. Meal £25.00-£30.00

Modernised crofthouse with large garden, enjoying fine views eastwards over the sea to islands of Fetlar, Unst and Skerries.

YETHOLM **Roxburghshire** Mrs Gail Brooker Bluntys Mill Yetholm Roxburghshire TD5 8PG Tel: (Yetholm) 01573 420288	Map 2 E7	COMMENDED	1 Twin	1 En Suite fac	B&B per person £16.00-£18.00 Single	Open Jan-Dec Dinner 1800-2030 B&B + Eve. Meal £22.00-£28.00	

Peaceful ground-floor accommodation in family home set in 6 acres of pasture.

Select your holiday accommodation with confidence,

use The Scottish Tourist Board's Grading and Classification Scheme

Book your accommodation anywhere in Scotland the easy way – through your nearest Tourist Information Centre.

A booking fee of £2.75 is charged, and you will be asked for a small deposit.

Local bookings are usually free, or a small fee will be charged.

 When you visit a Tourist Information Centre you are guaranteed a welcome by people who really know their country.

For information, maps, holiday reading, accommodation bookings and much more, look for the information $\boxed{i}$

ABERFELDY

OAKBANK
KENMORE STREET, ABERFELDY PH15 2BP
Telephone: 01887 820206
This comfortable Victorian home is close to all amenities. Shops, restaurants, swimming pool, golf course and many historical and natural areas of interest are available, many sporting activities are available as well as our own instructor/guide for walks. Archery and children's activities.

BALLOCH

Cameron Cottage
OLD LUSS ROAD, BALLOCH G83 2NQ
Telephone: 01389 759779
Attractive cottage in pleasant setting in own grounds overlooking the *Bonnie Banks of Loch Lomond*. Spacious comfortable rooms with colour TV, off-street parking, evening meal on request and most rooms with ensuite facilities. Ideal location for touring *The Trossachs*, *Stirling* and *Glasgow*.

BOAT OF GARTEN

GLENSANDA
Mullingarroch, Boat of Garton, Inverness-shire PH24 3BY
Telephone: 01479 831494
Modern custom built home designed with comfort in mind. Bright spacious TV lounge with open fire to relax in after enjoying the many ammenities the area offers. Ideal base for touring, angling, golfing, birdwatching, ski-ing, off-road driving and more. All bedrooms have en-suite shower room, heating, tea/coffee tray.

LARGS

WHIN PARK
16 Douglas Street, Largs, Ayrshire KA30 8PS
Telephone: 01475 673437
Personally managed by Mrs Henderson and situated close to the seafront in an attractive area of Largs. It is convenient for access to the islands of the Clyde and to Argyll within easy reach of many other scenic areas of West Scotland and Glasgow International Airport.
AA selected QQQQ.

Mulberry's Bed & Breakfast

HIGH STREET, MOFFAT DG10 9RS
Telephone: 01683 209000

Prime central position with unlimited free parking, adjoining family-run licensed restaurant with full A-la carte menu and supper specialities. En-suite rooms with TV, coffee and tea facilities. Large guests lounge.

GARYBUIE

4 Balmeanach, Glenhinnisdale, Snizort, Isle of Skye IV51 9UX
Telephone: 01470 542310

Cosy 1931 croft house/tea room in scenic glen. Good walking, Totternish Ridge, salmon fishing. B/B/evening dinners. Off A856 at Hinmisdal Bridge, along riverside to telephone box, house adjacent, four miles from ferry to Harris, Lewis. Area famous for connection with '45 Rebellion and Flora MacDonald's courageous action.

Taigh Na Mara
Vegetarian Info Centre

The Shore, Lochbroom, Nr Ullapool IV23 2SE
Telephone and Fax: 01854 655282

Taigh Na Mara Vegetarian Information Centre for the Scottish Highlands. Set on the shore of legendary Lochbroom near Ullapool, it is the most secluded, idyllic, stressfree base to discover all of the best of the Highlands. From Loch Ness right up to the North Coast of Sutherland and over to the Black Isle. Highly recommended by all discerning publications from BBC, *Veg Good Food* magazine through to *Scotland on Sunday, Independent, Observer* etc. 24hr information plus credit card hotline for vegetarian travellers. Guides available. Look out for our New Scottish Gourmet Vegan Cookbook. **I don' think so!** £19.95. incl. P+P.

286

Accommodation providing facilities for visitors with disabilities

The Scottish Tourist Board, in conjunction with the English and Wales Tourist Boards, operates a national accessible scheme that identifies, acknowledges and promotes those accommodation establishments that meet the needs of visitors with disabilities.

The three categories of accessibility, drawn up in close consultation with specialist organisations concerned with the needs of people with disabilities, are:

CATEGORY 1	CATEGORY 2	CATEGORY 3
Unassisted wheelchair access for residents	Assisted wheelchair access for residents	Access for residents with mobility difficulties

Category 1
Airlie Mount
  Holiday Services
2 Albert Street
Alyth, Blairgowrie
Perthshire
PH11 8AX

Ardgarth Guest House
1 St Mary's Place
Portobello, Edinburgh
EH15 2QF

Mr J G Bristow
56 Dumbreck Road
Glasgow
G41 5NP

Mrs Borrett
Cruachan, Dalmally
Argyll
PA33 1AA

Old Coaching Inn
Westwood House
Houndwood
Eyemouth
Berwickshire
TD14 5TP

Category 2
Auchendinny Guest House
Treaslane
Skeabost Bridge
Isle of Skye
Inverness-shire
IV51 9NX

Mr D McKenzie
Alban House
Bruce Gardens
Inverness
IV3 5ED

Mill Croft Guest House
Lawrence Road
Old Rayne
Insh
Aberdeenshire
AB52 6RY

Mrs C A Murphy
Orchard House
298 Annan Road
Dumfries
DG1 3JE

Old Pines Restaurant
By Spean Bridge
Inverness-shire
PH34 4EG

Category 3
Abbeylodge Guest
  House
137 Drum Street
Edinburgh
EH17 8RG

Averon Guest House
44 Gilmore Place
Edinburgh
EH13 9NQ

Avondale Guest House
Newtonmore Road
Kingussie
Inverness-shire
PH21 1HF

Mr D Barclay
Burnock Water
Haywood Road
Moffat
Dumfriesshire
DG10 9BU

Mrs Bennett
Mossgiel
Doune Road
Dunblane
Perthshire
Fk15 9ND

Mrs P J Borland
Knoydart
Windhill, Beauly
Inverness-shire
IV4 7AS

Clarke Cottage
   Guest House
139 Halbeath Road
Dunfermline
Fife
KY11 4LA

Mrs M Cooper
Lynwood
Golf Road
Brora
Sutherland
KW9 6QS

Craiglinnhe Guest
   House
Ballachulish
Argyll
PA39 4JX

Mrs P Davey
Soluis Mu Thuath
Braeintra
Achmore
Strome Ferry
Ross-shire
IV53 8UN

Dromnan Guest House
Garve Road
Ullapool
Ross-shire
IV26 2SX

Mrs Fife
Beehive Cottage
Kingston
North Berwick
East Lothian
EH39 5JE

Hayfield Equestrian
   Centre
Hazelhead Park
Aberdeen
Aberdeenshire
AB1 8BB

Mrs M Hutcheson
Mardon
37 Kenneth Street
Inverness
IV3 5DH

Innis Mhor
Ardheslaig
near Shieldaig
Strathcarron
Ross-shire
IV54 8XH

Kinross House Guest
   House
Woodside Avenue
Grantown-on-Spey
Moray
PH26 3JR

Mrs I Knight
Hopefield House
Main Street
Gullane
East Lothian
EH31 2DP

Mrs S Bowie, Aberchirder, by Huntly
Mrs A Hay, Aberchirder, by Huntly
Mrs Fiona Anderson, Aberdeen
Mr & Mrs Bisset, Aberdeen
Mrs Butler, Aberdeen
Mrs J Davidson, Aberdeen
Mrs M Esson, Aberdeen
H Florence, Aberdeen
Mrs J Kelly, Aberdeen
Mr and Mrs J A G McHardy,
    Aberdeen
Mrs Muir, Aberdeen
Mrs E Noble, Aberdeen
Mrs H Price, Aberdeen
Mrs D Spalding, Aberdeen
Mrs M Templeton, Aberdeen
Mr & Mrs Thomson, Aberdeen
Mr & Mrs A W Walker, Aberdeen
Mr & Mrs G L Allan, Aberdeen
Mrs Rhona Chalmers, Aberdeen
Mrs K Algie, by Aberdeen
Hazel Leslie, by Aberdeen
Mrs J M Petrie, by Aberdeen
Major David A Robertson,
    by Aberdeen
Mrs Willis, by Aberdeen
Mr & Mrs Hermiston, Aberfeldy
Mrs Kennedy, Aberfeldy
Mrs Ross, Aberfeldy
Mrs P Orr, by Aberfeldy
Mrs A Jennings, Aberfoyle
Mrs Fiona Oldham, Aberfoyle
Mrs C Robertson, Aberfoyle
Mrs A Dyer, The Sidings, Aberlady
Mrs A Hodge, Abington
V P Metcalfe, Aboyne

Mrs Brodie, Acharn, by Kenmore
Mrs S M Blackmann, Alford
A L Colliar, Alford
Mrs Henderson, Alford
Mrs Forrest, by Annan
Mrs J Caldwell, Arbroath
Mrs MacBean, Ardersier
Rosemary McAllister, Ardrishaig
Michael & Monica Farka,
    Ardrishaig, by Lochgilphead
Mrs Hamilton, Ardrishaig,
    by Lochgilphead
Mrs Barton, Ardvasar, Sleat
Mrs R Houlton, Ardvasar, Sleat
Miss Jan Harvey, Arrochar
Mrs Marion Russell, Ashkirk
F Wallace, Auchencairn,
    by Castle Douglas
Mrs F M Cannon, Auchencairn,
    by Castle Douglas
Mrs Gillian Matthews, Auchterarder
Mrs P MacRae, Aultbea
Mrs Edmondson, Aviemore
Mrs Ann Gambles, Ayr
J I Hamilton, Ballachulish
Mrs M Cameron, Balloch
Mrs M Cannon, Balloch
Mrs Margot Foulger, Balloch
Mr M Harris, Balloch
Mrs G McKinney, Balloch
P O Nichols, Balmaha, by Drymen
Mrs Wilson, Banchory
Mrs P Mallen, by Banchory
Mrs Maureen Watt, Banff
Mrs K MacDonald, Barvas
Mrs MacAulay, Bernera

Mrs D MacLeod, Bernisdale, by Portree
Mr & Mrs P Brotherstone, Biggar
Mrs M A Stewart, by Blairgowrie
Mrs S Lyons, Boat of Garten
Mrs B Kirk, Bo'ness
Mrs MacLean, Borve, by Portree
Mrs A E MacKinnon, Braemar
Mrs J Goddard, Braes, by Portree
D & K Ovenstone, Braemar
Mr Ian Dunsire, Bridge of Earn
Mrs Barbara Christie, Broadford
Mrs MacRae, Broadford
Mrs Sikorski, Broadford
Mrs A MacDonald, Bruichladdich
Mrs V Golding, Buchlyvie
Mrs Marion McKay, Buckie
Mrs Elizabeth H MacMillan, Buckie
Mrs A B Mair, Buckie
Mrs Davina Wright, Buckie
Mrs Acey, Bunessan
Mrs W B Donnelly, Burnmouth
Mr E M Weaving, Burrelton
Mrs J Donald, Callander
Mrs J MacFarlane, Callander
Mrs Bell, Campbeltown
Mrs J. Scott-Dodd, Campbeltown
Mr Riley, Canonbie
Fiona Paterson, Cappercleuch
Wendy Ebblewhite, Carnoustie
Mrs A Malcolm, Carnoustie
Mrs J Orr, Carnwath
Mrs P Bailey, Carrbridge
Mrs Shirley Campbell, Carrbridge
Mrs F Ritchie, Carrbridge
Mr & Mrs Stampfer, Carrbridge
Mrs F Borland, Castle Douglas

Mrs J C Herbertson, Castle Douglas
Mrs J E McMorran, Castle Douglas
Mrs M Mathie, Castle Douglas
Mrs A Muir, Castle Douglas
Mrs Rennie, Castle Douglas
Mrs M Robertson, Castle Douglas
Mrs C Smith, Castle Douglas
Mrs M Chrisp, Ceres
Mrs S C Lindsay, Chryston, by Glasgow
Mrs C Allan, Clarkston, Glasgow
Mrs J McCay, Clydebank, Glasgow
Mrs M McEwan, Clynder
Cul-Na-Sithe, Coldingham
Mrs Rosemary Scott, Coldingham
Mrs M W Hawkins, Colvend
Mr J Duncan, Cornhill
Mrs S Rawlings, Cornhill, by Banff
Mrs Joan F Grant, Cortachy, by Kirriemuir
Mrs B Croy, Craigellachie
Mr and Mrs F Donaghy, Craigellachie
Mrs S Allan, Craignure
Mrs Rosemarie Auld, Craignure
Mr J C W Christie, Crianlarich
Mrs Hancox, Crieff
Mrs Haseltine, Crieff
Mrs C E Murray, Crieff
Mrs Gladys Clarke, Crimond,
    by Fraserburgh
Mrs F Ricketts, Cromarty
M MacLeod, Crossbost
Mrs A Mair, Cullen
Mrs Frances Stewart, Cupar
Mrs P M Dennis, Dalbeattie
Mrs Helen S Eadie, Dalgety Bay
Mrs Dorothy Stevenson, by Dalkeith
Mrs E Seton, Darvel

Alex & Margaret Hutcheson, Daviot
Mrs M Lees, Daviot
Mrs Barbara Kinnear, Daviot East
The Topps, Denny
Mrs J Fairbairns, Dervaig
Mrs W Goulden, Dervaig
Pamela Taylor, Dolphinton, West Linton
Mrs O Robin, Dornie, by Kyle
Joyce Everitt, Dornoch
Mr & Mrs D Paice, Dounby
Mrs Rose Colclough, Drumnadrochit
The Haining, Drumnadrochit
Miss C C MacDonald, Drumnadrochit
Mrs J Duncan, Dullatur, Glasgow
Mrs Conaghan, Dumfries
Mrs Sheena Maxwell, Dumfries
Mrs Stradmeycr, Dumfries
Mrs Gardner, Dunbar
Mrs Elizabeth J Duncan, Dunblane
Mrs I Fraser, Dundee
Mrs J Hill, Dundee
Mrs E Pirie, Dundee
Mr & Mrs B Wallace, Dundee
Julia K Brown, by Dundee
Mrs A Dowds, Dunoon
Mrs K Fraser, by Duns
Mrs A Prentice, by Duns
Mrs Zan Kirk, Dunscore
Mrs Margaret Armstrong, Dunsyre
Mrs M MacDonald, Dunvegan
Mrs Sherlock, Eaglesfield, by Lockerbie
Mrs E Pope, Earlston
Mrs L Richardson, Earlston
Mrs E Campbel, East Linton
Mrs Norah Aitchison, Edinburgh
Mrs Linda J Allan, Edinburgh

T V Carey, Edinburgh
Helen Charles, Edinburgh
Robert & Helen Clephane, Edinburgh
Mrs S Crichton, Edinburgh
Mrs V Darlington, Edinburgh
Mrs Maureen Diggin, Edinburgh
Mrs J Ferguson, Edinburgh
Mrs C Forsyth, Edinburgh
Hubert H Fortune, Edinburgh
E. Fulton, Edinburgh
Mrs Greig, Edinburgh
Mrs Mary Hanson, Edinburgh
Mrs M Holmes, Edinburgh
Mrs Jameson, Edinburgh
Mrs C A King, Edinburgh
Mrs S MacKay, Edinburgh
Mrs U McLean, Edinburgh
Mrs I Millar, Edinburgh
Mrs Margaret Miller, Edinburgh
Mrs Maureen Miller, Edinburgh
Mrs E Nicholson, Edinburgh
Mrs Elizabeth Smith, Edinburgh
Susan Smith, Edinburgh
Mrs Susan Berkengoff, Edinburgh
Mrs Liz Collie, Edinburgh
Mrs Scott, Edzell
Mrs Sandra Asher, Elgin
Mrs C.C. Ann Cartmell, Elgin
Mrs I. McGowan, Elgin
Mrs Elizabeth Smith, Elgin
Mrs Margaret Craig Ward, Elgin
Mrs Linda Philip, by Elgin
Mrs Betty Stevenson, Ellon
Mrs I Jamieson, by Ellon
Mr K Thorpe, by Ellon
Mrs J Catterall, Enochdhu, by Pitlochry

Mrs Lilly Bernard, Ettrick Valley
Mrs E Blades, by Eyemouth
Mrs Helen Jones, Falkirk
Mr & Mrs J Nicol, Fallin, Stirling
Mrs E Clapham, Fearnan, Aberfeldy
Mrs Margaret J Tointon, Findhorn
Mrs M P Loades, Findochty
Mrs A Tait, Finstown
Mrs Alexia Shand, by Fochabers
Mrs Leith, Fordyce, by Portsoy
Mrs K Kilgour, Forfar
Mrs Kirby, by Forfar
Mr & Mrs John Cousens, Forres
Mrs Jean Dean, Forres
Mrs Isobel Ferguson, by Forres
Mrs J M Paterson, Fort Augustus
Mrs S E Buxton, Fort William
Mrs Campbell, Fort William
Mrs Elaine Corbett, Fort William
Mrs A Edwards, Fort William
Mrs J Ellison, Fort William
Mrs A Heger, Fort William
Patricia Jordan, Fort William
Mrs F Junor, Fort William
James Kennedy, Fort William
B Lytham, Fort William
Wilma & Jim McCourt, Fort William
Mrs Angela MacIntyre, Fort William
Mrs McKay, Fort William
Mrs MacLean, Fort William
Mrs S MacPherson, Fort William
Mrs M Ross, Fort William
Mrs Waugh, Fort William
Mrs Cumming, Fraserburgh
Mrs R M Largue, Fyvie
Mrs M Wyness, Fyvie

Mrs Barbara Hitchon, Gairloch
Mr & Mrs Reid, Galasheils
Mrs Adam, Galashiels
Mr & Mrs Findlay, Galashiels
Ken Gray, Galashiels
Mrs Janice Richardson, Galashiels
Bill & Sheila Salkeld, Galashiels
Jennifer Scott, Galashiels
Auchenlarich House, Gartocharn
Mrs Lindsay, Gartocharn
Mrs W Johnstone, Gatehouse-of-Fleet
Mrs D McFadzean, Gatehouse-of-Fleet
Mrs J Davies, Giffnock, by Glasgow
Mrs I Melville, Girvan
Mrs L Alexander, Glasgow
Mrs E Anderson, Glasgow
Mrs R Chalmers, Glasgow
Eight Marlborough, Glasgow
Mrs Joan Garner, Glasgow
Mrs C McArdle, Glasgow
Mr & Mrs C & A Malcolm, Glasgow
Mrs C Mill, Glasgow
Ms E MacLellan, Glasgow
Mrs K Rodger, Glencoe
Mrs L A Karisson, Mo Dhachaidh,
    Glendale
M V Butler, Glenhinnisdale
S J Evans, Glenisla
Mrs Jo R Durno, Glenlivet
Mrs B Murray, by Golspie
Mrs Jeanna Holl, Gordon
Mrs M. Lawson, Grantown-on-Spey
Crois Ailien Lodge, Gravir
Mrs S Slater, Greenlaw, Duns
Mrs V Nelis, Greenock
Mrs M F Mallinson, Gretna

Mrs M E Wormald, Haugh of Urr
Mr D N Cormack, Hawick
Mrs Lynette Evans, Hawick
Mrs E Herbert, Hawick
Mrs J M Needham, Hawick
Mrs D M Park, Hawick
Mrs M Irving, by Hawick
Mr & Mrs Witten, by Hawick
Mrs Janet Cowie, Helensburgh
Mrs N F McPherson, Hopeman
Mrs J Harris, Hownam, by Kelso
Mrs L Budge, Hoy
Mrs Leslye Budge, Hoy
Mr I Forbes, Huntly
Mrs Gent, Huntly
Mrs E Thomson, Huntly
J. Bailie, by Huntly
Mrs Doreen Ingram, by Huntly
I & P M Rees, by Huntly
Mrs Stewart, by Huntly
Mrs J Caird, Innerleithen
Mrs Alice Lumsden, Insch
Mrs Jane Croy, Inverinate, Glenshiel
Mrs Russell, Inverkip
Mrs M J Cameron, Inverness
M Colven, Inverness
Mr L P Cook, Inverness
Mrs M. Cook, Inverness
Crathie, Mrs J Miller, Inverness
Mrs A Davidson, Inverness
Mrs C Davidson, Inverness
Mr & Mrs W Y Findlay, Inverness
Mrs C Forsyth, Inverness
Mrs H Fraser, Inverness
Mrs M Green, Inverness
Mrs Joan Hendry, Inverness

J M Hogg, Inverness
Mrs P Lamb, Inverness
Mrs D MacDonald, Inverness
E A Mackay, Inverness
Mrs Fiona M MacNeil, Inverness
Mrs C McQueen, Inverness
Mrs Jane A MacRury, Inverness
Melness, Inverness
Mrs G Moffat, Inverness
Mrs Ann Petrie, Inverness
Mrs Mary Pritchard, Inverness
Donna Smith, Inverness
Mrs Taylor, Inverness
The Linn, Inverness
Mr L H Zeffert, Inverness
Mrs J Fountain, by Inverness
Mrs Munro, by Inverness
Mrs Alison Parsons, by Inverness
Mrs W Brinklow, Invershin, by Lairg
Mrs Milne, Inverurie
Mrs S McGhie, by Inverurie
Mrs Bathgate, Jedburgh
Mrs Ann Booth, Jedburgh
Mrs Doris Ferguson, Jedburgh
Mrs Margaret Harrison, Jedburgh
Mrs Deborah Henry, Jedburgh
Mrs Margaret Poloczek, Jedburgh
Mrs P Boyd, by Jedburgh
Mrs C. Keatinge, by Jedburgh
Mrs Hulton, Johnshaven, by Stonehaven
Mrs I Caffrey, Johnstone
Mrs Barbara Allan, Keith
T A Smith, Keith
Mrs E Blackie, Kelso
Ms Olive Gordon, Kelso
Mrs Isobel Liddle, Kelso

Mr and Mrs A C Robertson, Kelso
Mrs Judy Cavers, by Kelso
Mrs Jan Ford, by Kelso
Mrs W Steel, Kilmaurs, by Kilmarnock
Mrs J Shuttlewood, Kilmichael Glassary, by Lochgilphead
Mrs Gillie, Kilmichael Glassery, by Lochgilphead
Mrs Dunlop, Kilsyth
Mrs Rita Campbell, Kingsburgh
Mrs A Johnstone, Kingussie
Garbhein House, Kinlochleven
G & L Muirhead, by Kinross
Mrs Young, by Kinross
Mrs Preece, Kintore
Mrs Sochacka, Kippford, by Dalbeattie
Mrs Linda Duffy, Kirkcaldy
Mrs Y Kelly, Kirkcudbright
Mrs M Aitken, Kirkwall
Mrs M Bruce, Kirkwall
Mrs Cooper, Kirkwall
Mrs J H Cursiter, Kirkwall
Mrs M Flett, Kirkwall
Mrs J Forsyth, Kirkwall
Mrs M Hourie, Kirkwall
Mrs J Hume, Kirkwall
Mrs V Hume, Kirkwall
Mrs M Muir, Kirkwall
Mrs Omand, Kirkwall
Mrs M Parkins, Kirkwall
Mrs M Rendall, Kirkwall
Mrs Tonge, Kirkwall
Mrs Wilson, Kirkwall
Mrs Margaret Campbell, Kirk Yetholm
Mrs Burgess, Kirkwall
Mrs Murchison, Kyle of Lochalsh

Mrs Bowness, Lagavulin, by Port Ellen
Mrs B M Paterson, Lairg
Mrs E Young, Lanark
Mrs S Geddes, Langholm
Elizabeth Mackey, Largs
Mrs Falconer, Latheron
Mrs M MacKay, Laxdale
Mrs B Clark, Lerwick
Mrs Gifford, Lerwick
Mrs Herculeson, Lerwick
Mrs J Hutchison, Lerwick
Mrs M Irving, Lerwick
Norma Reid, Leurbost
Mrs C MacKenzie, Leverburgh
Mrs A Hay, Linlithgow
Mrs M A Johnston, Lochinver
Mrs V McMeechan, Lochwinnoch
Mrs Dempster, Lockerbie
Mrs Z Peace, Longniddry
Mrs Margaret C Cameron, Lossiemouth
Mrs I Harris, Lossiemouth
Mrs Margaret Stephen, Lossiemouth
Mrs Maggie Thomson, Lossiemouth
Mrs Dobson, Luib, by Broadford
Mrs Baxter, Lumsden
Mrs M MacLeod, Luskentyre
Mr G C Brittain, Macduff
Mrs J Crocket, Mallaig
Mrs P Aitken, Melrose
Mrs E G R Buchanan, Melrose
Sally & Bob Capo, Melrose
Mrs E M Cripps, Melrose
Mrs E Haldane, Melrose
Mrs Susan Christie, by Melrose
Mrs T Davison, by Melrose
Mrs Mary Strathie, by Melrose

J Neish, Memsie, by Fraserburgh
Mrs M MacKay, Mey
Mrs E J Chapman, Milngavie, Glasgow
Mrs O Daly, Milngavie, Glasgow
Grainneag, Milngavie, Glasgow
Mrs L Forrester, Moffat
Robert H Jackson, Moffat
Mrs J Milne, Moffat
I Toni, Moffat
Mrs Alison Boon, Moniaive
Mrs K Melville, Montgreenan,
    by Kilwinning
Mrs M Docherty, Montrose
Mrs C A Finch, Morar, by Mallaig
Mrs Emma MacDonald, Muir of Aird
Mrs H Fraser, Nairn
Mrs W McCluskey, Nairn
Southlea House, Newburgh
Mrs A Harvey, Newburgh
Mrs Taylor, Newmachar
Mrs S Limbrey, Newton Stewart
Mr S A Rankin, Newton Stewart
Mrs M Auld, North Berwick
Mrs L Morrison, North Berwick
Mrs B Pope, North Berwick
Mrs E Wood, North Mainland
Briarbank Bed & Breakfast, Oban
Mundi Cooper, Oban
Mrs J Driver, Oban
D MacCalman, Oban
Mrs S Scott, Oban
Mrs Morven Wardhaugh, Oban
Mr & Mrs A Hunter, Old Kilpatrick
Mr K Miller, Old Kilpatrick
Mrs J Grainger, Orphir
Mrs Dawn Wishart, Orphir

Mrs Morag Davis, Peebles
Mrs Fawcett, Peebles
Mrs E Gray, Peebles
Mrs Jane Lambley, Peebles
Mrs Pauline McLean, Peebles
Mrs O'Hara, Peebles
Mrs M Dennison, by Peebles
Mrs C M Hobbs, Penicuik
Mr Gallacher, Perth
Mr & Mrs Livingstone, Perth
Mr A P Normand, Perth
Mr & Mrs J Wilson, Perth
Mrs Linda Watson, Peterhead
Mr & Mrs MacLennan, Plockton
Mrs M MacLeod, Poolewe
Mrs M I Wood, Port Charlotte
Theresa & Iain Campbell, Portnalong
Mrs Effie Bain, Port of Menteith
Mrs Rhona Millar, Port of Menteith
Catriona MacLeod, Port of Ness
Mrs Boyd, Portree
Mrs MacFarlane, Portree
Mrs J Wardrope, Prestwick
Mr & Mrs G A W Henry, Reawick
Jill Jones, Redburn, Belivat
Mrs Nicolson, Rendall
Ms Gillian Chadwick, Roberton,
    by Abington
Mrs J Corbett, Rogart
Mrs Rae Stephen, Roslin
Mrs E K Anderson, Rothesay
Mrs M Coull, St Andrews
Mrs Crichton, St Andrews
Mrs E L Finlay, St Andrews
Mrs Nina Johnstone, St Boswells
Mrs A M Tyrer, St Boswells

Other quality assured Bed and Breakfasts

Mrs A Brown, St Margaret's Hope
Mrs M Cromarty, St Margaret's Hope
Mrs Gunn, St Margaret's Hope
Mrs C Spence, St Ola, by Kirkwall
Mrs C Stephens, Salen
Mrs Elizabeth Chalmers, Sandend,
   by Portsoy
Mrs Kirkpatrick, Sandwick
Mrs Poke, Sandwick
Mrs N Hedges, Scalloway
Marie Bowers, Selkirk
Mrs Alison M Scott, Selkirk
Mrs H Murray, Selkirk
Mrs Wallace, Shapinsay
E P Mills, Shiskine
Mrs J Jenner, Skellister, South Nesting
Mrs A Cromarty, South Ronaldsay
Mrs Smales, South Ronaldsay
Mrs Duberley, Spean Bridge
Mrs M McDonald, Staffin
Mrs Scott, Stenness
Mrs Swannie, Stenness
Mr and Mrs Dunbar, Stirling
Mrs E Paterson, Stirling
XI Victoria Square, Stirling
Mrs Sheila Mitchell, Stonehaven
Mrs Dowie, Stornoway
Mrs A Hughson, Stornoway
Mrs J MacKenzie, Stornoway
Mrs Marie Maclennan, Stornoway
Mrs A Bark, Stranraer
Mrs F Hull, Stranraer
Mrs O M Kelly, Stranraer
Mrs Goodwillie, Strathaven

Iain & Mary Edgar, Strathdon
Mr & Mrs G M Hardie, Strathdon
Mrs Kornelia Inverarity, Strathkinness,
   by St Andrews
Mrs E Coupland, Strathpeffer
Mrs J C Dewar, Stromness
Mrs R Laidlow, Stromness
Mrs O M Ritch, Stromness
Mrs D MacPherson, Strontian
Mrs H Wrigh, Suladale, by Portree
Mrs Marshall, Tarbert, Loch Fyne
Mrs McIlroy, Tarbet, by Arrochar
Mr J Rawle, Tarbet, by Arrochar
Mrs MacKie, Thornhill
Mrs Norma McLardy, Troon
Mrs Margaret Beattie, Turriff
Mrs F Sloan, Twynholm
Mrs Campbell, Uig
Mrs Downey, Ullapool
Mr G Bremner, Unst, Island of
Mrs S J Firmin, Unst, Island of
Mrs M Williamson, Upper Urafirth
Mrs B Leask, Walls
Mrs Joyce Muir, West Linton
Mrs R Keith, Westmuir, Kirriemuir
Mrs L Dodd, Whitebridge
Mrs E Forsyth, Whithorn
Mrs M Forsyth, Whithorn
Rowallan, Whiting Bay
Mrs H Turnbull, Yarrow
Mrs L S Hurst, Yetholm